CATALOGUE OF

BOOKS *and* Pamphlets

Principally Relating

TO

AMERICA

1870

NY

PREFATORY NOTE.

A time-honored custom demands a formal introduction of every volume to its readers; and, in deference to its requirements, this volume is thus presented to the collectors of books for their examination.

The Collection of Books of which this volume is a Catalogue, is an important one, and not without attractions to the intelligent bookbuyer. As a collection of Local Histories; of the Publications of Societies; of Biographies; of works on the North American Indians; of Washingtoniana; of Election, Thanksgiving, and Fast-Day Sermons; of Trials; of Early New England Theology; of Controversial Tracts on Banking, Theology, Politics, Law, Medicine, Temperance, etc.; of Fourth of July Orations; of College Publications; of Lincolniana; of works on the Rebellion and Slavery; of Sermons, etc., it may be said, truly, to have been surpassed in extent, variety, and value, by very few of even the most elaborate and best selected Libraries.

Of the Local Histories, including Centennial Discourses of Churches, Schools, Societies, etc., which it contains, not even a brief mention of them in detail can be made without encumbering this note and tiring the reader. Every page is sprinkled with their titles, and every State, and very often, every county of the several States, is represented in the list. The Index, at the close of the volume, refers to many, but not nearly to all of them; to which the reader's careful attention is respectfully directed.

Of the PUBLICATIONS OF SOCIETIES, the titles of which extend from page 148 to page 161, besides single specimens scattered elsewhere through the Catalogue, under the names of their several authors and of their peculiar localities, the Collection is unusually complete and valuable, as those who have sought such works will fully understand after having examined its pages.

Of the BIOGRAPHIES, in which may be included, not only the ordinary volumes of Biography, but *Diaries*, *Journals*, *Personal Narratives*, *Funeral and Ordination Sermons*, *Trials*, and other works of similar character, the Collection is very large and very important, containing not only those which are agreeable, but those which are notorious and depreciating in their tendencies.

Of the great variety of works on the NORTH AMERICAN INDIANS, embracing not only the more elaborate volumes of Adair, McKenny, Catlin, Schoolcraft, etc., but the numerous Personal Narratives, War Histories, Vocabularies, etc., especial mention cannot be made in detail; but an examination of the Index will indicate how numerous their titles are, and how important the Collection is to every lover of Bibliography.

The WASHINGTONIANA is described by their titles on pages 430–452; and even a passing glance will indicate the great variety and unusual importance of that portion of the Collection.

There are many other lines, however, scattered through the catalogue under the titles of their respective authors' names, which add to the interest of this specially attractive department; and those who are adding the works of this particular class to their libraries, will be repaid by a close examination of other portions of the Catalogue than that to which reference has been made.

The ELECTION SERMONS of Massachusetts extend with tolerable regularity, from 1720 until 1869, and those of Connecticut from 1766, with some deviation, to 1830; the THANKS-

GIVING SERMONS, extending from 1786 until a recent date, are various and desirable; and the FAST-DAY SERMONS, range from 1753 until our own day. Without claiming any notable degree of perfection in these departments, the works which they contain will serve an excellent purpose in making complete many collections which are lacking in particular works.

The TRIALS number, among others, many of the most notable, including those of the British soldiers at Boston, Aaron Burr, Judge Blount, Joshua Hett Smith, Major Andrè, Ephraim Wheeler, E. C. Delavan, Alexander Whistelo, Levi Weeks, Rev. John N. Maffit, John C. Colt, Bishops Doane and Onderdonk, Sir Henry Vane, the Forrest Case, William Hone, Doctor S. F. Jarvis, Horace Greeley, the Prophet Matthias, Alexander McLeod, the Parrish and Lawrence Will Cases, D. E. Sickles, Prof. Webster, Rev. William Parkinson, etc., and it will be seen that those who have an inclination to this class of works, will enjoy a rare opportunity for extending their collections.

Of EARLY NEW ENGLAND THEOLOGY AND HISTORY the specimens are quite numerous, and generally of great variety. Without naming all, the works of such men as John Checkley, John Cotton, Thomas Hooker, Cotton and Samuel Mather, Benjamin Colman, John Dunton, Thomas Prince, Nathaniel Appleton, Thomas Sheppard, John Josselyn, John Davenport, Captain Thomas Wheeler, will be found in this Collection.

The CONTROVERSIAL TRACTS number many hundreds; and the particular subjects on which they treat are numerous and of every conceivable character; and the same remarks will apply, with equal propriety, to the hundreds, if not thousands, of *Sermons* which are clustered in this Collection.

Of FOURTH OF JULY ORATIONS the variety is very large; and many specimens will be found which will add immeasurably to the joys of those local collectors whose interests are centered in whatever relates to some particular places.

Of the PUBLICATIONS BY, OR CONCERNING COLLEGES, there are many which will serve to complete files, which, hitherto, have almost defied completion. There is no subject, however, (unless it may be its Washingtoniana) which this Collection can more honestly boast of than its LINCOLNIANA and PUBLICATIONS CONCERNING SLAVERY AND THE WAR OF SECESSION—the former numbering more than a hundred and fifty distinct publications and the titles of the latter ranging, not including the unarranged works, from page 303 to page 357.

But we need not continue this survey of the thousands of works which constitute this Collection. Every book-buyer will examine the Catalogue for himself; and every one will measure the merit of the Collection by a standard of his own selection.

The Catalogue was made and carried through the Press by the owner of the Collection, after the regular business of the day had been closed; and it makes no pretension whatever to bibliographical erudition. It was made for use rather than for show; and, although it is not without errors, it is believed to be very well adapted for the purpose for which it was prepared—the honest instruction of its readers concerning the character of the Collection.

The Books which are described in this Catalogue are generally in excellent condition; and they will be sold, at the time and place designated, without reserve.

The subject is now left in the hands of those whose tastes and opportunities shall lead them to attend this sale, with the assurance that what can be done, either by the owner of the Collection or by those who shall represent him, will be done to make the sale agreeable and satisfactory.

PREFATORY.

A time-honored custom demands a formal introduction of every volume to its readers; and, in deference to its requirements, this volume is thus presented to the collectors of books for their examination.

The Collection of Books of which it furnishes a brief description, is *not* offered as a "Private Library" which has been collected from every quarter of the world, at an enormous expense, for the especial use of its liberal owner, and is now offered for sale because of "the now more matured taste" or the "advanced views" of that gentleman; nor is it such a conglomerate "Private Library" as is too often exposed for sale, in the auction rooms, after it has failed to attract purchasers, in detail, on the shelves of the booksellers, by whom in concert it has been brought to the hammer, as a "Private Library" of choice books.

It is, in fact, nothing more nor less than a collection of Books which has been made by its owner during several years, for his own amusement, but not without an eye to pecuniary profit; and it is offered for sale simply because its owner is pleased to offer it, at the designated time and place, and without any pretensions on his part of unusual virtue of mushroom growth, or of regret at parting with these treasures of his hearth and home.

The Collection of Books of which this volume is a Catalogue, notwithstanding the peculiarities to which reference has been made, is an important one, and not without attractions to the intelligent book-buyer. As a collection of LOCAL HISTORIES; of the PUBLICATIONS of SOCIETIES; of BIOGRAPHIES; of works on the NORTH AMERICAN INDIANS; of WASHINGTONIANA; of ELECTION, THANKSGIVING and FAST-DAY SERMONS; of TRIALS; of EARLY NEW ENGLAND THEOLOGY; of CONTROVERSIAL TRACTS on Banking, Theology, Politics, Law, Medicine, Temperance, etc.; of FOURTH OF JULY ORATIONS; of COLLEGE PUBLICATIONS; of LINCOLNIANA; of works on the REBELLION and SLAVERY; of Sermons, etc., it may be said, truly, to have been surpassed in extent, variety, and value, by very few of even the most elaborately puffed "Private Libraries" of Nassau Street or the West.

Of the LOCAL HISTORIES, including Centennial Discourses cf Churches, Schools, Societies, etc., which it contains, not even a brief mention of them in detail can be made without encumbering this Note and tiring the reader. Every page is sprinkled with their titles, and every State, and, very often, every County of the several States, is represented in the list. The INDEX, at the close of the volume, refers to many, but not nearly to all of them; and the careful reader is respectfully referred to the numbers arranged in the order of States in that place.

Of the PUBLICATIONS OF SOCIETIES, the titles of which extend from page 147 to page 161, besides single specimens, scattered elsewhere through the Catalogue, under the names of their several authors and of their peculiar localities, the Collection is unusually complete and valuable, as those who have sought for such works will fully understand after having examined the Catalogue.

Of the BIOGRAPHIES, in which may be included, not only the ordinary volumes of Biography, but *Diaries*, *Journals*, *Personal Narratives*, *Funeral and Ordination Sermons*, *Trials*, and other works of similar character, the Collection is very large and very important, containing not only a great variety of those which are agreeable, but of those which are scandalous and depreciating in their tendencies.

Of the great variety of works on the NORTH AMERICAN INDIANS, embracing not only the more elaborate volumes of *Adair*, *McKenney*, *Catlin*, *Schoolcraft*, etc., but the numerous Personal Narratives, War Histories, Vocabularies, etc., especial mention cannot be made in detail; but an examination of the Index will indicate how numerous their titles are, and how important the Collection is to every collector of this class of historical literature.

The WASHINGTONIANA is described by its titles on pages 430–452; and even a passing glance will indicate the great variety and unusual importance of that portion of the Collection.

There are many other lines, however, scattered through the catalogue under the titles of their respective authors' names, which add to the interest of this specially attractive department; and those who are adding the works of this particular class to their libraries, will be repaid by a close examination of other portions of the Catalogue than that to which reference has been made.

The Election Sermons of Massachusetts extend with tolerable regularity, from 1720 until 1869, and those of Connecticut from 1766, with some deviation, to 1830; the Thanksgiving Sermons, extending from 1786 until a recent date, are various and desirable; and the Fast-Day Sermons range from 1753 until our own day.

Without claiming any notable degree of perfection in these departments, the works which they contain will serve an excellent purpose in making perfect many collections which are lacking in particular works.

The Trials number, among others, many of the most notable, including those of the British soldiers at Boston, Aaron Burr, Judge Blount, Joshua Hett Smith, Major André, Ephraim Wheeler, E. C. Delevan, Alexander Whistelo, Levi Weeks, Rev. John N. Maffit, John C. Colt, Bishops Doane and Onderdonk, Sir Henry Vane, the Forrest Case, William Hone, Doctor S. F. Jarvis, Horace Greeley, the Prophet Matthias, Alexander McLeod, the Parrish and Lawrence Will Cases, D. E. Sickles, Prof. Webster, Rev. William Parkinson, etc., and it will be seen that those who collect this class of works, will enjoy a rare opportunity for extending their collections at the sale of this.

Of Early New England Theology and History the specimens are quite numerous, and generally of great variety. Without naming all, the works of such men as John Checkley, John Cotton, Thomas Hooker, Cotton and Samuel Mather, Benjamin Colman, John Dunton, Thomas Prince, Nathanael Appleton, Thomas Sheppard, John Josselyn, John Davenport, Captain Thomas Wheeler, Roger Clap, etc., will be found in this Collection.

The Controversial Tracts are numbered by hundreds; and the particular subjects on which they treat are numerous and of every conceivable character; and the same remarks will apply, with equal propriety, to the hundreds, if not thousands, of *Sermons* which are clustered in this Collection.

Of Fourth of July Orations the variety is very large; and many specimens will be found which will add immeasurably to the joys of those local collectors whose interests are centered in whatever relates to some particular places.

Of the Publications by, or Concerning Colleges, there are many which will serve to complete files, which, hitherto, have almost defied completion. There is no subject, however, (unless it may be its Washingtoniana,) which this Collection can more honestly boast of than its LINCOLNIANA and PUBLICATIONS CONCERNING SLAVERY AND THE WAR OF SECESSION—the former numbering more than a hundred and fifty distinct publications, and the titles of the latter ranging, besides the unarranged works, from page 303 to page 357.

But we need not continue this survey of the thousands of works which constitute this Collection. Every book-buyer will examine the Catalogue for himself; and every one will measure the merit of the Collection by a standard of his own selection. A few, very few, whose "matured tastes" and "advanced views," either real or fictitious, serve to make them more ridiculous than reliable, will probably turn up their sweet faces in well imitated disgust, that there is nothing "unique" in this Collection; while others, not more numerous or more respectable, may sneer at the Catalogue, ridicule its homespun integrity of descriptions, and prophecy the effect of its author's sturdy disregard of the marketable bibliography which he has bravely permitted to hang before his eyes without touching it.

The Catalogue was made and carried through the Press by the owner of the Collection, after the regular business of the day had been closed; and it makes no pretension whatever to bibliographical erudition or the clap-trap of modern illiterate pretenders. It was made for use rather than for show; and, although it is not without errors, it is believed to be very well adapted for the purpose for which it was prepared—the honest instruction of its readers concerning the character of the Collection.

The Books which are described in this Catalogue are generally in excellent order and condition, although not always new and fresh copies; and they will be sold, at the time and place designated, without reserve, or the assistance of packed bidders, or the insolent impertinence of an amateur salesman.

The subject is now left in the hands of those whose tastes and opportunities shall lead them to attend this sale, with the assurance that what can be done, either by the owner of the Collection or by those who shall represent him on the stand, will be done to make the sale agreeable and satisfactory.

CONDITIONS OF SALE.

I. The highest Bidder to be the Buyer; and if any dispute arise between two or more Bidders, the Lots so disputed to be immediatety put up again and re-sold.

II. The Purchasers to give in their names and Places of Abode, with a sufficient Deposit, if required, in Part Payment of the Purchase-money; in Default of which the Lot or Lots so purchased shall be immediately put up again and re-sold.

III. The Lots to be paid for and taken away at the Buyer's Expense and Risk, within six days from the conclusion of the Sale, or settled for to the satisfaction of the Auctioneers on or before delivery; in default of which the Auctioneers will not hold themselves responsible, if the Lots be lost, stolen, damaged, or destroyed, but they will be left at the sole risk of the Purchaser.

IV. The sale of any Book or Books, or Lot of Pamphlets is not to be set aside on account of any Stained or Short leaves of Text or Plates, want of List of Plates, or on account of the Publication of any subsequent Volume, Supplement, Appendix, or Plates. All Magazines, Reviews, Books in Lots, Pamphlets in Lots or Volumes, described as being in any way imperfect, will be sold with all Faults, Imperfections, and Errors of Description. The sale of any lot of Prints or Drawings in Illustrated Books or otherwise, is not to be set aside on account of any error in the enumeration of the numbers stated, or for any error of description therein.

V. Upon failure of complying with the above Conditions, the money deposited in part Payment shall be forfeited; and all Lots left uncleared in conformity with these Conditions, may be re-sold by public or private Sale without further notice; and the Deficiency (if any) arising from such re-sale, shall be made good by the Defaulters at this Sale, together with all charges attending the same. The Condition is without prejudice to the right of the Auctioneers to enforce the contract made at this Sale, without such re-sale, if they think fit.

CATALOGUE.

CATALOGUE.

BADDON'S Steam Engine Calumny delineated ; to which is subjoined the Infernal Triumvirate oppression, depression and extortion. By a Lover of Mercy. 12*mo, sheep*. *Philadelphia*, 1817

2 ABINGTON, MASS. HISTORICAL SKETCH OF. By Aaron Hobart. 8*vo, cloth. With an appendix*. *Boston*, 1839

3 ACTON, MASS. An Address delivered at, July 21, 1835 ; being the first Centennial Anniversary of the Organization of that Town. With an Appendix.

In which the honors of the Concord Fight, claimed by some late publications, for Maj. Buttrick and other Officers, belonging to Concord, particularly so far as they are supposed to belong to the memory of Capt. Isaac Davis of Acton, are considered ; with some reasons why a proposed monument should not be placed over the *two* British soldiers who were buried in one grave at the north bridge ; and some notice of the agitated question as to the place where the first resistance was made ; accompanied by the testimony of two of the surviving members of Capt. Davis's Company, and of his surviving widow ; and a Map of the scene of the Concord Fight as it was at the time.

By Josiah Adams. 8*vo pamphlet*, 48 *pages, rough edges ; very scarce ; fine copy*. *Boston*, 1835

4 ACTON, ME. THE HISTORY OF. By Joseph Fullonton.

"This shall be written for the generation to come,"

Sm. 8*vo, paper cov.*, 36 *pages ; fine copy ; scarce*. *Dover, N.H.*, 1847

Contains its Geographical, Civil and Ecclesiastical History, and Biographical Sketches of its prominent men.

5 ADAIR, JAMES. (*Trader with the Indians and Resident in their Country for Forty Years.*) THE HISTORY OF THE AMERICAN INDIANS, particularly those Nations adjoining the Mississippi, East and West Florida, Georgia, South and North Carolina and Virginia : containing an Account of their Origin, Language, Manners, Religious and Civil Customs, Laws, Form of Govern-

ment, Punishments, Conduct in War and Domestic Life, etc., etc., sufficient to render it a Complete Indian System; with Observations on former Historians, etc. Also, an Appendix, containing a Description of the Floridas, etc. With a new Map of the Country. *4to, full polished mottled calf, gilt. Bound by W. Pratt. Clean, perfect copy; very rare. London*, MDCCLXXV.

"Adair was an English Trader who had certainly a most intimate knowledge of the Indians. The great object of his work appears to be to prove that the Aborigines of America are descended from the Jewish Race."

6 ADAMS, JOHN. A Selection of Patriotic Addresses to the President of the United States. With the President's Answers. *8vo, sheep; fine copy. Boston*, 1798

7 Adams, John Quincy. Poems of Religion and Society. With Notices of his Life and Character. By John Davis and T. H. Benton. *8vo, cl. Auburn*, 1850

8 Adams, J. T. The White Chief among the Red Men; or, Knight of the Golden Melice. *8vo, cl. New York*, 1859

9 Addison Co., Vt. Statistical and Historical Account of. By Samuel Swift. *8vo; fine copy; scarce. Middlebury*, 1859

10 "Admirari Nil." The Trollopiad; or, Travelling Gentleman in America. A Satire. *8vo, cl. New York*, 1837

11 ÆSOP. The Fables of. With a Life of the Author. Illustrated with One Hundred and Eleven Engravings, from Original Designs by Herrick. *8vo; sheets folded; tinted paper. New York, Hurd and Houghton*, 1865

12 African Meth. Epis. Church. Minutes of the General and Annual Conferences for 1839–40. *Sm. 8vo, 47 pages. Brooklyn*, 1840

13 AGASSIZ, LOUIS. Lake Superior: its Physical Character, Vegetation and Animals, compared with those of other and similar regions. With a Narrative of the Tour, by J. Elliott Cabot. And Contributions by other Scientific Gentlemen. *Elegantly illustrated; large 8vo, cl. Boston*, 1850

14 ALBACH, JAMES R. Annals of the West: embracing a concise account of principal events which have occurred in the Western States and Territories, from the Discovery of the Mississippi Valley to the year eighteen hundred and fifty. Compiled from the most authentic sources. *Large 8vo, sheep. St. Louis*, 1852

15 ALBACH, JAMES R. Annals of the West. *Pittsburgh*, 1856

16 Albany, N. Y. Random Recollections of, from 1800 to 1808. *8vo pamphlet, 57 pages; scarce; fine copy. Albany*, 1849

17 ALBANY, N. Y. Address before Young Men's Association, Feb. 7, 1854. By Wm. Kent. *8vo pamphlet. New York*, 1854

18 ALBANY. Annals of the Medical Society of the County of, from 1806–1851, with Biographical Sketches of Deceased Members. By Sylvester D. Willard. *8vo, cl. Albany*, 1864

19 Aldrich, Thomas Bailey. The Ballad of Babie Bell and other Poems. *Third edition. 12mo, cl. New York*, 1860

20 ALEXANDER, Archibald. Biographical Sketches of the Founder and Principal Alumni of the Log College (*Bucks Co., Pa.*)

Together with an Account of the Revivals of Religion under their Ministry. *12mo, cloth.* *Philadelphia,* [1851]

21 ALEXANDER, JOHN H., Memoir of. By William Pinkney. Read before the Maryland Historical Society, May 2, 1867. *8vo, 33 pages, uncut.* *Baltimore,* 1867

22 ALLEN, COL. ETHAN. MEMOIR OF, containing the most interesting Incidents connected with his Private and Public Career. By Hugh Moore. *12mo, cloth.* *Plattsburgh, N. Y.,* 1834

23 ALLEN, COL. ETHAN. ALLEN'S CAPTIVITY, being a Narrative of, containing his Voyages, Travels, etc. Written by himself. *With plate; 12mo, boards, frontispiece.* *Boston,* 1845

24 ALLEN, COL. ETHAN. A Narrative of the Captivity of. *8vo, boards; 4th edition, with notes.* *Burlington,* 1846

25 ALLEN, COL. ETHAN. Narrative of Capture of Ticonderoga. *Fifth edition; 8vo, uncut; fine copy.* *Burlington,* 1849

26 ALLEN, ETHAN. Who were the Early Settlers of Maryland? *8vo, pamphlet; 18 pages.* *Baltimore,* 1866

27 ALLEN, WILLIAM. WUNNISSOO, or the vale of Hoosatunnuk: A Poem with Notes. *Cloth, 12mo, Portrait of Dr. Allen.* *Boston,* 1856

28 ALLSTON, WASHINGTON. The Sylphs of the Season. With other Poems. *8vo, boards, uncut; scarce.* *Boston,* 1813

29 AMES, FISHER. American Principles. A Review of Works of, compiled by a number of his friends. *8vo pamphlet; uncut, 56 pages; very scarce.* *Boston,* 1809

30 AMERICA. Travels through the Interior Parts of, in a Series of Letters. By Thomas Anburey. *New edition, in two vols., with map and engravings; 8vo, sheep.* *London,* 1791

The author served under Gen. Burgoyne. This work gives the best account extant of the Campaign which ended at Saratoga, and the subsequent fortunes of the surrendered army.

31 AMERICA. AN HISTORICAL, GEOGRAPHICAL, COMMERCIAL AND PHILOSOPHICAL VIEW of the United States and of the European Settlements in America and the West Indies. By W. Winterbotham. *In four vols., 8vo, boards, uncut; portraits; beautiful copy.* *London,* 1795

32 AMERICA, THE ANNALS OF, from the Discovery by Columbus in the year 1492, to the year 1826. By Abiel Holmes. *Second edition. 2 vols. Full dark blue cr. lev. extra, gilt top, uncut. Bound by R. W. Smith.* *Cambridge,* 1829

A magnificent copy. Every leaf having been examined with the utmost care, and all imperfections removed. Clean and spotless.

33 AMERICA. THE ANNALS OF. *8vo, bds., uncut; in fine condition.*

34 AMERICA. TRAVELS IN. By George Fibbleton, Ex. Barber. *Cl. 12mo.* *New York,* 1833

35 AMERICA. Ancient History and Discovery of, before the Time of Columbus. By John B. Newman. *8vo pamphlet; 48 pages, uncut; very scarce.* *New York,* 1848

36 AMERICA, its Realities and Resources; comprising important details connected with the present Social, [etc.] State of the Country, its Laws and Customs, together with a Review of the Policy of the United States that led to the War of 1812, and

Peace of 1814, the "Right of Search," the Texas and Oregon questions, etc. By Francis Wyse. 3 *vols., 8vo, cloth, uncut.* *London,* 1846

37 AMERICA. Antiquities of. The First Inhabitants of Central America, and the Discovery of New England by the Northmen, Five Hundred Years before Columbus. By A. Davis. *8vo pamphlet,* 32 *pages; fine copy; scarce.* *Buffalo,* 1849

> "Thither came in times afar
> Stern Lochlin's sons of roving war;
> The Northmen trained to spoil and blood"—

38 AMERICA. The History of Ancient America, anterior to the time of Columbus: proving the identity of the Aborigines with the Tyrians and Israelites; and the introduction of Christianity into the Western Hemisphere by the Apostle St. Thomas. By Geo. Jones. *Third edition; royal* 8*vo, cloth; engraved title-page. Medallion of Count Joannes.* *London, etc.,* 1843

39 AMERICAN REVOLUTION, MEMOIRS OF THE, so far as it related to the States of North and South Carolina and Georgia. Compiled from the most authentic materials, the Author's personal knowledge of the various events, and including an epistolary correspondence on public affairs, with Civil and Military Officers of that period. By Wm. Moultrie. *In two volumes, portrait; 8vo, sheep.* *New York,* 1802

40 AMERICAN REVOLUTIONARY WAR. A MILITARY JOURNAL during the, from 1775 to 1783; Describing interesting events and Transactions of this period; with numerous Historical Facts and Anecdotes, from the original MSS. To which is added an Appendix, Containing Biographical Sketches of several General Officers. By James Thatcher. *8vo, sheep; second edition; fine copy, scarce.* *Boston,* 1827

41 AMERICAN NAVY. A Compilation of Biographical Sketches of Distinguished Officers of the American Navy, with other interesting matter. By Benj. Folsom. *8vo, boards, frontispiece.* *Newburyport,* 1814

42 AMERICAN SUNDAY SCHOOL UNION. Minutes of the Debate in the Legislature of Penn., on the Bill to Incorporate the American S. S. Union. *8vo, Pamphlet,* 25 *pages; curious and interesting.* *Phila.,* 1828

43 AMERICAN GEOGRAPHICAL and STATISTICAL SOCIETY BULLETIN. Vol. II. for 1856. *8vo, paper, uncut.* *New York,* 1857

44 AMERICAN INSTITUTE of N. Y. Eighth Annual Report. *8vo, cl., Portrait of James Tallmadge.* *Albany,* 1850

45 AMERICAN'S OFFERING. A Recitative Ode on Events of Revolutionary Times. Dedicated to the American People. By a Mechanic. In Five Cantos, with Historical Notes. *8vo.* *Philadelphia,* 1849

46 AMERICAN PHILOSOPHICAL SOCIETY, Phila. Transactions of the Historical and Literary Com. of. Containing an Account of the History, Manners and Customs of the Indian Nations who once inhabited Pennsylvania and the neighboring States. By John Heckwelder. *8vo, half mor.* *Phila.,* 1819

47 AMERICAN PIONEER. A MONTHLY PERIODICAL, devoted to the

objects of the Logan Historical Society: or to collecting and publishing sketches relative to the early settlement and successive improvement of the Country. *In Two Volumes, half cr. lev. mor., gilt top, rough edges.* *Cincinnati,* 1844

48 AMHERST, MASS. CHARITY INSTITUTION. I. Address delivered at the laying of the corner stone of. By Noah Webster. II. Sermon delivered on the same occasion. By Rev. Dan'l A. Clark. III. Brief account of the origin of the Institution. *8vo, orig. cov., 48 p., uncut; fine copy.* *Boston,* 1820

49 AMHERST, N. H. Historical Sketch of, from the First Settlement to the present time. By John Farmer. *8vo; fine copy; very scarce.* *Amherst,* 1816

50 ANACREON. Select Odes of, with Critical Annotations. To which are added Translations and Imitations of other Ancient Authors. By Rev. Hercules Younge. *8vo; sheets folded; frontis.* *London,* 1802

51 ANDOVER, MASS. HISTORY OF, from its settlement (1634) to 1829. By Abiel Abbot. *8vo, cloth, uncut.* *Andover,* 1829

52 ANDOVER, MASS. MEMORIAL OF the Semi-Centen. Celebration of the Founding of the Theological Seminary at. *8vo, cl.* *Andover,* 1859

53 ANDOVER THEOLOGICAL SEMINARY. Sermon delivered Sept. 22, 1818, at the Dedication of the New Edifice erected for the use of. By Ebenezer Porter. *8vo, orig. cov., 30 p. uncut; fine copy.* *Andover,* 1818

54 ANDRÉ, MAJOR. ORATION PRONOUNCED before the young men of Westchester County on the completion of a monument erected by them to the Captors of Major André at Tarrytown, Oct. 7, 1853. By Henry J. Raymond. *8vo pamphlet; rare.* *New York,* 1853

55 ANDRÉ, MAJOR JOHN. Minutes of a Court of Inquiry upon the case of. With accompanying Documents, published in 1780 by Order of Congress. With an additional appendix, containing copies of the papers found upon Maj. André when arrested, and other documents relating to the subject. *4to, orig. cov., rubric titles. With portrait.* 100 *copies printed.* *Albany, Munsell, N. Y.,* 1865

56 ANDRÉ, MAJOR JOHN. VINDICATION OF THE CAPTORS OF. By Egbert Benson. *8vo, half polished cf., rough edges. Extra Illustrations.* 200 *copies printed.* *New York, Joseph Sabin,* 1865

57 ANDRÉ, MAJ. JOHN. LIFE AND CAREER OF. By Winthrop Sargent. *8vo, cl. Portrait, map.* *Boston,* 1861

58 ANDRÉ, MAJOR JOHN. The Life and Career of, Adjutant-General of the British Army in America. By Winthrop Sargent. LARGE PAPER. 75 *copies printed.* *8vo, cl., uncut.* *Boston,* 1861

59 ANDROS TRACTS. BEING A COLLECTION OF PAMPHLETS AND OFFICIAL PAPERS issued during the period between the overthrow of the Andros Government and the establishment of the second charter of Mass. Reprinted from the Original Editions and Manuscripts. By W. H. Whitmore. 2 *vols., paper, uncut.*

THE PUBLICATIONS OF THE PRINCE SOC. Vols. I. and II.

With Votes upon the grant of the second charter. 150 *copies printed. Sm. p. Portrait.* *Boston,* 1860

60 ANDROS TRACTS. BEING A COLLECTION OF PAMPHLETS, ETC. LARGE PAPER. *Only* 20 *copies.*

61 ANNAPOLIS, ANNALS OF. Comprising Sundry Notices of that old City, from the period of the First Settlements in its vicinity in the year 1649, until the War of 1812 ; together with various incidents in the History of Maryland, derived from Early Records and Public Documents. With an Appendix, containing a number of Letters from Gen. Washington and other Distinguished Persons. By David Ridgely. 8*vo, in sheets, folded.* *Baltimore,* 1841

62 ANTHON, HENRY. "Parish Annals." A Sermon, giving Historical Notices of St. Mark's Church in the Bowery, New York (from A. D. 1795 to 1845), delivered May 4, 1845. 8*vo pamphlet.* *New York,* 1845

63 ANTRIM, N. H. History of the Town of, for a Period of one Century, from 1744 to 1844. By John M. Whiton. 8*vo, paper cov.,* 95 *pages ; fine copy ; scarce.* *Concord, N. H.,* 1852

64 APES, WILLIAM. The Experience of, a Native of the Forest. Written by himself. *Bds.,* 12*mo. Second Ed.* *New York,* 1831

65 APES, WILLIAM. Indian Nullification of the unconstitutional laws of Mass., relative to the Marshpee Tribe ; or, the pretended riot explained. 12*mo, cl. With plate.* *Boston,* 1835

66 APPLETON, SAMUEL. Memorial of. With Genealogical notices of some of his Descendants. By Isaac Appleton Jewett. *Roy.* 8*vo, cl. ; engravings.* *Boston,* 1850

67 ARIZONA, Terr. Its Resources and Prospects. By R. C. McCormick. 8*vo pamphlet.* *New York,* 1865

68 ARKANSA, TERRITORY. A JOURNAL OF TRAVELS IN, during the year 1819, with occasional observations on the manners of the Aborigines. With a map and other engravings. By Thomas Nuttall, F.L.S. 8*vo, bds., uncut ; very scarce ; fine copy.* *Philadelphia,* 1821

69 ASSOCIATION OF 1774. Printed by order of Gov. R. F. W. Allston. 8*vo pamphlet.* *Charleston, S. C.,* 1859

70 ATTLEBOROUGH, MASS. SKETCH OF THE HISTORY OF, from its settlement to the present time. By John Daggett. 8*vo, paper cov.,* 136 *p. ; fine copy ; very scarce.* *Dedham,* 1834

71 ATWATER, CALEB. REMARKS made on a Tour to Prairie Du Chien, thence to Washington in 1829. 12*mo, sheep.* *Columbus, O.,* 1831

72 AUBURN, N. Y. The History of St. Peter's Church. Sermon, March 29th, 1868. Being the last occasion of worship in the old church. By Rev. John Barnard. *Stiff covers ;* 80 *pages, square* 12*mo.* *Auburn,* 1868

73 AUDUBON, JOHN J. A Story of Meadville. August 28, 1824. *Boston,* 1846

74 AUSTIN, IVERS J. An Address delivered before the Corps of Cadets at West Point, June, 1842. 8*vo ; fine copy ;* 18 *pages.* *New York,* 1842

75 AUTOGRAPHS for Freedom. Compiled for "The Rochester Ladies' Anti-Slavery Society." *8vo, cl.* *Boston*, 1853

76 AYRES, J. A. LEGENDS OF MONTAUK, with an Historical Appendix. *Cl., 8vo ; scarce.* *New York*, 1849

PAMPHLETS.

77 Miscellaneous. [*Thirteen.*]

Africa, Southern. Narrative of Travels in the Interior. By J. Barrow. *London*, 1802

Andy's Trip to the West, with Life of its Hero. By Petroleum V. Nasby.

Abbey, Henry L. Ralph and other Poems. *New York*, 1866

Allan, William. Commemorative of. By Wm. B. Sprague. *Albany*, 1868

Austin, L. A. Memorial of Mary W. Wicker. Ticond., Aug. 26, 1865.

Aladdin. Letters on Monetary Science. *London*, 1848

Alexander, A. Discourse occasioned by Burning of Theatre in Richmond. *Phila.*, 1812

Addicks, Barbara, O. S., Mrs. Essay on Education. *New York*, 1837

Atticus. Few Considerations, in Relation to the Choice of President. 1822

Arbuckle, James. The Sabbatical Institute: an Oration, Oct. 28, 1828. *New York*, 1828

Account of the very Important Debate in the House of Commons, July 9, 1782, on the Question of American Independence. *2d Edition.* *London*, 1782

Authentic Copies of the Provisional and Preliminary Articles of Peace between Great Britain and the United States of America. *London*, 1783

Account of, and Directions for using Coal Tar and Varnish. *New York*, 1788

78 Miscellaneous. [*Thirteen.*]

Avery, David. Sermons on Nature and Evil of Professors of Religion not Bridling the Tongue. *Boston*, 1791

Andros (of Jersey Prison-Ship's fame). Sermon on Death of his Wife. *Providence*, 1798

Austin, David. A Prophetic Leaf. *New Haven*, 1798

——— ——— The Dawn of Day. *New Haven*, 1800

Andrews, John. Sermon at the Interment of Rev. Thomas Cary. *Newburyport*, 1808

Abercrombie, James. Two Sermons (National Fast). *Philadelphia*, 1812

Allen, Stephen. Observations on Penitentiary Discipline add. to William Roscoe. *New York*, 1827

Aladdin's Lamp. *New York*, 1833

Alleghany County, Address to the Citizens of. By E. Pentland. *Pittsburgh*, 1836

Abridgment of the Evidence on Bribery and Corruption in Parliament. *London*, 1837

Ayrault, Charles. Habits of Mind or Character. A Lecture. *Geneva*, 1839

Alien List returned to Court Martial in 1839.

Address, Pastoral, to Young Women, by Rector of St. Timothy's Church. *Philadelphia*, 1843

79 Miscellaneous. [*Thirteen.*]

Atkinson, Rev. Thos. Sermon in Reference to Catastrophe on U. S. Ship Princeton, Feb. 28, 1844. *Baltimore*, 1844

Alverson, Laban. Lectures by the Clairvoyant. Part I., No. I. *Ann Arbor*, 1847

Anglican Church. List of Printed Books. *London*, 1850

Andrews, Wm. W. Sermon preached in Kent, Conn., May 20, 1849. *New York*, 1851

Adshead, Joseph. On Juvenile Criminals' Reformatories. *Manchester*, 1856

Abbott, The Messrs. New Seminary for Young Ladies at No. 45 La Fayette Place. *New York*, 1843

Ackermann's Patent Movable Axles. Obs. on. *London*, 1819

Address to the People of Ohio on the Subject of the next Presidency. *Cincinnati*, 1824

Address to the Republicans and People of New York, Penn. and Virginia upon the state of Presidential Parties. *New York*, 1824

Advice to a certain Lord High Chancellor, etc., in which all the rules of modern practice are laid down. *Dublin*, 1792

Arkansas, Supreme Court of, Jan., 1859. No. 181.

Auburn Prison, N. Y. Letter from E. King and T. J. Wharton, with a Communication from the Agent of. *Harrisburg*, 1829

Ancient and Honorable Artillery Company, Disc. before. By T. Baldwin. *Boston*, 1807

80 Miscellaneous. [*Thirteen.*]

Alton Outrage. Discourse on, at Peacham, Vt., Dec. 17, 1837. By L. Worcester. *Concord, N. H.*, 1838

Australian. Adventures of Three Travellers in search of the marvellous, giving an account of the discovery, capture and semi-civilization of the wild Australian children. *New York*, 1864

An account of the Great Whig Festival held in the City of Baltimore, Nov. 12, 1835.

Algiers, a short account of, and its several wars against Spain, etc. Added, a copious Appendix. *Phila.*, 1794

Acadie. Proofs considered of the Early Settlement of, by the Dutch. By J. Watts De Peyster.

Auction System. Remarks on the. *New York*, 1831

Age of Credulity. Letter to Nathan B. Halhead. *Phila.*, 1796

Appeal to the Candid. No. II.

Ames, Mr. Speech of, April 28, 1796. *Boston*, 1798

Allyn, John. Election Sermon by. *Boston*, 1805

Abercrombie, James. Charge to Senior Class of Phila. *Philadelphia*, 1808

Address on Approaching Election of Pres. *New York*, 1800
" of Friends of Domestic Industry. Oct. 26. *Baltimore*, 1831

81 Adams, John. [*Sixteen.*]
——— Correspondence between Wm. Cunningham and ———, beginning in 1803, ending in 1812. *Boston*, 1828
——— Review of, etc. By T. Pickering. 2*d ed.* *Salem*, 1824
——— Correspondence between Adams and several citizens of Mass. 2*d ed.* *Boston*, 1829
——— and Lewis' Conduct. Report on the minority of the Committee on Manufactures. *Boston, Feb.* 28, 1833
——— Letters on the Militia, addressed to. *Boston*, 1823
——— Address at Charleston, on Death of. By Edward Everett. *Boston*, 1826
——— and Jefferson. Eulogy on the Character of. By J. L. Tillinghast. *Prov.*, 1826
——— Deeds and other Documents relating to the several pieces of Land presented to the Town of Quincy, together with a Catalogue of his Books. *Cambridge*, 1823
——— Review of the Correspondence between Adams and Wm. Cunningham, from 1803–'12. By T. Pickering. 1824
——— and Thos. Jefferson. The First Jubilee of Amer. Indep. and Tribute of Gratitude to. *Newark, N. J.*, 1826
——— and Jefferson, Disc. on Death of. Delivered by John Stanford. *New York*, 1826
——— Inadmissible Principles. *Boston*, 1809
——— and Thos. Jefferson. Oration in Com. of. By John Sergeant. *Phila.*, 1826
——— Corresp. between, and Saml. Adams. *Boston*, 1801
——— Corresp. concerning British Doc. of Impressment, *Baltimore*, 1809
——— The Political Reformer, and Strictures on Defence of the Const. of U. S. *Phila.*, 1797

82 ADAMS, JOHN QUINCY. ORATIONS, EULOGIES, ETC. [*Sixteen.*]
——— Sketch of life and services of. 1827
——— Eulogy on the life and char. of Jas. Munroe, Aug. 25, 1831
——— "Dermot MacMorrogh"; or, The Conquest of Ireland. 1832
——— Report on manufactures, Feb. 28, 1833. *Boston*, 1833
——— Oration on the life and char. of Lafayette, Dec. 31, 1834
——— Eulogy on James Madison. *Boston*, 1836
——— Oration 61st Anniv. of the Dec. of In., July 4, 1837.
——— Correspondence between Adams and several citizens of Mass. *Boston*, 1829
——— Address Norfolk County Temp. Soc. *Boston*, 1842
——— Lecture before the Franklin Lyceum. *Prov.*, 1842
——— Token of a nation's sorrow, Feb. 23, 1848.
——— Disc. on Death of. By J. Henry Allen. *Washington*, 1848
——— Disc. on Death of. By F. A. Farley. *Brooklyn*, 1848
——— Remarks and Criticisms on Adams' letter to Harrison Gray Otis. *Boston*, 1808

ADAMS. Verdict of condemnation on an appeal of H. G. Otis, for a decision of their controversy with. *New York, Feb.* 27, 1829
——— Speech of. *New York,* 1828

83 Adams, John Quincy. [*Seventeen.*]
——— Inauguration, at [his] installation as Boylston professor of rhetoric [etc.] at Harv. Coll. *Boston,* 1806
——— Address [on the] anniversary of Independence at Washington, July 4, 1821 *Cambridge,* 1821
——— Oration, [at] Quincy, July 4, 1831 *Boston,* 1831
——— Oration on the life of G. M. de Lafayette, Dec. 31, 1834. 12*mo* *Trenton,* 1835
——— The same. 8*vo* *Washington,* 1835
——— Jubilee of the constitution, a disc. before the N. Y. Hist. Soc., 30th of April, 1839 *New York,* 1839
——— Letters on the entered apprentice's oath *Boston,* 1833
——— Notice of Mr. Adam's eulogium on the life and character of James Monroe *Washington,* 1832
Disc. at interment of J. Q. Adams. By W. P. Lunt *Washington,* 1848
Letters and opinions of Masonic institutions. By J. Q. Adams *Cincinnati,* 1851
Oration on Life and Char. of Lafayette. By John Q. Adams *Boston,* 1835
Address, July 4, 1821. By John Q. Adams *Washington,* 1821
Remarks on Address deliv. July 4, 1821. By John Q. Adams *Baltimore,* 1821
Correspondence between John Q. Adams and Several Cit. of Mass. *Washington,* 1829

Adams, Chas. Francis. Pamphlets.
Reflections upon the Currency in the U. S. *Boston,* 1837
Address, July 4th, at Quincy *Boston,* 1869

84 Agricultural Society Pamphlets. [*Ten.*]
Berkshire Agric. Soc., Hist. of Rise, Progress, and Existing State of. By Elkanah Watson. *Valuable.* 1819
——— ——— Address. By Jesse Buel, Oct. 5, 1837. *Pittsfield*
Jefferson Co. Agric. Soc. (N. Y.) Authentic Documents relative to the Black River and St. Lawrence Countries. By Rich'd Burr *Philad.,* 1820
Massachusetts Agric. Soc. Nat. Hist. of the Slug Worm. By Wm. D. Peck. *Ptate.* *Boston,* 1799
——— ——— Inquiries by *Boston,* 1800
——— ——— Papers on Agriculture *Boston,* 1801
——— ——— do do do 1803
Agric. College, Consid. on estab. an, etc. *Albany,* 1819
——— Soc. Address deliv. at Brattleborough, Vt., by John A. Andrew *Boston,* 1866
Aquidneck Agric. Soc. Address. By J. P. Hall, Sept., 21, 1854

85 Albany Pamphlets. [*Fourteen.*]
Albany, Report by the Mayor to the common council of, upon Licences *Albany*, 1846
—— The Fancy Ball *Albany*, 1846
—— Report of the special committee to submit a plan for supplying the city with Water *Albany*, 1846
—— Bridge Question Speech. By Daniel E. Sickles, March, 1856
Albany Society. For promotion of useful arts. Address by S. R. Beck, Feb. 3, 1813. *Valuable* 5
—— Ladies' Society. For relief of distressed Women and Children. By Frederic Beasley, Jan. 10, 1808
—— Female Academy. Lecture by Alexander Watson, Apr. 2, 1845
—— Quarterly, Animadversions on the *Phila.*, 1833
—— —— Extra, on the Cholera
—— Young Men's Assoc. Address by Rev. E. D. Allen *Albany*, 1841
—— Academy. Celebration of Semi-Centen. Anniv., June 23, 1863
—— Recollections of. Address before the Young Men's Assoc. by Wm. Kent
—— Regency. Short appeal from the decrees of King Caucus and the Albany Regency *New York*, 1854
Albanian. Original Poems, with imitations of Horace. *Albany*

86 Almanacs. [*Fourteen*].
—— American Naval, for 1815, by J. Sharp *Phil.*
—— Gramer's Pittsburg Magazine, 1815, by J. Taylor *Pittsburg*
—— Franklin, for 1839, by C. F. Egelmann *Baltimore*
—— Nord-Amerikain, for 1849, by C. F. Egelmann *Phil.* 10
—— Poor Richard's, for 1851 *New York*
—— Angler's—Fisher's Vade Mecum—for 1851 *New York*, 1851
—— Scobies Canadian, for year 1851 *Toronto*
—— Uncle Sam's do 1852 *Phil.*
—— Blunt's Nautical do 1855 *N. Y.*
—— The Churchman's do 1835 *N. Y.*
—— Democrat's, do 1840 *N. Y.*
—— United States, by Robt. De Silver, for 1826
—— do do do do 1827
—— do do do do 1832

87 Amer. B'd of Com. for Foreign Missions. [*Ten.*]
1. Sermon. Ordination of Missionary to Asia. By L. Woods.
2. Sermon. By T. Dwight *Boston*, 1813
3. Report, Sept. 12–13, 1822 *Boston* 6
4. Instructions to Missionary for Sandwich Islands, 1823
5. Sermon. By Dr. Miller *Boston*, 1835
6. Letter in reply to a recent pamphlet. By Bishop Southgate *N. Y.*, 1845
7. Statis. hist. of contrib. past sixteen years. Sept., 1852
8. Annual Sermon before. By G. W. Bethune. Oct., 1856

9. Historical Sketch of Missions *New York,* 1861
10. Sermon before. By J. P. Thompson *Boston,* 1867

88 American Institute of N. Y. [*Sixteen.*]

——— Address deliv. before the. Oct. 14, 1831. Edward Everett.
——— do do Oct. 17, 1833. J. P. Kennedy.
——— do do Apr. 14, 1841. Henry Colman.
——— do do Oct., 1843. James Tallmadge.
——— do do Oct. 20, 1848 do
——— Lecture on the origin of varieties in Animals and Plants. Apr. 21, 1857. By Dr. Waterbury
——— Address on the Smithsonian Institute. By William Barlow *New York,* 1847
——— Address. Oct. 9, 1834. Baldwin
——— do Jan. 8, 1835. Wakeman
——— do Oct. 19, 1837. Dewey
——— do Oct. 15, 1840. Mason
——— do Oct. 21, 1841. Choules.
——— do Oct. 26, 1841. Tallmadge
——— do Oct. 20, 1842. Colby
——— do Oct. 20, 1843. Barnard
——— do Jan. 7, 1845. Mapes

89 American Institute. [*Sixteen.*]

——— Address. Oct. 24, 1845. Tallmadge
——— do Oct. 6, 1846. Westervelt
——— do Oct. 23, 1846. Chandler
——— do Feb. 10, 1847. Barlow
——— do Sept. 6, 1847. Burchard
——— do Oct. 11, 1849. Woodbury
——— do Oct. 20, 1853. Seward
——— do Oct. 25, 1855. Marsh
——— do July 4, 1828. Western
——— do Oct. 7, 1845. Mapes
——— do Oct. 18, 1844. Stuart
——— do of Gen. James Tallmadge at Twentieth Annual Fair of the *N. Y.* 1847
——— do by Edward Everett, Oct. 14, 1831. 50 p.
——— do by J. H. Griscom, Dec. 30, 1844
——— do by Wm. Sullivan *Boston,* 1833
——— Documents on Manufacture of Silk *N. Y.,* 1845

90 *Twenty-one Pamphlets.*

American Temperance Union, Report of. *New York,* 1844
——— ——— Appeal to Public. *New York,* 1853
——— Temperance Society Address and Eighth report. 1835
——— Museum, for August, 1787. *Uncut.* *Phila.*
——— Magazine, for January, 1788. *Uncut.* *New York.*
——— ——— conducted by H. G. Spofford. Vol. 1. Nos. 2–12, 1815.
——— Educational Monthly, for Jan., 1868. *New York*
——— Education Society. Examination of the strictures upon, in the Biblical Repertory. By M. Stuart. 1829
——— Mental Picnic, Sept. 21st, 1839. *Uncut.* *New York*
——— Home Miss. Soc. Sermon, May, 1849. *New York*

American, Bible Union, 4th Annual report, Oct. 6th, 1855. *New York*

——— Tract Society. Responsibilities of the publishing committee, Feb., 1858.

——— Baptist Pub. Soc. 25th Annual Report, 1859

——— Christian Expositor. Vol. II. No. 12. April 1, 1833

——— Quarterly Register, Feb. 1841. *Boston*, 1841

——— Historical Society, Discourses before. By the Hon. Lewis Cass. Jan. 30th, 1836. *Washington*, 1836

——— Institute of Instruction, Lecture on moral education before. By Jacob Abbott. *Boston*, 1831

——— Sunday School Union, 20th Annual Report, May 21, 1844. *Phila.*, 1844

——— Union, Report of the executive committee, March 25, 1836. *Boston*, 1836

——— Academy of Fine Arts, Charter and By-laws. *New York*, 1817

——— Peace Society, Address by Charles Sumner. *Boston*, 1854

91 *Twelve Pamphlets.*

America, Dispute with, in a series of letters from a Cosmopolite to a clergyman. *London*, 1812

——— Treaty with French Indemnity.

——— (North), Memoir, Hist. and Polit. on the Northwest coast of, and the Adjacent Terr. By Robt. Greenhow. *Washington*, 1840

American Colonies, History of the issue of paper money in, Anterior to the Revolution. *(Scarce.)* *St. Louis*, 1851

America (Central), Memoir of an Eventful Expedition in, resulting in the discov. of the idolatrous city of Iximaya, and the possession of two remarkable Aztec children, etc., By J. J. Stevens. *New York*, 1850

America (U. S. of). The Commercial Conduct of considered, and the true interest thereof attempted to be shown by a citizen of N. Y. *Printed by S. & J. Loudon, New York*, 1786

America, (Central), Antiquities of, and Disc. of N. Eng. by the Northmen, Five Hundred yrs. before Columbus. By A. Davis. 9th ed. *Boston*, 1842

America. Exposition of the conduct of France towards. By Lewis Goldsmith. *New York*, 1810

America, (Spanish), and the U. S. ; or views of the actual commerce of the U. S. By a Merchant of Philadelphia. 1818

America, (South). Brief and correct Account of an Earthquake which happened in. *G. A. Gardner*, *Poughkeepsie*, 1820

American Character, European Delineation of, as contained in a letter of a Foreign Traveller in N. Y. to his Friend in London. *New York*, 1820

America, (U. S. of) and Eng. Being a reply to a criticism on Inchiquin's Letters. *New York, Jan.*, 1814

92 *Twelve Pamphlets.*

America, Lecture on the discovery of, by the Northmen. By A. Davis, 3d ed. *Rare.* *New York*, 1839

America. Antiquedades de Christoval Colon. *Habana.*
——— (Central), and transit between the ocean. By M. P. Sampson, April 1850. *New York*
——— Imminent Danger to Free Institution of U. S., through Foreign Immigration. *New York*, 1835
Americans. North, Freeman's address to. 1840
American Notes. Change for the. By an Amer. Lady. *New York*, 1843
——— Party, Principle and Objects of the. *New York*, 1855
——— Pulpit, Series of Sermons by Carlton Chase. *Boston*, 1831
America is not Free. By E. B. Runnell. *New York*, 1841
——— Oration on Prospects of Young Men of. *Boston*, 1818
American Bards. A satire. *Phila.*, 1820
America. Cursory view of Spanish Amer. By W. D. Anderson. *Georgetown, D. C.*, 1815

93 *Seven Pamphlets.* [*Splendid lot.*]
American Archeology, Observations on Aboriginal Monuments of Miss. Valley. By E. G. Squier. *Very scarce.* *New York*, 1847
America, Minutes of a Conspiracy against the Liberties of. *Philadelphia*, 1865
——— Disc. on the Tenth Century. By Charles C. Rafn. *Very scarce.* *New York*, 1838
American dialogues of the dead, and dialogues of the American dead. *Philadelphia*, 1814
America. Antiquities of, the first inhabitants of Central Amer. and the discovery of New England, by the Northmen. Lectures by A. Davis. *New York*, 1847
——— Oration on the Discovery of, deliv. in London, Oct. 12, 1792. Containing also a description of the City of Washington. By E. Winchester. *London*, 1792
——— Descriptive Catalogue of those Maps, Charts and Surveys relating to, which are mentioned in Vol. III. of Hakluyt's great work. By J. G. Kohl. *Scarce.* *Washington*, 1857

94 Amherst College. [*Twelve.*]
Clark, Daniel A. Address before Alexandrian Soc. *Amherst*, 1827
Verplanck, Gulian. Disc. Aug. 27, 1834.
Everett, Edward. Address before Literary Soc. of, Aug. 25, 1836.
Cushing, Caleb. Oration before Literay Soc. of, Aug. 23, 1836
Stebbins, Rufus P. Address before Peace Soc. of, July 4, 1838
Humphrey, Heman. Disc. on Sixth Commandment, March, 11, 1838.
Barnes, Albert. Address "Choice of a Profession," Aug. 21, 1838.
Cheever, Geo. B. Address before Soc. on inquiry on Missions. *New York, Aug.*, 1843
Catalogue of Plants growing without Cultivation in the vicinity of Amherst Col. By E. Hitchcock, 1829.

Kellogg, E. H. Oration before Social Union Soc. of Amherst, 1836.

Oration delivered before Phi Beta Kappa. 1861

Humphrey, Heman. Address delivered at Boston, 1823.

95 Andover. [*Twelve.*]

Theo. Sem. Consti. and Associate Statutes. *Boston*, 1808

——— Outlines of study in Theo. By J. Murdoch. 1822

——— Disc. deliv. Aug. 17, 1823. By J. Murdoch. 1823

——— Lecture deliv. Sept. 2, 1823. By L. Woods. 1824

——— Disc. deliv. Sept. 5, 1843. By I. Lewis. 1843

——— Sermon deliv. Sept. 28, 1808. By E. Pearson. 1808

——— Address deliv. Sept. 11, 1832. By T. H. Skinner. *Boston*, 1832

——— Address deliv. Sept. 21, 1824. By J. Edwards.

——— Disc. deliv. 1830. By Edw. U. Hooker.

——— Sermon at inaug. of Rev. E. Porter. By A. Holmes *Boston*, 1812

——— Poem, before the Porter Hist. Soc. of. By R. H. Dana. *Boston*, 1829

Andover Association, serious call to Family religion. *Cambridge*, 1802

BACON, E. Recollections of Fifty Years Since; with glances at the present aspects and future portents of the age and times. A Lecture delivered in Utica, Feb. 2, 1843. *8vo pamphlet, 43 p.; scarce.* *Utica*, 1843

97 Bailey, Isaac. American Naval Biography. *12mo, sheep.* *Providence*, 1815

98 Balance, and Columbian Repository. *Four volumes.* 1802–3–4–5. *Half cf., 4to.* *Hudson*, 1802

Edited by Harry Croswell. Contains an account of the death of Alex. Hamilton.

99 BALDWIN, EBENEZER. "The Duty of Rejoicing under Calamities and Afflictions." Considered and Improved in a Sermon at Danbury, Nov. 16, 1775, a day set apart for Thanksgiving in the Colony of Conn. *8vo pamphlet; very rare.* *New York*, 1776

100 BALDWIN, SIMEON. Oration pronounced before the Citizens of New Haven, July 4, 1778, in commemoration of the Declaration of Independence and Establishment of the Constitution of the United States of America. *New Haven*, 1788

101 BALTIMORE. Report of the Committee of Grievances and Courts of Justice of the House of Delegates of Maryland, on the Subject of the recent Mobs and Riots in the City of Baltimore, together with the Depositions taken before the Committee. *Very scarce; 8vo, unbound, uncut.* *Annapolis, printed by Jonas Green*, 1813

102 BALTIMORE. A Complete View of. With a Statistical Sketch of all the commercial, manufacturing, etc., institutions and establishments in the same and in its vicinity for fifteen miles around. To which is added a Detailed Statement of an Excursion on the Baltimore and Ohio Rail Road to the Point of Rocks, etc., and an Advertising Directory. By Charles Varle. *12mo, red mor.; map and engravings.* *Baltimore*, 1833

103 BALTIMORE, Annals of. By Thomas W. Griffith. *8vo; sheets folded.* *Baltimore*, 1824

104 BANCROFT, AARON. The Nature and Worth of Christian Liberty. Illustrated in a Sermon delivered before the Second Cong. Church and Soc. in Worcester, June 23, 1816. With an

Appendix, containing strictures on the attempt to establish consociation in Mass. *8vo, orig. cov., 35 p.; fine copy; very scarce.* *Worcester*, 1816

105 BARBER, J. WAR LETTERS of a Disbanded Volunteer. Embracing his experiences as Honest Old Abe's bosom Friend and unofficial adviser. *12mo, bds., uncut.* *New York*, 1864

106 BARCLAY, SIDNEY. Personal Recollections of the American Revolution. A Private Journal. Prepared from Authentic Domestic Records. Together with Reminiscences of Washington and Lafayette. *12mo, cl.* *New York*, 1869

107 BARD, SAMUEL A. Waikna; or, Adventures on the Mosquito Shore. With sixty illustrations. *8vo, half crim. cr., lev. mor., gilt. Bound by R. W. Smith.* *New York*, 1855

108 BARLOW, JOEL. THE COLUMBIAD, a Poem. *2 vols. 12mo, sheep.* *Philadelphia*, 1809

109 BATH, N. H. Address delivered to the inhabitants of, on the 23d of Jan. 1854, being the Fiftieth Anniversary of the author's first preaching in the Town. By Rev. David Sutherland. With an Historical Appendix by Thomas Boutelle. *8vo Pamphlet, 135 p.; scarce.* *Boston*, 1855

110 BARTLETT, JOSEPH T. An Oration written for the Youth's Celebration in the City of Bangor, July 4, 1840, and delivered by him. *8vo; fine copy; 12 pages; very scarce.* *Bangor*, 1840

Written and delivered by one of the "Youth."

111 BARTLETT, JOHN RUSSELL. THE PROGRESS OF ETHNOLOGY. An account of recent Archæological, Philosophical and Geographical Researches in various parts of the Globe tending to elucidate the Physical History of Man. *8vo, paper, uncut.* *New York*, 1847

112 BARTLETT, JOHN RUSSELL. THE LITERATURE OF THE REBELLION. A Catalogue of books and pamphlets relating to the Civil War in the United States, and on subjects growing out of that event; together with works on American Slavery, and Essays from Reviews and Magazines on the same subjects. 250 *copies in roy. 8vo, half mor., gilt top, rough edges.* *Boston*, 1866

113 BARTON, W. S.. Epitaphs from the Cemetery on Worcester Common, with occasional notes and references, and an Index. *8vo pamphlet, 36 pages.* *Worcester*, 1848

"Reader,
Keep Death and Judgment
Always in your eye,
Non's fitt to live,
But who is fitt to die."

114 BARTON, JAMES L. Address on the Early Reminiscences of Western New York, and the Lake Region of Country. Delivered before the Young Men's Assoc. of Buffalo. *8vo pamphlet.* *Buffalo*, 1848

115 BAXTER, RICHARD. AN | ABRIDGMENT | of | Mr. Baxter's HISTORY | of his | LIFE and TIMES. | With an ACCOUNT of many | others of those *Worthy Ministers* who | were Ejected, after the Restauration | of King CHARLES the Second. | Con-

taining the Grounds of their *Non-Conformity*, etc. By Edmund Calamy. *8vo, orig. old binding; portrait of Baxter.* *London*, 1702

116 BAYLIES, FRANCIS. AN HISTORICAL MEMOIR of the Colony of New Plymouth, from the Flight of the Pilgrims into Holland in 1608, to the union of that Colony with Massachusetts in 1692. With some corrections, additions and a *copious index*. By Samuel G. Drake. 2 *vols.*, *8vo, in sheets. Maps and plates.* *Boston*, 1830. *Wiggins & Lunt*, 1866.

117 BAYLEY, PETER, Jun., Esq. Poems by. *Philadelphia, Pa.*, 1804

118 BAYLEY, REV. J. R. A BRIEF SKETCH of the History of The Catholic Church on the Island of New York. *8vo, cl.* *New York*, 1853

119 BEACH, SAMUEL B. Escalala; an American Tale. *12mo, bds. uncut.* *Utica, N. Y.* 1824

120 BEARDSLEY, LEVI. REMINISCENCES; Personal and other Incidents, Early Settlement of Otsego County; Notices and Anecdotes of public men; judicial, legal and legislative matters; field sports; dissertations and discussions. *Portrait; 8vo, cl.* *New York*, 1852

121 BECKWOURTH, JAMES P. LIFE OF, Mountaineer, Scout and Pioneer and Chief of the Crow Nation of Indians. *With illustrations.* Written from his own dictation, by T. D. Bonner. *12mo, cl.* *New York*, 1858

122 BEDFORD, N. H.—An Address delivered at, on the One Hundreth Anniversary of the Incorporation of the Town, May 19th, 1850. *Paper covers*, 45 *pages; scarce.* *Boston*, 1850

123 BEDFORD, N. H. HISTORY OF, being statistics compiled on the occasion of the One Hundredth Anniv. of the incorporation of the Town, May 19th, 1850. *Cl. 8vo; map.* *Boston*, 1851

124 BEESON, JOHN. A PLEA FOR THE INDIANS, with facts and features of the late war in Oregon. *12mo, paper cover.* *New York*, 1858

125 BELCHERTOWN, MASS. HISTORICAL SKETCHES OF THE CONGREGATIONAL CHURCH, from its organization, 114 years, with notices of the Pastors and Officers and list of Communicants chronologically arranged, tracing Genealogies, Inter-marriages and Family Relatives,—also, embracing numerous facts and incidents relating to the first settlers, and Early history of the Place. By Hon. Mark Doolittle. *8vo, cl., port.* *Northampton*, 1852

126 BELDEN, L. W. An Account of Jane C. Rider, the Springfield Somnambulist. The Substance of which was delivered as a Lecture before the Springfield Lyceum, Jan. 22, 1834. *12mo, cl.* *Springfield*, 1834

127 BELFAST, ME. HISTORY OF, with introductory remarks on Acadia. By William White. *12mo, bds. Very rare.* *Belfast*, 1827

128 BELKNAP, JEREMY. AMERICAN BIOGRAPHY; or, an Historical account of those Persons who have been distinguished in America as Adventurers, Statesmen, Philosophers, Divines, Warriors Authors and other remarkable characters, comprehending a recital

of Events connected with their Lives and actions. 2 *vols.* 8*vo, sheep.*
Printed at Boston by Isaiah Thomas and Ebenezer T. Andrews. Faust's Statue, No. 45 *Newbury Street.* 1794 and 1798

129 BELKNAP, Jeremy. The Foresters ; an American Tale, being a sequel to the History of John Bull, the Clothier. 16*mo, full-crushed, dk. blue lev. mor. gt. By R. M. Smith.* *Exeter, N.H.* 1831

130 Belville, Jacob. Address at the Inauguration of the Hatborough Monument, Commemorating the Battle of the Crooked Billet, Dec. 5, 1861. 8*vo pamphlet,* 12 *pp. very scarce ; fine copy.* *Doylestown, Pa.,* 1862

131 BENNINGTON, Vt. Memorials of a Century, embracing a record of Individuals and Events chiefly in the Early History of Bennington, Vt. and its first Church. By Isaac Jennings. 8*vo, cloth ; maps and plates.* *Boston,* 1869

132 BERKSHIRE Co., Mass. A History of, in two Parts. The First, being a General View of the County ; the second, an account of the several Towns. By Gentlemen in the County, etc., 8*vo, sh., scarce ; maps, etc. fine copy.* *Pittsfield,* 1829

133 BERKSHIRE Co., JUBILEE. Celebrated at Pittsfield, Mass., Aug. 22nd and 23rd, 1844. 8*vo, plates.* *Albany,* 1845

134 BERGEN, N. J. Annals of the Classis of the Reformed Dutch Church, and of the Churches under its care, including the Civil History of the Ancient Township of Bergen. By Benjamin C. Taylor. 12*mo, cl., plates.* *New York,* [1857]

135 BEVERLY, Mass. History of, Civil and Ecclesiastical, from its settlement in 1630, to 1842. By Edwin M. Stone. 12*mo, bds. uncut ; with plates.* *Boston,* 1843

136 Beverley, Mass. An Address delivered in the First Parish, Oct. 2, 1867, on the Two Hundredth Anniversary of its Formation. By Christopher T. Thayer. 8*vo pamphlet,* 79 *p., fine copy* *Boston,* 1868

137 BIBB, HENRY. Narrative of the Life and Adventures of, an American Slave, written by himself. With an Introduction by Lucius C. Matlack. 12*mo, cloth* *N. Y.,* 1849

138 BIBLE. (Mohawk Language.) Isaiah. Ne Kaghyadonghsera ne Royadadokenghdy ne Isaiah. 18*mo, cloth.* *New York,* 1839

139 BIBLIOTHECA AMERICANA NOVA. A Catalogue of Books relating principally to America, printed between the years 1500 and 1700. Parts I. and II. 8*vo, half mor., marbled edges* *London: O. Rich,* 1832

140 BIBLIOTHECA AMERICANA NOVA. A Catalogue of Books relating to America, in various languages, including Voyages to the Pacific and Round the World, and collections of Voyages and Travels, printed since the year 1700. *Vol. I.,* 1701–1800. 8*vo, half mor., marbled edges. London : O. Rich,* 1835. *Containing also Supplement and Index, with additions and corrections,* 1701–1800. *Part I.* *London,* 1841

141 BIBLIOTHECA AMERICANA NOVA. A Catalogue of Books relating to America, in various languages, including Voyages to the Pacific and Round the World, and collections of Voyages and

Travels, printed since the year 1700. *Vol. II.*, 1801–1844. *With Index. 8vo, half mor., marbled edges. London: Rich & Sons*, 1846

142 BIBLIOTHECA AMERICANA NOVA. A Catalogue of Books relating principally to America, printed between the years 1500 and 1700. *Parts I. and II. 8vo, paper, uncut*
London: O. Rich, 1832

143 BIBLIOTHECA AMERICANA NOVA. A CATALOGUE OF BOOKS in various languages, relating to America, printed since the year 1700. *8vo, cloth. Vol. I.*, 1701–1800. *London: O. Rich*, 1835. *With Supplement and Index, containing additions and corrections. Part I.*, 1701–1800, *inclusive* *London*, 1841

144 BIBLIOTHECA AMERICANA NOVA. A CATALOGUE OF BOOKS RELATING TO AMERICA, in various languages, including Voyages to the Pacific and Round the World, and collections of Voyages and Travels, printed since the year 1700. *Vol. II.*, 1801–1844. *8vo, cloth. With Index* *London: Rich & Sons*, 1846

145 BIDWELL, BARNABAS. Oration on the Death of Roger Newton, Junior, Tutor in Yale College. *8vo pamphlet* *New Haven*, 1789

146 BILLERICA, MASS. AN HISTORICAL MEMOIR OF. Containing Notices of the Principal Events in the Civil and Ecclesiastical Affairs of the Town, from its Settlement to 1816. By John Farmer. *8vo pamphlet. Pr. Title cov., uncut ;* 36 *pages ; beautiful copy of this extremely rare History* *Amherst, N. H.*, 1816
See Woodward's Catalogue.

147 BILLERICA, Mass. Celebration of the One Hundredth Anniversary of the Incorporation of. May 29, 1855. *8vo pamphlet*, 152 *p. ; scarce.* *Lowell*, 1855

148 BISHOP, CAPT. JOHN S. A Concise History of the War. *With map. 12mo, boards* *Indianapolis*, 1864

149 BLACK HAWK. LIFE OF MA-KA-TAI-ME-SHE-KIA-KIAK. Embracing the Tradition of his Nation—Indian Wars in which he has been engaged. With an Account of the Cause and History of the late War, his Surrender and Confinement at Jefferson Barracks, and Travels through the United States. Dictated by himself. *12mo, bds., front.* *Boston*, 1834

150 BLAND, COL. THEODORICK, JR. THE BLAND PAPERS : Being a Selection from the Manuscripts of. To which are prefixed an Introduction and a Memoir of Col. Bland. Edited by Charles Campbell. In Two Volumes. *8vo, half dk. blue cr. lev. mor., gilt top. Bound by R. W. Smith* *Petersburg*, 1840

151 BLATCHLY, C. C. The Pleasures of Contemplation and Causes of Popular Poverty. 8vo, *bds, uncut ; sheep* *Philadelphia*, 1817

152 BLENNERHASSETT, HARMAN ; The Life of. Comprising an authentic narrative of the Burr Expedition, and containing many additional facts not heretofore published. By William H. Safford. *12mo, cloth ; plates* *Chilicothe, O.*, 1850

153 BLOODGOOD, S. DE WITT. THE SEXAGENARY ; or, Reminiscences of the American Revolution. *8vo, half crim. lev. mor. ; gilt top ; edges rough* *Albany: Munsell*, 1866

154 BLOOMINGTON, MINN. TERR. ; Sketch of the Town of. By William Brewster. *12mo, paper ; map.* *St. Paul (M. T.)*, 1857

155 BLISS, GEORGE. An Address to the Members of the Bar of the

Counties of Hampshire, Franklin and Hampden, at Northampton (Mass.), Sept., 1826. *8vo, uncut ; pamphlet, 85 pages ; fine copy ; scarce* *Springfield*, 1827

156 BONAPARTE, CHARLES LUCIAN. The GENERA OF NORTH AMERICAN BIRDS, and a synopsis of the Species found within the United States. Extracted from the Annals of the Lyceum of Natural History of New York. *8vo, paper, uncut. New York*, 1828

157 BONNER, T. D. The Mountain Minstrel, containing a collection of Temperance Songs, Hymns and Glees suitable for all Total Abstinence Societies. Original and Selected. *12mo, paper* *Concord*, 1847

158 BOON, COL. DANIEL ; LIFE AND ADVENTURES OF. Comprising an account of his first excursion to Kentucky, in 1769, and of his various encounters with the Indians. Written by himself. To which is added a narrative of the most important incidents of his life, from the latter period until the period of his death. Annexed is an Eulogy on Col. Boon, by Lord Byron. *8vo, full dark blue lev. mor., gilt top, uncut ; bound by Bradstreet ; very scarce ; full length portrait of Col. Boon in Hunting Costume* *Providence*, 1824

159 BOONE, DANIEL. BIOGRAPHICAL MEMOIR OF, the First Settler of Kentucky, interspersed with Incidents in the Early Annals of the Country. By Timothy Flint. *12mo, calf.* *Cincinnati*, 1846

160 BOONE, COL. DANIEL. LIFE AND TIMES OF. Comprising History of the Early Settlement of Kentucky. By Cecil B. Hartley. To which is added Col. Boone's Autobiography complete. Illustrated. *8vo, half crim. lev. mor., gilt. Bound by R. W. Smith.* *Philadelphia*, 1860

161 BOONE, DANIEL. LIFE AND ADVENTURES OF, the First Settler of Kentucky, interspersed with Incidents in the Early Annals of the Country. By Timothy Flint. *New edition.* To which is added an account of Captain Estill's Defeat. *16mo. With portrait. In sheets, folded.* *Cincinnati*, 1868

162 BOQUET, COL. HENRY. *Historical Account of Boquet's Expedition*, against the Ohio Indians in 1764. With preface by Francis Parkman, and translation of Dumas' Biographical Sketch of General Boquet. *Gr. cl., 8vo, uncut ; maps, plates.* *Cincinnati*, 1868

163 BOSCAWEN, N. H. A CHRONOLOGICAL REGISTER OF, from the First Settlement of the Town to 1820. In Three Parts : Descriptive, Historical and Miscellaneous. By Ebenezer Price. *8vo. Printed Title Cov., uncut, 116 pages ; beautiful copy ; extremely scarce.* *Concord, N. H.*, 1823

164 BOSTON. FEMALE ASYLUM. A Discourse by Joseph Eckley, Sept. 24, 1802. *8vo, 22 pages.*

Discourse. By Samuel Parker, Sept 23, 1803. *8vo, 32 pages.*

Discourse. By William Emerson, Sept. 20, 1805. *8vo, 30 pages.*

Discourse. By Thos. Baldwin, Sept. 26, 1806. *8vo, 31 pages.*

Discourse. By Jedidiah Morse, Sept. 25, 1807. *8vo, 24 pages.*
5 pamphlets in fine order, and now scarce.
Boston, 1802–7

165 BOSTON. Orations delivered at the request of the Inhabitants of the Town of, to Commemorate the evening of the Fifth of March, 1770. Second edition. *8vo, half dk. blue cr. lev. mor., gilt top, rough edges. Bound by R. W. Smith.* *Boston*, 1807

166 BOSTON. Orations delivered at the request of the Inhabitants of the Town of, to Commemorate the evening of the Fifth of March, 1770, when a number of citizens were killed by a Party of British Troops quartered among them in a Time of Peace. *Second edition. 8vo, bds., uncut.* *Boston*, 1807

167 BOSTON. A Topographical and Historical Description of, from the First Settlement of the Town to the Present Period; with some account of its environs. By Charles Shaw. *8vo, plates, bds., uncut.* *Boston*, 1817

168 BOSTON and its Vicinity. Extracts from a Journal of Travels in North America. By Ali Bey. *8vo, bds., uncut.* *Boston*, 1818

169 Boston Prize Poems, and other specimens of Dramatic Poetry. *8vo, bds., uncut.* *Boston*, 1824

170 BOSTON. A History of, from its Origin to the Present Period; with some account of the environs. By Caleb H. Snow. *8vo, bds., uncut, engravings; beautiful copy; quite scarce.* *Boston*, 1825

171 Boston Mechanics' Institution. First Annual Report of, Jan. 7, 1828. With the Constitution and List of Members. *8vo; good copy; 24 pages; scarce.* *Boston*, 1828

172 BOSTON. Picture of ; or, the Citizens and strangers' guide to the metropolis of Massachusetts and its environs. By Abel Bowen. *12mo, bds. uncut.* *Boston*, 1829

173 Boston. An Address to the Citizens on the 17th of Sept., 1830, the close of Second Century from the first settlement of the City. By Josiah Quincy. *8vo pamphlet, uncut, 68 p.; beautiful copy; scarce; autograph of Quincy.* *Boston*, 1830

174 BOSTON. A Geography of, and the Adjacent Towns. With Historical Notes. By C. H. Snow. *12mo, bds., rough edges, maps, plates.* *Boston*, 1830

175 Boston. An Ode: pronounced before the inhabitants of, Sept. 17, 1830, at the Centennial Celebration of the Settlement of the City. By Chas. Sprague. *8vo pamphlet, uncut, 22 pages.* *Boston*, 1830

176 BOSTON. Geography of, and the adjacent Towns. With Historical Notes. By C. H. Snow, M.D. *With maps and plates. 12mo, bds. First edition.* *Boston*, 1830

177 BOSTON. History of the Old South Church. In Four Sermons, delivered May 9 and 16, 1830. Being the First and Second Sabbaths after the Completion of a Century, from the First Occupancy of the Present Meeting House. By Benjamin B. Wisner. *8vo, paper, uncut.* *Boston*, 1830

178 BOSTON. A History of King's Chapel. The First Episcopal Church in New England, comprising notices of the Introduction

of Episcopacy into the Northern Colonies. By F. W. P. Greenwood. *8vo, cl., uncut, plates ; fine copy.* *Boston*, 1833

179 Boston Morning Post. Selections from the Court Reports, originally published in the. Arranged and Revised by the Reporter of the Post. *Cl., 12mo ; good copy ; scarce.* *Boston*, 1837

180 BOSTON. A Trip to. In a Series of Letters to the Editor of the U. S. Gazette. By E. C. Wines. *8vo, cl.* *Boston*, 1838

181 BOSTON. Picture of ; or, the citizen's and stranger's guide to the metropolis of Massachusetts and its environs. To which is affixed the Annals of Boston. By Abel Bowen. *Embellished with engravings. Third edition. 12mo, morocco.* *Boston*, 1838

182 BOSTON FEMALE ASYLUM. Reminiscences of. *Printed, not published. 8vo, bds.* *Boston*, 1844

183 BOSTON. Notions. Being an authentic and concise account of that Village, from 1630 to 1847. By Nathaniel Dearborn. *8vo, cl., illustrated.* *Boston*, 1848

184 BOSTON. A Short Narrative of the Horrid Massacre in ; perpetrated in the evening of the Fifth Day of March, 1770, by Soldiers of the 29th Regiment, which with the 14th Regiment were then quartered there, with some observations on the state of things prior to that catastrophe. *8vo, cl, frontis. Printed by order of the Town of Boston*, 1770. *Re-Published, N. Y.*, 1849

185 BOSTON. History of the Siege of, and of the Battles of Lexington, Concord and Bunker Hill. Also an account of Bunker Hill Monument. With Illustrative Documents. By Richard Frothingham, jr. *Second Ed. roy. 8vo., half crim. lev. extra, gt. top, rough edges ; remarkably large and fine copy.* *Boston*, 1851

186 BOSTON. History of the Siege of, &c. *8vo, cl ; 1st Ed.* *Boston*, 1849

187 BOSTON. New Guide to the city of, and vicinity. By Abel Bowen. *12mo, cl ; engravings.* *Boston*, [1849]

188 BOSTON. History of the Siege of, and of the Battles of *Lexington, Concord*, and *Bunker Hill*, and also an account of the Bunker Hill Monument. With Illustrative Documents. By Richard Frothingham, jr. *8vo, cl* *Boston, Mass.*, 1849

189 BOSTON. Epitaphs from Copp's Hill Burial Ground. With notes. By Thomas Bridgman. *8vo, sheets folded ; front.* *Boston*, 1851

190 BOSTON. Reminiscences of, and guide through the city and environs. By Nath'l Dearborn. *12mo, cl. ; plates.* *Boston*, [1851]

191 BOSTON. Sketches of, Past and Present, and of some few places in its vicinity. *Cl., 12mo ; 120 engravings.* *Boston*, 1851

192 BOSTON ANTHENÆUM. The History of, with Biographical Notices of its Deceased Founders. By Josiah Quincy. *Roy. 8vo, cl.* *Cambridge*, 1851

193 BOSTON. History of the Second Church ; or, Old North in Boston. To which is added, A History of the New Brick Church. By Chandler Robbins. *With engravings, 8vo, cl.* *Boston*, 1852

194 BOSTON. Memorials of the Dead in Boston ; containing exact transcripts of inscriptions, on the sepulchral monuments in the King's Chapel Burial Ground, with copious historical and bio-

graphical notices of many of the early settlers of the metropolis of New England. By Thomas Bridgman. 12*mo*, *cl.* *Boston*, 1853

195 BOSTON COMMON. The Great Tree on. By G. C. Warren. 8*vo*, *cl. frontispiece.* *Boston*, 1855

196 BOSTON. Tri-Mountain; or, the early history of. 16*mo*, *cl.*, *wood cuts.* *Philadelphia*, [1855]

197 BOSTON. The Pilgrims of, and their descendants; with an introduction by Hon. Edward Everett; also, inscriptions from the monuments in the Granary Burial Ground, Tremont street. By Thomas Bridgman. 8*vo*, *cl; portraits; eng.* *New York*, MDCCCLVI.

198 BOSTON. Notices of Histories of. By Sigma. 8*vo pamphlet*, *uncut*; 7 *p.*, *dbl. col.* *Boston*, 1857

199 BOSTON AND SUBURBS. Lights in; or, Guide to the Strangers. By R. L. Midgley. 8*vo*, *cl; illlus.* *Boston*, 1857

200 BOSTON SIGHTS; or, Hand-Book for Visitors. By R. L. Midgley. 8*vo.*, *cl*; *engravings; map.* *Boston*, 1859

201 BOTSFORD. Mrs. M. "Viola;" Heiress of St. Valverde. An Original Romance. To which is annexed a variety of original Poetical Pieces. 24*mo*, *sh.* *Philadelphia*, 1829

202 BOUDINOT, ELIAS. A Star in the West; or, a Humble Attempt to Discover the Long Lost Ten Tribes of Israel. 8*vo*; *unbound; fine large copy.* *Trenton, N. J.*, 1816

203 BOUDINOT, ELIAS. A Star in the West; or, a Humble Attempt to Discover the Long Lost Ten Tribes of Israel, preparatory to their return to their beloved city, Jerusalem. 8*vo*; *half calf.* *Trenton, N. J.*, 1861

204 BOUQUET, HENRY. Historical Accounts of Bouquet's Expedition against the Ohio Indians, 1764. With Preface by Francis Parkman. And a Translation of Dumas' Biographical Sketch of General Bouquet. 8*vo*, *cl*; *maps and plates.* *Cincinnati, Robert Clark & Co.*, 1868
[Ohio Valley Historical Series.]

205 BOUTON, Nathaniel. Discourse preached on the 25th anniversary of his settlement over the First Cong. Church, and Soc. in Concord, N. H. 8*vo*, *orig. cov.*; 54 *p*; *valuable appendix; scarce.* *Concord*, 1850

206 Bower, John. Description of the Abbeys of Melrose and old Melrose. With their Traditions. 8*vo*; *third edition improved; boards; uncut.* *Edinburgh*, 1827

207 BOYLSTON, Mass. A Brief Historical Sketch of the Town of, from its first Settlement to the Present Time. By Matthew Davenport. 8*vo*, *paper cov.*, *uncut*, 28 *pages; fine copy; very scarce.* *Lancaster, Mass.*, 1831

208 Brackenridge, H. M. Journal of a Voyage up the River Missouri. *Second ed.* *Bds.*, *uncut; scarce in this condition.* *Baltimore*, 1816

209 BRACKENRIDGE, H. M. History of the late war between the United States and Great Britain; comprising a minute account of the various military and naval operations. *With plates.* 8*vo*, *sh.* *Philadelphia*, 1846

210 Braddon, M. E. Lady Audley's Secret! *8vo, wall paper covers. Confederate publication.* *Mobile,* 1864

211 Bradford, Mass. A Discourse delivered in East-Parish, Dec. 22, 1820, Two Hundred Years after the First Settlement in New England; containing a History of the Town. By Gardner B. Perry. *8vo pamphlet,* 72 *p.; fine copy; scarce.* *Haverhill,* 1821

Presentation copy to Hon. Wm. Lincoln from the Author, signed G. B. Perry, contains a lengthy Memoir of Rev. Z. and Thos. Symms.

212 BRADFORD, ALEXANDER W. American Antiquities and Researches into the Origin and History of the Red Race. *8vo, cl.* *New York,* 1841

213 BRADSTREET, ANNE. The Works of, in prose and verse. Ed. by John Harvard Ellis. *L. 8vo, cl., uncut. With plates.* 250 *copies printed. No.* 182. *Rubric title.* *Charleston, Mass.,* 1867

214 Brainard, John G. C. The Literary Remains of. With a Sketch of his Life. By J. G. Whittier. *8vo, bds., rough edges.* *Hartford,* 1832

215 Brainard, John G. C. Occasional Pieces of Poetry. 12*mo, bds., uncut.* *New York,* 1825

216 Branch, William, Jr. Life: a Poem, in three books. Dedicated to the social and political welfare of the *people* of the United States. *Half mor.,* 12*mo.* *Richmond,* 1819

217 BRANAGAN, THOMAS. A Preliminary Essay on the oppression of the Exiled Sons of Africa. Consisting of animadversions on the impolicy and barbarity of the deleterious commerce and subsequent slavery of the Human Species; also, a desultory Letter written to Napoleon Bonaparte, 1801. 16*mo. sheep, frontispiece; rare.* *Phil.,* 1804

Anti-Slavery Book. The Author was a Slave-Trader for many years.

218 BRIDGEWATER, Mass. History of the Early Settlement of, including an extensive Family Register. By Nahum Mitchell. *8vo, bds., uncut; very scarce in any condition.* *Boston,* 1840

219 Bridgewater, Mass. Celebration of the Two Hundredth Anniversary of the Incorporation of the Town, June 3, 1856, including the Address by Emory Washburn, etc. With an Appendix. *8vo pamphlet,* 167 *p.; beautiful copy; scarce.* *Boston,* 1856

220 Briggs, C. F. and Augustus Maverick. The Story of the Telegraph and History of the Grt. Atlantic Cable; a complete record of the Inception, Progress and Final Progress and Final Success, etc. 4*to, cl.; abundantly and beautifully illustrated.* *New York,* 1858

221 Brisbane, A. H. Ralphton; or, the Young Carolinian of 1776. 12*mo, bds.* *Charleston,* 1848

222 Bristol, R. I. An Account of the Settlement of the Town of, and of the Congregational Church therein; with the succession of Pastors, from its Origin to the present time. Together with the Act of Incorporation of the Catholic Congregational Society. *8vo, blue cov.,* 16 *pages; fine copy; very scarce.* *Providence: printed by Bennett Wheeler.* 1785

223 British Partizan. A Tale of the Olden Time. By a Lady of South Carolina. 16*mo, paper. Confederate publication.* *Macon, Ga.,* 1864

224 BRITISH POETS. The Aldine Edition. Comprising the works of

Chaucer, . . .	6 vols.	Dryden, ...	5 vols.
Pope, ...	3 vols.	Shakespeare, . .	1 vol.
Thomson, . . .	2 vols.	Burns, ...	3 vols.
Butler, ...	2 vols.	Wyatt, ...	1 vol.
Gray, ...	1 vol.	Young, ...	2 vols.
Churchill, . . .	2 vols.	Milton, ...	3 vols.
Swift, ...	3 vols.	Goldsmith, . . .	1 vol.
Spencer, ...	5 vols.	Beattie, ...	1 vol.
Prior, ...	2 vols.	Falconer, ...	1 vol.
Parnell, ...	1 vol.	White, ...	1 vol.
Earl of Surrey, . .	1 vol.	Cowper, ...	3 vols.
Collins, ...	1 vol.	Akenside, . . .	1 vol.

52 *vols., full pol., cf. gt. tops, rough edges. Bound by Bedford.* London: *Bell and Daldy, Fleet Street,* 1866.

225 Broadhead, John Romeyn, and Horatio Seymour. Addresses deliv. before Clinton Hall and Mercantile Library Association, at their Celebration, June 8, 1854. *8vo, orig. cov.,* 40 *p.; good copy.* *New York,* 1854

226 BROOK, BENJAMIN. The Lives of the Puritans; Containing a Biographical Account of those Divines who distinguished themselves in the cause of Religious Liberty, from the Reformation under Queen Elizabeth, to the act of uniformity, in 1662. 3 *vols. 8vo, bds., uncut; very rare and beautiful copy.* *London, Eng.,* 1813

227 Brooks, J. G. and Mary E. The Rivals of Este and other Poems. *12mo, bds., uncut.* *New York,* 1829

228 Brookfield, Mass. An Historical Discourse, delivered Nov. 27, 1828. By Joseph J. Foot. *8vo, uncut,* 64 *p.; fine copy; very scarce.* *Brookfield,* 1829

229 BROOKFIELD, Mass. Sermon, delivered by Rev. Dr. Snell, on the last Sabbath in June, 1838, which completed the Fortieth Year of His Ministry; containing a Brief History of, and especially of the Church and Parish of North Brookfield, from 1798 to the present time. *8vo, pamphlet.* *Brookfield,* 1838.

230 Brookfield, Mass. Mr. Foot's Historical Discourse; to which is annexed Capt. Wheeler's Narrative of Capt. Hutchinson's Expedition to Brookfield, the depopulation and burning of the Town by the Indians, &c., and additional notices of occurrences in the Town. *8vo pamphlet,* 96 *pages; fine copy; very scarce.* *West Brookfield,* 1843

231 Brookfield, Mass. A Sermon, preached on the last day of the year 1775; together with some Marginal Notes, giving an account of the first Settling of the Town in the year 1660; its Desolations by the Indians in Philip's War in 1675; its Distresses in Queen Anne's War; and its Increase and Improvements to the present time. By Nathan Fiske. *8vo, reprint from the Boston ed.* 1776. *West Brookfield,* 1860

232 Brookline, Mass. An Address at the Opening of the Town Hall, 14th Oct., 1845. By John Pierce. *8vo pamphlet;* 52 *p. scarce.* *Boston,* 1846

233 BROOKLYN, N. Y. First, Second, Third, Fourth, Fifth and Sixth Reports of the Commissioners of Prospect Park, Jan. 28, 1861, to Jan. 1866. 2 *vols. in paper, bal. in* 1 *vol., cl.* *Brooklyn*, 1861–66

234 BROOKLYN City, and King's County Record; a Budget of General Information. With a Map of the City, an Almanac, and an Appendix. 12*mo, bds.* *Brooklyn*, 1855

235 Brooks, Rev. C. Tornado of 1851, in Medford, West Cambridge and Waltham, Middlesex County, Mass. 12*mo, cl., portrait.* *Boston*, 1852

236 BROOME COUNTY, N. Y. History of, From 1806 to 1867. 8*vo, paper.* *Syracuse*, 1867

237 BROTHERHEAD, W. American Notes and Queries. Vol. 1. Nos. 1 to 4. 8*vo, paper; uncut,* 4 *parts, all published.* *Philadelphia, Pa.*, 1857

238 BROWN UNIVERSITY, A Catalogue of the Library of, with an Index of Subjects. 8*vo. cl.* *Providence*, 1843

239 BRUNSWICK, Me. Description of, In Letters by a Gentleman from S. C. *Uncut, pamphlet.* *Brunswick*, 1823

240 Brutus. Foreign Conspiracy against the United States. Originally published in the New York Observer. Revised and cor. with notes by the author. 12*mo, cl.* *New York and Boston*, 1835

241 Brown, Capt. Chas. H., Narrative of the Imprisonment and Escape of, from the Chilian Convicts. 12*mo, cloth, front.* *Boston*, 1854

242 Brownell, Howard. War Lyrics and other Poems. 8*vo, cl.* *Boston*, 1866

243 BUCHANAN, JAMES. Sketches of the History, Manners and Customs of the North American Indians, with a Plan for their Melioration. 2 *vols., bds. uncut.* *New York*, 1824

244 Budington, Wm. I. "Our Puritan Fathers our Glory." A Sermon preached in Commem. of the 220th Anniversary of the Founding of the First Church in Charlestown, Mass., Nov. 14, 1852. 8*vo, orig. cov.,* 32 *p.; clean copy.* *Charlestown*, 1852

245 Budington, Wm. I. Farewell Discourse, preached in the First Church, Charlestown, Mass., Sept. 17, 1854. 8*vo, orig. cov.,* 24 *p.; fine copy.* *Philadelphia*, 1854

246 Buell, Samuel. A Sermon preached at Brook-Haven, on Long Island, Oct. 23, 1754, at the Ordination of Mr. Benjamin Tallmadge, with a Discourse on Ordination; the Charge and Exhortation to the People. *Small* 4*to, rough edges, fine copy; rare.* *New York*, 1755

247 BUFFALO. First Unitarian Church of. Its History and Progress, Rev. Dr. Hosmer's Quarter Centennial Discourses, "The Parish, The Pulpit." An Account of the Quarter Centennial Celebration, Oct. 16, 1867. 8*vo cl. Printed for Private Circulation.* *Buffalo*, 1861

248 BUFFALO, An Authentic and Comprehensive History of, with some account of its early Inhabitants, both savage and civilized, comprising Historic notices of the six nations, or Iroquois Indians, including a sketch of the Life of Sir William Johnson,

and other prominent white men—long resident among the Senecas. Arranged in Chronological order, in 2 vols. 8vo. By William Ketchum. *Half Roxburghe, gilt top, rough edges.* *Buffalo*, 1864

249 Bulkeley, John and John Cummins. A voyage to the South Seas in the years 1740–1. Containing a faithful narrative of the Loss of his majesty's Ship the Wager, etc., etc., things not published in the first edition. *The Second Edition, with additions, 8vo, London, Printed. Philadelphia; Re-printed by James Chattin for the Author.* 1757.

250 BULLOCK, W. Sketch of a Journey through the Western States of No. America in 1827. With a description of Cincinnati. By B. Drake and E. D. Mansfield. *8vo, bds. uncut; maps.* *London*, 1827

251 BUNKER HILL; or, the Death of General Warren. An Historic Tragedy. In Five Acts. By John Burke. 44 *pages*, 12*mo, full cr. crim. lev. mor., rough edges; bound by Bradstreet.* *New York*, 1817

252 BUNKER HILL. Account of the Battle of. By H. Dearborn; with a letter to Maj. Gen. Dearborn repelling his unprovoked attack on the character of Maj. Gen. Israel Putnam. By Daniel Putnam. *8vo, pamphlet, fine copy, very rare.* *Boston*, 1818

253 BUNKER HILL, The Battle of; or, The Temple of Liberty. An Historic Poem in Four Cantos. By Richard Emmons. *Second Edition.* *8vo, bds.* *Boston*, 1841

254 BURGOYNE'S CAMPAIGN; an Original, Compiled and Corrected Account of, and the memorable Battle of Bemis's Heights, Sept. 19, and Oct. 7, 1777, from the most authentic sources of information, including many interesting incidents connected with the same, and a map of the battle-ground. By Charles Nielson, Esq. 12*mo, cl.* *Albany, N. Y.*, 1844

255 Burleigh, William Henry. Our Country; its Dangers and its Destiny. Pronounced before the Allegheny Lit. Soc., Sept. 2, 1841. 12*mo, cl.* *Allegheny, Pa.*, 1841

256 BURNET, JACOB. Notes on the Early Settlement of the North Western Territory. *8vo, cl.* *N. Y.*, 1847

257 BURR, AARON. A Full Statement of the Trial and Acquittal of. Containing all the Proceedings and Debates that took place before the Federal Court at Frankfort, Ken., Nov. 25, 1806. By John Wood. *8vo, half calf, uncut; extra illustrations and autograph of Burr.* *Alexandria*, 1807

258 BURT, JOHN. A Sermon Preached at Bristol, in the Colony of Rhode Island, October the 25th, 1759, upon a Thanksgiving, for the Reduction of Quebeck, the Capital of Canada, to the Crown of Great Britain, by an Army under the Command of his late Excellency, James Wolf, Esq., Major-General, etc. (who was slain in Battle) covered by a Fleet under the Command of Admiral Saunders. *8vo pamphlet, very rare, good copy in excellent condition. NewPort, Rhode Island: Printed by J. Franklin, at the Printing Office, near the Middle of the Parade,* (1759)

259 Burton, R. A Journey to Jerusalem, containing the Travels of Fourteen Englishmen, in 1667, to the Holy Land and other

memorable places noted in Scripture. To which is prefixed Memorable Remarks upon the Ancient and Modern State of the Jewish Nation. Together with a relation of the Great Council of the Jews in the Plains of Hungary, in 1650, to examine the Scriptures concerning Christ. By Samuel Burt, an English Gentleman there present. With an Account of the Wonderful Delusion of the Jews by a False Messiah at Smyrna, 1666. Collected by R. Burton. 12*mo*, *bds*. *Hartford: Printed by J. Babcock*, 1796

260 BURRILLVILLE, R. I. As it Was, and As it Is. By Horace A. Keach. 8*vo*, *cl.*, *scarce*. *Providence*, 1856

261 Butler, B. F., N. Y. "The Military Profession in the United States," etc. An Address delivered before the Cadets of West Point, June 19, 1839. 8*vo*, 46 *pages*, *fine copy*, *scarce*. *New York*, 1839

262 Butler, Caleb. "Truth and Character Vindicated"—being a Review of Hon. Caleb Butler's History of the Ecclesiastical Affairs of Pepperell. By a Committee of the Church in that Place. 8*vo pamphlet*, 49 *p.*, *scarce*. *Boston*, 1849

263 BUTLER, B. F. General Butler in New Orleans. History of the Administration of the Department of the Gulf in 1862; with an account of the Capture of New Orleans, and a Sketch of the Previous Career of the General, Civil and Military. By James Parton. 8*vo*, *cl.*, *portraits*. *New York, etc.*, 1864

264 Buxton, George Frederic. Life in the Far West. *Cl.*, 12*mo*. *New York*, 1849

265 BYRON, Lord. Journal of Correspondence and Conversations between Lord Byron and the Countess of Blessington. 8*vo*, *paper*, *uncut*. *Cincinnati*, 1851

PAMPHLETS.

266 Miscellaneous. [*Twelve.*]

Badger, A. G. Illustrated History of the Flute. *New York*, 1853

Bayley, T. H. Psyche, or Songs on Butterflies. *Malton, (Eng.)* 1828

Balmanno, Mrs. Poems by *London*, 1830

Banco; or, The Tenant of the Spring—a Legend of the White Sulphur. *Phila.*, 1839.

Banting, Wm. Letter on Corpulence. 2d ed. *London*, 1863

Bard, (a Country) Epistle to the General Convention. 1847

Baltimore, Pastoral Letter of the Archbishop of. *Baltimore*, 1855

——— Address at the Laying of the Corner-Stone of the City Hall, by J. H. B. Latrobe. 1867

Blanchard, Calvin. Hell on Earth. *N. Y.*, 1858

Branch, H. Stephen. Life of *N. Y.*, 1857

Brattleboro', 1848. Systematic Report of 392 Cases treated Hydropathically, by Drs. R. Wesselhoeft and Wm. Grau. *N. Y.*, 1849

Brantly, Rev. W. T. Total Abstinence from Intoxicating Liquors the Only Safeguard. *Phila.*, 1833

267 Miscellaneous. [*Twelve.*]

Bache, Prof. Alex. D. Eulogy on Hon. James A. Pearce. *Washington*, 1863

Badger, Henry C. Discourse on Death of George Livermore. *Cambridge*, 1865

Banyer, Miss, and Miss Jay. Funeral Sermon of, By Rev Samuel Cooke. *N. Y.*, 1857

Ballou, Hosea. Discourse at Ordination, by T. F. Fisk. *Phila.*, 1828

Baptizo, defined, and the mode of Baptism proved from Scripture. *Albany*, 1840

Baldwin, Thomas. Christian Baptism as delivered to Churches by Evangelists and Apostles. *Boston*, 1812

Balch, Wm. S. Lecture in review of Bishop Hughes' Catholic Chap. in Hist. of U. S. *N. Y.*, 1852

Barnes, Rev. Albert. Discourse, "The Throne of Iniquity." *Phila.*, 1852

Barry, William. Farewell Discourse before So. Cong. Soc. in Lowell, July 12, 1835.

Brady, Rev. John. Correspond. between Rev. Mr. Edelen and. *Wash. City*, 1819

Barnes, Albert. Address—"Choice of a Profession." *Amherst*, 1838

Barker, Jacob. Letters developing the Conspiracy, in 1826, for his Ruin.

268 Miscellaneous, [*Twelve.*]

Bank of the United States—Congress—House of Representatives, April 13, 1830.

——— Commissioners' Report to the General Assembly. *Hartford*, 1839.

Bankrupt Law of the United States. *N. Y.*. 1841

Bankruptcy. An act to establish a Uniform System of—through the United States. *N. Y.*, 1842

Bank Note Reporter—Autographical Counterfeit Detector—Companion to, by J. Thompson. *N. Y.*,1852

Barker, Jacob—ads. the People—Court of General Sessions, June 6, 1822.

——— Letters developing the Conspiracy formed, in 1826, for his Ruin.

——— Speeches of—and his Counsel on the Trial for Consp. *N. Y.*, 1827

Bathurst, Rt. Hon. Lord. Ruinous Tendency of Auctioneering. *N. Y.*, 1828

Barnum's Parnassus—Confidential Disclosures of Prize Com. on Jenny Lind Song. *N. Y.*, 1850

——— New Year's Address. *N. Y.*, 1851

——— Improvements for Preventing Steam Vessels from Sinking. *N. Y.*, 1859

269 Miscellaneous. *Valuable Lot.* [*Twelve.*]

Bailey, Appleton, R. Life of, and Narrative of his Adventures, Imprisonments, &c. *Rochester*, 1848

Baker, Rachel, Surprising Case of—who Prays and Preaches in her Sleep. By Charles Mais. *N. Y.*, 1814

Baldwin, Thomas. Sermon at Ordination of Rev. Wm. Collier. *Boston*, 1799

——— ——— Sermon at Installation of Rev. Elisha Williams. *Boston*, 1803

Bancroft, Aaron. Sermon delivered in Worcester, at end of Fifty Years of his Ministry. *Worcester*, 1836

——— George. Oration before the Democracy of Springfield, July 4, 1836.

Barnard, John. Zeal for Good Works Excited and Directed in a Sermon. *Boston*, 1742

——— Daniel D. Lecture on Character and Services of Jas. Madison. *Albany*, 1837.

Barton, Prof. Memoir concerning the Fascinating Faculty of Serpents. *Rare.* *Phila.*, 1814.

Blair, John. Essays on Sacrament, Regeneration and Grace. *Uncut.* *N. Y., printed by John Holt*, 1771.

Bradbury, Thomas. A Comparison between the Tribes of Issachar and Dan, in their regard for Civil Liberty. *Boston*, 1768

Bradley, Abraham. A New Theory of the Earth. *Very rare.* *Wilkesbarre, Penn.*, 1801.

270 Miscellaneous. *Valuable lot.* [*Eight.*]

Baltimore. The First Baron of. By E. B. D. Neill. 1869

Barnstable, Centennial Disc., by Palfrey, *Sept.*, 1839

Billerica Cent. Celeb., May 29, 1855. *Lowell*, 1855

Bridgewater. Bi-Cent. Celeb. June 3, 1856.

Brookfield. Sermon by Nathan Fisk, Dec. 31, 1775. *Very scarce.* *West Brookfield*, 1860

Brookline. Reminiscences of forty years, by Dr. Pierce. *Very scarce.* *Boston*, 1837

——— Jubilee Disc., by Dr. Pierce. *Boston*, 1847

271 Banking and Currency Pamphlets. [*Fourteen.*]

An impartial enquiry into the conduct of Gov. Lewis and of the Legislature in relation to the Merchants' Banks, with an appendix. By Politicus. *New York, Jan.* 1806

Considerations on the approaching dissolution of the U. S. Bank. By Jesse Atwater. *New Haven*, 1810

Letter to the Secretary of Treasury on the Commerce and Currency of U. S. By Aristides. *New York*, 1819

Letter to M. Sterling on the expediency of adopting a uniform system of Bankruptcy in U. S. *New York*, 1822

Caution to Banks and Merchants, and an appeal to the Public. *Philadelphia*, 1823

Observations on the state of the currency with suggestions for equalizing its value and reducing to uniformity the Banking system in the U. S. *Boston, Jan.* 1, 1829

Memorial of Reuben M. Whitney into the affairs of the Bank of the U. S. *Washington*, 1832

Short History of Paper Money and Banking in the U. S. By William M. George. 2d Ed. *New York*, 1835

What is a Monopoly? or, some considerations upon the subject of Corporations and Currency. *New York*, 1835

Jeremy Bentham and the Usury Law. *Albany*, 1837

Articles of association of the Stuyvesant Banking Company, April 18, 1388.

Answers to the questions: What constitutes Currency? What are the causes of unsteadiness of the currency? By H. C. Carey. *Philadelphia*, 1840

Defence of Francis W. Edmonds against the charges preferred against him by its President and Assistant Cashier. *N. Y.*, 1855

How to detect Counterfeit Bank Notes, &c. By George Peyton. *N. Y.*, 1856

272 Miscellaneous. *Valuable lot.* [*Eighteen.*]

Belchertown Election. Report of the Case of the. By David Everett. *Boston*, 1811

Bentham, Jeremy. Table of the Springs of Action. *London*, 1817

Breckinridge, John. Address before Eucleian and Philomathean Soc. *N. Y.*, 1836

Brent, John C. Letters on the National Insti., Smithsonian Legacy, Fine Arts &c. *Wash.*, 1844

Berkshire Jubilee. Sermon deliv. at Pittsfield, Aug. 22, 1844. By Mark Hopkins. *Albany*, 1845

Bedell, Rev. G. Thurston. Sermon in Ch. of Ascension, Dec. 14, 1851. *N. Y.*, 1852

Berg, Joseph F. Farewell Words to First Ger. Reformed Ch. *Philadelphia*, 1852

Beale Dr. Stephen T. Trial and Conviction of. *Philadelphia*, 1855

Beck, Theodric R. Eulogy on Life and Character of. By Frank H. Hamilton. *Albany*, 1856

Berkley. Proceedings of Eclesiastical Council in Town of. *Taunton*, 1831

Berkley. Strictures on Publication entitled, Proc. of the Ecclesiastical Council in.

Benjamin, W. S. Great Epidemic in New Berne and Vicinity. *New Berne*, 1865

Benjamin, Park. Poetry. A Satire pronounced before Mercantile Lib. Assoc., 22d Anniv. *N. Y.*, 1842

Bellamy, Joseph. A letter to. Concerning Qualifications for Christian Communion. *N. London*

——— ——— Blow at the Root of Refined Antinomianism, by. *N. Y.*, 1812

Bellows, Henry W. Discourse on the Death of Dr. Channing. *N. Y.*, 1842

Bellows, Henry W. The Leger and the Lexicon. Oration before Phi Beta Kappa Society of Harvard University. *Cambridge*, 1853

——— —— Historical Sketch of Col. Benjamin Bellows. *N. Y.*, 1855

273 Beecher Pamphlets. [*Eleven.*]

Beecher, Lyman. Sermon at Newark, during the session of Synod of New York and New Jersey, Oct. 1808. 2d ed. *N. Y.*, 1809

——— Same. 3d ed. *Boston*, 1813

——— Letters of the Rev. Dr. Beecher and Rev. Mr. Nettleton, on the "New measures" in conducting revivals of religion. *N. Y.*, 1828

——— The Remedy for Duelling. Sermon delivered before the Presbytery of L. I. *N. Y.*, *April* 16, 1806

——— Sermon delivered at New Haven on the 27th Oct. (second Ed.) *Andover*, 1814

——— Sermon at Funeral of Tapping Reeve. *Litchfield, Conn.*, 1827

——— Letters of, and Rev. Mr. Nettleton on the new measures in conducting revivals of religion. *N. Y.*, 1828

——— Sermon at Ordination of Mr. Sereno E. Dwight. *Andover*, 1818

——— Sermon at Ordination of Rev. Loammi J. Hoadly. 2d ed. *Boston*, 1824

——— Sermon deliv. at Newark, N. J., during Session of the Synod of N. Y. & N. J. 7th ed. *Boston*, 1827

Beecher, Henry Ward. Discourse deliv. at Plymouth Ch., Brooklyn, N. Y., on Thanksgiving Day, Nov. 25, 1847. *N. Y.*, 1848

274 Miscellaneous. *Valuable Lot.* [*Eighteen.*]

Bianco ; or, the Enchanted Sword, a Fairy Pantomime in Ten Tableaux. By Jerome Ravel. *N. Y.*, 1857

Bigelow Monument. Ceremonies at Dedication in Worcester, Mass., Apr. 19. *Boston*, 1861

Bigham, T. J. Argument of. In House of Representatives.

Bingham, Caleb. Astronomical and Geographical Catechism for use of Children. 15th ed. *Boston*, 1818

Billiard Player's Hand Book. *London*

Bibliographical Tracts. Number one. *Boston*, 1865

Birmingham Inspector. Jan. 25. 1817

Blith, Walter. The English Improver, or a new Survey of Husbandry. *London*, 1649

Bridgewater, North. History of. By Bradford Kingman. *Boston*, 1866

Brigham, John C. Discourse on Life and Services of. By Rev. Wm. Adams. *N. Y.*, 1863

Bright, John. Life of. By John McGilchrist. *N. Y.*, 1869

Brisbane Albert. Concise Exposition of the Doctrine of Association. 8th ed. *N. Y.*, 1844

British Aristocracy. Suppressed Facts; being Nobility Unveiled. *N. Y.*, 1843
Bristol Academy. Discourse on Education, deliv. at Dedication of. By Simon Doggett. *New Bedford*, 1797
——— College. The Laws of. 1834
Bishop, Abraham. Oration on Extent and Power of Political Delusion. *Albany*, 1801
——— ——— Oration on Extent and Power of Political Delusion. 2d ed. *Newark*, 1800
Biddle, Hon. Richard. Eulogy on Life and Char. of David Ritchie. *Pittsburgh*, 1847

/ 275 Bible Society Pamphlets. *No Duplicates; rare lot.* [*Seven.*]
Bible Society, Address and the constitution of the. The First Report of the Board of Managers, of Bible Soc. of New York. *N. Y.*, 1811
Bowen, Nath'l. Sermon before Bible Soc. of New York, March 1, 1812.
Sixth Report of the Board of Managers of. *N. Y.*, 1815
Hobart, John Henry. Address delivered before the Auxiliary Bible Soc. New York, March 8, 1816.
First Annual Report of the Managers of the Auxiliary, etc. *N. Y.*, 1817
How, Thos. T. Address deliv. before the Managers of the Auxiliary, etc. *N. Y.*, 1817
Second Annual Report of the Managers of the Auxiliary, etc. *N. Y.*, 1818

/ 276 Bible Society Pamphlets. *No Duplicates; rare lot.* [*Seven.*]
McVickar, John. Address deliv. before the Auxiliary, N. Y. Bible Soc. *N. Y.*, 1818
Eighth Annual Report of the managers of the Auxiliary N. Y. Bible Soc. *N. Y.*, 1824
Constitution of the Amer. Bible Soc. formed by a convention of delegates. New York, May, 1816.
First Annual Report of the Board of Managers of the American Bible Soc. May 8, 1817. With an appendix. *N. Y.*, 1817
Third Report of the Amer. Bible Soc. New York, May 13, 1819
Second Report of the Amer. Bible Soc. *New York*, 1830
Address of the Board of Managers of the Amer. Bible Society. *New York*, 1829

/ 277 Bible Society Pamphlets. *No Duplicates; rare lot.* [*Seven.*]
Report of the Marine Bible Soc. of N. Y. April 21, 1817.
Address to Seamen. Deliv. at Portland. By Edw. Payson. N. Y., Oct. 28, 1821.
Eighth Annual Report of the Managers of the Marine Bible Soc. New York, Apr. 19, 1824.
Bible and Common Prayer Book Soc. Sermon before. By Benj. Moore. *N. Y.*, 1810
——— Society. Address to the Auxiliary. By John Bristed. *N. Y.*, 1813

Bible Society. Portland Auxiliary, Maine. Adressed to Seamen. By Edward Payson. *Portland*, 1821

——— —— of University of Virginia. Address by Henry L. Pinckney. March 11, 1835. *Richmond*, 1835

278 Bible Society Pamphlets. *No Duplicates; rare lot.* [*Seven.*]

——— American. Reasons why distilled Spirits should be Banished from the Land. Address by Wm. Goodell. *N. Y.*, 1830

——— Annual Report of the Young Men's, New York, with Constitution. *N. Y.*, 1837 3

Bible Explained and Infidelity Vindicated. By a Lover of Truth. *N. Y.*, 1852

——— Great Discussion on Origin, Authority and Tendency of. Between Rev. J. F. Berg of Phila., and Joseph Barker of Ohio. *Boston*, 1854

——— Society of Co. of Greene, N. Y. Histor. Disc. at Semi-Cen. Anniv. By Rev. C. H. Rockwell. *N. Y.*, 1865

——— —— Second Annual Report of the N. Y. *N., Y.*, 1811

——— —— Fourth Annual Report of the N. Y. *N. Y.*, 1813

279 Bible Society Pamphlets. *No Duplicates; rare lot.* [*Seven.*]

——— Constitution of the Auxiliary, N. Y. Founded June 28, 1813. *N. Y.* 1813

——— Constitution of the Auxiliary, N. Y. Founded June 28, 1813. *N. Y.*, 1814

——— Portland Aux., Maine. Address to Seamen. By Edward Payson. *Portland*, 1821 /

Address of the N. J. Bible Soc. to the Public. With an appendix. *New Brunswick*, 1810

Sermon before Mass. Bible Soc. By Thos. Baldwin. Delivered June 4, 1812.

Communications relative to the Progress of Bible Soc. in the U. S. *Phila.*, 1813

Sermon deliv. at Concord before the Bible Soc., Mass. By Chas. Stearns. *Cambridge*, 1815

280 Bible Society Pamphlets. *No Duplicates; rare lot.* [*Seven.*]

Sermon deliv. at Newburyport, before the Merrimack Bible Soc. By Daniel Dana. July 27, 1815.

Sixth Report of the Bible Soc. of Phila. May 4, 1814.

Fifth Report of the Bible Soc. of Oneida. Utica, Jan. 17, 1816. 5

Sixth Annual Report of the Managers of the Orange Bible Soc. Goshen June 10, 1817.

Report of the directing committee of the Conn. Bible Society. *Hartford*, 1818

Fifteenth Report of the Bible Soc. of Phila. May 7, 1823.

Sermon before the Onondaga Bible Soc. Deliv. by C. Gold Lee. *Syracuse*, 1845

281 Miscellaneous. [*Ten.*]

Boylston, Thomas Esq. The Will of. Late of London. (*Scarce*) 5

Bollman, Erick. Plan of an improved system of Money Concerns of the Union. *Phila.*, 1816

Bonaparte, Napoleon. Remarks on Character of. *N. Y.*, 1831

Bogart, David S. Discourse in New Church in No. Hemp stead, Queens Co., Nov. 5, 1818. *N. Y.*, 1833

Brooke, Charles W. Reply to the Communication signed, D. H. Mulvany. *Norristown*, 1835

Bowen, Wm. W. Answer to the Exposition of Thomas H. Lewis. *New Orleans*, 1839

Bourn, Mehetabel H. Copy of a Communication made to Rev. John Dyer.

Boone, Bp. Wm. J. Memorial Sermon by Wm. B. Stevens. *Phila.*, 1865

Boone, Wm. J. Address in behalf of the China Mission. *N. Y.*, 1837

Bolles, James A. Valedictory Sermon preached in Trinity Ch. Ohio, July 31. *Boston*, 1859

282 Miscellaneous. [*Eleven.*]

Bolivar, Libertador Simon. Memorias Sobre La Vida. Parte II.

Boucher, J. Sydney. 39 Articles on Pew-Rents, Appropriation and Weekly Offertory. *London*, 1866

Boundary, No. Eastern. Reports and Resolves in Relation to. 1838

Boundaries, No. Eastern, and Eastern. History of the Negotiations in refer. to, of U. S. *N. Y.* 1841

Brown, J. Letter to Rev. Dr. Lowth. *Newcastle-upon-Tyne*, 1766

Brown, John. Translation of First Epistle of the Apostle Peter. *Edinburgh*, 1848

Brown, John. Suggestions on Heating a House. *N. Y.* 1867

Bowdoin College. Charter, etc., and By-Laws of the Overseers. *Brunswick*, 1850

Bowdoin College. Address before the Phi Beta Kappa Soc., by Wm. B. Sprague. *Albany*, 1850

Bowden, John. Letters to Rev. Ezra Stiles from. *Rare.* *New Haven*, 1788

Bowder, Metcalf. Treatise on Agriculture and Practical Husbandry. *Providence*, 1786

283 Boston Pamphlets. *Valuable lot, no duplicates.* [*Fifteen.*]

Sumner, Charles. "True Grandeur of Nations." An Oration, July 4, 1845.

——— ——— Remarks upon an Oration by. July 4, 1845.

——— ——— "True Grandeur of Nations." An Oration. July 4, 1845. Stereotype Edition.

Greenough, Wm. W. "The Conquering Republic." An Oration. July 4, 1849.

Celebration of the Introduction of the Water of Cochituate Lake into the City of Boston, Oct. 25, 1848.

Boston Soc. of Natural History. Act of Incorp, and Consti. and By-Laws, 1832.
—— List of Persons, Co-partnerships and Corporations, Taxed in the City of. For 1834.
—— City Document, No. 15. Annual Appropriations, 1843
—— Common. 1843.
—— Social Loiterings and Visits in the vicinity of. 1845
—— and Worcester, and Western Railroads, a Chart and Description of. By Wm. Guild, 1847.
—— Oration Deliv. before the Municipal Authorities of. Seventy-ninth Anniv. of Amer. Inde. By Rev. A. A. Miner. July 4, 1855.
—— Theological Seminary. Annual Report of. 1868.
—— Athenæum. List of Books added to the Library of the. 1868.
—— Young Men's Christian Union.

284 Boston Pamphlets. *Valuable lot, no duplicates.* [*Fourteen.*]
Boston. Oration before Muni. Autho. of. Ninety-third Anniv. Amer. Ind. By Ellis W. Morton. 1869.
—— Report of Com., in relation to Lands in the Back Bay. *Boston,* 1857
—— Thirty-first Annual Report of Fragment Soc. of. *Boston,* 1843
—— Remarks on Project of supplying the Inhab. of, with Pure Soft Water. By Henry B. Rogers. *Boston,* 1845
—— Report of a Railroad from, to Hudson River and Providence. *Boston,* 1829
—— Oration before the City Authorities, by T. Bigelow, July 4, 1853.
—— Oration before the City Authorities, by G. Sumner, July 4, 1859.
—— Oration before the City Authorities, by E. Everett, July 4, 1860.
—— Oration before the City Authorities, by S. Eliot, July 4, 1868.
Boston Epis. Char. Soc. Hist. Memoirs of, by J. Boyle. *Scarce.* 1840.
—— Chil. Aid Soc. First report of. 1865.
—— Numismatic Soc. Address by Dr. Lewis, Jan. 5, 1865.
—— City Hospital, Third Annual Report of. *Boston,* 1867
—— Present. of Statue of Alex. Hamilton, by Thos. Lee. *Boston,* 1865

285 Botanical Pamphlets. *Valuable lot.* [*Seven.*]
Marshall, Humphrey. "Arbustrum Americanum." The American Grove; or, an Alphabetical Catalogue of Forrest Trees and Shrubs, Natives of the Amer. U. S. *Scarce.* *Phila.,* 1785
Hosack, David. Facts relative to the Establishment and Progress of the Elgin Botanic Garden. *New York,* 1811
Hosack, David. Hortus Elginensis, Catalogue of Plants, Indi-

genous and Exotic, cultivated in the Elgin Botanic Garden. Plates. *New York*, 1811

Anderson, Andrew. Inaugural dissertation on the Eupatorium Perfoliatum of Linnæus. *Scarce.* *New York*, 1813

Patterson, Henry S. Address "The Character and Labors of Linnæus," before the Penn. Linnæan Assoc. *Gettysburg, Sept.* 20, 1848

Smyser, Daniel M. An Address deliv. before the Linnæan Assoc. of Penn College on "The Study of Nat. Hist." *Gettysburg, Sept.* 19, 1849

Celebration at Flushing, of the Birth-day of Linnæus, by the N. Y. Branch of the Linnæan Soc. of Paris. May, 1824. *Scarce.*

286 Brown University. [*Six.*]

Brown University. History and Laws of the Library. *Prov.*, 1843

Brown University. Disc. designed to explain the doctrines of atonement, by John Maxcy. Delivered Nov. 11–25, 1796.

Brown University. Catalogue of Books in the Library of. *Prov.*, 1826

Brown University. Address to the Phi Beta Kappa Soc. of. By Theron Metcalf, Sept. 5, 1832.

Brown University. Address to the Phi Beta Kappa Soc. of. By Wm. G. Goddard, Sept. 7, 1836.

Brown University. Poem on Pleasures and Advantages of True Religion, by Rev. Dan. Huntington. Deliv. before United Brothers Soc. in. *Prov.*, 1819

287 Miscellaneous. [*Sixteen.*]

Buchanan, Rev. Claudius. Memoir of the expediency of an Ecclesiastical Establishment for British India. *Cambridge*, 1811

Buchanan, Rev. Claudius. The Healing Waters of Bethsaida. *Boston*, 1812

Buchanan, Rev. Claudius. Christian Researches in Asia. 3d ed. *Edinburgh*, 1812

Buchanan, Rev. Claudius. Journal of Man. No. II., vol. III., May 31. *Cincinnati*, 1852

Buchanan, Rev. Claudius. Sermon for benefit of Soc. of Missions. *Newark*, 1809

Burlington College. Address on Seventy-eighth Anniv. of American Ind. and Eighth Anniv. of the Insti. By Rev. George W. Doane. *Burlington*, 1854

Burdett, Sir Francis. Speech of, in the House of Commons, May 20, 1817. *London*

Burke, Master. Biography of the Irish Roscius. 7th ed. *Philadelphia*

Bullions, Dr. Case of, Fairly Stated. By an Observer. *N. Y.*, 1835

Butler, Benjamin F. The Military Profession. Address at Westpoint. *N. Y.*, 1839

Byrne, Alexander S. Observations on Best Means for Propelling Ships. 2d ed. *N. Y.*, 1841
Baltimore. Commem. Discourse deliv. in First Indepen. Ch. on Death of F. W. P. Greenwood, by George W. Burnap. *Baltimore*, 1843
Buffalo. Report of the Harbor Committee of. *Buffalo*, 1847
Buntline, Ned. Life, Career and Character of. *N.* Y., 1849
Brunner, A. Alphonse. Concise Rules for acquiring Genders of French Nouns. *Cincinnati*, 1852
Bryan Gallery of Christian Art. Companion to. *N. Y.*, 1853

288 Miscellaneous. [*Sixteen.*]

Burlington and Miss. R. R. in Iowa. Exhibit of Condition. *N. Y.*, 1856
Burges's, Mr., Two Speeches; Abstract of Debate in House of Rep. *N. Y.*, 1831
Burges, Mr. Speech of, in Case of Samuel Houston. *Washington*, 1832
Burns, Robert. Tam O'Shanter and Souter Johnny. Beautiful illustr. *London*, 1830
——— The Centenary of the Birthday of. *Boston*, 1859
Burton Henry. The Sounding of the Two Last Trumpets, the Sixth and Seventh. Digested by Henry Burton during his Banishment and close imprisonment in the Isle of Guernsey. *London*, 1641
——— Sermon at the Ordination of Rev. Thomas A. Merrill. *Middlebury, Vt.*, 1806
Bushnell, Horace. The Fathers of New England. Oration by. *N. Y.*, 1850
——— Twentieth Anniv. Commem. Disc. in North Ch. *Hartford*, 1853
——— Parting Words. Discourse, July 3, in North Ch. *Hartford*, 1859
Bush Geo. Letters to a Trinitarian *Boston*, 1850
——— "Gold for Brass." *N. Y.*, 1853
——— "The Valley of Vision." *N. Y.*, 1844
Burke Edmund. Letter from, to a Noble Lord. *N. Y.*, 1796
——— Letter from, to His Grace Duke of Portland. *Phila.*, 1797
——— Two Letters on Proposals for Peace with Regicide Directory of France, by. *Phila.*, 1797

289 Bunker Hill Pamphlets. *Valuable lot; no duplicates.* [*Seventeen.*]

Webster's Address on Bunker Hill. 4th ed. *Boston*, 1825
Address deliv. at laying of Corner stone of Bunker Hill Mon't. By D. Webster. *Boston*, 1825
Webster's Address deliv. at Completion of Bunker Hill Mon't. *Boston*, 1843
History of the Battle of Breed's Hill. By Charles Coffin. *Portland*, 1835
Command in the Battle of Bunker Hill. By R. Frothingham. *Boston*, 1850

Oration on the Seventy-fifth anniv. of Battle of Bunker Hill. By Edw. Everett. *Boston*, 1850

Proceedings of the Bunker Hill Mon't Assoc. *Boston*, 1862

Proceedings of the Bunker Hill Mon't Assoc. *Boston*, 1864

Who was the Commander at Bunker Hill? By S. Swett. *Boston*, 1850

D. Webster's Address at laying of Corner Stone of Bunker Hill Mon't. 5th ed. *Boston*, 1825

Hist. of Bunker Hill Battle. With a plan. 3d ed. By S. Swett. *Boston*,, 1837

Bunker Hill Battle. 2d ed. By S. Swett. *Boston*, 1836

Account of Battle of Bunker Hill. By a Citizen of Boston. 1825

Account of Battle of Bunker Hill. 2d ed. By a Citizen of Boston. 1825

Original planning and construction of Bunker Hill Mon't. By S. Swett. *Albany*, 1863

Webster, Daniel. Address deliv. at the laying of the Corner Stone of the Bunker Hill Monument, July 17, 1825. *Boston*, 1843

Particular Account of the Battle of Breed's Hill on the 17th June. 2d ed. *Boston*, 1825

290 Miscellaneous. [*Two.*]

Byron. Ode to Napoleon Bonaparte. *Newburyport*, 1814

——— Remarks on the Talents of and Tendencies of Don Juan.

CAIRO, Ill. ; The Past, Present and Future of the City of— in North America. With Reports, Estimates and Statistics. *8vo, paper.* *Portland,* 1858

291 Calhoun, J. C. The Carolina Tribute to Calhoun. Edited by J. P. Thomas. *8vo, cl. With portrait.* *Columbia, S. C.,* 1857

292 Calhoun, Rev. Geo. A. Celebration at North Coventry, Conn., March 10, 1859, of the Settlement of—over the Church and Society in that place, March 10, 1819. *8vo pamphlet, 40 p.* *Hartford,* 1859

293 California. Its History, Population, Climate, Soil, Productions and Harbors. And an account of the Revolution and Conquest of the Country by the United States. By John T. Hughes. *8vo, paper, uncut.* *Cincinnati,* 1849

294 California. Its History, Population, Climate, etc., from Sir George Simpson's "Overland Journey Round the World." An account of the Revolution in California and Conquest of the Country by the United States. By John T. Hughes. *Bds., 12mo, uncut.* *Cincinnati,* 1850

295 California, The Wonder of the Age. By Thomas Butler King. *8vo, paper.* *New York,* 1850

296 California, Lower. Historical Outline of. By Jacob P. Leese. *8vo, paper.* *New York,* 1865

297 Callendar, James Thompson. The American Annual Register ; or, Historical Memoir of the United States, for 1796. *8vo, bds., uncut.* *Phila.,* 1797

298 Calvert, Geo. Discourse on the Life and Character of—the First Lord Baltimore — made Dec. 9, 1845. By John P. Kennedy. *8vo pamphlet, fine copy, very scarce. Presentation copy to R. C. Winthrop by the author.* *Baltimore,* 1845

299 Cambridge, Mass. The History of. By Abiel Holmes. *8vo, blue cov., uncut ; 67 pages ; fine copy ; extremely rare.* *Boston,* 1801

Abiel Holmes' Copy, with Autograph. The Genuine First Ed. subsequently pub. in the Mass. Hist. Soc. Col.

300 CAMBRIDGE. Epitaphs from the Old Burying Ground. With Notes by William T. Harris. *8vo, bds., uncut, very fine copy.* *Cambridge,* 1845

301 Camden, N. J.; A Local History of. Commencing with its Early Settlement, Incorporation, and Public and Private Improvements, brought up to the present day. By L. F. Fisler. 12*mo*, *frontis.*, 62 *p.* *Camden*, 1858

302 Camden, Me.; Sketches of the History of, including Incidental References to the Neighboring Places and adjacent Waters. By John L. Locke. 12*mo*, *cl.* *Hallowell*, 1859

303 Campaign of 1860, comprising the speeches of Abraham Lincoln, William H. Seward, Henry Wilson, Benjamin F. Wade, Carl Schurz, Charles Sumner, William M. Evarts, etc. 8*vo*, *cl.* *Albany*, 1860

304 Canada, Upper; A Geographical View of the Province of, and Promiscuous Remarks upon the Government. In two parts, with an appendix, containing a complete description of the Niagara Falls. By M. Smith. 12*mo*, *paper*. *Hartford*, 1813

305 Canada, The Conquest of. Second Edition. In two volumes. By J. Eliot Warburton. 8*vo*, *cl.*, *rough edges*; *portraits* *London*, 1850

306 Candia, N. H; History of—once known as Charmingfare—with notices of some of the Early Families. By F. B. Eaton. 8*vo* *pamphlet*, *illustrated*, 152 *p.*; *scarce.* *Manchester, N. H.*, 1852

307 Canot, Capt.; or, Twenty Years of an African Slaver—being an account of his career and adventures on the Coast, in the Interior, on Shipboard, and in the West Indies. Written out and edited from the Captain's Journals, [etc.] by Brantz Mayer. 12*mo*, *cl.*; *woodcuts.* *New York, etc.*, 1854

308 Cape Anne, The Landing at; or, the Charter of the First Permanent Colony of the Territory of the Massachusetts Company. Now discovered and first published from the original manuscript. With an inquiry into its authority and history of the colony, 1624–1628. Roger Conant, Governor. By John Wingate Thornton. 8*vo*, *cl.* *Boston*, *New York*, 1854

309 Cape Cod. A Description of the Eastern Coast of the County of Barnstable, from Cape Cod, or Race Point to Cape Malebarre, etc. By James Freeman. *Pamphlet*, *uncut*; 15 *pages*; *scarce.* *Boston*, 1802

310 Cape Cod, Mass. A Discourse pronounced, Barnstable, Sept. 3d, 1839, at the celebration of the Second Centennial Anniversary of the settlement of Cape Cod, By John G. Palfray. 8*vo* *Pamph.*; 71 *p*; *scarce*; *fine paper copy* *Boston*, 1840

Cape Cod. Another copy, 50 p. Same date.

311 Cape Cod. Centennial Celebration at Barnstable. Sept. 3, 1839. On the Incorporation of that town—1639. 8*vo* *Pamph*; 92 *p*; *fine copy*; *scarce.* *Barnstable*,, 1840

312 Carolana. A Description of the *English Province* of, by the *Spaniards* call'd Florida, and by the *French*, *La Louisiane*. To which is added: A large and accurate *Map* of *Carolana*, and of the River *Meschacebe*. By Daniel Coxe, Esq. 8*vo*, *cf.* Printed for and sold by *Olive Payne*, at *Horace's* Head in *Pope's Head Alley*, *Cornhill*, opposite the Royal Exchange, 1741.

313 CAROLINA SOUTH. In the Revolutionary War. Being a reply to certain misrepresentations and mistakes of recent writers, in relation to the course and conduct of this State. By a Southron. 12*mo, paper.* *Charleston, S. C.*, 1853

314 CARTIER, ST. LEGER L. Nugæ, by Nugator ; or, Pieces in Prose and Verse. 16*mo, cl.* *Baltimore, Md.*, 1844

315 Cartwright, Dr., Portrayed, in his visit to Brooklyn, 1861 ; speeches and anecdotes, and correspondence with the Devil. With observations on Dr. Cartwright. By Dr. Abel Stevens. With portrait. 12*mo., cl.* *New York*, 1861

316 CASS, LEWIS. A discourse pronounced in the Hall of Representativesbefore the Amer. Hist. Soc. Jan. 30, 1836. 8*vo. Pamph.* 58 *p* ; *scarce.* *Washington*, 1836

317 Catalogue dès ouvrages relatifs a L'Amerique qui ont paru depuis dicouverte jusqu'a l'an 1700. Par H. Ternaux. 12*mo, half clf.* *Paris*, 1837

318 CATALOGUE of an exceedingly valuable collection of Books entirely relating to America, most of which are from the library of S. G. Deeth, Esq., of Washington. *L. P.* ; *uncut ;* 50 *cop.* *New York.*

319 CATALOGUE of an American Library. Chronologically arranged. Part I. 8*vo, paper cov., important titles.*

320 CATALOGUE of a Rare, Curious and Valuable collection of books on the History of America ; embracing the most Scarce and Standard works. Also, Voyages of all the Principal Navigators. Also, Peter Martyr's Decades ; Linsehoten's Discourse ; Eden's History of Travayle, Vaughn's Golden Fleece, Whitbourne's Newfoundland ; and others. By Champlain, Herrera, Acosta, &c. With Rare Early Treatises on Navigation, by Martin Cortes, Norman, Blundevil, Gilbert, &c. Works on Early New England History ; Backus' History of New England, 3 vols. ; John Cotton's Bloody Tenent ; and many others of equal rarity and interest. 8vo, *paper.* *N. Y.*, 1853

321 CATALOGUE of an extraordinary collection of original documents connected with the *British Army* ; its movements and expenses during the struggle that ended in the *Independence* of the *United States* of *America* and other *wars* consequent thereon ; containing also a few *Autograph letters*, &c., of the *leaders* of the *American Army.* For sale by John Gray Bell. 8*vo, paper.* *Manchester, Eng.*, 1857

Withdrawn from circulation ; *scarce.*

322 CATALOGUE of the Library of Wm. H. Corner, of Baltimore, Md. Composed almost exclusively of Books referring to the History of America. Many of great Rarity. Nearly 500 Washington Portraits. *Large Paper*, 4*to ; uncut ; Priced ; scarce.* *Baltimore, W. K. Boyle.* (*n.d.*)

323 Catalogue Raisonne of Curious Manuscripts, Early Printed. And other *Rare Books.* A. A. SMETS. Printed for *Private Circulation.* 8*vo, uncut.* *Savannah*, 1860

324 Catalogue of the Theatrical and Miscellaneous Library of W. E. BURTON. Comprising an immense assemblage of Books relating

to the Stage. *Prepared by Jos. Sabin, large paper, 8vo; partly priced; half morrocco gilt tops; rough edges. Port. N. Y.*, 1860

325 Catalogue of an Important and Valuable Collection of Books relating to the Discovery, Early History, and Religious and Political Controversies of America and the West Indies, &c. *8vo, paper; uncut; priced.* *London*, 1860

326 Catalogue of the choice collection of Books forming the Library of Zelotes Hosmer. Illustrative of Early English Literature and Standard Authors. *Large Paper. Uncut* *Boston*, 1861

327 Catalogue of the very choice collection of Books forming the Library of W. F. Fowle. *Interleaved Copy. 8vo, uncut. Paper Covers, (only few printed.) Cambridge, Riverside Press*, 1864.

328 ——— ——— The same L. P. Only 85 copies.

329 Catalogue of the Library of A. Wight, of Philadelphia. Prepared by J. Sabin. *8vo, large paper, priced; half morrocco; gilt top; rough edges.* *N. Y.*, 1864

330 Catalogue of the Most Valuable, Interesting and Highly Important Library of Geo. Daniel, together with his collection of Original Drawings and Engraved Portraits of Distinguished Actors and Actresses, Beautiful water-color Drawings, of the first quality. *8vo, paper covers; priced; uncut. Scarce.* *London*, 1864

331 Catalogue of the Books, Autographs, Engravings, and Miscellaneous articles, belonging to the Estate of John Allan, Esq. *roy. 8vo, L. P. Portrait. Priced and Purchasers' Names. Prepared by Jos. Sabin.* *New York*, 1864

332 Catalogue of a rare and extensive collection of Joel Munsell Books, principally relating to America, comprising a portion of the Private Library of Joel Munsell. *L. P. uncut.* *New York*, 1865

333 A Catalogue of a valuable Collection of Books, Pamphlets, Manuscripts &c., Illustrating the History and Geography of North and South America and the West Indies. By John Russell Smith. *8vo, half mor.; rough edges.* *London*, 1865

334 Catalogue of the entire Private Library of Mr. William J. Davis. *L. P. 4to, orig. cov., uncut, rubric title.* *New York*, 1865

335 Catalogue of the Library and Antiquarian Collection of John Allan, Esq. With the names of purchasers and the price each article sold for, preceded by a few Introductory Remarks, by William Gowans, Esq. *Sheets, folded.* *New York: William Gowans*, 1865

336 Catalogue of the entire Private Library of the late Mr. Henry Whitmore. Prepared by T. H. Morrell. *L. P., interleaved copy; only* 30 *copies; paper cov., uncut.* *New York*, 1865

337 Catalogue of the Rare, Curious, and Valuable Collection of Books, Tracts, Autographs, MSS., Engravings, &c. By E. B. Corwin. *8vo, unb., L. P., uncut.* *New York*, 1866

338 Catalogue of the Private Library of William A. Whiteman, Esq., of Philadelphia. A very select collection of books, etc., many very rare works relating to America. *8vo, paper; priced.* *New York*, 1866

339 Catalogue of the entire Private Library of T. H. Morrell, comprising a choice collection of Works on America, its History and Antiquities, etc. *8vo, uncut ; or. cover. Priced.* *New York*, 1866

340 Catalogue. Bibliotheca Americana. Catalogue of the Valuable Library belonging to R. W. Roche. *Priced. 8vo, paper, uncut.* *New York*, 1867

341 Catalolgue of a Fine Collection of Books, etc., etc. F. M. Josselyn. *Priced.* *Boston*, 1867

342 Catalogue. A Supplement to a Catalogue of Books on North and South America and the West Indies. *London: J. Russell Smith*, 1867

343 Catalogue of a Magnificent Private Library. *8vo, paper, uncut.* *New York: J. W. Bouton*, 1868

344 Catalogue of the Private Library of A. A. Smets, comprising one of the most valuable and extensive Collections of Books ever offered to the American Public. *8vo, paper, uncut.* *New York*, 1868

345 Catalogue of an Exceedingly Interesting Collection of Autograph Letters, American and Foreign. *8vo, paper, uncut.* *N. Y.: J. W. Bouton*, 1868

346 Catalogue of an extraordinary Collection of Books and Manuscripts, almost wholly relating to the History and Literature of North and South America, particularly Mexico. *8vo, cl., uncut ; printed prices.* *London*, 1869

347 Catlin, Geo. Letters and Notes of the Manners, Customs, and Conditions of the North American Indians. Written during eight years' travel amongst the wildest tribes of Indians in North America. In 1832 to 1839. 2 *vols., 8vo, cl., uncut.* 400 *illustrations, engraved from original paintings.* *London: Published by the Author*, 1841

348 Catlin, George. Adventures of the Ojibbeway and Ioway Indians in France, England and Belgium ; being notes of eight years' travels and residence in Europe with his North American Indian collection. In two volumes. Third edition. *8vo, half gr. cr. lev. mor., gilt top, rough edges ; bound by R. W. Smith.* *London*, 1852

349 CATSKILL, N. Y. Catskill Association, formed for improving the Town of. Dec. 28, 1836. 12*mo, cl., map, uncut ; scarce.* *N. Y.*, 1837

350 CHAMPLAIN, Samuel. Narrative of a Voyage to the West Indies and Mexico in the years 1599–1602, with maps and illustrations. Translated from the Original and unpublished Manuscript, with a biographical notice and notes by Alice Wilmere, edited by Norton Shaw. *8vo, cl., rough edges.* *London: Printed by the Hakluyt Society*, 1859

351 CHANDLER, T. B. The Appeal Farther Defended ; in Answer to the Farther Misrepresentations of Dr. Chauncy. *8vo, paper, uncut, very scarce, fine copy* *New York: Hugh Gaine*, 1771

Chandler wrote, under the signature of A. W., several letters to Hamilton.

352 Chambers, William. American Slavery and Color. *8vo, with map, unbound.* *London*, 1857

353 Chandler, Elizabeth Margaret; The Poetical Works of. With a Memoir of her Life and Character. By Benjamin Lundy. *8vo, sheep* *Phila.*, 1836

354 Chandler, Peleg W. American Criminal Trials. In two volumes. *8vo, cl., scarce* *Boston & London*, 1844

355 Channing, Henry. A Sermon preached at New London, Dec. 20, 1786, occasioned by the execution of Hannah Ocuish, a Mulatto Girl, Aged 12 Years and 9 Months, for the Murder of Eunice Bolles, Aged 6 Years and 6 Months. *8vo pamphlet, fine copy; curious.* *New London*, 1788

356 Chapman Family; or, The Descendants of Robt. Chapman, one of the First Settlers of Say-Brook, Conn.; with Genealogical Notes of Wm. Chapman, who settled in New London, Conn.; Edw. Chapman, who settled at Windsor, Conn.; John Chapman, who settled at Stonington, Conn.; Rev. Benjamin Chapman, who settled at Southington, Conn. By F. U. Chapman. *8vo, cl.; portraits; fine copy; very scarce.* *Hartford*, 1854

357 CHAPPELL, LIEUT. EDWARD. Narrative of a Voyage to Hudson's Bay, containing some account of the North-Eastern Coast of America and of the Tribes inhabiting that remote region. Map and plates. *8vo, half gr. crim. lev. mor., gilt; bound by R. W. Smith.* *London*, 1817

358 Charlemont, Mass. "Charlemont as a Plantation." An Historical Discourse at the Centen. Anniversary of the Death of Moses Rice, the first Settler of the Town, deliv. June 11, 1855, by Joseph White. *8vo, orig. cov., 48 p., clean copy.* *Boston*, 1858

359 Charleston. A Peep into the Past by an Ancient Lady. *Cloth, 12mo.* *Charleston*, 1853

360 Charleston, Reminiscences of. By J. N. Cardoza. *8vo, paper.* *Charleston*, 1866

361 Charlestown, Mass. History of the First Church in, in nine Lectures with Notes. By Wm. I. Budington. *8vo, cl. port.* *Boston*, 1845

362 Charlevoix, P. de. Journal of a Voyage to North America, undertaken by order of the French King, containing the Geographical Description and Natural History of the Country, Particularly Canada, together with an account of the Customs, Characters, Religion, Manners and Traditions of the original Inhabitants. In two volumes. *Calf, 8vo.* *London*, 1761

363 Charlevoix, Father. A Voyage to North America; undertaken by Command of the present King of France. Containing the Geographical Description and Natural History of Canada and Louisiana. With The Customs, Manners, Trade and Religion of the Inhabitants; a Description of the Lakes and Rivers, with their Navigation and Manner of passing Great Cataracts. Illustrated with a number of curious Prints and Maps not in any other Edition. In two volumes. *8vo, calf.* *Dublin*, 1766

364 Chase, Rev. B. C. Address deliv. at Camden, Maine, Sept. 11, 1855, at the Expiration of Half a Century from the Organiza-

tion of the First Cong. Church in that Town. Also, a brief sketch of the Revival there in 1836; names of Members, etc. *8vo pamphlet, 28 p.; clean copy.* *Boston,* 1855

365 Chase, Francis, M. A. Gathered sketches from the early history of New Hampshire and Vermont; containing vivid and interesting accounts of the adventures of our forefathers, and of other Incidents of Olden Time. Original and selected. With plates. 12*mo, cl.* *Claremont, N. H.* 1856

366 Chastellux, Marquis De. Travels in North America in the years 1780–81–82. Maj. Gen. in the French Army, serving under Count de Rochambeau. Translated from the French, with Notes. 2 *vols.* 8*vo, bs. uncut, fine copy.* *London,* 1787

367 Chatham Artillery of Savannah. Celebration of the Seventy-Fifth Anniversary, May 1, 1861. Oration by Chas. C. Jones. 65 *pages,* 8*vo, orig. cov., fine copy; very scarce.* *Savannah,* 1861

The Oration contains an interesting account of the part taken by this Corps in the Sepulture of Gen. Nathl. Green, in June 1786, also Biog. Sketches of the different Commanders, from its organization, also of its actions during the Revolution, and a Roll of its Members.

368 Chaudron, A. De V. Spelling book. *Fifth edition.* 12*mo, wall paper covers, woodcuts. Confederate.* *Mobile,* 1865

369 CHECKLEY, JOHN. The Speech of, upon his Tryal, at Boston in New England, for publishing the Short and Easy Method with the Deists, etc. To which is added the Jury's Verdict, etc. 8*vo, full crushed crim. lev. mor. gt. Bound by R. M. Smith.* *London,* 1730

370 Checkley, Mr. John. The Speech of, upon his Trial at Boston, in 1724. With an Introduction by Rev. E. H. Gillett, D. D., of Harlem, N. Y. 8*vo, uncut. Priv. prin. by H. B. Dawson.* *Morrisania, N. Y.,* 1868

371 Cheever, George B. The Journal of the Pilgrims at Plymouth in New England, in 1620; Re-printed from the Original Volume. With Historical and Local Illustrations of Providences, Principles and Persons. 8*vo, cloth, rough edges.* *New York,* 1848

372 CHELMSFORD, Mass. The History of, from its origin in 1653, to the year 1820. Together with an Historical Sketch of the Church and Biographical notices of the Four First Pastors. To which is added a Memoir of the Pawtuckett Tribe of Indians. With a large Appendix. By Wilkes Allen. 8*vo, bds.; uncut,* 192 *pages, beautiful copy of this extremely rare work.* *Haverhill,* 1820

373 Chester, N. H. Facts relating to the Early History of, from the settlement in 1720, until 1784. Collected by Chas. Bell, 1851. 8*vo pamphlet,* 73 *pages.* *Concord,* 1863

374 CHESTER, N. H. History of, from 1719 to 1869. By Benjamin Chase. 8*vo, sheets folded; portraits and maps.* *Auburn, Me.,* 1869

375 Cherry Valley, Otsego Co., N.Y. The Centennial Celebration at, July 4th, 1840. The Addresses of Wm. W. Campbell, Esq., and Gov. W. H. Seward, with Letters, Toasts, &c., &c. 8*vo, cl.; fine copy; very scarce.* *N. Y.,* 1840

376 Chester, N. H. Facts relating to the Early History of, from the Settlement in 1720, until the formation of the State Constitution in 1784. By Charles Bell. *8vo, paper.* *Concord,* 1863

377 Chicago. Annals of. A Lecture delivered before the Chicago Lyceum, Jan. 21, 1840. By J. N. Balestier. *8vo,* 24 *p.; fine copy; scarce.* *Chicago,* 1840

378 Chicopee, Mass. Centennial Disc. deliv. before the First Cong. Soc. in, Sept. 26, 1852. By E. B. Clark. *8vo, orig. cov.,* 23 *p.; fine copy.* *Springfield,* 1852

379 [Childs, Mrs. L. M.] First Settlers of New England; or, the Conquest of the Pequods, Narragansetts and Pokanokets. *12mo, bds., uncut; plate.* *Boston* 1829

380 Churches, Cong. Debates and Proceedings of the Nat. Council of, held at Boston, June 14–24, 1865. From the Phonographic Report by J. M. W. Terrinton and Henry M. Parkhurst. *8vo, sheets folded.* *Boston, Mass.,* 1866

381 Church, Esq., Benj. Entertaining Passages relating to Philip's War, which began in the Month of June, 1675; as also of Expeditions more lately made Against the Common Enemy and Indian Rebels in the Eastern Parts of New England: with Some Account of the Divine Providence towards Benj. Church, Esq. By T. C. *Boston,* 1716. Reprinted with an introduction and notes. By Henry Martyn Dexter. *Boston,* 1865 2 *Parts. Sm. paper, map, paper cover.* 250 *copies. No.* 68. *Library of New-England History, No. II.*

382 ——— ——— *Same. L. P.* No. 5.

383 Churchman, John. An Account of the Gospel Labors and Christian Experiences of. To which is added a short Memorial of the Life and Death of Joseph White, late of Bucks County, Pa. *8vo, sheep.* *London,* 1780

384 CINCINNATI. Natural and Statistical View, or Picture of, and the Miami Country. With an Appendix containing observations on the late Earthquakes, the Aurora Borealis and South-West Wind. By Daniel Drake. *Red tur., gilt top, uncut; fine copy; illus. by maps; very scarce.* *Cincinnati,* 1815

385 CINCINNATI. Spring Grove Cemetery. Its History and Improvements. With observations on Ancient and Modern Places of Sepulture. *8vo, col. frontispiece.* *Cincinnati: Robt. Clarke & Co.,* 1869

386 "CINCINNATI." Society of, in Mass. An Oration delivered to, July4, 1789. By Doct. Samuel Whitwell. *Sm. 4to, uncut,* 20 *p.; very scarce. Printed by Benjamin Russell, State Street, Boston,* 1789.

387 "CINCINNATI." Connecticut Society of. "The True Means of establishing Public Happiness." A Sermon delivered before the Conn. Soc. of Cinci., on the 7th of July, 1795. By Timothy Dwight. *8vo pamphlet,* 40 *pages; fine copy; very scarce. New Haven: printed by T. & S. Green, and sold by J. Beers at his Book Store.* 1795.

388 CINCINNATI. Conn. Soc. of. An Oration at New Haven, July 7th, 1801. By Theo. Dwight. *8vo,* 43 *pages, uncut; scarce.* *Hartford,* 1801

389 CINCINNATI. The Institution of the Society of, formed by the Officers of the Army of the United States, for the laudable Purposes therein mentioned. 15 *p.* *8vo; engraved frontis., designed and drawn by Geo. Graham; very scarce.* Published for the R. I. Members. *Boston,* 1802

390 CINCINNATI. Observations on a late Pamphlet entitled, "Considerations upon the Soc. or Order of the Cincinnati," clearly evincing the Innocence and Propriety of that Honorable and respectable Institution. By an Obscure Individual. *8vo pamphlet. Excessively scarce.* *Phila.,* 1783

391 CINCINNATI. The Institution of the Society of, formed by the Officers of the Army of the United States, for the laudable Purposes therein mentioned. *8vo; excessively scarce.* *Samuel Loudon, New York,* MDCCLXXXIV.

392 Cincinnati. The Institution of the Society of, formed by the Officers of the American Army of the Revolution, at the Cantonment on the Banks of the Hudson River, May, 1783. Together with some of the Proceedings of the General Society and of the New York State Society. Also, a List of the Officers and Members of the New York State Society, from its Organization to the Year 1851. *8vo, cl.* *New York,* 1851

393 CINCINNATI. Conn. Soc. of. An Oration at Hartford, July 6th, 1802. By Benj. Silliman. *8vo, uncut,* 34 *pages; fine copy.* *Hartford,* 1802

394 CINCINNATI. Conn. Soc. of. A Valedictory Discourse in Hartford, July 4, 1804, at the Dissolution of the Society. By D. Humphreys. *8vo, uncut,* 60 *p.; good copy; very scarce.* *Boston,* 1804

395 Cincinnati in 1841. Its Early Annals and Future Prospects. By Charles Cist. *8vo, cl.; engravings.* *Cincinnati,* 1841

396 Cincinnati, Ohio, in 1826. By B. Drake and E. D. Mansfield. *With plate.* *12mo, bl. mor.* *Cincinnati,* 1827

397 Cincinnati. Sketches and Statistics of, in 1859. By Charles Cist. *8vo, cl.* *Cincinnati,* 1859

398 "Citizen." The Marriage of a Deceased Wife's Sister vindicated, in a Letter from a Citizen to a Friend. *8vo,* 30 *p.; fine copy; scarce.* *New York,* 1797

399 Clairborne, Nathaniel Herbert. Notes on the War in the South, with Biographical Sketches of the Lives of Montgomery, Jackson, Sevier, the late Gov. Clairborne and others. *Sheep. 8vo.* *Richmond,* 1819

400 Clapp, Samuel C. Selections in Prose and Verse. *8vo, boards.* *Boston,* 1832

401 Claremont, War History, April, 1861 to April, 1865; with Sketches of New Hampshire Regiments and a Biographical Notice of each Claremont Soldier, etc. By Otis F. R. Waite. *8vo, in sheets, folded.* *Concord, N. H.,* 1868

402 CLARK, J. V. H. Lights and Lines of Indian Character and Scenes of Pioneer Life. Portrait. *8vo, half crim. lev. mor., gilt; bound by R. W. Smith.* *Syracuse,* 1854

403 CLARK, JOSHUA V. H. Onondaga; or, Reminiscences of Earlier and Later Times; being a series of Historical Sketches relative to Onondaga. With notes on the several Towns in the County, and Oswego. 2 *vols., in sheets, folded,* 8*vo, portraits and maps.* *Syracuse,* 1849

404 Clark, Rev. George H. The Union. Sermon in St. John's Church, Savannah, Fast Day, Nov. 28, 1860. 8*vo, paper.* *Savannah,* 1860

405 Clark, Rev. George H. The Liturgy of the Episcopal Church. Sermon delivered in St. John's Church, Savannah, Nov. 18, 1860, 8*vo, paper.* *Savannah,* 1860

406 Clark, Col. George Rogers. Sketch of his Campaign in Illinois, 1778–9, with an Introduction by Hon. Henry Pirtle of Louisville, and an Appendix, containing the public and private Instruction to Col. Clark, and Major Bowman's Journal of the taking of Post St. Vincents. *Cloth,* 8*vo, portrait; uncut.* *Cincinnati,* 1869

407 CLARK, J. V. H. Lights and Lines of Indian Character and Scenes of Pioneer Life. 8*vo, cloth; scarce.* *Syracuse,* 1854

408 Clark, McDonald. Sketches. Part II. 12*mo, boards.* *New York,* 1826

409 Clark, Samuel A. The Episcopal Church in the American Colonies. The History of St. John's Church, Elizabethtown, N. J., from the year 1703 to the present time—compiled from original documents, etc. 12*mo, cl.; with plate.* *Phila.,* 1857

410 CLAVERACK, N. Y.; History of the Reformed P. D. Church of. A Centennial Address by Rev. F. N. Zabriskie. *Paper.* *Hudson, N. Y.,* 1867

411 Clay, J. C. Annals of the Swedes on the Delaware. To which is added the Charter of the United Swedish Churches. With portrait of N. Collin. 24*mo, cl., scarce.* *Phila.,* 1835

412 CLEVELAND, Ohio; Early History of—including original papers and other matter relating to the adjacent country; with Biographical Notices of the Pioneers and Surveyors. By Col. Charles Whittlesey. *L.* 8*vo, cl.; gilt top.* *Cleveland, O.* 1867

413 Cleveland, Neh. The First Century of Dummer Academy. A Historical Discourse delivered at Newbury, Byfield Parish, August 12, 1863. With an Appendix. 8*vo, cl.* 115 *p.* *Boston,* 1865

414 CLIFTON, Staten Island; Description of, at the Narrows. With a map of the same. 8*vo,* 24 *pages; good copy.* *New York,* 1838

415 Clinton, Charles A. Biographical Sketch of the Clinton Family. *New York,* 1859

416 Clinton, De Witt; The Life and Writings of. By William W. Campbell. 8*vo, cloth, portrait.* *N. Y.,* 1849

417 Coates, D.; Beecham, J.; Ellis, W. Christianity the Means of Civilization, shown in the Evidence on Aborigines. 8*vo, cl., uncut.* *London,* 1837

418 Cockburn, John. The Unfortunate Englishmen; or, A Faithful Narrative of the Distresses and Adventures of John Cockburn, and Five other English Mariners, who were taken by a Spanish

Guarda Costa, in the John and Anne, Edward Burt, Master, and set on shore at Porto-Cavallo, naked and wounded ; containing a Journey over Land from the Gulph of Honduras to the Great South Sea. As also an Account of the Manners, Customs, and Behaviour of the several Indians inhabiting a Tract of Land of 2400 Miles ; particularly of their Dispositions toward the Spaniards and English. The third edition. 16*mo, half mor.; frontispiece.* *London,* 1773

419 CODMAN, JOHN. "Review of the Past." Sermon deliv. in Dorchester, Dec. 7, 1845; being the 37th Anniversary of the Author's Ordination. 8*vo, orig. cov. ;* 27 *p. ; clean copy.* *Boston,* 1846

420 COHOES, N. Y. Laws relating to the Incorporation of Villages and the By-Laws of Cohoes. 8*vo pamphlet, uncut,* 68 *pages.* *Cohoes,* 1855

421 COLCHESTER, CT. ; EXTRACTS FROM THE RECORDS OF—with some transcripts from the recording of Michaell Taintor, of "Brainford," Conn. Transcribed by C. M. Taintor. 12*mo, cl., scarce.* *Hartford,* 1864

422 COLE, SAMUEL W. The Muse ; or, Flowers of Poetry—a choice collection of favorite Odes, Poems, Songs, Elegies, Dirges, Epitaphs, Epigrams, Elegant Extracts, etc. 12*mo, bds.* *Cornish, Me.,* 1827

423 COLMAN, GEORGE. Broad Grins, comprising, with New Additional Tales in Verse, those formerly published under the title of "My Night-gown and Slippers." 12*mo, unbound, scarce.* *Worcester : Isaiah Thomas,* 1804

424 COLTON, GEORGE H. Tecumseh ; or, The West Thirty Years Since. 16*mo, bds.* *New York,* 1842

425 COLUMBIA CO., N.Y.; Biographical Sketches of the Distinguished Men of—including an account of the most important offices they have filled in the State and General Governments, and in the Army and Navy. By Wm. Raymond. 8*vo, half red mor. corners and back.* *Albany,* 1851

426 COLUMBIA, District of; A Chorographical and Statistical description of. With an engraved Plan of the District and View of the Capitol. By D. B. Warden. 8*vo, sheep ; maps ; fine copy.* *Paris,* 1816

427 CONCORD, N. H.; ANNALS OF THE TOWN OF, from its First Settlement, in the year 1726, to the year 1823 ; with several Biographical Sketches. To which is added a Memoir of the Penacook Indians. By Jacob B. Moore. 8*vo, paper cov. ; engraved wood cut view of Capitol, uncut ;* 112 *pages ; beautiful copy ; very scarce in this condition.* *Concord, N. H.,* 1824

"Rev. Jos. B. Felt, from J. B. Moore, Esq."—Autog.

428 CONCORD, New Hampshire ; The History of, from its first grant, in 1725, to the city government in 1853 ; with a history of the Ancient Pennacooks. The whole interspersed with numerous interesting incidents and anecdotes, down to the present period, 1855 ; embellished with maps ; with portraits of distinguished citizens, and views of ancient and modern residences. By Nathaniel Bouton. 8*vo, cl. Scarce.* *Concord,* 1856

429 CONCORD, N.H.; Annals of the Town of, from its First Settlement, 1726 to 1823; with several Biographical Sketches. To which is added a Memoir of the Penacook Indians. By Jacob B. Moore. *8vo, uncut.* *Concord*, 1824

430 CONCORD, N.H. Two Sermons delivered Nov. 21, 1830, in Commemoration of the Centennial Anniversary of the Establishment of the First Church. By Nathaniel Bouton. *8vo, paper cov., uncut; with map; fine copy, scarce.* *Concord N. H.*, 1831

431 CONCORD, MASS. A HISTORY OF THE FIGHT AT CONCORD ON THE 19th OF April, 1775, with a particular account of the Military Operations, and interesting events of that ever Memorable day; showing that then and there the First Regular and Forcible Resistance was made to the British Soldiery, and the First British blood was shed by armed Americans, and the Revolutionary war thus commenced. By Rev. Ezra Ripley, D. D., with other Citizens of Concord. *8vo, paper cov.. uncut, 60 pages, beautiful clean copy of the extremely rare First Ed.* *Concord*, 1827

432 CONCORD, MASS. A Historical Discourse delivered before the Citizens of, Sept. 12, 1835, on the Second Centennial Anniv. of the Incorporation of the Town. By Ralph Waldo Emerson. *8vo. paper cov., uncut; 52 pages, fine copy; scarce.* *Concord*, 1835

433 CONCORD, MASS. History of, from its earliest settlement to 1832; and of the adjoining towns, Bedford, Acton, Lincoln and Carlisle; containing various notices of County and State history not before published. By Lemuel Shattuck. *8vo, cl.; uncut. Very scarce.* *Boston and Concord*, 1835

434 CONFEDERATE STATES ALMANAC for 1864, the 4th year of the Independence of the Confederate States of America. Calculations made at the University of Alabama. *8vo.* *Mobile*

435 CONFEDERATE STATES. Regulations for the Army of, with a full Index. By Authority of the War Department. *Richmond, Va.*, 1864

436 CONGRESSIONAL GLOBE. Containing the debates and proceedings of Congress, 37th and 38th. *Parts* 1 and 2, 1862–3. *Parts* 1, 2, 3, and 4, 1863–4. *Parts* 1 and 2, 1864–5. *8 vols, 4to, half calf.* *Washington*, 1862–5

437 CONNECTICUT. GENERAL HISTORY OF, from its first settlement under George Fenwick, to its latest period of Amity with Great Britain prior to the Revolution. Including a description of the Country and many Curious and interesting Anecdotes. With an Appendix, pointing out the cause of the Rebellion in America; together with the particular part taken by the people of Connecticut. By Samuel Peters. London, 1781.

To which is added a Supplement, veryfying many important statements made by the Author. Illust., with eight engravings. *8vo, sh. Fine copy. Scarce.* *New Haven*, 1829

438 CONNECTICUT, ACADEMY OF ARTS AND SCIENCES. A Statistical Account of the Towns and Parishes in the State of Conn. *Vol. I. No. I.; all published. 8vo, fine copy; 83 pages.* *New Haven*, 1811

Contains an account of New Haven, by Timothy Dwight.

439 CONN. History of the Indians of, from the Earliest known Period to 1850. By John W. De Forest. *8vo, cl., with map ; plates.* *Hartford, Conn.*, 1853

440 CONNECTICUT. Narrative of the Missions to the New Settlements according to the appointment of the General Association of the State of, together with an account of the Receipts and Expenditures of the money contributed by the people of Connecticut in May, 1793, for the support of the Missionaries. *8vo pamphlet ; uncut.* *New Haven*, 1794

441 CONNECTICUT. Continuation of the Narrative of the Mission to the New Settlements, according to the appointment of the General Association of the State of, together with an account of the Receipts and Expenditures of the money contributed for the support of the Missionaries. *8vo, uncut.* *New Haven*, 1797

442 CONNECTICUT. Complete History of, Civil and Ecclesiastical, from the emmigration of its first Planters from England in 1630 to 1713. By Benj. Trumbull. *8vo, sh. ; with map and portraits of John Winthrop and others. Vol. I. all published.* *Hartford*, 1797

443 CONNECTICUT Academy of Arts and Sciences. Memoirs of. *Vol. I, Part I. 8vo, bds., uncut.* *New Haven*, 1810

444 CONNECTICUT. Sketch of, Forty years since. *Half red mor., gilt top, uncut.* *Hartford*, 1824

445 CONNECTICUT. A General History of, from its first settlement under George Fenwick to its latest period of amity with Great Britain prior to the revolution, including a Description of the country, and many curious and interesting anecdotes. With an appendix, pointing out the causes of the rebellion in America, &c. By a gentleman of the province. (Rev. Samuel Peters.) London, 1781. To which is added a supplement, verifying many important statements made by the author. *12mo, sheep ; eight plates.* *New Haven, Conn. : republished*, 1829

446 CONNECTICUT. The Code of 1650 : being a compilation of the earliest Laws and Orders of the General Court of Connecticut. Also, the Constitution or Civil compact entered into and adopted by the Towns of Windsor, Hartford and Wethersfield in 1638–9. To which is added some extracts from the Laws and Judicial Proceedings of the New Haven Colony, commonly called the Blue laws. *12mo, bds. ; frontispiece.* *Hartford*, 1836

447 CONN. Letters from the English Kings and Queens to the Governors of the Colony ; together with the Answers thereto, from 1635 to 1749. And other Original Ancient, Literary and Curious Documents. By R. R. Hinman. *8vo, cl.* *Hartford*, 1836

448 CONNECTICUT. The Blue Laws of New Haven Colony, usually called Blue Laws of Connecticut ; Quaker Laws of Plymouth and Massachusetts ; Blue Laws of New York, Maryland, Virginia and South Carolina. First Record of Conn. ; interesting extracts from Conn. Records ; cases of Salem Witchcraft ; Charges and Banishment of Roger Williams, &c. Compiled by an Antiquarian. *12mo, cl.* *Hartford*, 1838

449 CONNECTICUT. The History of the Episcopal Churches in, from the

Settlement of the Colony to the present time. By E. E. Beardsley. 2 *vols. 8vo, cl.; rough edges. 2d ed.* *Cambridge: Riverside Press,* 1869

450 CONNECTICUT. History of, from the First Settlement to the Present Time. By Theodore Dwight, Jr. *Cl.,* 12*mo. New York,* 1841

451 CONNECTICUT. THE HISTORY OF, from the First Settlement of the Colony. By G. H. Hollister. In 2 vols. *Half Roxburghe, gilt top, edges uncut.* 2*d ed., enlarged and improved.* *Hartford,* 1857

452 CONSIDERATIONS on the Measures carrying on with respect to the British Colonies in N. A. The Second Edition, with Additions and an Appendix relative to the present State of Affairs on that Continent. By Matthew Robinson. 8*vo, cl. London,* 1774

453 CONSTABLE'S POCKET-BOOK; or, a Dialogue between an Old Constable and a New. Being a guide in Serving all Warrants, Observing Orders of Courts, Summoning Town Officers and Town Meetings, Collecting Rates and Assessments, Serving Writs, &c., in their Keeping the Peace, &c. By N. B. *Second edition, corrected.* 12*mo, sheep; rare.* *Boston: printed, and are to be sold at the Bible in Cornhill,* 1727

454 COOK, Capt. JAS. A Journal of Captain Cook's last Voyage to the Pacific Ocean, and in quest of a North-West Passage between Asia and America; performed in the years 1776, '77, 78 and '79. Faithfully narrated from the original M.S. of Mr. John Ledyard. 12*mo, sheep, with map; excessively scarce. Hartford: printed and sold by Nathaniel Patten, a few rods north of the Court House.* MDCCLXXXIII

455 COOK, WILLIAM. Twenty-one Poems by. 8*vo, paper, uncut.* *Salem,* 1851–1864

456 COOPER JAMES FENIMORE. Memorial of. By G. P. Putman. 4*to, cl.; portrait.* *N. Y.,* 1852

457 COOPERSTOWN, N. Y. The Chronicles of, &c. 8*vo, full cr. crim. lev. mor., gt. top; rough edges. By R. W. Smith.* *Cooperstown, Phinney,* 1838

458 COOPERSTOWN, N. Y. CONDENSED HIS. OF, with a Biograph. Sketch of J. Fenimore Cooper. By Rev. S. T. Livermore. 8*vo, cl.; scarce.* *Albany: J. Munsell,* 1862

459 COPWAY, GEORGE (KAH-GE-GA-GAH-BOWH). The Life, History and Travels of, a Young Indian Chief of the Ojibwa Nation; with a Sketch of the Present State of the Ojibwa Nation. Written by Himself. *With plate.* 8*vo, cl. Albany, N. Y.,* 1847

460 COOS COUNTRY AND VICINITY, N. H. Historical Sketches of the Discovery, Settlement and Progress of Events in, between the years 1754 and 1785. By Rev. Grant Powers. 8*vo, sheep; excessively scarce.* *Haverhill, N. H.,* 1841

461 COPWAY, GEO. The Ojibway Conquest, a Tale of the Northwest. By Kah-ge-gah-bowh. 12*mo, cl.; with portrait. New York.* 1850

462 COPWAY, G. The Traditional History and Characteristic Sketches of the Ojibway Nation. 8*vo, cl.; with illustrations.* *Boston, (n. d.)*

463 CORNARO, LEWIS. (A Noble Venetian.) Discourses on a sober and temperate Life by, wherein is demonstrated, by his own exam-

ple, the method of preserving health to extreme old age. Translated from the Italian. To which is added, Physic of the golden age, a fragment. 12*mo, bds.* *Middletown, N. J.* 1836

464 CORNWALL, VT. History of the Town of. By Rev. Lyman Matthews. 8*vo, cl.; seven portraits and plates.* *Middlebury,* 1862

465 CORTES, HERNANDO. The Despatches of, the Conqueror of Mexico, addressed to the Emperor Charles V., written during the Conquest, and containing a Narrative of its Events. Now First Translated into English from the Spanish, with an Introduction and Notes. By George Folsom. *L. P. bds., uncut; scarce.* *New York. London,* 1843

466 CORWIN, EDWARD TANJORE. Manual of the Reformed Protestant Dutch Church in North America. 4*to, cl.* *New York,* 1859

467 COTTON, JOHN. The | Churches Resurrection, | or, the | Opening of the | Fift and Sixt verses of the 20th Chap. | of the | Revelation. | By that Learned and Reverend, | John Cotton. | Teacher to the Church of Boston in | New England, and there corrected | by his own hand. | *Small 4to, full green cr. lev. mor., bound by Hayday. Beautiful copy.*
London: | Printed by R. O. & G. D. for Henry Overton, | and are to be sold at his shop, in Popes-Head-Alley. | 1642. |

468 COVENTRY, NORTH, Conn. The Celebration at, March 10, 1859, of the Settlement of Rev. George A. Calhoun, over the Church and Society in that place, March 10, 1819. 8*vo, paper.* *Hartford,* 1859

469 COVENTRY, VT. A History of Coventry, Orleans Co., Vt. By Pliny H. White. 8*vo pamphlet,* 68 *pages; very scarce.* *Irasburgh, Vt.,* 1860

"Posterity delights in details."

470 COVENTRY MECHANICS' INSTITUTION. "The Influence of the Mind on Health." A Lecture delivered to the Members of. By a Medical Man. 8*vo, fine copy;* 25 *pages.* *London,* 1838

471 CRAIG, NEVILLE, B. The OLDEN TIME: a monthly publication, devoted to the Preservation of Documents and other Authentic Information in relation to the Early Exploration, and the Settlement and Improvement of the Country around the Head of the Ohio. *Vol. I., Nos.* 1 *to* 8 *incl., and No* 10. 9 *Nos. in parts, as originally pub. Roy. 8vo, uncut; plans, maps and plates..* *Pittsburgh, Pa.,* 1846

472 CRAIK, GEORGE L. Compendious History of English Literature, and of the English Language, from the Norman Conquest. 2 *vols. l. 8vo, half mor., gilt top, rough edges.* *New York,* 1864

473 CRESAP, CAPT. MICHAEL. A Biographical Sketch of the life of. By John J. Jacob. 4*to, rubric. ti., uncut., or. cov.* *Re-print, Cincinnati, Ohio,* 1866.

474 CROSBY, ENOCH, *alias* HARVEY BIRCH. THE SPY UNMASKED; or, Memoirs of, the Hero of Mr. Cooper's Tale of the Neutral Ground; being an authentic Account of the secret services which he rendered his country during the Revolutionary War. Taken from his own lips in short hand. Comprising many interesting facts and anecdotes never before published. By H.

L. Barnum. *Roy. 8vo, full crushed crim. lev. mor., gilt top, uncut; beautiful copy, embellished with engravings. By R. W. Smith.* *New York*, 1828

475 CROYDON, N. H. An Historical and Statistical Sketch of, from its Incorporation to the year 1832. Containing much local information which must be highly interesting to every inhabitant of the Town. By John Cooper. *8vo, 52 pages; scarce.* *Concord*, 1852

476 CROWTHER, JONATHAN. A True and Complete Portraiture of Methodism; or, the History of the Wesleyan Methodists; with the whole Plan of their Discipline, and a Description of Class-meetings, Bands, Love-feasts, etc., *12mo, sh.* *New York*, 1813

477 CURRIE, HELEN. Poems by. *Sheep, 12mo.* *Philadelphia*, 1818

478 CUMBERLAND, ANNALS OF THE ARMY OF THE, comprising Biographies, [etc.,] also its Police Record of Spies, [etc.] Together with Anecdotes, Incidents, Reminiscences and Official Report of the battle of Stone River. By an Officer. *Illustrated with Steel Portraits, Wood Engravings and Maps; l. 8vo, cl.* *J. B. Lippincott, Phila.*, 1864

479 CUSHMAN, ROBT. W. A Discourse delivered in Plymouth at the Cushman Festival, Aug. 15, 1855, on the 235th Anniv. *8vo pamphlet, 31 pages.* *Boston*, 1855

Plymouth Rock:
"The Rock whence we were hewn."

480 "CRYSTALINA." A Fairy Tale. By an American. *Bds., 12mo, uncut.* *New York*, 1816

PAMPHLETS.

481 Miscellaneous Pamphlets. [*Fifteen.*]

Cato. Examination of Treaty of Amity, Commerce and Navigation between U. S. and Great Britain.

Cass, Gen. Lewis. Biography of. *New York*, 1843

——— ——— France. Its King, Court, and Government. *New York*, 1848

Cathewood, F. Description of View of Jerusalem.

———Description of View of Temple of Karnak and City of Thebes.

Carey Mathew. Account of Malignant Fever in Phil., 1793.

——— ——— Desultory reflec., excited by calamitous fate of John Fullerton. *New York*, 1802

——— Thomas and Mr. Andrew's sermon to First Ch. and Soc. in Newburyport, Sept. 27, 1801.

Cheever, George B. Dependence of Evidences of Christianity on acknowl. of Fundamental Doctrines of the Gospel. *N. Y.*, 1835

Croton Aqueduct, description of, by John B. Jervis. *New York*, 1842

Carthagena. Account of the expedition to. *London*, 1743

Convention, Nat. Proc. of for protection of Amer. Int. Apr. 5, 1841. *N. Y.*

Connery, Edward D .Amer lib. vindic., and right of Foreigners to share its blessings, defended. Oration. *N. Y.*, 1844

Codman, John. Sermon 57th Anni., deliv. Dec, 7, 1845. *Boston*, 1846

Controversy between Drs. Wainwright and Potter. "Can there be a church without a bishop?" *New York*, 1844

482 Miscellaneous. [*Fifteen.*]

Clapton, Capt. Hist. and descrip. of Steamship Great Britain, built at Bristol. *New York*, 1845

Cortland Academy, Jubilee of, celeb. at Homer, N. Y., July 7, 8, 1846.

Colwell, Stephen. Position of Christianity in U. S. *Phila.*, 1854

Chase, S. P. Argument for the Supreme Court of U. S., Dec., 1846, in the case of Jones *vs.* John Vanzandt. *Cairo*, 1847

Chalmers, Thomas. Miscellanies, embracing Reviews, Essays, and Addresses. *New York*, 1847

Corn Acts. Abstracts of, with extracts from the report of the select committee. *London*, 1785

Carlyle, Thomas. Latter-Day Pamphlets—No. I, "The Present Time." March, 1850.

Champlain, M. B. Speech of, on impeachment of John C. Mather. In Assembly, June 15, 1853.

Cady, Daniel P. Farewell Sermon preached to Evan. Church and Soc. in Westboro', Mass., Jan. 27, 1856.

Caird, John. Sermon—Religion in common life—before Her Maj. the Queen and Prince Albert. *Phila.*, 1856

Commercial Agency. Annual, for 1857, by Tappan & McKillop.

Chipman, Samuel. Rep. of Exam. of Poor-Houses, Jails, &c., in N. Y. *Albany*, 1835

Cemetery. Exposition of Plan and Objects of Greenwood. *N. Y.*, 1839

Craik, Rev. James. Essay on the Divine Life and New Birth. *N. Y.*, 1850

Creesey, Rev. E. H. Sermon on Fifth Sunday after Trinity.

483 Miscellaneous. [*Sixteen.*]

Chesapeake, calm and dispassionate Enquiry into the Question of the, and necessity of war, 1807.

Cobb, Oliver. Sermon by E. Dexter, Jan. 18, 1809. *New Bedford.*

Corbett, William. Address, Nov. 13, 1844. *Boston*, 1815

Crowell, Robert. Sermon at Ipswich, July 23, 1818. *Andover.*

Crowninshield, Benj. Address deliv. Jan. 9, 1826. *Salem.*

Contostavlos, Alex. Narrative of material facts relative to building of the Two Greek Frigates. *New York*, 1826

Carlile, Richard. Sermon on subject of Deity, Sept. 9. *London*, 1827

Cogswell, Wm. Valedictory disc., Dec. 20, 1829. *Boston*, 1830

Cambridge Divinity School, Disc. by F. W. P. Greenwood, Jan., 1830, on Theology of.

Craig, James. Hist. of case of spectral illusion (from "Edin. Med. and Surg. Journal," No. 129).
Cobb, Alvin. Sermon in Attleboro' and Seekonk, Dec. 26, 1832.
Chipman, D. Speech, deliv. at Montpelier, Jan. 6, 1836. *Middlebury*, 1837
Campbell, John. Consid. and Arguments proving the inexpediency of an Internat. Copyright Law. *New York*, 1844
Cheever, Ezekiel. Elementary Grammar for study of Latin Language. *Boston*, 1838
Chinese collec., descrip. catalogue of, in Phil., by Nathan Dunn.
Canton, descrip. of city of; with appendix, containing an account of population of Chinese Empire, weights and measures. *Canton*, 1839

484 Miscellaneous. [*Sixteen.*]

Castlereagh, Lord. Spirit of Despotism. Dedicated to, *London*, 1821
Catechism of Man, pointing out the Rights and Duties of every Rational Being. *London*, 1794
Cooper, J. G. Essay on Comets. *Phila.*, 1832
Corrector, or Independent American, No. 2. *New York*, 1816
Croes, Rev. John. Sermon before Conven. of Prot. Epis. Ch., Phila., May 23, 1814.
Cape Cod, History of. Annals of Barnstable Co., by Frederick Freeman. No. 6. *Boston*, 1862
Chapter of Modern Chronicles.
Cevallos, Don Pedro. Exposition of the Practices and Machinations which led to the Usurpation of Crown of Spain. *N. Y.*, 1808
Currency Gold Note. Short Essays on. *New York*, 1858
Coolidge, J. I. T. Farewell disc. deliv. at 13th Cong. Ch., July 4, 1858, Boston.
Corning, J. L. Disc. Thanksgiving, deliv. Nov. 18, 1858.
Century Club. Twelfth night at the, 1859.
Campe, F. F. F. Philanthropic letters to the Million. *N. Y.*, 1859
Cambridge. Mayor's address at the organiz. of city government, and reports, 1859.
Cox, Richard. Farewell Sermon in Zion Ch., N. Y., June 12, 1859.
Cushman Monument. Proc. at the consecration of, Sep. 16, 1858.

485 Miscellaneous. [*Seventeen.*]

Cemetery, Mount Auburn. Catalogue of the lots in, &c., 1860.
Callaway, B. C. Remedies of, for the diseases of horses. *Trenton*, 1860
Clemson, Thos. G. Notes on the character of Mines.
Chenango. Boiler Explosion,—Coroner's Inquest,—Two verdicts, 1864.
Crosby, Howard. Sermon in 4th Avenue Pres. Ch., Sept. 11, 1864.

Catlin, Geo. The Breath of life, by. *New York*, 1865

Chauncey, N. Conditions of success in Genealogical Investigations, illus. in char. of. By W. C. Fowler, 1866.

Coombe, F. Splendid discovery. A beautiful plan to give every man a nice house and lot. *New York*, 1868

Canonization, Comedy of, in four scenes. *New York*, 1868

Chemistry in its application to Agric. and Phys., by Justin Liebeg. *Phil.*, 1845

——— Animal or Organic, in its applica. to Physiology and Pathology, by Wm. Gregory. *Phil.*, 1847

Christian Observer, Jan., 1817.

Club-Room, The. Nos. 1, 2, 3, Feb., March, April, 1820.

Colden, C. Campbell. Identities of Light and Heat, of Caloric and Electricity. *Phila.*, 1848.

Cooper, Judge. Opinion of, on Effect of a Sentence of a Foreign Court of Admiralty, by Alex. J. Dallas. *Phila.*, 1810

——— J. Fennimore. Letters to his Countrymen. *N. Y.* 1834

Cooper, Thomas. Fabrication of the Pentateuch proved in the Anachronisms. *New Jersey*, 1840

486 Miscellaneous. [*Fourteen.*]

Clark, Jefferson. Address delivered before Franklin Typographical Society, Jan. 7, 1826.

Coriolanus. Remarks on Late Infraction of Treaty at New Orleans. *New York*, 1803

Colman, Henry. Discourse on Proper Character of Religious Institutions. *Salem*, 1825

Callender, T. J. Political Progress of Britain. *Phila.*, 1795

Considerations which demand Attention of Farmers, Mechanics, &c. *New York*, 1828

Comptroller, Report of the, on Finances of the City. *New York*, 1826

Cutbush, James. Oration on Education. *Phila.*, 1812

Cincinnati. Fourth and fifth annual reports of the board of directors and treasurer of the Theolog. and Religious Library Association. *Cincinnati*, 1868

Crito's Letters to the Electors of the U. S. on Commercial Representation and the Seat of Government. *Phila.*, 1807

Commentary on Duties of the Public Ministry.

Claybaugh, Rev. Joseph. Introd. Address to Students of the Theological Sem. of Second A. R. Synod of the West, Nov. 9, 1840. *Oxford.*

——— —— Address. Nov. 1, 1841. *Rossville.*

——— —— Address. Nov. 13, 1843. *Rossville*

——— —— Address. Nov. 10, 1844. *Rossville*

487 Miscellaneous. [*Twelve*].

Calvinistic Doctrine of Predestination Unmasked. *Boston*, 1828

Camillus. Defence of Treaty of Amity, Commerce and Navigation between U. S. of America and G. Britain, by. *New York*, 1795

Colman, Henry. Disc. on the proper character of religious Institutions. Dec. 7, 1824. *Salem*

——— ——— Sermon, Review of. *Salem*, 1825

Colton, Walter. Remarks on Duelling. *New York*, 1828

——— ——— Reply to allegations of Bishop Kenrick on Public Schools. *Phila.*, 1844.

Coffin, Robt. S. The Eleventh Hour; or, Confessions of a Consumptive. *Boston*, 1827

——— ——— Oriental Harp, Poems of. 1826

China, To and Back. Diary of Albert Smith. 1859

Carthagena. Remarks on Canal, or "Dique" of. *New York*, 1855

Chicago. Report of Com. on Statistics for City of. *Chicago*, 1863

Colenso, Bishop. Reply to. Attack on the Pentateuch, by the Hebrew Wood Chopper. *San Francisco*, 1863

488 Miscellaneous. [*Fifteen.*]

Carey, M. Review of Evidence of a General Conspiracy of the Roman Catholics of Ireland to Massacre all Protestants that would not join them, Oct. 23, 1641. *Philadelphia*, 1834

Custom House Officers.

Childe Martin. Epic Poem. *New York*, 1840

Clayton, John. Sermon on Duty of Christians to Magistrates. *London*, 1791

China. Our Commercial and Political Relations with. *Washington*, 1855

Campbell, John. Considerations and Arguments proving the Inexpediency of an International Copyright Law. *New York*, 1844

Cato. Examination of the Treaty of Amity, Commerce and Navigation between the U. S. and G. Britain, by. 1795

Congress, Cautionary Hints to, Respecting Sale of Western Lands belonging to the U. S. *Second Ed.* *Phila*, 1796

Clarke, Adam. Letter to a Methodist Preacher on his entrance into the Work of the Ministry, by. *Second Ed.* *Lond.*, 1800

Columella. Inquiry into the Effects of our Foreign Carrying Trade, by *New York*, 1806.

Chalmers, Thomas. Sermon, April 18, 1813. *New York*, 1817

Conwell, Rev. Dr. H. True Copy of Excommunication of Church of Rome, by, against Rev. Wm. Hogan. *Phila.*, 1821

Cumming, Rev. F. H. The Spiritual Character of the Liturgy of Prot. Epis. Church. *Second Ed.* *New York*, 1832

Comets, Tract on, by John Farrar. *Boston*, 1832

Camp-Meetings Described and Exposed. "Strange Things" Stated.

489 Miscellaneous. [*Fourteen.*]

Cheetham, James. Reply to the Memorial of Thomas Storm, John Hone, and Peter J. Monro. *New York*, 1804

——— ——— Peace or War? or Thoughts on our affairs with England. *New York*, 1807

Cheetham, James. Dissertation concerning Political Equality and the Corporation of New York. *New York*, 1800

Colden, Cadwallader D. Answer of Mr. Sullivan to Letters and Misstatements of *Troy*, 1823

——— ——— Letters to, from Wm. A. Duer. *Albany*, 1817

——— ——— Speech of, on Repeal of Laws prohibiting Private Banking. *Albany*, 1825

Clay, Henry. Address containing certain Testimony in Refutation of Charges made against him by Gen. Andrew Jackson. *New Brunswick*, 1828

——— ——— Life of, by N. Sargent. *Phila.*, 1844

——— ——— Life and Public Services of, by Epes Sargent. *New York*, 1844

——— ——— Fifty reason why he should be elected President of the U. S., by George C. Collins. *Balt.*, 1844

Caisson, A. E. Second appeal to the Sons of Israel. *London*, 1827

——— ——— Third appeal to the Sons of Israel. *London*, 1827

Central Park. Communication to the Commissioners of, by A. H. Green. *New York*, 1866

——— ——— Few Remarks on.

490 Miscellaneous. (*Valuable lot.*) [*Sixteen.*]

Cairo, (N. A.) Past, Present, Future of the City of. *Portland, Sept.* 29, 1858

Calvert, George. Review on life and character of. Discourse by John P. Kennedy. *Baltimore*, 1846

Calvert, George H. Oration on Fortieth Anniversary of battle of Lake Erie, delivered in Newport, R. I., by. *Sept.* 10, 1853

Clap, Thomas. Essay on the nature and foundation of moral virtue and obligation. *New Haven*, 1765

Carver, William. A letter to the Rev. E. Burne. *Newark*, 1820

Cleveland. Inaug. of Perry Statue at. *Sept.* 10, 1860

Catskill Mountains, Scenery of, as described by Irving, Cooper, Bryant and others. 1864

Carey, Samuel. Address to Merrimack Humane Society, Sept. 2, 1806.

Cushman, R. Sermon. Sin and danger of Self-Love. Being the first sermon ever delivered in New England. Reprinted from the London edition, 1721. *Stockbridge, Mass.* 1804

Church, J. H. First Settlement of New England. Sermon delivered April 5, 1810.

Clark, M'Donald. Afara; or, the Belles of Broadway. *New York*, 1829

——— ——— The Same. Part III.

Carver, William. Select pieces in prose and verse, on various subjects. *New York*, 1834.

——— ——— A bone to gnaw for Grant Thorburn. *New York*, 1836

491 Miscellaneous. [*Fourteen.*]

Clarke, Uriah. Lectures on city life and char. *Lowell,* 1849

Cumming, Cooper. Sermon on divinity of our Lord and Saviour Jesus Christ. *Delivered in Albany,* 1823

Cumming, T. G. Description of bridges over Menai strait, Conway and Thames Rivers, with views. *London,* 1828

Cummings, George D. Discourse delivered in Trinity Church, Sept. 9, 1855. *Washington*

Comet. The Theo. and Polit.; or, Free-thinking Englishmen. August 28, 1819.

——— An Essay on.

——— The. May, 1833.

Constituzione-della Societá Italiana in Nuova York. 1840.

Constitution of the United States and acts of Naturalization. *Rochester, N. Y.,* 1855

Constitucion de la Sociedad Democratica de los Amigos de America. *Nueva York,* 1864

Calhoun, Mr., of South Carolina. Speech of, on report of Mr. Grundy, of Tennessee, Feb. 5, 1840. *Washington*

——— John C. Private life of, by Mary Bates. *Charleston,* 1852

——— ——— Life of, and History of Political events from 1811–1843. *New York.*

——— ——— Speech of, March 16, 1846.

492 California Pamphlets. [*Eight.*]

California. Burns Ranche Gold Mining Company; account of its location, title, mineral riches, etc. Dec., 1851.

——— Volcano Quartz Mining Company. *N. Y.,* 1852

——— Governor's Annual Message to the Legislature. Jan. 2, 1854. *Benicia*

——— Second Inaug. Address of his excellency, John Bigler. Jan. 7, 1854. *Benicia*

——— Gold Mines of. By G. G. Foster. *New York*

——— The Pioneer; or, Cal. Monthly Magazine, Oct., 1854. *San Fran.*

——— Diary of a Physician in. By Jas. L. Tyson, N. Y. *Phila.,* 1850

——— Upper; Geographical Memoir upon. By J. C. Fremont. *Washington,* 1848

493 Canal Pamphlets. No duplicates. [*Twenty.*]

Serious Appeal on the subject of a Canal communication between the Western Lakes and the Hudson. By a Friend to his Country. *N. Y.,* 1816

Considerations on the Great Western Canal, from the Hudson to Lake Erie. 2*d Ed.* *New York, Oct.,* 1818

Report of the Secretary of War relative to Roads and Canals. *Washington, Jan.* 14, 1819

Ploughshare, Peter. Considerations against continuing the Great Canal west of the Seneca. *N. Y.*, 1819

Tacitus. The Canal Policy of the State of New York. *Albany*, 1821

Troup, Robt. Letter to the Hon. Brockholst Livingston on the Lake Canal Policy of N. Y. *Albany*, 1822

Report of the commissioners of N. J. for the purpose of exploring the route of a Canal to unite the Delaware and Passaic Rivers, near Newark. *Morristown*, 1823

Proceedings at a general convention of delegates held in Washington on the subject of the Chesapeake and Ohio Canal. *Wash., Nov.*, 1823

Cunning, F. H. Address deliv. at the laying of the Cap Stone of the Ten Combined Locks at Lockport, June 24, 1825.

Tibbetts, George. The Finances of the Canal Fund of N. Y. *Albany*, 1829

Tower, R. Appeal to people of N. Y. in favor of the construction of the Chenango Canal. *Utica*, 1830

Remarks on the Sodus Canal and its Probable, Immediate, and Prospective Revenue. *N. Y.*, 1832

Appeal to the people of the State of N. Y. in favor of constructing the Genessee and Alleghany Canal. *New York*, 1833

Seward, Wm. H. Address deliv. at commencement of the Auburn and Owasco Canal, Auburn Oct. 14, 1835.

Charter of the Portage Canal and Manufacturing Co. *New York*, 1837

Remarks on the Canal or "Dique" of Carthagena, New Granada. *N. Y.*, 1855

The Practicability of a Ship Canal to connect the Atlantic and Pacific Oceans. *N. Y.*, 1855

Canal Co. An Act to Incorp. the Black River. *N. Y.*, 1828

Canal Commissioners, Annual Report of; Jan. 25, 1819. *Albany*

Canal Communication. Serious Appeal to the Wisdom and Patriotism of Legislature of N. Y. on subject of a Canal between Great Western Lakes and the Hudson. 1816

494 Catalogues. [*Ten.*]

Peale's Museum; A Scientific and Descriptive Catalogue of. *Phila.*, 1796

Priestley, Dr.; A Catalogue of Books written by. *London*

Buckminster, J. S.; A Catalogue of the Library of. *Boston*, 1812

Paff, M.; Catalogue of. Gallery of Paintings. *N. Y., May* 15, 1812

Hobart, Bp.; Catalogue of Books of Library of. *N. Y., Oct.*, 7, 1831

Morrison Educ. Soc.; Catalogue of Books of Library of. *Canton, Jan.* 1, 1838

Catalogue of Natural Productions and Curiosities of Cabinet of Natural History in N. Y., 1804.

Catalogue of Officers and Cadets of American Literary, Scientific and Military Academy. *Middletown, Ct.*, 1826
Catalogue of Collection of Rare Minerals for Study of Crystallography. *N. Y.*, 1829
Catalogue of Rare, Scarce and Valuable Books from Libraries of Dukes of York, Gloucester, Grafton and others. *N. Y.*, 1839

495 Catholic Pamphlets. No duplicates. [*Seventeen.*]

Wharton, Chas. H. A Short Answer to a True Exposition of the Doctrines of the Catholic Church, touching the Sacrament of Penance, etc. *Phila.*, 1814
Address of the Lay Trustees to the Congregation of St. Mary's Church. *Phila.*, 1822
Letter to the Roman Catholics of Philadelphia and the United States, by a Friend. *Phila.*, 1822
Smith, Samuel B. Renunciation of Popery. *6th Ed.* *Phila.*, 1833
Thomas, John. Examination of the Seven Sacraments of the Church of Rome. *Phila.*, 1834
The Roman Catholic Congressional Exposed, in three letters to a late cabinet minister. *Dublin*, 1837
Kenrick, Francis P.; Letter to. By W. R. Whittingham. *N. Y.*, 1841
Backus, M. M. Calvin on Romish Relics. *N. Y.*, 1844
Murray, N. The decline of Popery and its causes. *N. Y., Jan.* 15, 1851
An Answer to Six Months in a Convent, exposing its falsehoods and absurdities. By the Lady Superior. *2d Ed.* *Boston*, 1835
Review of the Lady Superior's Reply, etc.; being a vindication of Miss Reed. *Boston*, 1835
A Letter to the Rev. Wm. V. Harold, on reading his late Reply to a "Catholic Layman." *Phila.*, 1822
Appendix to the Address of the Lay Trustees of St. Mary's Church, etc. *Phila.*, 1823
Philalethe's Exposition of the principles of the Roman Catholic Religion, etc. *Hartford*, 1830
Catholics, Roman; Reply to an Address to the. *Phila.*, 1785
Catholics, Roman; Address to the. By a Catholic Clergyman. *Annapolis*, 1784
Convent, Answer to Six Months in a. By the Lady Superior. *Boston*, 1835
Convent, Review of Lady Superior's Reply to Six Months in a; being a Vindication of Miss Reed. *2d Ed.* *Boston*, 1835

496 Channing Pamphlets. [*Fourteen.*]

Channing, Wm. E. Sermon on Public Fast. *Boston, April* 5, 1810
——— Two Sermons on Infidelity. *Boston*, 1813
——— Sermon deliv. in Boston, Sept. 18, 1814.
——— Letter to Rev. Samuel C. Thatcher. *3d Ed.* *Boston*, 1815

Channing, Wm. E., Letter to — on subject of Letter to Rev. Samuel C. Thatcher, by Samuel Worcester. 2*d Ed.* *Boston*, 1815

——— Letter to—on subject of Letter to Rev. Samuel C. Thatcher, by Samuel Worcester. 3*d Ed.* *Boston*, 1815

——— Letter to—Remarks on Rev. Dr. Worcester's letter to. *Boston*, 1815

——— Second Letter to—by Rev. Samuel Worcester. *Boston*, 1815

——— Second Letter to—by Rev. Samuel Worcester. 3*d Ed.* *Boston*, 1815

——— Remarks on Rev. Dr. Worcester's Second Letter to. *Boston*, 1815

——— Third Letter to—by Samuel Worcester. *Boston*, 1815

——— Sermon at Ordi. of Rev. Mr. Gannet. *Boston*, 1824

——— Sermon at Ordi. of Rev. Jared Sparks, May 5, 1819. 2*d Ed.* *Baltimore*

——— Letters to—by Moses Stuart. *Andover*, 1819

497 Channing Pamphlets. [*Fifteen.*]

Channing, Wm. E. Sermon—Annual Election, May 26, 1830. *Boston*

——— Sermon at Ordi. of Charles F. Barnard and Frederick T. Gray. *Boston*, 1834

——— Sermon on War. *Boston*, 1835

——— Discourse before Benev. Fraternity of Churches—First Anniv., Boston, April 9, 1835.

——— Sermon by—April 5, 1810. Day of Public Fast.

——— Disc. on, deliv. from Military Despotism, June 15, 1814.

——— Sermon at Ordin. of J. Sparks, May 5, 1819. *Boston*

——— Sermon at Ordin. of J. Sparks. 7*th Ed.* May 5, 1819. *Boston*, 1821

——— Disc. deliv., Installation of M. J. Motte, May 21, 1828.

——— Sermon on War, deliv. Jan. 25, 1835. *Boston*

——— Disc. at Dedication of Sec. Congre. Unitarian Church. *N. Y.*, 1826

——— Disc. at Ordi. of Rev. Fred. A. Farley. *Boston*, 1828

——— Walter. Thoughts on Temperance Reform. *Boston*, 1834

——— Henry. Sermon at Funeral of Mrs. Anna Strong, March 22, 1789. *Hartford*

——— Dr. Remarks on Slavery, by an Abolitionist. *Boston*, 1826

498 Church Centennial Celebrations. *Valuable lot.* [*Five.*]

Albany, N. Y. Acts and Proceedings of the central Synod of Reformed Dutch Ch. in N. A., June and April, 1828. *New York*

Albany, N. Y. Disc. deliv. in the Dutch Ch. before the Northern Missionary Soc. of N. Y., at their Organization, by J. B. Smith.

Barre, Mass. Disc. on Fiftieth Anniver., Jan. 11, 1854 ; by J. Thompson.

Beverly, Mass. Articles of Faith and Form of Covenant adopted by Joseph Emerson. *Boston*, 1807

Bolton, Lancaster, Sterling and Stow ; Confession of Faith and Covenant of Evang. churches of. *Mar.*, 1830

499 Church Centennial Celebrations. *Valuable lot.* [*Twenty-two.*]

Boston, Mass. Mount Vernon Ch., 1847.

——— Mount Vernon Church ; Catalogue of—Feb. 1, 1848.

——— Park St. Ch. The Articles of Faith and the Covenant. *Boston*, 1841

——— Park St. Ch. The Articles of Faith and the Covenant. *Boston*, 1850

——— Park St. Ch. The Articles of Faith and the Covenant. *Boston*, 1859

——— Union Ch., Essex St. Confession of Faith and Covenant. *Boston*, 1830

——— Pitts St. Ch. Letter to the Ch. and Soc. at, Dec. 31, 1838.

——— New Cong. Ch. Confession of Faith and Covenant of the new Con. Ch., June, 1, 1842. *Boston*

——— Disc., Dec. 28, 1823. *Boston*, 1824

——— Disc. deliv. in West Church in—by Chas. Lowell. *Cam.*, 1845

——— Disc. deliv. by Thomas Baldwin, Jan. 1824.

——— Two Discourses, containing the History of the Old North and New Brick Churches, deliv. May 20, 1821, by Henry Ware.

——— History of the Old South Church in, 1830 ; by Benj. Wisner.

——— History of the Old South Church, in four sermons, by Benj. Wisner. *Boston*, 1830

——— (Old South.) Reasons for Investigating Prudential Affairs of, with copies of Mrs. Norton's Deeds. 1859.

——— Commem. Disc. in New South Church, Dec. 25, 1864. *Boston*, 1865

——— Sermon preached to the Chand. Soc. in Brattle St., Dec. 29, 1779, occasioned by the completion of a century, by Peter Thatcher. *Boston*, 1800

——— Bowdoin St. Ch. Articles of Faith and Covenant of. *Boston*, 1843

——— Bowdoin St. Ch. Articles of Faith and Covenant of. *Boston*, 1856

——— Salem St. Ch. Articles of Faith and Covenant of, June 1, 1853.

——— Sermon preached to the First Church on the twentieth Anniv., by N. L. Frothingham. *Boston*, 1835

——— Sermon preached in First Ch., May 10, 1868, by Rufus Ellis.

500 Church Centennial Celebrations. *Valuable lot.* [*Thirteen.*]
Cambridge, Mass. 25th Anniv. commem. of Settlement of, J. A. Albro. *Cam.* 1860
——— Disc. on the Ch. gathering in 1636, deliv. in First Ch. Feb. 22, 1846, by Wm. Newell. *Boston,* 1846
Charlestown, Mass. Two disc. in Harvard Ch., Mar. 15, 1840, by G. E. Ellis.
——— Articles of Faith and Covenant of First Ch. *Bost.,* 1842
Chelsea, Mass. Hist. disc. deliv. at twenty-fifth Anniv. of the Winnisimmet Cong.Ch., by Isaac P. Langworthy. *Chelsea,* 1866
Chicopee. Centen. disc. before 1st Cong. Soc. in, Sept. 26, 1852, by E. B. Clark. *Springfield,* 1852
Churches, Reformed. Centurial Jubilee celebration by all, Oct., 1517. 12½
Church, Holy Roman. A New Defence of, against Heretics and Schismatics. *London,* 1816
Clark, Samuel. The Fatal Vespers. True and full narrative of that judgment of God upon the Papists by the fall of the house in Black Friers. *London,* 1817
Cohasset, Mass. Articles of Faith and the Covenant, 2nd Cong. Ch. in, Nov. 24, 1824.
Concord, Mass. Half Century Disc. deliv. Nov. 16, 1828, by Ezra Ripley. *Very scarce.*
Concord, N. H. Disc. on Forty years' Minist., March 23, 1865, by Nath'l Bouton. *Very scarce.*
——— Two Sermons, 1st Ch., Nov. 21, 1830, Commem. of Organiz. of and settlement of First Minist., Nov. 18, 1730, by Nath'l Bouton. *Scarce.*

501 Church Centennial Celebrations. *Valuable lot.* [*Twelve.*]
Deerfield, Mass. 1st Ch. in. Fiftieth Anniv. disc., by S. Willard. *Greenfield,* 1858
Dorchester, Mass. Memorial of the First Church in, from its first settlement to the end of sec. century, July 4, 1830, by Thaddeus Mason Harris. *Scarce.* *Boston,* 1830
East Boston, Mass. Manerick Church, Articles of Faith and Covenant of. *Boston,* 1844
Elizabeth-Town. Three Sermons deliv. by David Magie. 1830.
Elizabeth-Town, N. J. Hist. notices of Saint John's Church, by John C. Rudd. *Very scarce.* *Elizabeth-Town,* 1825 12½
Elizabeth, N. J. Parish Statis. of Christ Ch. and Third Annual Address of E. A. Hoffman. 1856
Fairfield, Conn. Hist. disc. delivered in Trinity Ch. in, by N. C. Cornwall.
Franklin, Conn. Half Century Sermon, March 18, 1832. *Norwich,* 1832
Grafton, Mass. Sermon. Hist. notices of the Cong. Ch., by Edmund B. Wilson, Dec. 27, 1846.
Great Barrington, Mass. Centen. anniv. of the Cong. Ch., Dec. 23, 1843, by John Todd.
——— Disc. 50th Anniv. Cong. Ch., by C. Durfee, May 13, 1866.
Groton, Mass. Result of an Eccles. Council, July 17, 1826.

502 Church Centennial Celebrations. [*Seventeen.*]

Hartford, Conn. Centen. disc. delivered in 1st Ch., June 26, 1836, by Joel Hawkes. *Hartford,* 1836

Haverhill, Mass. Disc. at the re-dedication of the Centre Church, by B. F. Hosford. *Boston,* 1860

Hopkinton, Mass. Sermon commem. of twenty-five years of the author's settlement, Dec. 20, 1863, by J. C. Webster.

——— Century Sermon, by Nath'l Howe, Dec. 24, 1815

Hingham, Mass. Sermon deliv. on June 28, 1856, on the Fiftieth Anni., by Josiah Richardson. *Hingham,* 1856

Massachusetts. Inquiry into the right to change the ecclesiastical constitution of the Cong. Ch. of. 1816.

Morris, Ill. Reminiscences of, and Hist. of the Cong. Ch. A discourse by E. B. Turner. *Chicago,* 1865

New York. North Presb. Ch. Manual, 1858.

——— Church of the Puritans. Reply of, to the Protest of Deacons, 1857.

——— Hist. Sketch deliv. at the closing services in St. Stephen's Ch., July 1866, by J. H. Price. *N. Y.,* 1866

Newbury, Mass. Sermon preached May 4, 1806, by J. S. Popkin. *Newburyport,* 1806

New York. Semi-Centen. by Wm. Berrian. *New York,* 1860

——— Madison Sq. Pres. Ch. Appeal of Charles Gould from the session of. *New York,* 1864

——— City. Hist. of the Presb. Church of Geneva, by Hubbard Winslow. *Scarce.* *Boston,* 1859

——— City. Semi-Centen. Disc. in South Dutch Ch., by J. M. Matthews. *N. Y.,* 1858

——— City. Disc. 150th Anni. of First Reformed Dutch Ch., Sept 12, 1866, by Francis M. Kip. *Scarce.* *New York,* 1866

New Jersey. Disc. Hist. notices of Saint Peter's church, in the city of Perth-Amboy, June 19–26, 1825, by J. Chapman. *Elizabeth-Town,* 1830

503 Church Centennial Celebrations. *Valuable lot.* [*Twelve.*]

Portland, Me. Disc. addressed to Bap. Ch. in, Mar. 30, 1828, by Thomas B. Ripley. *Boston*

——— Articles of Faith, &c., St. Lawrence St. Ch., Nov. 1858.

Plymouth. Semi-Centen. disc. Oct. 1, 1851. Commem. of the organiz. of Third Church, by C. S. Porter. *Boston,* 1851

Portsmouth, N. H. Disc. deliv. at the re-opening and dedication of the North Church in, Jan. 31, 1838, by E. Holt.

Pepperell, Mass. Centen. disc. deliv. before the Church of Christ and Second Parish, by D. Andrews. 1847.

Pomfret, Conn. 150th Anni. of the organization of the First Ch. of Christ in, Oct. 20, 1865. *Danielsonville,* 1866

Providence, R. I. Centen. Sermon by Mark Tucker. *Prov.,* 1845

Providence City. 24th Annual Report of Ministry at large in, Jan. 21, 1866, by E. M. Stone. *Prov.,* 1866

Providence, R. I. Disc. on Hist. of 1st Cong. Church, June 19, 1836.

Philadelphia, Penn. Sermon. Centen. Celeb. of the opening of St. Peter's Church, Sept. 4, 1861, by Wm. Heathcote de Lancy *Phil.*, 1862

——— Century Sermon delivered in, Oct. 6, 1807. *Phil.*

——— Proceedings of an Ex-Parte Council, held at the First Cong. Church, Nov. 18th to 20th, 1868. *Phil.*, 1868

504 Church Centennial Celebrations. *Valuable lot.* [*Eleven.*]

Quincy, Mass. Disc. by E. P. Twing, Feb. 19, 1865.

——— Church Manual of the Evang. Cong. Ch, 1863.

——— Articles of Faith and covenant of the Evang. Ch. *Boston*, 1835

——— Disc. deliv. in the First Cong. Ch., Sept. 15, 1850, by William P. Lunt. *Boston*, 1850

——— Disc. deliv. Sept. 29, 1839, on two hundredth anni. of First Cong. Church in, by Wm. P. Lunt. *Boston*, 1840

Rehoboth, Mass. Narrative of the Origin of difficulties in the Cong. Ch. in, and Measures taken to dismiss Rev. Otis Thompson. *Prov.*, 1826

——— Facts and Doc. of 2d Ex-Parte Council, Nov. 1, 1825.

——— Facts and Doc. of 3d Ex-Parte Council, Nov. 29, 1825.

Richmond, W. Disc. deliv. in Grace Ch. in N. Y. *London*, 1830

Rindge, N. H. Confession of Faith and Catalogue of Members of. Jan. 1848. *Keene.*

Roxbury, Mass. Eliot Ch. Art. of Faith, &c. Dec. 31, 1857. *Boston.*

505 Church Centennial Celebrations. *Valuable lot.* [*Ten.*]

Salem, Mass. Address at the re-dedication of First Ch., Dec. 8, 1867.

——— Second Century Lecture of 1st Ch., by C. W. Upham. 1829.

——— Did the First Church of Salem originally have a Confession of Faith distinct from their Covenant? By J. B. Felt. *Boston*, 1856

——— Disc. delivered on the First Centen. Anniv. of the Tabernacle Church, by Samuel M. Worcester. *Salem*, 1835

Saybrook, Conn. Half Cent. Sermon, Sept. 22, 1833, by W. Hotchkiss.

San Francisco, Cal. Decade sermons: two Hist. disc. occasioned by the close of the first ten years' ministry in, March, 1859, by Sam. H. Willey. *San Fran.*, 1859

St. Albans, Vt. Hist. disc. on the rise and progress of the 1st Cong. Ch., by L. L. Dutcher. *St. Albans*, 1860

Stratford, Conn. Christ Church. Historical Disc., March 28, 1855, by Rev. John Paddock.

Troy, N. Y. Brief account of the origin and progress of the divisions in the First Pres. Ch. in 1827.

Topsham, Me. Hist. disc., fiftieth Anni., Sept 2, 1865, by A. Wilson.

506 Church Centennial Celebrations. *Valuable lot.* [*Ten.*]

Templeton, Mass. Sermon in Commem. of 50th Anniv. of the ordination of Rev. Chas. Wellington, Feb. 25, 1807. *Boston*, 1857

United States. Address to the ministers, elders, &c., of the Presb. Church of. *New York*, 1836

Wenham, Mass. Two Sermons deliv. on Second Centen. Anni. of the organiz. of First Ch., by Daniel Mansfield. *Andover*, 1845

West Brookfield. Semi-Centen. disc. March, 1851, by M. Stone.

Wrentham, Mass. Anniv. Sermons deliv. June 14, 1846, by E. Fisk.

Worcester, Mass. Fortieth Anni. of the settlement of Alonzo Hill, March 28, 1867, before the Second Cong. Soc.

——— Hist. disc. on Semi-Centen. Anni. in 1st Bap. Ch., Dec. 9, 1862, by Isaac Davis.

——— Semi-Centen. disc. in First Bap. Church, by I. Davis, 1862.

Westminster, Vt. Sermon. Centen., June, 1867, by P. H. White, 1867.

Watertown, Mass. Three disc. before Cong. Soc. in, by C. Francis. *Cambridge*, 1836

507 Clinton, De Witt, Pamphlets. *Scarce lot.* [*Seven.*]

——— Speech of, January 31, 1809—in Senate. *Albany*, 1809

——— Discourse on Character and Scientific Attainments of. By Samuel L. Mitchell. *N. Y.*, 1828

——— Discourse on Character and Services of. By James Renwick. *N. Y.*, 1829

——— Discourse before Literary Philosophical Society of New York. May, 1814.

——— Discourse Delivered at Schenectady before New York Alpha. July 22, 1823. *Albany.*

——— Address to Benefactors and Friends of Free School Society of New York. *N. Y.*, 1810

——— Sermon on Death of. By Rev. James Wilnor. *N. Y.*, 1828

508 College Pamphlets. [*Nine*].

Burlington College, N. J. Second Baccal. Add. by Bishop Doane. Sept. 29, 1851.

Marshall College, Mercersburg, Pa. Oration by B. Champneys. *Lancaster*, 1837

——— Mercersberg, Pa. Address by J. M. Porter. *Phil.* 1838

People's College, Havana, N. Y., Laying the Cornerstone of. Sept. 2, 1858.

Randolph, Macon College, Va. Discourse by Beverley Tucker. June 16, 1840.

St. John's College, Annapolis, Md. Address by John T. Lomax. Feb. 22, 1842.

Washington College, Conn., Remarks on.

Williams College, Mass. Address by Edward Everett. Aug. 16, 1847.

New Jersey College. Address by W. L. Dayton. April 26, 1843,

509 Columbia College. [*Fifteen*].

——— Statutes of. June 13, 1811. *N. Y.*, 1816

——— Catalogue of the Officers and Students of, with Graduates since 1844; founded 1754. *N. Y.*

——— Statutes of. Nov. 6, 1810. *N. Y.*, 1811

——— do May, 1848. *N. Y.*

——— A Defense of, from the Attack of S. P. Ruggles, by Gouverneur M. Ogden. *N. Y.*, 1854

——— Statutes of. June 13, 1811. *New York*,

——— Inaug. Discourse by James Renwick. January 4. 1821. *N. Y.*

——— Address to the Citizens of New York. Jan. 18, 1830.

——— Address by Gulian C. Verplanck. *N. Y.*, 1830

——— Anniv. Address by Ogden Hoffman. May 12, 1832.

——— Discourse by R. Bunner. Oct. 8, 1834. *New York.*

——— Address by J. McVickar. Oct. 4, 1837. *New York.*

——— Address by N. F. Moore. March 16, 1844. *New York.*

——— Address by W. A. Duer. July 24, 1848. *New York.*

——— Address and Poem. Oct. 27, 1858. *New York.*

510 Columbian College Pamphlets. [*Sixteen.*]

——— Catalogue, with a List of all Academical Honors, 1758 to 1836. *N. Y.*, 1836

——— Catalogue, with a List of all Academical Honors, 1758 to 1844. *N. Y.*, 1844

——— Address before the Alumni, 3d of May, 1826, by Wm. Bard. *N. Y.*, 1826

——— Discourse May 3, 1827, before the National Academy of Design, by S. F. B. Morse. *N. Y.*, 1827

——— Address before the Alumni, May 2, 1832, by Ogden Hoffman. *N. Y.*, 1832

——— Influence of Woman upon the Destiny of a People; Oration, October 3d, 1837, by N. W. Chittenden. *N. Y.*, 1837

——— Political Duties of Scholars. Address before the Alumni, October 7, 1840, by S. G. Raymond. *N. Y.*, 1840

——— Address before the Philolexian and Peithologian Societies, by E. P. Livingston. *N. Y.*, 1831

——— Address before the Philolexian Society, by J. McKnight. *N. Y.*, 1808

——— Address before the Philolexian and Peithologian Societies, August 2, 1830. *N. Y.*, 1830

Columbian College, D. C. Address by Wm. Staughton, January 9, 1822.

——— Address by Tobias Watkins, January 7, 1826.

——— Address by S. L. Southard, December 31, 1827.

——— Address by S. Chapin, March 11, 1829.

——— Address by S. Chapin, April 6, 1835.

——— Address by Edgar Snowden, July 4, 1837.

511 Connecticut Pamphlets. [*Thirteen.*]

——— Catalogue of the First Puritan Settlers of the Colony of, from 1635 to 1665—Nos. 2, 3, 4, 5. By R. R. Hinman. *Very Scarce.*

——— Missionary Society of. Address, with Narrative on the Subject of Missions, 1802. *Hartford,* 1803

——— Missionary Society of, Narrative on the Subject of, for 1807.

——— Exam. of Remarks on considerations of a Second College in. *Hartford,* 1825.

——— Letters on the Present State and probable Results of Theo. Spec. in. 1832.

——— Eastern Assoc. Vindication of Proc. of, in Fairfield County. 1794.

——— Minutes of the General Assoc. of, at their 156th Annual Meeting in New Britain, June 20–22, 1865.

——— Minutes of the General Assoc. of, at their 157th Annual Meeting in West Winsted, June, 19–21, 1866.

——— Laws of the State of, Relating to Education. 1868.

——— "Speech for Conn." Being an Hist. Estimate of the State, by Horace Bushnell. *Hartford,* 1851

——— Catalogue of the First Puritan Settlers of the. By R. Hinman. Nos. 5 and 6. *Hartford,* 1856

——— "The United States Elevated to Glory and Honor." Sermon, by Ezra Stiles. *Scarce. Worcester,* 1785

——— Address of General Assoc. of Pastors of the Consociated Churches of Colony of, to the Consociated Pastors and Churches in said Colony. *N. Y.,* 1776.

512 Controversial Pamphlets. [*Fifteen.*]

Correspondence between Com. Stephen Decatur and Com. James Barron. *Washington,* 1820

——— between Granville S. Pattison and Dr. N. Chapman. 2nd Ed., with Explan. Remarks. *Phila.,* 1821

Woods, Leonard. Remarks on Dr. Ware's Answer. *Andover,* 1822

Fatio, L. C. F. Appeal to People of U. S. against J. K. Paulding

Norton, Andrews. Thoughts on True and False Religion. *Cambridge,* 1823

Pulaski Vindicated from an Unsupported Charge, Inconsiderately or Malignantly introduced in Judge Johnson's Sketches of Life and Correspondence of Maj. Gen. Nathaniel Greene. *Very scarce. Corners' sale,* $7.50 *Baltimore,* 1824

The Washington Miracle Refuted; or, Review of Rev. Mr. Matthews' Pamphlet. *Georgetown,* 1824

Scott, Job. The Knowledge of the Lord, the Only True God, to which is added, Remarks upon the Doctrine of Perseverance. *Phila.,* 1824

Grew, Henry. Letters to Mr. Elias Lee, on his Remarks on

Dr. Millard's Late Publication and on his Strictures on Mr. Grew's Pamphlet on the Character of the Son of God. *Hartford*, 1825

Serious Conference, by Letters on Subject of Religious Worship and of the Church of God. *'St. John, N. B.*, 1826

Channing, W. E. Review of a Disc. preached at Dedication of Sec. Congre. Unitarian Church, N. Y. *Boston*, 1827

Collection of Facts and Documents relating to Eccles. Affairs in Groton, Mass. *Boston*, 1827

Brockway, J. Delineation of Characteristic Features of a Revival of Religion in Troy, in 1826 and 1827. *Troy*, 1827

Whitman, Bernard. Review of Disc. before Sec. Religious Soc. in Waltham. *Boston*, 1827

Morse, Samuel F. B. Reply to Article in No. American Review, entitled "Academies of Arts," etc. *N. Y.* 1828

513 Controversial Pamphlets. [*Fifteen.*]

Vindication of the Rights of the Churches of Christ. *Boston*, 1828

Review of a Pamphlet on the Trust Deed of the Hanover Ch. *Boston*, 1828

Common Sense Addresses to the Citizens of the Southern States. By a Citizen of Phila., 4th Ed., *Phila.*, 1829

Brief Summary of some of the Principal Incidents relative to Life of Ursula Newman and the Intercourse between her and Richard Johnson. *Curious.* *N. Y.* 1829

Gibbons, Wm. Exposition of Modern Scepticism, a Letter addressed to the Editors of the Free Enquirer. *Wilmington*, 1829

Controversy between the First Parish in Cambridge and Rev. Dr. Holmes, Pastor. *Cambridge*, 1829

Whitman, Bernard. Two Letters to Rev. Moses Stuart, on Subject of Religious Liberty. *Boston*, 1830

Notes on the Sayings and Doings of Dr. Lacey and his Three Friends. By Philo Cor-Rector, Esq., *Albany*, 1830

Marsh, John. Exhibition of Religious Sentiments of Presbyterian, Baptist and Methodist Denominations. *Buffalo*, 1831

Howell, R. B. C. Letter to Rev. Henry W. Ducachet, in reply to his "Examin. of Mr. Howell's Review," under the Signature of "An Episcopalian." *Norfolk*, 1832

Result of an Ex-Parte Council, Convened in Providence, June 2, 1832. *Providence*, 1832

Fleming, Lorenzo D. The Young Man's Reply, on Doctrine of the Trinity. Series of Letters addressed to Elder Amos Chase. *Rochester*, 1833

Reply to Rev. John Gibson and others. *N. Y.* 1833

Musgrave, Rev. G. W. Vindication of Religious Liberty; or, the Nature and Efficiency of Christian Weapons. *Baltimore*, 1834

Letter from Edmund Burke to a noble lord, on the attacks made upon him and his pension, in the House of Lords. *Lond.* 1796

22½ 514 Controversial Pamphlets. [*Fifteen.*]

Blatchford, Samuel. Validity of the Presbyterian ordination maintained, a letter to Rev. W. Smith. *New Haven*, 1798

Dialogue, between a Churchman and a Methodist, on the writings of Swedenborg. *London*, 1802

Affectionate address to the clergy, on the theol. writings of Swedenborg. *London*, 1802

Inglesby, John. Letter to Mr. Wm. Parkinson, added, a Dialogue between two brothers, illustrating a doctrine, which by him, is charged with striking at the foundation of a sinner's hope. *New York*, 1808

Letter from a Churchman to his friend in New Haven, containing a few strictures on a pamphlet signed J. R. O. *New Haven*, 1808

Niles, N. Letter to a friend, concerning the Doctrine which teaches that impenitent sinners have natural power to make themselves new hearts. *Windsor*, 1809

Barlow, Joel. Letter to Henry Gregoire, in reply to his letter on the Columbiad. *Washington*, 1809

Ely, Rev. Ezra Stiles. History of ecclesiastical proceedings, relative to the Third Presbyterian Church in Phila. *Phila.*, 1814

Inquiry into the right to change the ecclesiastical constitution of the Congreg. churches of Mass. *Boston*, 1816

Interesting correspondence, between the Rev. John Johnson and Miss Elizabeth Jones, relative to the change in her opinions, which occasioned her dismissal from his ch. *N. Y.* 1817

Rayner, Rev. Menzies. Review of the Rev. Mr. Taylor's sermon on Regeneration. *New Haven*, 1817

Laune, S. de. A plea for the Non-Conformists. In three parts. *London*, 1733

Whitaker, N. Two sermons: on the doctrine of reconciliation. With an Appendix, in answer to a dialogue wrote to discredit the main truths in these discourses, by W. Hart. *Salem*, 1770

Hopkins, Samuel. An inquiry into the nature of true holiness. With an Appendix; containing an answer to the Rev. Mr. Wm. Hart's Remarks on Pres. Edwards's Dissert. on the nature of true virtue, etc. *Newport*, 1773

Examination of a book, entitled, The true Sonship of Christ investigated. *Edinb.*, 1778

20 515 Controversial Pamphlets. [*Fifteen.*]

Conferences on Baptism, between a querist and an apologist. By the Rev. Aaron Kinne. *New London*, 1787

Hopkins, Samuel. An inquiry, concerning the future state of those who die in their sins. *Newport, R. I.* 1783

Second Letter from John Bowden, to Doctor Stiles, in [which] the Rev. Dr. Chauncy's Compleat View of Episcopacy is considered. *New Haven*, 1789

Important, An, Case argued: in three dialogues, between Dr. Opium, Gallio, and Discipulus. 6th ed. *London*, 1790

Modern Gratitude. [Correspondence between Luther Martin and R. R. Keene.] *No title page.*

Emmons, Nathanael. Dissert. on the Scriptural qualifications for admission and access to the Christian Sacraments. *Worcester*, 1793

Observations on, 1st. The chronology of Scripture. 2d. Strictures on the Age of Reason. 3d. The evidence which Reason, unassisted by Revelation, affords us with respect to the nature and properties of the soul of man. 4th. Arguments in support of the opinion, that the soul is inactive and unconscious from death to the Resurrection, derived from Scripture. *New York*, 1795

Examination of Cadwallader D. Colden's Book, entitled a Life of Robert Fulton. By a friend of John Fitch. 1818

Burns, Rev. Robert. Letter to the Rev. Dr. Chalmers, on the distinctive characters of the Protestant and Roman Catholic Religions. *Paisley*, 1818

Birkbeck, Morris. Extracts from a suppl. letter from the Illinois, Jan. 31, 1819. Address to British Emigrants, July 13, 1819. Reply to W. Cobbett, July 31, 1819. *New York*, 1819

Gray, Rev. Frederick T.; Letter to—being Strictures on Two Sermons preached by him. *Boston*, 1842

Douglass, D. B.; Further Statement of Facts and Circumstances of Removal of—from Presidency of Kenyon College. *Albany*, 1845

Graham, John L. Appeal from the Decision of the Auditor of the Post Office Department.

Spencer, Hon. John C. Review of a Pamphlet entitled, Report to the Vestry of St. Peter's Ch., Albany. *N. Y.*, 1846

Proc. of the Trustees of the Greene Foundation in relation to the Election of an Assistant Minister of Trinity Church. *Boston*, 1847

516 Controversial Pamphlets. [*Fifteen.*]

Address of Prot. Epis. Soc. in Western N. Y., for Promotion of Evangelical Knowledge. *Rochester*, 1848

Reply of Vestry of St. Paul's Ch., Castleton, to a pamphlet entitled the "Case of the Prot. Epis. Ch., at New Brighton, Staten Island." *N. Y.*, 1849

Communications from James Boorman to the Stockholders of the Hudson River R. R. Co., in Reply to Mr. A. C. Flagg. *N. Y.*, 1849

Barr, Oliver. Truth Triumphant; or, A Candid Exam. of the Trinitarian Doctrine. *N. Y.*, 1834

Narrative of Recent Occurrences in Eastern Subordinate Synod of Ref. Presb. Church. *N. Y.*, 1834

McDowall, J. R. Charges Against the N. Y. Female Benev. Soc. and the Auditing Com., by. *N. Y.*, 1836

——— History of Prelim. Proc. of Third Presbytery in Case of, including the Charges, Specifications, Sentences, &c. *N. Y.*, 1836

Norton, Andrews. Remarks on a Pamphlet entitled, "The Latest Form of Infidelity Examined." *Cambridge*, 1839

Humphrey, Rev. Dr. The Question—Will the Christian Religion be Recognized as the Basis of the System of Public Instruc. in Mass., discussed in Four Letters to. *Boston*, 1839

Statement of Facts Relating to Controversy between the English St. Matthew's Congre. and the United German Lutheran Churches in N. Y. *N. Y.*, 1840

Correspondence between a Committee and the Pastor of Hollis St. Soc., on Subject of a Second Eccles. Council. *Boston*, 1840

Bacon, Leonard. Seven Letters to Rev. George A. Calhoun, concerning the Pastoral Union of Connecticut and its Charges against the Ministers and Churches. *N. Haven*, 1840

——— An Appeal to the Congre. Ministers of Conn. against a Division. With an Appendix containing Short Notes on Mr. Calhoun's Letters. *N. Haven*, 1840

Exposition of the Peculiarities, Difficulties, and Tendencies of Oberlin Perfectionism. *Cleveland*, 1841

Result of an Eccles. Council. Exeter, N. H. *Boston*, 1842

517 Convention Sermons. [*Fifteen.*]

Barnard, John. Sermon deliv. to Assembly of Ministers, &c. *Boston*, *June* 1, 1738

The Testimony and advice of an Assembly of Pastors in N. E. By order of the Assembly. *Boston*, *July* 7, 1743

Appleton, Nath'l. Sermon before Ministers of Mass. Bay in N. E. Annual Convention. *Boston*, *May* 26, 1743

Barnard, Edward. Sermon before annual convention of Ministers of Mass. Bay, N. E. *Boston*, *May* 27, 1773

——— Thomas. Sermon before convention of Ministers of Commonwealth of Mass. *Boston*, *May* 30, 1793

Belknap, Jeremy. Sermon before convention of Clergymen of Mass. *Boston*, *May* 26, 1796

Osgood, David. Disc. before annual convention of Ministers of Mass. *Boston*, *May* 31, 1798

Dana, Joseph. Sermon before annual convention of Ministers of Mass. *Boston*, *May* 28, 1801

Emmons, Nath'l. Sermon before convention of Ministers in Boston. *Boston*, *May* 31, 1804

Puffer, Reuben. Sermon at annual convention of Ministers of Mass. *Boston*, *May* 30, 1811

Channing, Wm. Ellery. Sermon on War before convention of Ministers of Mass. *Boston*, *May* 30, 1816

Ware, Henry. Sermon before convention of Ministers in Mass. *Boston*, *May* 28, 1818

Holmes, Abiel. Sermon before the convention of Ministers of Mass., in Boston. *Boston*, *May* 27, 1819

Parish, Elijah. Sermon before the convention of Ministers of Mass., in Boston. *Boston May* 30, 1821

Codman, John. Sermon before Pastoral Association of Mass. *Boston*, *May* 24, 1836

ACOTAH ; or Life and Legends of the Sioux around Fort Snelling. By Mrs. Mary Eastman, with preface by Mrs. C. M. Kirkland. *8vo., cl.* *New York*, 1849

519 Dalcho, Frederick, M. D. An historical account of the Protestant Episcopal Church in South Carolina, from the first settlement of the Province, to the War of the Revolution ; with notices of the present state of the church in each parish : and some account of the Early Civil History of Carolina, never before published. Added, The Laws relating to Religious Worship ; the Journals and Rules of the Convention of South Carolina ; the Constitution and Canons of the Protestant Episcopal Church, and the course of Ecclesiastical Studies : with an Index and List of Subscribers. *8vo., sh.* *Charleston*, 1820

520 Dana, James. Sermon Preached April 29, 1789, at his Installation. *8vo., pamphlet.* *New Haven*, 1789

521 Daniel, D. V., Jr. A Vindication of Edmund Randolph. New Ed., with a preface. *16mo., half morocco.* *Richmond*, 1855

522 DANVERS, (Mass.) History of the Town of, from its Early Settlement to 1848. By J. W. Hanson. *12mo., cl., fine copy.* *Danvers*, 1848

523 Danvers Plains, (Mass.) Historical Sketch of School District number Thirteen, North Danvers, or by its ancient name, Porters' Plains. By Geo. Osgood. *8vo. pamph., 32p.* *Salem*, 1855

524 DANVERS, (Mass.) Proceedings at the Reception and Dinner, in honor of George Peabody, Esq., of London, by the citizens of, Oct. 9, 1856, to which is appended an Historical Sketch of the Peabody Institute, with the exercises of the corner-stone, and at the dedication. *Cl. 8vo. Port. of Geo. Peabody and engravings.* *Boston*, 1856

525 Darby William. A Tour from the city of New York to Detroit, in the Michigan Territory, made between the 2d of May and the 22d of September, 1818. *Map, 8vo., unb., uncut.* *New York*, 1819

526 Darby, William. Lecture on the Discovery of America, and the Colonization of North America by the English. *12mo., bds., uncut.* *Baltimore*, 1828

527 Darnell, Elias. A Journal containing an accurate and interesting account of the Hardships, Sufferings, Battles, Defeat and Captivity of those Heroic Kentucky Volunteers and Regu-

lars commanded by General Winchester, in 1812–13; also Two Narratives by Men that were Wounded and taken Captive by the Indians on the river Raisin. 12*mo., half boards.* *Philadelphia,* 1854

528 Dartmouth, Mass. Proceedings in connection with the Celebration at New Bedford, Sept. 14, 1864, of the Two Hundredth Anniversary of the incorporation of the Town. 8*vo pamph.,* 129 *pages.* *New Bedford, Mass.,* 1865.

529 Davenport, (Ia.,) Past and Present; including the Early History and Personal and Anecdotal Reminiscences of, together with Biographies, Likenesses of its Prominent Men; Compendious articles upon the Physical, Industrial, Social and Political Characteristics of the City; Full Statistics of every Department of Note or Interest, &c., by Franc B. Wilkie. 8*vo., cl., Ports.* *Davenport,* 1858

530 Davis, Samuel. Religion and Patriotism the Constituents of a good Soldier. A sermon preached to Capt Overton's Independent Company of Volunteers, raised in Hanover County, Virginia, Aug. 17, 1775. 8*vo., Rox.; fine copy.* *London,* 1756

531 Davis, Adjt. P. M. The four principal battles of the late war; being a full detailed account of the Battle of Chippeway, Fall and Destruction of the City of Washington &c. 8*vo pamph.,* 32 *pages; quite scarce.* *Harrisburg,* 1832

532 Davis, A. Lecture on the Antiquities of Central America, and of the Discovery of New England by the Northmen, five hundred years before Columbus, delivered in New York, Washington, Boston, and other cities. 6*th Ed.* *New York,* 1840.

533 Davis, Rev. Thomas. A Biographical Sketch of, Missionary of the Society for Propagating the Gospel in Foreign parts, in several of the Towns of Litchfield Co., Conn., from the year 1761 to the year 1776. By a minister of the county. 12*mo., bds.; with portrait.* *New Haven, Conn.,* 1843

534 DAVIS, WILLIAM JACKSON. In Memoriam. Memorial, written by Henry B. Dawson, Esq. 4*to, Photograph, uncut, scarce.*

535 Davis, Jefferson, and Stonewall Jackson. Life and Imprisonment of, together with the Life and Military career of Stonewall Jackson, from authentic sources. With portraits of Jeff. Davis, Stonewall Jackson and Gen. R. E. Lee. 12*mo, cl.* *New York,* 1866

536 Dawes, Rufus. The Valley of the Nashaway, and other Poems. 8*vo, cloth.* *Boston,* 1830

537 Dawson, Henry B. Gleanings from the Harvestfield of American History, Part VI. Major-General Israel Putnam. A Correspondence on this Subject with the editor of the "Hartford Daily Post," by "Selah," of that city, and Henry B. Dawson. 4*to, paper.* *No.* 104. *Morrisania,* 1860

538 Dawson, Henry B. Gleanings from the Harvestfield of American History, Part XI. The Assault on Stony Point, by Gen. Anthony Wayne, July 16, 1779. Prepared for the N. Y. Historical Society, and read at its regular monthly meeting, April 1, 1862. With a map, fac-similes, and illustrative notes. 4*to, cl., rubric title, uncut.* 250 *copies.* *No.* 39. *Morrisania, N. Y.,* 1863

539 Dawson, Henry B. The Federalist. A Collection of Essays, writ-

ten in favor of the New Constitution, as agreed upon by the Federal Convention, September 17, 1787. [By Alexander Hamilton and others.] Reprinted from the original text, with an Historical Introduction and Notes, by Henry B. Dawson. In two volumes. *Vol.* 1; *large* 8*vo., bds.; with portrait of Hamilton; rubric title. Only* 250 *copies printed. No.* 246.
Morrisania, N. Y., 1864

540 DEARBORN, GEN. HENRY. Defence of, against the attack of Gen. Wm. Hull. By H. A. S. Dearborn. 8*vo, uncut; Pamp.; fine copy; very scarce;* 28 *p., dble. col.* *Boston*, 1824

541 DEDHAM, MASS. Two Discourses: the First, delivered on taking leave of the Old Meeting-house, February 26th, and the Second, at the dedication of the New House, March 1, 1809. By Tho's Thacher. *Pamphlet,* 32 *pages; scarce.* *Dedham*, 1809

542 DEDHAM, MASS. A Sermon, containing a brief History of the South Church and Parish in Dedham. Delivered June 23, 1816, by Wm. Cogswell. 8*vo Pamphlet,* 23 *pages; fine copy; scarce; uncut.* *Dedham*, 1816

543 DEDHAM, MASS. THE HISTORY OF, from the beginning of its settlement, in Sept. 1635, to May, 1827. By Erastus Worthington. 8*vo; sheets folded; very scarce.* *Boston*, 1827

544 DEDHAM MASS. An Historical Address, delivered before the Citizens of the Town of, on the 21st of Sept., 1836; being the Second Centennial Anniv. of the Incorp. of the Town. By Samuel F. Haven. 8*vo; paper cover; uncut;* 79 *pages; beautiful copy; scarce.* *Dedham*, 1837

545 DEDHAM PULPIT, or Sermons by the Pastors of the First Church in Dedham, in the XVIIth and XVIIIth Centuries; with a Centennial Discourse, by the present Pastor (E. Burgess). 8*vo, cl.; scarce; fine copy.* *Boston*, 1840

546 DEDHAM. HISTORICAL ANNALS OF, from its settlement, in 1635, to 1847. By Herman Mann. 8*vo, sheets folded.*
Dedham, 1847

547 DE KAY, JAMES E. Anniversary address on the progress of the natural sciences in the United States; delivered before the Lyceum of Natural History of New York, Feb., 1826. 8*vo, bds.; scarce.* *New York*, 1826

548 DELAWARE. HISTORY OF THE ORIGINAL SETTLEMENT ON, from its Discovery, by Hudson, to the Colonization under Wm. Penn. To which is added an account of the Swedish settlers, and a History of Wilmington, from its settlement to the present time. By Benj. Ferris. *Illus., cl.,* 8*vo; scarce.* *Wilmington*, 1846

549 DELAWARE COUNTY, (PENN.) HISTORY OF, from the Discovery of the Territory included within its limits to the present time; with a notice of the Genealogy of the County and Catalogues of its Minerals, Plants, Quadrupeds and Birds. By George Smith. 8*vo, cl.; maps and plates. Scarce.* *Phila.*, 1862.

550 DEMAREST, DAVID D. History and Characteristics of the Reformed Protestant Dutch Church. 2*d ed.;* 16*mo, cloth; with plates.* *New York*, 1856

551 DE RIEDESEL, MADAME. Letters and Memoirs relating to the War

of American Independence, and the Capture of the German Troops at Saratoga. *8vo, bds., uncut.* *New York*, 1827

552 De Roos, Hon. F. Fitzgerald. Personal Narrative of Travels in the United States and Canada, in 1826 ; with remarks on the present state of the American Navy. *3d ed.; with plates ; 8vo ; uncut ; unbound.* *London*, 1827

553 De Tocqueville, A. Democracy in America. Translated by Henry Reeve. Edited, with notes, by Francis Bowen. 2 *vols., 8vo ; cl. ; uncut.* 100 *copies printed.* *Cambridge*, 1804

554 Deux Ponts, Count Wm. De. My Campaigns in America : 1780–'81. Translated from the French Manuscript, with an Introduction and Notes. *S. P.*, *8vo.* By Samuel Abbott Green. *Boston*, 1868

555 Devotion, John. A Sermon preached April 8, 1788, at the Interment of Madam Ursula Griswold, Consort of his Excellency Matthew Griswold. *New Haven*, 1788

556 De Witt, Thomas. A Discourse delivered in the North Reformed Dutch Church (Collegiate), in the City of New York, on the last Sabbath in August, 1856. *8vo, cl., Plates.* *New York*, 1857

557 Dexter, Timothy, Life of. Embracing sketches of the eccentric characters that composed his Associates. *12mo, cl., plates.* By Samuel L. Knapp. *Boston*, 1823

558 DIBDIN, THOS. FROGNALL. Bibliomania ; or, Book-Madness : A Bibliographical Romance. Illustrated with cuts. New and Improved Edition, to which are now added preliminary observations and a supplement, including a Key to the assumed characters in the Drama. Engraved Title, wood cuts, and rubricated borders, etc. Large paper. *Half Roxburghe, gilt top, rough edges.* *London, Bohn*, 1842

559 DIBDIN, T. F. A Bibliographical, Antiquarian, and Picturesque Tour in France and Germany. 3 *vols., Imp. 8vo, cf., uncut.* *London, Shakespeare Press*, 1821

560 DIBDIN, THOS. FROGNALL. Bibliophobia. Remarks on the present languid and depressed state of Literature and the Book-trade. In a letter addressed to the author of the Bibliomania. By Mercurius Rusticus. With notes by Cato Parvus. *8vo, bds., uncut.* *London*, 1832

561 Dibdin, Thos. Frognall. A Series of Groups, Illustrating the Physiognomy, Manners, and Character of the People of France and Germany. *Royal 8vo, bds., uncut. With plates.* By Geo. Lewis. *London*, 1823

562 Dibdin, Rev. Thomas Frognall. A Series of Groups, Illustrating the Physiognomy, Manners, and Character of the People of France and Germany. *L. P. cop., or. cov., uncut, 4to,* 3 *parts ; as originally pub.* *London, Eng.*, 1823

563 Dinsmore, Robert. Incidental Poems, accompanied with Letters. And a few Select Pieces, mostly Original, for their Illustration. Together with a Preface and Sketch of the Author's Life. *8vo, bds., uncut.* *Haverhill*, 1828

564 Disclosures Relating to the "A. B. C." Affair. From the Essex Register. *8vo, curious.*

565 Disraeli, Isaac. Curiosities of Literature. With a View of the Life and Writings of the Author by his Son. In four volumes.

8vo, Roxburghe, gilt top, uncut. With portrait and rubricated title page. Privately printed, Riverside Press, Cambridge, 1864

566 DISRAELI, ISAAC. AMENITIES of Literature, consisting of Sketches and Characters of English Literature. A New Edition Edited by his Son, B. Disraeli. In two volumes. *8vo, Roxburghe, uncut. Privately printed, Riverside Press, Cambridge*, 1864

567 DISTURNELL, JOHN. The Western Traveller, embracing the Canal and Railroad Routes from Albany and Troy, to Buffalo and Niagara Falls. Also, the Steamboat Route from Buffalo to Detroit and Chicago. *12mo, cl., plate. N. Y.*, 1844

568 DOCUMENTS Relative to the claims of Mrs. Decatur, with her earn est request that Congress will do her the favor to read them. *8vo, uncut*, 52 *p. Autograph of Edward Everett. Washington*, 1834

569 DODD, WILLIAM. Thoughts in Prison. In five parts: the Impris onment, the Trial, the Retrospect, Futurity, Public Punishment. To which are added Miscellaneous Pieces. Odiorne's Edition. *12mo, sh. Exeter*, 1794

570 DORCHESTER, MASS., Proceedings of the Second Church and Parish in, Exhibited in a Collection of Papers. *8vo, unbound*, 124 *p., fine copy, scarce. Boston*, 1812

Contains much valuable, early Ecclesiastical History.

571 DORCHESTER, MASS., a Discourse Delivered at, June 17, 1830, to Commemorate the Completion of the Second Century from its Settlement by our Pilgrim Fathers. By John Pierce. *8vo, uncut, fine copy, very scarce*, 36 *pages. Boston*, 1830

572 DORCHESTER, MASS. The Sexton's Monitor and Dorchester Memorial. Second Edition. By Daniel Davenport. *12mo pamph.*, 36 *p., scarce. Boston*, 1838

573 DORCHESTER Antiquarian and Historical Society. Number 1.—Memoirs of Roger Clap: 1630. No. 2.—Annals of the Town of Dorchester. By James Blake: 1750. No. 3.—Journal of Richard Mather: 1635. His Life and Death: 1670. 3 *vols., 12mo, bds., scarce. Boston, Mass.*, 1844, 1845, 1846

574 DORCHESTER, Mass. ANNALS OF THE TOWN OF, to 1750. By James Blake. *Half Rox., 12mo, uncut. Boston*, 1846

575 DORCHESTER. Historical Discourse delivered Jan. 2, 1848, on occasion of the Fortieth Anniversary of the Second Church. By Wm. Allen. *8vo pamphlet*, 30 *p., clean copy. Boston*, 1848

576 DORCHESTER, Mass., Recovery of Some Materials for the Early History of. By Samuel G. Drake. *8vo, cl., engravings and map. Boston*, 1851

577 DORCHESTER, Mass., in 1630, 1776, and 1855. An Oration delivered fourth of July, 1855, by Edward Everett. *8vo pamph.*, 158 *p. Boston*, 1855

578 DORCHESTER, Mass., History of the Town of. By a Com. of the Dorc. Ant. Hist. Soc. *8vo, Roxburghe, gilt top uncut. Boston*, 1859

579 DORCHESTER, Mass., Epitaphs from the Old Burying Ground in. *8vo pamphlet, orig. cov.*, 21 *p., uncut. Boston Highlands*, 1869

580 DRAKE, BENJAMIN. Life and Adventures of Black Hawk, with Sketches of Keokuk, the Sac and Fox Indians, and the Late Black Hawk War. *12mo, cl., 7th ed., plates. Cincinnati*, 1846

581 Drake, Benjamin. Life of Tecumseh and of his Brother the Prophet: with a Historical Sketch of the Shawnoe Indians. *12mo, cl., plates.* *Cincinnati,* 1856

82 Drake, Daniel. Discourse on the History, Character, and Prospects of the West: delivered to the Union Literary Society of Miami University, Oxford, Ohio, September 23, 1834. *8vo, paper cov., fine copy, with valuable appendix of notes, very scarce, 56 pages.* *Cincinnati,* 1834

583 DRAKE, DANIEL. Remarks on the Valley of the Mississippi. *8vo pamph., very scarce and important.* *Louisville.* 1833

584 DRAKE, DANIEL. Discourse on History, Character, and Prospects of the West. *8vo pamph., fine copy, very scarce and valuable.* *Cincinnati,* 1834

585 Drake, Daniel. Memoirs of the Life and Services of, Physician, Professor and Author; with Notices of the Early Settlement of Cincinnati, and some of its Pioneer Citizens. By Edward D. Mansfield, LL. D. *8vo., cl.; portrait of Drake.* *Cincinnati,* 1855

586 Drake, Samuel G. The History of Philip's War, commonly called the great Indian War, 1675–1676; also of the French and Indian Wars at the Eastward, in 1689. By Thomas Church, Esq., with numerous Notes, also an Appendix, containing an account of the treatment of the Natives, &c. *Second Ed., with plates; 12mo., hf. mor.* *Exeter, N. H.,* 1829

587 Drake, Samuel G. Indian Biography, containing the lives of more than two hundred Indian Chiefs: Also such others of that race as have rendered their names conspicuous in the History of North America from its first being known to Europeans to the present period. Giving at large their most Celebrated Speeches, memorable sayings, numerous anecdotes and a History of their wars. *8vo, cl.; engravings.* *Boston,* 1832

588 Drake, Samuel G. Biography and History of the Indians of North America; comprising a General account of them, also a History of their Wars; likewise exhibiting an analysis of the most Distinguished as well as Absurd Authors, who have written upon the great question of the First Peopling of America. *3d. ed., 8vo, sh.; plates.* *Boston,* 1834

589 Drake, Samuel G. Biography and History of the Indians of North America, from its first discovery to the present time; comprising a history of their wars, massacres, and depredations, with an account of their Antiquities, Manners and Customs, Religion and Laws. *Seventh Ed., with engravings; 8vo, cloth.* *Boston,* 1837

590 Drake, Samuel G. The Book of the Indians; or, Biography and History of the Indians of North America, from its First Discovery to the year 1841. *8th Ed., plates; 8vo, cl., rough edges.* *Boston,* 1841

591 Drake, Samuel G. A Review of Winthrop's Journal, &c. *8vo., uncut, 23 p., scarce.* *Boston,* 1854

592 Drake, Samuel G. The History of Philip's War, commonly called The Great Indian War of 1675–1676, also of the French and Indian Wars at the Eastward in 1689. By Thomas Church,

Esq., with numerous Notes, also an Appendix, Containing an Account of the treatment of the Natives, &c. *2d. Ed., with plates; 12mo, sheep.* *Boston,* 1860

593 Drake, Samuel G. News from New England, Being a true and last Account of the present Bloody Wars carried on betwixt the Infidels, Natives, and the English Christians and Converted Indians of New England, declaring the many dreadful battles fought betwixt them; As also the many Towns and Villages burnt by the merciless Heathens. And also the true number of all the Christians slain since the beginning of that War, as it was sent over by a Factor of New England to a Merchant in London. London, 1676. *Boston, N. E., reprinted* 1850

In same volume, two Catalogues of Rare and useful Books, chiefly Historical, relating principally to New England. *Half calf, 8vo., rough edges.* *Boston,* 1864–66

594 Drake, Samuel G. The Witchcraft Delusion in New England, its Rise, Progress, and Termination, as exhibited by Dr. Cotton Mather, in "The Wonders of the Invisible World," and by Mr. Robert Calef, in his "More Wonders of the Invisible World." With a Preface, Introduction, and Notes. *3 vols., sm. p.; 8vo, rubric;* 280 *copies printed, No.* 109. *Printed for W. Elliot Woodward.* *Roxbury, Mass.,* MDCCCLXVI

——— ——— *The Same, L. P.*

595 Drake, Samuel G. The Old Indian Chronicle; being a collection of Exceeding Rare Tracts, written and published in the Time of King Philip's War, By Persons residing in the Country. To which are now added an Introduction and Notes. *No.* 36, *4to, large paper; paper covers, map.* *Boston,* 1867

596 ——— ——— *The Same, S. P., cl., uncut; half mor., gilt top, uncut.*

597 Dudley, (Mass.) An Anniversary Discourse, delivered March 20, 1853, with Topographical and Historical Notices of the Town. By Joshua Bates. *8vo, cloth;* 58 *pages.* *Boston,* 1853

598 DUNBARTON, (N. H.) History of the Town of, from the Grant by Mason's assigns, in 1751 to 1860. By Caleb Stark. *8vo., cl.* *Concord,* 1860

599 Dunbarton, (N. H.) Address at the Centennial Celebration. By Rev. A. W. Burnham, D. D. *8vo pamph.* *N. H.,* 1865

600 Dunbarton, (N. H.) Record of the Centennial Celebration of the Incorporation of the Town of, Sept. 13, 1865. *8vo pamph.,* 124 *pages; scarce.* *Manchester, N. H.,* 1866

601 Duncan, John M. Travels through part of the United States and Canada, in 1818–19. In two volumes. *Full calf, 8vo.* *Glasgow,* 1823

602 Dunham, Capt. Jacob. Journal of Voyages, containing an account of the author's being twice captured by the English, and once by Gibbs, the pirate; his narrow escape when chased by an English war schooner, as well as his being cast away and residing with the Indians. *Cl., 12mo; with illustrations.* *New York,* 1850

603 Dunshee, Henry Webb. History of the School of the Reformed Protestant Dutch Church in the City of New York, from 1633

to the present time. With an Introduction by Rev. Thomas De Witt, D.D. 12*mo., cloth.* *New York*, 1853

604 DUNSTABLE, (Mass.) History of the Old Township of, including Nashua, Nashville, Hollis, Hudson, Litchfield, and Merrimac, N. H.; Dunstable and Tynsborough, Mass. By Charles J. Fox. 12*mo, cloth; with plates.* *Nashua*, 1846

605 DUNTON, JOHN. THE POST ANGEL, in Five distinct Parts. Viz.: I. The Remarkable Providence (of Judgment and Mercy). II. The Lives and Deaths of the most eminent Persons. III. A New Athenian Mercury; resolving the most nice and curious questions proposed by the most Ingenious of either Sex. IV. The Publick news at Home and Abroad. V. An Account of books lately Publish'd. With A Spiritual Observatory upon each Head. To be continu'd Monthly. From January to December, 1701, inclusive. 2 *vols. in one, 4to, calf. All Published.* *London*, 1701

606 DUNTON, JOHN. Letters written from New England, A. D., 1686. In which are described his voyages by Sea, his travels on Land, and the characters of his friends and acquaintances. Now First Published from the Original Manuscript, In the Bodleian Library, Oxford. With Notes and an Appendix, by W. H. Whitmore. *Twenty copies, L. P., No.* 9, *paper covers, 4to. Publications of the Prince Soc.* *Boston*, 1867

607 DUQUESNE, OLD FORT. A Tale of the Early Toils, Struggles and Adventures of the First Settlers at the Forks of the Ohio, 1754. 8*vo pamphlet; scarce.* *Pittsburgh*, 1844

608 DURAND, R. JAMES. The Life and Adventures of. During a Period of Fifteen Years. In which time he was Impressed on board the British Fleet, and held in detestable Bondage for more than seven years. 8*vo, bds., rare.* *Rochester, N. Y.* 1820

609 DURFEE, JOB. Whatcheer; or, Roger Williams in Banishment. A Poem. 16*mo, cl. uncut.* *Providence*, 1832

610 DURFEE, HON. JOB. The Complete Works of the Late Chief Justice of Rhode Island; with a Memoir of the Author. Edited by his Son, Thomas Durfee. 8*vo, cl.* *Providence—Boston*, 1832

611 DURHAM, CONN. The History of, from the first grant of land in 1662 to 1866. By William Chauncy Fowler, L. L. D. With an appendix. 8*vo, cl.* *Hartford*, 1866

612 DURRIE, DANIEL S. Bibliographia Genealogica Americana. An Alphabetical Index to American Genealogies and Pedigrees, contained in state, county and town histories, printed genealogies and kindred works. 8*vo, cl., uncut.* *Albany*, 1868

613 DUXBURY, MASS. HISTORY OF THE TOWN OF. With Genealogical Registers. By Justin Winsor. *Large* 8*vo, bds., uncut; port.* *Boston*, 1849

614 DWIGHT, TIMOTHY. The Conquest of Canaan. A Poem, in Eleven Books. 8*vo, sh.* *Hartford*, 1785

615 DWIGHT, TIMOTHY. Discourse on some events of the Last Century, delivered in Brick Church in New Haven, Jan. 7, 1801. *New Haven*, 1801

616 DWIGHT, THEODORE W. AND GEO. P. MARSH. Inaugural Addresses of, in Columbia College, N. Y. 8*vo, cloth.* *New York*, 1859

617 Dyer, Mary M. A Portraiture of Shakerism, Exhibiting a general view of their Character and Conduct, from the First Appearance of Ann Lee in New England, down to the present time. *Bds., 8vo.* *Concord, N. H. ; printed for the Author,* 1822

618 Dyer, Mary M. [now Marshall.] Rise and Progress of the Serpent in the Garden of Eden, to the present day : with a disclosure of Shakerism, exhibiting a general view of their real character and conduct from the first appearance of Ann Lee. Also, the Life and Sufferings of the author. 12*mo, sh. ; portrait of the Author.* *Concord,* 1847

PAMPHLETS.

619 Miscellaneous. [*Twelve.*]

Duffield, George. In Memoriam, by Rev. Wm. A. McCorkle. *Detroit,* 1868

Drink. The Influence of Wholesome Drink.

Dale's Patent Crevice Searcher for obtaining a Register of Oil Wells. *Elmira,* 1868

Dimmock, S. R. Review of Rev. Marvin R. Vincent's Essay and Rev. Washington Gladden's Sermon, by. 2nd Ed. *Syracuse,* 1867

Dickinson, Daniel S. Testimonial of Respect of the Bar of N. Y. to. *N. Y.,* 1866

Davis, Henry W. Oration on Life and Character of, by John A. J. Creswell. *Wash.,* 1866

Dawson, Henry B. Current Fictions tested by Uncurrent Facts. *N. Y.,* 1864

Douglas, Stephen A. Address on Death of, July 9, 1861. *Wash.,* 1861

Dadmun, J. W. Revival Melodies. *Boston,* 1858

Dayton, Aaron O. Memorial of Life and Character of, by Wm. Berrian. *N. Y.,* 1858

Doane, Bishop. Address at the Funeral of Rev. Dr. Ogilby. *N. Y.,* 1851

Dexter, Lord Timothy. A Pickle for the Knowing Ones. *Newburyport,* 1848

620 Miscellaneous. [*Thirteen.*]

Denison, Charles W. Defence of. Showing the Interest of Elder Nathaniel Culver. *Boston,* 1846

Dow, Jr. Short Patent Sermons. Vol. I. *N. Y.,* 1845

Duncan, Mr. Speech of, on General Appropriation Bill for 1840. *N. Y.*

Dial, The. A Magazine for Literature, Philosophy and Religion. No. II. Oct. 1840.

Dean, Paul. Discourse deliv. at Bulfinch St. on taking leave of the Soc. *Boston,* 1840

Davidson, Richard Oglesby. Description of the Plan of Construction and Mode of Operation of the Aerostat. *St. Louis,* 1840

Doran, Joseph M. Account of Celebration of St. Patrick's Day. *Phil.*, 1837
David and Uriah. Drama in five acts. *Phil.*, 1835
Danver's Discussion. Report of, between M. P. Braman and Thos. Whittemore, Nov. 6, 1833. *Boston*, 1833
Davis, Adjutant P. M. Battles of Chippeway, Washington, Baltimore and New Orleans. *Very scarce.* *Harrisburg*, 1832
Davison, David. Sermon preached in Old Jewry Chapel, Oct. 31, 1830. *London* 1830
Drew, Samuel. Arguments to prove the Divinity of Christ. *Trenton*, 1825
Daggett's Mr., Argument before General Assembly Conn., Oct. 1804. *Valuable.* *New Haven*, 1804

621 Miscellaneous. [*Twelve.*]

Dartmouth College. Discourse commem. of Daniel Webster, by Rufus Choate. *Boston*, 1853
——— Report on a Memorial of the Alumni. *Boston*, 1858
——— Poem before the Zeta Psi Fraternity, by Henry B. Atherton. *Concord*, 1861
Dickerson, Edward N. Argument of, in the Case of Sickles *vs.* Borden. *N. Y.*, 1856
——— Speech in Case of Mattingly *vs.* the Washington and Alexandria Steamboat Company. *N. Y.*, 1864
Dewey, Rev. Orville. Sermon on Moral Importance of Cities. *N. Y.*, 1836
——— Sermon deliv. under the Old Elm Tree in Sheffield. *N. Y.*, 1856
Dymond, Jonathan. An Inquiry into the Accordancy of War with the Principles of Christianity. *Phila.*
——— An Inquiry into the Accordancy of War with the Principles of Christianity. *N. Y.*, 1847
Domesticus. Remarks on the Letter of, by Veritas. *N. Y.*, 1827
——— Doctrine of Incest Stated. *N. Y.*, 1827
——— Dissertation on Incestuous Marriage, by Philip Milledoler. *N. Y.*, 1843

622 Miscellaneous. [*Twelve.*]

Dwight, Timothy. Disc., July 4, 1798. *New Haven*
——— Disc. on the genuineness and authenticity of the New Testament, Sept. 10, 1793. *N. Y.*
——— "The Nature and Danger of Infidel Philosophy." In two disc's, deliv. Sept. 9, 1797.
——— Greenfield Hill: a Poem in seven parts. *Scarce.* *N. Y.*, 1794
——— Disc. on some events of last century, deliv. Jan. 7, 1801. *Very scarce.* *New Haven.*
Dunlap, Wm. Review of Biographical Sketch of John Vanderlyn. *Very scarce.* *N. Y.*, 1838
Defence of Christianity against Deism and Infidelity. *Trenton*, 1810

Doane, George W. Sermon before the Prayer Book and Homily Soc. *Boston*, 1831

——— Sermon before the Sunday School Union. *Boston*, 1831

Dewey Orville. Disc. deliv. at dedication of Ch. of Messiah. *N. Y.*, 1839

Dwyer, Alex. Disc. on the structure of the Poetry of Hebrews. *Utica*, 1830

Doty, John. Farewell Sermon and Address to the Right Rev. Jacob, Bishop of Quebec, Oct. 24, 1802.

623 Miscellaneous. [*Twelve.*]

Dayton, Jonathan. Public Speculation Unfolded, in Sixteen Letters, addressed to F. Childs and J. H. Lawrence. *Scarce, and interesting.* *N. Y.*, 1800

Doggett, Simeon. Discourse preached to Congrega. Soc. in Norton. *Providence*, 1796

Duer, W. A. Eulogy on John Adams and Thomas Jefferson, July 31. *Albany*, 1826

Duer, John. Lecture on the Evils, Social, Moral and Political that flow from Party Div. *N. Y.*, 1841

Dudley Observatory. Inauguration of, at Albany, Aug. 28, 1856.

——— and the Scientific Council. *Albany*, 1858

Dog Cart. An Excursion of. *N. Y.*, 1822

Dogo-Graphy. Life and Adventures of the Celebrated Dog, Tiger, by Francis Butler. *N. Y.*, 1856

Derby, John B. Sketch of the Origin and History of the "Statesman Party." *Boston*, 1835

——— Sketch of the Origin and History of the "Statesman Party." Part 2. *Boston*, 1835

Drake, Samuel G. Review of Winthrop's Journal. *Boston*, 1854

Dearborn, H. A. S. Defence of Gen. Henry Dearborn against Gen. Wm. Hull. *Very Scarce.* *Boston*, 1824

624 Miscellaneous. [*Twelve.*]

Dearborn, H. A. S. Address on the Life and Character of, by George Putnam. *Roxbury*, 1857

Duane, W. Sampson against the Philistines. *Philadelphia*, 1805

——— Politics for American Farmers. *Washington*, 1807

Democratic Reformer. Embodying Documents concerning Governmental Reformation in New York. *Albany*, 1844

Democratic Review, United States. New Series. Vol. XLIII. Apr. 1859. No. I. *N. Y.*

Dwight, Timothy. Discourse at Funeral of Elizur Goodwich. *New Haven*, 1797

——— Sermon on Duelling, preached in Yale Col. Jan. 21. *N. Y.*, 1805

——— Sermon preached at Ordination of Eliphalet Pearson, Sept. 28, 1808. *Boston*, 1808

Dorchester. History of the Town of. Nunber one. *Boston*, 1851

——— Epitaphs from the Old Burying Ground in. *Boston Highlands*, 1869

Dana, Daniel. Address at Anniv. of Phi Beta Kappa Soc., Dart. Col., Aug. 26, 1817. *Exeter*, 1817

625 Dedication Pamphlets. [*Seventeen.*]

Appleton, Jesse. Sermon deliv. to the Congre. Soc. in Hampton, Nov. 14, 1797, at Dedication of New House for Public Worship. *Newburyport*, 1797

Lyman, William. Sermon deliv. at Lebanon at Dedica. of New Brick Meeting House, Jan. 21, 1807. *Hartford*, 1807

Griffin, Edward D. Sermon, Jan. 10, 1810, at Dedication of Park St. Church, Boston.

Thacher, Samuel C. Discourse at Dedication of a New Church on Church Green, Summer St. *Boston*, 1815

Porter, Ebenezer. Sermon, Sept. 22, 1818, at Dedica. of New Edifice for Use of Theological Seminary in Andover.

Palfrey, John G. Sermon. Dedication of Twelfth Congre. Church in Boston, Oct. 13, 1824. *Boston*, 1825

Willard, Samuel. Sermon. Dedication of New Meeting House in First Parish in Deerfield, Dec. 22, 1824. *Historical, and very Scarce.* *Greenfield*, 1825

Upham, Charles W. Sermon, Nov. 16, 1826, Dedica. of House of Public Worship of First Congre. Soc., Salem.

Gilman, Samuel. Sermon. Dedica. of Unitarian Church in Augusta, Geo., Dec. 27, 1827. *Charleston*, 1828

Sabine, James. Sermon. Dedica. First Presb. Church, Boston, Jan. 31, 1828.

Lowell, Charles. Sermon. Dedica. South Congre. Church, Natick, Nov. 20, 1828. *Boston*, 1829

Bancroft, Aaron. Sermon. Dedica. of Second Congre. Church, Worcester, Aug 20, 1829.

Farley, Frederick A. Sermon. Dedica. of Westminster Church in Providence, R. I., March 5, 1829. *Boston*, 1829

Story, Joseph. Address. Dedica. of Mt. Auburn Cemetery, Sept. 24, 1831. *Boston*, 1831

Johnston, James R. Discourse. Dedication of Presbyterian Church, Hamptonburgh, Feb. 26, 1845. *Goshen*, 1845

Virginia Theological Seminary. Services and Addresses in connection with Recent Dedication at. *Richmond*, 1859.

Stewart, Charles. Sermon. Ded. of St. Paul's Ch., St. Armaud, L. C. *Montreal*, 1811

626 Miscellaneous. [*Eleven.*]

Directions for the use of Anthracite Coal. By an Amateur.

Documents and Facts showing the fatal effects of interments in populous cities. *N. Y.*, 1822

Davis A. Lecture on the discovery of America. *N. Y.*, 1840

Diller J. W. Farewell disc. *Brooklyn*, 1842

Duelist, The. 1825.

Duelling. Essay on. *Y. Y.*, 1830.

Doddridge, Philip. Plain and Serious Address by. *Hartford*, 1777

——— Plain and Serious Address by. *Hartford*, 1778

——— Sermons on the religious education of children. *Stockbridge*, 1804

Dwight, Timothy. Memoir of, by Joseph P. Thompson. *New Haven*, 1844

Dwight, Sereno E. Greek Revolution. Address by. *Boston*, 1824

627 Miscellaneous. *Very fine lot.* [*Seven.*]

Dorchester. Disc. delivered at, June 17, 1830—Bi-Centen.—by J. Pierce. *Very scarce.* *Boston*, 1830

——— Disc. fiftieth anniversary second church of, Jan. 3, 1858, by Rev. Jas. Howard Means. *Boston*, 1858

Dedham. Hist. Address delivered before citizens of town of, Sept. 21, 1836, being second Centennial Anniversary, by S. F. Haven. *Very scarce.* *Dedham*, 1837

Danvers. Centen. Celebration, June 16, 1852. *Boston*, 1852

——— (North) Hist. Sketch of school district number thirteen of, by George Osgood. *Salem*, 1855

Danbury. Century Sermon deliv. at, Jan. 1, 1801, by T. Robbins. *Danbury*, 1846

Dartmouth (College). Class of Alumni, in 1813. *Boston*, 1854

628 Miscellaneous. [*Thirteen.*]

Day, Jeremiah. Sermon deliv. at Bethlehem, Jan. 4, 1774. *Very scarce.* *New Haven*

——— Sermon before Gen. Assoc. of Conn., June 22, 1831. *New Haven*

Dwight, Timothy. Two disc.—"The nature and danger of Infidel Philosophy"—Sept. 9, 1797. *New Haven*

——— Disc., July 23, 1812, Yale College. *Boston*

Dewey, Orville. The Unitarian Belief. *N. Y.*, 1835

——— Sermon on occasion of late fire in N. Y. *N. Y.* 1836

——— Disc. at ordination of Geo. Putnam, July 7, 1830. *Boston*

Dickinson, Moses. Answer to two important questions. *Scarce.* *New Haven*, 1770

Devotion, John. Sermon at interment of Ursula Griswold, by, April 8, 1788 *Very scarce.* *New Haven*, 1788

Dell, Wm. The doctrine of Baptism, by *N. Y.*

Decalogue. The lawful use of the moral law proving the, or ten commandments given by God as the rule of a believer's life. Southark.

Dow, John. Disc. deliv. July 4, 1806, at Belleville. *Newark, N. J.*

Dearborn, Alex. Oration deliv. at Salem, July 4, 1806. *Salem*

629 Miscellaneous.. [*Thirteen.*]

Devot, Mr. The Go-Between, or Two-edged sword. *N. Y.*, 1807

Danvers, Jno. T. Picture of a republican magistrate of the new school. *N. Y.*, 1808

Doctrines. The peculiar, of the gospel. *New Haven*, Feb. 23, 1809

Dorchester. Proc. of the second church and parish. 2d ed. *Boston*, 1812

Dehon, Theo. Disc. deliv. May 21, 1814. *Phila.*
Delaplaine's Repository. The author turned critic, or the reviewer reviewed, being a reply to an attack on. September, 1816. *Very scarce.*
Dexter, Franklin. Oration, July 4, 1819, by. *Boston*
Duane, W. The foul charges of the Tories against the editor of the Aurora, 1798.
"Domesticus." The doctrine of incest stated. *N. Y.*, 1827
——— the Argument of, on the doctrine of incest, by Clericus. *New York*, 1827
——— Reasons in favor of the erasure of the law on the doctrine of incest, by Clericus. *N. Y.*, 1827
——— The Opinions of a Layman on the Method of treating on the Doctrine of Incest. *New York*, 1827
Dean, Amos. Address deliv. before the Young Men's Assoc. of N. Y., Sept. 2, 1841. *Albany*

630 Miscellaneous. [*Thirteen.*]

Dean, Amos. Introductory Lecture deliv. Dec. 7, 1848. *Albany*
Dartmouth College. Catalogue of the members of the N. H. Alpha, Aug. 1812. *Hanover*
——— Opinion of the Superior Court of the State of N. H., in the case of the trustees of. *Concord*, 1818
——— Catalogue, 1822.
——— Address deliv. at anniv. of assoc. Alumni, Aug., 1833. *Boston*
Daggett, Nath'l. Sermon, Yale College, on death of Job Lane, one of the tutors in, Sept. 16, 1768. *Very scarce.* *New Haven*, 1768
——— Sermon at ordination of Ebenezer Baldwin, Sept. 19, 1770. *Very scarce.* *New Haven*, 1770
——— Sermon at ordination of Joseph Howe, May 19, 1773. *Very scarce.* *Boston*, 1773
——— David. Oration by, July 4, 1799. *Rare.* *New Haven*, 1799
Dana, James. Sermon on death of Chauncey Whittelsey, July 29, 1787. *Scarce.* *New Haven*, 1787
——— Sermon at his installation, April 29, 1789. *New Haven*
——— Disc. deliv. in Yale College, Nov. 23, 1794. *New Haven*
——— Sermon at ordination of Daniel Huntington, Oct. 17, 1798. *Scarce.* *Litchfield*, 1798

ASTBURN, JAMES WALLIS. Yamoyden, a Tale of the Wars of King Philip ; in six cantos. *8vo, bds., uncut ; illust.* *N. Y.*, 1820

632 EASTHAM, Mass. A comprehensive History, Ecclesiastical and Civil, of Eastham, Wellfleet and Orleans, Barnstable Co.; from 1644 to 1844. By Rev. Enoch Pratt, of Brewster. *8vo, cl., scarce.* *Yarmouth, Mass.*, 1844

633 EAST-HAMPTON, L. I. A Sermon, containing the General History of the Town of East-Hampton, from its first settlement to the present time, delivered Jan. 1, 1806. By Lyman Beecher. 8*vo pamphlet, uncut;* 40 *pages ; very fine copy and extremely scarce.* *Sag Harbor, N. Y.: printed by Alden Spooner*, 1806

634 EASTHAMPTON, Mass.; Historical Sketch of—delivered before the Young Men's Association, Oct. 7, 1851. By Luther Wright. 8*vo pamph.;* 32 *p.* *Northampton*, 1852

635 EASTHAMPTON, MASS.; History of. Its Settlement and Growth; its Material, Educational and Religious Interests — with a Genealogical Record of its Original Families. By P. W. Lyman. 8*vo, sheets, folded.* *Northampton*, 1866

636 EDSALL, JOHN; Incidents in the Life of. 12*mo, sheep.* *Catskill*, 1831

637 EDWARDS, JONATHAN, D.D. A SERMON at the Execution of Moses Paul, an Indian, who had been guilty of Murder; preached at New Haven, in America, by Samson Occom, a Native Indian, and Missionary to the Indians. To which is added a short account of the Late Spread of the Gospel among the Indians, also Observations on the Language of the Muhhekanew Indians. 8*vo, uncut, scarce.* *London*, 1789

638 EDWARDS, JONATHAN. A Careful and Strict Inquiry into the Modern Prevailing Notions of Freedom of Will. The fourth Edition. 8*vo, sheep.* *Wilmington*, 1790

639 ELLET, MRS. E. F. Domestic History of the American Revolution. 12*mo, cl.* *New York*, 1851

640 ELLIOTT, COM. JESSE D.; A Biographical Notice of—containing a Review of the Controversy between him and the late Com. Perry; and a History of the Figure-Head of the U. S. Frigate "Constitution." By a Citizen of New York. 12*mo, bds.* *Philadelphia*, 1835

641 ELLIOTT, Rt. Rev. STEPHEN. God's Presence with the Confederate States. A Sermon preached in Christ Church, Savannah, 13th of June, [1861]. *8vo, paper.* *Savannah,* 1861

642 ELLIOTT, Rt. Rev. STEPHEN. "The Silver Trumpets of the Sanctuary." Sermon preached to the Pulaski Guards in Christ Church, Savannah, on the second Sunday after Trinity. Being the Sunday before their departure to join the Army in Virginia. *8vo, paper.* *Savannah,* 1861

643 ELLIOTT, Gen. STEPHEN. In Memoriam. [Proceedings in the Legislature of South Carolina on the Death of, and address of W. H. Trescott.] *Large 8vo, paper, uncut.* *Columbia,* 1866

644 EMMONS, NATH'L. A Discourse addressed to the Norfolk Auxiliary Society in Dorchester, June 11, 1817. Second edition. *8vo,* 23 *pages.* *Providence,* 1825

645 EMMONS, NATH'L. Discourse delivered, Oct. 13, 1813, before the Mendon Assoc. Second edition. *8vo, uncut,* 36 *pages, fine copy.* *New York,* 1826

646 EMMONS, CHAS. P. Sketches of Bunker Hill Battle and Monument, with Illustrative Documents. 12*mo, cloth.* *Charlestown,* 1843

647 EMMONS, RICHARD. The Fredoniad, or Independence Preserved. An Epick Poem on The Late War of 1812. In four volumes. *8vo, bds., uncut.* *Boston,* 1827

648 EMMONS, RICHARD. Defence of Baltimore and Death of General Ross. Portrait of Charles Carrol. 3d ed. *Bds.* *Washington,* 1831

649 EMMONS, RICHARD. The Battle of Bunker Hill, or the Temple of Liberty; an Historic Poem, in four cantos. 12*mo, cl., with portraits, very scarce.* *New York,* 1839

650 ENGLISH, GEORGE BETHUNE. Five Pebbles from the Brook; being A Reply to "A Defence of Christianity," by Edward Everett. *8vo, bds., uncut.* *Phila.,* 1824

651 EPSOM, N. H.; A TOPOGRAPHICAL AND HISTORICAL SKETCH OF. By Jonathan Curtis. *8vo pamphlet, uncut;* 18 *pages; very scarce; beautiful copy.* *Concord,* 1823

With an Appendix, giving list of names of those who served in the regular army in the Revolution.

652 EQUIANO, OLAUDAH; The Interesting Narrative of the Life of; or, Gustavus Vassa, the African. Written by himself. First American ed. 12*mo, calf,* 2 *vols. in* 1. *Frontis.* *N. Y.,* 1791

653 ERIE Co., Penn.; The History of. By Laura G. Sanford. With port. and maps. 12*mo, cl.* *Phila., Pa.,* 1862

654 ESSEX Co., Mass. Memorial for 1836. Embracing a Register of the County. By James R. Newhall. *8vo, cl., scarce.* *Salem,* 1836

655 ESSEX, MASS.; History of the Town of—from 1634 to 1700. By Robert Crowell. *8vo, cl., map and engravings, very scarce.* *Boston,* 1853

656 ESSEX, MASS.; History of the Town of—from 1634 to 1868. By the late Robert Crowell. With Sketches of the Soldiers in the War of the Rebellion. By David Choate. *L. 8vo, cl.* *Essex,* 1868

656*ESSEX INSTITUTE Historical Collections. Vol. 1, No. 5. Nov., 1859. *Salem,* 1859

657 Estvan, B. War Pictures from the South. 12*mo, cl., rough edges.* *N. Y.*, 1863

658 Evarts, Jeremiah; Memoir of the Life of. By E. C. Tracy. 8*vo, cl.; portrait.* *Boston*, 1845

659 Everett, Moses (Father of Edw. Everett). Sermon preached Lord's-day Eve, Feb. 1, 1778, to Two Religious Societies of Young Men in Dorchester, Mass. 8*vo pamphlet,* 27 *p.; fine copy; very scarce; uncut.* *Boston*, 1779

660 Everett, Edward. An Address delivered before the Citizens of Worcester, July 4, 1833. 8*vo pamphlet, uncut;* 40 *p.; scarce.* *Boston*, 1833

661 Everett, Edward; A Memorial of—from the City of Boston. *L.* 8*vo. cl. Portrait and medallion. L. P., cl.* *Boston*, MDCCCLXV

662 Eyre, John. The Life of Gregory Lopez, a Hermit in America. 12*mo, cl.* *N. Y.*, 1841

663 Miscellaneous. [*Sixteen.*]

Essay to answer that *Most* Concerning and *All* Concerning Inquiry What must I do to be Saved? *New Haven*, 1765

Ely, Richard. Sermon at Ordi. of Rev. David Ely. *New Haven*, 1774

Enquiry into Principles on which a Commercial System for U. S. of America should be founded. *Phila.*, 1787

Ewing, Rev. Dr. Sermon at Ordi. and Instal. of Rev. Ashbald Green. *Phila.*, 1787

Extracts from writings of Divers Eminent Authors of Different Religious Denominations. *Phila.*, 1789

Eagle Fire Co., of N. Y. Act to Incorporate the. *N. Y.* 1806

Ellsworth, Oliver. Sermon at Funeral of, by Henry A. Rowland. *Hartford*, 1808

Essex Junta Exposed. The Whole Truth; by Hancock. *N. Y.*, 1809

Erasmus. Plea of Reason, Religion and Humanity against War. *N. Y.*, 1813

Examination of British Doctrine which subjects to Capture a Neutral Trade not open in Time of Peace.

Emott, Hon. James. Speech, Jan. 12, 1813. *Boston*, 1813

Evidences for the Truth of Christianity. *Boston*, 1813

Eustaphieve, Alexis. Memorable Predictions of Late Events in Europe. *Boston*, 1814

English Practice. Statement showing some of the Evils and Absurdities of the Practice of the English Common Law. *N. Y.* 1822

Empie, Adam. Remarks on the Distinguishing Doctrine of Modern Universalism. *N. Y.* 1825

Eaton, John H. Candid Appeal to the American Public, in Reply to Messrs Ingham, Branch and Berrien. *Washington*, 1831

664 Miscellaneous. [*Sixteen.*]

Election, The. *N. Y.* 1822

Election Law.

Eliot, Andrew. Sermon on Public Fast, April 19, 1753. *Boston.*
——— Sermon at Ordina. of Andrew Eliot, Jr. *Boston,* 1774
——— Sermon at Ordina. of John Eliot, his Brother. *Boston,* 1780
Edwards, Jonathan. Misrepresentation Corrected, and Truth vindicated. *Boston,* 1752
——— Sermon at Ordi. of Timothy Dwight. *N. Haven,* 1783
——— Remarks on his Notion of the Freedom of the Will and System of Universality. *Wilmington,* 1796
——— Sermon on Injustice and Impolicy of the Slave Trade. *New Haven,* 1791
Erskine, Hon. Thomas. View of Causes and Consequences of Present War with France. *Phila.,* 1797
——— College. Oration before Euphemian and Philomathian Soc. of. Sept. 15, 1847, by Wm. T. Hamilton. *Charleston.*
Emmons Nathaniel. Disc. concerning the Process of the General Judgment. *Providence,* 1783
——— Disc. Annual Fast in Mass. *N. Y.* 1801
——— Disc. Annual Fast in Mass. *Providence,* 1804
——— Sermon, Interment of Hon. Jabez Fisher. *Providence,* 1807
——— William. Oration and Poem, July 4, 1826 *Boston.*

665 Edward Everett Pamphlets. [*Eleven.*]
Oration deliv. at Concord, April 19, 1825. *Scarce.* *Boston.*
Address deliv. at Charlestown, Aug. 1, 1826. In commemoration of J. Adams and T. Jefferson. *Boston.*
Oration deliv. at Cambridge, July 4, 182–. *Boston.*
Remarks deliv. at Mass, April 25, 1826, on the bill for the relief of revolutionary officers. *Cambridge.*
Lectures deliv. at Charlestown, Oct. 6, 1830, on the Working Men's Party. *Boston.*
Eulogy on Lafayette, deliv. Sept. 6, 1834. *Boston.*
Oration, Charleston, July 4, 1828.
Address deliv. at Bloody Brook, Sept. 30, 1825, in commem. of the fall of the "Flower of Essex" at that spot, in King Philip's War, Sept. 18, 1675. *Scarce.* *Boston.*
Oration deliv. July 4, 1835, at Beverly.
Address deliv. April 19–20, 1835, at Lexington. *Scarce.*
Address deliv. Oct. 14, 1831, at N. Y. City, before Amer. Inst.

666 Edward Everett Pamphlets. *Scarce and valuable lot.* [*Thirteen.*]
Oration pronounced at Cambridge, before Phi Beta Kappa Soc., by Edward Everett, 1824.
Oration deliv. at Plymouth, Dec. 22, 1824, by Edward Everett. 1825
Oration deliv. at Cambridge, on Fiftieth Anniv. of Declar. of Ind., by Edward Everett. 1826
Address on Bi-Centen. Anniv. of Arrival of Gov. Winthrop, by Edward Everett. 1830
Eulogy on Lafayette, Sept. 6th, 1834, by Edward Everett. *Boston,* 1834

Eulogy on Lafayette, Sept. 6, 1834, by Edward Everett. 2nd Ed. *Boston*, 1834
Address deliv. at Lexington, April 19, 1835, by Edward Everett. 2nd *Ed.* *Boston*, 1835
Oration Deliv. at Beverly, July 4, 1835, by Edward Everett. 1835
Oration on Dedication of Statue of Daniel Webster, by Edward Everett. 1859
Oration deliv. before City Authorities of Boston, July 4, by Edward Everett. 1860
Address deliv. before United States Naval Academy, by Edward Everett. 1863
Address on the Inauguration of Union Club, April 9, by Edward Everett. 1863
Sermon on death of Edward Everett, Jan. 22, by C. A. Bartol. 1865

667 Edward Everett Pamphlets. *Scarce and valuable lot.* [*Thirteen.*]
Address on Life and Services of Edward Everett, by Richard H. Dana, Jr. 1865
Memorial of Edward Everett, by Nathaniel Hall. *Boston*, 1865
Sermon on Life, Services and Character of Edward Everett, by Rufus Ellis. *Boston*, 1865
Discourse on Edward Everett, deliv. Ch. of First Parish, Brookline, by F. H. Hedge. 1865
Disc. in Commem. of Edward Everett, by Charles Wiley. *Geneva*, 1865
Sermon in Memory of Edward Everett, by John E Todd. *Boston*, 1865
Sermon on Death of Edward Everett, by A. P. Putnam. *N. Y.*, 1865
Edward Everett in the Ministry of Reconciliation. Sermon preached in South Congregational Church, by Rev. Edward E. Hale, Boston, Jan. 22, 1865.
Discourse in Memory of Edward Everett, by Samuel Osgood. *N. Y.*, 1865
Oration on Seventy-fifth Anniv. of Bunker Hill, by Edward Everett. *Boston*, 1850
Remarks of, on the French Question. *Boston*, 1835
Address at Worcester, by Edward Everett, July, 4, 1833.
Address on erection monument to J. Harvard, by E. Everett. *Boston*, 1828

668 Miscellaneous. [*Ten.*]
Emmons, Nathanael. Discourse on Annual Fast in Mass., April 9, 1801. *N. Y.*, 1801
——— Sermon at Ordina. of Rev. Joseph Emerson, September 21, 1803.
——— Discourse, November 25, 1813, on Annual Thanksgiving. *Dedham*, 1813
Essex County Lyceum, Address before the, by Daniel A. White. *Salem*, 1830
——— South Conference. Review of the Result of an Eccle-

siastical Council Convention at Salem, Mass., Dec. 4, 1849. *Boston*, 1850

Emerson Brown. Discourse on Fiftieth Anniv. of Ordination. *Boston*, 1855

Ely, Ezra Stiles. Sermon for the Rich to Buy. *N. Y.*, 1810

Episcopal Church, Prot., Address to Students of Gen. Theological Seminary of the, by Samuel R. Johnson. *N. Y.*, 1851

Emerson, Joseph. Disc. on Female Education. *Boston*, 1822

Europe, Remarks on, Relating to Education, Peace, and Labor. *N. Y.*, 1846

669 Miscellaneous. [*Twelve*].

Eastern Railroad Company, a brief Statement relative to the Claim on the, to pay its indebtedness to the Commonwealth in gold.

Economy Club, Proceedings at the Commemorative Dinner of. 1868.

Edwards, Jonathan. The Necessity of Atonement and the Consistency between that and the Free Grace in Forgiveness. Illustrated in Three Sermons. *New Haven*, 1785

—— True Grace distinguished from the Experience of Devils, preached before the Synod of New York, Sept. 28, N. S., 1752. *Elizabethtown*, 1791

—— Discourse on Death of, by Robert Smith, Aug. 3, 1801. *Albany*, 1801

Eastburn, Manton. Sermon before Annual Convention of Diocese of N. Y. *N. Y.*, 1838

—— Sermon at Consecration of Rev. Henry W. Lee. *Rochester*, 1854

Episcopalians, The Resolutions of Certain, at Mechanics' Hall, Considered.

Episcopalians, Protestant, Reply to the Review of Dr. Wyatt's Sermon and Mr. Spark's Letters on the Prot. Epis. Ch., by a. *Boston*, 1821

Episcopal Register, Extra, No. 1, Middlebury, Vt., June, 1826.

—— Protestant Church, Defense of the Convention of, against Editorial Statements of Paper called "The Banner of the Church." *Boston*, 1832

—— Pulpit, Sermon by Rev. J. M. Wainwright. Vol. V., No. 11. *N. Y.*, 1835

670 Miscellaneous. [*Twelve*].

Episcopal Protestant Society, Charter and By-Laws. *N. Y.*, 1850

—— Church, Address of Rt. Rev. Stephen Elliott, to Thirty-Ninth Annual Convention. *Savannah*, 1861

Emmons, Nathanael, Sermon by, Sprinkling the Proper Mode, and Infants Proper Subjects of Christian Baptism, September 7, 1794. *Worcester*, 1795

Exposition of the Motives founded upon the Laws of Nations which determined the King of Prussia to lay an Attachment upon the Capital Funds, which his Majesty had promised to the Subjects of Great Britain in Virtue of the Peace-Treatise of Breslau and Dresden. *London*, 1752

Every Man His Own Law-Maker ; or, The Englishman's Complete Guide to Parliamentary Reform. *3d ed.* *London*, 1785

Erskine, Thomas. View of Causes and Consequences of the Present War with France. 16*th ed.* *London*, 1797

Ely, Zebulon. Sermon Delivered at Ordination of the Rev. Shubael Bartlett. *Hartford*, 1804

Emerson, Mrs. Eleanor. Memoirs of Life, Conversion, and Happy Death. *N. Y.*, 1817

Ellingwood, John W. Sermon at Ordination of Rev. Isaac Weston, June 10, 1818. *Portland*, 1818

Everett, Alexander H. Oration before Citizens of Boston, July 5, 1830. *Boston*, 1830

Emigrant ; or, Reflections while Descending the Ohio. A Poem. *Cincinnati*, 1833

Examiner, Causes of the Present Crisis Shown by an.

671 Miscellaneous. [*Twelve*].

English, Thomas C. Zephaniah Doolittle. A Poem. 2*d ed.* *Phila.*, 1838

Edwards, Monroe, Life of, by a Texan. *Boston*, 1842

England, The Women of, by Mrs. Ellis. *N. Y.*, *1844*

Edson, Rev. Theodore. Lecture in St. Anne's Church, Nov. 24. *Lowell*, 1844

Eothen ; or, Traces of Travel brought Home from the East. *N. Y.*, 1845

Ewbank, Thomas. Specimens of Ancient Oracular and Fighting Eolipiles, with Remarks on Other Fire Breathing Monsters. *N. Y.*, 1845

Estes, Benjamin H. Essay on Necessity of Correcting the Errors which have crept into the Washingtonian Temp. Movement. *N. Y.*, 1846

Edmonds, John W., Address on the Constitution and Code of Procedure. *N. Y.*, 1848

England in 1850. By A. D. Lamartine. Translated by W. Charles Ouseley. *N. Y.*, 1851

Elections, Practical Directions for the Holding of. *N. Y.*, 1852

Ellis, George E. Discourse Preached in Harvard Ch., Feb. 5, 1860. *Charlestown*, 1860

Ephrata, Pencillings About. By a Visitor. *Phila.* 1860

672 Educational Pamphlets. [*Fifteen.*]

Cutbush, James. Oration on Education. *Phila.* 1812

Bristed, John. Oration on the Utility of Literary Establishments. *N. Y.*, 1814

Warren Baptist Association, Constitution of the Education Soc. of the. *Boston*, 1817

Griscom, John. Discourse on the Importance of Character and education in the United States. *N. Y.*, 1823

Jardine, George. Outlines of Philosophical Education. *Glasgow*, 1825

Carter, James G. Essays on Popular Education. Particular Examination of Schools of Mass. *Boston*, 1826

Powers, Rev. H. P. Address Anniv. of Newark Institute for Young Ladies. *Newark*, 1826

Consequences of a Scientific Education to the Working-Classes. Theories of Mr. Brougham on that subject confuted, in a Letter to Marquis of Lansdown. *London*, 1826

Burroughs, Charles. Address on Female Education. *Portsmouth*, 1827

Manning, Joseph B. Epeography, or Notations of Orthoepy, to which is prefixed Lektography for Representing Sounds of Words. *Boston*, 1829

Broadhead, Jacob. Discourse on Education. *N. Y.*, 1831

Parkhurst, John L. Lecture on the Means to Stimulate the Student without the aid of Emulation. *Boston*, 1831

Essay on the Intellectual, Moral and Religious Instruction of the Youth, by means of Common Schools. *Troy*, 1834

Beecher, Catherine E. Essay on Education of Female Teachers. *N. Y.*, 1835

Pinney, Norman. The Principles of Education as Applied in Mobile Institute. *Mobile*, 1836

673 Educational Pamphlets. [*Fifteen.*]

Young, Samuel. Suggestions on Best Mode of Promoting Civilization and Improvement; or, Influence of Woman on Social State. *Albany*, 1837

Worcester, Mr. Address on Female Education.

Addicks, Mrs. Barbara O. Essay on Education. *N. Y.*, 1837

Rantoul, Robert. Remarks on Education.

Benedict, Erastus C. Address First Anniv. of Free Academy. *N. Y.*, 1850

Report on System of Popular Education. *N. Y.*, 1851

Proc. of First Session of the American Assoc. for the Advancement of Education. *Phila.*, 1852

Barnard, Frederick A. P. Letters on College Government. *N. Y.*, 1855

Bacon, Leonard. Sermon Sixth Anniv. of Auxil. Education Soc. of Young Men, Boston, Feb. 6, 1825. *Boston*, 1825

Seventh Annual Report of Board of Directors of the Presb. Educa. Soc. *N. Y.*, 1825

Blagden, G. W. Address Brighton School Fund Corpor. March 30, 1828. *Boston*, 1828

First Annual Report of Morrison Education Society. *Canton, China*, 1837

Manesca, John. Examin. of Mr. Dufief's Philosophical Notions. With a Criticism upon his System and Mode of Teaching Languages. In four Letters. *New York*, 1825

Soler, Mariano Cubi I. Observations on a Practical System of Translation. *Boston*, 1828

Surault, Francois M. J. Grammatical Dissertation on the Italian Language. *Boston,* 1835

674 Election Sermons. Ancient and Honorable Artillery. [*Twelve.*]
For the following years: 1773, 1789, 1803, 1814, 1826, 1828, 1855, 1861, 1862, 1864, 1865, 1867.

675 Election Sermons. Conn. [*Fifteen.*]
For the following years: 1777, 1779, 1791, 1798, 1800, 1805, 1806, 1807, 1808, 1809, 1811, 1812, 1813, 1814, 1818.

676 Election Sermons. Conn. [*Sixteen.*]
For the following years: 1766, 1779, 1783, 1785, 1787, 1788, 1789, 1790, 1792, 1793, 1794, 1796, 1797, 1817, 1823, 1830.

677 Election Sermons. Mass. [*Fourteen.*]
For the following years: 1720, Stone; 1723, Colman; 1729, White; 1734, Barnard; 1736, Holyoke; 1737, Loring; 1738, Webb; 1739, Clark; 1740, Cooper, Wm.; 1742, Appleton; 1743, Eells; 1744, Allen; 1747, Chauncy; 1748, Lewis.

678 Election Sermons. Mass. [*Fifteen.*]
For the following years: 1751, Welsteed; 1754, Mayhew; 1756, Cooper, S.; 1757, Pemberton; 1758, Frink; 1759, Parson; 1760, Dunbar; 1761, Stevens; 1762, Williams; 1763, Barnard; 1765, Eliot, A.; 1766, Barnard; 1767, Bridge; 1768, Shute; 1769, Haven.

679 Election Sermons. Mass. [*Ten.*]
For the following years: 1770, Cook; 1771, Tucker; 1772, Parson; 1773, Turner; 1774, Hitchcock; 1776, West; 1777, Webster; 1778 Payson; 1779, Stillman; 1780, Howard.

680 Election Sermons. Mass. [*Seventeen.*]
For the following years: 1783, Cumings; 1784, Hemmenway; 1786, West; 1787, Lyman; 1788, Parsons; 1789, Bridge; 1790, Foster; 1791, Robbins; 1792, Tappan; 1793, Parker; 1794, Deane; 1795, Fobes; 1796, French; 1797, Mellen; 1798, Emmons; 1799, Coffin; 1800, McKeen.

681 Election Sermons. Mass. [*Eleven.*]
For the following years: 1801, Bancroft; 1802, Baldwin; 1803, Puffer; 1804, Kendal; 1805, Allyn; 1806, Shepard; 1807, Bentley; 1808, Allen, T.; 1809, Osgood; 1810, Parish; 1811, Thacher, Thos.

682 Election Sermons, Mass. [*Fourteen.*]
For the following years: 1812, Foster; 1813, W. Allen; 1814, Appleton; 1815, Flint; 1816, Kirkland; 1817; 1818, Moore; 1819, Eaton; 1820; 1821, Ware; 1822; 1823, Thayer; 1824, Sharp; 1825, Sprague.

683 Election Sermons, Mass. [*Seventeen.*]
For the following years: 1826 Dewey; 1827, Stuart; 1828, Walker; 1829, Fisk; 1830, Channing; 1831, Withington;

1832, Dean ; 1833, Peabody; 1834, Yeomans ; 1835, Wainwright : 1836, Bigelow ; 1837, Dana ; 1838, Stone ; 1839, Hopkins ; 1840, Codman ; 1841, Damon ; 1842, Gannett.

684 Election Sermons, Mass. [*Twenty-five.*]

For the following years : 1843, Jackson ; 1844, Chapin ; 1845, Braman ; 1846, Putnam ; 1847, Bisbee ; 1848, Vinton ; 1849, Pierce ; 1850, Hitchcock ; 1851, Parke ; 1852, Neale ; 1853, Wolcott ; 1854, Raymond ; 1855, Lothrop ; 1856, Seeley ; 1857, Pike ; 1858, Huntington ; 1859, Hale ; 1861, Phelps ; 1862, Alger ; 1863, Walker ; 1864, Stearns ; 1865, Stone ; 1866, Quint : 1868, J. F. Clarke ; 1869, B. F. Clark.

685 Election Sermons, New Hampshire and Vermont. [*Four.*]

New Hampshire : 1810, 1818.

Vermont : 1822, 1825.

AIRFIELD, SUMNER L. The heir of the World and lesser poems. *Bds., 12mo.* *Philadelphia,* 1829

687 Fall River, Mass. An Historical Sketch of, from 1620 to the present time; with notices of Freetown and Tiverton. In three discourses, delivered Jan. 24, 1841. By Orin Fowler. *8vo, paper cov., 64 pages, and Genealogical Plate of the Borden Family; fine copy; scarce.* *Fall River,* 1841

688 FALL RIVER, Mass. History of, with notices of Freetown and Tiverton, as published in 1841. By Rev. Orin Fowler. With a sketch of the life of Rev. Orin Fowler; an Epitome of the Mass. and Rhode Island Boundary question; an account of the Great Fire of 1843; and Ecclesiastical, Manufacturing and other Statistics. *8vo, bds.; scarce.* *Fall River,* 1862

689 FARMER, JOHN. A Genealogical Register of the First Settlers of New England; containing an Alphabetical list of the Governors, Deputy-Governors, etc. To which are added various genealogical and biographical notes, collected from Ancient Records, Manuscripts and Printed Works. *8vo, bds., uncut.* *Lancaster,* 1829

690 Farmington, Conn. A Historical Discourse, delivered by request, before the Citizens of, Nov. 4, 1840, in commemoration of the original settlement of the Ancient Town in 1640. By Noah Porter, Jr. *8vo pamphlet, 99 p.; scarce.* *Hartford,* 1841

691 FARMINGTON, Me. History of, from its settlement to 1846. By Thomas Parker. *8vo, half mor.; very scarce; fine copy.* *Farmington,* 1846

692 Faux, W. Memorable Days in America: being a Journal of a Tour to the United States, principally undertaken to ascertain, by positive evidence, the Condition and probable prospects of British Emigrants; including accounts of Mr. Birkbeck's settlement in the Illinois, and intended to show Men and Things as they are in America. *8vo, bds., uncut; frontispiece.* *London,* 1823

693 Fay, Rev. Cyrus H., of Phila. An Address on "The Changes of a Century," delivered before the Members of Norwich University,

Aug. 21, 1839. *8vo pamphlet, rough edges,* 31 *pages ; fine copy ; very scarce. Historical.* *Newport, N. H.,* 1839

694 FAYETTEVILLE, N. C. Centenary Sermon deliv. before the Presbytery of, at Bluff Church, October 18, 1858. By Rev. Neill McKay. Also, A Centennial Historical Address. By James Banks. *8vo, orig. cov.,* 19 *and* 24 *p. ; fine copy ; very scarce.* *Fayetteville N. C.,* 1858

The Centennial Disc. by Banks is replete with Revolutionary incidents and the struggles of this Church with the Indians on the Frontiers of the State.

695 FELLOWS, JOHN. The Veil removed ; or, reflections on David Humphrey's Essay on the Life of Israel Putnam. Also, notices of W. B. Peabody's life of the same, S. Swett's sketch of Bunker Hill Battle, etc. *12mo, cl.* *New York,* 1843

696 FELTMAN, Lieut. WILLIAM. The Journal of, of the First Pennsylvania Regiment, 1781–1782, including the March into Virginia and the Siege of Yorktown. *8vo, bds., uncut.* *Philadelphia, Pa.,* 1853

697 FILLMORE COUNTY, Minnesota. History of, with an outline of her Resources, Advantages, &c. By J. W. Bishop. *Chatfield, Minn.,* 1858

698 FIRMIN, GILES. The Real Christian ; or, a Treasure of Effectual Calling. *Sheep, 12mo. Printed by Rogers and Fowle.* *Boston,* MDCCXLII.

699 FISHER, WILLIAM. An Interesting account of the voyages and travels of Capt's Lewis and Clarke in the years 1804–5 and 6, giving a faithful description of the river Missouri and its source; of the various tribes of Indians through which they passed ; manners and customs ; soil, climate, commerce ; gold and silver mines ; animal and vegetable productions. Interspersed with very entertaining anecdotes ; to which is added a complete dictionary of the Indian tongue. *Sheep 12mo, plates.* *Baltimore,* 1813

700 FISHER, E. T. Report of a French Protestant Refugee in Boston, 1687. Translated from the French. *Sm. 4to, orig. cov., rubric ti. ; only* 125 *copies printed ; uncut.* *Brooklyn N. Y.,* 1868

701 FISHKILL, N. Y. A Discourse delivered on the 12th of September, 1866, at the Celebration of the 150th Anniversary of the First Reformed Dutch Church—with an Appendix, furnishing a brief Historical Sketch of the Associated Churches of Hopewell, New Hackensack, Fishkill Landing and Glenham. *8vo,* 64 *pages, stiff covers ; illust.* *New York,* 1866

702 FITCHBURG AND LUNENBURG, MASS. History of the Town of Fitchburg and also of Lunenburg, from its first settlement to the year 1764. By Rufus C. Torrey. *8vo, paper cov., rough edges ;* 111 *pages ; very scarce ; beautiful copy.* *Fitchburg, Mass.,* 1836

"Few Town Histories will ever be written a second time. The pains are too great and the praise is too little."

703 FLETCHER, JOHN. Studies on Slavery in Easy Lessons, compiled

into eight studies, and subdivided into short lessons for the convenience of readers. *Sheep, large 8vo.* *Natchez,* 1852

704 Flint, Micah P. The Hunter, and other Poems. *8vo, bds., uncut.* *Boston,* 1826

705 FLINT, TIMOTHY. Recollections of the last Ten Years, in the Valley of the Mississippi. A series of letters to the Rev. James Flint. *8vo, bds., uncut.* *Boston,* 1826

706 FLINT, TIMOTHY. A condensed Geography and History of the Western States, or the Mississippi Valley. In two volumes. *8vo, half mor.* *Cincinnati,* 1828

707 FLINT, TIMOTHY. Indian Wars of the West; containing Biographical Sketches of those Pioneers who headed the Western Settlers in repelling the attacks of the Savages. Together with a View of the Character, Manners, Monuments and Antiquities of the Western Indians. *12mo, sheep. With map.* *Cincinnati,* 1833

708 Floridas, The; An Original Memoir on. With a General Description. By a Gentleman of the South. *Uncut.* *Baltimore,* 1821

709 Florida, The War in—being an Exposition of its Causes and an accurate History of the Campaigns of Generals Clinch, Gaines and Scott. By a Late Staff Officer. *Cloth, 12mo, rough edges; plates.* *Baltimore,* 1836

710 FLUSHING, L. I. Past and Present. A Historical Sketch. By G. Henry Mandeville. *Fine copy; cloth, 12mo; plates; scarce.* *Flushing, L. I.,* 1860

711 FORCE, PETER. Tracts and other Papers relating to the Origin, Settlement, and Progress of the Colonies in North America; from the Discovery of the Country to the year 1776. *4 vols., cl., uncut; imp. 8vo.* *Washington,* 1836–'46

712 Forster, John Reinhold. History of Voyages and Discoveries made in the North. Translated from the German, and elucidated by a new and original map of the Countries situated about the North Pole. *8vo, half sheep. With map.* *Dublin,* 1786

713 Fort Hill; The Story of—giving an account of many interesting Adventures between the Whites and Indians, previous to the Settlement of Auburn, N. Y. By Frederick Prince. *8vo pamph.; 50 p.; dble. col.; fine copy.* *Auburn,* 1859

714 Fort Duquesne, Oration delivered at the Centennial Celebration of the Evacuation of—Nov. 25, 1858. By A. W. Loomis. *l. 8vo, cl.; fine copy; 33 p.* *Pittsburgh,* 1859

715 Fort Wayne, Ind.; History of—from the earliest known accounts of this Point to the present period. Embracing an extended view of the aboriginal tribes of the north-west, including, more especially, the Miamies of this locality, their habits, customs, etc. With a sketch of the life of Gen. Anthony Wayne; including also a lengthy biography of the late Samuel Hanna. Together with short sketches of several of the early pioneer settlers of Fort Wayne. Also of the manufacturing, mercantile and railroad interests of Fort Wayne and vicinity. By Wallace A. Brice. *8vo, or. cov., uncut.* *Fort Wayne, Ind.,* 1868

716 Fox, Ebenezer; The Revolutionary Adventures of—of Roxbury, Mass. 12*mo, cl.; plates.* 1*st Ed.* *Boston,* 1838

717 Fox, Ebenezer; Adventure of—in the Revolutionary War. Illustrated. *Cloth,* 12*mo.* *Boston,* 1847

718 Franklin, Benjamin; Life of. Written by himself. *Bds.,* 12*mo.* *Phila.,* 1811

719 Franklin, Dr. Benjamin; The Works of—consisting of Essays, Humorous, Moral and Literary; with his Life, written by himself. 18*mo, sh.; with portrait.* *New York,* 1825

720 Franklin, Dr. Benjamin; The Works of—consisting of Essays, Humorous, Moral and Literary; with his Life, written by himself. 16*mo, cl., gilt front.* *London,* 1843

721 Franklin, Benjamin; Life of. By Jared Sparks. In 12 parts, as orginally issued. 8*vo, paper; with illustrations, uncut.* *Boston,* 1844

722 FRANKLIN, JOHN. Narrative of a Journey to the Polar sea, in 1819, 20, 21, 22. With an Appendix on various subjects relating to the science and natural history. Illustrated by numerous plates and maps. 4*to, cf.: scarce; fine copy.* *London,* 1823

723 FRANKLIN, JOHN. Narrative of a second expedition to the shores of the Polar sea, in 1825, 1826, and 1827. Including an account of the progress of a detachment to the Eastward by John Richardson. Illustrated by numerous plates and maps. 4*to, cf.* *London,* 1828

724 (French, J. C., and Carey, Edward.) The trip of the Oceanus to Fort Sumter and Charleston, S. C. Comprising the incidents of the Excursion, the Appearance at that time of the City, and the entire Programme of Exercises at the Re-raising of the Flag over the ruins of Fort Sumter, April 14th, 1865. 8*vo, or. cov., with plate.* *Brooklyn, N. Y.,* 1865

725 Frost, Barzillai. Discourse deliv. at Dedication of the New Church of the First Parish in Concord, Mass., Dec. 29, 1841. 8*vo pamphlet,* 31 *p., good copy.* *Boston,* 1842

726 Frost, John. Historical Sketches of the Indians. Exhibiting their Manners and Customs on the Battlefield and in the Wigwam. 8*vo, cl., col'd plates.* *Hartford,* 1857

727 Fryeburg, Me. The Scene of Lovewell's Fight. An Address delivered on the Commemoration at Fryeburg, May 19, 1825, by Charles S. Davis. 8*vo, paper cov.;* 64 *pages, uncut: beautiful copy, rare.* *Portland,* 1825

728 Fryeburg, Me. The Centennial Celebration of the Settlement of, with the Historical Address, by Rev. Samuel Souther. *Paper cover,* 79 *pages, fine copy.* *Worcester,* 1863

729 Fuller, S. M. Summer on the Lakes, in 1843. 8*vo, cl. plates.* *Boston,* 1844

730 FULLER, THOMAS, D. D. The Holy State, and the Profane State. New edition. With notes, by James Nichols. 8*vo, full polished calf, gilt top, edges rough* *London, Tho's Tegg,* 1841

731 FULLER, THOMAS, D. D. The Church history of Britain, from the birth of Jesus Christ until MDCXLVIII. New edition, by the

Rev. J. S. Brewer. Reprinted from London edition of 1655. 6 *vols. 8vo, full polished calf, gilt top, edges rough.* *University Press, Oxford*, 1845

732 FULTON CITY, (Ill.) Sketches of the Early History and present advantages of, showing its resources and prospects ; to which is added a brief Sketch of Whiteside Co. *8vo*, 32 *p. Scarce.* *Fulton City*, 1856 150

733 "FUNKS, PETER." The Mock Auction, Ossawattomie Sold, a Mock Heroic Poem ; with Portraits and Tableaux. *8vo, cl.* *Richmond, Va.*, 1860 100

734 FURMAN, WOOD. A History of the Charleston Association of Baptist Churches in the State of South Carolina, with an appendix. *8vo, sh.* *Charleston, S. C.*, 1811 10

PAMPHLETS.

735 Fast-Day Sermons. [*Twenty-three.*]

Abercrombie, James. Sermon, in Phila., July 30, 1812. *Phila.*, 1812

——— Sermon, in Phila., Aug. 20, 1812. *Phila.*, 1812

——— Two sermons: the first, July 30 ; the second, Aug. 20 , 1812. *Phila.*, 1812

Channing, W. E. Sermon, Aug. 20, 1812. *Boston*, 1812

Parish, E. A protest against the war. A disc. at Byfield, July 23, 1812. *Newburyport*, 1812

Giles, John. Two Discourses, in Newburyport, Aug. 20, 1812. With a copious Appendix. *Haverhill*, 1812

Austin, Sam'l. "The Apology of Patriots, or the heresy of the friends of the Washington and peace policy defended." Sermon, Aug. 20, 1812. *Worcester*, 1812

Colman, Henry. Sermon, Aug. 20, 1812. *Bingham* 5

Worcester, Noah. Sermon, Aug. 20, 1812. *Salisbury, N. H.*

Parish, Elijah. Discourse, April 8, 1813. *Byfield*

Stevens, John H. Discourse, April 8, 1813, Stoneham, Mass. *Windsor, Vt.*, 1814

——— Discourse, April 8, 1813, Stoneham, Mass. *N. Y. ed.*

Bemis, Stephen. Two Discourses at Harvard, Aug. 20, 1812. *Harvard*, 1814

Stevens, John H. Discourse, Stoneham, Mass., April 7, 1814. *Boston*, 1814

Parish, Elijah. Discourse, Byfield, Mass., April, 7, 1814. *Newburyport ed.*

Porter, Ebenezer. Sermon, Theol. Sem., Andover, April 3, 1823.

Wayland, Francis. Two Discourses, at Boston, April 7, 1825.

——— Two Discourses, at Boston, April 7, 1825. 2d ed.

Palfrey, John G. Discourse, at Boston, Aug. 9, 1832.

Mitchell, John. Sermon, at Northampton, Sept. 1, 1837.

Hopkins, Albert. Sermon, at Williamstown, Mass., March 28, 1839.
Bushnell, Horace. Discourse, Hartford, 1844. 3d ed.
Clowes, Rev. J. Sermon, Public Fast. *Manchester*, 1809

20 736 Fast Day Sermons. *Valuable.* [*Eighteen.*]

Eliot, Andrew. Sermon, April 19, 1753. *Boston*, 1753
Duché, Jacob. "The American vine," a sermon, July 20, 1775. *Very scarce.* *Phila.*, 1775
Price, Richard. Sermon delivered to a congregation of Protestant dissenters, at Hackney, 10th Feb., 1779, 3rd ed. *London*, 1779
Tappen, David. Disc. at Newbury, May 15, 1783. *Salem*, 1783
Mason, John M. Sermon, Sept. 20th, 1793, in N. Y., on account of a malignant and mortal fever in Phila. *New York*, 1793
Smith, Samuel S. Disc. on the nature and reasonableness of fasting, at Princeton, 6th Jan., 1795. *Phila.*, 1795
Barnard, Thomas. Sermon, at Salem, March 31, 1796. *Newburyport*, 1796
Miller, Samuel. Sermon, May 9, 1798. *New York*, 1798
Linn, William. Disc. on national sins. *New York*, 1798
Belknap, Jeremy. Sermon, 9th May, 1798. *Boston*, 1798
Dana, Joseph. Disc. in two parts, April 25, 1799. *Boston*, 1799
M'Donald, J. Danger of America delineated. Address at Cooperstown, April 25, 1799. *Very scarce.* *Cooperstown*, 1799
M'Donald, J. Duty of America enforced. An exhortation at Cooperstown, April 26, 1799. *Very scarce.* *Cooperstown*, 1799
Clowes, J. The protection mark, a sermon at Manchester, 27th Feb. *Manchester*, 1799
Morse, J. Sermon, at Charlestown, April 25, 1799. *N. Y.* 1799
Emmons, N. Disc. April 9, 1801. *Salem*, 1802
Channing. W. E. Sermon, April 5, 1810. *Boston*, 1810
Lathrop, Joseph. The prophecy of Daniel, relating to the time of the end, opened, in two discourses, April 11, 1811. *Springfield*, 1811

20 737 Miscellaneous. [*Twenty-one.*]

Frothingham, N. L. Sermon at ordination of. By J. M'Kean. 1815
——— Plea against religious controversy, deliv. Feb. 8, 1829. *Boston.*
——— Sermon preached to First Ch., April 10, 1842.
Frothingham, O. B. Sermon, "Plea for Frankness," May 6, 1866. *N. Y.*
Franklin, B. Cicero's Cato Major; or a disc. on Old age. *Phila.*
Franklin, B. Lecture on the life of. By John B. Murray. *Scarce.* Nov. 17, 1841.
Frankin Soc. Charter, Constitution and By-Laws of. *St. Louis*, 1837

Friends. An Epistle from. *Scarce.* *Phila.*, 1788
Friends. Documents issued by the Conference of. *Phila.*, 1849
Fleming, Dr. Letters on the state of Religion in Newfoundland to Dr. A. O'Connell. *Dublin*, 1844
Fleming, Robert. Disc., Rise and Fall of Papacy. *Phila.*, 1848
Franklin Institute. Charter of Incorporation, Consti. and By-laws. *Phila.*, 1824
Fraternal Assoc. Constitution of U. S. Naval. *N. Y.*, 1820
Facts for Consideration of Ship Builders, Seamen, Merchants, etc. *N. Y.* 1828
Feltus, Dr. Henry J. Lines on Death of. *N. Y.* 1829
Farmington. Hist. Discourse before Citizens of, by Noah Porter, Jr. *Very scarce.* *Hartford*, 1841
Fanny, Continued. *Very scarce.* *N. Y.* 1820
French Government. Letter on Genius and Dispositions of the. *Boston*, 1810
Force, Peter. Historical Library. Report of. *Washington*, 1867
Friends. Vindication of Society of, by Enoch Lewis. *Phila.*, 1834
France. Remarks on State of Naval Forces of. *Boston*, 1844

738 Miscellaneous. [*Sixteen.*]

Faugers, Margaretta A. Belisarius. A Tragedy. *N. Y.*, 1795
Fox, Capt. Joseph. Disc. deliv. at Fitchburg on Death of, Feb. 28, 1797. By Thomas Noyes. *Leominster.*
Frank; or, Who's the Croaker? *New York*, 1820
Flint, James. Sermon deliv. on Death of Abiel Abbott. 1828
Fisk, T. "The Pleasures of Sin." Disc. deliv. Dec. 16, 1827. *Phila.*
Females. Condition and Character of, in Pagan and Mohammedan Countries.
Fansher, Sylvanus. Treatise on Electricity. *New Haven*, 1830
Frick, Wm. Address in the University of Maryland. 1831
Forrest, Edwin. Oration deliv. 62nd Anniv. of Independence of U. S., July 4, 1838. *New York.*
Fisher, Samuel. Divine Sovereignty and Human Accountability. Sermon, May 16, 1839. *Phila.*
Fawcett, Henry. The Bachelor's Guide. Familiar commentary on the indiscretions arising from Human Frailty; in which the Symptoms and Baneful effects of self-abuse, Intemp. and Libertinism are explained in an easy manner, to which are added very extensive practical observations of sexual debility, and its attendant sympathies, addressed to Youth and Maturity. *New York*, 1840
Free Churches. *N. Y.* 1843
French without a master, by A. H. Monteith. *N. Y.* 1843
Fourier Assoc. Self exposed as to its principles and aims. By Donald C. M'Lauren. 1844
France. Remarks on the States of Naval Forces of. 1844
Fisch, G. Evangelical Ch. of Lyons. Brief notice of. 1845

739 Miscellaneous. [*Thirteen.*]

Fletcher, Abel. Address. The Hist. Objects and Princ. of the order of The Sons of Temperance. 1844

Fairchild, J. H. Statement and review of the whole case of. *Scarce.* *Boston,* 1845

Ferguson, Peter K. Ugliness and its Uses. Lecture before Y. L. Circulating Library Assoc. 1852

Felt, J. B. Who was First Gov. of Mass. ? *Scarce. Boston,* 1853

Firmin, Giles. Brief Memoirs of one of the ejected ministers of 1662. By John Ward Dean. *Boston,* 1866

Fontaine, J. A. A. Improved Aerial R. R. new system of Aero Locomotion. *New York,* 1867

Field, Henry M. Atlantic Telegraph. *New York,* 1867

Fremont, John C. Report on an exploration of the country, between the Missouri river and Rocky Mts. *Very scarce.* *Washington,* 1843

Fremont, John C. Life, Explorations and Public Services of. *N. Y.* 1856

Fremont, J. C. Life of. *New York,* 1856

Francis, Convers. Address on commem. of Amer. Ind. of July 4, 1828. *Cambridge.*

Francis, John W. Eulogy on, by A. K. Gardner, March 7, 1861. *N. Y.*

Fowler, O. S. Matrimony ; or, Phrenology and Physiology applied to the selection of congenial companions for life. *New York,* 1847

740 Miscellaneous. [*Fourteen.*]

Fowler, L. N. Synopsis of Phrenology and Physiology, and description of Functions of Body and Mind. *New York,* 1847

Finney, C. G. Sermons on Various Subjects. Nos. 1 to 7. *New York,* 1835

Foster, John. Sermon, Annual Fast, April 11, 1811. *Cambridge,* 1811

Foster, John. Sermon, Annual Fast, Jan. 12, 1815. *Boston,* 1815

Foster, John. Disc. deliv. Baptist Miss. Soc., Sept. 1818. *Taunton.*

Foster, Luke B. Sermon deliv. at Northborough, Mass. 1814

Fuller, S. W. Sermon deliv. before the 2nd Univ. Soc., Jan. 24, 1836.

Fuller, S. W. Biographical Sketch of, by S. Fuller, Jr. *Scarce.* 1843

741 Funeral Sermons. [*Twelve.*]

Onderdonk, Benj. T. Sermon, Funeral of Rev. John H. Hobart. *N. Y.,* 1830

Reed, John. Sermon, Death of Rev. John H. Hobart. *N. Y.,* 1830

Schroeder, John F. Disc., Character of Rev. John H. Hobart. *N. Y.,* 1830

Anthon, Henry. Sermon, Death of Rev. John H. Hobart. *N. Y.,* 1830

Wainwright, Jno. M. Sermon, Death of Rev. John H. Hobart. *N. Y.*, 1830
Pickering, John. Eulogy on Nathaniel Bowditch. *Boston*, 1838
Young, Alexander. Disc. on Life of Nathaniel Bowditch. *Boston*, 1838
Frothingham, N. L. Sermon, Death of John Adams. *Boston*, 1826
Rowan, Stephen N. Address, Funeral Obsequies of John Adams and Thomas Jefferson. *N. Y.*, 1826
Adams, John Q. Eulogy on Life and Character of James Madison. *Boston*, 1836
Whipple, Thomas J. Eulogy on James Madison. *Woodstock*, 1837
Croswell, Rev. Harry. Disc. on Death of Wm. H. Harrison. *New Haven*, 1841

742 Funeral Sermons. [*Thirteen.*]
Carpenter, Hugh S. Eulogy on Wm. H. Harrison. *N. Y.*, 1841
Cooke, Rev. Parsons. Disc. on Death of Wm. H. Harrison. *Lynn*, 1841
Potter, Rev. Horatio. Disc. on Death of Wm. H. Harrison. *Albany*, 1841
Lunt, Wm. P. Disc. on Interment of John Q. Adams. *Boston*, 1848
Adams, John Q.; Addresses in Congress of U. S. on Death of. *Wash.*, 1848
Everett, Edward. Eulogy on Life and Char. of J. Q. Adams. *Boston*, 1848
Woodbury, Levi. Eulogy on Life and Char. and Public Services of Ex-Pres. Polk. *Boston*, 1849
Baldwin, Oliver P. Eulogy on Life and Charac. of Gen. Zachary Taylor. *Richmond*, 1850
Adams, John Q. Oration on Life and Charac. of Gilbert Motier De Lafayette. *Washington*, 1835
Adams, John Q. Oration on Life and Charac. of Gilbert Motier De Lafayette. *New York*, 1835
Dayton, Aaron O. Eulogy on Lafayette. *New York*, 1835
Milnor, Rev. James. Sermon, Death of De Witt Clinton. *N. Y.*, 1828
Conkling, Alfred; Disc. Commem. of Talents, etc., of De Witt Clinton. *Albany*, 1828

743 Funeral Sermons. [*Nine.*]
Knapp, Samuel L. Disc. on Life and Char. of De Witt Clinton. *Washington*, 1828
Moreau, Funeral Oration at St. Petersburg in honor of. *N. Y.*, 1814
Moreau, Funeral Eulogy at St. Petersburg in honor of. *N. Y.*, 1814
Dwight, Timothy. Sermon, Death of Mr. Ebenezer G. Marsh. *Hartford*, 1804

Fowler, Bancroft. Oration, Death of Mr. Ebenezer G. Marsh. *Hartford*, 1804
Dyer, Rev. Palmer. Disc., Death of Wm. H. Harrison. *Whitehall*, 1841
Woods, Leonard. Sermon, Death of Moses Brown. *Andover*, 1827
Whitney, Eli. Oration on Death of Robert Grant. *New Haven*, 1792
Burroughs, Charles. Discourse, Interment of Rev. James Morss. *Portsmouth*, 1842

7 744 Funeral Sermons. [*Twelve.*]

Dashiell, A. H. Sermon on Life and Character of Rev. Joseph Eastburn. *Phila.*, 1828
Wylie, Rev. A. Sermon on Death of Mrs. Elizabeth Brady. *N. Y.*, 1829
Feltus, Rev. Dr. Henry J.; Lines occasioned by Death of. *N. Y.*, 1829
M'Elroy, Joseph. Sermon on Death of Rev. John M. Mason. *N. Y.*, 1830
Palfrey, John G. Sermon on Death of Hon. Isaac Parker. *Boston*, 1830
Pascalis, Felix. Eulogy on Life and Character of Hon. Samuel L. Mitchill. *N. Y.*, 1831
Hawes, Joel. Sermon, Funeral of Rev. Elias Cornelius. *Hartford*, 1832
Knox, Rev. John. Sermon, Death of Rev. Gerardus A. Kuypers. *N. Y.*, 1833
Rowan, Stephen N. Tribute to Memory of Alex. McLeod. *N. Y.*, 1833
Cuyler, Cornelius C. Disc., Death of Rev. Gilbert R. Livingston. *Phila.*, 1834
McVickar, John. Address, Death of Wm. M. De Rham. *N. Y.*, 1834
Smith, Hon. Nathan; Proc. at Funeral of, and Discourse. *New Haven*, 1834

7 745 Funeral Sermons. [*Thirteen.*]

Kennedy, John P. Disc. on Life and Character of Wm. Wirt. *Scarce.* *Baltimore*, 1834
Sewall, Samuel. Sermon at Funeral of Rev. Samuel Stearns. *Boston*, 1835
Fay, Warren. Sermon at Funeral of Rev. Benj. B. Wisner. *Boston*, 1835
Beck, T. Romeyn. Eulogium on Life and Services of Simon De Witt. *Albany*, 1835
Story, Joseph. Disc. on Life, Character and Services of Hon. John Marshall. *Boston*, 1835
Doane, George W. Sermon in Commem. of Rev. Wm. White. *Burlington*, 1836
Onderdonk, Rev. Henry U. Disc. at Funeral of Rev. Wm. White. *Phila.*, 1836

Bowen, Nathaniel. Sermon on Death of Rev. Wm. White. *Charleston*, 1836

Hopkins, Mark. Discourse on Death of Edward D. Griffin. *Troy*, 1837

Welch, B. T. Discourse on Death of Elder Alanson C. Covell. *Albany*, 1837

Preston, W. Discourse occasioned by Destruction of Steam Packet Pulaski. *Savannah*, 1838

Emmons, Nathanael. Extract from a Discourse at Funeral of Rev. Elisha Fish. *N. Y.*, 1797

Stiles, Ezra. Sermon at Funeral of Chauncey Whittelsey. *Very scarce.* *New Haven*, 1787

746 Funeral Sermons. [*Twelve.*]

Lord, Nathan. Discourse on Character of Stephen Chase. *Hanover*, 1851

Parker, Theodore. Discourse on Death of Daniel Webster. *Boston*, 1853

Hawley, Fletcher J. Tribute to Memory of Rev. F. S. Mines, Rev. Edmund Richards and Rev. John Wade. *St. Croix*, 1853

Doane, Bp. Words at Funeral of Mrs. Bradford. *Burlington*, 1854

Wakely, Joseph B. The Ethics of Funerals. Vindication of Meth. Epis. Ch. with regard to funeral of Wm. Poole. *N. Y.*, 1855

Taylor, Wm. J. R. Disc. in Commem. of Rev. Henry G. Livingston. *Phila.*, 1855

Bethune, George W. Disc. on Death of Rev. Jacob Brodhead (frontispiece). *N. Y.*, 1855

Norton, Rev. S. H. Memorial of Isaac Hayes. *N. Y.*, 1857

Wayland, Francis. Disc. on Life and Charac. of Hon. Nicholas Brown. *Boston*, 1841

Onderdonk, Benj. T. Sermon at Funeral of Rev. Lewis P. Bayard. *N. Y.*, 1841

Bellows, Henry W. Disc. on Death of Wm. E. Channing. *N. Y.*, 1842

Peers, Rev. Benj. O.; Obituary of. *Louisville*, 1841

747 Funeral Sermons. [*Thirteen.*]

Cox, Samuel H. Sermon at Funeral of Mrs. Mary L. Stafford. *N. Y.*, 1843

Vermilye, Thomas E. Discourse at Funeral of Mrs. Cornelia Van Rensselaer. *N. Y.*, 1844

Robbins, Rev. Royal. Sermon at Funeral of Mrs. Ruth Hart. *Hartford*, 1844

Greenleaf, Simon. Disc. on Life and Charac. of Hon. Joseph Story. *Boston*, 1845

Gadsden, Bp.; Sketch of Life and Character of.

Wayland, Francis. Discourse on Life and Services of Wm. G. Goddard. *Providence*, 1846

Zandt, Rev. B. Van. Sermon at Funeral of Rev. Jacob Sickles. *Kinderhook*, 1846

Reason, Charles L. Eulogy on Life and Character of Thomas Clarkson. *N. Y.*, 1847

Ventura, Padre. Funeral Oration on Daniel O'Connell. *Boston*, 1847

Thompson, James W. Tribute to Memory of Rev. Henry Colman. *Boston*, 1849

Grafton, Joseph. Sermon on Death of Miss Sally Grafton. *Boston*, 1805

Stillman, Samuel. Discourse at Interment of Rev. Hezekiah Smith. *Boston*, 1805

Shurtleff, Roswell. Discourse at Funeral of Mrs. Mary Woodward. *Hanover*, 1807

748 Funeral Sermons. [*Thirteen.*]

Eliot, Andrew. Sermon at Funeral of Rev. John Webb. *Boston*, 1750

Buell, Samuel. Sermon on Death of Charles J. Smith. *New London*, 1770

Inglis, Charles. Sermon on Death of John Ogilvie. *N. Y.*, 1774

Webster, Samuel. Sermon on Death of Two Young Men. *Newburpyort*, 1784

Marsh, John. Sermon at Funeral of Mrs. Lydia Beadle. *Middleborough*, 1788

Fobes, Peres. Sermon on Death of Rev. James Manning. *Providence*, 1791

Eames, Jno. Sermon on Death of Rev. John Tucker. *Newburyport*, 1792

Thornton, John; Disc. on Death of. *Providence*, 1794

Dutch Ebenezer; Disc. on occasion of Numerous Deaths in his Parish. *Haverhill*, 1795

Rodgers, John. Sermon on Death of Rev. John Witherspoon. *Very scarce.* *N. Y.*, 1795

Cary, Thomas. Sermon on Death of Rev. Samuel Webster. *Newburyport*, 1796

Morse, Jedidiah. Sermon on Death of Thomas Russell. *Boston*, 1796

Smith, Samuel S. Sermon at Funeral of Rev. Gilbert T. Snowden. *Phila.*, 1797

749 Funeral Sermons. [*Fourteen.*]

Thacher, Peter. Sermon at Funeral of Rev. John Clarke. *Boston*, 1798

Kirkland, John T. Sermon at Funeral of Rev. Jeremy Belknap. *Boston*, 1798

Griswold, Stanley. Two Disc. on Death of Rev. Nathanael Taylor. *Litchfield*, 1801

Barnard, Thomas. Sermon at Funeral of Rev. Phillips Payson. *Charlestown*, 1801

Morse, Jedidiah. Sermon at Funeral of Miss Mary Russell. *Charlestown*, 1806

Griffin, Edward D. Sermon at Funeral of Rev. Alex. Macwhorter. *N. Y.*, 1807

Andrews, John. Sermon at Funeral of Rev. Thomas Cary. *Newburyport*, 1808

Dwight, Timothy. Disc. on Death of Jno. Trumbull. *New Haven*, 1809

Buckminster, Joseph S. Sermon on Death of James Sullivan. *Boston*, 1809

Burhans, Daniel. Sermon on Death of Asahel Lewis, also James Clark. *New Haven*, 1809

Parish, Elijah. Eulogy on John Hubbard. *Hanover, N. H.*, 1810

Buckminster, Joseph S. Sermon at Funeral of Rev. Wm. Emerson. *Boston*, 1811

Green, Ashbel. Sermon at Funeral of Rev. Wm. M. Tennent. *Phila.*, 1811

Baldwin, Amos G. Sermon at Funeral of James Wetmore. *Utica*, 1812

750 Funeral Sermons. [*Thirteen.*]

Whitlock, Rev. Henry. Sermon, Funeral Rev. Bela Hubbard. *N. Haven*, 1812

Lathrop, John. Discourse, Death of Rev. John Eliot. *Boston*, 1813

Prince, John. Sermon, Death of Rev. Thomas Barnard. *Salem*, 1814

Prentice, Joseph. Sermon, Death of Hon. Samuel Dexter. *Boston*, 1816

Hobart, John H. Address, Funeral of Rev. Benjamin Moore. *N. Y.*, 1816

Silliman, Benjamin. Eulogy, Pres. Dwight. *N. Haven*, 1817

Allen, Samuel C. Eulogy on Hon. John Wheelock. *Hanover*, 1817

Kendall, James. Sermon, Death of Deacon Ephraim Spooner. *Boston*, 1818

Frothingham, N. L. Sermon, Funeral Rev. Joseph McKean. *Boston*, 1818

Perkins, Cyrus. Eulogy on Hon. William H. Woodward. *Hanover*, 1818

Smith, Daniel. Sermon, Funeral of Rev. Amzi Lewis. *Poughkeepsie*, 1819

Fisk, Ezra. Sermon, Funeral of Rev. George Stewart. *Goshen*, 1819

Lyman, Joseph. Sermon, Funeral of Hon. Caleb Strong. *Northampton*, 1819

751 Funeral Sermons. [*Thirteen*].

Fletcher, Nathaniel. Sermon, Funeral of Rev. Paul Coffin. *Kennebunk*, 1821

Sparks, Jared. Sermon, Death of Hon. William Pinkney. *Baltimore*, 1822

Holmes, Abiel. Sermon, Funeral of Rev. David Osgood. *Cambridge*, 1822

Kirkland, John T. Discourse, Death of Hon. George Cabot. *Boston*, 1823

Allen, Wm. Sermon, Funeral of Rev. Samuel Eaton. *Brunswick*, 1823

Wisner, Benjamin B. Sermon, Death of Mrs. Miriam Phillips. *Cambridge*, 1823

Kinnersley, T. Selection of Sepulchral Curiosities, with a Biographical Sketch on Human Longevity, containing Epitaphs taken from Monuments and Gravestones in England, Ireland, Scotland, and the United States ; *scarce.* *N. Y.*, 1823

Spring, Gardiner. Funeral Sermon, Death of Rev. Philip M. Whelpley. *N. Y.*, 1824

Merwin, Samuel. Funeral Sermon, Death of Rev. John Summerfield. *Baltimore*, 1825

Livingston, John H., Eulogy on Life and Character of. *N. Y.*, 1825

Shepherd, Rev. Wm. Sermon, Death of Rev. John Yates. *Liverpool*, 1826

Pierpont, John. Discourse, Death of Horace Holley. *Boston*, 1827

Mitchell, Samuel L. Discourse on Life and Character of Thomas A. Emmet. *N. Y.*, 1828

752 Funeral Sermons. [*Eight.*]

Clap, Mrs. Mary, Disc. delivered at Funeral of, by Chauncey Whittelsey ; *very scarce.* *New Haven*, 1769

Colman, Dr. Sermon after Funeral of Mr. Wm. Cooper. *Boston*, 1744

Campbell, Wm. H. Funeral Discourse on Death of A. Yates, Nov. 17, 1844.

Clark, Orin. Funeral Address delivered at Interment of the Hon. John Nicholas, Jan. 2, 1820.

Collins, Levi. Discourse at Funeral of Mrs. Mary Sexton. *Hartford*, 1807

Crossman, Joseph W. Discourse at Funeral of Wm. L. Strong. *Hartford*, 1805

Cunningham, Eliza, Monument to Memory of. *Phila.* 1796

Colton, Lucretia, Sermon deliv. at Interment of, with a Sketch of Her Life. *Hartford*, 1821

753 Fourth of July Orations. [*Eighteen.*] *Rare lot.*

Everett, Alex. H. Defence of the Char. and Prin. of Mr. Jefferson, at Weymouth, Mass., July 4, 1836.

Emery, Moses. Oration, Saco, Mass., July 4, 1839.

Upham, Chas. W. Oration, Salem, Mass., July 4, 1842.

Smith, J. C. Discourse, Washington, July 4, 1844, on the Religion and Patriotism of '76.

Miner, Charles. The Olive Branch ; or, The Evil and the Remedy. Address, July 4, 1821. *Priv. Printed.* *Phil.* 1856

Adams, Charles Francis. Address, Quincy, July 4, 1856.

——— Oration, Fall River, July 4, 1860.

James, Henry. Oration, Newport, R. I., July 4, 1861.

Eliot, Samuel. Oration, Boston, July 4, 1868.

Gardiner, John. An Oration delivered July 4, 1785, at the re-

quest of the Inhabitants of the Town of Boston, in celebration of the Anniversary of American Independence. *4to, uncut, very rare.* *Boston: Printed by Peter Edes, State Street.*
The First 4th of July Oration Delivered in Boston.

Snell, Thos. Oration, at Brookfield, July 5, 1813.

Cummings, Hooper. Oration, July 4, 1823. *Newark.*

Cheever, George B. Address at Relig. Celebration in Salem, July 4, 1833. *Boston*, 1833

Cooley, James. Oration delivered at Granville, July 4, 1813; *scarce.* *Hartford*, 1813

Caldwell, Charles. Oration delivered before Amer. Repub. Soc. of Phila., July 4, 1810; *scarce.*

Clark, Thomas M. Oration, 84th Anniv. of Amer. Ind., July 4, 1860.

Cummings, Hooper. Oration, Commem. Amer. Ind., delivered July 5, 1824, in the Bowery Church. *N. Y.*

Custis, Geo. Washington Parke. Oration June 5, 1813; *very scarce.* *Georgetown, D. C.*

754 Fourth of July Orations. [*Sixteen.*]

Andrews, Josiah. Oration at Perry Village, N. Y., July 4, 1831.

Wells, John. Oration at St. Paul's Ch., N. Y., July 4, 1798.

Lewis, Zechariah. Oration at Conn. Soc. of Cinn., N. Y., July 4, 1799; *scarce.*

Bancroft, George. Oration at Northampton, Mass., July 4, 1826.

Armstrong, Robert G. Address at Smithfield, N. Y., July 4, 1825.

Burges, Tristram. Oration at Providence, R. I., July 4, 1831.

Mallory, R. C. Oration at Whitehall, N. Y., July 4, 1817.

Mayo, H. B. Address at Oxford, Ohio, July 4, 1839.

Brownson, O. A. Address at Dedham, Mass., July 4, 1834.

Holmes, John. Oration at Alfred, Maine, July 4, 1815; *scarce.*

Morris, Gouverneur. Oration delivered before Washington Benevolent Soc., New York, July 5, 1813; *scarce.*

Perkins, Charles. Oration delivered at Norwich Conn., July 4, 1822.

Rutledge, Edward. Address delivered at Stratford, Conn., July 4, 1827.

Evarts, Jeremiah. Oration delivered at Charlestown, Mass., July 4, 1812.

Cushing, Caleb. Oration delivered at Newburyport, Mass., July 4, 1832.

Linn, Wm. Sermon, "The Blessings of Amer." N. Y. City, July 4, 1794; *scarce.*

755 Fourth of July Orations. [*Sixteen.*]

Austin, I. J. Oration delivered at Boston, Mass., July 4, 1839.

Wendover, P. H. "Nat. Deliv." Oration, N. Y. City, July 4, 1806; *scarce.*

Key, Francis S., Oration delivered by. Washington, July 4, 1831.

Johnson, John B. Discourse, "The Dealings of God with Israel and America." July 4, 1798 ; *scarce.* *Albany.*

Dwight, Theo. Oration delivered at New Haven, July 7, 1801, before the Soc. of the Cincinnati for the State of Conn., to Celebrate the Anniversary of American Independence ; *scarce.* *Hartford.*

Bartlett, Joseph. The Fourth of July Anticipated. An Add. Delivered at the Exchange Coffee House, on the evening of the 3d of July, 1823. Also, including a Poem—an Ode—and the New Vicar of Bray ; *curious.* *Boston,* 1823

Holmes, Abiel. Address delivered before Washington Benev. Soc. at Cambridge, July 5, 1813 ; *scarce.*

Quincy, Josiah. Oration delivered July 4, 1826. *Boston.*

Paine, Thomas. Oration at Boston, Mass., July 17, 1799 ; *scarce.*

Lee, Chauncey. Oration at Colebrook, Conn., July 4, 1800 ; *scarce.*

Whitman, Ezekiel. Oration at New Gloucester, Maine, July 4, 1801.

Ringwood, Thomas. Oration at New York, July 5, 1802.

Sullivan, Wm. Oration at Boston, Mass., July 4, 1803.

Pickering, John. Oration at Salem, Mass. July 4 1804.

Evans, Richard. Oration at Portsmouth, N. H., July 4, 1805.

Dunbar, John D. Oration at Pembroke Mass., July 4, 1805.

756 Fourth of July Orations. [*Sixteen.*]

Lincoln, Daniel W. Oration at Worcester, Mass., July 4, 1805.

Ritchie, Andrew. Oration at Boston, Mass., July 4, 1803.

Barlow, Joel. Oration at Washington, D. C., July 4, 1809.

Knapp, Samuel L. Oration at Newburyport, Mass., July 4, 1810.

Dana, Daniel. Oration at Newburyport, Mass., July 4, 1814.

Merrick, Pliny. Oration at Worcester, Mass., July 4, 1817.

Pickering, Timothy. Observations Introductory to Reading the Declaration of Independence, at Salem, July 4, 1823 ; *rare.*

Adams, G. W. Oration at Quincy, Mass., July 4, 1824 ; *uncut.*

Sprague, Charles. Oration at Boston, Mass., July 4, 1824 ; *uncut.*

Codman, John. Oration at Dorchester, Mass., July 4, 1826 ; *uncut.*

Colman, Henry. Oration at Salem, Mass., July 4, 1826 ; *uncut.*

Everett, E. Oration at Charlestown, Mass., July 4, 1828 ; *uncut.*

Austin, Jas. T. Oration at Boston, Mass., July 4, 1829 ; *uncut.*

Baylies, Francis. Oration at Taunton, Mass., July 4, 1831 ; *uncut.*

Cheever, Geo. B. Oration at Salem, Mass., July 4, 1833 ; *uncut.*

Rantoul, Robert. Oration at Gloucester, Mass., July 4, 1833 ; *uncut.*

757 Fourth of July Orations, etc. *Rare lot.* [*Twenty-one.*]

Avery, Joseph. Oration at Holden, July 4, 1806. *Boston,* 1806

Binns, John. Oration before the Democratic Societies of the City and County of Phila., 4th July, 1810. *Phila.*, 1810

Burnet, James. Oration, 1799, at Weston. *Scarce.* *Newfield*, 1799

Dwight, Timothy. The duty of Americans at the present crisis. Disc., fourth July, 1798. *Scarce.* *New Haven*, 1798

Green, Rev. Ashbel. Oration, July 4, 1789, at Phila. *Phila.*, 1789

Everett, Alex. H. Oration at Boston, July 5, 1830. *Boston*, 1830

Henry, Symmes C. Oration before the Cincinnati Soc. of N. J., July 5th, 1824. *Very scarce.* *Trenton*, 1824

Langdon, Chauncy. Oration in Poultney, July 4th, 1804. *Salem*, 1804

Linn, W. "The blessings of America." A sermon preached at the request of the Tammany Soc., 4th July. *Scarce.* *N. Y.*, 1791

Maclay, Wm. B. Oration before the Literary Assoc., 4th July, 1836. *N. Y.*, 1836

Magaw, Samuel. Sermon in St. Paul's ch., 4th July, 1786. *Scarce.* *Phila.*, 1786

Quincy, Josiah, jr. Oration, July 4, 1832. *Boston*, 1832

Seymour, T. H. Oration before the citizens of Middletown. *Middletown*, 1827

Odes to be sung at the Juvenile patriotic festival, July 4, 1839.

Baldwin, Simeon. Oration at New Haven, July 4, 1788. *Scarce. Uncut.*

Atkinson, Wm. King. Oration at Dover, N. H., July 4, 1791. *Uncut.*

Allen, Paul. Oration at Providence, Mass., July 4, 1796.

Quincy Josiah, Oration at Boston, Mass., July 4, 1798.

Austin, Samuel. Oration at Worcester, Mass., July 4, 1798. *Uncut.*

Newcomb, Rich'd E. Oration at Greenfield, Mass., July 4, 1799. *Uncut.*

Marcy, Jno. Oration at Providence, R.I., July 4, 1799. *Uncut.*

758 Miscellaneous. [*Fifteen.*]

Farley, Fred. A. Christian consolation for bereaved parents. A sermon, preached at Brooklyn, N. Y., Aug. 8, 1841. *Brooklyn*, 1841

——— Disc. at the dedication of Westminster church in Providence, R. I., Mar. 5, 1829. *Boston*, 1829

Ferguson, John. Letters to Rev. Moses Thacher; with the results of an ecclesiastical council at North Wentworth, Dec. 14, 1830. *Boston*, 1831

Fish, Joseph. Sermon at the ordination of the Rev. Mr. William Vinal, in Newport, R. I., Oct. 29, 1746. *Scarce.* *Newport*, 1747

Fisher, Samuel. Two sermons preached at Morris-Town, N. J.; annexed, an address to the Presbyterian congregation. *Morris-Town*, 1814

Fleming, Peter. Report to the president and directors of the Mohawk and Hudson railway company. *New York*, 1829

Flint, Abel. Sermon at East-Hartford, Nov. 3, 1806, at the funeral of Mrs. Mary Yates. *Hartford,* 1806

Fobes, Peres. Sermon at Taunton, Nov. 11, 1784, upon the day of the execution of John Dixon for burglary. *Scarce.* *Providence* [1784]

Follen, Charles. Address introd. to the fourth course of the Franklin lectures, Nov. 3, 1834. *Boston,* 1835

Ford, John. Sermon, Apr. 4, 1820, at Orange, New Jersey, before the exec. comm. appointed by the Presbyterian education Soc. *Newark,* 1820

Foxcroft, Thomas. Sermon at the Old Church Lecture in Boston, Thursday, Jan. 1, 1746–7. *Scarce.* *Boston,* 1747

Fowler, O. S. Temperance, founded on phrenology and physiology. *New York,* 1848

——— Phrenology and physiology applied to the cultivation of memory.

France : its king, court and government. Third ed. *New York,* 1848

French fraternity and French protection as promised to Ireland. 18th ed. *Dublin,* 1798

759 Miscellaneous. *Valuable lot.* [*Nine.*]

Franklin Benjamin. Eulogium on, by W. Smith, Mar. 1, 1791. *Very scarce.* *Phila.,* 1792

Frelinghuysen. Speech on his resolution concerning Sabbath mails, May 8, 1830. *Washington,* 1830

Friends, Soc. of. Further salutation of brotherly love, from the monthly meeting of. *Phila.,* 1795

Frothingham, N. L. Plea against religious controversy, Feb. 8, 1829. *Boston,* 1829

——— "The ruffian released." A sermon, 21st of Feb., 1836. *Boston,* 1836

——— Two hundred years ago. Sermon preached to the First Church on the close of their second century. *Valuable.* *Boston,* 1830

Fulford, Francis. Address in the chapel of the Gen. Theol. Seminary of the Prot. Episc. Ch., Nov. 13, 1852. *New York,* 1852

Fulton, Robert. Opinions of the Judges of the supreme court, in the court of errors, in the case of R. R. Livingston and R. Fulton *vs.* J. Van Ingen and others. *Very scarce and valuable.* *Albany,* 1812

Furness, Wm. H. Disc. at the dedication of the First Congreg. Unit. Ch., Phila., Nov. 5, 1828. *Phila.,* 1828

ADDIS, MAXWELL PIERSON. Foot-prints of an Itinerant. *Cl.* 12*mo; portrait.* *Cincinnati*, 1855

761 Gallagher, James. The Western Sketch-Book. 8*vo, cl.* *Boston*, 1850

762 Garden, Alexander. Anecdotes of the Revolutionary War in America; with sketches of character of persons the most distinguished in the Southern States for civil and military services. *Bds.*, 4*to*, 3 *vols.* 150 *copies. No.* 119. *Charleston*, 1822. *Reprint. T. W. Field, Brooklyn*, 1865

763 Garden, Alexander. Anecdotes of the Revolutionary War in America; with Sketches of Character of Persons the most Distinguished in the Southern States for Civil and Military Services. 8*vo, hf. mor., gilt top, uncut. With portraits. First series. Thirty plates inserted.* *Charleston, S. C.*, 1822

764 Garden, Alexander. Anecdotes of the Revolutionary War in America; with Sketches of Character of Persons the most Distinguished in the Southern States for Civil and Military Services. 8*vo, hf. cf.* *Charleston, S. C.*, 1822

765 Garden, Alexander. Anecdotes of the American Revolution, Illustrative of the Talents and Virtues of the Heroes and Patriots who acted the most conspicuous parts therein. 2d series. 12*mo, boards, uncut.* *Charleston, S. C.*, 1828

766 Gardiner, Me. History of Gardiner, Pittston and West Gardiner; with a sketch of the Kennebec Indians and New Plymouth Purchase, comprising Historical matter from 1602 to 1852; with Genealogical Sketches of many Families. By J. W. Hanson. 12*mo, cl.; plates.* *Gardiner*, 1852

767 GARDNER, Mass. History of, from its Earliest settlement to 1860. By Lewis Glazur. 12*mo, cl.; rare.* *Worcester*, 1860

768 Garrard, Lewis H. Wah-To-Yah and the Taos Trail; or, Prairie Travel and Scalp Dances; with a look at Los Rancheros from Muleback and the Rocky Mountain Campfire. 8*vo, cl.* *Cincinnati*, 1850

769 G. A. S. Original Poetic Effusions: Religious, Moral and Sentimental. 16*mo, bds., uncut.* *Boston*, 1822

770 Gaskill, Edward. The National Portrait Gallery of Distinguished Americans, with Biographical Sketches. 4 *vols., in* 30 *Nos. complete, as originally issued.* *Philadelphia*, 1852

771 Gass, Patrick. Journal of the Voyages and Travels of a Corps of Discovery under the Command of Capt's Lewis and Clarke during the years 1804, 1805 and 1806. With six engravings. 12*mo, sheep.* *Philadelphia*, 1812

772 General Orders affecting the Volunteer Force, Adjutant General's Office, 1861. 8*vo, cl.* *Washington*, 1862

773 Georgia, Statistics of. Including an account of its Natural, Civil, Ecclesiastical History; together with a particular Description of each County, Notices of the Manners and Customs of its Aboriginal Tribes, and a *map*. By Geo. White., *Cloth*, 8*vo.* *Savannah*, 1849

774 Georgia. Historical collections of, containing the most interesting facts, traditions, biographical sketches, anecdotes, &c., relating to its history and antiquities, from its first settlement to the present time. Illustrated by nearly one hundred engravings of public buildings, relics of antiquity, &c. 3d ed. By George White. *Cloth*, 8*vo.* *New York*, 1855

775 Gettysburg, Pa. Address of Edw. Everett, at the Consecration of the National Cemetery at Gettysburg, 19 Nov., 1863; with the Dedicatory Speech of Abraham Lincoln, and the other exercises of the occasion. 8*vo, cloth.* *Boston*, 1864

776 Giles, Wm. F. The Annual Address delivered before the Maryland Historical Society, December 17, 1866. 8*vo pamph,* 29 *p.* *Treats of libraries and manuscripts in Maryland.* *Baltimore*, 1867

777 Gilley, William B. The Olio; being a collection of Poems, Fables, Epigrams, &c., including Tributes to the Memory of Lieut. Allen, the Hon. Wm. W. Van Ness, and the Hon. Brockholst Livingston. *Bds.*, 12*mo.* *New York*, 1823

778 GILMANTON, (n. h.) History of. Embracing the Proprietary, Civil, Literary, Ecclesiastical, Biographical, Genealogical and Miscellaneous History, from the First Settlement to the Present time; including what is now Gilford, to the time it was disannexed. By Daniel Lancaster. 8*vo, bds; map; very scarce.* *Gilmanton*, 1845

779 Glastenbury, Conn.—for Two Hundred Years. A Centennial Discourse, May 18, 1853. With an Appendix, containing Historical and Statistical papers of Interest. By Alonzo B. Chapin. 8*vo pamph.*, 252 *p.; fine copy.* *Hartford*, 1853

780 GLOUCESTER, (Mass.) History of the Town of, including the Town of Rockport. By John J. Babson. *Large* 8*vo, half lev. mor., gt. top, rough edges.* [Most of the edition was destroyed by the great fire of Feb., 1864.] *Gloucester*, 1860

781 Gloucester, (Old.) Reminiscences of, or Incidents in the History of the Counties of Gloucester, Atlantic, and Camden, New Jersey. 8*vo, cl., uncut.* *Phila.*, 1845

782 Gleig, Rev. G. R. A Narrative of the Campaigns of the British Army, at Washington and New Orleans, under Gens. Ross,

Packenham, and Lambert, in the years 1814 and 1815; with some Account of the Countries Visited. 8*vo, half muslin.* *London*, 1821

783 (GLEIG, G. R.) A Subaltern in America; comprising his Narrative of the Campaigns of the British Army at Baltimore, Washington, &c., &c., during the late War. 8*vo, bds., uncut.* *Phila.*, 1833

784 GOODRICH, S. G. History of the Indians of North and South America. 8*vo, cl.; engravings.* *Boston*, 1844

785 GOODWIN, NATHANIEL. Genealogical Notes, or Contributions to the Family History of some of the First Settlers of Connecticut and Massachusetts. 8*vo, cl.* *Hartford*, 1856

786 GOODWIN, THOMAS S. The Natural History of Secession; or, Despotism and Democracy at Necessary, External, Exterminating War. 12*mo, cl.* *New York, etc.*, 1864

787 GORHAM, Me. An Address, delivered on the 26th of May, 1836, the Centennial Anniv. of the settlement of, by Josiah Pierce. 8*vo pamphlet,* 36 *pages, rare, fine copy.* *Portland*, 1836

788 GORHAM, Me. HISTORY OF THE TOWN OF, by Josiah Pierce. [Contains considerable matter relating to the Indians.] 8*vo, cl., scarce.* *Portland*, 1862

789 GOWANS, WILLIAM. Catalogue of English and scarce American Books, Nos. 5 to 20 inclusive, and Nos. 24 and 24½, from 1846 to '67. 17 *nos., uncut,* 8*vo.* *New York*, 1866

790 GRAFTON, Mass. An Address delivered before the Inhabitants of, on the First Centennial Anniversary of that Town, April 29, 1835, by Wm. Brigham. 8*vo pamph.,* 40 *p., uncut, fine copy, very scarce.* *Boston*, 1835

791 GRANBY, Conn. History of the Copper Mines and Newgate Prison at; also of Captivity of Daniel Hayes, by the Indians, in 1707. By Noah A. Phelps. 8*vo pamph.* *Hartford*, 1845

792 GRANT, MRS. Memoirs of an American Lady; with sketches of Manners and Scenery in America, as they existed previous to the Revolution. 12*mo, sh.* *New York*, 1809

793 GRANT, ASAHEL, M. D. The Nestorians, or the Lost Tribes; contrining evidence of their identity, an account of their Manners, Customs, and Ceremonies; together with sketches of travel in ancient Assyria, Armenia, Media, and Mesopotamia; and Illusi trations of Scripture prophecy. 12*mo, cl., with map.* *New York*, 1841

794 GRAYDON, ALEX. Memoirs of a Life, chiefly passed in Pennsylvania, within the last sixty years; with occasional remarks upon the general occurrences, character and spirit of that eventful period. 12*mo, cl., sp.* *Harrisburgh*, 1811

795 GRAYDON, ALEX. The Life of an Officer, written by himself, during a residence in Pennsylvania; with Anecdotes of the American War. 8*vo, bds., uncut.* *Edinburgh*, 1828

796 GREGG, Right Rev. ALEXANDER. HISTORY OF THE OLD CHERAWS; containing an account of the Aborigines of the Pedee, the First White Settlements, their subsequent progress, changes,

etc. Extending from about A. D. 1730 to 1810, with notices of Families and Sketches of Individuals. *8vo, cl. ; maps ; scarce.* *N. Y.* 1867

797 [Green, Jos., *alias.*] Entertainment for a Winter's Evening. Being a full and true Account of a Very Strange and Wonderful Sight Seen in Boston, on the Twenty-seventh of December, 1749, at Noonday. By Me, the Hon. B. B. *Uncut, paper ; scarce.* *Boston,* 1795

798 Greene, Nathaniel. An Examination of some statements concerning Maj. Gen. Greene, in the ninth volume of Bancroft's History of the U. S. By Geo. W. Greene. *Paper, 8vo.* *Boston,* 1866

799 Greenough, Horatio. A Memorial of. Consisting of a Memoir, Selections from his Writings and Tributes to his Genius. By Henry T. Tuckerman. *8vo, cl.* *New York,* 1853

800 Greenwood, James. Curiosities of Savage Life. With woodcuts and designs by Harden S. Melville ; engraved by H. Newsom Woods. And colored illustrations from water-color drawings by F. W. Keyl and R. Huttula. *8vo, cl. ; gilt edges.* *London,* 1863

801 Greenfield, Mass. History of. By D. Willard. *12mo, cl. Very scarce.* *Greenfield,* 1838

802 Greig, Alexander M. Fate of the Blendenhall, with an account of her wreck, and the sufferings etc., endured by the survivors, for six months, on the desolate Islands of Tristan D'Acunha. From a Journal kept on the Islands, and written with the blood of the Penguin. *12mo, sh. ; with plate.* *New York,* 1847

803 Grigsby, Hugh Blair. "The Virginia Convention of 1776." A Discourse delivered before the Virginia Alpha of the Phi Beta Kappa Soc., July 3, 1855, at Williamsburg. *8vo, cl. ; 206 p., fine copy ; rare.* *Richmond,* 1855

804 GROTON, Mass. History of the Town of, including Pepperell, and Shirley, from the First grant of Groton Plantation in 1655. With Appendices containing Family Registers, Town and State Officers, Population and other statistics. Autograph of the Author and Abbot Lawrence. By Caleb Butler. *8vo, full mor., illust. ; very scarce.* *Boston,* 1848

805 Guest, Moses. Poems, on several occasions. To which are added extracts from a Journal kept by the author while he followed the sea, and during a Journey from New Jersey to Montreal. *8vo, blue pol. cf., gt. ; by R. M. Smith.* *Cincinnati,* 1823

806 Guiana, S. America. An Essay on the Natural History of, containing a Description of Productions in the Animal and Vegetable Systems, together with an account of the Religion, Manners and Customs of several Tribes of its Indian Inhabitants. By Edward Bancroft. *8vo, sh., plate.* *London,* 1769

807 GUILD, REUBEN A. The Librarian's Manual. A Treatise on Bibliography, comprising a Select and Descriptive List of Bibliographical Works. To which are added, Sketches of Public Libraries. *Illustrated with Engravings. 4to, bds., rough edges. 500 copies.* *N. Y.* 1858

808 Gurowski, Adam. Diary, from November 18, 1862, to October 18, 1863. *8vo, cl. ; In two volumes. Vol. 2nd.* *N. Y.* 1864

PAMPHLETS.

809 Miscellaneous. [*Eleven.*]

Guilford Spring. *Boston*, 1868

Georgetown College. Annual Celebration of Philodemic Soc., July 2, 1867. *Baltimore*, 1867

Gold Mining Company. First National, of New York and Colorada. *N. Y.*, 1866

Glover, Gen. John. Memoir of, by Wm. P. Upham. *Very scarce. Salem*, 1863

Guion, Thomas T. Sermon in Memory of, by Edward Jessup. *N. Y.*, 1862

Gilman, Edward W. Sermon on day of Resignation, at Cambridge, Oct. 24, 1858.

Groton, Mass. Jubilee of Lawrence Academy, July 12, 1854. *N. Y.*, 1855

Gray, Alonzo. Address on Female Education *N. Y.*, 1854

Gerard, J. W. London and New York; their Crime and Police. *N. Y.*, 1853

Gladstone, Hon. W. E. Two Letters to Earl of Aberdeen, on State Prosecutions of the Neapolitan Government *N. Y.*, 1851

Greeley, H. Lecture on Formation of Character.

810 Miscellaneous. [*Twelve.*]

Grattan, H. P. The Battle; a Poem. *N. Y.*, 1848

Gaspee. Destruction of. Documentary Hist., by Wm. R. Staple. *Scarce. Providence*, 1845

Gardwell, Godek. Currency, the Evil and the Remedy. 5th ed. *N. Y.*, 1844

Goodwin, Frederick J. Farewell Sermon on Resignation, St. George's Church, Flushing, L. I. *Flushing*, 1844

Gatchell, Joseph. The Disenthralled; being Reminiscences of the Life of. *Troy*, 1843

Geology. Eight Lectures on, by Charles Lyell. *N. Y.*, 1842

George the Third. Pulling down the Statue of. *N. Y.*, 1835

Geneva College. Discourse before Euglossian and Alpha Phi Delta Societies of, by C. S. Henry. *N. Y.*, 1840

Gourlie John H. Address before Mercantile Library Association. *N. Y.*, 1839

Gouge, Wm. M. Short History of Paper Money and Banking. 2nd ed. *N. Y.*, 1835

Grigg, Rev. John. Sermon at Trinity Church. *Hudson*, 1832

Galveston Bay, and Texas Land Company. Address to Reader of Documents of. *N. Y.* 1831

811 Miscellaneous. [*Twelve.*]

Gibbons, Wm. Exposition of Modern Scepticism, in a Letter to the Editors of the Free Enquirer. *Wilmington*, 1829

Greeks. The Suffering.
Gay, Ebenezer. Discourse, on Birth Day of. *Scarce.* *Salem*, 1822
Gaston, Wm. Speech of, on Bill to Authorise a Loan of Twenty-five Millions of Dollars. *Washington*, 1814
Gleason, Benjamin. Address in Commem. of Anniv. of John the Baptist. 2nd ed. *Boston*, 1802
Granville, Lord. Grand Question discussed. *London*, 1744
German Society. Charter and By-laws of, with list of Members. *N. Y.*, 1808
Germany. Account of Distresses in, occasioned by late war on the Continent. *Burlington*, 1815
Greenwood Cemetery. Exposition of the Plan and Objects of. *N. Y.*, 1839
Greenwood. Rambling Reflections, with Description, in 1853, by Campeador. *N. Y.*, 1853
Gardiner, J. S. J. Sermon. Fast. *Boston*, 1810
Gardiner, J. S. J. Sermon, Fast. *Boston*, 1812

812 Miscellaneous. [*Twelve.*]
Girard College for Orphans. Account of Laying the Corner Stone, by Nich. Biddle. *Phila.*, 1833
Girard Stephen. Will of, and Biography. *Scarce.* *Phila.*, 1848
Griswold, Alexander V. Sermon at Meeting of Conven. of Eastern Diocese. *Boston*, 1811
Griswold, Alexander V. Sermon at Opening of Gen. Conven. of the Protestant Episcopal Church. *N. Y.*, 1817
Griswold, Bishop, on the Reformation, No. 2. 5th ed. *Boston*, 1844
Griswold, Rufus W. Statement of Relations of, with Charlotte Myers, Elizabeth T. Ellet and Ann S. Stephens. *Very interesting and scarce.* *Phila.*, 1856
Green, Rev. T. L. Sermon on Transubstantiation. 2nd Ed. *London*, 1831
Green, Andrew H. Address on his Re-election as Pres. of Board of Education. *London*, 1857
Green, Jonas. The Crown Won but not Worn ; or, M. Louise Green. *Boston*, 1867
Green's Pamphlet. Libel Refuted, a Reply to. *Lewiston*, 1868
Green, Jonas. A Rejoinder to Reply on the Kent's Hill Tragedy. *Lewiston*, 1868
Gannett, Ezra S. The State of the Country. *Boston*, 1856

813 Miscellaneous. [*Twelve.*]
Gannett, Ezra S. The Atlantic Telegraph. Discourse by. *Boston*. 1858
Groton Heights. Address in commem. of, Sept. 6, 1777. Spoken on Sept. 6, 1825, by Wm. F. Brainard. *Scarce and valuable.*
Gifford, John. A Letter to Thos. Erskine, containing some strictures on his view of causes and consequences of war with France. *Phila.*, 1797

Gifford, John. Letter to the Earl of Lauderdale, containing strictures on his Lordship's letters to the Peers of Scotland. *London*, 1800

Geneva. Description of, View of City and Lake of, by R. Burford. *N. Y.*, 1829

Green, Beriah. Address deliv. at Whitesborough, by. *Utica*, 1833

Gallatin, Albert. Views of Public Debt, Receipts and Expenditures of U. S. *N. Y.*, 1800

Gardinier, Barent. Speech of, on Foreign Relations. *Georgetown*, 1809

Griffin, Edward D. The Kingdom of Christ. Missionary Sermon. *Phila.*, 1805

Gregg's Improved Excelsior Steam Brick Press. *N. Y.*, 1867

Guinea, Northern. Superstitious Notions of. *Princeton*, 1855

Girard College. Constitution and Plan of Education for, by Francis Lieber. *Philadelphia*, 1834

814 Miscellaneous. [*Eleven.*]

Green, Beriah. Valedictory Address, deliv. Sept. 13, 1837. *Whitesboro*

Gardiner, J. S. J. Disc. deliv. April 9, 1812. *Boston*

Garnage, G. A. The Garland of Fugitive Poetry. *N. Y.*, 1825

Gallatin, Albert. Considerations on the currency and banking system of the U. S. *Phila.*, 1831

Griswold, Roger. An Eulogium on. Oct. 29, 1812. By David Daggett.

Gannet, Ezra S. Disc. deliv. at ordination of Artemas Muzzey, June 10, 1830. *Boston.*

Goodrich, Elizur. Sermon deliv. at ordination of Matthew Noyes, Aug. 18, 1790. *New Haven*

Giles, John. Two disc. deliv. Aug. 20, 1812. *Bridgeport.*

Gregory, Dr. A Father's Legacy to his daughter, by. *Boston*, 1779

Gunn, Alex. Sermon on Intemperate Drinking. *N. Y.*, 1813

Gillett, Francis. Address deliv. in Windsor, Conn. Feb. 10, 1830. *Hartford*

815 Miscellaneous; [*Eleven.*]

Goddard, Kingston. Sermon deliv. Dec. 8, 1842. *Brooklyn.*

Gore, Gov. Speech deliv. June 7, 1809, in Legis. of Mass.

Gordon, G. W. Lecture on subject of Lotteries, March 12, 1833.

Griffin, E. D. Sermon at inauguration of, June 21, 1809, Andover, by Samuel Spring. *Boston*

——— Sermon at ded. of Park st. ch., Jan. 10, 1810. *Boston*

——— Sermon bef. an. conven. of Mass, May 29, 1828. *Boston*

Grimke, T. S. On the Character of the accomplished orator, Jan. 28, 1809. *Charleston*

——— Appeal to the Christian women of the South.

——— Address, March 29, 1831. *Phila.*

——— Address, May 6, 1832. *Hartford*

Greenwood, F. W. P. Disc. deliv. at ordination of Wm. Newell, May 19, 1830. *Cambridge*

HADLEY, Mass. Celebration of the Two Hundredth Anniversary of the Settlement of the Town, June 8, 1859; inclnding the address by Prof. F. D. Huntington. *8vo pamphlet, 89 p.; scarce.* *Northampton,* 1859

817 HADLEY, Mass, History of; including the Early History of Hatfield, South Hadley, Amherst and Granby. By Sylvester Judd. With Family Genealogies, by Lucius M. Boltwood. *8vo, cl; fine copy.* *Northampton,* 1863

818 HALE, Capt. NATHAN. Life of, the Martyr-Spy of the American Revolution. By J. W. Stuart. With illustrations. Second edition, enlarged and improved. *12mo, cl.* *Hartford,* 1856

819 Haliburton, Thomas C. The Letter-Bags of the Great Western; or, Life in a Steamer. *12mo, bds.* *Philadelphia,* 1840

820 HALL, MISSES FRANCIS AND ALMIRA. Narrative of the Capture and Providential Escape of Two Respectable Young Women (sisters), of the ages of 16 and 18, who were taken prisoners by the Savages at a Frontier Settlement near Indian Creek, in May last, when fifteen of the Inhabitants fell victims to the bloody Tomahawk and Scalping-Knife; among whom were the parents of the unfortunate females. Likewise is added, the Interesting Narrative of the Captivity and Sufferings of Philip Brigdon, a Kentuckian, who fell into the hands of the merciless Savages on their return to their settlement three days after the Bloody Massacre. Communicated by persons of respectability living in the neighborhood of the captives. *8vo, hf. morocco, plate; very scarce; fine copy.* *New York,* 1832

821 Hall, James. Notes on the Western States, containing descriptive sketches of their soil, climate, resources and scenery. *12mo, cl.* *Philadelphia,* 1838

822 Hall, James. The West: its Commerce and Navigation. *8vo, cl.* *Cincinnati,* 1848

823 Hall, Edwin. The Puritans and their Principles. *8vo, cl. Sec. ed. Very scarce.* *New York,* 1846

824 Hall, Lieut. Francis. Travels in Canada and the United States in 1816 and 1817. *8vo, bds., uncut.* *Boston,* 1818

——— The same. *8vo, hf. cf.; map.* *London,* 1818

825 HALLECK, FITZ-GREENE. Alnwick Castle, with other Poems. 12*mo*, *uncut sheets.* *New York*, 1845

826 HALLECK, FITZ-GREENE. Lines to the Recorder. 4*to*, *paper cov.* *Ed. of* 70 *copies for W. L. Andrews. No.* 34. *N. Y.*, 1866

827 HALLECK, FITZ-GREENE. Fanny, with other Poems. 12*mo*, *cl.* *New York*, 1839

828 ——— The same. 8*vo*, *cl.* *N. Y.*, 1846

829 ——— The same. 70 *copies for W. L. Andrews. N. Y.*, 1866

830 HALLECK, FITZ-GREENE. DRAKE, JOSEPH RODMAN. The Croakers. First Complete Edition. Large 8*vo*, *sheets. With portraits.* 150 *copies. No.* 54. *New York*, 1860

Bradford Club.

831 HALLECK, FITZ-GREENE. Young America: A Poem. 12*mo*, *bds.*, *frontis.* *New York*, 1865

832 HAMILTON, ALEXANDER. A Letter from Phocion to the Considerate Citizens of New York on the Politics of the Day. 8*vo pamph.* *very scarce.* *New York printed; Newport reprint*, 1784

833 HAMILTON, SCHUYLER. History of the National Flag of the United States of America. 8*vo*, *cl.* *Phila.*, 1852

834 HAMOR, RAPHE. A True Discourse of the Present Estate of Virginia, and the Successe of the Affairs there till the 18th of June, 1614. Together with a Relation of the severall English Townes and Fortes, the assured hopes of that Countrie, and the Peace concluded with the Indians. The Christening of Powhatan's Daughter and her Marriage with an Englishman. *Fol. paper cov. Printed at London*, 1615. *Reprinted at Richmond, Va.* 200 *copies printed.*

835 HAMPDEN Co., Mass. Sketches of the Churches and Pastors, and also an Address delivered to the Pastors, by Rev. T. M. Cooley, D.D., at Mettineague, September 13, 1853. 12*mo*, *cl.; scarce.* *Westfield*, 1854

836 HAMPTON, N. H. An Historical Address delivered on the 25th of December, 1838, in Commemoration of the Settlement of that Town: Two Hundred Years having elapsed since that event. By Joseph Dow. 8*vo*, *paper cover*, 44 *p.*, *fine copy; scarce.* *Concord*, 1839

837 HANBURY, BENJAMIN. Historical Memorials Relating to the Independents or Congregationalists: from their Rise to the Restoration of the Monarchy, A. D. 1660. 3 *vols.*, 8*vo*, *cl.*, *uncut*, *scarce* *London, Eng.*, 1839–1844

838 HANCOCK, JOHN, Ten Chapters in the Life of. First Published (Boston) 1789 (under the title, "The Writings of Laco, as Published in the Massachusetts Centinel, February and March, 1789.") 8*vo*, *cl.* *New York*, 1857

839 HANGER, Col. GEO., Life and Adventures and Opinions of. Written by Himself. 2 *vols.* 8*vo*, *bds.*, *uncut.* *London*, 1801

840 HANOVER. Mass., Historical Sketch of the Town of, with Family Genealogies. By John S. Barry. 8*vo*, *cl.*, *engravings.* *Boston*, 1853

841 HARBISON, MASSY, A NARRATIVE OF THE SUFFERINGS OF, &c., from Indian Barbarity, giving an Account of her Captivity, the

Murder of her Two Children, her Escape, &c. Communicated by Herself. Together with some account of the History, Laws, Religion, Wars, and Cruelties of the Indians, &c, in the Western Country. Fourth Edition, much enlarged. *Full red tky., gilt top, rough edges, very scarce.* *Beaver, Pa.*, 1836

842 HARDWICK, Mass. An Address at the Centennial Celebration, November 15, 1838. By Lucius R. Paige. *8vo Pamph.*, 76 *p.*, *fine copy ; scarce.* *Cambridge*, 1838

843 HARRIS, THAD. MASON. Valedictory Discourse, preached to the First Church and Society in Dorchester, Oct. 23, 1836. Also, a Disc. preached Oct. 30, 1836, by Nath'l Hall. *8vo pamphlet*, 41 *pages, good copy, uncut.* *Boston*, 1836

844 HARRISON, WILLIAM HENRY ; a Historical Narrative of the Civil and Military services of, and a vindication of his Character and Conduct as a Statesman, a Citizen, and a Soldier. With a detail of his negotiations and wars with the Indians, until the final overthrow of the Celebrated Chief Tecumseh, and his Brother the Prophet. By Moses Dawson. *8vo, sheep ; fine copy; scarce.* *Cincinnati, Ohio*, 1824

845 HART, Rev. JOSEPH ; A Sermon occasioned by the death of. Preached in Jewin-street, June 5, 1768. By John Hughes. And an Oration delivered at his Interment, by Andrew Kinsman. *8vo pamphlet.* *London*, 1768

846 HART, LEVI. Discourse addressed to the Second Congregational Church, Newport, R. I., at Ordination of Rev. Wm. Patten, May 24, 1786. *8vo pamphlet ; scarce.* *Providence : Printed by John Carter*, 1786

847 HART, LEVI. Discourse occasioned by the death of the Hon. Jabez Huntington, Esq., delivered at Norwich, Oct. 8, 1786. *8vo pamph.* *New London : Printed by T. Green*, 1786

848 HARTFORD, CONN. An Address delivered at the request of the Citizens of Hartford on the 9th of November, 1835, the Close of the Second Century from the First Settlement of the City. By Joel Hawes. *Sm. 8vo, cl., uncut ; fine copy ; scarce.* *Hartford*, 1833

849 HARTFORD in the Olden Time : its First Thirty Years. By Scæva. Edited by W. M. B. Hartley. With Illustrations. *8vo in sheets, stitched. Engraved frontispiece.* *Hartford*, 1853

850 HARVARD UNIVERSITY ; The History of. By Josiah Quincy, LL.D. 2 *vols., royal 8vo, rough edges.* *Cambridge*, 1840

851 HARWINTON, Conn ; The History of. By R. M. Chipman. *8vo, paper cov. ;* 142 *pages ; fine copy.* *Hartford*, 1860

852 HATFIELD, EDWIN F. Twenty Years in the Seventh Presbyterian Church, New York City ; two Sermons, deliv. July 1st, 1855. *12mo, stiff cl. cov. ;* 66 *p. ; fine copy.* *New York*, 1855

853 HAVERHILL, MASS. ; THE HIST. OF. By B. L. Mirick. *8vo, bds., uncut ; very scarce.* *Haverhill*, 1832

This Copy is in the finest possible original condition. It contains a View of Haverhill at that time, from a sketch by a Lady.

854 HAVERHILL, Mass. ; The History of—from its first settlement, in

1640, to the year 1860. By George Wingate Chase. *Royal 8vo. In sheets. With plates, portraits, maps, etc.* *Haverhill*, 1861

855 HAZELIUS, ERNEST. History of the American Lutheran Church, from its Commencement, 1685, to 1842. To which several Appendices are added. *12mo, cl.* *Zanesville, O.*, 1846

856 HAZLITT, W. CAREW. Hand-Book to the Popular, Poetical, and Dramatic Literature of Great Britain, from the Invention of Printing to the Restoration. 11 Parts complete. *L. P. Royal octavo, paper covers.* *London*, 1867

——— —— The same. *S. P. Part XI. only.*

857 HEARD, ISAAC V. D. History of the Sioux War, and Massacres of 1862 and 1863; with portraits and illustrations. *8vo, cl.* *N. Y.*, 1864

858 HEATH, MAJ.-GEN. WILLIAM; Memoirs of, containing Anecdotes, Details of Skirmishes, Battles, and other Military Events, during the American War. Written by himself. *8vo, sh.; scarce; beautiful copy.* *Boston*, 1798

859 HECKEWELDER, JOHN. Narrative of the Mission of the United Brethren, among the Delaware and Mohegan Indians, from its commencement, in the year 1740, to the close of the year 1808. Comprising all the remarkable Incidents which took place at their Missionary Stations during that period. Interspersed with Anecdotes, Historical Facts, Speeches of Indians, and other Interesting Matter. *Portrait, 8vo, bds., uncut; very fine copy; scarce.* *Philadelphia*, 1820

860 HEDGE, FRED. H. A New Year's Discourse, preached at Brookline Jan., 1858—"1758 and 1858." *8vo pamph.; 20 p.; very interesting.* *Boston*, 1858

861 HEPWORTH, GEORGE H. The Whip, Hoe, and Sword; or, the Gulf Department in '63. *8vo, cl.* *Boston*, 1864

862 HERBERT, CHARLES. A RELIC OF THE REVOLUTION, containing a full and particular account of the sufferings and privations of all the American Prisoners captured on the High Seas, during the Revolution of 1776, etc. *8vo, full red turkey, gilt. By R M. Smith. Frontispiece; scarce.* *Boston*, 1847

863 ——— —— The same. *8vo, cl.*

864 HERKIMER COUNTY, N. Y.; History of—including the Upper Mohawk Valley, from the earliest period to the present time; with a brief notice of the Irquois Indians, the Early German Tribes, the Palatine immigrations into the Colony of New York, and Biographical sketches of the Palatine Families, the patentees of Burnetsfield in the year 1725. Also Biographical notices of the most prominent public Men of the county. With important statistical information. By Nathaniel S. Benton. *8vo, cl.; maps and plates.* *Albany*, 1856

865 HERNDON, Lieut. WM. LEWIS. Exploration of the Valley of the Amazon, made under direction of the Navy Department. Part I., by Lieut. Herndon, with maps accompanying. *8vo, cl.; plates.* *Washington*, 1853

866 Herring, Jas. and Longacre, J. B. National Portrait Gallery of Distinguished Americans. 4 *vols., 4to, L. P. cl., uncut. With portraits; fine copy.* *Phila., N. Y., and London,* 1836

867 Herring, Jas. and Longacre, James B. The National Portrait Gallery of Distinguished Americans. In four volumes. *4to, paper covers, as orginally published in Nos., lacking three Nos.; in fine condition.* *N. Y. and Phila.,* 1834–'5–'6–'9

868 Heustis, Capt. Daniel D. Narrative of Adventures and Sufferings of, and his Companions, in Canada and Van Dieman's Land, during a long captivity. With Travels in California, and Voyages at Sea. *2d ed. 8vo, paper.* *Boston,* 1848

869 Heuvel, J. A. El Dorado; being a Narrative of the Circumstances which gave rise to Reports, in the Sixteenth Century, of the Existence of a Rich and Splendid City in South America, to which that name was given, and which led to many enterprises in search of it; including a defence of Sir Walter Raleigh, in regard to the relations made by him respecting it and a nation of Female Warriors in the vicinity of the Amazon, in the Narrative of his Expedition to the Oronoco, in 1595. With a map. *8vo, half cloth.* *New York,* 1844

870 Hickey, W. The Constitution of the U. S. of America, with an alphabetical analysis. The Declaration of Independence: the Articles of Confederation; the Prominent Political Acts of Geo. Washington; Electoral votes for all the Presidents and Vice-Presidents; Chronological Narrative of the several States, &c. *Seventh ed. 8vo, cloth.* *Philadelphia,* 1854

871 [Higginson, F. J.] Remarks on Slavery and Emancipation. *12mo, bds.* *Boston,* 1834

872 Hill, Rev. Ebenezer. Memoir of, Pastor of the Congregational Church in Mason, N. H., from November, 1790 to May, 1854; with some of his Sermons, and his Discourse on the History of the Town. By John B. Hill. *8vo, cl.; with portrait.* *Boston,* 1836

873 Hill, Ira. Antiquities of America explained. *12mo, sh.; very scarce and interesting.* *Hagerstown,* 1831

874 Hill, Alonzo. Sermon, preached March 28, 1867, before the Second Cong. Soc. in Worcester, on the Fortieth Anniversary of his settlement. Together with an account of the Exercises on that occasion. *Large 8vo, orig. cover; 66 p., uncut. Portrait of Mr. Hill.* *Cambridge,* 1867

875 Hillsborough, N. H. Annals of the Town of, from its First Settlement to the year 1841. By Cha's James Smith. *8vo, paper cover, 72 pages; very scarce, fine copy.* *Sanbornton, N. H.,* 1841

876 Hingham, Mass. An Address delivered before the Citizens of the Town of, on the 28th of Sept., 1835, being the Two Hundredth Anniversary of the Settlement of the Town, by Solomon Lincoln. *8vo pamph., 63 p., fine copy, very scarce.* *Hingham,* 1835

877 Hinman, Royal. A Historical Collection from Official Records, Files, &c., of the part sustained by Connecticut during the War

of the Revolution. With an Appendix, containing important Letters, Depositions, &c. With portrait. *8vo, cl.*
Hartford, 1842

878 Historical Research, respecting the Opinions of the Founders of the Republic on Negroes and Slaves, as Citizens and as Soldiers. By George Livermore. *4th ed., 8vo, cloth.* *Boston*, 1863

879 Hitchcock, Enos. Memoir of the Bloomsgrove Family, in a series of Letters to a Citizen of Philadelphia; containing sentiments on a mode of domestic education in the United States, interspersed with a variety of interesting anecdotes. 2 *vols. 8vo, sh., fine copy.* *Boston*, 1790

880 Hitchcock, Reuben. Funeral Oration on the Death of Mr. Elizur Belden, of Wethersfield. *8vo pamph.* *New Haven*, 1786

881 Holden, Mass. The History of, 1667–1841. By Samuel C. Damon. *8vo, paper cover, frontis.,* 155 *pages, fine copy, scarce.*
Worcester, 1841

882 Holliston, Mass. View of, in its First Century. A Century Sermon, delivered on Dec. 4, 1826, by Charles Fitch. *8vo, paper cover, uncut,* 36 *pages, fine copy, scarce.* *Dedham*, 1827

883 Holloway, William. The Peasant's Fate: a Rural Poem, with Miscellaneous Poems. *12mo, sh., frontispiece.*
Wilmington, Del., 1803

884 HOOKER, THOMAS. A | survey | of the Summe of | Church Discipline. | Wherein, | the Way of the *Churches* of | *New England* | is warranted out of the Word, | and all Exceptions of weight, which | are made against it, answered: Whereby | also it Will appear to the Judicious Reader, | that something more must be said, then | yet hath been, before their prin|ciples can be shaken, or they | should be unsettled in | their practice. *4to, cf. London: Printed by A. M., for John Bellamy, at the Three Golden Lions | in Cornhill, near the Royall Exchange, MDCXLVIII.*

In same Volume—

Cotton, John. The way of | *Congregational* | *Churches* | *Cleared*; | in two *Treatises.* |

In the former { From the Historical Aspersions of Mr. | Robert Baylle, in his Book, called (A | Dissuasive from the Errors of the Time.)

In the latter { From some Contradictions | of | *Vindicæ Clavium.*

And from.... { Some Misconstructions of Learned Mr. | *Rutherford* in his Book intituled (The | Right due the Right of Presbyteries.)

By Mr. *John Cotton*, sometime Preacher at *Boston* | in *Lincolnshire*, and now Teacher of | the Church at *Boston* in | *New England.* |

London: | *Printed by Matthew Simmons for John Bellamie* | *at the sign of the three Golden Lions* | *in Cornhill*, 1648.

885 Holm, Thomas Campanius. Description of the Province of New Sweden, now called, by the English, Pennsylvania, in America.

Compiled from the Relations and Writings of persons worthy of credit, and adorned with maps and plates. Translated from the Swedish, for the Historical Society of Pennsylvania. With notes, by Peter S. Du Ponceau. *8vo, bds., uncut.* *Philadelphia*, 1834

886 HOLMES, Rev. JOHN. Historical Sketches of the Missions of the United Brethren for Propagating the Gospel among the Heathen, from their Commencement to the year 1817. *2d. ed. 8vo, bds., uncut.* *London*, 1827

887 HOLMES, OLIVER WENDELL. Poems by. *8vo, cl., rough edges.* *London, O. Rich & Sons*, 1846

888 HOOD, GEORGE. HISTORY OF MUSIC IN NEW ENGLAND, with Biographical Sketches of Reformers and Psalmists. *8vo, cl., rough edges.* *Boston*, 1846

889 HOPKINS, SAMUEL. The Youth of the Old Dominion. *12mo, cl.; scarce.* *Boston*, 1856

890 HORNII, GEORGII. De Originibus Americanis Libri Quatuor. *24mo, sh., eng. title.* *Hemipoli Sumptibus Joannis Mulleri Bibl. Anno.* 1669

891 HOWE, NATHANAEL. A Century Sermon delivered in Hopkinton, Mass., on Lord's Day, December 24, 1815. Second Edition, revised and corrected. *8vo pamph.* *Very scarce.* *Andover*, 1817

892 HOYT, E., Esq. Antiquarian Researches: Comprising a History of the Indian Wars in the Country bordering the Conn. River and Parts Adjacent, and other Interesting Events, from the First Landing of the Pilgrims, to the Conquest of Canada by the English in 1760, with Notices of Indian Depredations and of the First Planting of Settlements in New England, New York, and Canada. *8vo, bds., uncut.* *Splendid copy, very scarce.* *Greenfield, Mass.*, 1824

893 HUBBARD, WILLIAM. A Narrative of the Indian Wars in, from the First Planting thereof in the year 1607 to the year 1677, containing a relation of the Occasion, Rise, and Progress of the War with the Indians in the Southern, Western, Eastern, and Northern Parts of the said Country. *12mo, hf. mor.* *Worcester, Mass.* 1801

894 HUBBARD, WILLIAM. A Narrative of the Indian Wars in New England, from 1607 to 1677. Containing the Rise, and Progress of the War with the Indians. *12mo, sheep.* *Very scarce, fine copy.* *Brattleborough*, 1814

——— The same. *8vo, bds.*

895 HUBBARD, WILLIAM. Narrative of the Indian Wars in New England, from the First Planting thereof in 1607 to 1677. Containing a relation of the Occasion, Rise and Progress of the War with the Indians in the Southern, Western, Eastern, and Northern parts of the Country. *12mo, bds.* *Printed by John Trumbull.* *Norwich.*

896 HUBBARD, W. The Present State of New England. Being a Narrative of the Troubles with the Indians in New England, from the First Planting thereof in the year 1607 to this present year, 1677. But chiefly of the late Troubles in the two last years, 1675 and 1676. To which is added a Discourse about the War

with the Pequods in the year 1637. London and [Boston], 1677. Carefully Revised and Accompanied with an Historical Preface, Life and Pedigree of the Author and Extensive Notes. By Samuel G. Drake. *Fifty copies L. P., No.* 43 ; 2 *vols. Map, 4to.* *Roxbury*, 1865

Woodward's Historical Series, No. 3.

897 ——— The same. *Small paper, No.* 77.

898 ——— The same. *Small paper, hf. mor., gt. top.*

899 Hubbardton, Vt., An Historical Address Delivered, on the 82d Anniversary of the Battle of Hubbardton, July 7th, 1859. By Henry Clark. *8vo pamphlet,* 16 *p. Scarce.* *Rutland*, 1859

900 Hubbardston, Mass. An Address in Commemoration of the 100th Anniversary of the Incorporation of the Town, June 13, 1867, by John M. Stowe. A Poem prepared by Eph. Stowe, with an Appendix. *8vo pamphlet,* 109 *p.* *Worcester*, 1867

901 Hudson River, N. Y., Letters About, and its Vicinity, written in 1835–1837. *Third Edition. Engravings. 8vo, cl.* *N. Y.*, 1837

902 Hudson, N. Y., Historical Sketches of. Embracing the Settlement of the City, City Government, Business Enterprises, Churches, Press, Schools, Libraries, &c. By Stephen B. Miller. *8vo, cl.* *Hudson*, 1862

903 Hudson, Charter of the City of, in the State of New Jersey. *8vo.* *Hoboken, N. J.*, 1855

904 Hudson, Charles. Doubts concerning the Battle of Bunker's Hill. *12mo, cl.* *Boston*, 1857

905 Hudson, N. Y., Historical Sketches of, embracing the Settlement of the City, City Government, &c. By Stephen B. Miller. *8vo, cl.* *Hudson*, 1862

966 Hudson, Henry. A Historical Inquiry concerning Henry Hudson, his Friends, Relatives, and Early Life, his connection with the Muscovy Company and Discovery of Delaware Bay. By John Meredith Read, Jr. *8vo, S. P.* *Albany*, 1866

907 Hudson, Henry. Sketch of. The Navigator. By Dr. G. M. Asher. *8vo pamph., uncut. Reprinted for Private Distribution.* *Brooklyn*, 1867

908 HUMPHREYS, DAVID. An Historic Account of the Incorporated Society for the Propagation of the Gospel in Foreign Parts, Containing their Foundation, Proceedings, and the Success of their Missionaries in the British Colonies in 1728. *8vo, sh. Maps.* *London*, 1730

909 Hunter, John D. Manners and Customs of Several Indian Tribes, located West of the Mississippi, including some Account of the Soil, Climate, and Vegetable Productions, and the Indian Materia Medica, to which is prefixed the History of the Author's Life, during a residence of several years among them. *8vo, sh.* *Phila.*, 1823

910 ——— The same. *3d Ed., 8vo, hf. mor., uncut.* *London*, 1824

911 Hunter, Rev. Joseph. Collections Concerning the Church Congregation of Protestant Separatists, founded at Scrooby, in North Nottinghamshire, in the Time of King James I., the Founders of New Plymouth, the Parent Colony of New England. *8vo, cl.* *London*, 1854

912 Hunt, Freeman. Lives of American Merchants. *8vo, cl. Portraits.* *N. Y.*, 1856

913 HUNT, Genealogy of the Name and Family of. Early Established in America from Europe. Exhibiting Pedigrees of Ten Thousand Persons. Enlarged by Religious and Historic Readings. Enriched with Indices of Names and Places. *4to, cl.* Authorized by W. L. G. Hunt. Compiled by T. B. Wyman. *Boston*, 1862–1863

914 HUNTINGTON Family, A Genealogical Memoir of, in this Country: Embracing all the known Descendants of Simon and Margaret Huntington, who have retained the Family Name, and the First Generation of the Descendants of other names. By Rev. E. B. Huntington, A. M. *8vo, cl. With portraits.* *Stamford, Conn.*, 1863

915 HUTCHINSON, FRANCIS. An Historical Essay Concerning Witchcraft. With Observations upon Matters of Fact, Tending to clear the Texts of the Sacred Scriptures, and confute the vulgar Errors about the Point. And also Two Sermons—One in Proof of the Christian Religion; the other Concerning Good and Evil Angels. Second Edition, with considerable Additions. *8vo., hf. calf. Fine copy.* *London*, 1720

PAMPHLETS.

916 Miscellaneous. [*Ten.*]

Hayns R. Prevention of Poverty. *London*, 1674
Haynes, A. Reflections of the relics of Ancient Grandeur. 1829
Hughes, Maria. Some Account of.
Hughes, Bp. Lecture on the importance of a Christian Basis for Polit. Econ. Jan. 17, 18, 1844. *N. Y.*
—— "Christianity the only Source of Moral, Social and Polit. Regeneration." Sermon, Dec. 14, 1847. *N. Y.*,
Hodge, Charles. Dissertation on the importance of Biblical Literature. *Trenton*, 1822
Hodges, Edward. Essay on Cultivation of Ch. Music. *N. Y.*, 1841
Hall, Robert. Modern Infidelity considered with respect to its Influence on Soc. *Charlestown*, 1801
—— Terms of Communion; with a particular view to the case of Baptists and Pædo-Baptists. *Boston*, 1816
Hall, Wm. W. Exposition of Obscure Passages of the Holy Scriptures. *Baltimore*, 1847

917 Miscellaneous. [*Ten.*]

Hall, Charles. Disc. on Life and Char. of, deliv. Jan. 1, 1854, by Asa D. Smith. *N. Y.*, 1854
Hudson. Remarks and Spirit of the Forum. Apr. 16, 1817. *Hudson, N. Y.*
Hudson River; with descrip. and illustration of City of N. Y.

Herttell, Thomas. Sherlock's Letter to. *N. Y.*, 1834
——— Spirit of Truth. *Boston*, 1845
Hamilton. Review of a Late Pamphlet, under signature of "Brutus," by —— *Charleston*, 1828
Hamilton College. Notices of the embarrassments and decline of, by Henry Davis, April 18, 1833.
Harrison, Wm. Henry. Life and Public Services of. *N. Y.*, 1839
Hasty Pudding. A Poem in Three Cantos. *Scarce.* *Brooklyn*, 1833
Hervey, James. Considerations affording Consolation to the Afflicted. *Phila.*, 1793

918 Miscellaneous. [*Eleven.*]
Hoge, W. J. Farewell disc. deliv. Pres. Ch. N. Y., July 21, 1861.
Hippopotamus. A Full and Interesting Account of. *New York*, 1861
Huntington, Rev. C. Sermon, Maryland, Sept. 28, 1863.
Hallam, Robert A. Sermon preached in St. John's Church, Bridgeport, Apr. 22, 1866.
Hicks, T. H. Addresses on Death of, deliv. Feb. 15, 1865. *Washington*
Hitchcock, Enos. Disc. deliv. at dedication of new Cong. Ch., in Providence, Nov. 10, 1795. *Brookfield, Mass.*
——— New-Year Sermon deliv. Providence, Jan. 1, 1797.
Hitchcock, Edward. Essay on Alcohol and Narcotic Substances as articles of common use. *Amherst*, 1830
Harris, Thomas L. Sermon—"The Single and Evil Eye," deliv. June 10, 1849. *New York.*
——— Sermon—"The Christian Idea of Life, Duty and Providence," deliv. May 6, 1849. *New York*
Harris, R. W. Sermon preached at opening of St. Mark's Ch., N. Y., Jan. 25, 1852. *New York*

919 Miscellaneous. [*Fifteen.*]
Harris, Thaddeus Mason. Sermon—"Pray for the Jews," delivered Aug. 15, 1816. *Boston*
——— Memorials of 1st Ch. in Dorchester, from its settlement in New England to the end of second century, deliv. July 4, 1830. *Boston*
——— Address deliv. April 7, 1842, at funeral of, by Nath'l Hall. *Scarce.*
Harrison, Wm. Henry. Sketch of the Life and Public Services of. *N. Y.*, 1839
——— Contrast; or, William Henry Harrison *versus* Martin Van Buren. *Boston*, 1840
——— Log-Cabin Song-Book. *N. Y.*, 1840
——— Funeral Sermon occasioned by Death of, deliv. April 25, 1841, by J. P. K. Henshaw.
——— Disc. on Death of, by H. Potter, deliv. April 25, 1841.
——— City of New York Funeral obsequies in memory of. Oration by T. Frelinghuysen.
——— Disc. on Nat'l Fast, May 14, 1841, on occasion of Death of, by Charles Upham. *Boston*

Harrison. Boiler Work. 1867.

Hobart Bp. Corruptions of the Church of Rome. *N. Y.*, 1818

——— The U. S. of America compared with some European countries. Disc. by. *N. Y.*, 1825

Hoffman, David. Hints on the Professional Deportment of Lawyers, &c. *Phil.*, 1846

Hoffman and Beach : their Lives and Services ; with Biographical Sketches of Oliver Bascom, David B. M'Neil and Edwin O. Perrin. *N. Y.*, 1868

920 Miscellaneous. [*Eleven.*]

Harris, R. W. Sermon preached at the opening of St. Mark's Church, Jan. 25, 1852. *N. Y.*

Hillyer, Asa. Sermon before Pres. Edu. Soc., May, 1820. *Newark*

Horne, Melville. Sermon before Soc. for Missions, June 4, 1811. *Morris-Town, N. J.*

Haskins, R. W. Examination of the Theory of a Resisting Medium. *N. Y*

Hudson Forum. Address deliv. before the Library Assoc. of Jan. 27, 1836, by Wm. H. Freeland. *Hudson, N. Y*

Hooker, Asahel. Sermon on day of General Elec. at Hartford Conn., May 9, 1805.

Hooker, Edward W. Address before Musical Assoc. of Pitts field, Dec. 25, 1837.

Hill, Rowland. Journal through the North of England anc parts of Scotland. *London*, 179

——— Answer to Wesley's remarks upon a pamphlet in de fense of characters of Whitefield and others. Oct 1, 1777. *Bristo*

Hall Joseph. Oration on Anniv. of Amer. Indep., July 4, 180C *Bosto*

Hall, Edwin. Sermon, Norwalk, Conn., Oct. 12, 1834. *New Yo*

921 Miscellaneous. [*Eleven.*]

Hall, M. Oration, July 4, 1815, at Saugus, Mass. *Bosto*

Holmes, Oliver W. "Urania :" a rhymed lesson, deliv. Oct. 4 1846. 2nd Ed. *Bosto*

Holmes, Abiel. Sermon deliv. May 27, 1819. *Cambrid*

Hawes, Joel. Centen. disc., June 26, 1836. *Scarce. Hartfo*

Hints to both Parties. *New York*, 180

Hartford Convention. Short account of. *Boston*, 182

Hole in the Wall ; or, peep at the creed-worshippers. 1828.

History of a little Frenchman and his bank notes. *Phila.*, 181

History of late ecclesiastical oppressions in N. E. and Vt. *Scarce* *Richmond*, 179

Hudson, N. Y. Oration in, July 4, 1808, by T. P. Grosvenor.

Harper, Robt. G. Observations on the dispute between th U. S. and France, May, 1797. *Bost*

922 Miscellaneous. [*Eight.*]

Harper, Robt. Goodloe. Speech on the Foreign intercourse bill, March, 1798.

——— Observations on the dispute between the U. S. and France. *Phila.*, 1798

Huntington, Enoch. Political Wisdom ; or, Honesty the Best Policy. Sermon, April 10, 1786. *Middletown*

Huntington, William. Advocates for Devils refuted. *Phila.*, 1796

Huntington, Gov. Sermon deliv. at Funeral of, by Joseph Strong. *Hartford*, 1796

Holley, Horace. Disc. deliv. in Hollis street church on death of, by John Pierpont. *Boston*, 1827

Howe, Nath'l. Century sermon, Dec. 24, 1815. *Andover*

Holstein, Madame De Stael. Appeal to the nations of Europe against the continental system, March, 1813. *London*

923 Miscellaneous. [*Eight.*]

Howard. Essays of ; or, Tales of the Prison. *N. Y.*, 1811

Hart, George. Life and confession of, June 25, 1811.

Hunter, Elijah. Sermon on Death of, by J. Stanford. *N. Y.*, 1817

Humphreys, Col. David. Poem on Industry, Oct. 14, 1794. *Phila.*

Hospital, St. Luke's. Appeal of the managers. *N. Y.*, 1852

Herttell, Thos. Remarks on the Law of Imprisonment for debt. *N. Y.*, 1823

Hare, Robert. Essays—chemical, electrical and galvanic.

Hodges, Jubal. A tract for the times. *Ogdensburg*, 1852

924 Miscellaneous. [*Eight.*]

Harrison, Wm. Henry. Eulogy on, by Edward D. Mansfield. *Cincinnati*, 1841

"Hambden." First Reflections on Pres. Message to Congress, Dec. 7, 1830. *Washington*, 1831

Huntington, Gen. Jedediah. Sermon at Funeral of, by Abel M'Ewen. *N. Y.*, 1813

Hart, John. (One of the Signers Decl. of Indep.) Oration at Dedication of Mon. to Memory of, by Gov. Parker. *Scarce.* *Trenton*, 1865

Harrison, Wm. Henry. Discourse on Death of, by Rev. Horatio Potter. *Albany*, 1841

——— Tippecanoe Text-Book, by Wm. O. Niles. *Phila*, 1840

Hutchinson, Abigail. Account of. *New York*, 1834

Heraldry. Plea for the Antiquity of, by Wm. S. Ellis. *London*, 1853

925 Miscellaneous. [*Sixteen.*]

Harvard Univ. Inaugural Oration deliv. by J. Q. Adams, June 12, 1806. *Boston*

——— Doc. relating to. *Boston*, 1820

——— Curiosity : a Poem, deliv. by C. Sprague, Aug. 27, 1829.

——— Age of Print : a Poem, deliv. by G. Mellew, Aug. 26, 1830.

Hart, Levi. Disc. at Funeral of N. Eells, July 3, 1786. *New London*

——— Disc. at Ordination of Abiel Holmes, Sept. 15, 1785. *Scarce.* *New Haven*

——— Sermon, Jan. 4, 1789. *New London*

Hamilton College. Address of Lewis Cass, of Mich. *Utica,* 1830

——— Address of Albert Barnes, July 27, 1836. *Utica*

——— Disc. of Simeon North, May, 8, 1839. *Utica*

——— Disc. of Azel Backus, Dec. 3, 1812. *Utica*

——— Disc. of Luther Hamilton, Oct. 7, 1830. *Utica*

——— Address of W. T. Hamilton, July 17, 1845. *N. Y.*

——— Disc. of W T. Hamilton, Dec. 8, 1831. *Newark*

Harvard Univ. Inaugural Address, deliv. Dec. 11, 1816, by Jacob Bigelow.

——— Letter to the Pres. of. *Boston,* 1849

926 Miscellaneous. [*Eleven.*]

Harrison, Wm. Henry. The Tippecanoe Text-Book, by William Ogden Niles. *Baltimore,* 1840

——— Tribute to the Memory of; by J. G. Robberds, April 11, 1847. *Manchester*

H.——— A.——— General Censure. *N. Y.,* 1811

Hosack, David. Hortus Elginensis. *New York,* 1811

——— Funeral Address, May 26, 1818. *New York*

Hall, O. A. A brief popular view of Astronomy and natural philosophy. 8th ed. *New York*

Harrison, Wm. Henry; Sketch of the Life and Public Services of.

——— Outline of the Life and Public Services of. *Newark,* 1840

Huron, Town of (Mich.); Sketch of. *N. Y.*

Harrison, Wm. Henry. The contrast, or plain reasons why Harrison should be elected Pres. of U. S., and Van Buren should not be re-elected.

——— The Tippecanoe Almanac for 1841. *Phila.*

927 Miscellaneous. [*Seven.*]

Hobart, John Henry. The corruptions of the Church of Rome contrasted with certain Protestant errors. *N. Y.,* 1818

——— The Churchman. *N. Y.,* 1819

——— Christian Sympathy. *N. Y.,* 1825

——— Tribute to Memory of. *N. Y.,* 1830

Hobart, Noah. Attempt to illustrate and confirm the Ecclesiastical Constitution of the Consociated Churches in the Colony of Conn., occasioned by a late "Explanation of the Saybrook Platform." *Very scarce.* *New Haven,* 1765

Hobart, John Henry. The origin, character, and situation of Prot. Epis. Ch. *Scarce.* *Philadelphia,* 1814

——— Sermon, deliv. Sept. 19, 1830, on Death of. *N. Y.*

928 Miscellaneous. [*Seventeen.*]

Hopkins, Samuel. Animadversions on Mr. Hart's late Dialogue. In a letter to his Friend. *Scarce.* *New London*, 1770

Hartley, David. Address to the Mayor of Hull, on Parliamentary Reform. *Scarce.* *London*, 1784

Hawkins, John. Disc. Odes for the Laureateship. *London*, 1785

Humphreys, Col. David. Poem on Industry, addressed to the Citizens of Philadelphia, Oct. 14, 1794. *Scarce.*

Hollinshead, Wm. Sermon, delivered March 21, 1798. *Charleston*

Hutchinson, Gen.; Adventures of—and Serinda. *London*, 1802

Hawles, Sir John. Duties and Rights of Jurymen according to Law. *Phila.*, 1806

Hanning, John. Rights of Women Vindicated. Sermon. New York, 1807. *Very early Woman's Rights doc.*

Hadley, Mass.; Sermon at Dedication of New Ch. in. By S. Austin, Nov. 8, 1808.

Haven's Nicodemus. Wonderful vision of the city of New York, wherein he was presented with a view of the situation of the world after the dreadful 4th of June, 1812, showing what part of N. Y. is to be destroyed. *Curious.*

Harold, W. V. Sermon on occasion of the consecration of Dr. John Cheverus, Nov. 1st, 1810. *Baltimore*

Holmes, Abiel. Sermon deliv. at ordination of Thomas Gannett, Ch. in Cambridgeport, Mass. 1814.

L'Histoire, De. Abrege de L'Englise Chretienne. 1817.

Halleck, Fitz Greene. Fanny: A Poem. *N. Y.*, 1819

Humphrey, Heman. Sermon at Ordination of Missionaries to Sandwich Islands. Sept. 29, 1819.

Hodgson, Wm. Commonwealth of Reason. *London*, 1820

Hunt, Mrs. Magdalen; Elegy on the Death of. By G. J. Hunt, Newark, N. J. *London*, 1823

929 Miscellaneous. [*Eighteen.*]

Henshaw, J. P. K. Sermon, 5th Annual Meeting, Oct., 1823. *Baltimore*

House of Refuge; Report of Committee for erecting an institution for. *New York*, 1824

Hammond, J. D. Letters on the Repeal of the Restraining Law. *New York*, 1836

Halstead, Mr. Speech on the Bill making Appropriations for civil and diplomatic expenses of the Government. 1838. *Washington*

Helms, J. B. Imposture and Deception detected and Observed. New York, Aug. 14, 1840.

Harvey's (Dr.) Quietus.

Hopkins, John Henry. Charge, deliv. Sept. 27, 1842.

Hewit, Rev. Dr. Correspondence with reference to Episcopacy tested by Scripture between Hewit and Rev. N. E. Cornwall. *Bridgeport*, 1843

Hook, Walter Farquhar. A call on the principles of the English Reformation. Sermon. *N. Y.*, 1843
Humane Soc.; Hist. of. *Boston*, 1845
Humboldt, Alex. Von. Cosmos: A Survey of the Gen. Physical Hist. of the Universe. *N. Y.*, 1845
Hancock, John; Life of. *Scarce.* *New York*, 1857
Hooper, Wm. Address. "The Sacredness of Human Life." *Raleigh*, 1857
Herald. New Church, and Monthly Repository, Feb., 1857.
Hedge, F. H. New Year's Disc. in Boston. 1858.
Heywood, J. H. Disc. on Evangelical Character of Unitarian Christianity, July 3, 1859. *Baltimore*
Humbug. A Look at some Popular Impositions. *N. Y.*, 1860
Hastings, Orlando. Disc. deliv. in Central Pres. Ch., March 22, 1861, by Rev. F. F. Ellinwood. *Rochester*

930 HAMILTON AND BURR PAMPHLETS. *Very valuable lot.* [*Twenty-seven*].
Letter from Hamilton concerning John Adams. *New York*, 1800
Examination of Charges against Aaron Burr, by Aristides. *N. Y.*, 1803
A Narr. of suppression by Col. Burr of Hist. of Adams' Admin. *N. Y.*, 1802
Antidote to John Woods' Poison. By Warren. *Very scarce.* *N. Y.*, 1802
Nine Letters on Burr's Polit. defection, by Jas. Cheetham. *N. Y.*, 1803
Speeches of Gen. Hamilton, Van Ness, etc., against H. Croswell, on indictment of Libel on T. Jefferson. *N. Y.*, 1804
Disc. on Death of Hamilton, by Dr. Nott. *Rare.* *Salem*, 1804
Answer to Clandestine Address to the Electors of N. Y. By Epaminondas.
Examination of Charges against Burr, by Aristides. *New York*, 1804
Examination of Charges against Burr, by Aristides. *Philadelphia*, 1803
Eulogy on Hamilton by Harrison G. Otis. *Boston*, 1804
Oration on Hamilton by Dr. Mason. *N. Y.*, 1804
View of Polit. Conduct of Burr, by W. Van Ness. *N. Y.*, 1802
Answer to Hamilton's Letter on Adams. *N. Y.*, 1800
Observations on certain doc. in Nos. V. and VI. of "The History of the United States for 1796." Phila., 1797. *Very rare.*
Correct Statement of the various sources from which the History of John Adams was compiled, &c. By John Wood. *N. Y.*, 1802
Letters to Alex. Hamilton, "King of the Feds." By Tom Callender. *N. Y.*, 1802
Full Exposition of the Clintonian Faction, by John Wood. *Exceedingly scarce.* *Newark*, 1802
The Examination of the President's Message. By A. Hamilton. Dec. 7, 1801.
Report of the Committee appointed to Examine into the State

of the Treasury Department, made to the House of Representatives of U. S. By Alex. Hamilton. *Phila.*, May 22, 1794

Disc. deliv. on death of Alex. Hamilton, July 29, 1804. By Dr. Nott. *Albany*

Letters addressed to the Yeomanry of U. S. By A. Hamilton. *Phila.*, 1792

A Letter from Phocion to the considerate Citizens of N. Y. on Politics of the Day. By A. Hamilton. *N. Y.*, 1784

Report of the Secretary of Treasury (Alex. Hamilton) on the subject of a Nat. Bank. Dec. 13, 1790. *N. Y.*

Letter from Alex. Hamilton concerning the public conduct and character of J. Adams. 3d ed. *N. Y.*, 1800

Letter to Aaron Burr, Vice-President of the U. S. of America, on the barbarous origin, the criminal nature and the baneful effects of duels occasioned by his late fearful interview with the deceased and much lamented Gen. Alex. Hamilton. By Philanthropos. *Exceedingly scarce.* *N. Y.*, 1804

An Examination of the late Proc. in Congress respecting the Official Conduct of the Secretary of the Treasury (Hamilton). *Very scarce.* *Printed within the U. S.* 1793.

931 Harvard College Pamphlets. [*Thirteen.*]

Wigglesworth, Edward. Two Discourses deliv. Public Lectures, Nov. 12 and 19, 1754. *Boston*, 1754

Chauncy, Charles. Discourse. Dudleian Lecture, May 12, 1762. *Boston*, 1762

Cooper, Samuel. Discourse. Dudleian Lecture, Sept. 1, 1773. *Boston*, 1774

Tucker, John. Discourse. Dudleian Lecture, Sept. 2, 1778. *Boston*, 1778

Puffer, Reuben. Discourse. Dudleian Lecture, May 11, 1808. *Cambridge*, 1808

Channing, W. E. Discourse. Dudleian Lecture, March 14, 1821 *Boston*, 1821

Brazer, John. Discourse. Dudleian Lecture, May 13, 1835. *Cambridge*, 1835

Everett, Edward. Oration. Phi Beta Kappa Soc., Aug. 26, 1824. *Boston*, 1825

Story, Joseph. Discourse. Phi Beta Kappa Soc., Aug. 21, 1826. *Boston*, 1826

Sprague, Charles. Poem. Phi Beta Kappa Soc., Aug. 27, 1829. *Boston*, 1829

Dewey, Orville. Oration. Phi Beta Kappa Soc., Aug. 26, 1830 *Boston*, 1830

Bushnell, Horace. Oration. Phi Beta Kappa Soc., Aug. 24, 1848. *Cambridge*, 1848

Bethune, George W. Oration. Phi Beta Kappa Soc., July 19, 1849. *Cambridge*, 1849

932 Harvard College Pamphlets. [*Twelve.*]

Harvard College. Constitution, with Appendix. *Cambridge*, 1812

Harvard College. Laws of. *Cambridge*, 1814

Harvard College. Catalogue. Second Ed. *Boston*, 1813

Harvard College. Catalogue of Phi Beta Kappa. *Cambridge*, 1814

Harvard College. Catalogue of. *Cambridge*, 1815

Harvard College. Catalogue of. *Cambridge*, 1821

Norton, Andrews. Inaug. Discourse, Aug. 10, 1819. *Cambridge*, 1819

Story, Joseph. Discourse, Inaug. of. *Boston*, 1829

Follen, Charles. Inaug. Disc. Sept. 3, 1831. *Cambridge*, 1831

Everett, Edward. Address at Inaug. of, as Pres., April 30, 1846. *Boston*, 1846

Sparks, Jared. Address at Inaug. of, as Pres., June 20, 1849. *Cambridge*, 1849

Appleton, Nathaniel. Exposition of Romans III. 20, etc., verses. *Boston*, 1749

932 Harvard College Pamphlets. [*Fourteen.*]

Tucker, John. Two Sermons, April 9, 1769. *Boston*, 1769

Dana, James. Two Discourses, May 10, 1767. *Boston*, 1767

Osgood, David. Disc., April 8, 1810. *Cambridge*, 1810

Harvard University. Oration and Poem. Departure of Senior Class, July 31, 1811. *Cambridge*, 1811

Popkin, John S. Two Disc., Oct. 8, 1815. *Newburyport*, 1816

America. Oration on the Prospects of Young Men of, July 14, 1818. *Boston*, 1818

Norton, Andrews. Address at Inter. of Prof. Frisbie, July 12, 1822. *Cambridge*, 1822

Ware, Henry. Introd. Address. Theological School, Oct. 18 and 25, 1830. *Cambridge*, 1830

Palfrey, John G. Sermon, July 13, 1834. *Cambridge*, 1834

Story, Joseph. Discourse, Aug. 23, 1842. *Boston*, 1842

Ticknor, George. Remarks on Changes lately proposed or adopted in H. U. *Boston*, 1825

Hollis. Facts and Documents relating to Harvard Col. *Boston*, 1829

Gray, F. C. Letter to Gov. Lincoln, from. 2nd ed. *Boston*, 1831

Norton, Andrews. Letter to, July 19, 1839, by an Alumnus. *Boston*, 1839

934 Harvard University. [*Twelve.*]

Harvard Univ. Oration before, July 21, 1796. By Timothy Bigelow. *Scarce.* *Boston*

Harvard Univ. Oration before, July 17, 1799. By Leonard Woods. *Boston*

Harvard Univ. Oration before, Sept. 16, 1794. By David Tappan. *Boston*

Harvard Univ. Oration before, April 8, 1810. By David Osgood. *Cambridge*

Harvard Univ. Oration before, March 14, 1821. By W. E. Channing. *Boston*

Harvard Univ. Memorials of the Graduates of. Aug. 1833

Harvard Univ. Curiosity. A Poem, deliv. Aug. 27, 1829. By Chas. Sprague.

Harvard Univ. Catalogue of. 1833

Harvard Univ. Disc., occasioned by recent Duel in Washington, deliv. March 4, 1838. By Henry Ware. *Cambridge*

Harvard Univ. Oration deliv. by George Putnam, Aug. 29, 1844. *Boston*

Harvard Univ. Oration deliv. by Horace Bushnell, Aug. 24, 1848. *Cambridge*

Harvard Magazine, June, 1855. *Cambridge*

935 Historical and Biographical Pamphlets. [*Fourteen.*]

Fuller, Samuel. Early Days of the Church in the Helderberg. Two Sermons on Death of. By his Son. *Very scarce.* *Andover*, 1843

Tyler, John. His Hist. Char. and Position. Port. *N. Y.*, 1843

Calhoun, John C. Life of. Port. *N. Y.* 1843

Cass, Gen. Lewis. Biog. of. *N. Y.* 1843

Butler, B. F., and Jesse Hoyt. Lives and Opinions of. By W. L. M'Kenzie. *Very scarce.* *Boston*, 1845

Thorburn, Grant. Sketches from the Note Book of Laurie Todd. Port. *N. Y.* 1847

Woodhull, Gen. Nath'l., and his monument. An Oration, by Luther R. Marsh. *Scarce.* *N. Y.* 1848

Green, J. H. Sketch of a Reformed Gambler.

Knickerbocker, Diedrich, Jr. The Manuscript of. *N. Y.*, 1824

Irving, Washington. Brief Remarks on the Wife of. *N. Y.*, 1819

Smith, Samuel B. Decisive Confirmation of the Awful Disclosures of Maria Monk, proving her residence in the Hotel Dieu Nunnery, etc. *Scarce.* *N. Y.*, 1836

Mais, Charles. Surprising Case of Rachel Baker who Prays and Preaches in her Sleep. *N. Y.*, 1814

Napoleon. Reply to Sir Walter Scott's History of. By Louis Bonaparte. *Phila.*, 1829

——— Historic doubts relative to, by R. Whateley. From the 4th Lond. ed. *Cambridge*, 1832

936 Historical and Biographical Pamphlets. [*Twelve.*]

Oldstyle, John. Letters of, by the author of the Sketch Book, with a Biog. Notice. *N. Y.*, 1824

Crawford, Wm. H. Sketches of the Life and Character of. By Americanus. *Albany*, 1824

Lee's Gen. Chas. Farewell Dinner, a Sketch of the Olden Time. By an Antiquary. *N. Y.*, 1829

Ponte, Lorenzo Da. Memoirs of. *N. Y.*, 1829

Gerard, Stephen. The Will of, with a short biog. of his Life. *Phila.*, 1832

Scott, Sir Walter. Tribute to the memory of, by J. M'Vickar. *N. Y.*, 1833

Parkes, Rev. Nathan. Memoir of, by Henry Ware.

Murell, John A. The Great Western Land Pirate. A Hist. of the detection, conviction, Life and designs of. Together

with his system of Villainy and Plan of exciting a Negro Rebellion, etc. 1836.
Madison, James. Lecture on the Char. and Services of. By D. Barnard. *Albany*, 1837
Rood, Parthena. Memoirs of. 1837
Rensselaer, Stephen Van. A Disc. on Life, Char. and Services of, with an Hist. Sketch of the Colony and Manor of Rensselaerwick. By Daniel D. Barnard. *Very scarce and important doc.; 144 pages.* *Albany*, 1839
Franklin, Benj. Lecture on Life of, by Hugh M'Neile. *Scarce.* *New York*, 1841

937 Historical and Biographical Pamphlets. [*Fourteen.*]
Iturbide, Agustin D. Emperor of Mexico, a statement of some of the principal events in the Public Life of, written by Himself. *London*, 1824
Iturbide, Agustin D. Narrative of the last moments of the Life of. By Col. Charles Beniski. *Scarce.* *N. Y.*, 1825
New York City. Wealth and Pedigree of the Wealthy Citizens of. 4th Ed. 1842
——— Wealth and Biog. of the Wealthy Citizens of. 6th Ed. *N. Y.*, 1845
——— The Aristocracy of. *N. Y.*, 1848
Lafayette, G. M. Oration on the Life and Character of. By J. Q. Adams, Dec. 31, 1834. 96 pp.
——— do do 94 pp.
Erskine Thomas and James Mingay, Sketches of the Characters of, Interspersed with Anecdotes, etc. *London*, 1794
Bowles, Gen. W. A. Life of. *Very scarce, contains incidents of Border Life and Indian Warfare.* *N. Y.*, 1803
Clark, Mrs. Joseph. Authentic and Interesting Memoirs of; likewise the charges relative to the Duke of York. Port. *Scarce.* *N. Y.*, 1809
Emerson, Mrs. Elinor. Memoirs of her Life, Conversion and Happy Death. *N. Y.*, 1817
Pedagogus, Dr. The Reformer, Sketch of Life and Character of. By Corrector. *N. Y.*, 1817
Murray, John Jr. Memoirs of. By Thomas Eddy. *N. Y.*, 1819
Elizabeth; or, The Exiles of Siberia. By Madam Cottin. *N. Y.*, 1823

938 Historical and Biographical Pamphlets. [*Ten.*]
Boston. Disc. at the dedication of a new ch. on Church Green, Summer St. By S. C. Thacher. *Boston*, 1815
——— Eliot, Rev. John, Character of. Disc. at the New North Ch. *Boston*, 1813
——— Histor. Notices of the New North Rel. Soc., with Anecdotes of Andrew and John Eliot. *Very scarce.* *Boston*, 1822
——— Disc. in the Second Baptist Meeting-House, Jan. 1824. By T. Baldwin. *Boston*, 1824
——— Sermon to the church in Brattle Sq., July 18, 1824. By John G. Palfrey. *Boston*, 1825

Boston. Address, Jan. 3, 1829, by Josiah Quincy, on taking final leave of the office of mayor. *Boston*, 1829

—— Address, on the Removal of the Municipal Government to the Old State House. By H. G. Otis. *Boston*, 1830

—— Ode, at the Centennial Celebration of the Settlement of. By Charles Sprague. *Boston*, 1830

—— Address, on the close of the Second Century, from the Settlement of. By J. Quincy. *Boston*, 1830

—— Sermon, to the First Church, on the close of their Second Century, Aug. 29, 1830. By N. L. Frothingham. *Boston*, 1830

939 Historical and Biographical Pamphlets. [*Ten.*]

California, from its Discovery, to the Present Time, with a Brief Description of the Gold Region. *N. Y.*, 1848

—— Sketches of. No title page. *N. Y.*, 1848

—— Gold Regions of. Edited by G. G. Foster. *N. Y.*, 1848

—— Notes of Travel in. From the Official Reports of Col. Fremont and Maj. Emory. *Scarce.* *N. Y.*, 1849

—— Four Months among the Gold Finders. By J. Tyrwhitt Brooks. *N. Y.*, 1849

—— Diary of a Physician, including Notes of the Journey. By James L. Tyson. *Scarce.* *N. Y.*, 1850

—— Report of Hon. T. Butler King on. *Washington*, 1850

—— Four Months in the Mines of. By S. Weston. 2d ed. *Providence*, 1854

Catskill, N. Y., Description and Natural Advantages of. *Map, very scarce local.* 1836

Chicago and her Railroads. Jan. 31, 1854.

940 Historical and Biographical Pamphlets. [*Nine.*]

Detroit, Trade and Commerce of, for 1857. By M. D. Hamilton. *Detroit*, 1858

Durham, Conn. Sermon at the Dedication of the South Cong. Ch., Dec. 29, 1847. By Rev. W. C. Fowler. *Amherst*, 1848

Elizabethtown, N. J. Histor. notices of St. John's Church. A Disc., Nov. 21, 1824. By John C. Rudd. *Scarce.* *Elizabethtown*, 1825

Florida. An Original Mem. on the Floridas. *Scarce.* *Baltimore*, 1821

—— Titles, of Lands, in East Florida, belonging to R. S. Hackley. *Very scarce.* *Brooklyn*, 1822

Galveston, Title to the City of. *N. Y.*, 1847

—— Articles of Assoc. of the City. *N. Y.*, 1847

Georgetown, Mass., Semi-Centennial Disc. in, June 7, 1847. By J. Braman. *Georgetown*, 1847

Grafton, Mass. Centennial Address, April 29, 1835. By Wm. Brigham. *Very scarce, fine copy.*

941 Historical and Biographical Pamphlets. [*Thirteen.*]

Hadley, Mass. Sermon, at the Dedication of the New Meeting-House in, Nov. 3, 1808. By S. Austin. *Worcester*, 1808

Hempstead, L. I. Sermon, in St. George's Church, Sept. 21, 1823. By Rev. Seth Hart. *N. Y.*, 1823

Lancaster, Mass. Sermon, Dec. 29, 1816, the last Lord's day in which there was Religious Worship in the Old Meeting-House. By N. Thayer. *Worcester*, 1817

Louisiana. Prospectus of Historical and Geog. Tracts. By Wm. Darby. New York, June 12, 1815. *Fine copy.*

Nahant; or, "The Floure of Souvenance." *Scarce. Philadelphia*, 1827

New-Brunswick, N. J. Record of Christ Ch. By Rev. Alfred Stubbs. *N. Y.*, 1850

Newbury, Mass., Sermon, Sept. 17, 1806, at the Dedication of the New Meeting-House of the First Parish in. By J. S. Popkins. *Newburyport*, 1806

——— Sermon, May 4, 1806, the Last Time of Assembling in the Old Meeting-House of the First Parish. By J. S. Popkins. *Newburyport*, 1806

Newburyport, Mass., Account of the Origin [etc.] of the Episcopal Ch. in. A Sermon, Jan. 6, 1811. By James Morss. *Newburyport*, [1816.]

Norfolk, Conn. A Half-Century Sermon, at, Oct. 28, 1811. By A. R. Robbins. 2d ed. *Very scarce.* *Hartford*, 1812

Oregon. Letters of Albert Gallatin, on the Oregon Question. *Washington*, 1846

——— Narrative of the Exploring Expedition to the Rocky Mountains, 1842, and to Oregon and North California, 1843–44. By J. C. Fremont. *Scarce. N. Y.*, 1846

Portsmouth. Histor. Sketch of the North Ch. Disc. Jan. 31, 1838. By E. Holt. *Portsmouth*, 1838

942 Historical and Biographical Pamphlets. [*Fourteen.*]

Sandusky, Ohio. Articles of Assoc., and a Sketch of its History. *Very scarce.* 1837

Sandwich, Mass., Sermon, Oct. 20, 1813, at the Dedication of the Meeting-House, for the Calvinistic Cong. Soc. in. By E. D. Griffin. *Boston*, 1813

St. Louis, History of. Commercial Statistics. *St. Louis*, 1854

Texas. Considerations on the Propriety of Annexing, to the United States. By a Revolutionary Officer. *Scarce N. Y.*, 1829

——— Address of the Hon. S. F. Austins, [on the Annexation.] [*N. Y.*,] 1836

——— Address of the Hon. W. H. Wharton, April 26, 1836. Address of S. F. Austin, 7th March, 1836, with other Docs. *N. Y.*, 1836

——— Texas: its Geography, Natural History, and Topogr. By W. Kennedy. *N. Y.*, 1844

——— Thoughts on the Annexation of. By T. Sedgwick, with the Add. of Alb't Gallatin. 2d ed. *N. Y.*, 1844

Virginia, Tour through part of, in the summer of 1808, including an Account of Harper's Ferry, etc. *N. Y.*, 1809

——— Laurie Todd's Notes, with a Chapter on Puritans, Witches, and Friends. By Grant Thorburn. *N. Y.*, 1848

Watertown, Mass., Hist. Sketch of. By Convers Francis. *Very scarce, and fine copy.* *Cambridge*, 1830

West Haven, Conn., Sermon, in Christ Ch., Aug. 11. 1839, the Hundredth Anniv. of Laying the Foundation of. By Rev. A. B. Chapin. *New Haven*, 1830

White Haven, Meeting-House, Conn. Report of a Com. 1813

Yonkers. St. John's in 1753 and 1853. Sermon at St. John's Church, March 13, 1853. By A. B. Carter. *N. Y.*, 1853

HISTORICAL SOCIETY PAMPHLETS.

943 American Historical Society. A Discourse pronounced in the Hall of Representatives, Jan. 30, 1836, by Lewis Cass. With Const. and Names of Officers. *8vo, orig. cov., fine copy,* 68 *pages. Very scarce.* *Washington*, 1836

944 American Historical Society. A Discourse pronounced in the Hall of Representatives, Jan. 20, 1837—Second annual meeting —by Levi Woodbury. *8vo, orig. cov., fine copy,* 67 *pages. Extremely scarce.* *Washington*, 1837

BUFFALO HISTORICAL SOCIETY.

945 SALISBURY, GUY H. Buffalo in 1836 and 1862 : a paper read before the Buffalo Hist. Soc., Feb. 6, 1863. *8vo, without title. Scarce.* 19 *pages.* Contains, also, Climatology of Buffalo. By Wm. Ives. 5 *pages.*

Extracted from Thomas's Buffalo City Directory.

946 HOSMER, GEO. W. The Physiognomy of Buffalo. Annual Address delivered before the Buffalo Historical Society, Jan. 13, 1864. *8vo,* 9 *pages.; scarce.*

947 MARSHALL, O. H. The Niagara Frontier : embracing Sketches of its Early History, and Indian, French and English Local Names. Read before the Buffalo Hist. Club, Feb. 27, 1865. *8vo, stiff paper cover,* 46 *pages. Printed for private circulation. Very scarce.*

---

948 Conn. Historical Society. The Charter of Incorporation and By Laws: with list of officers, and an address to the public. *8vo, orig. cov.; fine copy;* 11 *pages.* *Hartford*, 1839

---

949 Chicago Historical Society. Biennial Report of, to the Governor of Ill. *8vo pamph.,* 14 *pages.* *Springfield, Ill.*, 1863

---

950 Essex Historical Society. Petition for Incorporation; with the Constitution. *8vo, uncut; clean, handsome copy;* 8 *pages.* 1821

FLORIDA HISTORICAL SOCIETY.

951 FAIRBANKS, GEO. R. An Intro. Lecture delivered before the Florida Historical Soc., April 15, 1857; with an Appendix, containing the Const. and List of Members, &c. *8vo, orig. cov., fine copy; very scarce and important;* 31 *pages.* *St. Augustine, Fla.*, 1857

The subject of the Address is "The Early History of Florida."

GEORGIA HISTORICAL SOCIETY.

952 Collections of, Vol. I., II., and Vol. III., Part I. *Vols. I. and II., in green cloth,* 8*vo, beautiful copies, almost uncut; and Vol. III. in orig. cov., fine condition, embracing* 88 *pages of Col. Benj. Hawkins's* "Sketch of the Creek Country, in the years 1798 and 1799." *Savannah*, 1840–'2–'7

Vol. I. is a presentation copy to Dr. Wm. Jenks, by the Society.

953 CONSTITUTION, BY-LAWS, AND LIST OF MEMBERS of the Georgia Historical Society. *8vo pamph.*, 15 *pages.* *Savannah*, 1859

954 ELLIOTT, REV. STEPHEN. A Reply to a Resolution of the Georgia Hist. Soc., read before the Society, Feb. 12, 1866, its anniv. *8vo, orig. cover*, 13 *pages, fine copy.* *Savannah*, 1866

Subject of the resolution, "The best method of increasing and extending the usefulness of the Society."

955 ELLIOTT, STEPHEN (Bp. of Dioc. of Georgia, and Prest. of Geo. Hist. Soc.) Eulogy on the Life and Character of, by Hon. Solomon Cohen. *8vo, orig. cov.*, 18 *pages, fine copy.* *Savannah*, 1867

956 ELLIOTT, STEPHEN. "A High Civilization the moral duty of Georgians:" a discourse delivered before the Georgia Historical Society, on its 5th anniv., Feb. 12, 1844. *8vo pamph., uncut, fine copy; very scarce;* 31 *pages.* *Savannah*, 1844

957 JACKSON, HENRY R. Eulogy upon the Life and Character of the Hon. Cha's J. McDonald, pronounced at Marietta, April 20, 1861. *8vo, orig. cov.*, 35 *pages; fine, clean copy.* *Atlanta, Geo.*, 1861

McDonald was Solic. General and Judge of Flint Circuit, in 1823–'5; Senator and Governor of the State; Judge of Supreme Court, &c., &c.

958 JONES, JOSEPH. Agricultural Resources of Georgia. Address before the Cotton Planters' Convention, at Macon, Dec. 13, 1860. *8vo, uncut*, 13 *p., double cols. Scarce.* *Augusta, Ga.*, 1861

959 JONES, CHARLES C. Ancient Tumuli on the Savannah River. *8vo.* "This tract was privately printed—15 copies only"—in the handwriting of the author. 14 *pages, beautiful typography,* with a Pen and Ink plan, showing the situation of Tumuli on the river. Well done, evidently by the author. Dated *New York, March* 7, 1868.

960 JONES, CHARLES C. Monumental Remains of Georgia. Part First. The Ancient Monuments near Augusta, Geo. *Large 8vo, uncut,* 119 *pages. Very scarce in this condition Beautiful copy.* *Savannah*, 1861

A most valuable record of the early aboriginal monuments and vestiges of Georgia.

961 JONES, CHAS. C. Historical Address delivered to the Liberty Independent Troop, upon its Anniversary, February 22, 1856. Printed by the Troop. *8vo, orig. cov.*, 63 *p.* *Fine copy, very scarce.* *Savannah*, 1856.

The Appendix to this pamphlet gives a list of its members from 1794 to 1856, and other interesting matter. The subject of the Address is on the "Early Use of Cavalry in this Country."

962 JONES, CHAS. C. Indian Remains in Southern Georgia. Address delivered before the Georgia Historical Society on its 20th Anniversary, February 12, 1859. *8vo, orig. cov.*, 25 *p.* *Fine copy, very scarce.* *Savannah*, 1859

963 LAW, WILLIAM. A Discourse Delivered before the Georgia Historical Society, Savannah, Feb. 12, 1840, on the Early Settlements and History of Georgia. *8vo pamph.*, 43 *p.* *Fine copy, very scarce.* *Savannah*, 1840

This is the first Intro. Address of the Soc., afterwards republished in the Society's Collections, Vol. I., page 1.

964 WARD, JOHN D. Addresses delivered before the Georgia Historical Society, on its 19th Anniversary, February 12, 1858. 24 *p.*, *8vo, orig. cov.* *Fine copy, scarce.* *Savannah*, 1858

965 WARING, JAMES J. Report of the Com. on Sewerage and Drainage of Board of Health, May 2, 1866. *8vo pamph.*, 20 *p.* *Savannah*, 1866

---

966 JUNIOR PIONEER ASSOCIATION of Rochester, N. Y. Historical Collections of. No. 1.—An Address by Ferd. De W. Ward, on the Progress and Improvement of Rochester, &c. *8vo, orig. cov.*, 48 *p.* *Scarce.* *Rochester*, 1860

---

967 LONG ISLAND HISTORICAL SOCIETY. Early History of Suffolk Co., by Henry Nicoll. 1866.
——— Long Island, by W. Alfred Jones. 1863.
——— Third Annual Report. Brooklyn, 1866.
——— Fifth Annual Report. 1868.
——— By-Laws. Certificate of Incorporation. 1863.
——— Second Annual Report. 1865.
——— First Annual Report. 1864.
——— Louis 16th and Eleazar Williams, by Francis Vinton. 1868.

MAINE HISTORICAL SOCIETY.

968 BOURNE, HON. EDW. E. An Address on the Character of the Colony founded by Geo. Popham, at the Mouth of the Kennebec River, Aug. 19 (O. S.), 1607, delivered in Bath on the 257th Anniversary of that Event. *8vo pamph.*, 60 *p.* *Fine copy.* *Portland*, 1864

969 CLEVELAND, PARKER, Address on the Life and Character of, delivered in Augusta, Jan. 19, 1859, before the Maine Historical Society. By Leonard Woods. *Second Edition.* *Portrait of Cleveland.* 80 *p.*, *uncut.* *Fine copy.* *Brunswick*, 1860

970 FOLSOM, GEORGE. A Discourse delivered before the Maine Historical Society, at its Annual Meeting, September, 6, 1846, on the

Early Discovery and Settlement of Maine. *8vo pamph., 80 p. Scarce.* *Portland*, 1847

971 PATTERSON, JAMES W. Responsibilities of the Founders of Republics. An Address on the Peninsula of Sabino, on the 258th Anniv. of the Planting of the Popham Colony, Aug. 29, 1865. *8vo. Only* 250 *copies printed, uncut, tinted paper.* *Boston*, 1865

972 POOR, JOHN A. The First Colonization of New England. An Address delivered at the Erection of a Monumental Stone in the Walls of Fort Popham, August 29, 1862, Commemorative of the Planting of the Popham Colony on the Peninsula of Sabino, August 19, 1607, Establishing the Title of England to the Continent. *8vo pamphlet, cov., 48 p. Scarce.* *New York*, 1863

973 POPHAM COLONY. A Discussion of its Historical Claims, with a Bibliography of the Subject. *8vo, 300 copies only printed, uncut.* *Boston*, 1866

974 THORNTON, JOHN WINGATE,—Colonial Schemes of Popham and Gorges—Speech of, at the Fort Popham Celebration, August 29, 1862, under the Auspices of the Maine Historical Society. *Large 8vo, half mor., bds., uncut, 20 p., double col.* *Boston*, 1863

975 WINTHROP, ROBT. C. An Address delivered before the Maine Historical Society at Bowdoin College, September 5, 1849. Biographical Sketch of the Bowdoin Family. *8vo pamphlet, cov., 68 pages.* *Boston*, 1849

976 WINTHROP, R. C., Address of, September 5, 1849. *8vo, double col., 15 pages. Another edition.* *Boston*, 1849

---

977 MARYLAND HISTORICAL SOCIETY. *Complete.* [*Thirty-six.*]

—— Constitution, By-Laws, etc., of the Soc., March 8, 1844.

—— Historical Discourse, Chas. F. Mayer, First Ann. Disc., 20th June, 1844.

Memoir of Benj. Banneker, the Colored Astronomer. By J. H. B. Latrobe.

Journal of Chas. Carroll of Carrollton. By Brantz Mayer.

Geo. Calvert. First Lord Baltimore. By J. P. Kennedy. Second Annual Disc.

Life and Character of Sir Walter Raleigh, By J. M. Harris. Third Ann. Disc.

Memoir of Maj. Sam. Ringgold. By Dr. J. Wynne.

Commerce, Literature, and Art. By Brantz Mayer.

American Colonial History. By Thomas Donaldson. Fourth Ann. Disc.

A Paper on California. By J. M. Harris.

Annual Report of the President. J. Spear Smith.

Origin and Growth of Liberty in Maryland. By G. W. Brown. Fifth Ann. Disc.

Life and Services of General Otho Williams. By Osmond Tiffany.

Memorial of Columbus, Etc. By Robt. Dodge.

Tah-gah-jute ; or, Logan and Cresap. By Brantz Mayer. Sixth Ann. Disc.

Maryland Two Hundred Years Ago. By S. F. Streeter. Seventh Ann. Disc.

Democracy in America. By Rev. Dr. G. W. Burnap. Eighth Ann. Disc.

Baltimore, Long, Long Time Ago, Etc. Poems. By W. B. Buchanan. 1853.

Annual Report of the President, J. Spear Smith, First May, 1854.

Catalogue of the Manuscripts, Medals, Maps, Etc. By Lewis Mayer, 1854.

Sketch of the Life of Benjamin Banneker. By Mrs. Tyson, October, 1854.

African Slave Trade in Jamaica. By Moses Sheppard. October, 1854.

Martin Behaim. By Rev. Dr. J. G. Morris. Ninth Ann. Discourse.

Memoir of Baron De Kalb. By Gen. J. Spear Smith, 7th Jan., 1858.

Report of the President, J. Spear Smith, Feb. 1858.

Origin of the Japan Expedition. By G. L. L. Davis, 1860.

Early Friends; or, Quakers in Maryland. By J. Saurin Norris, 6th March, 1862.

Who were the Early Settlers of Maryland? By Ethan Allan, Oct., 1865.

The Maryland Historical Society and the Peabody Institute. By Brantz Mayer, April, 1866.

Tenth Ann. Discourse. By the Hon. Wm. Fell Giles, 17th Dec., 1866.

Memoir of Jared Sparks. By Brantz Mayer, 7th February, 1867.

History, Possessions and prospects of the Soc. Inaug. Disc. of Brantz Mayer. 7th March 1867.

Review of J. P. Kennedy's Disc. on the Life of George Calvert, 1846.

Reply of J. P. Kennedy to the Review of his Discourse on Calvert, 1846. *Excessively Scarce.*

Remarks of the United States Catholic Magazine on the Discussion between J. P. Kennedy and his Reviewer. *Very scarce.*

A paper on Rosas and the Argentine Republic, by Sebastian F. Streeter, July Number, 1849, of the North American Review.

978 Maryland Pilgrim Soc. Oration by Rev. John McCaffrey. 1842

—— Discourse by Rev. P. Correy. 1849

—— Discourse by Enoch Louis Lowe. 1845

—— Discourse by George H. Miles, Esq. 1847

—— Oration by Hon. Joseph Chandler. 1855

—— Oration by William George Read. 1842

MASSACHUSETTS HISTORICAL SOCIETY.

979 APPLETON, HON. NATHAN ; Memoir of. Prepared agreeably to a Resolution of the Mass. Hist. Soc. By Robt. C. Winthrop. With an Introduction and Appendix. *8vo, orig. cov. ;* 79 *pages ; fine copy ; portrait ; only few copies printed for the Members. Boston,* 1861

" Hon. Edward Everett, with the kindest regards of Robt. C. Winthrop." —Autog.

980 APPLETON, HON. WILLIAM ; Memoir of. Prepared agreeably to a Resolution of the Mass. Hist. Soc. By Chandler Robbins, D.D. With an Appendix. *Large 8vo, orig. cov. ;* 64 *pages. Portrait ; fine copy ; only few copies printed for the Members. Boston,* 1863

981 Aspinwall, Thomas. Remarks on the Narragansett Patent. Read before the Mass. Hist. Soc., June, 1862. *8vo, orig. cov. ;* 41 *pages ; fine copy. Boston,* 1863

The Narragansett Patent purports to be a grant, dated Dec. 10, 1643, from the Parliamentary Com. to the Gov. of the Colony of Mass., of the Territory now constituting Rhode Island.

982 BELL, LUTHER V. ; Memoir of. Prepared by vote of the Mass. Hist. Soc. By George E. Ellis. *Roy. 8vo, uncut ; orig. cov. ;* 75 *pages. Portrait ; beautiful copy. Only few copies printed for Members. Boston,* 1863

" Hon. John G. Palfrey, from Geo. E. Ellis."—Autograph.

983 Emerson, Geo. B. Education in Massachusetts: Early Legislation and History. A Lecture of a Course, by Members of the Mass. Hist. Soc., delivered Feb. 16, 1869. *8vo, orig. cov. ;* 36 *pages. Boston,* 1869

984 FRANCIS, CONVERS ; Memoir of. By Rev. Wm. Newell, D.D. *8vo, orig. cov. ;* 23 *pp. Contains list of Dr. Francis' publications. Cambridge,* 1866

985 HARRIS, THADDEUS MASON ; Memoir of. By Nathaniel L. Frothingham. *8vo, orig. cov. ; fine copy ;* 28 *pages. With a list of his publications. Cambridge,* 1855

986 LAWRENCE, HON. ABBOTT ; Memoir of. Prepared for the Mass. Hist. Soc. By Hon. Nathan Appleton. *8vo, orig. cov. ;* 21 *pages ; fine copy. Boston,* 1856

987 Livermore, George. An Historical Research, &c. *Third edition. 8vo, uncut ; fine copy. Boston : A. Williams & Co.,* 1863

988 LIVERMORE, GEORGE. An Historical Research respecting the opinions of the founders of the Republic on Negroes as Slaves, as Citizens, and as Soldiers. Read before the Mass. Hist. Soc., Aug. 14, 1862. *First edition. 8vo, stiff covers, uncut; fine copy ;* 215 *pages. Boston*

989 MASON, REV. CHAS. ; Memoir of. Prepared agreeably to a Resolution of the Mass. Hist. Soc. By Rev. A. P. Peabody. With an Appendix. *Large 8vo, orig cov. ;* 39 *pages ; fine copy ; with port. Only a few copies printed for Members. Boston,* 1863

990 Parker, Joel. The Origin, Organization, and Influence of the

Towns of New England; a Paper read before the Mass. Hist. Soc., Dec. 14, 1865. *8vo, orig. cov.; fine copy; 54 pages.* *Cambridge*, 1867

991 PELHAM, PETER; Notes concerning, the earliest Artist Resident in New England, and his successors, prior to the Revolution. By Wm. H. Whitmore. *8vo, orig. cov.; rough edges; fine copy; 31 pages.* *Cambridge*, 1867

992 PRESCOTT, WM. HICKLING; Proceedings of the Mass. Hist. Soc. in Respect to the Memory of. Feb. 1, 1859. *8vo, stiff covers, tinted paper; 59 pages; fine copy.* *Boston*, 1859

993 PROCEEDINGS of the Mass. Hist. Soc. at its Annual Meeting, April 12, 1855. *8vo, orig. cov.; 15 pages.* *Boston*, 1855

994 QUINCY, JOSIAH; MEMOIR OF. By James Walker, D.D. *8vo, orig. cov.; 76 pages; fine clean copy; with port. Only few printed for the Members.* *Cambridge*, 1867

995 REPORT OF A COMMITTEE Appointed by the Mass. Hist. Soc. on Exchanges of Prisoners, during the American Revolutionary War. Dec. 19, 1861. *8vo, orig. cover; 26 pages; scarce.* *Boston*, 1861

996 REPORT of the Proceedings at the Annual Meeting of the Mass. Hist. Soc. Address of Robt. C. Winthrop and the Remarks of Edward Everett. With a Description of the Dowse Library. April 9, 1857. *8vo pamphlet, uncut; 8 pages; double column; scarce.* *Boston*, 1857

Presented to Rev. Dr. Jenks, by R. C. Winthrop.—Autograph.

997 STURGIS, HON. WILLIAM; MEMOIR OF. Prepared agreeably to a Resolution of the Mass. Hist. Soc. By Charles G. Loring. *Large 8vo, orig. cov. Thick paper, uncut; beautiful copy; 64 p. Only a few copies printed for Members.* *Boston*, 1864

998 THE ACT OF INCORPORATION, with the additional Acts and By-Laws of the Mass. Hist. Soc. *8vo, stiff cloth cover; 19 pages.* *Boston*, 1857

999 WASHBURN, EMORY. The Origin and Sources of the Bill of Rights declared in the Constitution of Mass. *8vo pamphlet; 22 pages. Only few printed for the Members.* *Cambridge*, 1866

1000 WILLARD, JOSEPH. Naturalization in the American Colonies, with more particular reference to Mass. Read before the Mass. Hist. Soc., July, 1859. *8vo pamphlet; 30 pages; fine copy; scarce.* *Boston*, 1859

MINNESOTA HISTORICAL SOCIETY.

1001 MATERIALS FOR THE FUTURE HISTORY OF MINNESOTA—being a Report of Minn. Hist. Soc. to the Legislative Assembly. *4to, paper cov.; 141 pages; fine copy; now quite scarce. Finely illustrated.* Contains in addition—ADDRESS at the 6th Anniv. of the Minn. Hist. Soc., delivered by H. H. Sibley, February 1st, 1856. 17 pages of Indian History. *St. Paul*, 1856

1002 ANNUAL REPORT of the Minnesota Historical Society. Jan. 20, 1868. *8vo, orig. cov.; 32 pages; fine copy.* *St. Paul*, 1868

1003 NEW ENGLAND HISTORICAL AND GENEALOGICAL SOCIETY PUBLICATIONS. *No Duplicates.* [*Twenty-seven.*]

Circular No. 2. April 1846.
Report on the Sudbury Fight, April 1676.
Address, by Wm. Jenks, March 1, 1852.
Address, by Wm. Whiting, Jan. 12, 1853.
Remarkable Providences, by John Dane. *Boston,* 1854
Circular No. 4, Constitution and By-Laws, 1858.
Address, by L. Sabine, Sept. 13, 1859. [*Uncut.*]
Sketches by Usher Parsons. *Albany,* 1862
Address, by Dr. Lewis, Jan. 1, 1862.
History of, by J. H. Sheppard, *Albany,* 1862
Genealogy of the Messinger Family.
Memoir of Dr. Lewis, by J. H. Sheppard. *Albany,* 1863
Life of Michael Wigglesworth, by John Dean. 1863
Sketch of Dr. Jonathan Potts, by E. D. Neill. 1863
Hist. Sketch of the Old Church, Quincy, by F. A. Whitney.
Notes on the Winthrop Family, by W. H. Whitmore.
Life and Character of Gen. David Cobb, by F. Baylies. 1864
Address, by Dr. Lewis, Jan. 6, 1864.
Address, by Dr. Lewis, Jan. 4, 1865.
Memoir of Gideon F. Thayer, April, 1865.
Will of Rev. Richard Mather, July 1866.
Embarkation of Cromwell for New England. *Boston,* 1866
Address, by John A. Andrews, Jan. 2, 1867.
Address, by Marshall P. Wilder, Jan. 1, 1868.
Genealogy of Martin Moore, July, 1868.
Genealogy of Vickar's, or Vickery Family.
Genealogy of Gale Family.
Valed. Add., by Dr. Lewis, Feb. 7, 1866.
Paper on N. E. Architecture, by N. H. Chamberlain, Sept. 4, 1858.
Sketch of Joshua Coffin, July, 1866.
Memoir of Andrew Henshaw Ward. *Albany,* 1863
Address, by Hon. Marshall P. Wilder. *Boston,* 1869
Thomas Gyles and his Neighbors, by John A. Vinton. *Boston,* 1867
In Memoriam, Edward Everett. *Boston,* 1865
Journal of Visits to the Indians, by Joseph Baxter. *Boston,* 1867

NEW HAMPSHIRE HISTORICAL SOCIETY.

1004 BARTLETT, RICHARD. Remarks and Documents relating to the Preservation of the Public Archives. *8vo, orig. cov., uncut; fine copy;* 72 *pages, very scarce.* *Concord, N. H.,* 1837

1005 BOUTON, NATHANIEL. "THE HISTORY OF EDUCATION IN NEW HAMPSHIRE." A Discourse delivered before the New Hampshire Hist. Soc., at their Annual Meeting in Concord, June 12, 1833. *8vo, orig. cov., uncut,* 36 *pages; beautiful copy, very scarce.* *Concord, N. H.* 1833

1006 BREWSTER, CHAS. W. A Lecture on Printing, delivered before the

Portsmouth Lyceum, April 11, 1835. *8vo pamphlet*, 16 *pages; double col., fine copy; scarce.* *Portsmouth*, 1835

1007 Burroughs, Rev. Chas. A Discourse on the "Preservation of Documents as the Materials of History," delivered before the New Hampshire Hist. Soc., at their Anniv., June 14, 1843. *8vo, orig. cov.*, 29 *pages very fine copy; scarce.* *Concord, N. H., n. d.*

1008 Constitution and By-Laws of the New Hampshire Hist. Soc., with the names of the Members and Officers. *12mo, stiff paper cover*, 18 *pages; scarce.* *Concord*, 1833.

1009 The Celebration of the Centennial Anniversary of introduction of the Art of Printing into New Hampshire, in Portsmouth, Octo. 6, 1856, with the Oration by A. P. Peabody, and Poem by B. P. Shillaber, (Mrs. Partington,) and Sketch of the Proceedings. Inserted also, a Fac-Simile of the First copy of the N. H. Gazette, Oct. 7, 1756. *8vo, orig. cov*, 60 *pages, fine copy, scarce.* *Portsmouth*, 1857

NEW JERSEY HISTORICAL SOCIETY.

1010 Proceedings of. Vol. I., 1845–1846. *8vo, orig. cov.*, 203 *pages; beautiful copy, very scarce in this condition.* *Newark*, 1847

1011 Proceedings of. Vol. II, 1846–47. *Roy. 8vo, uncut, fine copy*, 198 *pages, very scarce.* *Newark*, 1848

1012 Proceedings of. Vol. III. 1848–49. *8vo, orig. cov., fine copy;* 201 *pages. Very scarce.* *Newark*, 1849

1013 Proceedings of. Vol. I., No. 2. (2nd series). 1868
——— Vol. X., No. 1. 1865
——— Vol. X., No. 2. 1865
——— Vol. X., Nos. 3–4. 1866
——— Vol. VIII., No. 4. 1859
——— Vol. IX., No. 3. 1862
Northern Boundary line of N. J., by W. A. Whitehead. 1859
First Ann. Add., by Bp. Doane. 1846
Address, by Richard S. Field, *Newark*, 1865

NEW YORK HISTORICAL SOCIETY.

1014 [*Nineteen.*]

Charter and by-laws, 1846, 1853, (revised 1858), 1862.

Proceedings, Jan. 5, 1847; June, 1847; Oct. 5, 1847; Oct., 1848; May, June, 1849; Nov., 1847; Dec., 1847; Jan, 1848; Jan., 1849; Feb., 1849; Nov., 1848; April, 1849; Dec., 1849; April, May, 1848; June, 1848.

1015 [*Eighteen.*]

Discourse, 6th Dec. 1811, by DeWitt Clinton. *New York*, 1812

Inaugural disc. 4th Sept., 1816, the 206th anniv. of the discovery of New York. By Gouverneur Morris. *New York*, 1816

Anniversary Discourse, Dec. 7, 1818, by G. C. Verplanck. *New York*, 1818

——— Dec. 28, 1820, by H. Wheaton. *New York*, 1821

——— Dec. 6, 1823, by W. Sampson. *New York*, 1824

Memorial, 1827.

The battle of Long-Island : a lecture, Feb. 7, 1839, by S. Ward. *New York*, 1839

Origin and nature of the representative and federative insts. of the U. S. Disc. by W. B. Lawrence. *New York*, 1832

Life and military services of Gen. James Clinton. Lecture, Feb. 1839, by W. W. Campbell. *New York*, 1839

Jubilee of the Constitution. A disc., 30th of April, 1839, by John Q. Adams. *New York*, 1839

Address, Feb. 23, 1852, by Daniel Webster. *New York*, 1852

Inaugural Address of the Hon. A. Gallatin. Feb. 7, 1843. *New York*, 1843

Memoir on the North-Eastern boundary, by Hon. A. Gallatin, with a speech on the same subject by Daniel Webster, April 15th, 1843. *New York*, 1843

Address, Feb. 23, 1852, by Daniel Webster. *New York*, 1852

Discovery and colonization of America. Lecture, 1st June, 1853, by E. Everett. *Boston*, 1853

Semi-Centennial Celebration, Nov. 20, 1854. *New York*, 1854

New York during the last Half Century. Disc. in commemoration of the fifty-third anniversary, by J. W. Francis. *New York*, 1857

Proceedings on the announcement of the death of William Hickling Prescott, Feb. 1859.

1016 [*Eighteen.*]

Henry Cruger : a paper read Jan. 4th, 1859, by Henry C. Van Schaak. *New York*, 1859

Annual report of the Committee on the fine arts. 1862

Declaration of Independence by the colony of Massachusetts Bay, May 1, 1776. Letter to Hon. L. Bradish, by H. B. Dawson, Jan. 7, 1862. 1862

Resident members, March, 1866.

Catalogue of the Museum and Gallery of Art. *New York*, 1866

Moral and intellectual influence of Libraries upon social Progress. Address, Nov., 12 1865, by F. de Peyster. *New York*, 1866

New York in the nineteenth century. A disc., Nov. 20, 1866, by S. Osgood. *New York*, 1866

Const. and Bye-Laws. *N. Y.*, 1839

Procès Verbal of ceremony, Inst. of President, N. Y. His. Soc., Feb. 8, 1820. *Burlesque.*

Address by J. R. Brodhead, Nov. 20, 1844. 1844

The Sons of Liberty, by H. B. Dawson. New York, 1859. 1859

Catalogue of Books, Maps and Paintings. *N. Y.*, 1840

Biog. Memoir of Hugh Williamson, deliv. Nov. 1819, by David Hosack.

Anniversary discourse, Dec. 6, 1828, by James Kent. *New York*, 1829

Memorial of the N. Y. Hist. Soc. to the Honourable the Legislature of the State of N. Y. *New York*, 1814

Hosack, David. Inaugural address deliv. before N. Y. Hist. Soc., N. Y., Feb 2, 1820.

——— Biographical Memoir of Hugh Williamson, before the N. Y. Hist. Soc., Nov. 1, 1819.

Treachery in Texas, the Secession of Texas, &c., by Maj. J. T. Sprague. *N. Y.*, 1862

ORLEANS COUNTY HIST. SOC., VT.

1017 SUMNER, SAMUEL. History of the Missisco Valley. With an Introductory Notice of Orleans County, by S. R. Hall. *8vo*, 75 *pages ; fine copy ; orig. cov. ; very scarce.* *Irasburgh, Vt.*, 1860

Contains much Revolutionary and Indian History, and Biog. Sketches of the Early Settlers of Orleans Co.

PENNSYLVANIA HISTORICAL SOCIETY.

1018 Ann. Disc. by W. P. Foulke. 1856

1019 Armstrong, Edward. An address delivered at Chester before the Historical Soc. of Pa., on the 8th of Nov. 1851, in celebration of the 169th Anniversary of the Landing of Wm. Penn at that place. With the page of Errata and Appendix, often wanting. *8vo, orig. cov. ; fine copy ; very scarce ;* 36 *pages.* *Phila.*, 1856

1020 Bulletin of the Historical Society of Pa. Vol. I., Nos. 7 and 8. Some Account of the British Army under the Command of Genl. Howe, and of the Battle of Brandywine, on the Memorable Septem. 11, 1777, and the Adventures of that day, which came to the knowledge and observation of Joseph Townsend, accompanied by a Notice of the Life of Joseph Townsend, and an Historical Sketch of the Battle. *8vo, orig. pamphlet, cov.,* 63 *pages, uncut ; very rare ; beautiful copy.* *Phila.*, 1846

Contains Map of the Battle, and two Plates representing "Birmingham Meeting House" and "Washington's Headquarters on the Brandywine."

1021 Chambersburg in the Colony and the Revolution. A Sketch, by Lewis H. Garrard. *Phila.*, 1856

1022 Coles, Edward. History of the Ordnance of 1787. Read before the Historical Soc. of Pa., June 9, 1856. *8vo, orig. cov ; fine copy ;* 33 *pages.* *Press of the Society*, 1856

1023 COLLECTIONS of the Pennsylvania Historical Society, Vol. I., Nos. 1, 2, 3, 4, 5, uncut, and No. 6, being for May and November, 1851, May and November, 1852, May and November, 1853. *Six numbers. 8vo, orig. cov. ; very scarce ; fine copies.* *Philadelphia*, 1851–3

Containing most interesting matter—"The March of the Paxton Boys," "An Essay on Indian Affairs," "Hist. of Moorland," &c. Papers never before printed.

1024 Denton, Daniel. A Brief Description of New York, formerly called New Netherlands, &c. Reprinted by the Historical Soc. of

Pa., from the London ed. of 1670. Edited by John Pennington. *8vo, uncut; very scarce; 16 pages.* *Press of the Hist. Soc.*, 1845

1025 Duane, William. Canada and the Continental Congress. Annual Address, Jan. 31 1850. *8vo, paper cov.*, 20 *pages; fine copy; very scarce.* *Phila.*, 1850

1026 Feltman, Lieut. William. The Journal of the First Pennsylvania Regiment, 1781, '82; including the March into Virginia and the Siege of Yorktown. *8vo, bds., uncut; fine copy.* *Phila.*, 1853

1027 Fisher, J. Francis. A Discourse delivered before the Historical Society of Penn., April 9, 1836, on "The Private Life and Domestic Habits of William Penn." *8vo pamphlet; orig. cov, fine copy*, 40 *pages. Very scarce.* *Phila.*, 1836

1028 Ingersoll, Jos. R. Memoir of the late Samuel Breck, &c. *8vo pamphlet;* 56 *pages; second edition; fine copy.* *Phila.*, 1863

1029 Ingersoll, Jos. R. Memoir of the late Vice-President of the Hist. Soc. of Pa. Read before the Society, Jan. 12, 1863. *8vo*, 56 *pages; fine copy. Very rare.* *Phila.*, 1863

This is of the greatest rarity; it is almost impossible to obtain it from any source at any price. It is a most interesting memoir.

1030 Jones, Horatio Gates. Report of the Committee of the Historical Society of Pennsylvania of their Visit to New York, May 20, 1863, at the Celebration of the 200th Birthday of Wm. Bradford, who introduced the art of Printing into the middle Colonies of British America. Read June 8, 1863. *8vo pamph., fine copy*, 14 *pages.* *Phila.*, 1863

1031 Jones, Horatio Gates. "Andrew Bradford, Founder of the Newspaper Press in the Middle States of America." An Address delivered at the Annual Meeting of the Historical Society of Pa., Feb. 9, 1869. *8vo, rubric title, or. cov. and title-page; tinted paper, uncut;* 36 *pages.* *Phila.*, 1869

1032 Latrobe, John H. B. The History of Mason and Dixon's Line; contained in an Address, delivered before the Historical Soc. of Pa., Nov. 8, 1854. *8vo, paper cov.*, 52 *pages; scarce.* *Press of the Society*, 1855

1033 Memoirs of the Historical Society of Pennsylvania, Vol. IV., Part I. *Royal 8vo, bds., uncut*, 212 *pages; beautiful copy: very rare.* *Phila.*, 1840

Contains Inaug. Disc. by Du Ponceau; Memoir of Wm. Rawle; Specimen of Aborig Eng.; Memoir of Roberts Vaux; Pennington's New Albion; and Inedited Letters of Wm. Penn.

1034 Proceedings of the Historical Soc. of Pa., Vol. I., No. 4—Dec., 1845—from pages 46–63 incl. *Uncut, 8vo, clean condition.*

1035 Proceedings and Speeches at the Dinner in Celebration of the Landing of William Penn, by the Historical Society of Penn., Dec. 8, 1852. *8vo pamphlet;* 42 *pages; beautiful, clean copy; scarce.* *Phila.*, 1853

1036 T. L. Kane. "The Mormons." 1850

1037 Tyson, Job R. Discourse, delivered before the Historical Soc. of Pa., Feb. 21, 1842, on the Colonial History of the Eastern and some of the Southern States. *8vo pamph; cov.*, 64 *pages, fine copy; scarce.* *Phila.*, 1842

1038 TYSON, JOB R. Annual Discourse delivered before the Historical Soc. of Pa., Oct. 24, 1831, on Pennsylvania, in the Revolution. *8vo, paper cov.*, 52 *pages; fine copy; very scarce.* *Phila.*, 1831

POPHAM SOCIETY.

1039 The Popham Colony. A discussion of its Historical Claims. *Boston*, 1866
Bourne's Address on Char. of Col. Delivered in Bath, Aug. 29. 1864
Patterson's Address. 250 copies printed. Aug. 29. 1865.

1040 QUEBEC LITERARY AND HIST. SOC. Island of Anticosti. J. Richardson. 1856

RHODE ISLAND HISTORICAL SOCIETY.

1041 ALLEN, ZACHARIAH. Memorial of Lafayette. Paper Read before the R. I. Hist. Soc., Feb. 4, 1861. 12*mo*, 19 *pages, good copy, scarce.* *Providence*, 1861

1042 DURFEE, JOB. A Discourse delivered before the Rhode Island Historical Society, Jan. 13, 1847. *8vo, orig. cov., fine copy,* 32 *pages, very scarce.* *Providence*, 1847

1043 GREENE, GEO. W. A Discourse delivered before the R. I. Hist. Soc., Feb. 1, 1849, on the "Progress of Historical Science." *8vo, orig. cov., fine copy,* 23 *pages, scarce.* *Providence*, 1849

1044 HALL, EDWARD B. A Discourse delivered before the R. I. Hist. Soc., Feb. 6, 1855, on the "Life and Times of John Howland," late President of the Soc. *8vo, orig. cov., fine copy,* 36 *pages, valuable Historical incidents.* *Providence*, 1855

1045 PITMAN, JOHN. A Discourse delivered at Providence, August 5, 1836, in Commemoration of the First Settlement of Rhode Island and Providence Plantations, being the Second Centennial Anniversary of the Settlement of Providence. *8vo*, 72 *pages, fine copy, scarce.* *Providence*, 1836

1046 SARMIENTO, D. F. North and South America. A Discourse delivered before the R. I. Hist. Soc., Dec. 27, 1865. *8vo, orig. cov., fine copy,* 44 *pages.* *Providence*, 1866

1047 STAPLES, WM. R. The Proceedings of the First General Assembly of the "Incorporation of Providence Plantations," and the Code of Laws adopted by that Assembly in 1647. With Notes Historical and Explanatory. *8vo, orig. cov. Fine clean copy,* 64 *p. Scarce.* *Providence*, 1847

1048 Battle of Lake Erie. 2d Ed. Dis. by Usher Parsons. 1854
Indian Names of places in R. I. by do. 1861
Address by Elisha R. Potter. 1851
Battle of Lake Erie. Dis. by Usher Parsons. 1853
Address by Wm. Gammell. 1844
Discourse by S. G. Arnold. 1853
Discourse on Ch. Justice Durfee, by R. G. Hazard 1848

SOUTH CAROLINA HISTORICAL SOCIETY.

1049 Literary and Philos. Soc. of S. C. Oration by Bp. England. *Baltimore, May* 9, 1832.

1050 Petigru, James L. Oration on Centennial Anniv. of, Jan. 13, 1848. *8vo pamph.; scarce.* *Charleston*, 1848

1051 Hanckel, Thomas M. Oration delivered on the 5th Anniv. of the South Carolina Hist. Soc., in Charleston, May 23, 1860. *8vo, orig. cov.*, 34 *pages, fine copy; very scarce.* *Charleston*, 1860

TENNESSEE HISTORICAL SOCIETY.

1052 Dix, William Giles. An Address delivered at Beersheba Springs, Aug. 19–22, 1859. Subject—"The University of the South." *8vo, orig. cov.*, 32 *pages, good copy; scarce.* *Nashville, Tenn.*, 1859

Ulster His. Soc. Vol. 1, Part 1. Collections. Kingston, 1860

——— — " 1, " 3. " " 1862

VERMONT HISTORICAL SOCIETY.

1053 Addresses of Geo. F. Edmunds, on "The Life, Character, and Services of Solomon Foot;" of Pliny H. White, on "Jonas Galusha," and of J. E. Rankin on "The Sources of New England Civilization." Delivered before the Vermont Hist. Soc., Oct. 16, 1866. Constituting a very interesting and important document. *8vo, uncut, orig. cov.*, 72 *pages.* *Montpelier*, 1866

1054 Butler, James Davie. "Deficiencies in our History." An Address delivered before the Vermont Historical and Antiquarian Society, at Montpelier, Oct. 16, 1846. With an Appendix, Containing Charter, Const., etc., of the Soc., Vermont Declaration of Independence, and the "Song of the Vermonters," in 1779. *8vo, orig. cov., fine copy*, 36 *pages; very scarce.* *Montpelier*, 1846

1055 Clark, Henry. An Essay on "Town Centennial Celebrations, their Historic Importance and Social Advantages." Delivered before the Vermont Historical Society, at Special Meeting, Jan. 22–23, 1862, together with the proceedings. *8vo*, 34 *pages, fine copy.* *St. Albans, Vt.*, 1862

1056 Collamer, Hon. Jacob. Memorial Address on the Life and Character of. By James Barrett. Read before the Vermont Historical Society, Oct. 20, 1868. *8vo, uncut, fine copy*, 27 *pages, dble. col.* *Rutland, Vt.*, 1868

1057 Constitution and By-Laws of the Vermont Historical Society, and a Catalogue of Officers and Members. *8vo, orig. cov.*, 16 *pages.* *Woodstock, Vt.*, 1860

1058 Proceedings of the Vermont Historical Society at Meetings held at Brattleboro, July 16–17, and at Montpelier, Oct. 14, 1862. *8vo, orig. cov.*, 59 *pages, fine copy.* *St. Albans, Vt.*, 1863

1059 Proceedings of the Vermont Historical Society at its 22nd Annual Meeting, holden at Montpelier, Vt., Oct. 15–16, 1861. *8vo, orig. cov.*, 17 *pages.* *St. Albans. Vt.*, 1861

1060 SKINNER, HON. RICHARD. The Life and Character of. A Discourse read before the Vermont Historical Soc., at Montpelier, Oct. 20, 1863. By Winslow C. Watson. *8vo, orig. cov., uncut, fine copy,* 30 *pages.* *Albany: J. Munsell,* 1863

1061 THOMPSON, DANIEL P. An Address pronounced before the Vermont Hist. Soc., Oct. 24, 1850, on "The History of the Settlement and Organization of the State." *8vo, orig. cov.,* 22 *pages, good copy.* *Burlington,* 1850

1062 TORREY, REV. JOSEPH. "The Discovery and Occupation of Lake Champlain." Annual Address delivered before the Vt. Hist. Soc., with the Proceedings at the 21st Annual Meeting, Oct. 16, 1860. *8vo, orig. cov., fine copy,* 27 *pages; scarce.* *Burlington,* 1860

1063 WHITE, PLINY H., AND ALBERT D. HAGER. "The Life and Services of Matthew Lyon," and "the Marbles of Vermont." Two Addresses, Oct. 29, 1858, before the Vermont Historical Society. *8vo, orig. cov., fine copy,* 16 *and* 26 *pages.* *Burlington, Vt.,* 1858

VINCENNES, IND., HISTORICAL AND ANTIQUARIAN SOCIETY.

1064 Address, Delivered February 22, 1839, by Judge John Law. *8vo, orig. cov.,* 48 *p.* *Fine copy, with map, often wanting. Very rare.* *Louisville, Ky.,* 1839

Subject of this Discourse—"The Early Settlement, Rise and Progress of Chippe-coke or Vincennes."—Presented "to Hon. Dan. Webster, with respects of Author."

VIRGINIA HISTORICAL SOCIETY.

1065 WASHINGTON, H. A. The Virginia Constitution of 1776: A Discourse delivered before the Virginia Hist. Society, January 17, 1852. *8vo pamph.,* 51 *p.* *Fine copy.* *Richmond,* 1852

1066 VIRGINIA HISTORICAL REGISTER, and Literary Advertiser. April, 1848. *8vo pamph, uncut, Vol. I., No. II.,* 47 *p.* *Richmond,* 1848

1067 VIRGINIA HISTORICAL REGISTER and Literary Companion. Edited by William Maxwell. Vol. VI., for 1853. *8vo, paper covers,* 240 *p.* *Very scarce.* *Richmond,* 1853

1068 WM. PENN SOCIETY. Discourse on the Indian Race, by Job. R. Tyson. 1836.

——— Discourse on the 150th Anniversary, by P. S. Duponceau. 1832.

——— Proc. on the 142d Anniv. Phila., 1824.

1069 WISCONSIN STATE HIST. SOC., First Annual Report. Madison, 1855.

1070 AMERICAN HISTORICAL MAGAZINE and Literary Record. January, February, April, May, and June. Vol. I., Nos. 1, 2, 4, 5, 6: Five Numbers as originally published—rough edges. *8vo. Very scarce, fine condition.* *New Haven,* 1836

Contains Biographical Sketches of Gen. Wooster, Nathan Hale, Gen. Putnam, &c., Revolutionary Papers, &c.,&c., comprising a valuable collection.

ILLINOIS, Gazetteer of. In three parts. Containing a General View of the State, each County and Town, Alphabetically arranged. By J. M. Peck. 12*mo, cl.* *Jacksonville*, 1834

1072 ILLINOIS AND WISCONSIN. Letters Written by John Kingman, while on a Tour, in the Summer of 1838. 8*vo*, 48 *p., pamph. Scarce.* *Hingham*, 1842

1073 IMLAY, GEORGE. TOPOGRAPHICAL DESCRIPTION OF THE WESTERN TERRITORY OF NORTH AMERICA: Containing a Succinct Account of its Soil, Climate, Etc. To which are added, the Discovery, Settlement, and Present State of Kentucky. And an Essay towards the Topography and Natural History of that Important Country. By John Filson. To Which is added: I.—The Adventures of Col. Daniel Boon, comprehending every important Occurrence in the Political History of that Province. II.—The Minutes of the Piankashaw Council, held at Post St. Vincent's, April 15, 1784. III.—An Account of the Indian Nations Inhabiting within the Limits of the Thirteen United States: their Manners, Etc. Illustrated with correct Maps of the Western Territory of North America; the State of Kentucky as divided into counties, from the latest surveys, and a Plan of the Rapids of the Ohio. The second edition, with considerable additions. 8*vo, bds., rough edges. Very fine copy.* *London*, 1793

1074 IMLAY, GILBERT. A TOPOGRAPHICAL DESCRIPTION OF THE WESTERN TERRITORY OF NORTH AMERICA. Containing a succinct Account of its Soil, Climate, Natural History, Etc. To which are added: I.—The Discovery, Settlement, and Present State of Kentucky. By John Filson, 1784. II.—An account of the Indian Nations, Inhabiting within the limits of the Thirteen States. III.—The Culture of Indian Corn, Etc., and other particulars in the Vegetable Kingdom. IV.—Observations on the Ancient Works, the Native Inhabitants of the Western Country, Etc., by Major Jonathan Heart. V.—Historical Narrative and Topographical Description of Louisiana and West-Florida, by Thomas Hutchins. VI.—Account of the Soil, Growing Timber, and other productions of several Lands now in Progress of being Settled. VII.—Remarks for the Information of those who wish to become Settlers in America, by Dr. Franklin. VIII.—Topographical Description of Virginia, Pennsylvania, Maryland, and North Carolina, by Mr. Tho. Hutchins. IX.—Mr. Patrick Kennedy's Journal of the Illinois River, Etc. X.—Description of the State of Tenasee, and of the South-western Territory, with the Constitution of Tenasee, established 1796, Etc., by Gilbert Imlay. Illustrated with correct Maps, from actual surveys by Elihu Barker ; a Map of the Tenasee Government, and a Plan of the Rapids of the Ohio. The Third Edition, with great additions. *8vo, sheep. Very scarce. London : Printed for J. Debrett, opposite Burlington House, Piccadilly*, 1797.

1075 INDIANA. Valley of the Upper Wabash, with Hints on its Agricultural Advantages, Etc. By Wm. Henry Ellsworth. 12*mo. cl. Map.* *New York*, 1838

1076 INDIANA, A History of, from its Earliest Exploration by Europeans, to the close of the Territorial Government in 1816 ; comprehending a History of the Discovery, Settlement, and Civil and Military Affairs of the Territory of the United States, North-west of the river Ohio, and a general View of the Progress of Public Affairs in Indiana, from 1816 to 1856. By John B. Dillon. *8vo, in sheets. With map, portraits, etc. Very scarce in this style.* *Indianapolis, Ind.*, 1859

1077 INGLIS, Rev. JOHN, Bp. of Nova Scotia. A Sermon at Halifax, on Behalf of the Society for Propag. the Gospel in Foreign Parts, February 19, 1832. *8vo. Fine copy*, 27 *pages. Historical.* *Halifax*, 1832

1078 IOWA, Constitution for the State of, Adopted in Convention, May 18, 1846. *8vo pamph.* *Iowa City*, 1846

1079 IOWA, As It Is, in 1855. Embracing a full Description of the State, her Agricultural, Mineralogical, and Geological Character, with numerous Illustrations. By N. Howe Parker. *8vo, cl.* *Chicago, Ill.*, 1855

1080 IPSWICH, ESSEX, AND HAMILTON, Mass., HISTORY OF, with The Appendix. By Joseph B. Felt. *Cl., 8vo. Portrait.* *Cambridge*, 1834

1081 IRVING, WASHINGTON, Brief Remarks on the "Wife." *8vo*, 18 *p. Curious, good copy, scarce.* *New York*, 1819

1082 ITHACA, N. Y., Views of, and its Environs. By an Impartial Observer. *8vo, uncut*, 44 *p. Scarce.* *Ithaca*, 1835

PAMPHLETS.

1083 *Pamphlets.* [*Sixteen.*]

Idaho. Six Months in the New Gold Diggings. By J. L. Campbell. *Chicago*, 1864

Ide, Jacob. Sermon at Ordination of Rev. John M. Putnam. *Boston*, 1820

Ide, Rev. Jacob. Sermon at Ordina. of Charles T. Torrey. *Providence*, 1837

Illinois, Proceedings of Board of Commis. of Public Works of· *Vandalia*, 1837
——— College, Address at Anniv. of Sigma Phi Soc., of. By Rev. L. Grosvenor. *St. Louis*, 1848
——— Central Railroad Company offer for sale, over 2,400,-000 Acres. *N. Y.*, 1855
——— Remarks on Retirement of Chief Justice Caton, from the Bench of Supreme Court of. *Chicago*, 1864
Infidel Society of United States. Minutes of. *Boston*, 1846
Indiana Medical College, Address before Officers and Students of. By John B. Niles. *Indianapolis*, 1846
Indiana University, Address before Athenian Soc. of. By Prof. J. W. Scott. *Oxford*, 1838
Insurance. The Hope Mutual Life. *N. Y.*, 1847
——— Mutual Life, Fifteenth Annual Report, of New York. *N. Y.*, 1859
——— Mutual Life, of New York.
——— The Great Western Life, of New York.
Italian Language, Grammatical Dissertation on. By Francois M. J. Surault. *Boston*, 1835
Inquiry into the Causes of Public Distress. *N. Y.*, 1834

¼ 1084 Miscellaneous. [*Twelve.*]

Irving, Washington. Remarks on the "Wife." *N. Y.*, 1819
Iron Dike. Tracts concerning the Reclamation of Swamp and Marsh Lands, and Strengthening of River Levees, etc. *N. Y*
Iliff, Frederick. Week-Day Prayers for use of Boarding-Schools. *London*
Ipswich Female Sem. Address by Daniel Dana, Jan. 15, 1834.
Inquirer, Christian. Olive Branch. Vol. I., No. 7, New York, June 28, 1828.
Inglis, Charles. Sermon on the Death of John Ogilvie. *N. Y.*, 1774
Ives, Rt. Rev. Levi S., Sermon on taking Leave of his Congregation. *N. Y.*, 1831
Ireland, Political History of. From 1172, to the present time. By Edwin Williams. *N. Y.*, 1843
——— Rev. John, Second Appeal to the Church, Containing Remarks and Strictures on the late violent proceedings of a pretended Ecclesiastical Court against. *Brooklyn*, 1811
Imray, J. W. Altamont, a Philosophical Drama, in 2 Acts. *London*, 1828
Iturbide, Don Augustine De. Narrative of the Last Moments of the Life of, Ex-Emperor of Mexico. By Col. Charles De Beneski. *N. Y.*, 1825
Indiana School Journal. George W. Ross. Vol. XIII., No. 3, March, 1868.

1085 Indian Pamphlets. [*Seven.*]

Indian, Statement of, Relations. Reply to Articles on Removal of the Indians. *N. Y.*, 1830
Indians. Speech of Hon. Mr. Storrs, on Seminole War.
——— Removal of the. Rep. No. 227. By Mr. Bell, Feb. 24, 1830.
——— Reform, Remarks on Practicability of. By Isaac M'Coy. *Boston*, 1827
——— Reform, Remarks on Practicability of. By Isaac M'Coy. (2d Ed.). *N. Y.*, 1829
——— Documents and Proc. Relating to Formation and Progress of a Board in New York, for Emig., Preservation and Improvement of. *N. Y.*, 1829
——— Disc. before Soc. for Prop. the Gospel among the. By E. Porter. *Boston*, 1808

1086 Indian Pamphlets. [*Thirteen.*]

No. 1. Indian Bulletin for 1867. By N. W. Jones. *N. Y.*, 1867
Stories of the Revolution. By Josiah Priest. *Scarce.* *Albany*, 1836
Catalogue of the Ind. Gallery. *Washington.*
Mosaic Account of the Unity of the Human Race.
Indian Names of places in R. I. By Usher Parsons. With Portrait. *Prov.* 1861
Report on the Sudbury Fight, April, 1676.
Darien Indians. By Dr. Cullen. 1865
Journal of Visits to the Indians on the Kennebec River. By the Rev. Joseph Baxter. *Boston*, 1867
Letter from John Ross to a Gentleman of Phil. 1837. *Scarce.*
A New Soc. for Benefit of Ind. *Washington*, 1822
Speech of Mr. Frelinghuysen. *Washington*, 1830
Speech of Jas. Talmadge, on the Seminole War. *N. Y.*, 1819
View of the Present Relations between the Government and the Indians.

1087 Indian Pamphlets. [*Thirteen.*]

Remarks of Mr. Stockton, on the Ind. Appro. Bill. *Washington*, 1852
Report of Visit to some of the Tribes of Ind. located West of the Mississippi. By Lang & Taylor. *N. Y.*, 1843
Edward Everett's Address at Bloody Brook, Sept. 30, 1835. *Very scarce.*
Organization of New Ind. Terri. By George Copway. *N. Y.*, 1850
Lincoln's Address at Bloody Brook, Aug. 31, 1838. *Very scarce.*
Monumental Remains of Georgia. By C. C. Jones. *Savannah*, 1861
Cherokee Almanac, 1836–'58. Union and Park Hill, Georgia.
Speech of Mr. Wild, of Georgia. *Washington*, 1830
The Abenaki Ind. By Frederic Kidder. *Poor copy.* *Portland*, 1859

Charles Gibbon's Address, before the Northern Lyceum of Philadelphia. 1839

Report on the Seneca Indians. *Boston*, 1840

Spelling-Book in the Seneca Language, Buffalo Creek Reservation.

Newspaper in the Seneca Language, "The Mental Elevator." Nos. 1 to 5 inclusive. 1841–42

1088 Indian Pamphlets. [*Nine.*]

Receipts of the Indian Dr. John Mackentosh, (Cherokee.) *N. Y.*, 1827

Plan for Civilizing the Indians of N. A. *London*, 1796

Origin of the Indians, etc. From Boston Monthly Magazine, Jan. 1826.

Cong. Doc. No. 74. Treaty with Florida Ind. 1826

Soc. for Prop. the Gosp. among the Ind. Disc. by Porter. *Boston*, 1808

Capt. J. Lovewell's Fight at Pequawket. *Concord* 1861

Life and Adventures of Henry Lanson. *London*, 1801

The Sioux War. By J. W. Taylor. *St. Paul*, 1862

Boston Two Hundred Years Ago; or, The Romantic Story of Miss Ann Carter and the Celebrated Indian Chief Thundersquall, with many Reminisences and Events of Olden Time. *Very scarce.* *Exeter*, 1831

1089 Indian Pamphlets. [*Nine.*]

Barr, Capt. James, Correct and Authentic Narrative of the Indian War in Florida, with a Description of Maj. Dade's Massacre. *Very scarce.* *N. Y.*, 1836

Soc. for Prop. Gosp. among Indians. Sermon. By Philip Furneaux. *London*, 1775

Sketch of Life of Apostle Eliot. By H. A. S. Dearborn. *Roxbury*, 1850

John C. Metcalf's Oration at Ind. Rock, July 4, 1823. *Scarce.* 1823

Cong. Doc. No. 10, on Ind. Trade, 1822. 1822

Oneida County and Mohawk Valley. Papers No. 18. From the New York Col. Hist.

Narrative of a Captivity among Mohawk Ind. A Description of New Netherland, 1642–43. By Father Isaac Joques, with a Memoir by John G. Shea. *Scarce.* *N. Y.*, 1857

The Moravian Church Miscellany. Vol. IV., No. 3, Containing a Report on Ind. 1853

Eulogy on King Philip. By Wm. Apess. 2d ed. *Scarce.* *Boston*, 1837

1090 Indian Pamphlets. [*Ten.*]

Eulogy on King Philip, by Wm. Apess. 1*st Ed.* *Very scarce.* *Boston*, 1837

Rambles among Araucanian Indians. *Thomaston*, 1851

Atlantic Journal, Vol. I., No. 3. American Tribes not Jews. By C. S. Rafinesque. *Scarce.* *Phila.*, 1832

Address on present condition of the Aboriginal Inhabitants of North America. By M. B. Pierce. *Very scarce.* *Steele's Press*, 1838

Address of Gov. Boutwell at Dedication of Monument to Memory of Capt. Wadsworth, at Sudbury. Nov. 23, 1852. *Very scarce. Autograph of Boutwell.*

Davis, A. Antiquities of America and the Discovery of New England by the Northmen. 9th Ed. *Boston*, 1842

Marriage of Pocahontas. By B. J. Lossing.

The Early Peopling of America. By John B. Newman. *New York*, 1848

Statement of the Indian relations. *New York*, 1830

Relations between Cherokees and U. S.

1091 Indian Pamphlets. [*Ten.*]

Appeal to Christian Community on prospects of N. Y. Indians. By N. T. Strong, Seneca Chief. *N. Y.*, 1841

Observations on the Aboriginal Monuments of the Mississippi Valley. E. G. Squier. *Scarce.* *New York*, 1847

Soc. for Prop. Gospel among Ind. Discourse by Dr. Lathrop, Jan. 19, 1804.

——— Discourse by L. Frisbie, Nov. 1, 1804.

——— Discourse by T. Barnard, Nov. 6, 1806. 55

——— Discourse by Abiel Holmes, Nov. 3, 1808.

——— Discourse by E. Parish, Nov. 3, 1814.

——— Discourse by D. Osgood, June 2, 1788.

Hist. Sketch of the formation of the Confed. with reference to the limits of the General Gov't. over Indian Tribes and the Public Territory. By Joseph Blunt. *Scarce.* *N. Y.*, 1825

Treaty of Six Indian Tribes. By Madison and Jefferson.

1092 Indian Pamphlets, &c. [*Fourteen.*]

Schoolcraft's Oneota, Nos. 1, 2, 3 (4). *Scarce.* *New York*, 1844

Apthorp's Consid. on the Soc. Prop. Gosp. *Boston*, 1763

Cong. Doc., Ind. Aff. Generally. Feb. 10, 1829.

——— Fur Trade. Feb. 9, 1829.

——— Trade. Feb. 11, 1822.

——— Treaty, Lewis Cass and Chippeways. Feb. 5, 1828. 12½

——— No. 122. Chickasaw Fund.

——— No. 519. Removal of the Chippewa, Ottawa, &c. May 29, 1844.

——— No. 86. Removal of the Choctaws. February 7, 1845.

——— No. 115. Chickasaw Fund. Feb. 9, 1844.

——— No. 152. Memorial on the Purchase of Catlin's paintings and curiosities. 1848.

1093 Indian Pamphlets, &c. [*Thirteen.*]

Cong. Doc. No. 41. Memorial of Coody and Drew. "Old Settlers" of the Cherokees. 1849.

——— 149. Report of Choctaw Bd. of Comm. 1845.

——— 149. Report on behalf of Milly, an Indian Woman. 1844.

——— 145. Memorial of the Cherokee Delegation. 1848.

——— 736. Ind. terri. west of the Miss. 1848.

147. Memorial of Tuckahatchee, Mico, and others. 1848.

——— 31. Letter of the 2d Auditor of Treasury. 1862.

——— 474. Com. on Ind. Aff. for estab. of West. Terri. 1834.

——— 8. Letter from Sec. of Treas. Statement of Money appropriated and paid for Indians since 1820.

——— 51. Letter from Sec. of Treas. relating to sale of lands to the United Brethren. 1822.

——— 47. Memorial of Soc. of Friends. 1818.

——— 10. Report of Comm. in relation to the treaty with the Creek and Cherokee Ind. 1822.

——— 102. Preserv. and Civiliz. of Ind. 1826.

1094 Indian Pamphlets. [*Thirteen.*]

Message No. 50, from Pres. Monroe. 1822.

——— 21, from Pres. Monroe. 1825.

——— 25, from Pres. Madison. 1816.

Soc. for Prop. the Gospel among the Ind.; Report of, Nov. 6, 1845.

——— Among the Ind., Report of, Nov. 7, 1850.

——— Among the Ind., Report of, May 31, 1855.

——— Among the Ind., Report of, May 30, 1861.

Soc. for Prop. Gospel. Sermon by Dr. Morse, Nov. 1, 1810.

——— Sermon by Dr. Eckley, Nov. 7, 1805.

——— Sermon by James Kendall, Nov. 7, 1811.

——— Sermon by Joshua Bates, Nov. 4, 1813.

——— Sermon by B. B. Wisner, Nov. 5, 1829.

Report concerning the Indians of Mass. No 96. 1861.

1095 Indian Pamphlets. [*Thirteen.*]

Disc. on Remnant of the Indian Race. By J. R. Tyson. *Very scarce.* *Phila.*, 1836

Removal of the Indians. *Boston*, 1830

Events in Life of Brant.

Journal of Peter Jacobs, Ind. Missionary. *Toronto*, 1853

Me-won-i-toc: A Tale of Frontier Life and Ind. Charac. *N. Y.*, 1867

Journal of a Tour in the Ind. Terr. *N. Y.*, 1844

Journal of Rev. Peter Jacobs. *N. Y.*, 1857

Thrilling Sketch of the Life of Okah Tubbee. By L. L. Allen. *New York*, 1848

Plea for the Ind. By John Beason. *N. Y.*, 1858

Essays on American Indians. By William Penn. *Boston*, 1829

Medical receipts of Col. John Wabash, Ind. Phys. to the Creek Nation. *Philadelphia*

Effort and Failure to Civilize the Aborigines. Letter to Hon. N. G. Taylor from Edward D. Neill. *Washington*, 1868

Memories of the Ind. and Pioneers of the Region of Lowell. By Charles Cowley. *Lowell*, 1862

1096 Indian Pamphlets. [*Fifteen.*]

Soc. for Propagating the Gospel among the Indians and others in N. A. Discourse by Joseph Eckley, Nov. 7, 1805. *Boston*

——— Discourse by Thomas Barnard; Charlestown, Nov. 6, 1806.

——— Sermon by James Kendall, at Anniv., Nov. 7, 1811. *Boston*, 1812

——— Sermon by Joshua Bates, at Anniv., Nov. 4, 1813. *Boston*, 1813

——— Sermon by Ebenezer Porter, Nov. 1, 1827. *Andover*, 1827

McCoy, Isaac. Remarks on Practicability of Indian Reform, embracing their Colonization. *Boston*, 1827

Documents and Proc. relating to the Formation and Progress of a Board for the Emigration, Preservation, and Improvement of the Aborigines. N. Y., July 22, 1829.

Indian Territory. Periodical Account of Baptist Missions within—for year ending Dec. 31, 1836.

——— Annual Register of Indian Affairs within the. By Isaac McCoy. Shawanoe Baptist Mission, Ind. Ter. 1837.

——— Annual Register of Indian Affairs. By Isaac McCoy. *Washington*, 1838

Chronicles of the N. American Savages. Vol I. May, 1835. No. 1.

Chronicles of the N. American Savages. Vol. I. June, 1835. No. 2.

Cherokees, The; Relations between, and the Gov't. of U. S.

Indian Territory, Journal of a Tour in the. *N. Y.*, 1844

Kah-ge-ga-gah-bouh, or Geo. Copway. Organization of a New Indian Territory, East of the Missouri River. *N. Y.*, 1850

JACKSON, ANDREW. Memoir of. By S. W. Putnam. *8vo, sh.*. *Hartford*, 1819

1098 JACKSON, THOMAS J. "Stonewall Jackson." The Life and Military Career of. By Markinfield Addey. *8vo, paper.* *New York*, 1863

1099 JACOBS, BELA. Second Annual Report of the Exec. Com. of the Western Baptist Educational Assoc., May 28, 1834. *8vo, 24 pages ; fine copy ; scarce.* *Boston*, 1834

1100 JACOBS, THOMAS. Scenes, Incidents and Adventures in the Pacific Ocean, or the Islands of the Australasian Seas, during the Cruise of the Clipper "Margaret Oakley," under Capt. Benjamin Morrell. *8vo, cl. ; rough edges ; illustrated.* *New York*, 1844

1101 JAMAICA. Its Past and Present State. By James M. Phillippo. *8vo, uncut ; pamphlet.* *Philadelphia*, 1843

1102 JAMES, WILLIAM. A Full and Correct Account of the chief Naval Occurrences of the Late War between Great Britain and the United States of America ; to which is added an Appendix ; with plates. *8vo, cl., uncut.* *London*, 1817

1103 JANNEY, SAMUEL M. The last of the Lenape and other Poems. *12mo, cl.* *Phila.*, 1839

1104 JAMESTOWN, Va. Celebration of the Two Hundred and Fiftieth Anniversary of the English Settlement, May 18, 1857. *8vo pamphlet, 32 p.* *Washington*, 1857

1105 JAY, WILLIAM. Remarks on the Character and Narrative of the Rev. John Clark, interspersed with brief sketches from the narrative. By another hand. *8vo, 94 p. ; uncut.* *Boston*, 1821

1106 JEANNETTE. A Poem, with Three Portraits. By Aeculapius Non Vinotus. *8vo, cl. ; free.* *New York*, 1857

1107 JEMISON, MARY. DEH-HE-WA-MIS ; OR, A NARRATIVE OF THE LIFE OF, otherwise called the White Woman, who was taken captive by the Indians in 1755, and continued with them 78 yrs. Containing an account of the murder of her Father and his Family, her marriage and sufferings. Indian Barbarities, Customs and Traditions. By James E. Seaver.
Also, The Life of Hiokatoo and Ebenezer Allen ; a sketch of

Gen. Sullivan's Campaign ; Tragedy of the "Devil's Hole," etc. Hist. Sketches of the Six nations, etc. By Ebenezer Mix. 12*mo, full cr. crim., lev. mor., gt. By R. M. Smith, very scarce.* *Batavia, N. Y.*, 1842

1108 Jersey City, Hoboken and Hudson. Combined Directories of, for 1854–55 : with an Appendix, containing various Statistical and Historical Information and a Map. 12*mo, bds.* *Jersey City*, 1854

1109 Jewett, C. C. Notices of Public Libraries in the United States of America. 8*vo, cl.* *Washington*, 1851

1110 Jewitt, John R. Narrative of the Adventures and sufferings of, only survivor of the Crew of the Ship Boston, during a Captivity of nearly 3 years among the Savages of Nootka Sound, with an account of the Manners, Mode of Living and Religious Opinions of the Natives. 12*mo, cl. ; plates.* *Ithaca, N. Y.*, 1851

1111 Johnson, Joseph. Traditions and Reminiscences, chiefly of the American Revolution in the South. Including Biographical Sketches, Incidents and Anecdotes, Particularly of Residents in the Upper Country. 8*vo, cl., fine copy ; very scarce.* *Charleston, S. C.*, 1851

1112 Johnson, Mrs. Thomazin, of Braintree, Mass. Memoir of, with an account of her Pious Lineage, from John Alden, the first Pilgrim Father who placed foot on Plymouth Rock. By her son, L. D. Johnson. 16*mo, cl.* *Boston*, 1835

1113 Jones, A. D. The American Portrait Gallery ; containing correct Portraits and brief notices of the principal Actors in American History, embracing Distinguished Women, Naval and Military Heroes, Civilians, Jurists, Divines and Artists ; together with celebrated Indian chiefs. From Christopher Columbus down to the present time. With portraits. 8*vo.* *New York*, 1867

1114 Jones, George. Tecumseh and the Prophet of the West ; An Historical, Israel-Indian Tragedy. In Five Acts, with Historical Notes. The Life and History of General Harrison, and the First Oration upon the Life, Character and Genius of Shakspeare. *In* 1 *vol.*, 8*vo, cl.* *London*, 1844

1115 Jones, Chevalier, John Paul. Life and Character of ; a Captain in the United States Navy during the Revolutionary War. By John Henry Sherburne. 8*vo, bds. uncut.* *Washington*, 1825

1116 Jones, John Paul. Life and Character of, a Captain in the United States Navy, during the Revolutionary War. By John Henry Sherburne. 8*vo, cloth,* 2*nd ed.* *New York*, 1851

1117 Jones, Paul. The Life and Adventures of. 8*vo, unbound.* *N. Y.*, 1848

1118 JONES, CHARLES C. Historical Sketch of the Chatham Artillery during the Confederate Struggle for Independence. 8*vo, red cl.* *Joel Munsell ; Albany*, 1867

1119 Jones, Samuel. A Century Sermon, delivered in Phila., before the Phila. Baptist Assoc., Oct. 6, 1807. Comprising a History of the Church at Lower Dublin, Phila., from the year 1688, and a general Hist. of the progress of the Baptist Church, etc., 8*vo,* 26 *pages, good copy ; scarce.* *Phila.*, 1807

1120 Joshua, The Books of, and Ruth, translated into the Choctaw language. 16*mo, unbound.* *New York,* 1852

1121 Josselyn, John. An account of Two Voyages to New-England, made during the years 1638, 1663. *Sm. 4to, cl., uncut.* Reprinted from the London edition of 1675. *William Veazie, Boston,* 1865

Only 25 copies printed.

1122 Josseylyn, John. New-England Rarities, Discovered in Birds, Beasts, Fishes, Serpents and Plants of that Country. With an Introduction and Notes by Edward Tuckerman, M. A. Reprinted from the London edition, 1672. *Sm. 4to, cl., uncut.* *William Veazie, Boston,* 1865

250 copies printed.

1123 "Juba." "United we stand; divided we fall." 12*mo, bds. uncut.* *New York,* 1812

1124 Juvenal. A new translation, with notes of the third satire of; to which are added, miscellaneous poems. 12*mo, sheep.* *New York,* 1806

PAMPHLETS.

1125 Miscellaneous. [*Thirteen.*]

Jenks, Capt. Robert W. The Brachial Telegraph. *N. Y.,* 1852
Jamaica. Description and History of the Island of, by W. Wemyss Anderson. *Kingston, Jamaica,* 1851
Jaeger. Prof. B. Life of North American Insects. *N. Y.,* 1853
Jahnsenykes, Rev. Williamson. Memoir of the Northern Kingdom. *Quebec,* 1901
Jewett, Charles C. In Memoriam. *Providence,* 1868
Jessup, Rev. Edward. The Dignity and Duty of a Minister of Christ. *N. Y.,* 1864
Jeffreys, Archdeacon. The Religious Objection to Tetotalism. *London,* 1840
Jacobinical Times. Progress of the Pilgrim Good Intent. *Stockbridge,* 1802
Jacobs, Rev. Bela. Report of his Tour in Western States. *Boston,* 1833
Jones, J. Thoughts on Literary Prospects of America. *Baltimore,* 1839
Jones, Rev. Cave. Solemn Appeal to the Church. *N. Y.,* 1811
Jones, Paul. Life, Travels, Voyages, &c. *London.*
Jones, Henry. Strange Phenomena of New England in the Seventeenth Century, including the Salem Witchcraft, 1692, from the Writings of Rev. Cotton Mather. *Very Scarce.* *N. Y.,* 1846

1126 Miscellaneous. [*Fourteen.*]

Jones, Thomas. Paradoxes of Debit and Credit Demolished, &c. *N. Y.,* 1859
Jones, Henry. Animal Magnetism—repudiated as Scorcery—not a Science. *N. Y.,* 1846

Jayne, Ebenezer. Letter to Ephraim Green. *Byram*, 1811
Jarvis, Sarah M. Petition for Divorce from her Husband, Rev. Samuel F. Jarvis. *Scarce.* *Hartford*, 1839
Jarvis, Samuel, F. Sermon before Annual Convention of Prot. Epis. Ch. *Boston*, 1822
Joncourt, R. De. Predestination Considered. *Newburgh*, 1811
Johnston, David. The Heinousness and Aggravation of Theft. *Edinburgh*, 1788
Junius. The Test; or, Parties tried by their Acts. *N. Y.*, 1843
——— The Tariff. *N. Y.*, 1843
——— The Currency. *N. Y.*, 1843
——— Life of Henry Clay. *N. Y.*, 1843
Jack, Charles J. Speech in favor of Re-annex. of Texas to U. S. *Phila.*, 1844
——— Review of Opinion of Hon. Edward King. *Phila.*, 1846
Judson, Adoniram. Sermon preached in La Bazar Chapel, Calcutta, Sept. 27, 1812. *Boston*, 1817

1127 Miscellaneous. [*Twelve.*]

Johnson, John B. Farewell Sermon, Sept. 26, 1802. *Albany*, 1802
Jordan, John. Serious Actual Dangers of Foreigners and Foreign Commerce in Mexican States. *Phila.*, 1826
Johnson, Rev. John. Correspondence between and Miss Elizabeth Jones. *Phila.*, 1817 25
Johnson, Col. Richard M. Speech on Imprisonment for Debt. *Boston*, 1823
Johnson, Hon. Mr. Review of Report of Com. on subject of Mails on the Sabbath. *Boston*, 1829
Johnson, A. G. History of Progress of Judicial Usurpation. *Troy*, 1863
Jay's, Mr., Treaty. Features of. *Phila.*, 1795
Jay's, Wm. Letter to Rt. Rev. Bishop Hobart. *N. Y.*, 1823
Jay, Wm. Essay on Marriage. *Utica*, 1814
Johnson, Oliver. Dissertation on Subject of Future Punishment. *Boston*, 1831
Jay's, Judge, Portrait at White Plains. *N. Y.*, 1863
——— Second Letter on Dawson's Introduction to the Federalist. *N. Y.*, 1864

1128 Miscellaneous. [*Eleven.*]

Japan and the Japanese. By Talbot Watts. *N. Y.*, 1852
——— By an Oriental Traveller. *N. Y.*, 1860 15
Judd, Gideon, N. Sermon on National Fast. *Newark*, 1828
Jefferson, Thomas. Address on Life and Character of. *Phil.*, 1800
——— Address on Inaug. of, by Tunis Wortman. *N. Y.*, 1801
——— Address on Life and Character of. 2nd Ed. *Worcester*, 1802
——— Observations on "Notes on Virginia." *N. Y.*, 1804

Jefferson, T. Documents relating to the Presidential Elec. in 1801, Aspersing the Character of the late James Bayard. *Phila.*, 1831

——— Answer to. Justification of his Conduct in Case of New Orleans Batture, by Edward Livingston. *Very scarce.* *Phila.*, 1813

Jefferson College. Annual Address, Philo. Lit. Soc. of, by Wm. T. Hamilton. *Pittsburgh*, 1849

Journal. Monthly American, of Geology and Natural Science. Vol. I., No. 3., Sept., 1831. *Phila.*

1129 Miscellaneous. [*Fourteen.*]

Jesuits. Secret Instructions of. *Phila.*, 1844

——— Interference with Domestic Affairs, by Wm. C. Byrne. *Galveston*, 1848

——— Lecture in Musical Fund Hall, by Joseph F. Berg. *Phila.*, 1851

Johns, Rev. Evan. Review of Layman's Essay on the Sabbath. *Canandaigua*, 1829

Johns, Henry V. D. Letter to, on Sermon entitled, "The Protestant Episcopal Pastor." *Baltimore*, 1842

Johns, Rev. J. Valedictory Address deliv. in Christ Church. *Baltimore*, 1842

Johnson, John B. A Farewell Sermon deliv. Sept. 26, 1802. *Albany*

Jefferson, Tho. A Series of Letters addressed to, by Tacitus. *Scarce.* *Phila.*, 1802

James, Wm. Warden Refuted ; Defence of British Navy. *London*, 1819

Johnson, Mr. Report on Sunday Mails. *Boston*, 1829

Jefferson, Thomas. Answer to. Justification of his conduct in case of the New Orleans Batture, by Edward Livingston. *Phila.*, 1813

Jackson, Andrew. Affidavit of, in Suit of Robert Mayo *vs.* Blair and Rives, by Robt Mayo. *Washington*, 1840

——— Sermon on Death of, by Rev. John N. M'Jilton. *Baltimore*, 1845

Jackson, Gen. Andrew. Memoirs of. *Bridgeton, N. J.*, 1824

1130 Miscellaneous. [*Fourteen.*]

Jackson, Gen. Andrew. Reflections on Charac. and Public Services of. *N. Y.*, 1828

——— First Invasion of Florida, and of his Immortal Defence of New Orleans, by Aristides. *Rare.* *N. Y.*, 1827

——— Memoirs of, with Letter of Sec. Adams. *N. Y.*, 1824

——— Oration on Life and Char. of, by Wm. L. Yancey. *Baltimore*, 1846

Jefferson, Thomas and John Adams. Discourse on Death of, by John Stanford. *N. Y.*, 1826

Jefferson, Thomas. Vindication of, against Charges contained in a Pamphlet entitled "Serious Considerations," by Grotius. *Scarce.* *N. Y.*, 1800

——— Pretensions of, to the Presidency examined, and the Charges against John Adams refuted. *Scarce.* *U. S.*, 1796

——— Observations on certain passages in "Notes on Virginia." *Scarce.* *New York*, 1804

Jackson, Gen. Reminiscences, or Extract from Catalogue of his Juvenile Indiscretions. *Curious and scarce.*

Jackson, Andrew. Letters of "Wyoming" in favor of Election of. *Phila.*, 1824

——— Supplement to Address of Henry Clay. *Washington*, 1828

——— Life of, by Wm. Cobbett. *Baltimore*, 1834

Jackson. Farmer, in N. Y.; or, the Tenn. Farmer. *N. Y.*, 1821

Jackson, Gen. Address of Repub. Genl. Committee of Young Men of N. Y. Friendly to Election of. *N. Y.*, 1828

1131 Jackson, Gen. Pamphlets relating to. [*Five.*]

Letters of Gen. Adair and Gen. Jackson relative to the charge of Cowardice made by the latter against the Kentucky Troops at New Orleans, Apr. 10, 1815. *Scarce.* 32½

Virginia. Anti-Jackson Conventions, Dec. 12, 1827.

Aristides. A concise narrative of Jackson's first invasion of Florida and of his immortal defence of New Orleans, with Remarks, &c. *Very scarce.* *New York*, 1827

Letters and Documents of distinguished Citizens of Tenn. on the buying and selling of Human Beings. *New York*, 1828

Truth's Advocate and Monthly Anti-Jackson Expositor, from Jan. to July, 1828, inclusive. *Cincinnati, Ohio.*

1132 Jew Pamphlets. [*Five.*]

Whitaker, E. W. Dissertation on the Prophecies relating to the Final Restoration of the Jews. *London*, 1784

M'Donald, John. A new translation of Isaiah, chap. xvii.: a remarkable prophecy respecting the restoration of the Jews. 12½ *Albany*, 1814

Nickelsburger, Jacob. Koul Jacob in defence of the Jewish Religion. *New York*, 1816

M'Chord, James. A Plea "For The Hope Of Israel" and the Hope of all the World. *Phila.*, 1817

Noah, M. M. Disc. on the restoration of the Jews. *N. Y.*, 1845

1133 Jew Pamphlets. [*Twelve.*]

Jews in the East, Persecution of the. *Phila.*, 1840

——— Dissertation on Future Restoration of the. By Jas. Wilson. *Providence*, 1828/

——— The Restoration of, to Jerusalem, by the year 1798, under their Revealed Prince and Prophet. Written by himself. Book First. *Scarce.* *Phila.*, 1795

Jews in the East. Extract from Report of Com. of London Society for Promoting Christianity amongst the, *Brooklyn*, 1811

—— Israel Vindicated. Refutation of Calumnious Prop. respecting the Jewish Nation, by an Israelite. *N. Y.* 1820

—— Sermon at Ordina. of Rev. Wm. G. Schauffler as Missionary to the, by Moses Stuart. *Andover*, 1831

—— Restoration of the. The Crisis of all Nations. By J. Bicheno. *London*, 1800

Jewish Chronicle, Vol. III., No. 7. Jan., 1847.

Jews. Friendly Address to the, by J. Bicheno. *London*, 1787

—— Remarks on Prophecies relating to the Restoration of, by M. S. M. *London*

—— Lecture on Conversion of. *N. Y.*, 1846

—— The Shekinah. By S. B. Brittan. Vol. 1, No. 1. *Bridgeport*, 1851

AMEHAMEHA III. Kanawai o ka moi ke alü o ko Hawaii pae aina i kaula e na Alii Ahaolelo A me ka poeikohoia iloko oka Ahaolela oka makahiki. *8vo, half cf.* *Honolulu*, 1853

1135 KEAPP, SAM'L. L. Oration before the Phi Beta Kappa, at Dartmouth College Aug. 19, 1824. *8vo, fine copy,* 32 *pages. Historical.* *Boston*, 1824

1136 KEATING, WM. H. Narrative of an Expedition to the source of St. Peter's River, Lake Winnepeek, Lake of the Woods, &c. ; performed in the year 1823, by order of the Hon. J. C. Calhoun, under the command of Stephen H. Long. In 2 vols. *8vo, bds., uncut ; engraving and map.* *London*, 1825

1137 KEEFER, JUSTUS. Slavery : its Sin, Moral Effects, and certain Death. Also, The Language of Nature, compared with Divine Revelation. With extracts from eminent Authors. *8vo, cl.* *Baltimore*, 1864

1138 KEENE, N. H. Annals of the Town of, from its settlement, in 1734 to the year 1790. By Salma Hale. *8vo, paper cover, uncut ;* 69 *pages ; the rare first ed., in beautiful condition.* *Concord, N. H.*, 1826.

J. B. Felt's copy and autograph.

1139 KEENE, N. H. ANNALS OF THE TOWN OF, from its First settlement, in 1734, to 1790. By Salma Hale. *8vo, cl., plain ; scarce.* *Keene*, 1851

1140 KELLOGG, ROB'T H. (*Sergt. Major* 16*th Regt. Conn. Volunteers.*) LIFE AND DEATH IN REBEL PRISONS. Giving a complete History of the inhuman and barbarous treatment of our brave soldiers by Rebel authorities ; inflicting terrible suffering and frightful mortality, principally at Andersonville and Florence ; describing plans of escape, arrival of prisoners, &c., and anecdotes of Prison Life. To which is added, an account of the Capture of Davis, and Life, Trial, and Execution of Wirz. Illustrated. *8vo, half dark blue lev. mor., gilt top ; bound by R. W. Smith.* *Hartford*, 1866

1141 KENNEBUNK PORT, (ME.) HISTORY OF, from its First Discovery, by Bartholomew Gosnold, May 14, 1602, to A.D. 1837. By Charles Bradbury. *12mo, clo. ; plate ; very scarce.* *Kennebunk*, 1837

1142 KENNEDY, J. P. Swallow Barn, or a Sojourn in the Old Dominion. *Twenty illustrations, by Strother.* 24*mo, cloth.* *New York*, 1853

1143 KENNEDY, THOMAS. Poems. *Washington, D. C.*, 1816

1144 KENTUCKY. AN EXCURSION to the Mammoth Cave and Barrens of, with some notices of the Early Settlement of the State. By R. Davidson. 12*mo, cl.; scarce.* *Lexington, Ky.*, 1840

1145 KENTUCKY. THE HISTORY OF, from its Earliest Settlement to the Present Time. By T. S. Arthur and W. H. Carpenter. 12*mo, cloth.* *Philadelphia*, 1853

1146 KENTUCKY. SKETCHES OF THE EARLY CATHOLIC MISSIONS OF, from their Commencement, in 1787, to the Jubilee of 1826–'7; embracing a summary of the early history of the State, &c., and of the general State of the Catholic religion in Kentucky. Compiled, with the assistance of the Rev. Stephen Theodore Badin, First Priest ordained in the United States. By M. J. Spalding, D. D. 12*mo, sh.* *Louisville, Ky.*, 1844

1147 KENTUCKY. RAMBLES IN THE MAMMOTH CAVE, in 1844. By a Visitor. 12*mo, hlf. moroc., cl. sides; with chart and plates.* *Louisville, Ky.*, 1845

1148 KENTUCKY. A HISTORY OF THE COMMONWEALTH OF. By Mann Butler. 1st Ed. *Port. of Geo. Roger Clarke. Full red Turkey, gilt. By R. M. Smith. Very scarce.* *Louisville Ky.*, 1834

1149 KETT, REV. HENRY. The Flowers of Wit, or a choice collection of Bon Mots. Two vols. 12*mo, half cf.* *London*, 1814

1150 KILBOURN, JOHN. THE OHIO GAZETTEER, or Topographical Dictionary; containing a description of the several Counties, Towns, Villages, Settlements, &c., &c., in the State; alphabetically arranged. Second ed., improved. *Pamph.*, 8*vo*, 114 *p.; fine copy, very scarce.* *Columbus*, 1816

1151 KINNE, AARON. A New Year's Gift; presented especially to the Young People in the First Society of Groton, Jan. 1, 1788. 8*vo pamph, scarce.* *New London*, 1788

1152 KIP, REV. WILLIAM INGRAHAM. THE EARLY JESUIT MISSION IN NORTH AMERICA; Compiled and Translated from the Letters of the French Jesuits, with Notes. Parts I. and II., complete. 8*vo, hf. mor.; very scarce.* *N. Y.*, 1846

1153 KIPP, FRANCIS, M., D.D. Historical Discourse delivered on 150th Anniversary of the First R. D. Church, Fishkill, N. Y. With an appendix furnishing a Brief His. Sketch of the Associated Churches of Hopewell, etc. *Plates.* 8*vo, fine copy; interesting.* *New York*, 1866

1154 KIRK, E. N. An Oration delivered before the Acad. of Sacred Music, in New York, May 14, 1841. 8*vo, fine copy*, 27 *pages.* *New York*, 1841

1155 KNIGHT, H. C. The Broken Harp. Poems. 12*mo, cl.* *Philadelphia*, 1815

1156 KNIGHT, MADAME, AND REV. MR. BUCKINGHAM. Journals of, from the Original Manuscripts. Written in 1704 and 1710. 12*mo, bds., uncut; scarce.* *New York*, 1825

1157 KNIGHT, CHAS. GALLERY OF PORTRAITS; with Memoirs. 7 *vols.* 4*to, rough edges. With portraits. Very fine copy; scarce.* *London*, 1833–37

1158 Knox County, Ohio, A History of, from 1779 to 1862 inclusive; comprising Biographical Sketches, Anecdotes and Incidents of men connected with the County from its first settlement; together with complete lists of the Senators, Commissioners, etc., also of those who have served in Military capacity from its first organization to the present time. And also a sketch of Kenyon College, and other Institutions of learning within the County. By A. Banning Norton. *With portraits, plates. 8vo, cl.; scarce.* *Columbus*, 1862

1159 Knox, Thomas W. Camp-Fire and Cotton-Field. Southern Adventures in time of War. Life with the Union Armies and Residence on a Louisiana Plantation. *8vo, bds.* *New York, Chicago*, 1865

1160 Kruger, K. The First Discovery of *America*, and its Early Civilization. Translated and enlarged. By W. L. Wagener. *12mo, cl.* *New York*, 1863

PAMPHLETS.

1161 Miscellaneous. [*Nine.*]

King, Rufus. Speech of, on the American Navigation Act, deliv. June, 1818. *N. Y.*

Kean, Laurence. Sermon. "The Diversity of Christ," deliv. Feb. 9, 1821. *N. Y.*

Keene, Rich'd R. Letter from, to L. Martin, Esq. *Scarce.* Baltimore, June, 1802.

Knickerbocker. April, 1839.

Kendall, James. Sermon deliv. at Ordination of Hersey B. Goodwin, deliv. Feb. 17, 1830, in Concord, Mass.

Kendall, Samuel. Sermon deliv. on termination of a century. Jan. 12, 1813. *Very scarce.* *Cambridge*, 1813

Kinne, Aaron. New Year's Gift presented to the young people of Groton, Jan. 1, 1788. *New London*, 1788

Kemp, James. Letter in defence of the clergy of the D. C., 1822.

Kenrick, F. P. Letter on Christian Union. *Phila.*, 1841

1162 Miscellaneous. *Valuable Lot.* [*Twelve.*]

Kip, Francis M. Discourse on 150th Anniv. of First Ref. Dutch Ch., Fishkill. *N. Y.*, 1866

Kennedy on Diseases of the Skin. *Roxbury.*

Kendall, R. C. Treatise on Perennial Cotton. *N. Y.*, 1862

Knox, Rev. John. Memorial of. Died Jan. 8, 1858.

Kent, Elisha Kent. Memoir and Eulogy of. By E. W. Andrews. *N. Y.*, 1857

Know-Nothings. Startling Facts for Native Americans. *N. Y.*, 1855

Kollock, Henry. Sermon before Gen'l Assembly Presb. Church. *Phila.*, 1803

Kemp, Francis Adrian Van Der. Oration at Presb. Church Commem. of Emancipation of Dutch from French Tyranny. *Very scarce.* *Utica*, 1814

Knickerbocker, Diedrich, Jr. Manuscript of. *Scarce.* *N. Y.*, 1824
Kirkland, Pres. Disc. on Life and Character of. By Alex. Young. *Boston*, 1840
Krauth. Charles P. Disc. on Popular Amusements. *Winchester*, 1851
Koszta. Correspondence bet. Wm. L. Marcy and Chev. Hulsemann.

2 1163 Miscellaneous. *Valuable Lot.* [*Twelve.*]
Kearney, Frederick. Treatise on Industry and False Pride. *London.*
Kossuth, Louis. Life and Public American Speeches of. *N. Y.*, 1852
Knoepfel's Schoharie Cave. Account of. *N. Y.*, 1853
Knapp, Martin. Human Liberty against Ultra-Temp. Intolerance. *N. Y.*, 1853
Kenyon College. Three Letters to Bishop Chase on Present Indebtedness of. By Rev. Samuel Chase. *Peoria*, 1843
——— ——— Reply of Trustees of, to Statement of D. B. Douglass. *Phila.*, 1844
——— ——— Statement of Facts and Circum. connected with Removal of D. B. Douglass. *Printed for private circulation.* 1844.
King, Edward. Considerations on Utility of National Debt. *London*, 1793
King, Wm. R. Obituary Addresses on Death of. *Washington*, 1854
King's Maiesties Declaration concerning Lawful Sports. *Phila.*, 1866
Keith, Isaac S. Charge at Ordination of Rev. James Adams. *Scarce.* *Charleston*, 1799
Kent, James. Dissertations by. *Scarce.* *N. Y.*, 1795

LACKAWANNA VALLEY, (Pa.) Contributions to the History of the *Lackawanna Valley.* 12*mo, cl. With portrait and map.* By H. Hollister, M. D. *New York*, 1857

1165 LAHONTAN, BARON. NEW VOYAGES TO NORTH AMERICA. Containing An Account of the several Nations of that vast Continent; and the various Adventures between the French and the Iroquese Confederates of England, from 1683 to 1694. A Geographical description of Canada. Also a Dialogue between the Author and a General of the Savages. To which is added a Dictionary of the Algonkine Language, which is generally spoke in North America. Illustrated with twenty-three Mapps and Cutts. Written in French by the Baron Lahontan. Done into English. In two volumes. A great part of which never Printed in the Original. 2*vols.*, 8*vo, cf., fine copy. Scarce.* *London*, 1703

1166 LAKE GEORGE and Lake Champlain, from their first discovery to 1759. Replete with incidents of the early French and Indian Wars, and Revolutionary History. By B. C. Butler. 12*mo, cl., maps.* *Albany*, 1868

1167 LAMB, GEN. JOHN. MEMOIR OF THE LIFE AND TIMES OF. An Officer of the Revolution who Commanded the Post at West Point at the time of Arnold's Defection, and his Correspondence with Washington, Clinton, Patrick Henry and other distinguished Men of his Time. By Isaac Q. Leake. 8*vo, cloth; fine copy.* *Albany: Joel Munsell*, 1850

1168 LANCASTER, (Mass.) TOPOGRAPHICAL AND HISTORICAL SKETCHES OF, furnished for the Worcester Magazine and Historical Journal. By Joseph Willard. 8*vo Pamphlet, uncut,* 90 *pages, beautiful copy; very scarce.* *Worcester*, 1826

1169 LANCASTER, (Mass.) An Oration delivered Feb. 21, 1826, in Commemoration of the one hundred and fiftieth Anniv. of the Destruction of that Town by the Indians. By Isaac Goodwin. 8*vo,* 15 *pages, uncut, very rare in any condition, fine copy.* *Worcester*, 1826

1170 LANCASTER, Mass. An Address in Commemoration of the Two Hundreth Anniversary of the Incorporation of Lancaster, with an Appendix. By Joseph Willard. 8*vo pamph.*, 270 *p. Fine copy, very scarce.* *Boston*, 1853

1171 LANDIS, JOHN. The Messiah: A Poem of the Birth, Mission, Sufferings, Resurrection, Ascension, and Second Advent of Our Lord Jesus Christ; with Original Hymns. 18*mo, bds.* *Chambersburg, Pa.*, 1838

1172 LANMAN, CHARLES. Essays for Summer Hours. 8*vo, cl.* *Boston*, 1842

1173 ——— Letters from the Alleghany Mountains. 12*mo, cl.* *New York*, 1849

1174 LANMAN, CHARLES. Adventures in the Wilds of the United States and British American Provinces. Illustrated by the Author, and Oscar Bessau. With an Appendix by Lieut. Campbell Hardy. 2 *vols.*, 8*vo, cl.* *Philadelphia, Pa.*, 1856

1175 LATHROP, JOSEPH. Century Sermon, delivered in West Springfield on the 1st day of the Nineteenth Century. 8*vo pamph.* *Scarce.* *Springfield*, 1801

1176 LAWSON, J. ONTWA. The Son of the Forest. A Poem. 12*mo, bds., uncut.* *New York*, 1821

1177 LAW, JOHN, Memoir of. The Mississippi Bubble. To which are added--Authentic Accounts of the Darien Expedition, and the South Sea Scheme. Translated and Edited by Frank S. Fiske. 8*vo, sheets, stitched.* *New York*, 1844

1178 LEAVITT, Rev. W. S. Sermon on the Anniversary of the Landing of the Pilgrims. Preached in the Eliot Church, Newton, Ms., December 22, 1850. 8*vo, paper.* *Boston*, 1851

1179 LEBANON, N. H. JULY FOURTH, 1761: An Historical Discourse in Commemoration of the One Hundreth Anniversary of the Charter of. By Rev. D. H. Allen. 8*vo, cl.* *Boston*, 1862

1180 LEDYARD, JOHN, Memoirs of the Life and Travels of. From his Journals and Correspondence. By Jared Sparks. 8*vo, bds. uncut.* *Scarce.* *London*, 1828

1181 LEE, MAJ.-GEN. CHARLES, "Mr. Lee's Plan, March 29, 1777," Treason of, Second in command in the American Army of the Revolution. By Geo. H. Moore. 8*vo, cl., uncut.* *With port.* *New York*, 1860

1182 LEE, CHAS., MAJ.-GENERAL, Second in Command to General Washington, the Life and Memoirs of, during the American Revolution. To which are added, his Political and Military Essays. Also, Letters to and from many Distinguished Characters, both in Europe and America. 12*mo, bds., uncut.* *New York*, 1813

1183 LEE, HENRY. MEMOIRS OF THE WAR IN THE SOUTHERN DEPARTMENT OF THE UNITED STATES. A new edition, with corrections left by the Author, and with Notes and Additions by H. Lee, the Author of the Campaign of '81. 8*vo, bds., uncut.* *Very scarce, fine copy.* *Washington: Printed by Peter Force*, 1827.

1184 LEE, NELSON. Three Years among the Camanches, the Narrative of the Texan Ranger, containing a Detailed Account of his Captivity among the Indians, his Singular Escape through the instrumentality of his Watch, and fully Illustrating Indian Life as it is. 12*mo, paper uncut.* *With portrait.* *Albany*, 1859

1185 LEES, THOMAS J. The Musing of Carol: Containing an Essay on

Liberty. The Desperado : A Tale of the Ocean, and other Original Poems. 12*mo, half mor.* *Wheeling, Va.*, 1831

1186 LEGGET, WILLIAM. Leisure Hours at Sea. Being a few Miscellaneous Poems. By a Midshipman of the United States Navy. 24*mo, half mor., very scarce.* *New York*, 1825

1187 LEOMINSTER, Mass., History of, or, the Northern Half of the Lancaster New or Additional Grant, from June 26, 1701, the date of the Deed from George Tahanto, Indian Sagamore, to July 4, 1852. By David Wilder. 8*vo, cl.* *Fitchburg*, 1853

1188 LESLIE, CHAS. A Short and Easie Method with the Deists, Etc. In a Letter to a Friend. The eighth edition. *Full cr. crim. lev. mor., gilt. By R. M. Smith.* *London*, 1723

1189 LEVERETT, SIR JOHN, Memoir, Biographical and Genealogical of, of Hon. John Leverett, and of the Family generally. 8*vo, cl., Portrait.* *Boston*, 1856

1190 Levin, Lewis C. Intemperance the Prelude to Gambling and Suicide, as Illustrated in the Life of Rev. C. C. Colton, Author of "Lacon." 8*vo pamph.*, 21 *p. Scarce.* *Phila.*, 1845

"Poor Colton. In Intellect, a God!
In Frailty, less than man!"

1191 Lewis, D. W. Oration on the Death of Mr. Eli Kelsey. A Senior in Yale College. 8*vo pamph.* *New Haven*, 1788

1192 Lewis, R. B. Light and Truth ; Collected from the Bible and Ancient and Modern History, containing the Universal History of the Colored and the Indian Race, from the Creation of the World to the present time. 12*mo, cl.* *Boston*, 1844

1193 LIBRARY COMPANY of Philadelphia. Charter, Laws and Catalogue of the books of, with a short account of the Library prefixed. 8*vo, paper, uncut.* *Phila.*, 1770

1194 LIGHTON, Rev. WILLIAM B. Narrative of the Life and Sufferings of, containing an Interesting and Faithful Account of his early Life, and enlistment into the British Army ; his experience while in the Service, and escape from his Regiment ; Capture, Imprisonment, Trial, and Condemnation to Death ; his subsequent sufferings, and final escape from Captivity and settlement in the United States. Written by himself. New and revised Edition, embellished with ten steel engravings. 12*mo cl.. very scarce.* *Boston*, 1843

1195 LINCOLN, HON. ABRAHAM, and Hon. Stephen A. Douglas, Political Debates in the Celebrated Campaign of 1858, in Illinois, including the preceding speeches of each at Chicago, Springfield, etc. Also, the two great Speeches of Mr. Lincoln in Ohio, in 1859. 8*vo, cl.* *Columbus*, 1860

1196 LINCOLN, ABRAHAM. History of the Administration of, including his Speeches, Letters, Addresses, Proclamations and Messages. With a preliminary sketch of his Life. By Henry J. Raymond. 12*mo cl. ; with portrait.* *New York*, 1864

1197 LINCOLN, ABRAHAM. His Life and Public Services. By Mrs. P. A. Hanaford. 12*mo, cl., with portrait and plates.* *Boston*, 1865

1198 LINCOLN, ABRAHAM. Political Tributes to the Memory of. 8*vo, cl,, portrait, rough edges.* *Phila.*, 1865

1199 LINCOLN, ABRAHAM. Our Martyr President, Voices from the Pulpit of New York and Brooklyn. Oration by Bancroft, and Oration at the Burial by Bishop Simpson. *8vo, half dk. blue, cr. lev. mor., gilt top, edges uncut; bound by R. M. Smith.* *New York*, 1865

1200 LINCOLN MEMORIAL. A Record of the Life, Assassination and Obsequies of the Martyred President. By John Gilmary Shea. *8vo, cl., with portrait.* *New York, Bunce & Huntington*, 1865

1201 LINCOLN, ABRAHAM. A Memorial of. By the City of Boston. *l. 8vo, cl.* *Boston*, 1865

1202 LINCOLN, ABRAHAM. A Tribute of Respect, by the Citizens of Troy to the Memory of. *4to, large paper, uncut; portrait of Lincoln.* *Albany, J. Munsell*, 1865

1203 LINCOLN, ABRAHAM. A Tribute of Respect by the Citizens of Troy to the Memory of. *Small paper 8vo, uncut.* *Troy*, 1865

1204 LINCOLNIANA. William V. Spencer. Only 250 copies printed. *4to, cl., rough edges.* *Boston*, 1865

1205 LINCOLN, ABRAHAM. Obsequies of, in the City of New York, under the Auspices of the Common Council. By David T. Valentine. *Roy. 8vo, cl.; portrait, frontispiece and plates.* *New York, E. Jones & Co.*, 1866

1206 Lindsay, William. View of America, comprehending a general description of the extent, limits, original inhabitants, etc., to which is prefixed a Narrative of a voyage, etc. *12mo, paper.* *Hawick*, 1824

1207 LINIGAN, GEN'L. An Address, occasioned by the Death of, who was murdered by the Mob at Baltimore. Delivered at Georgetown, Sept, 1, 1812. By Geo. Washington Parke Custis. *8vo, uncut*, 16 *p.; very scarce.* *Boston*, 1812

1208 Leppard, George; Life and Choice Writings of. With portrait. *8vo, cl.* *New York*, 1855

1209 Litchfield, Conn. Centennial Celebration, Aug. 13 and 14, 1851. Address by Samuel Church. Poem by John Pierpont. Discourse by Horace Bushnell. Letters, Speeches, Poems, &c. *8vo pamphlet;* 212 *p.; frontis. Presentation Copy and Autograph of John Pierpont.* *Hartford*, 1851

1210 LIVINGSTON, EDWARD; Life of. By Charles Havens Hunt. With an introduction by George Bancroft. Portraits on India paper of Livingston and General Jackson. *Imp. 8vo, cl., uncut.* *N. Y.: D. Appleton & Company*, 1864

Large paper, only 100 copies printed.

1211 Loguen, Rev. J. W. A Narrative of Real Life as a Slave and as a Freeman. *8vo, cl., portrait.* *N. Y.*, 1859

1212 Lomax, Judith. The Notes of an American Lyre. *12mo, bds.* *Richmond*, 1813

1213 London Missionary Soc.; An Account of. To which is added the State of Religion at Sierra Leone, Africa. With an Evangelical Hymn, composed in the Bengal Language. 1788. By Ram Ram Boshoo. *8vo*, 16 *p., scarce.* *Phila.*, 1796

1214 LONDONDERRY, N. H. A CENTURY SERMON delivered in the East Parish Meeting House, Londonderry, New Hampshire, April 22, 1819, in Commemoration of the First Settlement of the Town—containing a Sketch of the History of the Town from its earliest settlement. By Edward L. Parker. *8vo pamphlet, uncut,* 44 *pages, scarce, fine copy.* *Concord, N. H.,* 1819

1215 LONDONDERRY, N. H.; HISTORY OF. Comprising the Towns of Derry and Londonderry. By Rev. Edward L. Parker. With a Memoir of the Author. *8vo, cl. Port. of E. L. Parker, and engravings; now scarce; good copy.* *Boston,* 1851

1216 LONG, J; VOYAGES AND TRAVELS OF, an Indian Interpreter and Trader, describing the Manners and Customs of the North American Indians; with an account of the Posts situated on the River St. Laurence, Lake Ontario, etc.; to which is added, a Vocabulary of the Chippeway Language, Names of Furs and Skins, in English and French. A List of Words in the Iroquois, Mohegan, Shawanee, and Esquimaux Tongues, and a Table, showing the Analogy between the Algonquin and Chippeway Languages. *4to, uncut, half mor. With map; very fine copy.* *London,* 1791

1217 LORETTE. The History of Louise, daughter of a Canadian Nun, exhibiting the interior of female convents. *2d Ed. 16mo, bds. Frontispiece and engraved title.* *New York,* 1834

1218 LOSSING, BENSON J. PICTORIAL FIELD BOOK OF THE REVOLUTION; or illustrations by pen and pencil, of the History, Scenery, Biography, Relics, and Traditions of the War for Independence; with six hundred engravings on wood, by Lossing and Barritt, chiefly from original sketches by the author. In thirty numbers as originally issued. *Roy. 8vo, paper, uncut.* *N. Y.,* 1850

1219 ——— ——— The same Edition in Two Volumes. *Royal 8vo, cloth.*

1220 LOSKIEL, GEORGE HENRY. HISTORY OF THE MISSION of the United Brethren among the Indians in North America. In Three Parts. *8vo half mor., gilt top, rough edges, fine copy.* *London,* 1794

1221 LOTHROP, SAMUEL H. Proceedings of an Ecclesiastical Council in the Case of the Hollis-street Meeting-House and Rev. John Pierpont. *8vo, bds.* *Boston,* 1841

1222 LOUISIANA, HISTORICAL COLLECTIONS OF. Embracing Translations of many Rare and Valuable Documents, relating to the Natural, Civil and Political History of that State. Compiled with Historical and Biographical Notes and an Introduction. Part III. By B. F. French. *8vo, sheets, folded.* *New York,* 1851

1223 LOUISIANA, Constitutions of—1812, 1845 and 1852. Also, the Constitution of the United States, with Amendments. Articles of Confederation and the Declaration of Independence *Confed. Pamphlet. 8vo, paper.* *New Orleans,* 1861

1224 LOUISVILLE, SKETCHES OF—and its Environs; including, among a great variety of miscellaneous matter, a Florula Louisvillensis, or, a Catalogue of nearly 400 Genera and 600 Species of Plants, that Grow in the Vicinity of the Town, etc. By H. McMurtrie. To which is added an Appendix, containing an Account of the Earthquake of Dec. 16, 1811, etc. *First edition. 8vo, boards, uncut; with maps of the Falls of Ohio; beautiful copy; very scarce.* *Louisville*, 1819

1225 LOVEWELL, Capt. JOHN. Historical Memoirs of the Late Fight at Piggwacket; with a Sermon, occasioned by the Fall of the Brave Capt. John Lovewell and several of his Valiant Company, in the late Heroic Action there. Pronounced at Bradford, May 16, 1725. By Thomas Symmes, V. D. M. Reprinted by Frederick Kidder. *Small paper*, 200 *copies printed.* *Boston*, 1865

1226 LOWELL, Mass. As it Was, and as it Is. By Henry A. Miles. 12*mo, cl.; map and plate.* *Lowell*, 1845

1227 LOWELL, Mass. Hand-Book for the Visitor. *Half mor.*, 12*mo*, 46 *p.* *Lowell*, 1848

1228 Lowell, Mass. A Hand-Book of Business in; with a History of the City. By Charles Cowley. 8*vo pamphlet;* 166 *p.; scarce.* *Lowell*, 1856

1229 LOWELL, Mass. Introduction of the Power Loom and Origin of Lowell. By Nathan Appleton. 8*vo pamphlet;* 36 *p., tinted paper copy.* *Lowell*, 1858

1230 LOWELL, Mass. Memories of the Indians and Pioneers of the Region of Lowell. By Chas. Cowley. 8*vo pamphlet;* 24 *pages; double column; scarce.* *Lowell*, 1862

1231 LOWELL, Mass.; History of. By Charles Cowley. 12*mo, cl. With plates.* *Boston*, 1868

1232 Lowell, James Russell. Poems. Second Series. 12*mo, cl., uncut.* *Cambridge, etc.*, 1848

1233 LOWNDES, WILLIAM THOMAS. The Bibliographer's Manual of English Literature, containing an account of rare, curious and useful books, published in, or relating to Great Britain and Ireland, from the invention of printing; with bibliographical and critical notices, collations of the rarer articles, and the prices at which they have been sold in the present century. In ten volumes. 8*vo, cl., rough edges.* *London*, 1857

1234 LYNCHBURG, Va. Sketches and Recollections of. By the Oldest Inhabitant. 12*mo, cl.* *Richmond*, 1858

1235 LYNN, Mass. History of. By Alonzo Lewis. 8*vo, sheep,* 1*st ed., very scarce.* *Boston*, 1829

1236 LYNN, Mass. The History of, including Nahant. By Alonzo Lewis. 8*vo, cl., plates,;* 2*nd ed., scarce.* *Boston*, 1844

Presentation Copy from the Author to Rev. Jos. B. Felt, with Autograph of Alonzo Lewis.

1237 LYNN, Mass. History of, including Lynnfield, Saugus, Swampscot and Nahant. By Alonzo Lewis and James R. Newhall. 8*vo, half mor., gilt top, uncut, very scarce, beautiful copy, engravings.* *Boston*, 1865

1238 LUDEWIG, HERMANN E. The Literature of American Local History. A Bibliographical Essay. 8*vo, paper, beautiful copy; quite scarce.* *N. Y.*, 1846

1239 LUDEWIG, HERMANN E. THE LITERATURE OF AMERICAN ABORIGINAL LANGUAGES. With additions and corrections, by Prof. Wm. W. Turner. Ed. by Nicolas Trubner. *Rub. title*, 8*vo*, *cl.*, *rough edges.* *London, Eng.*, 1858

PAMPHLETS.—Lincoln Eulogies, Sermons, Addresses, etc.

1240 *Very fine lot.* [*One hundred and Fifty-seven.*]

Assassination and History of the Conspiracy. *Cin.*, 1865
Assassination and History of the Conspiracy. German. *Cin.*, 1865
Abbott, A. A. Assas. and Death. *N. Y.*, 1865
Abbott, A. A. Assas. of A. Lincoln. *Phila.*, 1865
Abraham, Africanus I. *N. Y.*, 1864
Allen, Ethan. Disc., June 1, 1865. *Balto.*, 1865
Athenæum Club. In Memoriam. *N. Y.*, 1865
Bird, M. B. Poem. *Kingston, Jamaica*, 1866
Briggs, G. W. Eulogy, June, 1, 1865. *Salem, Mass.* 1865
Birch, E. P. Devil's Visit to Old Abe. *La Grange, Ga.*, 1865
Butler, C. M. Address, April 19, 1865. *Phila.*, 1865
Blackburn, Wm. M. Sermon, April 16, 1865. *Trenton*, 1865
Brooks, Phillips. Sermon, April 23, 1865. *Phila.*, 1865
Boston, City Council of. April, 17, 1865. *Boston*, 1865
Bartlett, D. W. Life of. *N. Y.*, 1860
Booth, Robert Russell. Sermon, April 23, 1865. *N. Y.*, 1865
Buffalo. In Memoriam. *Buffalo, N. Y.* 1865
Bliss, T. E. Disc., April 23, 1865. *Memphis, Tenn.* 1865
Babcock, Samuel D. Disc., April 19, 1865. *Dedham*, 1865
Benjamin, S. G. W. Ode. *Boston*, 1865
Badger, Henry C. Disc., April 23, 1865. *Boston*, 1865
Butler, J. G. Sermon. *Washington, D. C.*, 1865
Boardman, H. A. Sermon. *Phila.*, 1865
Bancroft, George. Address, Feb. 12, 1866 *L. paper.* *Wash.*, 1866
Boyd, Andrew. A Poem, with an illustration from the London Punch. [Re-published.] Seventy-five copies printed, No. 21. *Cl.* *By Joel Munsell.* *Albany, N. Y.*, 1868
Chamberlain, N. H. Sermon, Apr. 19, 1865. *N. Y.*, 1865
Colfax, Hon. Schuyler. Address, Apr. 24, 1865. *Phila.*, 1865
Crane, C. B. Sermon, April 16, 1865. *Hartford*, 1865
Coit, T. W. Disc., June 1, 1865. *Troy*, 1865
Crozier, H. P. Disc., April 19, 1865. *N. Y.*, 1866
Crocker, S. L. Eulogy, June 1, 1865. *Boston*, 1865
Dyer, D. Disc., April 19, 1865. *Albany*, 1865
Daggett, O. E. Sermon, Apr. 16, 1865. *Canandaigua*, 1865
Dunning, H. Address, Apr. 19, 1865, *Balto.*, 1865
Duane, B. B. Sermon, Apr. 19, 1865. *Providence*, 1865
Dix, Morgan. Sermon, April 19, 1865. *Cambridge*, 1865
Deming, H. C. Eulogy, In Memoriam, *Hartford*, 1865
Demund, I. S. Sermon, May, 1865. *N. Y.*, 1865

Dunning, H. Disc., May 7, 1865. *Balto.*, 1865
Davidson, J. Address, Apr. 19, 1865. *N. Y.*, 1865
Darling, H. Discourse. *Albany*, 1865
Davidson, B. Disc., April 19, 1865. 2nd ed. *Huntington, L. I.*, 1865
Everett, C. C. Eulogy, June 1, 1865. *Bangor*, 1865
El'Rey, J. H. Mac. Two disc., Wooster, Ohio, 1865. *Wooster, O.*, 1865
Eddy, R. Three Sermons, April 16–17, June 1. *Phila.*, 1865
Farquhar, J. Sermon. *Lancaster*, 1865
Fowler, H. Disc., Apr. 28, 1865. *N. Y.*, 1865
Fowler, John. Address, April 20, 1865. *N. Y.*, 1865
Guthrie, W. E. Oration. *Phila.*, 1865
Ginhorn, David. Eulogy, April 19, 1865. *Phila.*, 1865
Gaddis, M. P. Sermon, April 16, 1865. *Cin.*, 1865
Gurley, P. D. Sermon, June 1, 1865. *Wash.*, 1865
Garrison, J. F. Address, April 19, 1865. *Camden, N. J.*, 1865
Glover, L. M. Discourse, April 23, 1865. *Jacksonville*, 1865
Gordon, W. R. Sermon, May 7, 1865. *N. Y.*, 1865
Hayden, C. A., Mrs. Poem. *Boston*, 1865
Hall, C. H. Disc., April 19, 1865. *Wash.*, 1865
Hopkins, T. M. Disc., April 19, 1865. *Bloomington, Ind.*, 1865
Hammond, C. Sermon, June 1, 1865. *Springfield*, 1865
Haven, Gilbert. Disc., April 23, 1865. *Boston*, 1865
Hornblower, W. H. Sermon, April 16, 1865. *Paterson, N. J.* 1865
Hodge, Dr. Essay, from the Princeton Review, July, 1865
Hall, Gordon. Sermon, April 19, 1865. *Northampton*, 1865
Hall, Newman. Sermon, May 14, 1865. *Boston*, 1865
Johnson, H. Disc., April 28, 1865. *Pittsburgh*, 1865
Jeffery, R. Sermon, June 1, 1865. *Phila.*, 1865
Lowe, C. Sermon, April 23, 1865. *Boston*, 1865
Lincoln, Abraham. Life of. *Phila.*, 1864
Lincoln Cathecism. *N. Y.*, 1864
Lincoln, A. Life of, and McLellan. *N. Y.*
——— Life of. *N. Y.*
——— Life, Speeches and Public Services of, *N. Y.*, 1860
——— Address of. *N. Y.*, 1860
——— In Memoriam. Paste-board. *N. Y.*, 1865
——— Sarcophagus raised. Card. *N. Y.*, 1865
——— President's Hymn. *N. Y.*, 1865
——— Broadside Caricature. *N. Y.*, 1865
Mayo, A. D. Two disc., Apr. 16–19, 1865. *Cin.*, 1865
Myers, L. Address, June 15, 1865. *Phila.*, 1865
Morgan, W. F. Sermon, In Memoriam. *N. Y.*, 1865
M'Cauley, J. A. Sermon, June 1, 1865. *Balto.*, 1865
M'Clintock, J. Disc., April 19, 1865. *N. Y.*, 1865
M'Donald, Disc., June 1, 1865. *N. Y.*, 1865
Murray, W. H. Address. *N. Y.*, 1865
Moore, R. Addresses. *Trenton*, 1867
Nason, Elias. Eulogy. *Boston*, 1865
Nelson, H. A. Two disc., May 7, 1865. *Springfield, Ill.*, 1865

Niles H. E. Address. *York, Pa.*, 1865
Niccolls, S. J. Disc., Apr. 23, 1865. *St. Louis*, 1865
Noble, M. Sermon. *Newport*, 1865
Newell, R. H. Poem. *New York*, 1865
Normandie, de, James. Sermon, Apr. 16, 1865. *Portsmouth, N. H.*
New York Legislature, April 15, 1865. *Albany*, 1865
New York Times for April 15–16–19–21–22–24, 1865.
New York Commercial Advertiser for April 15, 1865.
Pulpit and Rostrum. Nos. 34, 35. *New York*, 1865
Post, Jacob. Disc., Apr. 23, 1865. *Oswego*, 1865
Paddock, W. F. Disc. *Phil.*, 1865
Potter, W. J. Four Sermons. *New Bedford*, 1865
Putnam, G. Address, Apr. 19, 1865. *Roxbury*, 1865
Preacher. The National. *New York*, 1865
Providence, City Council of. *Providence*, 1865
Robinson, C. S., Apr. 16, 1865. Sermon. *N. Y.*, 1865
Rankin, J. E. Disc., April 19, 1865. *Boston*, 1865
Robinson. T. H. Sermon, June 1, 1865. *Harrisburg*, 1865
Rice, N. L. Sermon, April 19, 1865. *New York*, 1865
Stoddard, R. H. Ode. *New York*, 1865
Sumner. C. Eulogy, June 1, 1865. *Boston*, 1865
Sears, H. Address. *Cin.*, 1865
Simpson, M. Address. *New York*, 1865
Stone, Andrew. Disc., Apr. 14, 1865. 300 copies printed. 1865
Steele, R. H. Sermon, June 1, 1865. *Newburn, N, J.*, 1865
Sample, R. F. Sermon, Apr. 30, 1865. *Phil.*, 1865
Southgate, Horatio. Sermon, Apr. 23, 1865. *New York*, 1865
Smith, Henry. Sermon. *Buffalo*, 1865
Speed, James. Opinion. *Washington*, 1865
Symmes, J. G. Address. *Cranbury, [N. J.,]* 1865
Swain Leonard. Sermon. *Providence*, 1865
Storrs, R. S. Oration. *Brooklyn*, 1865
Seiss, J. A. Sermon. *Phil.*, 1865
Sedgwick. Eulogy. *Syracuse*, 1865
Tapley, R. P. Eulogy, April 19, 1865. *Biddeford*, 1865
Thompson, J. C. Disc., In Memoriam. *Phil.*, 1865
Thomas, A. G. Disc., Apr. 19, 1865. *Phil.*, 1865
Trial of Abraham Lincoln. *New York*, 1863
Thayer, W. M. Character of. *Boston*, 1864
Townsend, G. A. Real Life of. *New York*, 1867
Tucker, J. T. Disc., June 1, 1865. *Holliston*, 1865
Thompson, J. P. Life of. *New York*, 1865
Thrall, S. C. Sermon. *New York*, 1865
Walden T. Sermon. *Phil.*, 1865
Webster, J. C. The Foe Unmasked. *New York*, 1865
Wilson, W. T. Sermon, Apr. 19, 1865. *Albany*, 1865
Wells, T. W. Sermon. *Jersey City*, 1865
Woodbury, A. Disc. June 1, 1865. *Providence*, 1865
——— Sermon, Apr. 16, 1865. *Providence*, 1865
White, E. Sermon, June 1, 1865. *New York*, 1865

Wortman, D. Disc. Apr. 16, 1865. *Albany*, 1865
Wilcox, G. B. Disc., In Memoriam. *New London*, 1865
Yard, R. B. Disc., June 1, 1865. *Newark, N. J.*, 1865
Vincent, M. R. Sermon, Apr. 23, 1865. *Troy, N. Y.*, 1865
Philadelphia. Proceedings of the Union League. *Phil.*, 1865
Washington, D. C. Proc. of meeting, Apr. 17. *Washington*, 1865
Bunker Hill Monument Assoc. Proc. of, June 17, 1865.
God Bless Abraham Lincoln. (Disc.,) 1863. *N. Y.*
Poore, Ben Perley. The Conspiracy Trial. Part I. *Boston*, 1865
Old Abe, The Miller ; or, the Campaign of Richmond.
Lincoln and Grant. *San Francisco*, 1864
Trial of the Assassins and Conspirators. *Phil.*, 1865
Lincoln Abraham. In History. "Atlantic Monthly," June, 1865.
——— From "Hours at Home," June 1865.
In Memoriam. Personal recollections of. "Hours at Home," June, 1865.
British Sympathy in our Affliction. "Hours at Home," July, 1865.
" A Nation on its Knees," by E. H. Gillett, D. D.
Storrs, R. S. Oration, June 1, 1865, before War Fund Committee. 100 copies. No. 60.
Celebration by the Col. People's Educa. Monument Assoc. in Memory of Abraham Lincoln, Wash., July 4, 1865.
Loyal Publication Society, No. 85. " Abraham Lincoln, His Life and its Lessons." Sermon deliv. by Joseph P. Thompson, Apr. 30, 1865. *N. Y.*

PAMPHLETS.

1241 Miscellaneous. [*Fourteen.*]
Lord, John C. Human Government and Laws. Discourse. *Buffalo*, 1852
——— Discourse on decease of Calhoun, Clay and Webster. *Buffalo*, 1852
——— Discourse on death of Rev. Norris Bull. *Buffalo*, 1852
——— Discourse on death of Hon. Samuel Wilkeson. *Buffalo*, 1848
——— Discourse on Presbyterianism. *Buffalo*, 1854
——— Sermon on Duties Men owe to God and Govt. *Buffalo*, 1851
Luther, Martin. Third Centennial Jubilee of Reformation. *N. Y.*, 1817
Lafayette, Gen. Principal Events in Life of. *Boston*, 1825
——— Impeachment of, by Wm. Cobbett. *Phila.*, 1793
——— Biography of. *Wilmington*, 1824
——— Principal Events in Life of. *Portland*, 1825
Lafayette College. Inaug. Charge by J. M. Porter, and Inaug. Ad. by Rev. George Junkin. *Easton, Pa.*, 1834

Lafayette College Literary Soc. Address by Joseph R. Ingersoll. *Phila.*, 1833

Letter from a Churchman, containing Strictures on a pamphlet signed J. R. O. *New Haven*, 1808

1242 Miscellaneous. [*Fourteen.*]

Lancaster, Joseph. Chief Events in Life of. *New Haven*, 1833

Logier, Mr. Strictures on Pamphlets of. *Dublin*, 1818

Lodi, Battle. Sketch of Gen. Bonaparte's Cam. in Italy. *N. Y.*, 1804

Linn, Wm. Discourse on National Sins by. *Scarce.* *N. Y.*, 1798

Lowe, Rev. Peter. Discourse at Funeral of, by Rev. I. P. Vanpelt. *N. Y.*, 1818

L. L., Mrs. The Proselyte. *N. Y.*, 1829

Lyman, Theodore, Jr. Oration, July 4, 1820. *Boston*, 1820

Leavitt, Joshua. Address at Funeral of Rev. John R. M'Dowall. *N. Y.*, 1837

Lancey, Wm. H. De. Sermon, June 23, 1833. *Phila.*, 1833

Louisiana. Report to Gen. Assembly of, by Edward Livingston. *N. Orleans*, 1822

Lowell, Charles. Sermon at Dedi. of So. Congre. Ch. in Natick. *Boston*, 1829

Lewis, Isaac. Sermon on Divine Mission of Jesus Christ. *N. Haven*, 1796

Lathrop, Joseph. Funeral Sermon of Mrs. Mary Gay. *Suffield*, 1797

Lamson, Alvan. Sermon at Ordi. of Charles C. Sewall. *Dedham*, 1827

1243 Miscellaneous. [*Eleven.*]

Lowell, Charles. Sermon at Ordi. of Robert F. Wallcut. *Boston*, 1830

Layman, A. Demonstration of Divinity of the Scriptures. (No. I.) *Boston*, 1811

Lysander. Annals of Corporation rel. to late Contested Elections. *N. Y.*, 1802

Leonidas. Reply to Lucius Junius Brutus. *N. Y.*, 1801

Leaming, Jeremiah. Dissertations on Various Subjects. *Litchfield*, 1798

——— The Evidences for Truth of Christianity. *N. Haven*, 1785

Letter to Wm. Roscoe. Con. Strictures on late Publication. *N. Y.*, 1808

Lee, Elias. Dissolution of Earthly Monarchies. Sermon by. *Danbury*, 1794

Laws relating to Landlord and Tenant. *N. Y.*

L'Ouverture, Toussaint. Life and Military Achievements of. 2nd Ed. 1805

Landaff. Letter to John, Lord Bishop of. By Wm. Livingston. *Very scarce.* *N. Y.* 1768

1244 Miscellaneous. [*Eleven.*]

Laune, Thomas De. Plea for Non-Conformists. *Scarce.* *London*, 1733

Langdon, Timothy. Sermon on Pleasure and Advan. of Church Music. *Curious.* *Danbury*, 1797

Luzerne Assoc. Report of Committee. *Wilkesbarre*, 1813

Lyman, Wm. Election Sermon. *Hartford*, 1806

Lockwood, James. Sermon at Ord. of Eleazer May. *N. Haven*, 1756

Livingston, John H. Funeral Disc. at Inter. of, by John De Witt. *Scarce.* *New Brunswick*, 1825

——— Address to Ref. German Churches. *New Brunswick*, 1819

Lowell, John. Oration, July 4, 1799. *Boston*, 1799

Lathrop, John. Sermon on National Fast. *Boston*, 1799

Lamson, Alvan. Sermon on Adaption of Christianity. *Dedham*, 1825

Love. Philosophy and Poetry of. *New York*, 1848

1245 Miscellaneous. [*Ten.*]

The Patent Laws of the United States, together with information to persons having business to transact at the Patent Office. *N. Y.*, 1845

U. S. Mail Steam Line. Proceedings in the Cir. Ct. of the U. S. in Equity, George Law, Marshall O. Roberts, etc. *N. Y.*, 1849

The Circuit Court of the U. S. in Equity, Albert G. Sloo, Complainant. George Law, Marshall O. Roberts and others, Defendants. *N. Y.*, 1849

Paige, Alonzo C. Address to the Graduating Class of the State and Nat. Law School. *Albany*, 1852

Louisville Lit. Assoc. Address on the Amelioration of the Social State. By Alex. Campbell. *Scarce.* *Louisville*, 1839

London Corresponding Soc. Address to the Nation. By Maurice Margarot and Thos. Hardy, July 8, 1793.

Litchfield Co. (Conn.) Centen. Celeb. at, 13–14 Aug., 1851. *Hartford*, 1851

Lowell, Mass., Introduction of the Power Loom, and Origin of. By N. Appleton. *Lowell, Mass.*, 1858

Lafitte ; or, The Greek Slave. *Selma, Ala.*, 1864

Legal Reform. Act concerning Costs and Fees in Courts of Law. *N. Y.*, 1840

1246 Miscellaneous. [*Eleven.*]

Locke, John. Thoughts concerning Education. Vol. I. *N. Y.*, 1869

Livermore, George, Discourse on Death of. By Henry C. Badger. *Cambridge*, 1865

Lamont, George D. Oration by, at City of Lockport. *Lockport*, 1865

Leavitt, T. H. Tracts about Peat, by. *Boston*, 1865

Lawton, Edward. Lectures on Science, Politics, Morals, etc. *St. Louis*, 1862

Langworthy, Isaac P. Farewell Sermon to Winnisimmet Congre. Ch. of Chelsea, Mass. *Boston*, 1858
Lehmann, M. The Elf-King ; or, Wealth and Poverty. *N. Y.*, 1856
Lawrence, The Families of. By Mercy Hale. *Boston*, 1856
Lawrence, Edward A. Inaugural Discourse, by. *Hartford*, 1854
Layman's Argument against Interdiction of Intox. Liquors. *Richmond*, 1853
Liguori, St. Alphonso M. Novena in Honor of the Adorable Heart of Jesus. *N. Y.*, 1851

1247 Miscellaneous. [*Twelve.*]

London. Adventures of Mr. and Mrs. Sandboys. By Henry Mayhew and George Cruikshank. *N. Y.*, 1851
Little, Rev. John, Obedience to Law, Sermon, by. *N. Y.*, 1851
Liebig on Evaporation in Plants, and Origin of Potato Disease. By Wm. Gregory. *Phila.*, 1850
Lester, C. Edwards. Social Life, and Natural Spirit of America. *Great Barrington*, 1849
Levin, L. C. Speech on Pro. Mission to Rome, Mar. 2, 1848.
L'Enclos, Ninon De. The Story of the Celebrated Aspasia of France. *Boston*, 1843
Louisville Literary Brass Band. The King of Angelo, a Tragico Comico ; or, Melo-Dramatico Burlesco, by.
Latrobe, John H. B. Address on Manual Labor School. *Baltimore*, 1840
Ladies' Garland, Vol. III., No. 1, July 20, 1839.
Literature, Greek, Synopsis of Course of Lectures on History of.
Leake, John G. Last Will and Testament of. *N. Y.*, 1837
Lyon Charles H. Lecture in Favor of Classical Studies. *N. Y.*, 1839

1248 Miscellaneous. [*Twelve.*]

Lundy, Rev. F. J. Metra Horatiana. *Burlington, Vt.*, 1838
Lamb, Charles, The Essays of Elia, by. *N. Y.*, 1836
Lillybridge, C. Appeal to the Community of Norfolk. *Norfolk*, 1832
Leland, John. Short Sayings on Times, Men, Measures, etc. *Pittsfield*, 1830
Long Island, Question of a South Ferry to. By A. Freeman. *N. Y.*, 1826
Louverture, Toussaint, History of. Buonaparte in the West Indies. Part III., 3d Ed. *London*, 1803
Lyman, Eliphalet. Two Discourses Preached at Woodstock. *Norwich*, 1794
Lindsey, Theophilus. Resignation Discourse. *London*, 1793
Law, Wm. Address to the Clergy. Account of Life and Character of. *Phila.*, 1786
Lunt, Wm. P. Discourse at Installation of Rev. George Whitney. *Boston*, 1836
——— Discourse at 1st Congre. Ch. Quincy. *Boston*, 1854
——— Discourse on Twentieth Anniv. of his Installation. *Boston*, 1855

1249 Miscellaneous. [*Twelve.*]

Lexington, Proc. of Coroner in Case of Steamer. *N. Y.*, 1840
——— Account of Loss of the. *Providence*, 1840
——— Sermon on Loss of the. By S. K. Lothrop. 3d ed. *Boston*, 1840
Lafayette, Gen. Oration Commem. of. By Wm. B. Sprague. *Albany*, 1834
——— Oration on the Life and Character of. By John Q. Adams. *Washington*, 1835
——— College, Address before the Literary Soc. of. By Joseph R. Ingersoll. *Philadelphia*, 1833
——— ——— Address before the Alumni of. By Edward F. Stewart. *Philadelphia*, 1854
——— ——— Address before the Literary Soc. of. By Daniel Dougherty. *Easton, Pa.*, 1859
Letter to Patriot Senator ———. *London*, 1783
——— on Parliamentary Representation, to John Sinclair. 3d ed. *London*, 1783
——— to Author of an Article entitled, The Liturgy of Prot. Epis. Ch. in America. *N. Y.*, 1843
Letters to Lord Stanley. By Rt. Rev. Bishop Maginn. *Boston*, 1850

1250 Miscellaneous. [*Eleven.*]

Library, Christian. Life of Wm. Cowper, by Thomas Taylor. No. 4. *Y., Y.*, 1835
——— ——— Life of Wm. Cowper, by Thomas Taylor. No. 5. *N. Y.*, 1835
——— ——— Complete Duty of Man, by Rev. Henry Venn. No. 37. *N. Y.*, 1836
——— Theological. Treatise on Consanguinity and Affinity between Christ and His Church, by Jas. Relly. Vol. I., No. 6. *Phila.*, 1843
——— Theological. Opinions and Phraseology of the Jews, by Hosea Ballou 2d. Vol. II., No. 1. *Phila.*, 1844
Luke's, St., Hospital. Appeal of the Managers of. *N. Y.*, 1852
——— ——— Account of. *N. Y.*, 1860
Livingston, Edward. Remarks on Expediency of Abol. the Punish. of Death. *Phila.* 1831
——— John. Portraits of Eminent Americans now Living; with Biographical and Historical Memoirs of their Lives and Actions. Part I., Vol. IV. *N. Y.*, 1854
London. Short History of the Tower of. *London* 1842
——— ——— of the Tower of, by Joseph Wheeler. *London*, 1850

1251 Miscellaneous. [*Eleven.*]

Lathrop, Joseph. Two Sermons on Death of Four Young Women. *Springfield*, 1809
——— John. Sermon at interment of Rev. Joseph Eckley. *Boston*, 1811

Lathrop, John. Sermon at Dedication of New South Meeting-House, Dorchester. *Boston*, 1813

——— Joseph. Sermon at Ordination of Rev. Thaddeus Osgood. *Brookfield*, 1821

Lee, Rt. Rev. Alfred. Sermon at First Commen. of Divinity School, Prot. Epis. Ch. *Phila.*, 1863

Lee, Rt. Rev. Henry W. Primary Charge to Clergy of the Prot. Epis. Ch., Iowa. *Davenport*, 1857

Lee, John. Letter to the President, on the Disputed Frontier. *Cambridge*, 1839

Laplace, M. Le Marquis De. Historical Eulogy, by R. W. Haskins.

Linn, Wm. Character of Simon the Sorcerer. *N. Y.*, 1793

Lind, Jenny. Programme of Concert.

Lafayette, Gen. Oration, by Jas. A. Hillhouse, Aug. 19, 1834.

1252 Law Pamphlets. [*Nine.*]

Wilson, James. Introductory Lecture to a course of Law Lectures. *Dedicated to Mrs. Martha Washington.* *Phila.*, 1791

An Enquiry into the constitutional authority of the Supreme Federal Court over the several States, in their political capacity.: being an answer to Observations upon the Government of the U. S. By James Sullivan. *Charleston*, 1792

Laws and ordinances for the good rule and government of the city of N..Y., passed and enacted in the Mayoralty of Edw. Livingston. *N. Y.*, 1803

Duane, Wm. Sampson against the Philistines, or the Reformation of Lawsuits. *Phila.*, 1805 4

Experience the test of Government, in Eighteen Essays. *Phila.*, 1807

Duane, W. J. The Law of Nations, investigated in a popular manner. Addressed to the Farmers of U. S. *Phila.*, 1809

Hall, John E. The American Law Journal, Vol. V., containing the proceedings of the Government of U. S., in maintaining the Public Right to the Beach of the Mississippi adjacent to N. O., against the intrusion of Edw. Livingston. Also, his reply. *Scarce.* *Baltimore*, 1814

Supreme Court of the U. S. Case on a Bill of Exceptions. Martha Bradstreet suit. *N. Y.*, 1816

Bowring, John. Observations on the restrictive and prohibitory Commercial System, from the manuscript of Jeremy Bentham. *London*, 1821

1253 Law Pamphlets. [*Eleven.*]

Laws of the Commonwealth of Mass., passed by the General Court. *Boston*, Jan. 16, 1812 5

Acts relating to circuit courts in Penn., with the rules established by the Judges of the Supreme Court. *Phila.*, 1826

Laussal, Anthony. An Essay on Equity in Penn. *Phila.*, 1826

Landlord and Tenant Statistics of State of N. Y.

Interest made Equity. Mr. McCulloch. *N. Y.*, 1826

Herttell, Tho's. The Demurrer; or, Proofs of Error in the decision of the Supreme Court of the State of New York, requiring Faith in particular religious doctrines as a legal qualification of witnesses. *N. Y.*, 1828

Leggett, Samuel. An explanation and vindication of, late President of the Franklin Bank in city of N. Y. 1831

Statement of facts in relation to the dismissal of Mrs. Martha Bradstreet's suits from the District Court of the U. S. for the Northern district of N. Y. *Albany*, Aug., 1831

Conkling, Alfred. Opinion of, in the case of Martha Bradstreet vs. Henry Huntington. 1834

In Chancery, N. Y. Life Insurance and Trust Co. Answer and Report. *N. Y.*, 1834

Copies of the original grant of land on the White River, lying in the States of Arkansas and Missouri, in the year 1793, by the Baron De Carondelet, to Capt. Don Joseph Valliere. Also, copies of the power of attorney, by the heirs of Valliere, to Creed Taylor, authorizing him to sell and dispose of the same, and a deed from him, as such, to John Wilson, for an undivided half thereof. *Scarce.* *N. Y.*, 1844

MACHIAS, Me. Memorial of the Centennial Anniversary of the Settlement of. May 20, 1863. *8vo pamph.*, 179 *p.*; *fine copy.* *Machias*, 1863

1255 MACK, DR. EBENEZER. The Cat Fight. A Mock Heroic Poem. Supported with Copious Extracts from Ancient and Modern Classic Authors. *8vo, bds., uncut.* *New York*, 1824

1256 MACKENZIE, SIR ALEXANDER. VOYAGES FROM MONTREAL, on the River St. Laurence, through the Continent of North America, to the Frozen and Pacific Oceans, in the year 1789 and 1793. With a preliminary Account of the Rise, Progress, and present state of the Fur Trade of that Country. With map. *8vo, sheep. Very scarce.* *Phila.*, 1802

1257 MACOMB, ALEXANDER. A Treatise on Martial Law and Courts-Martial, as practised in the United States of America. *8vo, bds., uncut.* *Charleston*, 1809

1258 MALDEN, Mass, An Oration delivered at, on the Two Hundreth Anniversary of the Incorporation of the Town, May 23, 1849. By James D. Green. *8vo pamphlet*, 53 *pages, uncut.* *Boston*, 1850

1259 MAINE, Sketches of the Ecclesiastical History of, from the Earliest Settlement to the Present Time. By Jonathan Greenleaf. *12mo, cf.* *Portsmouth*, 1821

1260 MAINE. FIRST REPORT OF THE GEOLOGY of the State of. *Paper, 8vo.* By Charles T. Jackson. *Augusta*, 1837

1261 MAINE, The Native Poets of. By S. Herbert Lancey. *Large 8vo, cl.* *Bangor*, 1854

1262 MAINE, ANCIENT DOMINIONS OF. Embracing the Earliest Facts, the Recent Discoveries of the Remains of Aboriginal Towns, the Voyages, Settlements, Battle Scenes, and other incidents of History. By Rufus K. Sewall. *Fine copy, cl., 8vo, plates. Scarce.* *Boston*, 1859

1263 MAN, THOMAS, Alias. Picture of a Factory Village, to which are annexed Remarks on Lotteries. *bds., 12mo.* *Providence*, 1833

1264 MANN, HERMAN. Human Prudence; or, The Art by which a Man and a Woman may be Advanced to Fortune, to Permanent Honor and to Real Grandeur. First American Edition. *8vo, sh.* *Dedham*, 1806

1265 Manuel, Pereira; or, The Sovereign Rule of South Carolina. With Views of Southern Laws, Life, and Hospitality. By F. C. Adams, 12*mo, cl., uncut.* *London,* 1852

1266 Mariners' Chronicle. Containing Narratives of the Most Remarkable Disasters at Sea: Such as Shipwrecks, Storms, Fires, Etc. Also, Naval Engagements, Etc. 12*mo, sh., with plates.* *New Haven, Conn.,* 1834

1267 MARION, Gen. FRANCIS, Life of. A Celebrated Partisan Officer in the Revolutionary War against the British and Tories in South Carolina and Georgia. By Brigadier-General P. Horry, and M. L. Weems. 12*mo, sh., with plates.* *Phila.,* 1841

1268 MARION, FRANCIS, the Life of. Illustrated. By Wm. Gilmore Simms. 8*vo, half gr. crushed lev. mor., gilt. Bound by R. W. Smith.* *New York.*

1269 MARLBOROUGH, Mass., History of, from its First Settlement in 1657 to 1861. With a brief Sketch of Northborough. A Genealogy of the Families in Marlborough to 1800, and an Account of Celebration of the Two Hundredth Anniversary of the Incorporation of the Town. By Charles Hudson. 8*vo, cl., portraits.* *Boston,* 1862

1270 MARTHA'S VINEYARD, Mass., Sketches of, and other Reminiscences of Travel at Home, &c. By Samuel A. Devens. 8*vo, cl. Scarce.* *Boston,* 1838

1271 Maryland Toleration; or Sketches of the Early History of Maryland to the year 1650. By Rev. Ethan Allan. 8*vo pamph.,* 64 *pages. Scarce.* *Baltimore,* 1855

1272 MARYLAND, Clergy in, of the Protestant Episcopal Church since the Independence of 1783. By Ethan Allan. 8*vo, cl.* *Balt.,* 1860

1273 MARYLAND, Sketches of the Early History of. By T. W. Griffith. Plate of the State House at Annapolis. 8*vo, unbound. Very rare.* *Baltimore,* 1821

1274 MARYLAND, The History of, from its First Settlement in 1633, to the Restoration in 1660. With a copious Introduction, Notes, and Illustrations. In two volumes. By John L. Bozman. 8*vo, sh. Fine copy.* *Balt.,* 1837

1275 Maryland, Message of the Governor of, Transmitting Reports in Relation to the Intersection of the Boundary Lines of the States of Maryland, Pennsylvania, and Delaware, 8*vo pamph.,* 87 *p. Scarce.* *Washington,* 1850

1276 MARYLAND, History of, from its Settlement in 1634 to the year 1848, with an Account of its first Discovery, and the various Explorations of the Chesapeake Bay, anterior to its Settlement; to which is added a copious appendix. By James McSherry, Esq. 12*mo, cl.* *Balt.,* 1852

1277 MARYLAND, Tragic Scenes in the History of, and the Old French War. By Joseph Banvard. 12*mo, cl. Illustrated.* *Boston,* 1856

1278 MASON. N. H., History of, from the First Grant in 1749 to 1858. By John B. Hill. 8*vo, cl.* *Boston,* 1858

1279 MASSACHUSETTS BAY. Collection of Original Papers Relative to the History of the Colony of. By Thomas Hutchinson. *8vo, hf. mor. Very Scarce. Boston, New England: Printed by Thomas and John Fleet,* 1769.

1280 MASSACHUSETTS BAY. A Collection of Original Papers relative to the History of the Massachusett-Bay. By Thomas Hutchinson. 150 copies S. P. No. 132. Prince Society Publications. 2 *vols., 8vo, paper.* *New York,* 1865

1281 MASSACHUSETTS-BAY, History of the Colony of. From the First Settlement thereof, in 1628, until its Incorporation with the Colony of Plimouth, Province of Main, &c., by the Charter of King William and Queen Mary in 1691. By Mr. Hutchinson. 8*vo, sheep.*
Boston, New England. Printed by Thomas and John Fleet, at the Heart and Crown, in Cornhill. 1764.

1282 MASSACHUSSETS, History of; from the first settlement in 1628 until 1750. By Thomas Hutchinson. 3*rd Ed. With notes and corrections.* 2 *vols.,* 8*vo, sheep.*
Printed at Salem and Boston, by T. C. Cushing, for Thomas and Andrews. 1795

1283 MASSACHUSETTS, The History of—from 1749 to 1774, comprising a detailed narrative of the origin and early stages of the American Revolution. By Thomas Hutchinson, Esq., LL.D., formerly Governor of the Province. Edited from the author's MS., by his Grandson, the Rev. John Hutchinson, M.A. 8*vo, bds., uncut.*
London: John Murray, Albemarle Street. 1828

1284 MASSACHUSETTS BAY, Continuation of the History of the Province of—from the Year 1748, with an Introductory Sketch of Events, from its Original Settlement. By George Richard Minot. 2 *vols., bds., uncut.* *Boston,* 1798

1285 MASSACHUSETTS, The History of. The Colonial, Provincial and Commonwealth. Periods 1492–1820. In three volumes. By J. S. Barry. 8*vo, half Roxburghe, gilt top, rough edges.* *Boston,* 1857

One of three copies, uncut.

1286 MASSACHUSETTS. The History of the Insurrection in the Year 1786, and the Rebellion Consequent thereon. By George Richards Minot. 2*d Ed.* 8*vo, cl., uncut.* *Boston,* 1810

1287 MASSACHUSETTS, A Geographical and Statistical View of. By Rudolphus Dickinson. 8*vo, bds., uncut.* *Greenfield,* 1813

1288 MASSACHUSETTS. Historical Letters on the First Charter. By Abel Cushing. *Full cr. crim. lev. mor., gilt top, uncut. By R. M. Smith.* *Boston,* 1839

1289 MASSACHUSETTS, WESTERN. History of the Counties of Hampden, Hampshire, Franklin and Berkshire. Embracing an outline of general history of the section, an account of its scientific aspects and leading interests, and separate histories of its one hundred towns. By Josiah Gilbert Holland. *In two volumes and three parts. With map and plates.* 12*mo, cl.*
Springfield: Samuel Bowles and Company. 1855

1290 MASSACHUSETTS CURRENCY, An Historical Account of. By Joseph B. Felt. 8*vo, sheets, folded.* *Boston,* 1839

1291 MASSACHUSETTS State Library, Catalogue of. *8vo, cl.* *Boston*, 1858

1292 MASSACHUSETTS, Annual Report of the Adjutant-General of. For the Years, 1862, 1863, 1864, 1865, 1866, 1867, 1868. *Seven Volumes. 8vo, in cl. and paper.* *Boston*, 1863–'69

1293 MASSACHUSETTS, Statistical Information relating to certain Branches of Industry in. For the year ending May 1, 1865. By Oliver Thorner. *8vo, cl.* *Boston*, 1866

1294 MASSACHUSETTS. Third Annual Report of the Board of State Charities, Jan., 1867. *8vo, paper.* *Boston*, 1867

1295 MATHER, INCREASE. THE PROPHET'S DEATH. Lamented and Improved in a SERMON, preached Sept. 1, 1723, to the North Church in Boston, on the Lord's Day, after the Funeral of their Venerable and Aged Pastor, Increase Mather, D.D. And now published at the Desire of Many in the Audience. By Benjamin Colman. *8vo, fine copy; very scarce.* *Boston: Printed by T. Fleet, for Nath. Belknap, at his Shop, near Scarlet's Wharfe.* 1723

1296 MATHER, SAMUEL. AN APOLOGY for the Liberties of the Churches in New England; to which is prefixed, a Discourse concerning Congregational Churches. *8vo, old cf. bdg.* *Boston: Printed for D. Henchman.* 1738

1297 MATHER, SAMUEL. Answer to an insidious Pamphlet, entitled, "Salvation for All Men." *2d Ed.* *Boston*, 1783

1298 MATHEWS, CORNELIUS. The Motley Book. A Series of Tales and Sketches of American Life. With Illustrations by Dick, Gimber and others. Third Edition. *8vo, cl.* *N. Y. and Boston*, 1840

1299 MATHEWS, J. M. Fifty Years in New York; a Semi-Centennial Discourse, preached in the South Dutch Church. *8vo, orig. cov.; 48 p.; fine copy.* *N. Y.*, 1858

1300 MATHEWS, ROBERT. "Matthias" and his Impostures, or the Progress of Fanaticism, as illustrated in the extraordinary case of, and some of his Disciples and Forerunners. By William L. Stone. *12mo, cl., uncut.* *N. Y.*, 1835

1301 MAUMEE VALLEY, Ind.; EARLY HISTORY OF. By H. L. Hosmer. *Paper, 8vo.* *Toledo*, 1858

1302 MAXWELL, WILLIAM; Poems by. *Bds., 12mo.* *Philadelphia*, 1812

1303 MAYER, BRANTZ. Journal of Charles Carroll, of Carrollton, during his Visit to Canada, in 1776; with Memoir and Notes. *8vo pamphlet; 84 p.; the rarest of the Collection of Md. Hist. Soc. Pub.* *Baltimore*, 1845

1304 MAYER, BRANTZ. TAH-GAH-JUTE; or Logan and Cresap, an Historical Essay. *8vo, sm. p., 200 copies.* *Albany*, 1867

1305 MAYER, BRANTZ. TAH-GAH-JUTE; or Logan and Cresap, an Historical Essay. *8vo, orig. cov. L. P.* *Albany, N. Y.*, 1867

1306 MAYER, BRANTZ. The History, Possessions and Prospects of the Maryland Historical Society. Inaugural Discourse, March 7, 1867. *8vo Pamph., uncut, 36 p.; contains complete list of Publications of this Soc. Very important.* *Baltimore*, 1867

1307 M'Call, P. Discourse delivered before the Law Acad. of Phila., Sept. 5, 1838. *8vo, fine copy*, 51 *pages; very scarce.* *Phila.*, 1838

Full of interesting matter, relating to And. Bradford, the First Newspaper Printer, etc., and the early Lawyers, from the first beginnings of the Colony. The Judicial History of Penn, etc.

1308 M'Carty, Wm. Songs, Odes, and other Poems on National subjects, compiled from various sources. Part 1st, Patriotic. Part 2nd, Naval. Part 3rd, Military. 3 *vols., cl.*, 12*mo.* *Philadelphia*, 1842

1309 M'Clung, John A. Sketches of Western Adventure, containing an account of the most interesting incidents connected with the Settlement of the West from 1755 to 1794. With an Appendix, engravings. 12*mo, cl.* *Dayton, Ohio*, 1852

1310 McCoy, Isaac. History of Baptist Indian Missions: embracing remarks on the former and present condition of the Aboriginal Tribes; their Settlements within the Indian Territory, and their Future Prospects. 8*vo, cl.; plate inserted.* *Washington and N. Y.*, 1840

1311 M'Crum, James. The Navigator; containing directions for navigating the Monongahela, Allegheny, Ohio and Mississippi Rivers, with an ample account of these much admired waters, from the head of the former to the mouth of the latter, and a concise description of their towns, villages, harbors, settlements, etc., with maps; to which is added an appendix, containing an account of Louisiana, and of the Missouri and Columbia Rivers, as discovered by the voyage under Capt. Lewis and Clark. 8*th Ed. Sh.* 12*mo. Plans and Charts.* *Pittsburg*, 1814

1312 McCulloh, J. H., M. D. Researches, Philosophical and Antiquarian, Concerning the Aboriginal History of America. 8*vo, bds., uncut With Map. Very scarce.* *Baltimore*, 1829

1313 McDonald, John. Biographical Sketches of General Nathaniel Massie, General Duncan McArthur, Captain William Wells, and General Simon Kenton, who were early settlers in the Western Country. 8*vo, sh.; with plates.* *Dayton, O.*, 1852

1314 McIntosh, John. The Origin of the North American Indians, with a faithful description of their Manners, and Customs, Religions, Languages and Dress, including various specimens of Indian eloquence. *New Ed. With plates.* 8*vo, cl.* *N. Y.*, 1843

1315 McKean, Joseph. Sermon preached at Dorchester, June 25, 1817, on occasion of organizing the Third Church, in that Town; and the Installation of Rev. Edw. Richmond as its Pastor. 8*vo pamphlet*, 35 *p., uncut; fine copy.* *Dedham*, 1817

1316 McKENNEY, THOMAS L. Sketches of a Tour to the Lakes. Of the Character and Customs of the Chippeway Indians, and of incidents connected with the Treaty of Fon du lac. Also a Vocabulary of the Algic, or Chippeway Language. 8*vo, bds., uncut. Illustrated with* 29 *Engravings—Ind. Likenesses, etc.* *Baltimore*, 1827

1317 M'KENNEY, THOS. L., AND HALL, JAS. History of the Indian Tribes of North America, with Biographical Sketches and Anecdotes of the Principal Chiefs. Embellished with One Hundred and Twenty Portraits, from the Indian Gallery in the Department of War, at Washington. 3 *Vols. in parts. Folio.* *Philadelphia*, 1838

Folio. Vol. I., pp. 204, 48 Col. Portraits. Vol. II., (1842), 48 Plates. Vol. III., (1844), 24 Plates.

"As early as 1824, the practice was begun of taking portraits of the principal Indians, who came to the seat of government, and of depositing them in the War Department. The project was approved and aided by the Executive, and under the management of Col. M'Kenney, then Superintendent of Indian Affairs, the number rapidly increased, till a very interesting gallery was formed. They were chiefly painted by Mr. King, an artist of high repute in this branch of the profession, who, by his long residence in Washington, and frequent opportunities of studying the subject of his pencil, has been remarkably successful in transferring to his canvas, the strong lineaments of the Indian countenance. Having this rare and curious collection before him, Col. M'Kenney conceived the plan of making it more valuable to the world by publishing a series of engraved portraits, exactly copied and colored from these paintings. With each portrait is connected a biographical sketch of the individual whom it is intended to represent, drawn from original materials, and interspersed with anecdotes and narrations, many of which are spirited and strikingly graphic. The work contains also a historical account of the various tribes of Indians within the borders of the United States, and particularly of those situate to the eastward of the Mississippi. This essay forms a rare and valuable contribution to Indian History."

1318 McKenney, Thomas L. Memoirs, Official and Personal; with Sketches of Travels among the Northern and Southern Indians; embracing a War excursion, and description of scenes along the Western Borders, and on the Origin, History and Rights of the Indians, with a plan for the Preservation and Happiness of the Remnants of that Persecuted Race. *Two volumes in one.* 8*vo, cl., plates.* *New York*, 1846

1319 McMaster, Gilbert. "The Obligations of the American Scholar, to his Country, and the World." An Address delivered before Hanover College, Sept. 28, 1841. 8*vo, twenty-four pages, good copy.* *Madison, Ind.*, 1841

1320 Means, J. H. Historical Discourse on occasion of the Fiftieth Anniversary of the Second Church, Dorchester, deliv., Jan. 3, 1858. 8*vo, orig. cov.*, 32 *p.*; *fine copy.* *Boston*, 1858

1321 Mease, James. A Geological account of the United States, comprehending a short description of their Animal, Vegetable, and Mineral productions, Antiquities and Curiosities. *Sh.*, 12*mo, plates.* *Philadelphia*, 1807

1322 MEDFORD, Mass. History of the Town of, from its First Settlement in 1630, to 1855. By Charles Brooks. 8*vo, cl.; with plates, portrait. Very scarce.* *Boston*, 1855

1323 MEDINA COUNTY, Ohio, Pioneer History of. By N. B. Northrop. 12mo, cl. *Medina, Ohio*, 1861

1324 MEDWAY, Mass. "A Pastor's Review." Discourse preached Nov. 2, 1864, on the Fiftieth Anniversary of the Author's Ordination and Settlement. By Jacob Ide. *8vo, orig. cov.; valuable appendix, 39 p. Sermon 33 p.; clean copy. Boston,* 1865

1325 MELROSE, Mass. MEMORIAL (THE) ANNALS OF. In the Great Rebellion of 1861–65. By Elbridge H. Goss. *4to, cl. Privately printed by subscription. Boston,* 1868

1326 ——— The same, *uncut; only a few copies.*

1327 MELVIN, JAMES. A JOURNAL of the Expedition to Quebec, in the year 1775, under the Command of Col. Benedict Arnold. By a Private. 100 *copies printed. 8vo, uncut, sheets. Philadelphia, Pa.; printed for the Franklin Club,* 1864

1328 MEMOIRS OF THE DEAD, and Tomb's Remembrancer. *12mo, sh. Very scarce, fine copy. Baltimore,* 1806

1329 MENDON ASSOCIATION, of Congregational Ministers. Centurial History of. With the Centennial Address delivered at Franklin, Mass., and Biographical Sketches of the Members and Licentiates. By Rev. Mortimer Blake. *8vo, cl. Boston,* 1853

1330 MENDON, Mass. An Address by Carlton A. Staples. A Poem by Henry Chapin, and other proceedings in Commemoration of the Two Hundredth Anniversary of the Incorporation of Mendon. *8vo pamph., 89 pages. Worcester,* 1868

1331 MERCANTILE LIBRARY ASSOC. N. Y. An Introd. Lecture, on the Evils, Social, Moral and Political, that flow from our Party Divisions, etc., delivered Feb. 2, 1841. By John Duer, Esq. *8vo, 27 pages, good copy. New York,* 1841

1332 MERIVALE, CHARLES. History of the Romans under the Empire. Fifth edition. *5 vols., 8vo, cl., uncut; with Map. London,* 1864

1333 MEXICO, AS IT WAS, AND AS IT IS. By Brantz Mayer. *8vo, cl., rough edges; illustrations on wood. New York,* 1844

1334 MICHIGAN. HISTORY OF, Civil and Topographical, in a Compendious Form; with a view of the surrounding Lakes. By James H. Lanman. With a map. *8vo, cl. New York,* 1839

1335 MICHIGAN. EMIGRANT'S GUIDE; or, Pocket Gazetteer of the Surveyed Part of. By John Farmer. *2d Ed. 24mo, paper. Albany,* 1831

1336 MIDDLEBOROUGH, Mass. Book of the First Church of Christ, in Middleborough, Plymouth County, Mass. With notices of other Churches in that Town. *8vo, cl. Boston,* 1852

Contains, Historical Notice of the First Church, and Two Discourses by Israel W. Putnam, also Chronological Notice and Descriptive Catal. of its Members, from 1695 to 1853.

1337 MIDDLEBURY, Vt. HISTORY OF THE TOWN OF, to which is prefixed a Statistical and Historical account of the County. Written at the request of the Historical Society. By Samuel Swift. *8vo, cl.; port's, plates. Middlebury,* 1859

1338 MIDDLESEX COUNTY, CONN.; A Statistical Account of. By David D. Field. *8vo pamph., uncut; very scarce; 154 p. Middletown, Conn.,* 1819

1339 MIDDLETOWN, Vt.; The History of. In Three Discourses. By Barnes Frisbie. *8vo pamphlet; 130 p.; scarce. Rutland,* 1867

1340 MIDDLETOWN, Conn. CENTENNIAL ADDRESS, by David D. Field,

D.D. With Historical Sketches of Cromwell, Portland, Chatham, Middle-Haddam, Middletown and its Parishes. 12*mo, cl.; with plates.* *Middletown, Conn.*, 1853

1341 MILLER, SAMUEL. A Brief Retrospect of the Eighteenth Century. In Two Volumes. Containing a Sketch of the Revolutions and Improvements in Science, Arts, and Literature, during that Period. 8*vo, sheep.* *New York*, 1803

1342 MILLER, WM. W. An Address for the Benefit of the Greeks, Jan. 13, 1824. 8*vo pamphlet; 23 p.; good copy.* *Newark, N. J.*, 1824

1343 MILLS, SAM'L. J.; Memoirs of—late Missionary to the S. W. Section of the U. S. By Gardiner Spring. 8*vo*, 247 *p.; scarce.* *New York*, 1820

1344 MILTON, Mass.; Address delivered before the Inhabitants of the Town of—on the 200th Anniversary of the Incorporation, June 11, 1862. By James M. Robbins. 8*vo pamph.; fine copy;* 76 *p.* *Boston*, 1862

1345 MILLSTONE, N. J. HIST. DISCOURSE on the Centennial Anniversary of the Ref. Dutch Church. 1866. By Edward Tanjore Corwin. 8*vo, cl.* *New York*, 1866

1346 MILWAUKEE, Wis.; CHRONICLES OF—being a Narrative History of the Town, from its Earliest Period to the Present. By A. C. Wheeler. 16*mo, cl.* *Milwaukee*, 1861

1347 MINISINK REGION, N.Y. A HISTORY OF THE MINISINK REGION, and includes the present towns of Minisink, Deerpark, Mount Hope, Greenville and Wayanda, in Orange County, New York, from their organization and first settlement to the present time; also, including a general History of the First Settlement of the County. By Charles E. Stickney. 12*mo, half mor., uncut; scarce.* *Middletown, N. Y.*, 1861

1348 MINNESOTA AND ITS RESOURCES, to which are appended camp-fire Sketches or Notes of a Trip from St. Paul to Pembina and Selkirk settlement on the Red river of the north. By J. Wesley Bond. *With plates*, 8*vo, cl.* *Chicago, Ill.*, 1856

1349 MINNESOTA TERRITORY, The History of; from the earliest French explorations to the present time. By Edward Duffield Neill. *Roy.* 8*vo, cl.; with map.* *Phila., Pa.*, 1858

1350 MINNESOTA, Minn. ITS ADVANTAGES TO SETTLERS. Being a brief synopsis of its History and Progress, Climate, Soil, Agricultural and Manufacturing Facilities, Commercial Capacities and Social Status. Its Lakes, Rivers and Railroads, &c. 8*vo pamph.* *St. Paul, Min.*, 1869

1351 MISSISSIPPI, THE CONSTITUTION OF THE STATE OF—as revised in Convention on the 26th of Oct., 1832. 8*vo*, 27 *pages; beautiful copy; very scarce.* *Jackson, Miss.: printed by Peter Isler*, 1832

1352 MISSOURI, GAZETTEER OF THE STATE OF. With a map of the State; to which is added an Appendix, containing Frontier Sketches, and Illustrations of Indian Character; with front. Compiled by Alphonso Wetmore. 8*vo, cl., rough edges; scarce.* *St. Louis*, 1837

1353 MISSISSIPPI VALLEY. NOTES ON THE NORTHWEST, or Valley

of the Upper Mississippi. Comprising the Country between Lakes Superior and Michigan, &c. By Wm. J. A. Bradford. 12*mo, cl.* *New York and London*, 1846

1354 MISSISSIPPI VALLEY, History of the Discovery and Settlement of—by Spain, France, and Great Britain, and the subsequent occupation, settlement, and extension of civil government by the United States, until 1846. By John W. Monette, M.D. In two volumes. 8*vo, cf., gilt, maps ; very scarce ; fine copy.* *New York*, 1848

1355 MISSISSIPPI VALLEY. History of the Discovery of the Valley of the. By Adolphus M. Hart. 8*vo, paper ; scarce.* *Saint Louis, Mo.*, 1852

1356 Monk, Maria. Awful Exposure of the Atrocious Plot formed by certain Individuals against the Clergy and Nuns of Lower Canada, through the intervention of Maria Monk. With an authentic Narrative of her Life, from her Birth to the present moment, and an account of her Impositions, &c. 12*mo, cl.* *New York*, 1836

1357 Monk, Maria; Decisive Confirmation of the Awful Disclosures of; proving her Residence in Hotel Dieu Nunnery and the existence of the Subterranean Passages. By Samuel B. Smith, *late a Popish Priest.* 8*vo*, 30 *pages ; curious plates ; fine copy ; scarce.* *New York*, 1836

1358 MONSON, Mass. Discourses and Speeches, deliv. at the Celebration of the Semi-centennial Anniversary of Monson Academy, July 18 and 19, 1854. 8*vo pamph. ;* 90 *p. ; good copy.* *New York*, 1855

Contains History of Monson, by Charles Hammond ; Disc., by Richard Storrs, on "Relation of Commerce to Literature ;" and an Account of the Jubilee of Monson Academy.

1359 Monson Academy, An Address deliv. at the Re-dedication of, July 12, 1864. By Chas. Hammond. 8*vo pamph. ;* 32 *p.* *Springfield*, 1865

1360 MONTPELIER, Vt. ; History of the Town of—from the time it was first Chartered in 1781 to the year 1860 ; together with Biographical sketches of its most noted deceased Citizens. By D. P. Thompson. 8*vo, cl.; port.* *Montpelier*, 1860

1361 MONTREAL. Hochelaga Depicta ; or the History and Present State of the City and Island of. Numerous Illustrations. Map. By Newton Bosworth. 8*vo, cl., uncut ; fine copy ; scarce.* *Montreal*, 1839

1362 Moore, Frank. Personal and Political Ballads ; 1 vol. Rebel Rhymes and Rhapsodies ; 1 vol. Songs of the Soldiers ; 1 vol. Lyrics of Loyalty ; 1 vol. 18*mo, half mor. ; 4 vols.* *New York*, 1864

1363 Moore, Frank. Heroes and Martyrs : Notable Men of the time. Biographical sketches of the Military and Naval Heroes, Statesmen and Orators, distinguished in the American crisis of 1861–2; with forty portraits on steel, from Original sources. 20 parts, complete. 4*to, paper covers.* *New York*, 1861

1364 MORGAN, Gen. DANIEL ; The Life of. Of the Virginia Line of the Army of the United States ; with Portions of his Correspondence. By James Graham. *8vo, cl. ; portrait.* *New York*, 1856

1365 MORRIS, Ill. Reminiscences of, and History of the Cong. Church. Discourse delivered December 4, 1864. By E. B. Turner. *8vo, orig. cov.*, 16 *p. Clean copy.* *Chicago*, 1865

1366 Morse, Jedediah, D.D. The American Gazetteer. Exhibiting in Alphabetical order a more full and accurate Account of the States, Cities, and Villages, Indian Tribes, Etc., on the American Continent, also of the West India Islands, with a Description of the Georgia Western Territory. With seven maps. *8vo, sheep.* *Printed in Boston*, 1797

1367 Morse, Rev. Jedidiah. A Report to the Secretary of War of the United States on Indian Affairs, comprising a Narrative of a Tour performed in the Summer of 1820. *8vo, sheep.* *New Haven*, 1822

1368 Morse, Jedidiah. Annals of the American Revolution. To which is prefixed a Summary Account of the First Settlement of the Country, and some of the Principal Indian Wars, and an Appendix containing a Biography of the principal Military Officers. *8vo, cl. Illustrated.* *Hartford, Conn.*, 1824

1369 MOTLEY, JOHN LOTHROP. The Rise and Fall of the Dutch Republic. A History. In three volumes. *8vo, cloth, rough edges.* *New York*, 1857

1370 MOULTRIE, WILLIAM. Memoirs of the American Revolution, so far as it Related to the States of North and South Carolina and Georgia. 2 *vols, 8vo, portrait, full cr. crim. lev. mor., gt. Very fine copy, scarce. By R. M. Smith.* *New York*, 1802

1371 MOUNT AUBURN, Cambridge, Mass., Dearborn's Guide Through, for the Benefit of Strangers. With Seventy-Six Engravings, and a Plan of the Cemetery. *Small 8vo pamph*, 53 *p.* *Boston*, 1856

1372 Mount Benedict, Chronicles of. A Tale of the Ursuline Convent of Charlestown, Mass. By Mary Magdalen. 12*mo, cl. Scarce.* *Boston*, 1837

1373 Muhlbach, L. Henry VIII., and his Court ; or, Catharine Parr. A Historical Novel. From the German. By Rev. H. N. Pierce, D. D. *8vo, wall paper covers. Confederate.* *Mobile*, 1865

1374 Munn, Lewis C. Autographs : Containing the Declaration of Independence, with the Fac-Similes of the Autographs of the Signers ; the Constitution of the United States, Washington's Farewell Address, &c. *6th ed.*, 12*mo, bds., uncut.* *Worcester*, 1866

PAMPHLETS.

1375 Miscellaneous. *Valuable.* [*Twelve.*]

Machias, Me. Memorial of the Centen. Anniv. of the Settlement of, May 20, 1863.

Madison, Wis. The Capital of Wisconsin—its Progress, Capabilities, and Destiny. 1854

Maine, Dist. of. Description of the Situation, Climate, Soil, and Productions of. 1794

——— Aroostook Ter., Report of an Exploration and Survey of, during the Spring and Autumn of 1838, by E. Holmes.

Malden, Mass., Oration, Bi-Centen. Anniversary, delivered at, May 23, 1849, by J. D. Green.

Marshfield, Mass., Memorial of, and Guide-Book to its Localities at Green Harbor. By Marcia A. Thomas. *Boston,* 1854

Maumee Valley, Early History of. By H. L. Hosmer. *Toledo,* 1858

Maryland. Discourse delivered Commem. of Landing of the Pilgrims in Maryland, May, 12 1845. By E. L. Lowe. *Gettysburg,* 1845

Medway, Mass., Centennial Sermon delivered at, Nov. 4, 1813. By Luther Wright. *Dedham,* 1814

Middlesex Co., Conn., Statis. Account of. By David D. Field. *Middletown,* 1819

Minnesota and Lake Superior. By Charles Sweetzer. *New York,* 1868

Mississippi, Valley of, History of the Discovery of. By A. M. Hart. *St. Louis,* 1852

1376 Miscellaneous. *Valuable.* [*Thirteen.*]

Massachusetts, History of the Insurrections in, and the Rebellion Consequent thereon. By G. R. Minot. 1810

Missionary Society, New York. Discourse, April 1, 1800. William Linn.

McLean, Charles B. Sermon at Funeral of Rev. Jairus Burt. *Hartford,* 1857

Missouri Question. By Daniel Raymond. *Baltimore,* 1819

Meeting of Mechanics and other Working Men. *N. Y.,* 1830

Mission, Historical Sketch of the Syria. By Rev. Thomas Laurie. *N. Y.,* 1862

Miller, Samuel. The Divine Appointment—Duties and Qualifications of Ruling Elders. Sermon by. *N. Y.,* 1811

Minnesota and Lake Superior. Tourist's Guide. By Charles S. Sweetser. *N. Y.,* 1868

Missouri, Report of Committee of Bank of. *Jefferson,* 1851

——— Address on Education before Two Houses of General Assembly of. By James Shannon. *Jefferson,* 1851

——— Report of Sup. of Com. Schools to Sixteenth General Assembly of. *Jefferson City,* 1851

Missionary Society, Sermon before the Foreign, of N. Y. and Brooklyn. By Rev. Walter Clarke. *N. Y.,* 1860

Masonic. Address Before Grand Lodge and Chapter of Maine on Festival of St. John the Baptist. *Boston,* 1844

1377 Miscellaneous. [*Eighteen.*]

Minto, Walter. Inaugural Oration on the Progress and Importance of the Mathematical Sciences. *Trenton,* 1788.

Macwhorter, Alexander. A Festival Discourse on 17th Anniv. of American Indep. *Scarce.* *Newark,* 1793

McKnight, John. The Divine Goodness to the United States of America. N. Y., Feb. 19, 1795.
Moore, Benj. The Duty of Fulfilling all Righteousness Explained. *N. Y.*, 1806
Mass., Legisl. of. The Patriotic Proceedings—Jan. 26 to March 4, 1809. *Boston.*
Morris, Governeur. Oration delivered June 29, 1814. *N. Y.*
Mais, Charles. The Surprising Case of Rachel Baker who Prays and Preaches in her Sleep. *N. Y.*, 1814
Macgowan, John. The Arians and Socinians' Monitor. *Baltimore*, 1819
Memoirs, Public and Private. Life and Adventures and Secret Amours of Mrs. C. M., late Mad. V——. *Free and easy.*
McLane, Louis. The British West-India Trade.
Meredith, William, Speech of, May 13, 1777. *London.*
Masonic, Anti. Address, Sep. 11, 1830, by Myron Holley. *Phila.*, 1830
Mephistopheles. Review of Mr. Cambreling's Report. *Baltimore*, 1830
Milligan, James. The Prospects of True Christians in a Sinful World. *Haverhill*, 1831
McMaster, Gilbert. The Moral Character of Civil Government of United States. *Albany*, 1832
Memorial of the Committee Appointed by the "Free Trade Convention," held at Philadelphia, September and October, 1831, to Prepare and Present a Memorial to Congress. *N. Y.*, 1832
Mathias Fanaticism. By W. L. Stone. *N. Y.*, 1835
Martineau. Two Discourses. By John Kenrick and James Martineau, Jan. 24, 1836. *London.*

1378 Miscellaneous. [*Twenty-four.*]
Magazine, National. For June 1, 1799. No. 1, Vol. I. By James Lyon.
——— For 1799. No. 4, Vol. I. By James Lyon.
——— Youth's. For 1818. Vol. I. N. Y., 1819.
——— Youth's. For December, 1818. Vol. I.
——— American Monthly. Jan. 1824. Vol. I., No. 1.
——— Farmers, Mechanics, Manufacturers, and Sportsman's. N. Y., May, 1826. No. 3, Vol. I.
Musical Review. Jan. 19, 1839. Vol. I., No. 25.
Magazine for the Million. Feb., 18, 1844. Vol. I., No. 1. By Edward Morley.
——— The Christian, of the South. June, 1847. Vol. V., No. 6.
——— English Spirit of. Feb. 1, 1824.
Madison, James, Northern Grievances Set Forth in a Letter to. *N. Y.*, 1814
——— Papers, Prospectus of. July, 1839. By Langtree and O'Sullivan.

Miller, Samuel. Sermon, May 9, 1798. *N. Y.*
——— Letter Addressed to. By T. J. How. *Utica,* 1808
——— Wm. W. Address for the Benefit of the Greeks, Jan. 13, 1824. *Newark, N. J.*
Mason, John M. Sermon, Feb. 19, 1795. *New York*
——— Sermon, May 31, 1801. *New York.*
——— Sermon, Nov. 1, 1801. *New York.*
——— Sermon, Jan. 10, 1830, New York, on Death of. By Joseph McElroy.
——— Lowell. Address on Church Music. Oct. 7, 1826. *Boston.*
——— Alfred, Address on Death of. By Charles A. Cheever. 1828
Missionary Soc. Edinburgh. Sermon, November 10, 1796. By J. Peddie.
——— Foreign, Sixth Report of, May 7, 1823. *N. Y.*
——— Cong. Church, Proc. of the Evangelical Consociation, and. R. I., June, 1835. *Providence.*

1379 Miscellaneous. [*Twenty.*]

Maxcy, Jonathan. Address at commencement of Rhode Island College, Sept. 3, 1794. *Providence.*
——— Sermon, preached Aug. 9, 1795 in Providence.
——— Funeral Sermon occasioned by Death of Rev. James Manning, deliv. July 31, 1791.
——— Sermon at dedication of Meeting-House, deliv. Sept. 14, 1796.
——— Sermon at Warren Association, Sept. 12, 1797.
——— Disc. to explain the Doctrine of Atonement, Nov. 25, 1796. 20
——— Address deliv. to Graduates of R. I. College, Sept. 5, 1798. *Providence*
——— Address deliv. in R. I. College, Sept. 2, 1801. *Wrentham*
——— Sermon deliv. in R. I. College, Sept. 3, 1800. *Providence*
——— Anniv. Sermon Address, Dec. 1, 1816. *Columbia, S. C.*
Miller, Jonathan. "The Jewish and Christian Church the Same."
Miller and his Men. Ry Wm. Cole. *London*
Miller, Samuel. Disc. deliv, before Literary and Philosophical Soc. of N. J., Sept. 27, 1825. *Princeton*
——— Letter to a Gentleman of Baltimore in reference to the Rev. Mr. Duncan. *Princeton Press,* 1826
——— Sermon deliv., Aug. 26, 1829, at installation of Wm. B. Sprague. *Albany, N. Y.*
Murray, Nicholas. Disc. "Lesson which Death teaches," deliv. at Death of Rev. D. M. Miller. *N. Y.,* 1855
Morse, Jedidiah. Sermon, Day of Nat. Fast. *Charleston,* 1797

Morse, Jedidiah. Sermon, Anniv. Thanks. *Charleston, Nov.*, 29, 1798

Morse, O. A. Vindication of the claim of Alexander M. W. Ball to the Authorship of the Poem, "Rock me to Sleep Mother." *N. Y.*, 1867

Missionary, Northern Soc. Sermon before, in Troy, Feb. 8, 1798. By Alexander Proudfit. *Scarce.*

1380 Miscellaneous. *Valuable.* [*Twenty.*]

Moreno Celso Cesare. Amer. Int. in Asia. *New York*, 1869

Merchants Union Law Co., for the Continent. 1869

Marshall, William. Speech on the question whether the marriage of a man to the neice of his former wife, is agreeable to Scripture. *N. Y.*, 1834

Marshall, Chief Justice. Judge Story's disc. upon the Life, Char. and Services of. *Scarce and valuable.* *Boston*, 1835

Marshall College, Address deliv. before the Literary Societies of, by John Frost, Sept. 28, 1841. *Phila.*

Marshall, John. Speech of, also the autobiography of. 1848

Mackenzie, Wm. L. Lives and opinions of B. T. Butler and Jesse Hoyt. *Very scarce.* 1845

Mackenzie, Henry. Story of La Roche. *Boston*, 1848

Madison, James. Letter addressed to. 1808

——— Memorial and Remonstrance of. *Boston*, 1819

——— Lecture on the character and services of. By Daniel D. Barnard. *Scarce.* 1837

Madison Papers. Prospectus of, by H. D. Gilpin.

McJimsey, John. Sermon, "Comfort for the afflicted," deliv. Aug. 22, 1852.

McJimsey, Wm. Sabbath Remembrance and Gospel Banner, containing Bible commentaries and Poems. *N. Y.*, 1852

Moore, Ely. Address deliv. before The General Trades Union of City of New York, Dec. 2, 1833. *N. Y.*

Moore, David. Funeral Sermons on the Death of, by Thurston Bedell and Robert Travis. *N. Y.*, 1856

Mills, Samuel J. Report of a missionary tour west of the Allegany Mts. *Very scarce.* *Andover*

Mills, J. Speech of, deliv. at British Forum. *London*, 1819

Mills, Robert. Guide to the Capitol of the U. S. *Washington*, 1854

Moonshine. By the Lunarian Soc. Nos. III. IV. V. July, 1807 *Baltimore*

1381 Miscellaneous. [*Fifteen*].

Messiah. The second, and glorious appearing of the, at the pass-over, 1855, By J. Chapman

M'Lellan, Maj. Gen. The Life and Public Services of. *Phila.*, 1864

Mexico. Proc. at dinner of Senor Matias Romero, March 29, 1864. *N. Y.*

Mass. Address, by C. A. Staples. *Worcester*, 1868

Hedding, Elijah. Sermon, "The supreme deity of Christ proved," deliv. in Bath, Maine, July 4, 1822. *Boston*

Exposition of the Methodist Conf, also a serious address. *Boston,* 1830

Ambler, J. L. Extracts from the minutes of the eight Annual Meth. Epis. conference, with a Sermon, April 10, 1838. *New York*

African Meth. E. Ch. Minutes of the general and annual conference of the Meth. Epis. Ch., from 1836–1839 inclusive. *Brooklyn, N. Y.* 1839

Minutes taken at the several annual conference of the Meth. Epis. Ch. for 1823. *N. Y.*

Barber, John W. Thoughts on some parts of the discipline of the Meth. Epis. Ch. *New Haven,* 1829

Missionary Soc. N. Y. Sermon, Apr. 6, 1802, by Samuel Miller. *N. Y.*

——— Sermon, Apr. 3, 1804. by J. Livingston. *N. Y.*

——— 21st Report, April 7, 1818. *N. Y.*

——— Proc. at 1st Anniv. *N. Y.* 1817

——— 4th Report of, Dec. 6, 1820. *N. Y.*

1382 Miscellaneous. [*Twenty-Three.*]

Magill, S. Two dis. on day of Nat. Thanksgiving. *Glasgow,* 1798

M'Knight. View of the Pres. State of Polit. and Relig. world, Jan. 1, 1802.

M'Clures, D. Sermon, deliv. interment of Thomas Potwine, Nov. 17, 1802.

Milledoler, P. Disc. deliv. March 23, 1806. *New York*

Magdalen Soc. First Annual Report of. *New York,* 1813

Moreau. Funeral, Oration pronounced at St. Petersburg in Honor of. *New York,* 1814

Manuscript, A True Copy of a MS. Found hanging on a Post at Gorham Corner, 1819. *Concord*

Maltby, Erastus. Sermon on Installation of Rev. Wm. M. Cornell, June 15, 1831. *Taunton*

Maryland Univer. Address deliv. by J. P. Kennedy, Jan. 3, 1831. *Balt.*

McVickar, J. Tribute to the Memory of Sir Walter Scott. 1833

Marie. The Bandit's Daughter. A Poem. *N. Y.,* 1834

Mathias. Memoir of the Prophet. *N. Y.,* 1835

Mallard, J. B. Account of Cong. Chat. Midway, Ga. *Very scarce.* 1840

McLeod, J. N. On capital punishment. *N. Y.,* 1842

Mermaids. Short Hist. of. *Boston,* 1842

Miles, J. W. Farewell Sermon by, Aug. 20, 1843. *Charleston*

M'Ilvaine, Bp. Earnest word from, in behalf of the church Institutions at Gambier, Ohio. *New York,* 1843

Milnor, James. Last Sermon in St. George's Church, N. Y., Apr. 6, 1845.

M'Mahon, Isaiah. Hebrew without a Master. *Pen Yann,* 1846

Mitchell, Joseph. Belcher, Charles. Memorial and Brief, on behalf of.

McKenney's, Col. Reply to Kosciusko Armstrong's Assault upon, narrative by Thomas McKenney. *Scarce.* *N. Y.*, 1847

Macdonald, A. J. Monuments, Gravestones, Burying Grounds, 1848

Macready, Mr. Rejoinder, "The Replies from England," etc. *Very scarce. Morell's sale,* $6. *New York,* 1849

3 1383 Miscellaneous. [*Sixteen.*]

Mississippi. The River, from St. Paul to New Orleans. *N. Y.*
Militia and Public defence. *New York,* 1851
Montes, Lola ; or, A Reply to the "Private History and Memoirs" of that celebrated Lady. *Free.* *N. Y.*, 1851
Muhlenberg, W. A. Two Protestant Sisterhoods. *New York,* 1856
Mystic-Hall Seminary. First Catalogue of the Teachers and Pupils. *Boston,* 1857
M'Lean, Charles B. Sermon preached at Funeral of Rev. James Burt, of Canton, Conn., Jan. 22, 1857.
Magruder, Col. J. Bankhead. Presidential Contest of 1856, in Three Letters. 1857
Mackinaw City. Expedition of the Natural Position of, and the Climate, Soil and Commercial Elements of, by E. D. Mansfield, Oct. 1857. *Cinn.*
Maumee Valley. Early History of, by H. L. Hosmer. *Toledo,* 1858
Mann, Horace. Biographical Sketch of, by H. Barnard, Dec. 1858.
Michigan Southern and Northern Indiana R. R. Co. Report of the Directors of, March 28, 1859. *N. Y.*
M., H. Outward reverence due to the Holy Eucharist, May 14, 1865. *London.*
Malta, The Sons of, exposed : being a complete exposé of the secret doings of the I. O. S. M. ; or, the Mysterious Order, by One who was "sold." 1860
M'Henry, George. Familiar Epistle to Robert J. Walker. 1863
Mariposa Company. Final Report of the Committee of the Bondholders of, June 4, 1868. *New York.*
Mayer, Joseph. Address to the Members of the Hist. Soc. of Lancashire and Cheshire. *Liverpool,* 1868

10 1384 Miscellaneous. [*Twenty-seven.*]

Missionary Soc.. New York. Two Sermons before, Apr. 24. *N. Y.*, 1799
——— Disc. by John N. Abeel, deliv. Apr. 6, 1801. *N. Y.*
——— Sermon by Samuel Miller, deliv. Apr. 6, 1802. *N. Y.*
Missionary Soc., Northern. Report of, for year 1811, by Wm. Jenkins.
——— Report of, for year 1813. *Albany.*
Missionary Soc., Mass. Sermon deliv. May 27, 1800. *Charlestown,* 1800

Missionary Soc., Mass. Bap. Sermon deliv. May 28, 1806, by William Collier.
Missionary Soc., United Foreign. Sermon deliv. May 11, 1828, by P. M. Whelpley.
Missionary Soc., Boston Bapt. Foreign. Sermon deliv. Oct. 26, 1823, by F. Wayland.
Missionary Soc., Hampshire. Sermon deliv. Aug. 24, 1815, by John Keep.
Missionary Soc., Foreign. Sermon deliv. Jan. 1, 1824, by B. B. Wisner.
——— Annual Report, Nov. 4, 1843. *Cincinnati*
Missions. General Hints on. 1842
Missions, Board of. Brief remarks on the Organization and Action of. *New York*, 1844
——— Brief remarks on the Organization and Action of. *N. Y.*, 1844
Mission to the Mahrattas. Hist. sketch of. *N. Y.*, 1862
Massachusetts, Char. Fire Soc. Address deliv. May 28, 1803, by J. H. Gardiner.
——— Proper Views of, by R. Dickinson. *Scarce. Greenfield*, 1813
Massachusetts Soc. Constitution of, for 1818. *Boston*
——— Address before the, delivered May 27, 1833. *Boston*
Massachusetts, Laws of. Remarks on some of the provisions of, March, 1822, by Josiah Quincy. *Cambridge*
Mass. Two months abroad; or, a trip to Eng., &c., Aug. and Sept., 1843, by a R. R. director of. *Boston*
——— Who was first Gov. of? By J. B. Felt. *Boston*, 1853
——— Fourteenth Report relating to the Registry of Births, Marriages and Deaths in, for 1855. *Boston*
——— Institute of Technology. *Boston*, 1862
——— Commonwealth of. No. 150.
——— Address of A. H. Bullock, Jan 3, 1868. *Boston*

1385 Miscellaneous. [*Twenty.*]

Mexico. Memorial on the Nat., Polit. and Civil State of the Province of Cohauila. *Cadiz*, 1812
——— Serious Actual Dangers of Foreigners and Foreign Commerce in the Mexican States, by J. Jordan. 1826
Mexico and Havanna. Voyage to. *N. Y.*, 1841
Mexico. Speech of Elias B. Holmes on subject of War in. 1846
——— Reports and Despatches exhibiting the operations of the U. S. Naval Force during the war with.
——— Its Geography, People and Institutions, by T. J. Farnham. *New York*
——— Campaign in, by "One who was Thar." *Phil.*, 1850
——— Marine Corps in, convened Sept. 1852. *Scarce. Washington*
——— and the Solidarity of Nations, by G. Clussert. *New York*, 1866

Mexico, Presidency of. Protest of Gen. Jesus Gonzales Ortega. *New York*, 1866

——— French in. The Speech of M. Billault, Feb. 7, 1863. *London*

Masonry Anti. Report upon the Subject of, by Mr. Patterson.

Masonry. Address of Benj. French, Nov. 5, 1850. *Washington*

Masonic Union. A Monthly Magazine, by F. M. King, Oct., 1851.

——— Ancient Tree. Address by T. Douglass. 1853

Masonry, Free, in N. Y. 1856

Masons, Free. "Exoteric duties of." Address by T. J. Corson, Dec. 12, 1859.

Mason, John M. "Living Faith." Sermon by. *N. Y.*, 1802

Mason, Dr. Speech relative to the resignation of his Pastoral Charge in the city of N. Y. *Phil.*, 1810

Mason, Erskine. Subject and Spirit. Sermon deliv. Oct. 16, 1838. *New York*

1386 Miscellaneous. [*Nineteen.*]

Message from the Pres. of U. S. on causes of Failure of Arms on Northern Frontier. *Albany*

——— from Pres. of U. S. in relation to our affairs with Spain, Dec. 28, 1818. *Washington*

——— from Pres. of U. S., March 9, 1820. *Washington*

——— from Pres. of U. S., Apr. 21, 1820. *Washington*

——— from Pres. of U. S. Dec. 11, 1862. *Washington*

——— from Pres. of the U. S. to the two Houses of Congress. 1867.

Murray, Lindley. First Book for Children, by. *N. Y.*, 1811

——— Biog. Sketch of Henry Tuke. 1816.

Murray, Patrick. Letters on the Philosophy of Plain Speaking, with specimens of False Speaking. *Dublin*, 1850

Murray, W. H. H. Faithfulness. *New York*, 1867

Murray, N. Decline of Popery and its causes. Address, Jan. 15, 1851. *New York*

Marsh, Herbert. Course of Lectures in Theological Learning. *Cambridge*, 1823

Marsh, Mr., of Vt. Speech of, on the bill for establishing The Smithsonian Insti., Apr. 22, 1846.

Milton, John. Remarks on the Char. and Writings of. *Boston*, 1826

——— On Marriage ; or, Marriage as it now is. *Phil., March*, 1841

Methodist Travelling Preacher. Original and Thrilling Sketch from the Diary of a. *N. Y.*, 1845

Methodist Epis. Ch. Proceedings of the Layman's Assoc. of the, held Dec. 14 and 15, 1857. *Rochester*

Methodism in New Haven. Disc. deliv. Nov. 24, 1859, by G. W. Woodruff.

McMaster, Gilbert. Moral character of civil government of U. S. 1832.

1387 Missionary Society. [*Nine.*]

Missions (Swiss) in Canada, A Plea for. Disc. deliv. Oct. 15, 1843, by N. S. S. Beman. *Troy*

Missionary Soc., Domes. and Foreign. Sermon by Bp. Onderdonk. *N. Y.*, 1829

Missions, Foreign. Report of the Amer. Board of, Sept. 14, 15, 16, 1836. *Boston*

Missionary, Domes. and Foreign, Soc. Sermon "On the Increase of the Ch.," Oct. 22, 1832, by Wm. White.

——— "An Appeal in behalf of Missions," May 12, 1829, by Alonzo Potter.

Missions, Foreign. Sermon—"The Power of Christian Gratitude," by Nehemiah Adams. *Boston*, 1855

——— Sermon deliv. before Amer. Board of Commiss. for, by P. Dwight. *Boston*

——— Sermon—"The Missionary Enterprise, dependent on the Religion of Principle for Success," Sept., 1844, by A. Barnes. *Boston*

Missionary Soc., R. I. Proceedings of the Evangel. Consos. for June, 1834. *Prov.*

1388 Miscellaneous Magazines, Reviews, etc. [*Twenty-Five.*]

Magazine. Free Will Baptist. Vol. I., No. 4. Feb. 1827

——— Blackwood's Edinburgh. No. XIV., Vol. III. May, 1818

——— Blackwood's Edinburgh. Supplement.

Review, Edinburgh. Feb., 1818. No. LVIII.

——— or Critical Journal. June, 1826. Sept., 1826. Vol. XLIV. No. 87.

The National Preacher. Vol. I. Nos. 1 and 2.

——— Vol. II. Nos. 2 and 8.

——— Vol. IV. Nos. 3 and 8.

——— Vols. VII. and VIII.

——— Vol. VII. No. 2.

——— Vol. IX. No. 6.

——— Vol. X. Nos. 1, 2 and 9.

——— Vol. XI. Nos. 10 and 11.

——— Vol. XIX. No. 10.

——— Vol. XX. No. 1.

Wright's Literary Gazette and Analytical Review. Vol. I. Nos. 1, 2, 3, 4 and 5.

1389 Miscellaneous Magazines, Reviews, etc. [*Twenty-Five.*]

The Columbian Parnassiad.

The Newport Female Evangelic Miscellany. No. II. 1806

The Baltimore Medical and Philosophical Lycæum. Vol. I. No. II. April, May and June, 1811

The Evangelical Record and Western Review. Vol. I. No. 12. *Scarce.* Dec., 1812

The American Bible Soc. Quarterly Extracts. No. II. Nov., 1818

The Washington Theological Repertory. No. XII. Vol. II. July, 1821

The Idle Man. No. II. *N. Y.*, 1821

The N. Y. City Hall Recorder. Vol. VI. No. 8. Sept., 1821

The Museum of Foreign Literature and Science. July, 1822

Pindar, Peter. No. I. The Vagabond, or New Looking-Glass, being an everlasting Magazine of Acrostical Biography. *N. Y.*, 1823

The American Evangelist. Vol. I. No. 3. *Boston,* Nov., 1827

The American Journal of Education. *Boston,* 1829

Theology, Views in. No. XV. Vol. IV. Nov. *N. Y.*, 1834

Medicine, The Electric Journal of. Vol. II. No. 3. Jan., 1838

Journal of Christian Education and Family and Sunday School Visitor. Vol. III. Nos. 11 and 12. Nov. and Dec., 1841

The Christian Observer. No. 62. Feb., 1843

The Peaceful Revolutionist. Vol. 2. No. 1. *Utopia,* May, 1848

The Protestant Quarterly. Vol. XI. No. 4. October, 1854

Review of American Unitarianism. *Boston.*

Review of N. America. No. 46. New Series. No. 21. Jan., 1825

The Literary Advertiser. March, 1827

U. S. Review and Literary Gazette. Vol. 1. From Oct. 1, to April 1, 1827

U. S. Review and Literary Gazette. Vol. 1. No. 6. March, 1827

U. S. Review of the American in Egypt. *N. Y.*, 1842

Magazine, The Lady's. May, 1771

1390 Magazines, etc. [*Thirty.*]

N. Y. Magazine, or Literary Repository. Oct., 1796

Magazine, The Experienced Christian's. April, 1797

——— Edinburgh Monthly. June, 1810

——— The European. April, 1819

——— American, of Wonders. Vol. 1.

——— Providence Theological. Vol. 1. From Sept., 1821, to Aug., 1822

Magazine, The Presbyterian. Jan., 1822
——— The Sailor's, and Naval Journal. Sept., 1828
——— Portland. No. 1. Vol. I. Oct. 1, 1834

Atlantic Journal and Friend of Knowledge. Vol. 1
Nos. 1 and 2. *Scarce.* *Phila.*, 1832

The Prot. Epis. Pulpit. Vol. II. No. IX. Sept., 1832

Rt. Rev. Benjamin Moore, Brief Memoir of.

Peace, The Friend of. Vol. III. No. XI.
——— Soc., Ninth Report of American. *N. Y.*, 1837
——— Advocate of. No. 1, 2, 3, 4, 5, 8, 9, 10.
——— ——— No. 10. Vol. II.
——— ——— Nos. 12 and 14.

Magazine, American Baptist, and Missionary Intelligencer.
No. 7. Vol. I. Jan., 1818
——— Vol. III. *Boston*, 1821
——— Free Will. Vol. I. 1826
——— ——— Vol. I. No. 3. Nov., 1826

Miscellaneous. [*Twelve.*]

Mass. Cong. Charitable Soc. Sermon in Boston. By Peter Thacher. *Boston*, Feb. 12, 1795

Mass. Charitable Fire Soc., Address to members of. By John Q. Adams. *Boston*, May 28, 1802

Mass. Charitable Fire Soc., Address to members of. By Peter Thacher. *Boston*, May 31, 1805

Mass. Christian Knowledge Soc. Sermon deliv. By Eliphalet Pearson. *Boston*, Nov. 27, 1811

Mass. Charitable Mechanic Assoc. Address By Wm. Hilliard. *Cambridge*, Oct. 4, 1827
——— Lecture on Rail-Roads. By Wm. Jackson. *Boston*, Jan. 12, 1829
——— Address By J. T. Buckingham. Oct. 7, 1830. *Boston.*

Morrison College. Address by Benj. O. Peers. *Lexington, Ky.*, 1833

Marietta College, O. Second Annual Report of the Trustees. Sept., 1835.

Proceedings of the Anti-Masonic State Convention of Mass. Boston, Dec. 30–31, 1829, and Jan. 1, 1830.

Address to the People of the U. S., on the subject of the Anti-Masonic Excitement, or New Party. *Albany*, 1830

Proc. of the Second U. S. Anti-Masonic State Convention. Sept., 1831. *Boston.*

1392 Missionary Society Pamphlets. [*Fourteen.*]

Missionary Soc. Boston Bapt. Foreign. Sermon deliv. Oct. 26, and before Salem Bible Trans. Soc., Nov. 4, 1823, by F. Wayland.

—— Northern. Sermon before, Troy, Feb. 8, by Alex. Proudfit. *Very scarce; relates to Indian missions.* *Albany*, 1798

—— United Domestic. Sermon. "Charity at Home," by John H. Rice. *N. Y.*, 1824

—— Boston Bapt. Foreign. Sermon deliv. Oct. 26, and before Salem Bible Trans. Soc., Nov. 4, 1823, by F. Wayland. *Boston*, 7th ed.

—— Bapt. Disc. by John Foster, Sept., 1818, Bristol, (Eng.) Printed in *Trenton*, 1822

—— Female. Report to the, March, 1817, N. Y., by Ward Stafford.

—— Female. Sermon on the Idolatry of the Hindoos, Nov. 29, 1816, by Samuel Nott. *Norwich*

—— Dumfries. Sermon, "The divine authority and encouragement of missions from Christians to the Heathens," by Bryce Johnson. *Dumfries*, Nov. 16, 1797

—— Edinburgh. Remarks on Mr. Dick's Sermon concerning the qualifications and call of Missionaries March 31, 1801, by G. Ewing. *Glasgou*

—— Marine, N. Y. Sermon, "The Claims of Seamen,' deliv. Nov. 7, 1819, by Edward D. Griffin. *New Yor*

—— Maine. Sermon deliv. before, July 5, 1809, by Wm Jenks. *Hallowel*

—— Mass. Report of a Miss Tour through the wester part of U. S., by S. J. Mills and D. Smith. *Andover*, 181

—— Mass. Sermon deliv. May 26, 1812, by L. Woods. *Bosto*

—— United For. Sermon, May 9, 1819, by E. D. Griffin *N. Y*

1293 Missionary Society Pamphlets. [*Sixteen.*]

Missionary Soc., N. Y. Disc. deliv. April 1, 1800, by Willian Linn. *N. Y*

—— For. N. Y. Sermon deliv. April 15, 1855, by Wm Adams. *N. Y*

—— Young Men's N. Y. Sermon, "Plea for a Standin Ministry," deliv. Dec. 28, 1817, by Alexander Mc Lelland. *N. Y.*, 181

—— N. Y. Sermon deliv. before, by S. Miller. *N. Y.*, 180

—— N. Y. Sermon deliv. before, by J. Livingston. *N. Y.*, 180

—— N. Y. Prot. Epis. Mission. Disc. delivered Jan. 1 1826, by C. R. Duffie. *N. Y*

Missionary. N. Y. Bapt. Miss. Soc. Report of, by their Board of Directors, 1815.

——— N. Y. Evangel. A Brief View of Facts which gave rise to. *N. Y.*, 1817

——— Magazine, N. Y. and Repository, of religious intelligence, July, 1803.

——— London. Report of the directors of, May 13, 1813.

——— African. Disc. on the occasion of forming the, delivered Aug. 10, 1828, by J. M. Wainwright.

——— African. Address of the executive committee of the. *Hartford*, 1828

——— African. Sermon, "The Star in the East," Feb. 26, 1809, by Claudius Buchanan. *Hartford*

——— African. Sermon, "The Star in the East," Feb. 26, 1809, by Claudius Buchanan. *Hartford*

——— African. Sermon, "The Star in the East," Feb. 26 1809, by Claudius Buchanan. To which is added a report of Dr. Kerr. *Boston*, 1809

——— Auxiliary. Address delivered before, Oct. 24, 1820, by William W. Miller. *Morristown*, 1820

——— Hampshire. Sermon, "The Missionary of Angels," August 19, 1813, by Theophilus Packard. *Northampton*

1394 Mormon Pamphlets. *Scarce lot.* [*Fourteen.*]

The Voice of Joseph, by L. Snow. *Liverpool*, 1852

Patriarchal order, or plurality of wives, by O. Spencer. *Liverpool*, 1852

Pearl of great price. Selections from the revelations, etc., of Joseph Smith. *Liverpool*, 1851

Marriage and morals in Utah, by P. P. Pratt. *Liverpool*, 1856

Series of Pamphlets, by O. Pratt. *Liverpool*, 1852

Startling disclosures of the Great Mormon Conspiracy, by I. McG. Van Deusen and his wife. *Curious plates.* *N. Y.*, 1849

Account of the massacre of Joseph Smith and Hyrum Smith, with a history of Mormonism, by G. T. M. Davis. *Very scarce.* *St. Louis*, 1844

The demoralizing doctrines of the Mormon hierarchy. *N. Y.*, 1866

Assassination of Joseph and Hyrum Smith, by J. S. Fullmer. *Liverpool*, 1855

Mormonism triumphant, by J. H. Flanigan. *Liverpool*, 1849

Bible view of Polygamy. Letter to Bishop Hopkins.

Testimonies for the truth: experience of B. Brown. *Liverpool*, 1853

Spiritual delusions, exposing the Spiritual wife system, by I. Van Deusen and his wife. *N. Y.*, 1856

Startling disclosures; by I. Van Deusen and his wife. *N. Y.*, 1850

1395 Miami University, Ohio. [*Eleven.*]

Bishop, R. H. Address delivered at Oxford, Ohio, containing his inaugural address to the graduates of the years 1829, '30, '31, '32, '33, '34, '35.

Olds, Chauncy N. Address before Soc. of inquiry of Missions of. *Oxford*, Feb. 26, 1837

McArthur, J. Address deliv. to Union Lit. Soc., Aug. 12, 1840.

Snow, Henry. Address deliv. to graduates of the Union Lit. Soc., Aug. 10, 1841.

Claybaugh, J. Address before Soc. of Inquiry of Miami Univ. *Rossville*, March 6, 1842

Campbell, A. Address to the members of the Union Lit. Soc. of. *Bethany*, 1844

Coke, Richard H. Address deliv. before the graduates of the Erodelphian Soc. of, *Oxford*, 1837

Thomas, F. W. Address before Erodelphian Soc. *Oxford*, 1838

Caldwell, William B. Address before Erodelphian Soc. *Oxford*, 1839

Third Triennial Catalogue of the Officers and Graduates of, *Oxford*, 1840

Temple, John B. Address deliv. to graduates of Erodelphian Soc. of Cin., Aug. 12, 1840.

1396 Miscellaneous. [*Nineteen.*]

Mitchell, Samuel L. Obsevation on the Canada Thistle, New York, July 20, 1810.

——— Disc. on the Character and Service of Thomas Jefferson as a promoter of Nat. and Phys. Science. New York, Oct. 11, 1826.

——— Disc. on the Life and Character of Tho's Addis Emmet, New York, March 1, 1828.

——— Eulogy on the Life and Character of. Deliv. by Felix Pascalis. New York, Oct. 15, 1831.

Miller, Samuel. Guilt, Folly, and sources of Suicide. In two Disc. New York, Feb. 1805.

——— Disc. before the Literary and Philosophical Soc. of N. J., Sept. 27, 1835. *Princeton*, 1835

——— Importance of mature preparatory study for the Ministry. Introd. Lect. at the Summer Sess. of the Theol. Seminary, at Princeton, N. J., July 3. *Andover*, 1830

MacMaster, E. D. Disc. at Ballston, N. Y., April 29, 1838. *Albany.*

Magazine. The Spiritual. Putney, Vt., June 1, 1847.

——— Popular, Nov. 7, 1846. *Phila.*

——— Parley's and Robert Merry's Museum, Sept. 1847.

Memorial Proposed to Congress of the U. S.

Memoirs of Distinguished Americans. *N. Y.*, 1853

McKean, Rev. Joseph. Eulogy on the. By Levi Hedge. *Cambridge*, 1818

Miller, Rev. Rodney A. Speech of, on the Plummer Professorship. *Boston*, 1855

Marcy, Secretary. Review of. Letter in reply to Lord Clarendon. By R. W. Russel. *New York*, 1856

Michelet, J. Priest, Women, and Families. 6th Ed. *London*, 1846

Merrick, Richard T. Oration, July 5, 1852, at Baltimore.

Moore, Gabriel. Address to Freemen of Alabama. *Washington*, 1835

1397 Massachusetts Horticultural Society. [*Eight.*]

Dearborn, H. A. S. Address deliv. before, on the Celebration of their First Anniv. Boston, Sept. 19, 1829.

Cook, Zebedee. Address deliv. before, in Commem. of its Second Annual Festival. Boston, Sept. 10, 1830.

Ward, Malthus. Address before, in Commem. of its Third Annual Festival, Sept. 21, 1831.

Harris, Thaddeus. Address before, Fourth Anniv., Oct. 3, 1832

Everett, Alex. H. Address before, Fifth Anniv., Sept. 18, 1833.

Gray, John C. Address before, Sixth Anniv., Sept. 17, 1834.

Russell, John L. Address before, Seventh Anniv., Sept. 17, 1835.

Constitution and Bye-Laws of Mass. Hort. Society. *Boston*, 1836

1398 Merrimac Humane Society. [*Seven.*]

Bass, Edward. Sermon at anniv. meeting of. Newburyport, 1803.

Dana, Joseph. Sermon at anniv. meeting of. Newburyport, Sept. 4, 1804.

White, Daniel A. Address to the members of. Newburyport, Sept. 3, 1805.

Cary, Samuel. Address to the members of. Newburyport, Sept. 2, 1806.

Spring, Samuel. Address to the members of. Newburyport, Sept. 1, 1807.

Andrew, John. Disc. to the members of. Newburyport, Sept. 1, 1812.

Lathrop, John. Disc. to the members of Mass. Humane Soc., Boston, June, 1787.

1399 Mass. Humane Soc. [*Seven.*]

Clark, John. Disc. deliv. before the members of, Boston, June 11, 1793.

Gardiner, J. S. J. Sermon deliv. before the members of, Boston, June 14, 1803.

Harris, T. M. Disc. deliv. before the members of, Boston, June 10, 1806.

Emerson, Wm. Disc. deliv. before the members of, Boston, June 9, 1807.

Danforth, Thomas. Disc. deliv. before the members of, Boston, June 14, 1808.

Colman, Henry. Disc. deliv. before the members of, Boston, June 9, 1812.

Kendall, James. Disc. deliv. before the members of, Boston, June 8, 1813.

1400 Medical Pamphlets. [*Fifteen.*]

Peale, Clarles W. Epistle on Means of Preserving Health,

Promoting Happiness, and Prolonging the Life of Man to its Natural Period. *Phila.*, 1803

Medical and Agricultural Register. Vol. I. Jan. 1806, to Aug. 1806 inclusive.

Windship, Charles W. Discourse on the Phenomena of Vitality, or Laws of Mobility and Motion in Animal Bodies. *Boston*, 1818

Dewitt, Benjamin. Lecture on Natural Philosophy. *New York*, 1818

Stearns, John. Address on Influence of the Mind upon the Body in the Production and Cure of Diseases. *Albany*, 1820

—— Address on the Function and Diseases of the Liver. *Albany*, 1821

Thompson, Samuel. Learned Quackery Exposed, or Theory according to Art. *Boston*, 1824

King, F. G. Catalogue of the Anatomical Museum in the College of Phys. and Surgeons. *New York*, 1825

Hosack, David. Observations on the Medical Character. *New York*, 1826

Mackenzie, Wm. Use of the Dead to the Living. *Glasgow*, 1824

Yates, Christopher C. Observations on the Epidemic called Asiatic or Spasmodic Cholera. *New York*, 1832

Manley, James R. Letters addressed to the Board of Health, and to Richard Riker, Recorder of City of New York. *New York*, 1832

Bedford, Gunning S. Address, Nov. 15, 1835. *N. Y.*, 1836

Stone, Wm. L. Letter to Dr. A. Brigham, on Animal Magnetism. *New York*, 1837

Reese, David M Introd. Lecture at opening of Albany Medical College, Jan. 2, 1839.

1401 Masonic Pamphlets. *Scarce.* [*Thirteen.*]

Mitchill, Samuel L. Oration before the Society of Black Friars, at their Anniv. Festival. *New York*, Nov. 11, 1793

Clinton, Dewitt. Address deliv. before Holland Lodge, on his Installation. *New York*, Dec. 24, 1793

Constitutions of the Ancient and Honorable Fraternity, or Free and Accepted Masons in the State of N. Y. 1794

Miller, Samuel. Disc. deliv. before the Grand Lodge of the State of N. Y. June 24, 1795.

Weems, M. L. Oration, "The True Patriot," or the Beauties and Beatitudes of a Republic. *Phila.*, Jan., 1802

Jenks, William. Disc. deliv. before Solar and United Lodges of Free and Accepted Masons, assembled at Bath, Maine, June 24, 1807.

Burrill, Wm. Oration delivered before Trinity and Benevolent Lodges of N. Y., Fortitude Lodge of Brooklyn, also an adress by John Vanderbilt. *N. Y.*, Jan. 11, 1808

Town, Salem. Masonic Address deliv. before Grand Royal Arch Chapter of the State of N. Y. Feb. 4, 1812.

Osgood, Samuel. Sermon, "The Tenets of Free Masonry," before Orient Lodge, Conn. *Hartford*, Sept. 25, 1822

Todd, Ambrose S. Address before the Members of Union Lodge on Death of Wm. Cooke, of Danbury. *New Haven*, 1822

Allen, B. Oration deliv. before Phœnix Lodge, proving the "Great Light of Masonry to be from God." Dec. 27, 1827.

Colden, Cadwallader, Letter of, upon the secret order of Freemasonry. *N. Y.*, April 21, 1829

Brief Report of the Debates in the anti-Masonic State Convention of Mass. *Boston*, Jan. 1, 1830

1402 Medical Pamphlets. *Very scarce lot.* [*Twelve.*]

Youle, Joseph. Inaug. Dissertation on Respiration. *Scarce.* *N. Y.*, 1793

Weldon, Walter. Observations on different modes of Puncturing the Bladder in Cases of Retention of Urine. *Scarce.* *Southampton*, 1793

Jones, Calvin. Treatise on Scarletina Anginosa, or Scarlet Fever or Canker Rash. *Very scarce.* *Catskill*, 1794

Wetmore, Timothy F. Inaug. Dissertation on the Puerperal Fever. *Scarce.* *N. Y.*, 1795

Stuart, James. Dissertation on Salutary Effects of Mercury in Malignant Fevers. *Scarce.* *Phila.*, 1798

Bulfinch, Thomas. Desultory Extracts and Observations, shewing the method of Treatment as related to Rules laid down by Hippocrates and Galen, Sydenham and Boerhaave. *Boston*, 1796

Holliday, John. Account of Origin, Symptoms and Method of Treating the Putrid Bilious Yellow Fever. *Boston*, 1796

Moore, Dr. John. Inaug. Dissertation on Digitalis Purpurea, or Fox Glove and its Uses. *Phila.*, 1800

Caldwell, Charles. Eulogium to Memory of Mr. George Lee, deliv. to Phila. Medical Soc., Feb. 24, 1802.

Caldwell, Charles. Oration on Causes of the difference in point of Frequency and Force, between the Endemic Diseases of the U. S. and those of Europe. *Very scarce.* *Phila.*, 1802

Klapp, Joseph. A Chemico-Physiological Essay, disproving the Existence of an Aeriform Function in the Skin. *Phila.*, 1805

Peale, Charles W. Epistle on means of Preserving Health, Promoting Happiness and Prolonging Life. *Philadelphia*, 1803

1403 Medical Pamphlets. *Very fine lot.* [*Twelve.*]

Biegler, Aug. P. Essay on Anatomy and Physiology of the Brain and Nervous System. *Albany*, 1840

Feuchtwanger, Dr. Lewis. The Mad Dog, or Hydrophobia. With all its various Symptoms, Causes, and Remedies. *N. Y.*, 1840

Lee, Charles A. Introd. Discourse on Medical Education. *Geneva,* 1844

The Dissector. Vol. II. October, 1845. No. IV.

Holmes, Oliver W. Introd. Lecture deliv. at Mass. Medical College, Nov. 3, 1847. *Boston*

Warren, John C. Address before the American Medical Association, at anniv. meeting, in Cincinnati, May 8, 1850. *Boston,* 1850

Brower, Jacob V. Popular Treatise, containing Observations concerning the Origin of Yellow Fever. *N. Y.,* 1805

Mitchell, George E. Inaug. Address on Puerperal State of Fever. *Phila.,* 1805

McCall, Edwin L. Inaug. Essay on Mutual Subserviences of the different parts of the Body. *Phila.,* 1806

Tucker, Wright. Inaug. Dissertation on the Operation of Cold. *Phila.,* 1806

Floyd, John. Experimental Enquiry into the Medical Properties of the Magnolia Tripetala and Magnolia Acuminta. *Phila.,* 1806

Medical College, Mass. Introductory Lecture. Nov. 6, 1850. By John Ware. *Boston*

1404 Medical Pamphlets. *Scarce lot.* [*Seventeen.*]

N. Y. University, College of Physicians and Surgeons; Historical Sketch of Origin, Progress, and Present State of. By Dr. Francis. *Scarce.* *N. Y.,* 1813

Hosack, David. Discourse on Theory and Practice of Physic and Tribute to Memory of Dr. Benjamin Rush. *New York,* 1813

Review of Essay on Bilious Epidemic Fever by Christopher C. Yates. *Albany,* 1813

N. Y. College of Physicians and Surgeons. Syllabus of Medical Lectures. *N. Y.,* 1814

Medical Soc., Anniv. Address to. By the President. *N. Y.,* 1815

Francis, John W. Letter on Febrile Contagion, to David Hosack. *N. Y.,* 1816

Delafield, Edward. Inaug. Dissertation on Pulmonary Consumption. *N. Y.,* 1816

Murray, John W. B. Eulogy on late Edward Post. *N. Y.,* 1816

Medico-Chirurgical Soc. of Univ. of N. Y., Report of Proc. of. *N. Y.,* 1818

Hosack, David. Tribute to Memory of the late Caspar Wistar. *N. Y.,* 1818

McNaughton, James. Disc. at anniv. meeting of Kappa Alpha Phi Soc. of College of Physicians and Surgeons. *Albany,* 1830

Southwick, Solomon. View of Origin, Powerful Influence and Pernicious Effects of Intemperance. *Albany,* 1832

Matlack, Charles F. View of Rise and Progress of Homœopathic Medicine. *Phila.,* 1833

Graham, Sylvester. Lecture on Epidemic Diseases generally, and the Spasmodic Cholera. *N. Y.*, 1833

Dunglison, Prof. Address to Graduates in Medicine at Annual Com. of University of Maryland. *Baltimore*, 1834

Proposal for altering the Eastern front of Phila., with view to prevent the recurrence of Malignant Disorders. According to the Original Design of William Penn. *Phila.*, 1820

Ducachet, Henry W. Biogr. Memoir of Samuel Bard. *Phila.*, 1821

1405 Medical Pamphlets. *Fine Lot.* [*Eighteen.*]

Mitchell, Samuel L., Discourse on Life and Character of Samuel Bard. *Scarce.* *N. Y.*, 1821

McClellan, George, Statement of Facts by. *Phila.*, 1822

Ducachet, Henry W. Tribute to Memory of Jacob Dyckman. *N. Y.*, 1823

Suckley, John L. Secretion the Source of Pleasurable Sensations. A Thesis. *N. Y.*, 1823

Mass., Gen. Hospital. Some Account of, and of the Medical School in Boston. *Boston*, 1824

MacNeven, Wm. J., Discourse on Application of Chemistry to Agriculture. *N. Y.*, 1825

Church, Dr. Wm. Analysis of the Waters of Bedford Mineral Springs. *Bedford, Pa.*, 1825

Jefferson Medical College. Representation of Conduct of the Trustees and Members of the Faculty and Circumstances in Relation to John Barnes. *Phila.*, 1828

Griffiths, Elijah. Observations on Fevers, &c. *Scarce.* *Phila.*, 1828

Beck, John B. Intro. Lecture deliv. at College of Phys. and Surgeons of N. Y., November 6, 1829.

Mott, Valentine. Biog. Memoir of Wright Post. *N. Y.*, 1829

Knight, J. Eulogium on Nathan Smith. *N. Haven*, 1829

Channing, Wm. Letters to Phys. of France on Homœopathy. By Count Des Guidi. Translated from French. *N. Y.*, 1834

Mayo, Herbert. Observations on Injuries and Diseases of the Rectum. *Washington*, 1834

Turnbull, Alexander. Investigation into the Remarkable Medicinal Effects resulting from the External Application of Veratria. *Washington*, 1834

Philip, A. P. W. Influence of Minute Doses of Mercury. *Washington*, 1834

Brodie, B. C. Observations on Diseases of the Joints. *Washington*, 1834

Blake, Andrew. Practical Essay on Delirium Tremens. *Washington*, 1834

1406 Medical Pamphlets. *Scarce Lot.* [*Twenty-one.*]

Cornell, Wm. M. Observations on Epilepsy. *Boston*, 1854

Dowler, Bennett. Tableau of Yellow Fever of 1853. *New Orleans*, 1854

Knapp, M. L, Discov. of Cause, Nature, Cure and Prevention of Epidemic Cholera. *N. Y.*, 1855

Harris, Elisha. Pestilential Diseases and Laws which Govern their Propagation. *Albany*, 1858

Jarvis, Edward. Tendency of Misdirected Education, &c., to produce Insanity. *Very curious doc.* *Dorchester*, 1858

Morton, Wm. T. G. Testimonial of Members of Medical Prof. *Phila.*, 1860

Clark, J. Henry. Medical Topography of Newark, N. J. *Scarce.* *N. Y.*, 1861

Strickland, A. Cholera, its Symptoms and Treatment. *Cincinnati*, 1866

Norwood, W. C. Authorship and Therapeutical Powers of Veratrum Viride. *Albany*, 1868

Markoe, Thomas M. Amputations at the Knee Joint. *N. Y.*, 1868

Manley, James R. Inaug. Address, Feb. 3, 1826.

Reports of the Medical Society of the City of New York, on Nostrums, or Secret Medicines. Part I. *N. Y.*, 1827

Dewees, Wm. P. Essay on Means of Lessening Pain and Facilitating Cases of Difficult Parturition. *Scarce.* *Philadelphia*, 1806

Simmons, Wm. H. Essays on some of the Effects of Contusions of the Head

N. Y. Medical Society. Report and Address by President to the Charter of College of Physicians and Surgeons. *N. Y.*, 1807

Low, Jacob. Dissertation on Lock-Jaw. *Edinburgh*, 1807

N. Y. Medical Society, By-Laws of. *N. Y.*, 1808

——— Transactions of, for 1808. *N. Y.*, 1809

Barton, Wm. P. C. Biographical Sketch of Professor Barton. *Scarce.* *Phila.*, 1810

Beck, Theodric R. Inaugural Dissertation on Insanity. *N. Y.*, 1811

Francis, John W. Inaugural Dissertation on Mercury. *N. Y.*, 1811

/0 1407 Medical Pamphlets. *Rare Lot.* [*Fourteen.*]

Medical Department. Lecture delivered at Opening of Columbian College, March 30, 1825. By Thomas Sewall. Second Edition. *Washington.*

Medical Society, An Inaugural Address delivered before, August 3, 1825. By John Onderdonk. *New York.*

Instructions and Observations concerning the Use of the Chlorides of Soda and Lime. By Jacob Porter. *New Haven*, 1829

Treatise on Malignant Fever. By I. Ffirth. *Very Rare.* *Philadelphia, June* 6, 1804

Complete Treatise on the Mineral Waters of Virginia. By J. Rouelle. *Scarce.* *Phila.*, 1792

An Account of the Malignant Fever in N. Y., 1805. By James Hardie. *Very scarce.* *N. Y.*, 1805

An Account of the Malignant Fever in N. Y. By James Hardie. *Very scarce.* *N. Y.*, 1799

Disc. on Epidemic Cholera Morbus, November 9, 1831. By J. M. Smith. *N. Y.*

Dissertation on the medical Properties and Injurious Effects of Use of Tobacco. By A. M'Allister. *Utica*, 1830

Carpenter's Annual Medical Advertiser for 1836. By G. W. Carpenter. *Phila.*

An Account of the Malignant Fever Lately Prevalent in Philadelphia. By Matthew Carey. Second Edition. *Phila., Nov.* 23, 1793

Remarks on Delirium Tremens. By John Watts. April 3, 1827. *N. Y.*

Discourse on Medical Education, April 6, 1819. By Samuel Bard. *N. Y.*

1408 Medical Pamphlets. [*Twenty-three.*]

Beakley, Prof. J. Valedic. Address at First Annual Commencement of the Homeopathic Med. College. *N. Y.*, 1861

Mass. Medical Society. Consumption in New Eng. By Henry I. Bowditch. *Boston*, 1862

R. I. Medical Society. Act of Incorp. and Medical Police, By-Laws, &c. *Providence*, 1838

Vermont Medical College. Catalogue of Trustees, Examiners, &c. *Woodstock*, 1843

Pargeter, Wm. Observations on Maniacal Disorders. *Very scarce.* *Reading*, 1792

Skinner, R. C. Treatise on the Human Teeth. *N. Y.*, 1801

McClellan, George. Statement of Facts, &c. *Phila.*, 1822

Haslam, John. Letters to Right Hon. Lord Chancellor on Moral Management of Insane Persons. *London*, 1823

Miner, Dr. Thomas. Typhus Syncopalis; or, Spotted Fever of N. Eng. *Very scarce.* *Middletown*, 1825

Warren, John C. Letter to Hon. Isaac Parker. Containing Remarks on the Dislocation of the Hip Joint. *Cambridge*, 1826

Reflections sur L'Ophthalmie. *Paris*, 1827

Francis, John W. Avon Mineral Waters. *N. Y.*, 1834

Morison, James. Essay on the Vitality of the Warm Blood and Air. *N. Y.*, 1834

Taylor, George. Enquiry into the Origin of Disease. *N. Y.*, 1839

Animal Magnetism. Report on Magnetic Experiments—Remarks on Col. Stone's Pamphlet. Second edition. *Phila.*, 1837

Electro-Magnetic—Brief Essay. By C. Griglietta. *Phila.*, 1838

Howe, J. M. To Consumptives: Information Respecting the Practice of F. M. Ramadge. *N. Y.*, 1840

Houston, James A. The New York Lancet. Volume I., No. 1. *N. Y.*, 1842

Du Cholera. A. M. Bureaud-Riofrey. *Paris*, 1847

Morehead, D. C. Cholera: Its Cure and Prevention. *N. Y.*, 1849

Wells, Dr. Horace. Discovery of Applicability of Nitrous Oxyde Gas, Sulphuric Ether, &c., in Surgical Operations. *Hartford*, 1850

London Medicated Vapor Bath Institution, Established 1822. *N. Y.*, 1850

Hossack, Alexander E. History of Case of John K. Rodgers. *Curious.* *N.* Y., 1851

7 1409 Medical Pamphlets. *Fine lot.* [*Twenty-two.*]

Medical College, Albany. Introductory Lecture at opening of, by David M. Reese. *Albany*, 1839

——— Address before the Grad. Class of, by A. J. Parker. *Albany*, 1851

Medical Society, Albany. Address on Semi-Cen. Anniv. by S. D. Willard. *Albany*, 1857

Medical Plants. Manual of Active Principles of Indigenous and Foreign.

Medicines. Specialties in, by Henry D. Noyes. *N. Y.*, 1865

Medical and Surgical Soc. Oration at Anniv. Meeting of, by G. W. Miltenberger. *Baltimore*, 1856

Hist. Sketch of the College of Physicians and Surgeons, by Dr. Francis. *Scarce.* *N. Y.*, 1813

Hosack, David. Introductory Discourse to Course of Lectures on the Theory and Practice of Physic, and Tribute to Mem. of Dr. Benj. Rush. *N. Y.*, 1813

Scudder, John. Inaugural Dissertation on Diseases of Old Age. *N. Y.*, 1815

College of Physicians and Surgeons. Secretion the Source of Pleasurable Sensations : a Thesis, by John L. Suckley. *N. Y.*, 1823

——— Disc. on Influence of Diseases on the Intellectual and Moral Powers, by Joseph M. Smith. *N. Y.*, 1848

——— Hist. of Art of Midwifery, by Augustus K. Gardner. *N. Y.*, 1852

Medical Society. Inaugural Address before, by John Onderdonk. *N. Y.*, 1825

Schroeder, John F. Address at opening of an Edifice erected by Trustees of N. Y. Dispensary. *N. Y.*, 1830

N. Y. Medical and Surgical Soc. Essay on Spinal Irritation, by John H. Griscom. *N. Y.*, 1840

N. Y. Medical College. Address on First Public Exhib., by Abm. L. Cox. *N. Y.*, 1850

Hospital, N. Y. By-laws and Regula. of, and Bloomingdale Asylum. *N. Y.*, 1833

Hempel, Charles J. Eclecticism in Medicine : Inaug. Thesis. *N. Y.*, 1845

Revere, John. Biographical Memoir of, by Valentine Mott. *N. Y.*, 1847

Francis, John W. Anniv. Disc. before the N. Y. Acad. of Medicine *N. Y.*, 1847

Medical Ethics, Code of, Adopted by Amer. Med. Assoc. and N. Y. Acad. of Med. *N. Y.*, 1848

Medicine, N. Y. Acad. of. Inaugural Address, by Thomas Cock. *N. Y.*, 1852

1410 Medical Pamphlets. [*Nineteen.*]

Graham, Sylvester. The Aesculapian Tablets of the Nineteenth Century. *Providence*, 1834

O'Beirne, James. New Views of the Process of Defecation. *Wash.*, 1834

Cutbush, Edward. Discourse at Opening of Medical Institution of Geneva College of N. Y. *Geneva*, 1835

Bigelow, Jacob. Discourse on Self-limited Diseases. *Boston*, 1835

Bedford, Gunning S. Address, Nov. 8, 1834. *N. Y.*, 1835

Fowler, Orin. Disquisition on Evils of using Tobacco. *Boston*, 1835

Delafield, Edward. Introd. Address to Students of College of Phys. and Surgeons of Univ. of N. Y., Nov. 7, 1837.

Wilson, Rev. James R. Address deliv. before Newburgh Library Assoc. on First Anniv., Dec. 29, 1836. *Newburgh*, 1837

American Medical Library and Intelligencer. 1836

Boston Medical and Surgical Journal, Dec. 20, 1837.

Knight, Jonathan. Lecture Introductory to Course of Instruction in Medical Institution of Yale College. *N. Haven*, 1838

Transylvania Medical Journal. Catalogue of Medical Graduates. *Lexington, Ky.*, 1838

Jefferson Medical College. Prof. Pattison's Intro. Lecture. *Phila.*, 1838

Medical Missionary Society in China. Address. *Canton*, 1838

Crossman, T. J. Extracts from a Work on Counter-Irritation. *Phila.*, 1839

Bucknell, William. Eccaleobion. Treatise on Artificial Incubation. *London*, 1839

Medical Convention of Ohio. Journal of Proc. of, at its Third Session, Cleveland, May 14, 15, 1839.

Wood, George B. Address to Medical Graduates of Univ. of Penn. *Phila.*, 1836

Bedford, Gunning S. Address, Nov. 15, 1835. *N. Y.*, 1836

1411 Medical Pamphlets. *Very scarce lot.* [*Sixteen.*]

Dunglison, Robley. Address to Medical Graduates of Jefferson Medical College. *Phila.*, 1837

Hamilton, Frank H. Intro. Lecture before Surgical Class of Geneva Medical College, Dec. 1, 1840.

Brandreth, Benjamin. Purgation; or, Brandrethian Method of Treating Diseases and Curing them. *N. Y.*, 1840

Webster, James. Lecture on Anatomy and Physiology. *Geneva*, 1840

Bryan, James. Lecture on Principles and Practice of Surgery in Vermont Academy of Medicine, March 12, 1840.

Huston, R. M. Introd. Lecture to Course of Obstetrics and Diseases of Women and Children. *Phila.*, 1840

N. Y. Medical Gazette, Dec 1, 1841.

M'Clintock, James. Introd. Lecture to Course on Anatomy and Physiology, April 7, 1841. *Castleton, Vt.*

Macgowan, Daniel J. Claims of the Missionary on the Medical Profession. Address by. *N. Y.*, 1842

M'Clintock, James. Introd. Lecture deliv. in Castleton Medical College, March 8, 1842.

Reese, David M. Introd. Lecture deliv. before the Medical Class in Castleton Med. College at opening of the Fall Session, 1842.

Post, Alfred C. Introd. Address at Commencement of Course of Lectures on Opthalmic Anatomy and Surgery. *Rutland*, 1843

Carr, Ezra S. Introd. Lecture at opening of Fall Session, 1843 *Albany*, 1843

Chemistry in its relations to Agriculture. *Edinburgh*, 1845

Draper, John W. Allotropism of Chlorine as connected with the Theory of Substitutions. *New Haven*, 1845

Silliman, B., Jr. Report of Chemical Exami. of Several Waters for City of Boston. *N. Haven*, 1845

1412 Medical Pamphlets. *Very scarce lot.* [*Eighteen.*]

Mitchell, Samuel L., and James M'Neven. Chemical Examination of the Mineral Water of Schooley's Mountain Springs. *Morristown*, 1845

Gibbs, Oliver W. Inaug. Dissertation on Chemical Classification. *Princeton, N. J.*, 1845

Trenor, John. Observations on Amalgam. *N. Y.*, 1847

Stearns, John. Address on assuming the Chair as President at First Regular Meeting of N. Y. Acad. of Medicine, Feb. 3, 1847.

Vaughan, Daniel. A New System of Vegetable Physiology. *Cincinnati*, 1848

Jackson, Charles T. Memorial addressed to Trustees of Mass. Gen. Hospital in behalf of, by Joseph L. and Henry C. Lord. *Boston*, 1849

Horsford, E. N. Service-pipes for Water. Investigation by. *Cambridge*, 1849

Stevens, Alex. S. Annual Address before N. Y. State Medical Soc. and Members of Legislature, Feb. 6, 1849. *N. Y.*

Salisbury, J. H. Analysis of Rhubarb. *Albany*, 1850

Chemical Exam. of the Urinary Calculi, in Transylvania Univ.

Gardner, Augustus K. History of Art of Midwifery. Lecture by. *N. Y.*, 1852

Marchand, R. F. and Th. Scheerer. Chemical Qualities of Magnesia.

Carey, Mathew. Account of the Malignant Fever lately prevalent in Phila., 1793.

Davidson, Robert G. W. Inaug. Dissertation on the Suffocatio Stridula, or Croup. *Phila.*, 1794

Sugrue, Charles. Dissertation on Respiration. *Edinburgh*, 1796

Church, John. Dissertation on Camphor. *Phila.*, 1797

Disborough, Henry. Dissertation on Cholera Infantum. *Phila.*, 1798

Stuart James. Dissertation on Salutary Effects of Mercury in Malignant Fevers. *Phil.*, 1798

NACK, JAMES. The Legend of the Rocks, and other Poems. 12*mo, half mor.* *New York*, 1827

1414 NAHANT, Mass. Guide through, containing a description of Swallow's Cave, etc., with an account of the First Inhabitants, etc. By Alonzo Lewis. 8*vo pamphlet*, 14 *p., scarce.* *Lynn*, 1851

1415 NAHANT, Mass. The Picture of. By Alonzo Lewis. 12*mo pamphlet*, 32 *p. Illust.* *Lynn*, 1855

1416 NANTUCKET, Mass. History of, being a compendious account of the first settlement of the Island by the English, with the rise and progress of the Whale Fishery ; and other Historical facts. By Obed Macy. With map. 8*vo, cl. very scarce.* *Boston*, 1835

1417 Narraganset, Chief. The Adventures of a Wanderer. 8*vo, bds.* *New York*, 1832

1418 NARRAGANSETT CLUB, Publications of. First Series, Vol. 3. Containing Reprint of the 1644 edition of the "Bloody Tenent, of Persecution, for causse of Conscience, Discussed in a Conference betweene Truth and Peace. Who in all tender Affection, present to the High Court of Parliament (as the result of their Discourse,) these (amongst other Passages) of highest consideration." Only 200 copies printed. Edited by Samuel Caldwell. 4*to, uncut, cl.* *Providence R. I.* 1867

1419 NATICK, Mass. A Sermon delivered Jan. 5, 1817, containing a History of said Town, from 1651 to the Day of delivery. By Martin Moore. 8*vo pamphlet, uncut*, 24 *pages, very scarce in this condition.* *Cambridge*, 1817

1420 NATICK, Mass. History of the Town of, from the days of the Apostolic Eliot, 1650, to the present time 1830. By William Biglow. 8*vo, paper cov.*, 87 *pages, uncut, very fine copy, scarce.* *Boston*, 1830

1421 NATICK, Mass. History of, from its First Settlement in 1651, to the Present Time, with Notices of the First White Families, and also an account of the Centennial Celebration, Oct. 16,

1851. Rev. Mr. Hunt's address at consecration of Dell Park Cemetery, etc. By Oliver N. Bacon. *8vo, cl., plates and ports. fine copy, scarce.* *Boston,* 1856

1422 NATIONAL INSTITUTION. Circular and address of, for promoting Industry in the United States, to their Fellow Citizens. *8vo,* 28 *pages, good copy.* *New York,* 1820

1423 NEAL, DANIEL. The History of the Puritans ; or, Protestant Non-Conformists. From the Reformation under King Henry VIII, to the Act of Toleration, under King William and Queen Mary, with an account of their principles, etc. In two volumes. The 2nd ed. corrected. *4to, cf.* *London,* MDCCLIV

Fine Portrait of Neal, after Ravenet.

1424 NEAL, DANIEL. The History of the Puritans ; or, Protestant Non-conformists, from the Reformation to the Act of Toleration in the Reign of King William and Queen Mary, in the year 1688. Containing an account of their Principles, their attempts for a further Reformation in the church, their sufferings, and the Lives and Characters of their principal Divines. A new edition, revised, corrected and enlarged, by Joshua Toulmin, D. D., to which are prefixed, some Memoirs of the Life and Writings of the Author. *8vo, sh.* 5 *vols., best edition. Bath: printed by R. Cruttwell.* *London,* 1793–1797

1425 NEAL, DANIEL. History of the Puritans ; or, Protestant Non-conformists, from the Reformation in 1517, to the Revolution in 1688. A New Edition, in Five Volumes : Re-printed from the text of Dr. Toulmin's Editon, with his Life of the Author and account of his Writings. Revised, corrected and enlarged. 5 *vols., 8vo, bds., uncut.* *London,* 1822

1426 Neal, John. The Battle of Niagara, with other Poems. 2nd ed. enlarged. *18mo, bds., uncut.* *Baltimore,* 1819

1427 NEEDHAM, Mass. Sermon Delivered, on the Termination of a Century since the incorporation of the Town. By Stephen Palmer. *8vo,* 40 *pages, uncut, scarce.* *Dedham,* 1811

1428 "Negro Pew." Being an Inquiry concerning the Propriety of Distinctions in the House of God, on account of Color. *Bds., 12mo.* *Boston,* 1837

1429 Nell, William C. The Colored Patriots of the American Revolution, with Sketches of several Distinguished Colored Persons, to which is added a brief survey of the Condition and Prospects of Colored Americans. With an Introduction by Harriet Beecher Stowe. *12mo, cl. With plates.* *Boston,* 1855

1430 NEW AMSTERDAM. History of ; or, New York as it was, in the days of the Dutch Governors. Together with papers on events connected with the American Revolution ; and on Philadelphia in the times of William Penn. *12mo, cl. With plates.* *New York,* 1854

1431 NEWARK Mechanics' Assoc. Address delivered on the 3d anniv., Jan. 25, 1831. By John Griscom. *8vo,* 39 *pages, fine copy.* Also, address by Samuel L. Southard, July 5, 1830. *8vo,* 27 *pages ; fine copy. Two pamphlets, scarce.* *Newark,* 1830–1

1432 NEWARK, N. J. Historical Discourses, in the First Presbyterian Church in Newark; delivered in the Month of Jan. 1851. By Jonathan F. Stearns, D. D. With notes and Illustrations. 12*mo, half mor.* *Newark, N. J.*, 1852

1433 NEW BEDFORD, (Mass.), History of, containing a History of the old Township of Dartmouth and the present Townships of Westport, Dartmouth, and Fair Haven, from their settlement to the present time. By Daniel Ricketson. 8*vo, cl.* *New Bedford*, 1858

1434 NEWBERRY, (S. C.), Annals of. Historical, Biographical and Anecdotal. By J. Belton O'Neall, LL. D. 12*mo, cl.; with portrait.* *Charleston, S. C.*, 1859

1435 NEW BOSTON, (N. H.), History of. By E. C. Cogswell. *Large* 8*vo, cl.*, 39 *portraits and engravings; scarce.* *Boston*, 1864

1436 NEWBURGH, (N. Y.), History of the Town of. By E. M. Ruttenber. *Illustrations by C. W. Tice. Royal* 8*vo, cl.; scarce.* *Newburgh*, 1859

1437 NEWBURYPORT, (Mass.), History and present state of the town of. By Caleb Cushing. 12*mo, bds., uncut, fine copy; very scarce.* *Newburyport*, 1826

1438 NEWBURYPORT, (Mass.), History of, from the earliest settlement of the country to the present time. With a Biographical Appendix. By Mrs. E. Vale Smith. 8*vo, cl.* *Newburyport*, 1854

1439 NEWBURY, NEWBURYPORT AND WEST NEWBURY, (Mass.), Sketches of the History of, from 1635 to 1845. By Joshua Coffin. 8*vo, cl. Plates. Portrait of Dr. John Clarke.* *Boston*, 1845

Jos. B. Felt's Copy. With Autograph.

1440 Newell, William. Discourse deliv. before the First Parish in Cambridge, May 27, 1855, on the completion of the 25th year of his Ministry. 8*vo, orig. cov., rough edges,* 28 *p. sermon;* 8 *p. appendix, which contains considerable Historical matter.* *Cambridge*, 1855

1441 NEW ENGLAND, The History of. Containing an Impartial Account of the Civil and Ecclesiastical Affairs of the Country, to the year of our Lord, 1700. To which is added the Present State of New England. With a new and accurate map of the country. And an Appendix, containing their Present Charter, their Ecclesiastical Discipline, and their Municipal Laws. In two volumes. By Daniel Neal. 8*vo, bds., uncut, with map; very rare in this condition.* *London, MDCCXX.*

1442 NEW ENGLAND, The History of. Containing an Impartial Account of the Civil and Ecclesiastical Affairs of the Country, to 1700. To which is added, The Present State of New England. With a new and accurate map of the Country. And an Appendix, containing their Present Charter, their Ecclesiastical Discipline, and their Municipal Laws. In two volumes. The Second Edition. With many additions by the Author. By Daniel Neal. 2 *Vols.,* 8*vo, cf.* *London, MDCCLXVII.*

1443 NEW ENGLAND. A Platform of Church Discipline, gathered out of the word of God, and agreed upon by the Elders and Messengers of the Churches assembled in the Synod at Cambridge, in New England. 12*mo, unbound.* *Boston*, 1772

1444 NEW ENGLAND, A Compendious History of. By Jed. Morse and Elijah Parish. 1*st Ed.* 8*vo, bds., uncut; map; very scarce in this condition.* *Charlestown*, 1804

1445 NEW ENGLAND, A General History of, from the discovery to MDCLXXX. By William Hubbard. 8*vo, bds., uncut; very scarce.* *Cambridge*, 1815

1446 NEW ENGLAND AND NEW YORK, Travels in. In four volumes. By Timothy Dwight. 8*vo, maps, bds., uncut; beautiful copy.* *New Haven*, 1821–22

1447 (NEW ENGLAND). The Witch of New England. A Romance. 12*mo, sheep.* *Philadelphia*, 1824

1448 NEW ENGLAND'S MEMORIAL; or, a brief relation of the most memorable and remarkable passages of the Providence of God, manifested to the Planters of New England, in America. With special reference to the First Colony thereof, called New Plymouth. By Nathaniel Morton. 8*vo, sh.; good copy.* *Plymouth*, 1826

1449 New England Village, Sketches of, in the Last Century. 12*mo, cl.* *Boston*, 1838

1450 NEW ENGLAND, Church History of, from 1620 to 1804. Containing a view of the Principles and Practice, Declensions and Revivals, Oppression and Liberty of the Churches, and a Chronological Table. With a Memoir of the Author. By Isaac Backus. 8*vo, sh.; good cond.* *Phila.*, 1839

1451 NEW ENGLAND, The Early History of. Illustrated by numerous interesting incidents. By Henry White. 12*mo, sh.* 2*d Ed.* *Concord, N. H.*, 1841

1452 NEW ENGLAND, Sketches of, or Memories of the Country. By John Carver, Esq. 8*vo, cl.* *New York*, 1842

1453 NEW ENGLAND. Chronology from the Discovery of the Country, by Cabot, 1497 to 1820. By Alden Bradford. 12*mo, cl.* *Boston*, 1843

1454 NEWGATE, Conn. A History of the Prison, its Insurrections, Massacres, etc., Imprisonment of the Tories, in the Revolution; the ancient and recent working of its Mines, etc. By Richard H. Phelps. 8*vo pamph.* 1*st Ed.* 24 *pages; very scarce.* *Hartford*, 1844

1455 NEW HAMPSHIRE Historical Society. Collections. Vols. I., II., III., IV., V., VI., VII., VIII. Provincial Papers, Vols. I.–II., being Vols. IX. and X. of the Collections. 8*vo, bds. and paper, uncut;* 10 *vols.; very scarce; fine copies.* *Concord and Manchester*, 1824–1868

1456 NEW HAMPSHIRE. Notes made during an Excursion to the Highlands of, and Lake Winnepiseogee, by a Gentleman of Boston. 8*vo, bds., uncut.* *Andover*, 1833

1457 NEW HAMPSHIRE. History of, from its settlement, in 1623, to 1833. Comprising notices of the memorable events and interesting incidents of a period of two hundred and ten years. By John M. Whiton. *8vo, cl.* *Concord,* 1834

1458 NEW HAMPSHIRE. History of, from its discovery, in 1614, to the Passage of the Toleration Act, in 1819. By George Barstow. *8vo, 2d ed., cloth.* *Boston,* 1853

1459 NEW HAMPSHIRE. Second Festival of the Sons of, celebrated in Boston, Nov. 2, 1853; including also an account of the Proceedings in Boston on the Day of the Funeral at Marshfield, and the subsequent obsequies commemorative of the death of Daniel Webster. *8vo, cl. Port.* *Boston,* 1854

1460 NEW HAVEN, (Conn.) Two Discourses. I. On the Commencement of a New Year. II. On the Completion of the Eighteenth Century. Delivered in New Haven—the former, Jan. 4: the latter, Jan, 11, 1801. By James Dana. *8vo pamphlet; 68 pages, uncut; fine copy, scarce.* *New Haven,* 1801

1461 NEW HAVEN, (Conn.) A Statistical Account of the City of, by Timothy Dwight. *8vo pamph; 83 p., rough edges; scarce.* *New Haven,* 1811

1462 NEW HAVEN, (Conn.) History and Antiquities of, from its earliest settlement to the present time. By J. W. Barber. *Cl., 12mo, illus., rough edges.* *New Haven,* 1831

1463 NEW HAVEN, (Conn.) History and Antiquities of, from its earliest settlement to the present time; with Biographical sketches and Statistical information of the Public Institutions, &c., &c. By John W. Barber. *With plates and engravings. 8vo, hlf. calf.* *New Haven,* 1856

1464 NEW IPSWICH, (Mass.) The History of, from its First grant, in 1736, to the present time. With Genealogical notices of the principal Families, and also the proceedings of the Centennial celebration, Sept. 11, 1850. By Frederic Kidder. *Royal 8vo, bds., uncut; 35 illlus.; scarce.* *Boston,* 1852

1465 NEW JERSEY. The History of the Colony of Nova Cæsaria, or New Jersey. Containing an account of its first settlement, progressive improvements, the original and present Constitution, and other events, to the year 1721, with some particulars since, and a short view of its present state. By Samuel Smith. *8vo., full crushed crimson levant mor., gt.; beautiful copy. Bound by R. W. Smith.* *Burlington, in New Jersey,* MDCCLXV.

1466 NEW JERSEY. Civil and Political History of, embracing a compendious History of the State, from its Early Discovery and Settlement by Europeans, brought down to the present time. By Isaac S. Mulford. *8vo, cl.; scarce.* *Phila.,* 1851

1467 NEW JERSEY. Historical Collections of, containing a general collection of the most interesting facts, etc., relating to its History and Antiquities, with Geographical descriptions of every Township in the State. By John W. Barber and Henry Howe. *Illustrated by 120 Engravings. 8vo, in sheets, stitched; very scarce.* *Newark, etc.,* 1860

1468 NEW JERSEY. Thirty days in New Jersey, ninety years ago: an essay, revealing new facts in connection with Washington and his Army, in 1776 and 1777. By C. C. Haven. *8vo, cl.; scarce.* *Trenton,* 1867

1469 NEW LONDON, (Conn.) History of, from its First survey of the coast, in 1612, to 1852. By Francis M. Caulkins. *Second edition. Continued to* 1860. *8vo, cl. Scarce and valuable local history.* *New London*, 1860

1470 NEW MEXICO. Report of Lieut. J. W. Abert, of his Examination, &c., of, in 1846–'7. *8vo, unb., with plates; paper uncut.* *n. d.*

1471 New Mirror for Travelers, and Guide to the Springs. By an Amateur. *8v, bds., uncut.* *New York*, 1828

1472 NEW ORANGE (Now New York); View of the City of—as it was in the Year 1673. With Explanatory Notes. By Joseph W. Moulton. *1st Ed. 8vo, very scarce.* *N. Y.*, 1825

1473 NEWPORT, R. I.; Sketches of—and its Vicinity; with Notices respecting the History, Settlement and Geography of Rhode Island. With plates. *12mo, cloth.* *New York*, 1842

1474 NEWPORT, R. I. The Controversy touching the Old Stone Mill. With Remarks, Introductory and Conclusive. *8vo pamph.; 91 p.; illust. Scarce.* *Newport*, 1851

1475 NEWPORT, R. I., Illustrated in a Series of Pen and Pencil Sketches. By the Editor of the Newport Mercury. Engravings. *12mo, cl.* *N. Y.*, 1854

1476 NEWPORT, R. I.; Re-union of the Sons and Daughters of. Aug. 23, 1859. By George C. Mason. *8vo, cloth.* *Newport*, 1859

1477 NEWPORT, R. I. Services at the Dedication of the School House, erected by the Trustees of Long Wharf, May 20, 1863. With an Appendix. *8vo, 106 pages.* *Newport*, 1863

1478 NEWTON, Mass.; A brief Notice of the Settlement of the Town of. Prepared by a Committee who were charged with the duty of erecting a monument to the memory of the First Settlers. Sept., 1852. 38 *pages, etc.; pamph.* *Boston*, 1852

1479 NEWTON, Mass.; History of the Early Settlement of—from 1639 to 1800; with a Genealogical Register of its Inhabitants prior to 1800. By Francis Jackson. *8vo, cl.; portrait.* *Boston*, 1854

1480 NEWTOWN, N. Y.; Annals of. Containing its History from its First Settlement, together with many interesting facts concerning the adjacent Towns; also a particular account of numerous Long Island Families, etc. By James Riker, Jr. *8vo, half mor., maps; scarce.* *N. Y.*, 1852

1481 NEVIN, Rev. ALFRED. Churches of the Valley; or, an Historical Sketch of the Old Presbyterian Congregations of Cumberland and Franklin Counties in Pennslyvania. *12mo, cl.* *Phila.*, 1852

1482 NEW YORK. Report of the Commissioners appointed by the Senate and Assembly, March 15, 1810, to explore the Route of an Inland Navigation from Hudson's River to Lake Ontario and Lake Erie. *8vo, fine copy;* 35 *pages; very scarce.* *Albany*, 1811

Report signed by Gouv. Morris, S. Van Rensselaer, W. North, De Witt Clinton, etc.

1483 NEW YORK. Report of the Commissioners appointed by the Legislature for the Consideration of all matter relating to the Inland Navigation of the State. *8vo, fine copy;* 40 *pages ; scarce.* *Albany,* 1812

This Report is signed by Gouv. Morris, De Witt Clinton, S. Van Rensselaer, S. De Witt, W. North and R. R. Livingston ; also copy of letter from Robt. Bowne, to Robert Fulton.

1484 NEW YORK CITY. Strangers' Guide to. To which is prefixed, an Historical Sketch, &c. With an Appendix. Embellished with a Plan of the City, and engravings of public buildings. By Edmund M. Blunt. 12*mo, sheep ; scarce.* *New York,* 1817

1485 New York, Anti-Auction Com. Facts important to be Known by the Manufacturers, Mechanics and all other Classes of the Community. 8*vo,* 39 *pages ; good copy.* *New York,* 1831

1486 NEW YORK. Sketches of the North River. 12*mo, cl. ; maps ; scarce.* *New York,* 1838

1487 New-York. A Familiar Conversational History of the Evangelical Churches of. 16*mo, cl. Woodcuts.* *New York,* 1838

1488 New York Mirror. A Weekly Journal, devoted to Literature and the Fine Arts. Embellished with Engravings and Music. 6 *vols. fol., half calf.* *New York,* 1838

Contains valuable views of the city, and portraits of Sprague, Halleck, Irving, and others.

1489 NEW YORK CITY. Pen and Ink Panorama of. By Cornelius Mathews. 12*mo, cl.* *New York,* 1853

1490 NEW YORK. A Discourse delivered in the North Reformed Dutch Church, on the last Sabbath in August, 1856. By Thomas Dewitt, D.D. Published by the Consistory of the Dutch Reformed Church. 8*vo, cl. With plates.* *New York,* 1857

1491 NEW YORK and CONNECTICUT. A Memorial of the Dedication of Monuments Erected by the Moravian Historical Society, to mark the sites of Ancient Missionary Stations, in New York and Connecticut. 8*vo, cloth.* *New York and Philadelphia,* 1860

1492 NEW YORK, The Women of. Written and Illustrated. By Marie L. Hankins. 8*vo, cl.; free.* *New York,* 1861

1493 NEW YORK (City) during the American Revolution. Being a collection of original papers (now first published) from the manuscripts in the possession of the Mercantile Library Association. 4*to, cl.. uncut ; rubric title. With map.* *New York: privately printed for the Association.* 1861

1494 NEW YORK. Old New York ; or, Reminiscences of the Past Sixty Years. By John W. Francis. With a Memoir of the Author, by Henry T. Tuckerman. 8*vo, cl. With portraits and plate ; uncut.* 100 *copies printed.* *N. Y.,* 1865

1495 NEW YORK Historical Society, Collections of—for the Year 1809. Vol. I. 8*vo, bds., uncut.* *N. Y.,* 1811

1496 NEW YORK Historical Society, Collections of—for the Year 1814. Vol. II. 8*vo, bds., uncut ; very scarce.* *N. Y.,* 1814

1497 NEW YORK Historical Society, Collections of. 2d Series. Vol. I. *8vo, cl., scarce.* *N. Y.*, 1841

1498 NEW YORK HISTORICAL SOCIETY. Discourse delivered before—at their anniversary meeting, 6th December, 1811. By De Witt Clinton. *8vo, half mor.; very scarce.* *N. Y.*, 1812

1499 NEW YORK Historical Society. Memoir read before the. Dec. 31, 1816. On the Dutch and Indian names of New York. By Egbert Benson. 2d Ed., with Notes. *8vo, bds., uncut; beautiful copy. Very scarce.* *Jamaica*, 1825

1500 NEW YORK, Manual of the Corporation of the City of. For the *years* 1842–'43. By D. T. Valentine. *12mo, maps, etc. Very scarce; fine copies.* *New York*, 1843

1501 NEW YORK, Manual of the Corporation of the City of. For the years, 1850, '58, '59, '62, '64, '65. By D. T. Valentine. *6 vols. Cl., 12mo, maps and plates.* *New York*, 1851

1502 NEW YORK, History of. From its First Discovery to the year 1732. To which is annexed, a description of the Country, with a short Account of the Inhabitants, their Religious and Political state, and the Constitution of the Courts of Justice in that Colony. With a continuation, from the year 1732, to the Commencement of the year 1814. By Wm. Smith. *L. 8vo, bds., uncut, scarce; fine copy.* *Albany*, 1814

1503 NEW YORK, The Natural, Statistical and Civil History of the State of. By James Macauley. *3 vols. 8vo, full clf.* *New York*, 1829

1504 NEW YORK CITY, A Summary Hist., Geog. and Statist. view of. *Together with some Notices of Brooklyn, Williamsburgh, etc., in its environs. Prepared to accompany the Topog. Map of the City and County of New York. 16mo, cl., plates.* *New York*, 1836

1505 NEW YORK. History of New Netherlands, Province of New York, and State of New York, to the adoption of the Federal Constitution. By William Dunlap. 2 vols. *With portraits and plates. 8vo, cl.; scarce.* *New York*, 1839

1506 NEW YORK, (WESTERN.) A History of the Purchase and Settlement of Western New York, and the Rise, Progress, and present state of the Presbyterian Church in that section. By James H. Hotchkiss. *8vo, cl.; with plates.* *New York*, 1848

1507 NEW YORK, (*St. Lawrence and Franklin Counties.*) A History of. From the earliest Period to the present time. By Franklin F. Hough. *Half Roxburghe, gilt top, edges uncut; fine copy.* *Albany*, 1853

1508 NEW YORK CITY, History of. By David T. Valentine. *8vo, cl.; with maps, plans and plates.* *New York*, 1853

1509 NEW YORK. History of New Amsterdam, or New York as it Was, in the days of the Dutch Governors. Together with papers on events connected with the American Revolution; and on Philadelphia in the Time of Wm. Penn. By Prof. A. Davis. *8vo, full red Turkey, glt. edges.* By *R. W. Smith. Fine copy; illustrated.* *New York*, 1854

1510 NEW YORK. A Lecture on the Topography and History of New York. By Horatio Seymour. *8vo pamphlet, 41 p. Scarce; fine copy.* *Utica*, 1856

1511 NEW YORK, History of the Five Indian Nations depending on the Province of. By Cadwallader Colden. Reprinted exactly from Bradford's New York edition (1727.) With an introduction, by John Gilmary Shea. *8vo, or. cov., uncut, rubric title, 125 copies, No. 98; with portrait.* *N. Y.*, 1866

1512 NEW YORK CITY, History of. From the Discovery, to the Present Day. By Wm. L. Stone. *8vo, cl.* *New York*, 1868

1513 NIAGARA, MONTREAL and QUEBEC, An account of Journey to. In 1765, or "'tis Eighty years since." *8vo pamphlet, 30 pages.* *New York*, 1846

1514 Nichols, Maj. Geo. Ward. The Story of the Great March. From the Diary of a Staff Officer. With maps and illustrations. *8vo, hlf. crim. cr., lev. mor., gilt top, edges uncut, bound by R. W. Smith.* *New York*, 1865

1515 NONANTUM and NATICK. By Sarah S. Jacobs. *8vo, cl., gilt; scarce, illustrated.* *Boston*, 1853

1516 NORFOLK, (Conn.) Half Century Sermon, deliv. Oct. 28, 1811. By Ammi R. Robbins. *2d ed.* *8vo pamphlet, 20 pages. Fine copy; scarce.* *Hartford*, 1812

1517 NORFOLK, (Conn.) A brief History of the Town of. From 1783 to 1844, and a Summary of Events which have occurred in this Town, from its First Settlement, Chronologically arranged, etc. By Auren Roys. *8vo pamph., 89 pages, fine copy; scarce.* *New York*, 1847

1518 NORFOLK, (*Va.*,) (and Vicinity,) Historical and Descriptive Sketches of. Including Portsmouth and the Adjacent Counties during a period of Two Hundred Years; also, Sketches of Williamsburg, Hampton, Suffolk, Smithfield, and other places, with descriptions of some of the principal objects of interest in Eastern Virginia. By William S. Forrest. *8vo, cl.* *Philadelphia*, 1853

1519 NORRIDGEWOCK and CANAAN, (Me.,) History of the Old Towns of. Comprising Norridgewock, Canaan, Starks, Skowhegan, and Bloomfield, from their early settlement, to the year 1849; including a sketch of the Abnakis Indians. By J. W. Hanson. *12mo, cl., with plates. Very scarce.* *Boston*, 1849

1520 NORRIDGEWOCK, (Me.,) The History of, Comprising Memorials of the Aboriginal Inhabitants and Jesuit Missionaries, Hardships of the Pioneers, Biographical notices of the early Settlers, and Ecclesiastical sketches. By Wm. Allen. *12mo, cl., with plates. Very scarce.* *Norridgewock*, 1849

1521 Norris, J. Saurin. The Early Friends; or, Quakers in Maryland. Read at the Meeting of Maryland Historical Society, March 6, 1862. *8vo pamph., 30 pages.* *Baltimore*, 1862

1522 NORTH AMERICA, Travels through the Interior Parts of. In the years 1766, 1767, and 1768. By J. Carver. Illustrated with copper plates. *8vo, cl.* *London, MDCCLXXVIII.*

1523 NORTH BROOKFIELD, Mass. A Sermon, delivered by Rev. Dr. Snell, June, 1838. Containing a brief History of the Town, and especially of the Church and Parish, from 1798 to the present time. *Pamphlet.* 55 *pages ; very scarce.* *Brookfield,* 1838

1524 NORTH BROOKFIELD, Mass. A Discourse Containing an Historical Sketch of the Town. By Thomas Snell. *8vo pamph.* 56 *p. ; very scarce ; fine copy.* *West Brookfield,* 1854

1525 NORTH BRIDGEWATER, (Mass.), History of, from its First Settlement to the present time, with Family Registers. By Bradford Kingman. *8vo, sheets, stitched.* 40 *illustrations.* *Boston,* 1866

1526 NORTH CAROLINA, A Defence of the Revolutionary History of, from the Aspersions of Mr. Jefferson. By Jos. S. Jones. *8vo, cloth, uncut.* *Boston,* 1834

1527 NORTH CAROLINA, Memorials of. By J. Seawell Jones, of Shocco. *8vo, unbd.* *New York,* 1838

1528 NORTH CAROLINA, The Moravians in. An Authentic History. By Levin T. Reichel. 12*mo, cloth ; scarce.* *Salem, N. C.,* 1857

1529 NORTH CAROLINA, Geological Survey. Part II., Agriculture. Containing descriptions, with many analyses, of the soils of the Swamp Lands. By Ebenezer Emmons. *8vo, paper covers.* *Raleigh,* 1860

1530 (NORTH CAROLINA). Geological and Natural History Survey. Part III., Botany : Containing a Catalogue of the Plants of the State, with Descriptions and History of the Trees, Shrubs, and Woody Vines. By M. A. Curtis, D. D. *8vo, paper.* *Raleigh,* 1860

1531 (NORTH PROVIDENCE. Centennial). Report of the Celebration at Pawtucket, North Providence, on the One Hundredth Anniversary of the Incorporation of the Town, June 24, 1865. With an address containing Historical Matters of Local Interest. *8vo, paper covers.* *Pawtucket,* 1865

1532 NORTH CAROLINA. Agricultural, Geological, and Descriptive Sketches of Lower N. C. and the similar adjacent Lands. By Edmund Ruffin. *8vo, orig. cov. ; scarce.* *Raleigh,* 1861

1533 NORTH-WESTERN TERRITORY, Notes on the Early Settlement of. By Jacob Burnet. *8vo, cloth. Portrait of J. Burnet.* *Cincinnati,* 1847

1534 NORTH-WESTERN REVIEW, and Commercial and Real Estate Reporter. Vol. 1, No. 1. June, 1856, to No. 11, April, 1858, inclusive. H. H. Belding Editor. *8vo, hf. shp. ; very scarce. Contains considerable local History.* *Keokuk, Iowa,* 1856–1858

1535 NORTHAMPTON, Mass., Historical Sketch of, from its first settlement. In a Sermon, delivered April 13, 1815. By Rev. Solomon Williams. 24 *p. uncut ; very scarce ; beautiful copy.* *Northampton,* 1815

1536 NORTHAMPTON, (Mass.). Register of the Deaths in, from the First Settlement of the Town, in 1653, to August, 1824. Copied from the Town Records, and from the Records of Dea.

Ebenezer Hunt, Rev. John Hooker, Rev. Solomon Williams, Doct. Eben. Hunt and Doct. David Hunt. *12mo, paper cov., 80 pages; very scarce.* *Northampton*, 1824

1537 NORTHAMPTON, (Mass.) An Address delivered Oct. 29, 1854, in Commemoration of the close of the Second Century, since the settlement of the Town. By William Allen. *8vo pamph., 56 p., scarce; fine copy.* *Northampton*, 1855

1538 NORTHBOROUGH, (Mass.), Historical Sketch of. By Joseph Allen. *8vo pamph., 10 p.*

1539 NORTON, (Mass.), History of, from 1669 to 1859. By George Faber Clark. *8vo, cl.* 19 *Portraits and Plates.* *Boston*, 1859

1540 Norton, Charles B. Literary Letter, comprising American Papers of Interest, and a Catalogue of Rare and Valuable Books relative to America. Bibliographies of Maine, New Hampshire and Vermont. *Sm. 4to, in 6 Nos. complete.* *New York*, 1857

1541 NORWICH, (Conn.), History of, from its Settlement, 1660, to January, 1845. By Miss F. M. Caulkins. *12mo, cl. Frontispiece. 1st Ed. Scarce.* *Norwich*, 1845

1542 NORWICH, (Conn.) The Norwich Jubilee, Report of the Celebration at, on the Two Hundredth Anniv. of the Settlement of the Town, Sep. 7th and 8th, 1859. With an Appendix, containing Historical Documents of Local Interest. By John W. Stedman. *8vo, hf. calf, marbled edges, map and plates; fine copy.* *Norwich*, 1859

1543 NORWICH, Conn., A Historical Discourse delivered in, Sept. 7, 1859, at the Bi-Centennial Settlement of the Town. Second ed., with additional Notes and Index. By Dan'l C. Gilman. *8vo pamph., 128 pages.* *Boston*, 1859

1544 NORWICH, (Conn.) Historical Discourse, deliv. at the Hundredth Anniversary of the Second Cong. Church, July 24, 1850. With an Appendix. By Alvan Bond. *8vo, orig. cov., 64 p., clean copy. Plan of the Church.* *Norwich*, 1860

1545 NORWICH, (Conn.), History of, from its possession by the Indians, to the year 1866. By Francis M. Caulkins. *2d Edition. 8vo. cl., portrait; scarce and important.* *Hartford*, 1866

1546 NOVA SCOTIA, An Historical and Statistical Account of. In two volumes, illustrated by a map of the Province, and several engravings. By Thomas C. Haliburton. *8vo, bds., uncut.* *Halifax*, 1829

1547 Nova Scotia, Considered as a Field for Emigration. By P. S. Hamilton. *8vo, paper.* *London*, 1858

1548 NORWAY, Me., History of Comprising a Minute Account of its First Settlement, Town Officers, the annual Expenditures of the Town, with other Statistical Matters; Historical Sketches, Narrative and Anecdote, and Occasional Remarks by the Author, &c. By David Noyes. *8vo, cloth; scarce.* *Norway*, 1852

1549 NORWALK, Conn. An Historical Discourse in Commemoration of the Two Hundredth Anniversary of the Settlement of Norwalk in 1651, delivered July 9, 1851, by Nathaniel Bouton. *8vo pamphlet, 80 pages. Fine copy; scarce.* *New York*, 1851

"One generation shall praise thy works unto another, and shall declare thy mighty acts."

1550 NORWALK, Conn., ANCIENT HISTORICAL RECORDS of, with Plan of the Ancient Settlements, and of the Town in 1837. Compiled by Edwin Hall. 12*mo*, *half morocco ; very scarce.* *Norwalk, Conn.*, 1865

1551 NOTT, REV. SAMUEL. Half Century Sermon preached at Franklin, March 13, 1832. 8*vo*, *original cover*, 28 *pages ; fine copy.* *Norwich*, 1833

1552 NOTT, REV. SAMUEL. Sixteenth Anniversary Sermon preached at Franklin, March 13, 1842. 8*vo*, *original cover*, 16 *pages ; fine copy ; very scarce.* *Norwich*, 1842

1553 NOTT, CHARLES C. Sketches of the War: a Series of Letters to the North Moore Street School. 8*vo*, *cloth.* *New York*, 1863

PAMPHLETS.

1554 Miscellaneous. *Very valuable lot.* [*Ten.*]

Native Americans, Address to. By J. T. Buckingham. Second edition. *Boston*, 1844
New-Englandism not the Religion of the Bible. *Hartford*, 1844
New England, Pages from Ecclesi. History of, between 1740 and 1840. *Boston*, 1847
North Carolina, Agriculture of. Part II. By Ebenezer Emmons. *Scarce.* *Raleigh*, 1860
——— Report of Progress of Geological Survey of. By Professor W. C. Kerr. *Raleigh*, 1867
New Hampshire. Sermon before His Excellency Samuel Bell, being Anniv. Elec. By Rev. James B. Howe. *Concord*, 1820
——— State of, in General Court. June 16, 1820
——— Festival of Sons of. By James W. Stowe. *Boston*, 1850
Nahant and other places on North Shore. *Boston*, 1848
New Jersey, Proposition to Extin. Exclusive Priv. in. *Princeton*, 1836

1555 Miscellaneous. *Very valuable lot.* [*Eleven.*]

New Jersey, First Annual Report of Geological Survey of, for 1854. *Very scarce.* *Trenton*, 1855
——— Third Annual Report of Geological Survey of, for 1856. *Trenton*, 1857
New York One Hundred and Seventy Years Ago. By Joseph Moulton. *Very scarce.* *New York*, Dec., 1843
——— Missionary Society, Sermon before. By Samuel Miller. *Scarce.* *N. Y.*, 1802
——— Report of Deaths in City and County of, for year 1818. *N. Y.*, 1819
——— Prices of Cut Stone and Marble in. *N. Y.*, 1811
——— Law Society—Laws of.
——— Young Men's Society. Professor Vethake's Lecture on Political Economy. *N. Y.*, 1833

Navy and Marine Corps, Proceedings of Convention of Officers of. *N. Y.*, 1820

North Carolina University, Address before. By Henry L. Pinckney. *Raleigh*, 1836

New York, State of, in Chancery. *N. Y.*, 1834

1556 New York State and City Pamphlets. [*Eleven.*]

New York Lyceum of Natural History, Discourse on Opening New Hall of. By John W. Francis. *N. Y.*, 1841

——— University, Ninth Annual Report of the Regents of. *Albany*, 1856

——— National Academy of Design. Address to Students of. By William Dunlap. *N. Y.*, 1831

——— National Academy of Design. Funeral Oration on Death of Thomas Cole. By Wm. Cullen Bryant. *N. Y.*, 1848

——— Typographical Society, Reply to a Report of the. *N. Y.*, 1829

——— Typographical Society, Address before, on Franklin's Birthday. By Peter C. Baker. *N. Y.*, 1865

——— General Society of Mechanics and Tradesmen, Charter and By-Laws. *N. Y.*, 1823

——— Mechanics' Institute, Lecture before. By Gulian C. Verplanck. *N. Y.*, 1833

——— Mechanics' Institute, Address, Report, &c., of. *N. Y.*, 1838

——— Law Institute, Discourse on Anniversary Celebration. By Henry Wheaton. *N. Y.*, 1834

——— Law Association, Address before. By Hon. James Kent. *N. Y.*, 1836

1557 New York State and City Pamphlets. [*Eight.*]

Nott, Eliphalet. Discourse before Ladies' Society for Relief of Distressed Women and Children. *Albany*, 1804

——— Sermon before General Assembly of Presbyterian Ch. *Phila.*, 1806

Naval Victories, Official Account of, during Present War Between United States and Great Britain. *Boston*, 1813

Navy of United States. History of Existing Controversy on Subject of Assimilated Rank. By W. S. W. R. *Philadelphia*, 1850

Newcastle, Duke of, Letter of, by His Majesty's Order, to Monsieur Michael, the King of Prussia's Secretary. *London*, 1753

Naturalization Laws, Imminent Dangers to Free Institutions of United States through Foreign Immigration and Present State of. By an American. *N. Y.*, 1835

Noah, M. M. Discourse on Restoration of the Jews. *Scarce.* *N. Y.*, 1845

Nevin, John W. Principle of Protestantism, as Related to Present State of the Church. *Chambersburg, Pa.*, 1845

1558 Miscellaneous. *Valuable.* [*Twenty.*]

Newman, John B. Ancient History and Discovery of America before the Time of Columbus. *Very scarce.* *N. Y.*, 1848

Naval Architecture, Progress of. By Darius Davison. *N. Y.*, 1852

Nall, Robert. Voice from Twenty Graves. Sermon. *Mobile*, 1854

Newburyport, Report of Proceedings of Reception of Sons of. By Joseph H. Bragdon. *Newburyport*, 1854

Nebraska: A Poem—Personal and Political. *Boston*, 1854

Nicaragua, Destiny of. Central America as it Was, Is, and May Be. *Boston*, 1856

Newburgh, History of. By E. M. Ruttenber. One Number. *Newburgh*, 1859

Newport, Foggy Night at. *St. Louis*, 1860

New Haven, History of City Burial Ground in. *New Haven*, 1863

Newell, Wm. Discourse on Death of Jared Sparks. *Cambridge*, 1866

Newark and New York Railroad Company, Report to Board of Directors of. By Alfred F. Sears. *Newark*, 1866 /2

Neill, Edward D. Virginia Co. of London. Extracts from Manuscript Transactions. *Washington*, 1868

——— Sir George Calvert created Baron of Baltimore in Co. of Longford, Ireland, and Projector of Province of Maryland. *Baltimore*, 1869

Narrative of Five Youth from the Sandwich Islands. *New Brunswick*, 1816

——— Promises Made to Officers of Continental Army for Services in the Revolutionary War. *Very scarce.* *Elizabethtown, N. J.*, 1826

New England Patriot. Being a Candid Comparison of Princ. and Conduct of the Washington and Jefferson Admin. *Boston*, 1810

——— Tracts. No. 1. Narratives of Reform in Canton and Norfolk Conn., in Four Letters. By Rev. Jeremiah Hallock.

——— Tracts. No. 2. Discourse by a New England Pastor, March 26, 1826.

——— Tracts. No. 3. Sermon by a New England Pastor on Fifty-fourth Anniversary of his Ordination, April 22, 1823.

——— And the West. By R. W. Haskins. *Buffalo*, 1843

1559 New York State and City Pamphlets. [*Twenty-four.*]

New York. Case of the Manufacturers of Soap and Candles in. *N. Y.*, 1797 5

——— Address of Republicans of City and Co. of. *N. Y.*, 1808

——— Review, or Critical Journal, March, 1809. *N. Y.*, 1809

New York. Letter on Use and Abuse of Incorporations. *N. Y.*, 1827
——— Female Benevolent Soc., Fourth Annual Report. *N. Y.*, 1837
——— Marine Temperance Society. Address on Anniv. of Amer. Ind. By John Marsh. *N. Y.*, 1840
——— Public School Soc. By-laws of Trustees of. 1841
——— Supreme Court, Garrit H. Striker, *vs.* Thomas Kelly. *N. Y.*, 1842
——— 170 Years ago, by Joseph W. Moulton. *Very scarce.* *N. Y.*, 1843
Is the Diocess of N. Y. Vacant?
New York. Wealth and Biography of the Wealthy Citizens of. 10th ed. *N. Y.*, 1846
——— Aristocracy of, who they are and what they were. Part I. *N. Y.*, 1848
——— Astor Pl. Opera House. Account of Terrific and Fatal Riot. *N. Y.* 1849
——— Plea for Church Hospital in. Two Lectures, by W. A. Muhlenberg. *N. Y.*, 1850
——— Response from Diocese of, to a letter from his Grace, the Archbishop of Canterbury. Third Semi-Cen. Jubilee of Soc. for the Propagation of the Gospel in Foreign Parts. *N. Y.*, 1851
——— Reports of Majority and Minority of Special Committee on Subject of Widening West St. *N. Y.*, 1851
——— Minutes of the General Assoc. of. *Madison*, 1848
——— Minutes of the Particular Synod of. *N. Y.*, 1856
——— The Sabbath in. Report. *N. Y.*, 1858
——— Memoir on the Danger and Defences of, addressed to John B. Floyd. By James St. C. Morton. *Wash.*, 1858
——— Address of Liquor Dealers and Brewers of the Metro. Police District to the People of. *N. Y.*, 1868
——— Communication of Mayor Clark in relation to Precautionary Measures at Recent Election in. *N. Y.*, 1839
——— Ordinance to Divide the City of, into Convenient Elec. Dis. *N. Y.*, 1859
——— Practical Directions for the Holding of Elections. *N. Y.*, 1860

1560 New York Pamphlets. [*Twenty-three.*]
New York. County of. Maps of Wards and District Divisions. *N. Y.*, 1868
——— Address to Ind. Federal Electors of. *Albany*, 1820
——— Discourse before the Alpha of Phi Beta Kappa of. By De Witt Clinton. 3rd Ed. *N. Y.*, 1823
——— Report of Exam. of Poor Houses, Jails, etc. 3rd ed. By Samuel Chipman. *Albany*, 1835

New York. Address of Dem. Rep. Young Men's Gen. Committee. *N. Y.*, 1838

——— and Harlem Rail Road Company, Case of. *N. Y.*, 1840

——— Vindication of the Canal Policy of. Samuel B. Ruggles. *Rochester*, 1849

——— The Anti-Rent Movement, and Outbreak in. By Daniel D. Barnard. *Scarce.* *Albany*, 1846

——— Address of N. Y. State Auxiliary Clay Mon. Assoc. to People of. *N. Y.*, 1853

——— Laws of, relating to Landlord and Tenant. *N. Y.*, 1858

——— State Inebriate Asylum, Ceremonies. *N. Y.*, 1859

——— State. In Assembly. No. 150. Report, Feb. 11, 1835.

——— State. In Senate. No. 32. Communication from Sec. of State, Jan. 27, 1847.

——— State. In Assembly. No. 201. Message from Gov., March 30, 1849.

——— State. In Assembly. No. 9. Report of Select Commit., Jan 2, 1850.

——— State. In Assembly. No. 136. Commu. from Sec. of State, April 6, 1854.

——— Mercantile Library Assoc. Thirty-first Annual Report of. *N. Y.*, 1852

——— Mercantile Library Assoc. Two Lectures on Political Economy, by Wm. B. Lawrence. *N. Y.*, 1832

——— Society Library. Lecture on Past, Present and Future of, by John McMullen. *N. Y.*, 1856

——— University. History of the Controversy in. *N. Y.*, 1838

——— University. Letter to the Councillors of the. *N. Y.*, 1838

——— University. Americanism. Address before the Euclean Society of, by Cornelius Matthews. *N. Y.*, 1845

——— University. Republican Homes. Address before the Assoc. of the Alumni of the, by Rev. Edward Hopper. *N. Y.*, 1861

1561 Miscellaneous. [*Fifteen.*]

Nahant; or, "The Floure of Souvenance." *Phila.*, 1827

Narrative of five youths from the Sandwich Islands, now receiving an education in this country. *New York*, 1816

Needham, John R. The pleasures of poverty; a poem. *New York*, 1837

Newburyport. Sunday School Society. Address, at their third anniversary, by R. C. Waterston. *Boston*, 1835

New Jersey College. American, Whig and Cliosophic Societies. Address, Sept. 29, 1840, by Rev. J. Johns. *Princeton*, 1840

——— Address, Sept. 29, 1835, by Wm. Gaston. *Princeton*, 1835

N. J. Col. Address, Sept. 26, 1837, by S. L. Stoddard. *Princeton*, 1837

——— Address, before Alumni association of Nassau Hall, Sept. 30, 1835, by N. Biddle. 3rd ed. *Princeton*, 1835

New Jersey Colonization Soc. Proceedings of, the first annual meeting. *Princeton*, 1825

New Jersey Lyceum. Paper No. 1, circular. *Princeton*, 1834

New Jersey. Congressional election. 1839

Niles, Wm. Ogden. The Tippecanoe Text-Book. *Baltimore*, 1840

North Carolina University. Address before the two Literary Societies of, by R. Strange. *Raleigh*, 1837

North American Coal Company. Sketch of the property belonging to, etc. *New York*, 1827

Notes on farming. *New York*, 1787

/ 1562 New York Societies. [*Twenty-two.*]

Asylum for lying-in women. 6th annual report. *N. Y.*, 1829

Bible Society. The three Bibles, an important discovery in religion.

Congregational Association. Constitution, etc. *N. Y.*, 1837

Dispensary. Charter and by-laws. *N. Y.*, 1818

Dispensary. Address, at the opening of an edifice erected by the trustees of, Jan. 11, 1830, by J. F. Schroeder. *N. Y.*, 1830

Lyceum of Natural History. Annals of. 1827

Horticultural Society. Inaug. Disc., 31st Aug. 1824, by D. Hosack. *N. Y.*, 1824

Horticultural Society. Address before, Aug. 29, 1826, by S. L. Mitchill. *N. Y.*, 1826

Horticultural Society. Address before, Aug. 28, 1827, by N. H. Carter. *New York*, 1827

Horticultural Society. Address before, Sept. 8, 1829, by J W. Francis. *N. Y.*, 1830

Literary and Philosophical Soc. Charter, etc. *N. Y.*, 1818

Naval School. Remarks on the home squadron and Naval school. *N. Y.*, 1840

Magdalen Society. First annual report. *N. Y.*, 1831

Presbytery. Address from the, to the churches under their care. *N. Y.*, 1805

Society for the prevention of pauperism. Report on the expediency of erecting an institution for the reformation of Juvenile delinquents. *New York*, 1824

Synagogue. Discourse at the consecration of, by M. M. Noah. *N. Y.*, 1818

University. Annual report of the regents. *Albany*, 1829

University. Letter to the councillors of. *N. Y.*, 1838

University. Exposition by the council of, respecting the late retrenchment. *N. Y.*, 1838

University College of Physicians and Surgeons. Circular, 1838–9. *N. Y.*, 1838

University College of Physicians and Surgeons. Hist. sketch of, by J. W. Francis. *Scarce.* *N. Y.*, 1813

University. Address before the Eucleian and Philomathean Societies, by J. Breckinridge. *N. Y.*, 1836

1563 Miscellaneous. [*Eighteen.*]

New York City. Board of Health Documents. *New York*, 1806

Appeal to the people on the proposed alteration of the charter of the city. *New York*, 1821

Address of the Board of Health to their Fellow-citizens. *New York*, 1824

Bank for Savings. 5th Report. *New York*, 1824

Doc. No. 44. Report upon supplying the city with pure water. 1835

Communication to S. Allen, Mayor, from T. Eddy. *New York*, 1823

Letter on the use and abuse of incorporations, to the delegation from the city. *New York*, 1827

Report of the committee on laws, on the subject of interment. *New York*, 1825

Wealth and biography of the Wealthy citizens of. *New York*, 1845

Address of the republicans of the city and county of N. Y. *New York*, 1808

Address of the Committee of Mechanics, etc. *New York*, 1830

New York State. Comparative view and exhibition of reasons opposed to the adoption of the New Constitution. *New York*, 1822

Address of the committee of vigilance of the City to the people of the State. *New York*, 1824

[Address] to the members of the legislature. *New York*, 1824

Let not the faith nor the laws of the commonwealth be violated. [On lotteries.]

History of the New York Kappa Lamba Conspiracy. *New York*, 1839

New South Ferry between New York and Brooklyn. Proceedings in relation to, Dec., 1825, to Jan., 1835. *New York*, 1835

New York and Erie Rail Road. Inquiry into the causes which have affected the prospects and condition of. *New York*, 1843

1564 Miscellaneous—Historical. *Very valuable.* [*Fifteen.*]

New York in olden time, by those who knew. *New York*, 1833

New York 170 years ago, with a view and explanatory notes, by Joseph W. Moulton. *Very scarce.*

New York. Progress of the city of, during the last fifty years. by Charles King. *N. Y.*, 1852

Wisconsin. Sketches of the West; or, the Home of the Badgers: comprising an early Hist. of. *Very scarce.* *Milwaukie*, 1847

Westminster, Mass. Celeb. of the One Hundredth Anni. of the incorporation of. Address by C. Hudson ; Poem by Wm. S. Heywood. *Boston*, 1859

Worthington, N. Y. Hist. of the town of, from its first settlement to the present time. *Very scarce.* *Albany*, 1853

Westfield, N. J. Sermon containing a general hist. of the Parish of, Jan. 1, 1839, by James M. Huntting. *Very scarce.* 1840

Watertown, Mass. Hist. sketch of, from the first settlement of the town to the close of its sec. century, by Convers Francis. *Very scarce.* 1830

Williams College. Sigma Phi Soc. Poem by S. E. Burrall. *Boston*, 1868

Yale College. 150th Anni. Hist. disc. by T. D. Woolsey. *New Haven*, 1850

Yale College Catalogue. *New Haven*, 1796

Maine. Rosier's narrative of Waymouth's voyage to the coast in 1605. *Scarce.* *Bath*, 1860

Boston and Charlestown. Considerations respectfully submitted to the citizens of, by J. Quincy, Sen. *Boston*, 1854

Boston. Bi-Centen. Address by Josiah Quincy. *Scarce.* *Boston*, 1830

America. Narrative of Journal of voyages and travels through North West Continent. *London*, 1802

1565 Miscellaneous—Historical. *Very scarce lot.* [*Seventeen.*]

New Haven, Conn. Bi-Centen. Anniv. Disc, by J. L. Kingsley. *Scarce.* 1838

——— Bi-Centen. Anniv. of the founding of the Hopkins Grammar School, July 24, 1860, by L. W. Bacon. 1860

——— Semi-Centen. Address to the Alumni of Yale College and Graduates of 1814, at their annual meeting July 27, 1864, by S. B. Ruggles. *New York*, 1864

New Foundland. Acts of the Island of, with the nature of its Trade and Fishery, by Capt. G. Williams. *Very scarce.* 1765

North Haven. Century sermon ; or, Sketches of the history of the eighteenth century, deliv. Jan. 1, 1801. *Very scarce.* *New Haven*, 1801

Newton Theological Institution. Address deliv. before the Soc. of Alumni, by Wm. Hague. *Boston*, 1835

Northampton, Mass. Address deliv. at, in commem. of close of second century, by William Allen, Oct. 29, 1854.

Northborough, Mass. Half Century Sermon, by J. Allen. *Cambridge*, 1867

Newburyport, Mass. Half Century Sermon, by D. Dana. *Newburyport*, 1845

New Brunswick. Early reminiscences : a Poem, by L. Scott. *New York*, 1864

Norfolk, Conn. Brief Hist. of Town of, from 1738 to 1844, by Auren Roys. *Scarce.* *New York*, 1847

A Few Days at Nashotah. *Albany*, 1849
New Brunswick. Disc. before Young Men's Assoc. Dec. 1, 1842, By William B. Lawrence. *Somerville*, 1845
New Orleans. Official and full detail of the great battle of, by Major P. M. Davis. *N. Y.*, 1836
Norwalk, Ct. Bi-Centen. Anniv. disc., by N. Bouton. *Scarce.* *New York*, 1851
Natick, Mass. Sermon deliv. at, Jan. 5, 1842, containing history of said Town from 1851 to day of delivery, by Martin Moore. *Rare.* *Cambridge*, 1817
——— Hist. of, from the days of the Apostolic Eliot, 1650, till the present time, by Wm. Bigelow. *Very scarce.*

1566 Miscellaneous. *Valuable lot.* [*Eighteen.*]
New Hampshire. Festival of the sons of, with speeches, Nov. 7, 1849, by James W. Stone. *Boston*, 1856
——— Repository devoted to Education, Literature and Religion, April, 1846. *Gilmanton*, 1846
——— First Annual Report on the Geology of the State of, by C. T. Jackson. *Very scarce.* *Concord, N. H.*, 1841
——— Hist. disc. before the general association of New Hampshire, Aug. 22, 1848, by N. Bouton.
——— General Assoc. Semi-Centen. Anni. Disc. by N. Bouton.
New York. University of. Address, May 20, 1837, by J. Talmadge.
——— Univ. of City. Serpents of, by Spencer F. Baird, *Scarce.* *Albany*, 1854
New York City. Seventh annual report of the regents of the University of, on the condition of the state cabinet of natural history, and the Hist. and Antiq. Collec., Jan. 18, 1854. *Albany.*
——— Union Theo. Sem. Sermons by Adams and Skinner, May, 1868.
——— Account of the terrific and fatal riot at the Astor Place Opera House. *New York*, 1849
Schenectady. Disc. Phi Beta Kappa, by De Witt Clinton. 1823
New York City. Report of Marine Bible Soc. of, Apr. 20, 1818.
——— Report of the Select Committee of the Senate on the Electoral Law, Feb. 24, 1824.
New York Typographical Soc. Proceedings at the Printers' Banquet, on Franklin's Birthday, Jan. 17, 1850.
New York Magdalen Soc. First annual report of the executive committee of, Jan 1, 1830.
——— Magdalen Tracts. No. I. Jan. 1862.
New York. Brief description of New York, formerly called New Netherlands, and places adjoining, by Daniel Denton. *New York*, 1845
——— Lecture of the Topography and Hist. of N. Y., by Horatio Seymour. *Very scarce.* *Utica, N. Y.*

1567 New York. Soc. Pamphlets. [*Eighteen.*]

N. Y. Orphan Asylum. Sermon by Bp. Hobart, Jan. 2, 1820.

N. Y. Female Benevolent Soc. Charges preferred by J. R. M'Dowall. *N. Y.*, 1836

——— Fifth Annual Report. 1837.

——— First Annual Report. 1834.

N. Y. Female Bethel Union. Const. and Cir., June, 1835.

N. Y. Young Men's Chris. Assoc. Address by Isaac Ferris May 28, 1852.

N. Y. Soc. Library. Address of the Trustees. 1833.

N. Y. Merc. Lib. Assoc. Lectures by E. S. Gould and J. H. Gourlie. 1836.

N. Y. Tract Soc. Seventeenth Annual Report. *N. Y.*, 1843

N. Y. Athenæum. Address by Henry Wheaton, Dec., 14, 1824

N. Y. Peace Soc. First Annual Report. 1838.

N. Y. Soc. for the Encouragement of Faithful Domestic Servants. Second Annual Report. *N. Y.*, 1827

N. Y. Soc. for Ref. of Juv. Delinq. Fourth Annual Report. *N. Y.*, 1829

N. Y. Academy of Sacred Music. Const. and Bye-Laws of. 1838

N. Y. Gen. Trade Union. Address by Ely Moore, Dec. 2, 1833.

N. Y. Mech. and Tradesmen's Soc. Address by M. M. Noah, Nov. 25, 1821.

N. Y. The Constitution of the State of. *N. Y.*, 1785

——— The Constitution of the State of. *Albany*, 1825

1568 New England Society Pamphlets of N. Y. [*Twenty-three.*]

Anniv. Celebrations. Dec. 22, 1839–1855–1863–1864–1865–1866–1867.

Discourses. 1847, Hall; 1857, Stone; 1846, Upham; 1822, Whelpley; 1857, Storrs; 1854, Evarts; 1842, Cheever; 1853, Hopkins; 1851, Hillard; 1820, Spring; 1849, Bushnell; 1841, Hadduck; 1838, Bacon.

N. Eng. Soc. of Columbus, O. Address by J. W. Andrews, Dec. 22, 1858.

Constitution and By-Laws, Dec. 5, 1843.

Remarks on the Charges made against the Religion and Morals of the People of Boston and Vicinity. By Rev. Gardiner Spring. *N. Y.*, 1820

1569 New England Pamphlets. *Valuable lot.* [*Eight.*]

Account of Discovery of an Ancient Ship. By Amos Otis. *Albany*, 1864

Prof. Park's Sermon on the Duties of the New England Clergy. *Andover*, 1844

Sermon, deliv. in Andover, April 5, 1810, Annual Fast, by John H. Church. *Very scarce.* *Sutton*, 1810

Mr. Albro's Discourse on the Fathers of New England. *Boston*, 1844

The Vassals of New England. By Edward D. Harris. *Albany*, 1862

Strange Phenomena of New England. By Henry Jones. *Scarce. N. Y.*, 1846

News from New England. *Boston: Reprinted for Samuel G. Drake.* April, 1850.

Pages from Ecclesiastical History of New England from 1740 to 1840. *Boston*, 1847

1570 New England Society Pamphlets. *Valuable lot.* [*Nine.*]

Nancrede, Joseph G. Address before N. E. Soc. of Philadelphia, May 1, 1820.

Furness, W. H. Oration, "The Spirit of the Pilgrims," before N. E. Soc. of Phila., Dec. 22, 1846.

Spring, Gardiner. Sermon, "Remarks on the Charges made against the Religion and Morals of the People of Boston and its Vicinity," before N. E. Soc. of N. Y. Dec. 22, 1820.

——— Sermon, "A Tribute to N. E.," deliv. before N. E. Soc. of N. Y. Dec. 22, 1820.

Bacon, Leonard. Address before N. E. Soc. of N. Y. Dec. 22, 1838.

Winthrop, Robert C. Address before the N. E. Soc. of N. Y. Dec. 23, 1839.

Webster, Daniel. Speech before N. E. Soc. of N. Y. Dec. 23, 1850.

Hopkins, Mark. Oration, "The Central Principle," before N. E. Soc. of N. Y. Dec. 22, 1853.

Anderson, Chas. Address on Anglo-Saxon Destiny, deliv. before N. E. Soc. of Cinn. Dec. 20, 1849.

1571 Miscellaneous. [*Nineteen.*]

Considerations upon the expediency and the means of establishing a Univ. in the City of N. Y. 1830

Butler, Benj. F. Plan for the organization of a Law Faculty in the City of N. Y. 1835

Breckinbridge, John. Address before the Eucleian and Philomathean Soc. of the N. Y. Univ. *N. Y.*, July 15, 1835

Tallmadge, James. Address Dedicatory. *N. Y.*, May 20, 1837

History of the Controversy of the Univ. of the City of N. Y., with original documents. 1838

Anthon, Geo. C. Narrative and Documents connected with the displacement of the Professor of the Greek Language and Literature in the Univ. of the City of N. Y. 1851

Newark Mech. Assoc. Address by S. L. Southard. July 5, 1830.

——— Address by John Griscom. Jan. 25, 1831.

New Brunswick, N. J., Theol. Sem. Address by H. Mandeville. May 13, 1847.

Townsend, Peter S. Anniv. Disc. before Lyceum of Nat. Hist. of N. Y. 1820

De Kay, James E. Anniv. Address on the Progress of the Nat. Sciences in the U. S., deliv. before the Lyceum of Nat. Hist. in New York. 1826

Mitchill Samuel L. Disc. on the Char. and Scient. attainments of De Witt Clinton. *N. Y.*, 1828

Address, by John W. Francis, deliv. Sept. 8, 1829. New York Horticultural Society.

New York Institution. Companion to American Museum. Catalogue of Fine Arts. *N. Y.*, 1823

New York State Medical Soc. Address before. By Alex. H. Stevens. *Albany*, 1849

New York College of Physicians and Surgeons. Discourse by Joseph M. Smith. *N. Y.*, 1846

New York College of Physicians and Surgeons. Address by Nicholas Romayne. *N. Y.*, 1808

Proceedings of the N. Y. Hor. Soc., at the Celebration of its Tenth Anniv. New York, Aug. 26, 1828.

Schroeder, John F. Anniv. Disc. at Annual Celebration. New York, Aug. 26, 1828.

BERLIN, WELLINGTON Rescue; History of. Compiled by J. R. Shipherd. With an Introduction by Prof. H. E. Peck, and Hon. R. Plumb. *8vo, paper.* *Boston, etc.*, 1859

1573 OBERLIN, Ohio. Its Origin, Progress and Results. An Address, prepared for the Alumni of Oberlin College, August 22, 1860. By J. H. Fairchild. *8vo,* 70 *pages; pamphlet.* *Oberlin*, 1860

1574 O'CALLAGHAN, E. B. A Brief and True Narrative of the Hostile Conduct of the Barbarous Natives towards the Dutch Nation. *8vo, paper, uncut.* *Albany: J. Munsell*, 1863

1575 O'Cataract, Jehu. Battle of Niagara, a Poem; and Goldan, or the Maniac Harper. 12*mo, boards., uncut.*

1576 O'Doherty, Sir Morgan. A Reply to the Libel of James Gordon Bennett on Daniel O'Connell. *8vo pamphlet;* 12 *pages; very rich, rare and racy.* *New York*, 1838

1577 OHIO. Journal of a Tour into the Territory northwest of the Alleghany Mountains; made in the Spring of 1803. With a Geographical and Historical account of the State of Ohio. Illustrated with original maps and views. By Thaddeus Mason Harris. *8vo, bds., uncut,* *Boston*, 1805
Baltimore, Md., 1818

1578 OHIO GAZETTEER, or Topographical Dictionary. Containing a description of the several counties, towns, villages, settlements, roads, rivers, lakes, springs, mines, &c., in the State of Ohio, alphabetically arranged. By John Kilbourn. 6th Ed. 12*mo, unbound.* *Columbus*, 1819

1579 Ohio. Letter of the Hon. John M. Goodenow on the subject of the Northern Boundary of Ohio. *8vo pamph.;* 15 *p.; double column; scarce.* *St. Clairsville*, 1835

1580 OHIO, History of the State of—Natural and Civil. By Caleb Atwater. First Edition. *8vo, sheep; very scarce.* *Cincinnati*, 1838

1581 OHIO. Biographical and Historical Memoirs of the Early Pioneer Settlers of. With Narratives of Incidents and Occurrences in 1775. By S. P. Hildreth, M. D. To which is annexed a Journal of occurrences which happened under the author's personal observation, in the detachment commanded by Col. Benedict Arnold, consisting of two battalions from the U. S. army at Cambridge, Mass., in 1775. By Col. R. J. Meigs. With portraits and plates. 8*vo, cl.* *Cincinnati, O.*, 1852

1582 OHIO. TRANSACTIONS OF THE HISTORICAL AND PHILOSOPHICAL SOCIETY OF. Part Second. Vol. I. Published by Order of the Society. 12*mo, half sheep.* *Cincinnati, Ohio*, 1839

1583 OHIO. Fugitive Essays upon interesting and useful subjects relating to the early history of its Geology and Agriculture; with a Biography of the first successful constructor of steam-boats. A dissertation upon the material universe, and other articles; being a reprint of various periodicals of the day. By Charles Whittlesey. 12*mo, cl.* *Hudson, Ohio*, 1852

1584 OGLE COUNTY, Ill., SKETCHES OF THE HISTORY OF, and the Early Settlement of the Northwest. 8*vo, paper.* *Polo., Ill.*, 1859

1585 OHIO, ATHENS Co., HISTORY OF, and Incidentally of the Ohio Land Company, and the First Settlement of the State at Marietta, with Personal and Biographical Sketches of the Early Settlers, Narratives of Pioneers, Adventures, etc. By Charles M. Walker. With map and portraits. *L.* 8*vo, cl., rubric. title, uncut.* *Cincinnati, O.*, 1869

1586 OLD FLAG. Fac-simile of a paper in imitation of print published during an Imprisonment of Thirteen Months at Camp Ford, Tyler, Smith Co., Texas. Vol. I., Nos. 1, 2, 3. With list of officers, prisoners at Camp Ford. By Wm. H. May. 4*to, p. cov.* *(Ford City, Texas*, 1864.) *Printed, New York.*

1587 ONDERDONK, JR., HENRY. DOCUMENTS AND LETTERS INTENDED TO ILLUSTRATE THE REVOLUTIONARY INCIDENTS OF QUEEN'S COUNTY; with connecting narratives, explanatory notes, and additions. 8*vo, full red Turkey, gilt top, rough edges. By R. M. Smith. Very scarce; beautiful copy.* *New York*, 1846

1588 ——— REVOLUTIONARY INCIDENTS OF SUFFOLK AND KINGS COUNTIES; with an Account of the Battles of Long Island, and the British Prisons, and Prison Ships at New York. 8*vo, full red Turkey mor., gilt top, rough edges. By R. M. Smith. Exceedingly scarce.* *New York*, 1849

1589 ONEIDA COUNTY, (N. Y.) ANNALS AND RECOLLECTIONS OF. By Pomroy Jones. 8*vo, cl. Very scarce.* *Rome, N. Y.*, 1851

1590 ONONDAGA; OR, REMINISCENCES OF EARLIER AND LATER TIMES. Being a Series of Historical Sketches relative to Onondaga; with Notes on the Several Towns in the County, and Oswego. By Joshua V. H. Clark. 2 vols. *Half crim. lev. mor., gt. top, rough edges; fine copy, scarce.* *Syracuse*, 1849

1591 OPIE, AMELIA. The Negro Boy's Tale. A Poem. To which are added, The Morning Dream, by Cowper, and other poems. *Sq.* 12*mo, frontis.* *N. Y., (n. d.)*

1592 OREGON TERRITORY. Travels in the Great Western Prairies, the Anahuac and Rocky Mountains, and in the Oregon Territory. By Thomas J. Farnham. 12*mo, cl.* *Poughkeepsie*, 1841

1593 OREGON TERRITORY, and British North American Fur Trade; History of, with an Account of the Habits and Customs of the

Principal Native Tribes of the Northern Continent. By John Dunn. *8vo, cl., rough edges; with map.* *London,* 1844

1594 OREGON TERRITORY. JOURNAL OF TRAVELS IN THE ROCKY MOUNTAINS, to the Mouth of the Columbia River; made during the years 1845 and '46: containing minute descriptions of Valleys of the Willamette, Umpqua, and Clamet; a general description of Oregon Territory; its Inhabitants, Climate, Soil, Productions, etc., etc.; a list of necessary outfits for emigrants, and a Table of Distances From Camp to Camp on the Route. Also, a letter from the Rev. H. H. Spalding, resident Missionary for the last ten years among the Nez Percé Tribe of Indians, on the Koos-koos-kee River; the Organic Laws of Oregon Territory; Tables of about three hundred words of the Chinook Jargon, and about two hundred words of the Nez Percé Language; a description of Mount Hood; incidents of Travel, etc., etc. By Joel Palmer. *12mo, or. cov., uncut.* *Cincinnati, O.,* 1852

1595 OREGON and CALIFORNIA, History of, and other Territories on the North-West Coast of North America, from their Discovery to the Present Day, accompanied by a Geographical View of those Countries, and a number of documents as proofs and illustrations of the history. By Robert Greenhow. *8vo, cl., 4th Ed.* *Boston,* 1847

1596 ORMOND. The Lay of the Last Pilgrim. *12mo, bds.* *Charlestown, S. C.,* 1832

1597 ORNE, CAROLINE F. Sweet Auburn, and Mount Auburn. With other Poems. *8vo, bds.* *Cambridge,* 1844

1598 OSSANDER. Miscellaneous Poems, on Moral and Religious subjects. *12mo, sheep.* *Hudson,* 1811

1599 OWEN, ROBERT DALE. Moral Physiology; or, A Brief and Plain Treatise on the Population Question. *12mo, full clf., front.* *New York,* 1831

PAMPHLETS.

1600 Ordination Sermons. [*Fourteen.*]

Backus, Charles. Sermon deliv. at ordination of Joseph Russel, in Princeton, Mass., March 16, 1796.

——— Sermon deliv. at ordination of Timothy Mather Cooley, in Granville, Feb. 3, 1796.

Edwards, Jno. Sermon deliv. at ordination of Timothy Dwight, in Greenfield, Nov. 5, 1783.

——— Sermon deliv. at ordination of Wm. Brown, in Glastenbury, June, 1792.

——— Sermon at ordination of Dan. Bradley, in Whitestown, N. Y., Jan. 11, 1792.

Channing, Wm. Ellery. Sermon at ordination of John Emery Abbot, Salem, Apr. 20, 1815.

——— Sermon at ordination of Jared Sparks, Baltimore, May 5, 1819.

——— Disc. deliv. at installation of Mellish Irving Motte, Boston, May 21, 1828.

——— Disc. deliv. at ordination of Frederic A. Farley, R. I., Sept. 10, 1828.

Greenwood, F. W. P. Sermon at ordination of Wm. P. Lunt, in the city of New York, June 19, 1828.

——— Disc. at ordination of Wm. Newell, Cambridge, May 19, 1830.

Beecher Lyman. Sermon at installation of the Rev. John Keyes, Woolcot, (Conn.,) Sept. 21, 1814.

——— Sermon at ordination of Sereno E. Dwight, as Pastor, and Elisha P. Swift and others as Missionaries to the Heathen, Boston, Sept. 3, 1817.

——— The same, 1827.

1601 Ordination Sermons. [*Thirteen.*]

Beecher, Lyman. Sermon at Worcester, at ordination of Loamine Ives Hoadly. 2d Ed. Boston, Oct. 15, 1823.

Harris, Walter. Sermon at installation of Stephen Chapin. Mount Vernon, N. H., Nov. 15, 1809.

Eastman, Tilton. Sermon at ordination of Samuel Bascom. Hanover, March 12, 1806.

Smith, John. Disc. deliv. at installation of Amasa Smith. North Yarmouth, Maine, Oct. 22, 1806.

Emmons, Nath'l. Disc. deliv. at ordination of Walter Harris, Dunbarton, R. I., Aug. 26, 1789.

Lyman, Joseph. Sermon at ordination of Eliphalet Lyman. Woodstock, Sept. 2, 1779.

Stillman, Samuel. Sermon at ordination of Tho's Waterman, at Charlestown, Oct. 7, 1802.

Parish, Elijah. Sermon at ordination of Nathan Waldo, in Williamstown, Vt., Feb. 26, 1806.

Cornelius, Elias. Sermon deliv. at ordination of E. Frost. Boston, 1823.

Coles, Thomas. Sermon at ordination of, by James Hinton. Charge by John Ryland. Bristol, 1801.

Carey, Samuel. Sermon, Jan. 1, 1809 ; being the Sabbath of his ordination. Boston.

Chapman, Robert H. Sermon deliv. at ordination and installation of Rev. J. Younglove. 1806.

Carey, Arthur. Examination and ordination of. New York, 1843.

1602 Ordination Sermons. [*Fifteen.*]

Bancroft, Aaron. Sermon deliv. at installation of Andrew Bigelow, Medford. Boston, July 9, 1823.

Brazer, John. Sermon deliv. at ordination of John Cole Kingston. Salem, Jan. 21, 1829.

Young, Alex. Dis. deliv. at ordination of James W. Thompson, Natick. *Historical and scarce.* Feb. 17, 1830.

Kendall, James. Sermon at ordination of Hersy B. Goodwin, as colleague pastor with Ezra Ripley. Concord, Feb. 17, 1830.

Maltby, Erastus. Sermon at installation of Wm. M. Cornell. Woodstock, Conn., June 15, 1831.

Furness, W. H. Sermon at installation of D. H. Barlow. Brooklyn, Sept. 17, 1834.

Blagden, G. W. Sermon at ordination of Robert B. Hall. Plymouth, Aug. 23, 1837.

Smith and Anthon, Drs. Statement of Facts relative to the recent ordination of Arthur Carey. N. Y., 1843.

Whittingham, Wm. R. Sermon at consecration of J. P. K. Henshaw, as Bp. of R. I. Aug. 11, 1843.

Sprague, Wm. B. Sermon at installation of Malcolm N. Mc Laren. Rochester, Aug. 27, 1845.

Chase, Carlton. Sermon at Consecration of John Mayhew Wainwright. New York, Nov. 10, 1852.

Messler, Abraham. Sermon at installation of John Steele. New Brunswick, 1853.

Hoge, Wm. J. Installation services of, as associate pastor. N. Y., May 22, 1859.

Walker, James. Sermon at installation of S. J. May. Boston, Nov. 5, 1823.

Walker James. Discourse at installation of Charles Robinson. Boston, Nov. 1, 1826.

1603 Ordination Sermons. [*Fourteen.*]

Dunbar, Samuel. Sermon at ordination of Ebenezer Grosvener. Boston, April 20, 1763.

Daggett, Nath'l. Sermon at installation of Nath'l Sherman. New Haven, May 18, 1763.

Woodward, Samuel. Sermon at ordination of John Marsh. New Haven, Jan. 12, 1774.

Ely, Richard. Sermon at ordination of David Ely. New Haven, Oct. 27, 1773.

Willard, Joseph. Sermon at ordination of Joseph McKeen. Mass., May 11, 1785.

Mellen, John Disc. at ordination of Levi Whitman. Plymouth, April 13, 1785.

Perkins, Nathan. Sermon at installation of Solomon Walcott, in Wintonbury. Hartford, May 24, 1786.

Magaw, Samuel. Sermon at the first ordination held by the Bp. of the Prot. Epis. Church. *Very scarce.* Phila., 1787.

Belknap, Jeremy. Sermon at installation of Jedediah Morse, in Charlestown. Boston, April 30, 1789.

Trumbull, Benj. Sermon at ordination of Tho's Holt, in Hardwick. Worcester, Mass., June 25, 1789.

Hitchcock, Enos. Disc. delivered at ordination of Abel Flint to the ministerial office. Hartford, April 20, 1791.

Dana, James. Sermon at Cambridge, at installation of Abiel Holmes. Boston, Jan. 25, 1792.

McDonald, John. Sermon in Stillwater, at ordination of Aaron Condict. Albany, Jan. 15, 1793.

Smith, Wm. Dis. delivered in New Haven, before Ecclesiastical Conven. of Conn., at consecration of Abraham Jarvis. Newfield, Oct. 18, 1797.

1604 Ordination Sermons. [*Thirteen.*]

Dwight, Timothy. Sermon at opening of Andover Theol. Institution, at ordination of Rev. Eliphalet Pearson. Boston, Sept. 28, 1808.

Milledoler, Philip. Sermon at installation of John B. Romeyn. New York, Nov. 9, 1808.

Hobart, John Henry. Sermon at Consecration of Trinity Church, by Bp. Moore. Newark, N. J., May 21, 1810.

Kewley, John. Sermon at institution of Henry Whitlock. New Haven, Aug. 29, 1811.

Woods, Leonard. Ordination of Missionaries to the Heathen in Asia. Boston, Feb. 6, 1812.

Whitlock, Henry. Sermon at ordination of Philander Chase. Hartford, June 2, 1812.

Baldwin, Tho's. Sermon at installation of James M. Winchell. Boston, March 30, 1814.

Flint, James. Sermon at ordination of Nath'l Whitman, as colleague with Henry Cummings, church in Billerica. Cambridge, Jan. 26, 1814.

Holmes, Abiel. Sermon deliv. at ordination of Tho's Brattle Gannett. Cambridgeport, Jan. 19, 1814.

Butler, David. Sermon at induction of Frederic Van Horn. Troy, Aug. 8, 1805.

White, Wm. Sermon at consecration of Thomas C. Brownell. New Haven, Oct. 27, 1819.

Humphrey, Heman. Sermon deliv. at Goshen (Conn.), at ordination of Hiram Bingham and Asa Thurston as missionaries to Sandwich Islands. Boston, Sept. 29, 1819.

Ware, Henry. Sermon at ordination of Wm. Ware. Cambridge, Dec. 13, 1821.

1605 Miscellaneous. [*Eighteen.*]

O'Gallagher, S. F. A Brief Reply to a short Answer to a true exposition of the Doctrine of the Catholic Church, on the Sacrament of Penance. *N. Y.*, 1815

Owen, Robert. Disc. exposing his system as practised by the Franklin Community, by J. McKnight. *N. Y.*, 1826

Ogilby, Jno. Essay on the right of Property in Land. *London*, 1780

Oedipus Tyrannus. Translated.

Old Things and New. A Satire. *Baltimore*, 1835

Oglethorpe Univ., Address deliv. before the Soc. of, by H. M. Charlton, Nov. 16, 1842. *Milledgeville.*

Obrien, Edward, The Lawyer. His Character and rule of Holy Life. *Phil.*, 1843

Olney, Lafayette W. Disc. "Politics in the Pulpit." Aug. 31, 1856. *N. Y.*

Odenheimer, W. H., The Primary Charge of. *Phil.*, 1862

O'Connell Club, Preamble, Constitution and By-Laws of. *N. Y.*, 1845

Ogilby, J. D. Address before Gen. Theo. Sem. "The Christian Athlete." *N. Y.*, 1847

Ormsby, W. L. Cycloidal Configurations, or the Harvest of Counterfeiters. *N. Y.*

Ouseley. W. C. England in 1850, by A. de Lamartine, translated by. *New York*, 1851

Otis' Letters in defence of Hartford Conven. and People of Mass. *Boston*, 1824

Otis', H. G., Address to City Council. *Scarce.* *Boston*, 1830

Onderdonk, Bp. Pastoral Letters. *N. Y.*, 1844

——— Pastoral Letter to the Laity of his spiritual charge. *N. Y.*, 1844

——— Report of the Committee on the sentence of. *N. Y.*, Jan. 8, 1845

1606 Onderdonk. [*Sixteen.*]

Onderdonk, Bp. The Trial Tried; or The Bp. and the Court at the bar of Public Opinion, by Lucius. *N. Y.*, 1845

——— The Proceedings of the Court, convened Dec. 10, 1844, by authority of the Court. *N. Y.*

——— A defence of the Ladies, and others, against the Bp. of Maryland and his aids, by J. G. Richmond. *N. Y.*, 1845

——— Verdict unsealed; being a review of the Testimony before the court for trial of. *N. Y.*. 1845 /2½

——— Statement of Bp. Meade, in reply to Bp. Onderdonk's statement of facts connected with his trial. *N. Y.*, 1845

——— Statement of Facts and Circumstances of trial of. *N. Y.*, 1845

——— The Voice of Truth; or an examination of the Proceedings on the trial of. Nos. I., IV. and V.

——— Jay's Pamphlet Reviewed. *N. Y.*, 1845

——— Conspiracy against, by J. C. Richmond. *N. Y.*, 1845

——— Mr. Richmond's Reply to statement of. *N. Y.*, 1845

——— Facts connected with the presentment of, by John Jay. *N. Y.*, 1845

——— Sermon. "The Change at the Resurrection," Deliv. Oct. 20, 1840. *N. Y.*

——— Funeral Sermon on Death of Lewis P. Bayard. 1841

——— Address, 59th Annual Conven. of Prot. Epis. Ch., Sept. 28, 1843. *N. Y.*, 1843

——— Sermon: "Witness unto the Truth," deliv. May 7, 1861, by S. Seabury. *N. Y.*, 1861

——— Obsequies and Obituary Notices of. *N. Y.*, 1862

3 1607 Miscellaneous. [*Sixteen.*]

Onderdonk, Henry U. Answer to a Letter addressed to the Author by the Wardens and Vestry of Conn. *N. Y.*, 1824

—— The Decisions of the Bishop, who united in the consecration of. *Phila.*, 1827

—— Some Remarks on a Pamphlet entitled, "Rev. Mr. M'Ilvaine in answer to," etc., by an Episcopalian of Maryland. *Baltimore*, 1829

—— Disc.: "Man Saved by Mercy." Oct. 21, 1830

—— Disc. at Funeral of Rev. Wm. White, delivered July 20, 1836 *Phila.*

—— Bp. Meade's Second Pamphlet in the case of. *Winchester*, 1854

Odd Fellows, Constitution, By-Laws and Rules of Order of the Right Worthy Grand Lodge of the Ind. Order of. *N. Y.*, 1851

—— Proceedings of the R. W. Grand Encampment of N. Y. Semi-Annual Session, 1856–7.

—— Kirk's exposition of Odd-Fellowship. Illus. *N. Y.*, 1857

Opdyke, George. Communication from his Honor the Mayor. Jan. 5, 1863. Doc. No. I. *N. Y.*

—— Libel Suit of, by Judge Mason. *N. Y.*, 1865

Ohio, State Bank of. An act to incorporate it and other banking companies, Feb. 24, 1845. *Columbus.*

—— Treasury, Defalcation of. March 30, 1867.

—— Bridge, Reports on, at Cin. Feb. 28, 1867.

Oregon Expedition. Circular to all people who wish to emigrate to, by H. J. Kelley. *Charlestown*, 1831

Oregon and N. Carolina, Narrative of an Exploring Expedition to, and Rocky Mts., by J. C. Fremont. 1843–1844.

35 1608 Miscellaneous. *Valuable.* [*Eighteen.*]

Oregon Title, Plain View of, by H. Berrian. *Washington*, 1846

Oregon Question. By Albert Gallatin. *N. Y.*, 1846

—— Speech of W. T. Colquitt, (Ga.), Feb. 17, 1846.

—— —— Mr. Hillard, (Alabama), Jan. 6, 1846.

—— —— Mr. Barrow, (La.), Senate U. S., March 30, 1846.

Onderdonk, Rev. Henry U., Reply to Letter remonstrating against the Consecration of. *Phila.*, 1827

Ontwa, The Son of the Forest, a Poem. *Very scarce.* *N. Y.*, 1822

Odofriede, the Outcast, by S. B. Judah. *Very scarce.* *N. Y.*, 1822

Onderdonk, B. T. Sermon at Funeral of J. H. Hobart, deliv. Sept. 16, 1830. *N. Y.*

Oldstyle, Jno., Letters of. *N. Y.*, 1824

Oglethorpe Univ. (Ga.) Oration—"Eloquence," by W. T. Hamilton, 1847.

Ohio, A brief topographical descrip. of Co. of Washington, in the State of, by J. Delafield, Jr. *Exceedingly scarce.* *N. Y.*, 1834

Ordination of Priests.

Osgood, David. Sermon. Nov. 20, 1794. *Boston*, 1795

Ogden, James De Peyster. Address deliv. Oct. 5, 1842. *Jamaica.*

Oregon Territory, History of, by Thomas J. Farnham. 2d ed. *N. Y.*, 1845

Ogle County, Ill., History of. *Very scarce.* *Polo*, 1859

Oxford, N. H. Centennial Celebration, Sept. 7. *Manchester*, 1865

PAINE, ROBERT TREAT, Jr., The Works in Verse and Prose of. With Notes; to which are prefixed Sketches of his Life, Character, and Writings. By Charles Prentiss. *8vo, bds, uncut. With portrait.* *Boston*, 1812

1610 PAINE, THOMAS. COMMON SENSE, Addressed to the Inhabitants of America. *8vo, bds. Second edition.* *Phila.*, 1776

1611 PAINE, THOMAS. Rights of Man. Part the Second, combining Principle and Practice. *8vo, uncut*, 120 *p. Scarce.* *Phila.*, 1792

1612 PAINE, THOMAS, The Life of. By James Cheetham. *8vo, hf. dk. gr. lev. mor., gilt top, rough edges. Bound by R. W. Smith.* *New York*, 1809

1613 PALMER, SAMUEL. THE NONCONFORMIST'S MEMORIAL. Being an account of the Ministers who were Ejected or Silenced after the Restoration, particularly by the Act of Uniformity, which took place on Bartholomew-day, August 24, 1662, containing a concise view of their Lives and Characters, their Principles and Sufferings, and printed Works. Originally written by Edmund Calamy. To which is prefixed an introduction, containing a brief History of the Times in which they lived, and the Grounds of the Nonconformity. Embellished with the Heads of many of those Venerable Divines. In two volumes. *Sheep, 8vo; fine copy, scarce.* *London, MDCCLXXV.*

1614 PALMER, SAMUEL. THE NONCONFORMIST'S MEMORIAL. Being an Account of the Lives, Sufferings, and Printed Works of the Two Thousand Ministers Ejected from the Church of England, chiefly by the Act of Uniformity, August 24, 1666. Originally Written by Edmund Calamy, D.D. Abridged, Corrected, and Methodized, with many Additional Anecdotes and Several New Lives. Second Edition. Embellished with Heads of the Principal Divines, chiefly from Original Plates. Three Volumes. *8vo, bds., uncut. Very scarce in this condition.* *London, Eng.*, 1802–3

1615 PALMER, Mass., AN HISTORICAL ADDRESS, delivered July 5, 1852, in Commemoration of the Centennial Anniversary of the Incorporation of the Town. By Thomas Wilson. *8vo pamph., 60 p. Scarce.* *Lowell*, 1855

1616 PALMER, RAY. Two Discourses on our Own Religious Affairs. *8vo, orig. cov.*, 61 *p. Clean copy.* *Albany, J. Munsell*, 1856

Two Historical Discourses on the First Congregational Church at Albany.

1617 PALMER, Rev. B. M. Thanksgiving Sermon—in New Orleans—November 29, 1860. *8vo, paper.* *Milledgeville, Ga.*, 1860

1618 PALMER, B. M. The South: Her Peril and Her Duty. A Discourse, in the First Presbyterian Church, New Orleans, November, 29, 1860. *8vo, paper.* *N. Orleans*, 1860

1619 PALMER, PETER S. HISTORY OF LAKE CHAMPLAIN, from its first Exploration by the French in 1609, to the close of the year 1814. *Large paper copy; uncut.* *Albany, J. Munsell*, 1866

1620 PARKER, DANIEL. Proscription Delineated; or, a Development of Facts appertaining to the Arbitrary and Oppressive Proceedings of the North Association of Litchfield County in Relation to the Author. 12*mo, full cf.* *Hudson*, 1819

1621 PARKER, Rev. SAMUEL. Journal of an Exploring Tour beyond the Rocky Mountains. Containing a Description of the Geography of the Country, and the Numbers, Manners, and Customs of the Natives, with a Map of Oregon Territory. Fifth Edition. 12*mo, cl., rough edges.* *Auburn*, 1846

1622 PARKINSON, WM. A Jubilee Sermon. Containing the History of the Origin of the First Baptist Church in the City of New York, and its Progress during the First Fifty Years since its Constitution. Also, a Sermon Delivered in the Meeting-House of the First Baptist Church in the City of New York, being a day recommended as a Day of Humiliation and Prayer on account of the late War—Mexico. 12*mo, cl. In one vol. Scarce.* *New York*, 1846

1623 PARKMAN, FRANCIS, Jr. HISTORY OF THE CONSPIRACY OF PONTIAC, and the War of the North American Tribes against the English Colonies after the Conquest of Canada. *Half Roxburghe, gilt top, rough edges.* *Boston*, 1866

75 copies. No. 56.

1624 PARKMAN, FRANCIS, Jr. FRANCE AND ENGLAND IN NORTH AMERICA. A Series of Historical Narratives. Part First.—Pioneers of France in the New World. *Half Roxburghe, gilt top, rough edges.* *Boston*, 1866

75 copies. No. 56.

1625 PATAGONIA. The Captive in Patagonia; or, Life among the Giants. A Personal Narrative, with Illustrations. By B. F. Bourne. *Cloth, 8vo.* *Boston*, 1853

1626 PATTIE, JAMES O., OF KENTUCKY, PERSONAL NARRATIVE OF, During an Expedition from St. Louis through the vast Regions between that place and the Pacific Ocean, and thence back through the City of Mexico to Vera Cruz, during Journeyings of Six Years; in which he and his father, who accompanied him, suffered unheard of hardships and dangers, had various conflicts with the Indians, and were made Captives, in which captivity his father died; together with a Description of the Country, and the various Nations through which they passed. Edited by Timothy Flint. 12*mo, sheep; fine copy, very scarce.* *Cincinnati,* 1833

1627 Pazos, Don Vicente. Letters on the United Provinces of South America. Addressed to the Hon. Henry Clay. Translated from the Spanish by Platt H. Crosby, Esq. 8*vo, bds., uncut. With map.* *New York,* 1819

1628 Peck, J. M. A New Guide for Emigrants to the West, containing Sketches of Michigan, Ohio, Indiana, Illinois, Missouri, Arkansas, with the Territory of Wisconsin and the adjacent parts. Second edition. *Cloth,* 12*mo.* *Boston,* 1837

1629 Pedder, James. Report made to the Beet Sugar Society of Philadelphia, on the Culture in France, of the Beet Root, &c. 8*vo,* 40 *p. Good copy.* *Phila.,* 1836

1630 Pelham, Peter. Notes concerning The Earliest Artist resident in New England and his successors prior to the Revolution. By Wm. H. Whitmore. 8*vo pamphlet.* *Cambridge,* 1867

1631 Pencil, Mark. The White Sulphur Papers; or, Life at the Springs of Western Virginia. 12*mo, cl.; rough edges, scarce.* *New York,* 1839

1632 Penhalow, Samuel. The History of the Wars of New England with the Eastern Indians; or, a Narrative of their continued Perfidy and Cruelty, from the 10th of August, 1703, to the Peace renewed, 13th of July, 1713. And from the 25th of July 1722, to their Submission, 15th December, 1725. Which was ratified August 5th, 1726. *Sm.* 4*to, cl.* *Printed, Boston,* 1736. *Re-printed, Cincinnati,* 1859

1633 Penn Company, for Insurance on Lives and granting annuities. An Address from the Pres't. and Directors of, to the U. S., on the beneficial objects of that Institution. 8*vo,* 45 *pages, scarce.* *Phila.,* 1814

1634 Penn, William. Life of, compiled from the usual Authorities, and also many Original Manuscripts. By Mrs. Hughs. 16*mo, bds.* *Phila.,* 1828

1635 PENNSYLVANIA. A Discourse on the Early History of, being an Annual Oration, before the American Philosophical Soc. held at Philadelphia. By Peter S. Du Ponceau. 8*vo, paper, uncut, scarce.* *Phila., Pa.,* 1821

1636 Pennsylvania. The Pictorial Sketch Book of; or, its Scenery, Internal Improvements, Resources and Agriculture. By Eli. Powen. Illustrated with over 200 Eng., and Maps. 8*vo, cl., gilt.* *Phila.,* 1852

1637 PENNSYLVANIA HISTORICAL SOCIETY. Memoirs of. Vol. 6, Contributions to American History, 1858. *Roy.* 8*vo, cl.* *Phila.,* 1858

1638 PENSILVANIA. HISTORICAL AND GEOGRAPHICAL Account of the Province and Country of, and of West New

Jersey in America. By Gabriel Thomas. *Cl.* 12*mo, maps, usually wanting.* *London*, 1698

Lithographed for H. A. Brady, Esq., 1848, who was lost at Sea in the Arctic.

1639 PEORIA, ILL. HISTORICAL VIEW OF. From the Discovery by the French Jesuit Missionaries, in the Seventeenth Century, to the Present Time. By S. De Witt Brown. 12*mo, cl., scarce.* *Peoria, Ill.*, 1850

1640 PEPPERELL, Sir WILLIAM. LIFE OF. By Usher Parsons. 8*vo, cl., rough edges.* *Boston*, 1855

——— The Same. 2d Ed. *London*, 1856

1641 PETERBOROUGH, N. H. An Address delivered at the Centennial Celebration, Octo. 24, 1839. By John H. Morrison. 8*vo pamph.*, 99 *p., fine copy ; very scarce.* *Boston*, 1839

1642 PETERSHAM, MASS. An Address delivered in, July 4, 1854, in Commemoration of the One Hundreth Anniversary of the Incorporation of that Town. With an Appendix. By Edward B. Willson. 8*vo pamph.*, 133 *p., fine copy, scarce.* *Boston*, 1855

1643 PHELPS, RICHARD H. NEWGATE OF CONN. Its Insurrections, Massacres, etc., imprisonment of the Tories in the Revolution, the ancient and recent working of its mines. Also, a Description of the State Prison at Wethersfield. 3d ed. 8*vo pamph.*, 24 *p., very scarce.* *Hartford*, 1844

1644 PHELPS, NOAH A. A HISTORY OF THE COPPER MINES and Newgate Prison, at Granby, Conn., also, of the Captivity of Daniel Hayes, by the Indians, in 1707. 8*vo pamph.*, 34 *p., fine copy, scarce.* *Hartford*, 1845

1645 PHILADELPHIA. THE PICTURE OF. Giving an account of its origin, increase and improvements in Arts, Sciences, Manufactures, Commerce and Revenues. With a view of its Societies, etc. By James Mease. 8*vo, bds., uncut, plate of Phila., fine copy.* *Phila.*, 1811

1646 PITTSFIELD, MASS. A HISTORY OF THE TOWN OF, with a map. By Rev. David D. Field. 8*vo pamph.*, 80 *p., uncut, scarce.* *Hartford*, 1844

1647 PITTSBURGH, PA. IN THE YEAR 1826, containing Sketches Topographical, Historical and Statistical, together with a Directory of the City and a View of its various Manufactures, Population, Improvement, etc., By S. Jones. 8*vo, bds., fine copy, very scarce. Engrav.* *Pittsburgh*, 1826

1648 PLAINFIELD, MASS. TOPOGRAPHICAL DESCRIPTION AND HISTORICAL SKETCH OF. May, 1834. By Jacob Porter. 8*vo pamph.*, 44 *p., uncut, very scarce.* *Greenfield*, 1834

"Land of brown heath and shaggy wood,
Land of the mountain and the flood."

1649 PLATFORM OF CHURCH DISCIPLINE, Gathered out of the Word of God, and agreed upon by the Elders and Messengers of the churches assembled in the Synod at Cambridge in New England. 8*vo, full polished calf, gt. By R. M. Smith.* *Boston*, 1772

1650 PLYMOUTH, Mass., History of the Town of, From its First Settlement in 1620, to the present time. With a Concise History of the Aborigines of New England, and their Wars with the English, &c.. Second edition, enlarged. By James Thatcher. *8vo, sheets folded; map. Very scarce in this condition.* *Boston,* 1835

1651 PLYMOUTH. Chronicles of the Pilgrim Fathers of the Colony of Plymouth, from 1602 to 1625. Now first collected from Original Records and contemporaneous printed documents, and illustrated with Notes. By Alexander Young. Portrait of Gov. Winslow. *8vo, cloth, rough edges. Very scarce.* *Boston,* 1841

——— Another copy. Second edition. 1844

1652 PLYMOUTH, Guide to, and Recollections of the Pilgrims. By Wm. S. Russell. *12mo, cloth. Illustrated.* *Boston,* 1846

1653 PLYMOUTH, New England. The Journal of the Pilgrims in 1620. With Historical and Local Illustrations of Providences, Principles, and Persons. By George B. Cheever. Second edition. *8vo, cl., rough edges.* *N. Y.,* 1849

1654 PLYMOUTH and the Pilgrims; or, Incidents of Adventure in the History of the First Settlers. By Joseph Banvard. *8vo, cloth, gilt edges. Engravings.* *Boston,* 1851

1655 PLYMOUTH and the Pilgrims; or, Incidents of Adventure in the History of the First Settlers. By Joseph Banvard. *12mo, cl.* *Boston,* 1851

1656 Poems on Moral and Religious Subjects. By a Lady. *12mo, bds., uncut.* *Woodstock, Vt.,* 1820

1657 Poems. The Genius of Erin; Columbia's Freedom; Flights of Fancy; Lucinda, &c., &c., &c. By a Citizen of South Carolina. *8vo, bds.* *Charleston, S. C.,* 1836

1658 Poems by a South Carolinian. *Cloth, 12mo.* *Charleston,* 1848

1659 Pollard, Edward A. Black Diamonds Gathered in the Darkey Homes of the South. *8vo, cl.* *N. Y.,* 1859

1660 POLLARD, EDWARD A. Southern History of the War. The First Year of the War. Corrected and Improved Edition. *8vo, cl. Portrait.* *New York,* 1863

1661 Pollard, E. A. Southern History of the War. In two volumes. Portrait of General Lee. Vol. I. All published. *8vo, paper, uncut.* *N. Y.,* 1866

1662 POMFRET, Conn., History of. A Discourse Delivered on the Day of Annual Thanksgiving, November 19, 1840. By D. Hunt. *8vo, paper cover,* 35 *pages, rough edges; fine copy. Very scarce.* *Hartford,* 1841

1663 POOLE, WM. FRED., A.M. An Index to Periodical Literature. *8vo, hf. mor., gilt top, rough edges; very scarce and important work of reference.* *New York,* 1853

1664 Pope, Major-Gen. John. Report of His Campaign in Virginia, to the Secretary of War. January 27, 1863. House of Representives, 37th Congress, 3d Session, Ex. Doc. No. 81. *8vo, cl.* *Washington,* 1863

1665 POPHAM COLONY. The First Colonization of New England. An Address delivered at Erection of a Monumental Stone in the

Walls of Fort Popham, Aug. 29, 1862, Commemorative of the Planting of the Popham Colony on the Peninsula of Sabino, Aug. 19th, O. S., 1607. Establishing the Title of England to the Continent. By John A. Poor. *8vo, uncut, pamph.* *N. Y.*, 1863

1666 POPHAM COLONY. MEMORIAL VOLUME of the Popham Celebration, August 29, 1862, Commemorative of the planting of the Colony on the Peninsula of Sabino, August 19, O. S., 1807, establishing the Title of England to the Continent. By Edwin Ballard. *Half cr. lev., extra, gilt top, rough edges. Fine copy.* *Portland*, 1863

1666*POPHAM COLONY. An Address on the Character of. Founded by George Popham, at the Mouth of the Kennebec River. Aug. 19 [O. S.], 1607. Delivered in Bath on the 257th Anniversary. By Hon. Edward Bourne. *8vo pamph., uncut.* *Portland*, 1864

1667 POPHAM COLONY. An Address on the Two-Hundred and Fifty-Eighth Anniversary of. By Hon. James W. Patterson. *Paper, uncut.* *Boston*, 1865

250 copies printed.

1668 POPHAM COLONY. A Discussion of its Historical Claims; with a Bibliography of the Subject. *Boston*, 1866

300 copies printed.

1669 PORTFOLIO, The, for March, 1818. Embellished with a plan of the Battle of Bunker's Hill. *8vo, half sheep; scarce.* *Phila., Pa.*, 1818

1670 PORTLAND, ME.; HISTORY OF—from its first Settlement; with Notices of the Neighboring Towns and of the Changes of Gov't. in Maine. By Wm. Willis. In Two Parts. *8vo, cl.; maps and engravings; scarce. 2 vols.; fine copy.* *Portland*, 1831

Rev. Jos. B. Felt's copy and Autograph.

1671 PORTLAND, Maine; THE HISTORY OF—from 1632 to 1864; with a Notice of previous Settlements, Colonial Grants, and Changes of Government in Maine. By William Willis. 2d ed., revised and enlarged. *Roy. 8vo. In sheets. With maps.* *Portland*, 1865

1672 PORTSMOUTH, N. H.; AN ACCOUNT OF THE SEVERAL RELIGIOUS SOCIETIES IN—from their first establishment, and of the Ministers of each to the first of January, 1805. By Timothy Alden, Jun. *8vo, bds., scarce.* *Boston*, 1808

1673 PORTSMOUTH, N. H.; ANNALS OF. Comprising a period of Two Hundred Years, from the first settlement of the Town; with Biographical Sketches of a few of the most respectable Inhabitants. By Nathaniel Adams. *L. 8vo, bds., uncut; fine copy; very scarce.* *Portsmouth*, 1825

1674 PORTSMOUTH, N. H.; RAMBLES ABOUT. Sketches of Persons, Localities, and Incidents of Two Centuries; principally from Tradition and Unpublished Documents. By Charles W. Brewster. *8vo, cl., very scarce.* *Portsmouth*, 1859

1675 POTTER, NATHANIEL. A Memoir on Contagion, more especially as it respects Yellow Fever, read in convention of the Medical and Chirurgical Faculty of Maryland, 3rd of June, 1817. 8*vo*, *bds., uncut.* *Baltimore*, 1818

1676 POTTER, RAY; Memoirs of the Life and Religious Experience of. 12*mo, half mor.* *Providence*, 1829

1677 POTTER, RAY. Admonitions from "The Depths of the Earth;" or, the Fall of Ray Potter. In twenty-four Letters. Written by himself to his Brother, Nicholas G. Potter. 12*mo, cl.* *Pawtucket*, 1838

1678 PRESBYTERIAN CHURCH in the Confederate States of America. Address of the General Assembly of—to all the Churches. 8*vo*, *paper.* *Augusta, Ga.*, 1861

1679 PRESCOTT, WILLIAM HICKLING. Proceedings of the Massachusetts Historical Society in respect to the Memory of. Feb. 1, 1859. 12*mo, cloth.* *Boston, Mass.*, 1859

1680 PRESCOTT, WILLIAM HICKLING; LIFE OF. By George Ticknor. *Imp.* 8*vo, cl. L. P.* *Boston*, 1864

1681 PRIEST, JOSIAH. American Antiquities and Discoveries in the West: being an Exhibition of the Evidence that an Ancient Population of partially Civilized Nations, differing entirely from those of the present Indians, peopled America many Centuries before its Discovery by Columbus, and inquiries into their Origin; with a Copious Description of many of their stupendous works, now in ruins; with conjectures concerning what may have become of them. Fourth Edition. 8*vo, sheep; plates.* *Albany*, 1834

1682 PRIEST, JOSIAH. American Antiquities and Discoveries in the West: being an Exhibition of the Evidence that an Ancient Population of partially Civilized Nations, differing entirely from those of the present Indians, peopled America many Centuries before its Discovery by Columbus, and inquiries into their Origin; with a Copious Description of many of their stupendous works, now in ruins; with conjectures concerning what may have become of them. Fifth Editon. 8*vo, sheep; with plates.* *Albany, N. Y.*, 1835

1683 PRINCE, THOMAS. A CHRONOLOGICAL HISTORY OF NEW ENGLAND in the Form of ANNALS: being A summary and exact Account of the most material Transactions and Occurrences relating to THIS COUNTRY, in the Order of Time wherein they happened, from the Discovery by Capt. Gosnold in 1602, to the Arrival of Governor BELCHER, in 1730. With an Introduction, containing A brief Epitome of the most remarkable Transactions and Events Abroad, from the CREATION, etc. 12*mo, full dark blue cr. lev. mor.*
Boston, N. E.: Printed by Kneeland & Green, MDCCXXXVI

1684 PRINCE, THOMAS. THE CHRISTIAN HISTORY, containing accounts of the Revival and Propagation of Religion in Great Britain and America. For the years 1743 and 1744. 8*vo, old cf.* 2 *vols., very scarce.*
Boston, N. E.: Printed by S. Kneeland and T. Green, for T. Prince, junr. 1744 '45

1685 PRINCE, THOMAS. A CHRONOLOGICAL HISTORY OF NEW ENGLAND, in the form of Annals ; with an Introduction. *In sheets, folded.* 8*vo.* *Boston, N. E.*, 1736. *Reprinted*, 1826

1686 PRINCE, THOMAS. CATALOGUE of the American portion of the Library of. With a Memoir, and List of his Publications. By Wm. H. Whitmore. 12*mo, paper cover. Port. Uncut.* *Boston*, 1868

1687 PRINCE, W. R. An Oration pronounced in the M. E. Church, Hempstead, L. I., July 4, 1831. 8*vo pamph.* ; 15 *p.* ; *scarce.* *Hempstead*, 1831

1688 PRINCETON, Mass. ; THE HISTORY OF—from its First Settlement ; with a sketch of the present Religious Controversy in that place. By Chas. Theo. Russell. 8*vo pamph.* ; 130 *p.* ; *fine copy* ; *scarce.* *Boston*, 1838

1689 PRINCETON, MASS. ; HISTORY OF—Civil and Ecclesiastical, from its First Settlement in 1739 to April, 1852. By Jeremiah L. Hanaford. 8*vo, cl., scarce.* *Worcester*, 1852

1690 PRINCETON, Mass. Celebration of the 100th Anniversary of the Incorporation of the Town, October 20th, 1859 ; including the Address of Chas. Theo. Russell, Poem of Erastus Everett, &c. 8*vo pamph.* ; 119 *p.* ; *scarce.* *Worcester*, 1860

1691 PRINCETON Theological Seminary. Discourse addressed to the Alumni of, Apr. 30, 1862, on Occasion of Completion of its First Half Century. By Wm. B. Sprague. With an Appendix. 8*vo pamph.* *Albany*, 1862

1692 PRITTS, J. MIRROR OF OLDEN TIME BORDER LIFE ; embracing a History of the Discovery of America, also History of Virginia, also History of the Early Settlement of Pennsylvania, Penn's Treaty with the Indians, and the Subsequent Warfare which marked the efforts to settle the Interior with Devastation, Blood and Suffering, until the final establishment of Peace. To which are added Personal Narratives of Captivities and Escapes, of Strange and Thrilling Adventures, Personal Prowess, etc. Together with numerous Sketches of Frontier Men, the Remarkable Achievements and Incidents in their career ; with numerous Miscellaneous Sketches of Daring Deeds, Remarkable Events, etc. 8*vo, full calf* ; *plates.* *Abingdon, Va.*, 1849

1693 PROCEEDINGS of the Convention of the Soldiers of the War of 1812 in N. Y., Oct. 17, 1856, in reference to their Claims, etc., and to Celebrate the Anniversary of Burgoyne's Surrender. 8*vo, uncut, fine copy* ; 34 *p.* *Albany : Munsell*, 1857

1694 PROVIDENCE. AN HISTORICAL DISCOURSE deliv. at celebration of the Second Centennial Anniv. of the First Bap. Church, Nov. 7, 1839. By Wm. Hague. *Cl.,* 8*vo* ; *fine copy.* *Boston*, 1839

1695 PROVIDENCE. ANNALS OF THE TOWN OF, from its First Settlement to the Organization of the City Government in June, 1832. By Wm. R. Staples. 8*vo, cl.* ; *scarce.* *Providence*, 1843

1696 PUFF, BREVET MAJOR PINDAR. The State Triumvirate : a Political Tale, and the Epistles of. 12*mo, bds., uncut.* *New York*, 1819

1697 PUTNAM, MAJOR-GENERAL ISRAEL. Life of. By Col. David Humphreys, with Notes and Additions. With an Appendix, containing an Historical and Topographical Sketch of Bunker Hill Battle. By S. Swett. *8vo, bds., uncut. Portrait. Very scarce in this condition.* *Boston*, 1818

1698 PUTNAM, ISRAEL. MEMOIRS OF THE LIFE, Adventures and Military Exploits of. *24mo, bds.; scarce; fine copy.* *Ithaca, N. Y.*, 1839

1699 PUTNAM PHALANX. EXCURSION OF, to Boston, Charlestown and Providence, Oct. 4, 5, 6, 7, 1859. *8vo, blue cl. Frontispiece.* *Hartford, Conn.*, 1859

1700 PUTNAM, ISRAEL W. "A Fifty Years Ministry." Two Disc. on the Fiftieth Anniversary of the Author's Ordination, Mar. 5th, 1815, deliv. in Middleborough, Mar. 19, 1865. *8vo, orig. cov., 34 p.; fine copy; uncut.* *Middleboro', Mass.*, 1865

1701 PUTNAM COUNTY, N. Y. THE HISTORY OF, with an enumeration of its Towns, Villages, Rivers, Creeks, Lakes, Ponds, Mountains, Hills and Geological Features; Local Traditions, and short Biographical Sketches of Early Settlers, etc. By William J. Blake. *12mo, cl.; scarce; fine copy.* *New York*, 1849

1702 [PYE, H. J.] Shooting: a Poem. [By H. J. Pye, Esq., Poet Laureat.] *4to, hf. cf., corners and back. With plates.* *London*, 1784

PAMPHLETS.

1703 Miscellaneous. *Valuable.* [*Twenty-one.*]

Price, Richard. Observations on the Nature of Civil Liberty, the Principles of Government, and the Justice and Policy of the War with America. *London*, 1776

——— Essay on Population of England from Revolution to the Present Time. *Scarce.* *London*, 1780

——— Discourse on the Love of our Country. *Boston*, 1790

Preston, W. Discourse on Destruc. of Steam Packet Pulaski. *Savannah*, 1838

Preston, Willard. Sermon. Savannah, Dec. 21, 1845. *Savannah*, 1846

Paine, Thomas. Dissertations on Gov., the Affairs of the Bank and Paper Money. *Scarce.* *Phila.*, 1786

——— Disser. on First Principles of Gov. *Paris.*

——— Agrarian Justice. *Phila.*

——— Answer to Rights of Man, by H. Makenzie. *Phila.*, 1796

——— Appendix to Theological Works. *Scarce.* *London*, 1820

——— Letters between Andrew A. Dean and. *Scarce.* *N. Y.*, 1823

——— Common Sense. *Dedham*, 1844

Pittsburgh Board of Trade. Speech of Walter Foward to Assoc. of. *Pittsburgh*, 1840

Philological Institute. Address before Thirteenth Anniv., by Robert Robb. *Pittsburgh*, 1841

——— Address before Fifteenth Anniv., by T. J. Bigham. *Pittsburgh*, 1842

——— Address before Fourteenth Anniv., by Wm. M. Shinn. *Pittsburgh*, 1842

——— Address before the Sixteenth Anniv., by John A. Willis. *Pittsburgh*, 1843

Parish, Elijah. Sermon at Byfield on Annual Fast. 2nd Ed. *Interesting and spicy.* *Newburyport*, 1811

——— Sermon at Byfield on Annual Fast. *Newburyport*, 1813

Parish Henry. Argument of John W. Edmonds on subject of Will of. *N. Y.*, 1857

Porter, John K. Argument of Parish Will Case. *Albany*, 1862

1704 Miscellaneous. [*Nineteen.*]

Porcupine, Peter. A rub from snub; or, a cursory analytical epistle. *Phila.*, 1795

——— Polit. Censor; or Monthly Review, by. *Phila.*, 1796

——— Prospect from the Congress Gallery during the Session, Dec. 7, 1795. *Phila.*, 1796

——— Life and Adventures of. *Phila.*, 1796

——— A Bone to Gnaw for the Democrats. *Phila.*, 1796, and 1795. *Parts* 1 *and* 2. *Scarce.*

——— The Rush Light. Nos. I., II., III., Feb. 15–28, March 15, 1800. *Scarce.* *N. Y.*

Prot. Epis. Church. Journal of the Proceedings of. *Scarce.* *N. Y.*, 1792

——— Sermon deliv. before convention of, Oct. 4, 1808, by Rev. Frederic Beasley. *N. Y.*

——— Constitution of the, in the Eastern Diocese of the U. S. of America.

——— Charge deliv. to the convention of, Oct. 5, 1808, by Benjamin Moore. *N. Y.*

——— Articles of Religion as established by, in Convention. *N. Y.*, 1802

——— Journal of the proceedings of the 46th Convention, 1831. *N. Y.*

——— Sermon by Benj. T. Onderdonk, Gen. Theo. Sem., 1831.

——— Sermon by J. Adams before Conven. of, Feb. 13, 1833. *Charleston*

——— Letter to—"Liturgy is no Danger," Oct., 1843. *N. Y.*,

——— Sermon deliv. at Diocesan Convention, May 19, 1847, by James May. *Winchester, Va.*

Panama R. R. Co. *N. Y.*, 1849

——— Communication of the Board of Directors to Stockholders. *N. Y.* 1853

Prattsville Tannery. Description of. Nov. 27, 1847.

1705 Miscellaneous. *Valuable lot.* [*Eighteen.*]

Porter, D. H. Disc., "Religion and the State," July 4, 1858. *Savannah, Ga.*

Porter, Mrs. S. T. Address at Funeral of, Nov. 15, 1858, by A. Dickinson.

Porter, Com. W. D. Defence of, before Naval Retiring Board, Nov. 1863.

Parker, G. G. Piratical Barbarity of the Female Captive, March 12, 1825. *N. Y.*

Parker, Theodore. Sermon of the moral dangers incident to prosperity, Nov. 5, 1854. *Boston.*

Parker, Joel. Opinion of, against Hoboken Land and Improvement Co. *Jersey City,* 1860

——— Inaugural Address of, deliv. Trenton, Jan. 20, 1863.

Palmer, A. H. Letter to C. J. Ingersoll on Foreign Relations. March 27, 1846. *N. Y.*

Palmer, Ray. "Study of Hist." Lecture, Dec. 4, 1835. *Bath.*

——— "The Highest civilization the result of Christianity and Christian learning." Disc., Nov. 15, 1865. *Albany.*

Porcupine, Peter. A Bone to Gnaw for the Democrats; or, observations on a Pamphlet entitled "The Political Progress of Great Britain." *Phila.*, 1795

——— The Democratiad: a Poem, in retaliation for the "Phila. Jockey Club." *Scarce.* *Phila.*, 1796

——— The Guillotina; or, a Democratic Dirge: a Poem. *Scarce.* *Phila.*, 1796

——— Political Progress of Britain. *Parts* 1 *and* 2. *Very scarce.* *Phila.*, 1795. (J. T. Callendar.)

——— A Rub from Snub, addressed to. *Phila.*, 1795

Plymouth. Articles of Faith and Form of Covenant of Third Cong. Ch. 1826.

——— Oration at Anniv., Dec. 22, 1802, by J. Q. Adams. *Very scarce.*

——— Sermon deliv. in Plymouth, by Wm. T. Torrey. *Scarce.*

1706 Miscellaneous. [*Twenty-five.*]

Pratt, Zadoc. Chronological Biog. of. *New York,* 1868

Presb. Educ. Soc. 7th Annual Report of, May 12, 1825. *New York.*

Parochial Schools. Report of Board of Educ. on, May, 1847. *Phila.*

Popery and Paganism. Exact conformity of, by C. Middleton. 1836

Pusey, E. Sermon before Oxford Univ., by. *N. Y.*, 1843

St. Patrick's Purgatory, by T. Wright. *N. Y.*

Pope Pius IX. Life and Reign of, with Portrait, by J. Dowling. *N. Y.*

Priest, Parish. Absolution; Mystery of the Kingdom of Heaven. *London,* 1854

Pitrat, John C. Review of the speech of J. R. Chandler, Jan. 10, 1855.

Parton, J. How N. Y. is governed. *Boston*, 1866

——— The Danish Islands. *Boston*, 1869

Philosopher. A Sentimental Fragment of a Journal of. *N. Y.*, 1809

Philosophy of Evil. *Phila.*, 1845

Philosophy of Modern Miracles, by a Dweller in the Temple. *N. Y.*, 1850

Potter, Horatio. Introductory Sermon, Albany, May 12, 1833

Pickering, Timothy. Letter from, addressed to James Sullivan. *Boston*, 1808

——— Sketch of Life of. Sermon, by Charles W. Upham. *Scarce.* *Salem*, 1829

Pickering, John. Lecture on Telegraphic Language. *Boston*, 1833

——— Eulogy on, by D. A. White, Oct. 28, 1846. *Cambridge*

Primer, Amer. Easy introduction to Spelling and Reading. *Phila.*, 1808

Primer of Reading and Drawing, by Mary T. Peabody. *Boston*, 1841

Porters, E. Annual Conven. Sermon, May 31, 1810. *Newburyport*, 1811

Pomfret. Sermon deliv. at, July 18, 1819, at Funeral of S. Cotton, by James Porter. *Providence*

Porter, W. D. Oration before Calhoun Monument Assoc., March, 18, 1854. *Charleston*

Porter, J. K. Argument on trial at Albany of Wm. Landon, acquitted July 21, 1855. *Albany.*

Miscellaneous. *Fine Lot.* [*Seventeen.*]

Plymouth, N. E. Sermon describing the Sin and Danger of Self-Love, preached 1621, by Robt. Cushman.

Plymouth, Mass., Result of an Ecclesiastical council convened at, Dec. 25, 1832. *Plymouth.*

Puritans, Disc. on the Characteristics of, deliv. Dec. 21, 1845, by David Dyer. *Dorchester.*

Plymouth. Disc. deliv., Dec. 22, 1848, by S. M. Worcester. *Salem.*

——— Oration deliv. Dec. 21, 1855, by Wm. H. Seward.

——— Disc. deliv. in, at Cushman Festival, Aug. 15, 1855, by Robt. W. Cushman. *Boston.*

——— Collection, Revival Hymns and Tunes selected from.

——— Sermon—"The Pilgrim Temple-Builders," Sermon, Dec 17, 1865, by John Milton Holmes. *N. Y.*

——— Memorial of the Pilgrim Fathers, by S. G. Buckingham.

Perkins, Erasmus. A few hints relative to the texture of mind, and the manufacture of Conscience. *London.*

Perkins, J. A. The Female Prisoner, a narrative of the Life and singular adventures of. *N. Y.*, 1839

Perkins, John, Speech of, on the transfer to the States by the general government. *Washington*, 1854

Panoplist and Missionary Magazine, June, 1812. Nos. 1, 2, 3 and 4.

Pitt, Wm., Letter to, upon the nature of Parliamentary Representation. *London*, 1784

——— Letter to, on the Anti-Aristocratical tendency of Burke's Letters. *London*, 1796

Preacher, Liberal. Monthly publication of Sermons, by living ministers, Feb., 1828, April, 1829. *Boston.*

——— National Amer. Original Monthly, by W. H. Bidwell, May, 1842–1847, June, 1844, Apr., 1846. *N. Y.*

7 1708 Miscellaneous. *Fine lot.* [*Nineteen.*]

Putnam's, Dr., Dis. deliv. at installation of Rev. D. Fosdick, March 3, 1846. *Boston.*

Parsons, C. B. Address on the Philosophy of Time, before the Anthon Lit. Soc., April 18,1847. *St. Louis.*

Pierce, John. Disc. deliv. in Brookline, March 15, 1847. *Scarce. Historical local.* *Boston.*

Pillow, Maj. Gen., Defence of, before Court of Inquiry. *Scarce.* *Maryland*, 1848

Penn, Wm., and T. B. Macaulay. Charges made in Macaulay's Hist. of Eng. against Penn, by W. E. Forster. *Scarce.* 1849

People, Amer. Journal. *N. Y.*, Feb., 1850

Pacific Telegraph and Railway, by J. Loughborough. *St. Louis*, 1849

Philoponos. Great Exhibition of 1851. *London*, 1851

Phelps, Anson G., Sermon on the Death of, by G. L. Prentiss. 1854

Pelt, Van P. J. Disc. July 4, 1851. *New York.*

Pool, William, True Life of. *New York*, 1855

Parris, Samuel, Account of the Life, Char., etc., of, by S. P. Fowler, Nov. 14, 1856. *Salem.*

Pulpit and Rostrum. Sermons, Orations, Popular Lectures, etc., by T. L. Cuyler. *N. Y.*, Nov. 15, 1858

Patrick, M. R. Address deliv. before Queens Co. Agri. Soc., Sept. 19, 1860.

Paine, Thomas. Origin of Free Masonry. *Very scarce.* *N. Y.*, 1810

Pauperism, Report of a Com. on Subject of. *N. Y.*, 1818

Philadelphia. Report of a Com. on the Pauper System. *Phila.*, 1827

——— Report of a Com. appointed by Guardians of the Poor, to visit Baltimore, New York, etc. *Phila.*, 1827

Poor-Houses, Report of an examination of, Jails, etc., in N. Y., by Samuel Chipman. 3d Ed. 96 *p.*, *fine copy, uncut.* *Albany*, 1835

1709 Miscellaneous. [*Twenty-One.*]

Postscript to Peter's Letters addressed to S. T. Coleridge. *N. Y.*, 1820

Pastoral Letters of Archbishop Carroll to the Cong. of Trinity Ch., etc. *Phila.*, 1819–1797

Patterson, G. S. Answer to a pamphlet entitled "Strictures on Mr. Pattison's Reply to certain Oral and Written Criticisms." *Relates to the affair of Pattison and Mrs. Ure.* *Baltimore*, 1820

Plain Sense on Nat. Industry, to People of U. S., Dec. 9, 1820. *N. Y.*

Prefatory Remarks of Proprietors of the Coal Mines, April 23, 1838.

Pelton, S. Reply to L. Kean's Vindication of Methodism, Oct., 1823.

Pindar, Peter. The Vagabond, or New Looking-Glass. Apr. 7, 1823.

Paterson, Charles. Address 12th exhibition of Amer. Academy of Fine Arts. *N. Y.*, 1826

Proposition for an Anthracite Coal Steam Power Boat and Barge Company for Passengers on North River, by J. L. Sullivan.

Piper. Tour of Wandering. *Portland*, 1833

Pious Family. *Edinburgh.*

Polish Revolution, History of, with latest atrocities of Russian Conquerors. *N. Y.*, 1834

Phrenology, Catechism of, by G. Combe. *Phila.*, 1835

Poyen, Charles. Letter to Col. Stone on Animal Magnetism. *Boston*, 1837

Phenix Bank, Exam. of Charges of Board of Trade against. *N. Y.*, 1838

Poinsett, Joel R. Disc. before the Nat. Institution for promotion of Science. Washington, 1840. 1st Anniv.

Peebles, C. Glen. The Reformer. No. I., on Temperance. *Baltimore*, 1841

St. Paul's College, account of the Grammar School or Junior department of. *N. Y.*, 1842

Pocahontas, Marriage of, by Benson J. Lossing. *Scarce.*

Pickett, Wm. V. New System of Architecture, developing the properties of Metals. *London*, 1845

Poetry of Animated Nature. Illustrated. *Phil.*, 1846

1710 Miscellaneous. *Fine Lot.* [*Twenty.*]

Pitman, Robt. C., Argument of, on License Bill, April 7, 1868. *Boston.*

Peckham, Joseph. Address at Funeral of Mrs. Catharine A. Prince, July 15, 1867.

Popham Colony, Biography of the subject. *Boston*, 1866

Poore, Ben Perley. Congressional directory for the 1st session of the 39th Congress of U. S. of America, 1866.

Phipps, Spencer. Instructions for treating with the Eastern Indians. *Boston*, 1865

Presbyter., Review of. A Pastoral Letter to the Clergy of N. Y., July, 1865.
Patents, Introductory Report of the Commissioners of, 1863.
Proudfit, John. Sermon—"The Sanctuary of God consulted in the Present Crisis." Apr. 21, 1861.
New Brunswick, 1861
Peel, George, "Menie Conceited Jests of." *Reprint. Scarce.*
London.
Penington, John. Inaugural dissertation on the Phœnomena, Causes and Effects of Fermentation. *Scarce.* *Phila.*, 1790
Pelew Islands, Account of, and Shipwreck of Antelope. *Curious wood cuts. Very early imprint.* *Catskill*, 1797
Packard, Hezekiah. Federal Republican. Two disc., April, 1799.
Pope, Alexander, The Imperial Epistle and the shade of.
Phila., 18
Potwine, Thomas, Sermon on Death of, by N. Prudden.
Hartford, 1803
Peacock at Home. Sequel to the Butterfly's Ball.
N. Y., 1808
Paley, William. Sermon, July 15, 1777.
Puffer, Reuben. Sermon, Annual Conven. of Cong. Ministers of Mass., May 30, 1811.
Persecution, Modern. A Poem. *London*, 1811
Pettibone's Economy of Fuel, with or without steam.
Phila., 1812
Porson, Prof. Catechism for use of Swinish Multitude.
London.

8 1711 Miscellaneous. *Fine lot.* [*Twenty-four.*]
Penn. Company. Address from Pres. and Directors of.
Phila., 1814
——— Brief View of System of Internal Improvement of, by M. Carey. *Phila.*, 1831
——— View of Anthracite Coal Trade of, by Caleb Cushing. *Boston*, 1836
——— Railroad Guide for, Information to Travelers.
Phila., 1855
——— Hospital. Report of Board of Managers of.
Phila., 1858
——— Hist. Sketch of Paper Money issued by.
Phila., 1862
——— College. Oration before Phrenakosmian Soc. of, at Third Anniv. Celebration. By Hon. J. Reid.
Gettysburg, 1834
——— Lyceum. Proc. of Education Convention, with Address from. *Phila.*, 1835
Philadelphia Law Academy. Address before, by Edward D. Ingraham. *Very valuable.* *Phila.*, 1828
——— Discourse before, by John K. Kane. *Very valuable.*
Phila., 1831
——— Address before, by Peter S. Du Ponceau. *Very valuable.* *Phila.*, 1831

Phil. Law Acad. Discourse on Nature and Study of Law, by Wm. Rawle. *Very valuable.* *Phila.*, 1832

——— Truth Unveiled, or Exposition of Origin and Cause of the Terrible Riots in. *Phila.*, 1844

——— Soc. for Promo. of National Industry. Address of. No. I. *Phila.*, 1819. (3d ed.)

Priestly, Joseph. Letters to Rt. Hon. Edmund Burke; occasioned by his Reflections on Revolu. in France. *N. Y.*, 1791

——— Observations on Emigration of. *N. Y.*, 1794

——— Continuation of Letters on Religion, in Answer to Mr. Paine's Age of Reason. *Scarce.* *Salem*, 1795

Peyster, Frederic De. History of the Tontine Building. *N. Y.*, 1855

——— J. Watts De. History of the Life of Leonard Torstenson. *Poughkeepsie*, 1855

——— J. Watts De. History of the Life of Carausius. *Poughkeepsie*, 1858

——— J. Watts De. Practical Strategy, as illus. by the Achiev. of the Austrian Field-Marshal Traun. *Catskill*, 1863

Parkinson, Wm. Two Sermons of a Series of Sermons, Nos. 3 and 4. *N. Y.*, 1828

——— Two Sermons, of a Series of Sermons, Nos. 7 and 8. *N. Y.*, 1828

Payne, John H. "Adeline, the Victim of Seduction." *Very free.* *N. Y.*, 1822

1712 Miscellaneous. *Scarce lot.* [*Sixteen.*]

Perry, David L. Sermon delivered at Funeral of Cotton Mather Smith, Nov. 27, 1806. *Hartford*

Porcupine, Peter. A little plain English, addressed to people of U. S. *Phila.*, 1795

Priestly, Joseph. The originality and superior excellence of the Mosaic Inst. *Northumberland*, 1803

Proudfit, Alex. Sermon at ordination of Mr. Henry Davis, Feb. 21, 1810. *Salem* 10

Price, Richard. Sermon on day of General Fast. 3rd Ed. *London*, 1779

Prince, Tho's. Sermon on Death of Tho's Cushing, April 11, 1746.

Presbytery. A second statement of facts relative to the session, etc. *N. Y.*, 1823

Presbyterian Church. Original draft of a Pastoral Address before. *New York*, 1832

——— Extracts from the minutes of the Synod. Aug. 3, 1825. Session XI.

——— Strictures on a pamphlet published by a minority of the eastern subordinate synod. By Rob't Gibson. *N. Y.*, 1832

——— Minutes of the General Synod of. Session XVI. Aug. 1833. *Phila.*

Presbyterian Church. Statement of some recent transactions in. *N. Y.*, 1833

——— Proc. of the General Synod of. Session XVI. Aug., 1833. *Phila.*

Phila. The ordination of the corporation of the city of Phila., 1805.

Parker, Addison. Oration deliv. July, 1829. *Southbridge*

——— Samuel. Disc. Sept. 23, 1803. *Boston*

1713 Miscellaneous. *Valuable lot.* [*Twenty-one.*]

Porcupine, Peter. Prospect from the Congress Gallery, during session, Dec. 7, 1795. *Phila.*

——— Political Censor, for March, 1797. *Phila.*

——— Political Censor of the most interesting Political occurrences relative to U. S. of Amer. Phil., 1796.

——— For March, April, May.

——— Paine, Tho's. Origin of Freemasonry. *Very scarce. N. Y.*, 1810

Pacificus, Philo. Solemn review on the custom of war. *Cambridge,* 1816

Puffer, Reuben. Disc. on revealed religion, deliv. May 11, 1808, by H. P. Dudley.

Plymouth. Oration deliv. Dec. 22, 1824, by Edward Everett. *Boston*

——— Oration deliv. Dec. 22, 1820, by Daniel Webster. *Boston*

——— Oration Deliv. Dec. 22, 1829, by Wm. Sullivan. *Boston*

Pœdagogus, Dr. Sketch of Life and character of. *N. Y.*, 1817

Peculiar Doctrines of the Gospel explained and defended.. *New Haven,* Feb. 23, 1809

Pennsylvania. Annual Disc. before the Academy of Fine Arts, Nov. 29, 1826, by Henry D. Gilpin. *Phila.*

Publicola. Strictures on Prof. McVickar's Pamphlet. *N. Y.*, 1829

Princeton Review. Perfect Sanctification. July, 1842. *Princeton*

Publicola. Letter to A. Gallatin, by. *N. Y.*, 1845

Pierson, Isaac. Vindication of the Currency of the State of N. Y. By Publicola. 1818

——— Remarks on Private Banking. *Albany,* 1818

Poem. "A Rhapsody." *Curious and scarce. N. Y.*, 1789

Philip, John. Letter from. *Princeton, N. J,* 1833

Perkins, Nathan. Disc. on ordination of Joab Brace, Jan. 16, 1805. *Hartford*

1714 Miscellaneous Pamphlets. Poetry and Tragedy. *Desirable lot.* [*Nineteen.*]

The Robbers. A Tragedy. From the German of Frederick Schiller. *N. Y.*, 1793

Francis the First. A Tragedy. Performed by Francis Ann Kemble. *N. Y.*, 1832

Euphemio of Messina. A Tragedy. From Italian of Silvio Pellico. *N. Y.*, 1834

Byron, Lord. English Bards and Scotch Reviewers. Satire, by. *N. Y.*, 1817

——— Lament of Tasso. 3d ed. *London*, 1817

——— Mazeppa. A Poem. A Fragment. *London*, 1819

———Lament of Tasso. *London*, 1817

Wesley, Charles. Epistle to Rev. George Whitefield. *London*, 1771

Democracy. An Epic Poem. By Aquiline Nimble-Chops, Democrat. *Very scarce political doc.* *N. Y.*

Irony, Solomon. Fashion, or the Art of making Breeches : an Heroi-Satiri Didactic Poem. *Very scarce.* *Phila.*, 1800

Frank ; or, Who's the Croaker? *Very scarce.* *N. Y.*, 1820

Bonaparte, The Storm at Sea, Madaline, and other Poems. *N. Y.* 1820

Athens, and other Poems. *Salem*, 1824

Mellen, Grenville. The Rest of the Nations. A Poem. *Portland*, 1826

Fanny. Poem. By Fitz-Greene Halleck. *N. Y.*, 1819

Alnwick Castle, with other Poems. *N. Y.*, 1827

Adams, John Quincy. Dermot MacMorrogh, or the Conquest of Ireland. Historical Tale of Twelfth Century. Four Cantos. *Boston*, 1832

Everest, C. W. Vision of Death. Poem. *Hartford*, 1837

——— Babylon. Poem. *Hartford*, 1838

Barn-Yard Rhymes: showing what opinions the Turkey, Cock, Goose, and the Duck entertain of Allopathia, Homœopathia, Electro-Galvanism, and the Animalcule Doctrines. *Curious.* *N. Y.*, 1838

1715 Miscellaneous. *Valuable.* [*Fifteen.*]

Report of the Delegation Appointed by Commis. of Public Schools of Baltimore to Represent the Board in the National Conven. of the friends of Com. Sch. Instruc. *Baltimore*, 1849

Report of School Com. for 1853. *Cambridge*, 1853

Webster, Noah, Jr. Letter to Gov., Instruc. and Trustees of Universities and Other Seminaries of Learning, on the Errors of English Grammars. *Scarce.* *New York*, 1798

Webster, Noah, Jr. Letter to Hon. John Pickering on Subject of his Vocabulary. *Very scarce and valuable.* *Boston*, 1817

Brown, Rev. Wm. Memoir relative to Itinerating Libraries. *Edinburgh*

Report of the Com. on the Library, in relation to the Donations from Paris. City Doc. No. 46. *Boston*, 1849

Mitchill, Samuel S. Discourse. Soc. for instructing the Deaf and Dumb. *N. Y.*, 1818

Miller, Sylvanus. Address in behalf of N. Y. Institution for

Instruc. of Deaf and Dumb, before N. Y. Forum. *N. Y.*, 1819

Akerly, Samuel. Address, Introduc. to Exercises of the Pupils of N. Y. Institu. for Instruc. of Deaf and Dumb. *N. Y.*, 1826

Premiums for Advantage of the British Colonies, by the Soc. Instituted at London for encouragement of Arts, Manufactures and Commerce. *London*, 1751

The Constitution of the Columbianum, or American Academy of the Fine Arts. *Scarce.* *Phila.*, 1795

Clinton, De Witt. Discourse. American Acad. of Arts. *N. Y.*, 1816

Catalogue of Paintings and Engravings, American Acad. of Arts. 9th Exhib. *N. Y.*, 1823

Lawrence, Wm. B. Address, Opening of American Acad. of Arts, May 10, 1825. *N. Y.*, 1826

Circular Letter of the Literary and Philosophical Soc. of N. Y., on the Subject of a Statistical Account of. *N. Y.*, 1815

1716 Miscellaneous Pamphlets. [*Sixteen.*]

Clinton, De Witt. Introd. Discourse. Literary and Philos. Soc. *Scarce.* *N. Y.*, 1815

Statement, Explanatory of the Resignation of Officers of the Regiment of Artillery of City and County of N. Y., 1797. *Very scarce.*

Duane, Wm. Hand Book for Infantry, containing First Principles of Military Discipline. Fifth ed. *Phila.*, 1813

Butler, Benj. F. Address. "The Military Profession in the U. S., and the Means of Promoting its Usefulness and Honor." *N. Y.*, 1839

Mordecai, Brev. Maj. Alfred. Sec. Report of Experiments on Gunpowder, made at Washington Arsenal, 1845, '47, '48. *Washington*, 1849

Annual Report of the Deaths in City and County of N. Y. for 1820. *N. Y.*, 1821

Report on Com. on Laws to Corpor. of N. Y., on Subject of Interment. *N. Y.*, 1825

Hicks, Elias. Substance of Two Discourses, Dec. 17, 1824. *N. Y.*, 1825

Hicks, Elias. Observations on Sermons of, in Several Letters to him, by a Demi-Quaker. *Phila.*, 1826

Hicks, Elias. Review of Testimony against, by Evan Lewis. *N. Y.*, 1829

Wetherald, Thomas. Sermons. Friends' Meeting, Wash., March, 1825. *Phila.*, 1825

Wetherald, Thomas. Sermons. Friends' Meeting, Baltimore, June 15, 1825. *Baltimore* 1825

Braithwaite, Anna. Sermon and Prayer. Friends' Meeting, Phila., Oct. 26, 1825. *Phila.*, 1825

Hopkins, Gerald T. Sermon and Prayer. Friends' Meeting, Balto., June 15, 1825. *Balto.*, 1825

Declaration of Yearly Meeting of Friends, respecting the Proc.

of those who have lately separated from the Soc., and also showing the Contrast between their Doctrines and those held by Friends. *N. Y.*, 1828

Lewis, Enoch. Vindication of Soc. of Friends, being a Reply to a Review of Cox on Quakerism. *Phila.*, 1834

1717 Peter Porcupine Pamphlets. *Valuable and scarce.* [*Ten.*]

Porcupine, Peter. The prospect from the Congress Gallery during the Session, Dec. 7, 1795. 2nd ed. *Phila.*

——— The prospect from the Congress Gallery during the Session, Dec. 7, 1795. *Phila.*

——— Observations on the emigration of Joseph Priestly, Feb. 8, 1795. *Phila.*

——— A New Year's Gift to the democrats; or, observations on a pamphlet entitled, " a vindication of Mr. Randolph's Resignation." *Very scarce.* *Phila.*, 1796

——— The Political Censor of the most interesting political occurrences, 1796. For March, May and Sept. *Phila.*

——— A Bone to Gnaw for the democrats. Parts I. and II. *Phila.*, 1796

——— A little plain English, addressed to the people of the U. S. *Phila.*, 1796

——— The Imposter detected, or a review of some of the writings of. *Phila.*, 1796

——— An answer to Paine's Rights of Man. *Phila.*, 1796

——— Life and Adventures of. *Phila.*, 1796

1718 "Peter Porcupine" Pamphlets. *Very scarce lot.* [*Seven.*]

A Twig of Birch for a butting calf; or, strictures upon remarks on the emigration of Doctor Joseph Priestly, etc. *New York*, 1795

Porcupine, Peter, A Rub from Snub; or, a cursory Analytical Epistle addressed to. *Phila.*, 1795

——— A New Year's Gift to the Democrats; or, observations on a pamphlet, entitled a Vindication of Mr. Randolph's Resignation. *Phila.*, 1796

——— The Scare-Crow, being an infamous letter sent to Mr. John Oldden. *Phila.*, 1796

——— A Roaster; or, a check to the progress of political blasphemy, intended as a brief reply to. By Sim Sans-culotte. *Phila.*, 1796

——— The polit. Censor, or monthly review of the most interesting polit. occurrences relative to the U. S. *Phila.*, 1796

——— Porcupine's polit. censor, containing the Remarks on the debates in Congress, etc. *Phila.*, 1796

1719 Plymouth Orations, Addresses, Etc. *Very scarce lot.* [*Thirteen.*]

Adams, John Quincy. Oration deliv. in 1802, Dec. 22, at Plymouth, at the anniversary commemoration of the landing of our ancestors at that place. *Scarce. Published for the first time by request in* 1820.

Webster, Daniel. Disc. deliv. at Plymouth, in commemoration of the first settlement of N. E. *Boston*, Dec., 22, 1820

——— Disc. deliv. at Plymouth in commemoration of the first settlement of N. E. Dec. 22, 1820

——— The same. 2d Ed.

——— The same. 3d Ed.

——— The same. 4th Ed.

Toney, Wm. T. Sermon deliv. in Plymouth, after the anniv. of the landing of the Fathers. *Very scarce.* *Boston*, Dec. 23, 1821

——— Disc. deliv. before the Charitable Soc., of Plymouth. *Boston*, Jan., 1822

Cushman, Robert. Sermon describing the "Sin and Danger of Self-Love." Preached at Plymouth, in N. E., in 1621. From an old edition. *Very scarce.* *Stockbridge*, 1822

Whitmore, Benj. Sermon deliv. at Plymouth, on Thanksgiving Day. *Dec.* 5, 1822

Everett, Edward. Oration deliv. at Plymouth. *Boston*, Dec. 22, 1824

Beecher, Lyman. Sermon, "The Memory of our Fathers," deliv. at Plymouth. Dec. 22, 1827

May, Samuel J. Letter to Joel Hawes, in review of his "Tribute to the memory of the Pilgrims." *Scarce.* *Hartford*, 1831

Blagden, Geo. W. Address, "Great Principles associated with Plymouth Rock, deliv. before the Pilgrim Society of Plymouth, Dec. 22, 1834.

1720 Pilgrim Soc., Plymouth and Puritan Pamphlets. *Very valuable lot.* [*Seventeen.*]

Sermon, Dec. 31, 1820, Bi-Cent. in Plymouth, by Dr. Emmons.

——— Dec. 22, 1820, Bi-Cent. in Hadley, by J. Woodbridge.

——— Dec. 22, 1827, in Plymouth, by Lyman Beecher.

——— Dec. 22, 1830, in Plymouth, by B. B. Wisner.

Tales and Jests of Mr. Hugh Peters. *London*, 1807

Defence of Hugh Peters. By J. B. Felt. *Boston*, 1851

Account of Pilgrim Celeb. at Plymouth, Aug. 1, 1853. *Boston*, 1853

The Pilgrim Fathers. Lecture. By Rev. H. S. Browne. *Manchester*, 1853

"A Finger point from Plymouth Rock." By Charles Sumner. *Boston*, 1853

Theology of Puritans. By Leonard Woods. *Boston*, 1851

Pictures of Embarkation of Pilgrims. *New York*, 1853

Memorial of Pilgrim Fathers. By S. G. Buckingham. *Springfield*, 1867

Disc. deliv. in Plymouth. By Robert W. Cushman. *Boston*, 1855

——— on Characteristics of Puritans. By David Dyer. *Boston*, 1846

——— Dec. 22, 1829, at Plymouth. By Wm. Sullivan.

——— Dec. 22, 1820, at Plymouth. By Daniel Webster.

——— Dec. 22, 1835, at Plymouth. Peleg Sprague.

1721 Paine Pamphlets. *Valuable lot.* [*Twelve.*]

Paine, Thomas. Dissertations on Government, the Affairs of the Bank, and Paper Money. *Very scarce.* *Phila.*, 1786

——— Dissertation on First Principles of Government. *Paris*

——— The Decline and Fall of the English System of Finance. *Paris*, 1796

——— The Decline and Fall of the English System of Finance. *Phila.*, 1796

——— Rights of Man. Part Sec., Combining Principle and Practice. *Albany*, 1792

——— Letter from, to People of France on his Election to National Convention; also, Letter from M. Condorcet to a Magistrate in Switzerland, respecting Massacre of the Swiss Guards, etc. *N. Y.*, 1793

——— Examination of the "Age of Reason;" or an Investigation of True and Fabulous Theology. By Gilbert Wakefield. *Scarce.* *N. Y.*, 1794

——— Observations on Pamphlet, entitled the Decline and Fall of the English System of Finance. By Ralph Broome. *London*, 1796

——— An Apology for the Bible, in a Series of Letters addressed to. By R. Watson. *Phila.*, 1796

——— An Apology for Christianity. Series of Letters. By R. Watson. *Phila.*, 1796

——— Examination of the passages in the New Testament; also, Essay on Dream, with an Appendix containing my Private Thoughts of a Future State. *Very scarce.* *New York.*

——— Two Letters. Correspondence between Andrew A. Dean and. *New York*, 1823

1722 Pamphlets relating to Universities, Libraries, Schools and Sunday-Schools. [*Fifteen.*]

Sunday-School Association of the City of Troy. First Annual Report. *Troy*, 1817

——— Union Soc., New York. Second Annual Report. *New York*, 1818

——— Hints for Conducting. Useful also for Day Schools.

Substance of Speech, by Rev. Thomas Smith, at Annual Meeting of Sheffield Sunday-School Union, June 11, 1821.

American Sunday-School Union. First Annual Report. *Phila.*, 1825

Alexander, Archibald. Suggestions in Vindication of Sunday-Schools. 1829

Speeches of Messrs. Webster, Frelinghuysen and others at the Sunday-School Meeting in Washington. *Phila.*, 1831

Considerations, Principles and Objects of the American Sunday-School Union. *Phila.*, 1845

Goram, Robert. Political Inquiries. To which is added a Plan for the General Establishment of Schools throughout the United States. *Very scarce.* *Wilmington*, 1791

Remonstrance and Answer of the Bethel Free School to the Memorial and Observations of Trustees of New York Free Schools. *New York*, 1824

Report of a Com. High Sch. Soc. of N. Y. Appointed to prepare a Plan of Instruction. *New York*, 1824

Irving, John T. Address. Opening of New York High Sch. for Females, Jan. 21, 1826. *New York*, 1826

Humphrey, Heman. Address. Opening of Convention of Teachers and Friends of Education. *Hartford*, 1831

Common School Advocate, Cincinnati, Feb. 1838. No. 14.

Hazard, Rowland G. Address. Washington Co. Assoc., for Improv. of Public Schools. *Providence*, 1845

1723 Pamphlets Relating to Music. [*Ten.*]

Peale Charles W. Discourse Introductory to a Course of Lectures on the Science of Nature. *With Original Music. Very Scarce.* *Philadelphia, Nov.* 8, 1800

Brown, Francis. Address on Music before the Handel Society, Dartmouth College, August, 1809.

The Words of the Dettingen Te Deum of Handel. *Philadelphia*, 1824

Hooker, Edward. Address delivered before the Society of Sacred Music in the Theological Seminary of West Windsor. New York, August 6, 1839.

——— E. W. Address delivered before the Hastings and Mason Musical Association, Pittsfield, December 25, 1837.

Worcester, Samuel. Address on Sacred Music, delivered before the Middlesex Musical Society, and the Handel Society of Dartmouth College, Concord, Sep. 19, 1810.

Rice, Luther. Address delivered before the Singing Society of the Second Baptist Church in Boston, at their Concert of Sacred Music, Boston, February 16, 1814.

Nevin, John W. Address on Sacred Music. *Princeton*, 1827

Enquiry into the Nature and Design of Music. *Boston*, 1831

First Annual Report of the Boston Academy of Music. *Boston*, 1833

1724 Protestant Epis. Ch. Pamphlets. [*Nine.*]

Kemp, James. Charge to Clergy in Diocess of Maryland at a Convention in City of Washington, June 5, 1822.

Address of Board of Trustees of Theological Seminary of Md. *Georgetown, D. C.*, 1822

Hobart, John H. The High Churchman Vindicated in a Fourth Charge to the Clergy. *N. Y.*, 1826

Address to Protestant Episcopalians on Subject of a Tract called "Origin of the Terms High and Low Churchmen."

Brownell, Thomas C. Christian Zeal—Sermon at Opening of General Convention, in St. James' Ch., Phila., Aug. 12, 1829 *N. Y.*, 1829

Manney, Solon W. Essay Demonstrating the Truth and Divine Original of Episcopacy. *Michigan*, 1841

Episcopacy Divine in its Origin and Unbroken in its Succession. *Providence*, 1843

Report of the Select Committee on the Alteration of Article III. of the Constitution, touching the Qualifications of Lay Delegates appointed by the Convention of 1847. *N. Y.*, 1848

Jarvis, Samuel F. A Voice from Connecticut, occasioned by the late Pastoral Letter of Bishop of North Carolina to the Clergy and Laity of his Diocese. *Hartford*, 1849

1725 Prot. Epis. Ch. Pamphlets. [*Fifteen.*]

Whittingham, Wm. Robinson. Sermon—The Charge to Feed the Lambs of Christ—on the Quarter Centennial Anniversary, 1851.

Leaming, Rev. Jeremiah. Address of Episcopal Clergy of Connecticut to Right Rev. Bp. Seabury, with his Answer, and a Sermon before Convention at Middletown, Aug. 3, 1785. Also Bishop Seabury's First Charge to Clergy of his Diocese. *Very scarce.* *New Haven*, 1785

Journal of Proceedings of the Annual Convention of the Protestant Episcopal Church in New York. *N. Y.*, 1804

——— Of the Bishops, Clergy and Laity of Protestant Epis. Church in United States of America in a Convention. *N. Y.*, 1804

An Office of Induction of Ministers into Parishes or Churches. *N. Y.*, 1804

Constitution and Canons of Prot. Episcopal Church, 1789 to 1804. *N. Y.*, 1805

Articles of Religion and Canons of Prot. Epis. Ch., Maryland; to which is prefixed a Pastoral letter from Bishop Thomas J. Claggett. *Baltimore*, 1805

Journal of Proc. of a Convention in New Jersey. *New Brunswick*, 1806

——— do do do do 1807

Beasley, Rev. Frederic. Sermon deliv. before Convention. *N. Y.*, Oct. 4, 1808

Journal of proc. of Ann'l Convention in New Jersey. *N. Brunswick*, 1809

Third Annual Report of Trustees of Society of Protestant Epis. Church for Advancement of Christianity in Pennsylvania. 1815.

Journal of Proc. of Bishops, Clergy, and Laity in a General Convention. *N. Y.*, 1817

Brownell, Thomas C. Charge to the Clergy. *New Haven,* 1821

Kemp, James. Pastoral Letter Addressed to Members of Protestant Epis. Church in Diocese of Maryland. *Baltimore,* 1822

1726 Prot. Epis. Ch. Pamphlets. [*Eleven.*]

Bishop Jarvis's Charge to the Clergy of his Diocese delivered immediately after his Consecration, together with the Address and Bishop's answer. *Newfield, Conn., Oct.* 18, 1797

Wilmer, Simon, Sermon delivered at the Convention of, in New Jersey. *Burlington, May* 1, 1811

Bowen, Nath'l. A Charge to the Clergy of. Sermon—The Moral Efficacy of the Christian Ministry, How Best Secured. Feb. 10, 1831

Brownell, Thomas C. A Charge delivered to the Clergy. *Hartford, Conn., Oct.* 11, 1836

Bowen, Nath'l. Address delivered at Commencement of the General Theological Seminary. *N. Y., July* 1, 1836

Whittingham, Wm. Rollinson. Sermon—Emanuel in the Eucharist. Preached in Baltimore, Dec. 5, 1842.

Onderdonk, Bishop. Worship : the Use of a Liturgy. A Charge to the Clergy. *Phila., May* 17, 1843

De Lancey, Wm. H. A Charge to the Clergy of the Diocese of West New York, on the Extent of Redemption. *Geneva, N. Y.,* Aug. 17, 1842

Henshaw, J. P. K. Two Lectures in answer to an Inquiry—What is the True Construction of the terms Priest, Altar, and Sacrifice. *Balt.,* Dec. 15, 1842

Reasons why I am a Churchman; or, the Episcopalian Armed againt Popular Objections. Second Edition. *Hartford,* 1844

Wainwright, J. M. Sermon—A Plea for Unity. November 27, 1850. *New York*

1727 Political Pamphlets. *Very valuable.* [*Twelve.*]

Seventh Essay on Free Trade and Finance. *Scarce. Philadelphia,* 1785

Honesty Shewed to be True Policy; or a General Impost Considered and Defended. By a Plain Politician. *Scarce. N. Y.,* 1786

Enquiry into the Principles on which a Commercial System for United States should be Founded. *Scarce. Phila.,* 1787

Observations Leading to a Fair Examination of System of Government proposed by the Late Convention, in a Number of Letters from the Federal Farmers to the Republicans. *Very scarce. Printed in the year* 1687

Attention! or, New Thoughts on a Serious Subject; being an Enquiry into the Excise Laws of Connecticut. *Hartford,* 1789

Lessons to a Young Prince by an Old Statesman on the Present Disposition in Europe to a General Revolution. Sixth Edition, with addition of a Lesson on French Revolution. By Hon. Edmund Burke. *N. Y.,* 1791

Barlow, Joel. Letter to the National Convention of France on the Defects in the Constitution of 1791 ; also, a Poem by, *N. Y.*

Strictures and Observations upon the Three Executive Departments of the Government of United States. *Printed in the United States of America*, 1792.

Madison, James. Speech, January 14, 1794, in Support of his propositions for the Promotion of the Commerce of the United States, and in Reply to Wm. Smith. *N. Y.*, 1794

Manlius, with Notes and References. No. 1. As published in the Columbian Centinel. Sept. 3, 1794.

Letters to the people of Great Britain respecting the Present State of their Public Affairs. *London*, 1795

Features of Mr. Jay's Treaty, to which is annexed a View of the Commerce of the United States as it Stands at Present. *Phila.*, 1795

1728 Political Pamphlets. [*Thirteen.*]

Treaty of Amity, Commerce and Navigation between Great Britain and the U. S. of America. *Phila.*, 1795

Examination of Treaty of Amity, Commerce and Navigation between the U. S. and Great Britain. By Cato. *N. Y.*, 1795

Official Notes from the Minister of French Republic to Secretary of State of the U. S. *Phila.*, 1796

Notes from Citizen Adet, Minister Plenipotentiary of the French Republic, to Secretary of State of U. S. *Phila.*, 1796

Ames's, Fisher, Speech of—on the Treaty between U. S. and Great Britain. April 28, 1796. *Phila.*, 1796

Burke, Rt. Hon. Edmund. Letter from—on the Attacks made upon him and his Pension. By Duke of Bedford and Earl of Lauderdale. *Dublin*, 1796

Fauchet, Joseph. Sketch of our Political Relations with the U. S. of America. *Phila.*, 1796

Boissière, C. C. Tanguy De La. Observations on the Dispatch, Jan. 16, 1797, by Mr. Pickering to Mr. Pinckney. *Scarce. Phila.*, 1797

Erskine, Hon. Thomas. View of the Causes and Consequences of the present War with France. *N. Y.*, 1797

Instructions to Charles C. Pinckney, John Marshall and Elbridge Gerry, Envoys Extraord. and Ministers Plenip. to French Republic. *Phila.*, 1798

Young, John. Essays on Government, Revolutions, British Constitution, &c. *Phila.*, 1798

Nicholas, George. Letter from—Justifying the Conduct of the Citizens of Kentucky, as to some of the late measures of the General Gov't., and Correcting Certain False Statements. *Phila.*, 1799

The Political Green-House for the Year 1798. *Scarce. Hartford*, 1799

1729 Political Pamphlets. *Valuable.* [*Fourteen.*]

Cooper, Thos., of Northumberland. Political Essays. *Phila.*, 1800

Serious Considerations on the Election of a President. *Trenton*, 1800

Windham, Wm. Speech of. Nov. 4, 1801. *London*

New York. Address to the Electors of. *Albany*, 1801

Wolcott, Oliver. Address to the People of the U. S. on the Subject of the Report of a Committee appointed to "Examine and Report whether Monies drawn from the Treasury have been faithfully applied to the Objects for which they were Appropriated, &c." *Relates to the imputed misuse of funds by Alex. Hamilton. Very scarce. Uncut.* *Boston*, 1802

Return of the whole numbers of Persons within the several districts of the U. S. For 1800. *Second Census.*

Return of the whole numbers of Persons within the several districts of the U. S. For 1791. *First Census of U.S.*

Duties on Goods, Wares, and Merchandise imported into the U. S. *N. Y.*, 1803

Duane, Wm. Mississippi Question. Report of a Debate in the Senate of U. S. 23, 24, 25 Feb., 1803. *Phila.*

Message of the President of the U. S. to the Senate and House of Representatives, Oct 17, 1803.

Treaty and Conventions entered into and ratified by the U. S. of America and the French Republic, relative to the cession of Louisiana. April 30, 1803. *Scarce.*

W. T. Political Economy, Founded in Justice and Humanity, 1804. *Washington*

Answer to War in Disguise. *N. Y.*, 1806

Impartial Enquiry into the Conduct of Gov. Lewis in relation to the Merchants' Bank. By Politicus. N. Y., Jan. 1806.

1730 Political Pamphlets. [*Ten.*]

Randolph, John. Speech on the Importation of British Goods into the U. S. March 5, 1806.

War without Disguise, or the Frauds of Neutral Commerce. *Scarce.* *Amer.*, 1807

Fessenden, Thos. Green. Some Thoughts on the Present Dispute between G. B. and Amer. *Phila.*, 1807

Cheetham, James. Peace or War? or Thoughts on our Affairs with England. *N. Y.*, 1807

Hints to both Parties, or Observations on the Proceedings in Parliament. *N. Y.*, 1808

Mr. Lloyd's Speeches in the Senate of the U. S. on Mr. Hillhouse's resolution to repeal the Embargo Laws. Nov. 21, 1808.

Report, in part, of the Committee appointed on the President's Message. *Phila.*, 1808

Mr. Pickering's Letter. Feb. 16, 1808. *Washington*

Memorials of Sundry Merchants relative to the Infringements of our Neutral Trade. Nov. 18, 1808. *Washington*

Communications on the next election for President of the U. S. and of the late measures of Fed. Admin. 1808

1731 Political Pamphlets. [*Eleven.*]

Reasons for Laying an Embargo. *New York*, 1808
Remarks on the Embargo Law. By Civis. *N. Y.*, 1808
To the Honorable the Legislature of the State of N. Y. *Albany*, 1808
New Crisis, or Appeal to the Nation. By Pericles. *Philad.*, 1809
Analysis of the late Correspondence between our Administration and Great Britain and France. *N. Y.*, 1809
Memoir concerning the Commercial Relations of the U. S. with England; also, an Essay on the Advantages to be Derived from new Colonies. *Boston*, 1809
Review of the Works of Fisher Ames. By his Friends. *Scarce.* *Boston*, 1809
Gardinier, Barent. Speech of—as relates to our Foreign Relations. March, 1809. *Georgetown, D.C.*
Hear both Sides, or an Address to all Impartial Men of all Parties. N. Y., Dec. 21, 1809.
Address to the People of Mass. March 1, 1809.
Cases and Queries Submitted to Citizens of U. S. *New York*, 1809

1732 Political Pamphlets. [*Thirteen.*]

Memorial of Merchants in Salem to Congress. *Salem*, 1820
Navy Yard Exposition and Abuses. By B. Phillips. *Curious doc't.* *Phila.*, 1820
Address to the Federal Electors of N. Y. on the election of Governor and Lt.-Gov. of that State. *Albany*, 1820
Three Letters on the present Calamitous State of Affairs, to J. M. Garnett. By M. Carey. *Phila.*, 1820
Van Buren, M. Speech of, on the Settlement of the Governor's Accounts. *Albany*, 1820
Observations upon certain Public Offices. *N. Y.*, 1822
Pell, A. S. Address to the Electors of N. Y. *Albany*, 1824
——— Address to the Electors of Duchess Co. (1824)?
Memorial to the Legislature of N. Y. By Myron Holly. 1826
Memorials to Congress in regard to transporting the Mails and keeping the Post Offices open on the Sabbath. *N. Y.*, 1829
Speech of Mr. Hayne on Public Lands. Jan. 21, 1830.
White, E. D. Speech of, on the Duty on Sugar. Feb., 1831.
Strictures on Nullification. *Boston*, 1832

1733 Political Pamphlets. [*Ten.*]

Thoughts on the Present Relations and Interests of U. S. *New York*, 1810
Perpetual War the Policy of Mr. Madison. Conscript Militia and a Local Volunteer Force. *Boston*, 1812
History of French Influence in the U. States. *Philadelphia*, 1812
Proceedings of Government of United States in Maintaining the Public Right to the Beach of the Mississippi adjacent to New Orleans against the Intrusion of Edw. Livingston. Prepared by Thomas Jefferson. *Very scarce.* *N. Y.*, 1812

Touchstone to the People of the United States on the choice of a President. *N. Y.*, 1812

Giles, Wm. B., Address of, to the People of Virginia. 1813

Treaties between United States and Great Britain. *Boston*, 1815

Address to the House of Representatives of United States on the War with Great Britain. *Phila.*, 1812

King, Rufus. Speech on the Navigation Act. *N. Y.*, 1818

——— Two Speeches on the Missouri Bill. *N. Y.*, 1819

1734 Political Pamphlets. [*Twelve.*]

Speech of Henry Clay in Defense of the American System. Feb. 1832.

Debate on the Nomination of Martin Van Buren as Minister of United States to Great Britain. *Interesting.* January 25, 1832.

Mr. Barnard's Speech, July 25, 1832. *Utica, N.Y.*

Journal of the Convention of the People of S. C. November 19, 1832. 131 *p. The First Nullification and Secession Convention.* *Columbia*, 1833

Proceedings of the Onondaga Whig Convention. *Syracuse*, July 4, 1834

Reply to J. F. Cooper. By one of His Countrymen. *Boston*, 1834

Report of the Union Committee in Relation to National Banks. *New York*, 1834

Cambreleng's Letter to the Democratic Committee.

Speech of Mr. Moore of New York, May 5, 1836, on public Monies of United States.

——— Silas Wright of New York, January 31, 1838, on public Monies of United States.

Oration of Edwin Forrest. July 4, 1838.

Address and Resolve of the Democratic Members of Mass. Legislature of 1838.

1735 Political. [*Eleven.*]

Letters from Jesse Hoyt to Secretary of the Treasury, &c. *Scarce.* *N. Y.*, 1842

Address of Whig Members of Senate and House of Representatives of Mass. *Boston*, 1845

Speech of Mr. McMurray on the Governor's Message, January, 1843.

——— S. F. Vinton on the Loan Bill. February 8, 1848.

Sinclair, John. Sermon on Great Britain and America. October 15, 1853.

The Great Clay Festival. June 9, 1842.

Speech of J. S. Bosworth on the Forty Million Debt.

Reply to the March Number of the Democratic Review, entitled "The Late Acting President." *Scarce.* *N. Y.*, 1845

An Appeal to the whole country for an Union of Parties. *United States*, 1850

Speech of Charles Sumner on the Fugitive Slave Bill, May 26, 1852.

—— Mr. Soule on the American Fisheries, August 12, 1852.

Pamphlets.

1736 Installation and Thanksgiving Discourses. [*Twenty.*]

1737 Miscellaneous pamphlets. Contains several Episcopal Convention Reports. [*Sixteen.*]

1738 Unitarian and Universalist Controversial pamphlets. [*Eight.*]

1739 Reports of Secretary of Treasury and N. Y. City Documents. [*Thirty-one.*]

1740 In the case of Ship Hunter—Joseph W. Brackett and Samuel Leggett. *Very scarce lot.* [*Seven.*]

1741 On Mails; Lotteries; Bristed's Oration on Literature; Samuel Farmer Jarvis's Address in N. Y.; Supreme Court, &c., &c. *Very scarce lot.* [*Twenty-three.*]

1742 Funeral Sermons. *Rare lot.* [*Twenty-six.*]

1743 Charges of the Bishops of the Protestant Episcopal Church—Bishops Ives, McIlvaine, Doane, White, Otey, Onderdonk, Brownell, De Lancey, Moore, and Others. [*Thirty.*]

1744 Channing Pamphlets. Comprising his Letter to Hon. Henry Clay, and Review of the same; and Professor Stuart's Letter on Religious Liberty; Duty of the Free States; Sermon on War, &c. [*Eleven.*]

1745 Temperance pamphlets. [*Sixteen.*]

1746 Unit. Assoc. Verplanck, Wardlaw, Deane, Small, &c. [*Twenty.*]

1747 Miscellaneous. *Valuable.* [*Thirteen.*]

Act to Abolish Imprisonment for debt and to punish Fraudulent Debtors, passed April 26, 1831. *N. Y.*, 1832

Reports on the Abolition of Capital Punishment. *Boston,* 1837

Vindication of the Separate System of Prison Discipline from the Misrepresentation of North American Review. *Phila.*, 1839

First Report of the Prison Association of New York. *N. Y.*, 1844

Patton, Benjamin. Jurisdiction of the Lakes. *Pittsburgh*, 1842

Payson, Thomas. Address, Oct. 10, 1816. *Boston.*

Porter, David. Sermon, Dec. 5, 1822. *Catskill.*

Pudding, Hasty: a Poem. *Very scarce.* *Brooklyn*, 1833

Political Green House, Jan. 1, 1799. *Hartford.*

Dwight, Timothy. Sermon on Duelling. *N. Y.*, 1805

—— —— —— *Hartford*, 1805

Authentic Account of the Fatal Duel Fought on Sunday the 21st March, 1830, near Chester, Penn., between Charles G. Hunter and Wm. Miller, the former midshipman of United States Navy and Latter Attorney at Law of Phila., 1830. *Very scarce.*

An Essay on Duelling. *N. Y.*, 1830

1748 Miscellaneous. *Valuable. Historical.* [*Seven.*]

Granby, Ct. History of the Copper Mines, and Newgate Prison. Also of the Captivity of Dan. Hayes by the Indians in 1707. By Noah A. Phelps. *Hartford,* 1845

Hadley, Mass. Bi-Cent. Celeb. of the Settlement of, June 8, 1859. *Northampton,* 1859

Hartford, Conn. Address delivered at close of Second Century, Nov., 1835.

Hingham, Mass. Bi-Centen. Annniversary Address, by S. Lincoln. *Very scarce.* *Hingham,* 1835

Hopkinton, Mass., Century Sermon in, December 24, 1815. By N. Howe. *Boston,* 1825

Tennessee, East, Its Agricultural and Mineral Resources. By John Caldwell. *N. Y.,* 1867

Texan Revolution, View of. By Dr. Joseph E. Field *Very scarce.* *Greenfield,* 1836

1749 Miscellaneous. [*Thirteen.*]

Dartmouth College. Address deliv. before Alumni Assoc. of. By Samuel C. Bartlett. *Boston,* 1865

——— Address deliv. before Alumni Assoc. of. By Samuel G. Brown. *Concord,* 1856

——— Catalogue, 1813.

——— Oration. By Samuel L. Knapp, Aug. 19, 1824.

——— Val. Lect. By Bénj. Hale. *Hanover,* 1835

——— Address. By J. K. Lord, July 24, 1844.

Derby Academy, Hingham. Disc. By Convers Francis, May 21, 1828.

Elder's Ridge Academy, Penn. Address. By A. B. Brown, Pittsburgh, Oct. 12, 1849.

Hamilton Lit. and Theol. Inst. Address. By G. W. Bethune, June 5, 1833, *Utica.*

Howard Benev. Soc. of Boston. Sermon. By R. S. Storrs, Jan. 12, 1820.

Hamilton and Rossville Mech. Ins't. Lecture. By D. Mc Dill. *Rossville, Ohio,* 1842

Princeton, N. J., Theol. Sem. Lecture. By Samuel Miller, July 3, 1829.

Pennsylvania, Debates of the Convention of State of, on the Constitu. proposed for the Govt. of the U. S. *Very scarce.* *Phila.,* 1788

1750 Miscellaneous. *Valuable.* [*Eleven.*]

Pennsylvania Coal Regions. By E. Bowen. *Pottsville,* 1848

——— Controversy between that State and Virginia, about Boundary Line. By Neville B. Craig. *Scarce.* *Pittsburgh,* 1843

Philadelphia. Report of the Board of Health. *Phila.,* 1868

Pittsburgh, As it Is. By George H. Thurston. *Pittsburgh,* 1857

——— The same, another edition.

Pittsfield, Mass., History of. By David D. Field. *Very scarce.* *Hartford*, 1844
Plainfield, Topographical Description and Historical sketch of. By Jacob Porter. *Very scarce.* *Greenfield*, 1834
Portsmouth, N. H. Centen. Anniv. of St. John's Lodge. By Charles W. Moore. *Boston*, 1836
Providence, N. H. Centen. Disc., Aug. 5. By John Pitman. *Scarce.* *Providence*, 1836
Fryeburg, Me. Address delivered at the commemoration, May 19, 1825. By Charles S. Daveis. *Very scarce.* *Portland*, 1825
——— Centen. Celeb. of the settlement of, with the Hist. address. By Rev. Samuel Souther. *Scarce.* *Worcester*, 1863

1751 Miscellaneous. [*Eighteen.*]

Parish Will Case. Mr. Evarts' Argument in Reply, in the Court of Appeals. *N. Y.*, 1862
Paine Thomas. Apology for the Bible, addressed to. By R. Watson. *Phila.*, 1796
Plymouth. Sermon deliv. by Stephen Chapin, Dec. 22, 1820. *Scarce.*
——— Oration deliv. by Edward Everett. *Boston*, 1828
Priestly, Joseph. The Doctrine of Philogiston Established. *Northumberland*, 1800
Paine, Thomas. The Ruling Passion. Poem. *Boston*, 1797
——— The Invention of Letters. Poem. *Boston*, 1795
Geneva, College. Baccalaureate address. By Benj. Hale. *Geneva, N. Y.*, 1847
——— Disc. deliv. by Gulian C. Verplanck. *N. Y.*, Aug. 7, 1833
——— Disc. By C. S. Henry, Aug. 5, 1840.
——— Address, by Samuel A. Foote, Aug. 1, 1832.
Gouverneur Wesleyan Sem. Oration, by W. W. Ninde, Lowville, Jan. 27, 1841.
Greenwood, F. W. P. Sermon at ordination of Wm. P. Lunt, June 19, 1828. *N. Y.*
——— Sermon, Twenty-fifth Anniv. of Boston Female Soc. Sept. 23, 1825. *Boston.*
——— Sermon at Funeral of James Freeman, Nov. 22, 1835. *Boston.*
——— Sermon at Funeral of Christopher Gore, March 11, 1827. *Boston.*
Gay, Ebenezer. Disc., Aug. 26, 1781. *Salem, reprinted*, 18—

QUAKERS. The History of the Rise, Increase, and Progress of the Christian People called Quakers, intermixed with several Remarkable Occurrences. Written Originally in Low Dutch, and by himself Translated into English. By Wm. Sewel. *4to, sh.* *London*, 1722

1753 QUARTERLY REGISTER AND JOURNAL of the American Education Society, Conducted by Rev. E. Cornelius and B. B. Edwards. Vols. I., (Nos. 1-7,) III to XV inclusive, 1827–42, 14 vols. in original numbers. *8vo, portraits.* *Boston*, 1829–42

Full of Historical and Biographical matter of great interest and value to the antiquarian.

1754 QUEBEC. A SERMON preached Oct. 25, 1759, for the success of the British Arms this year; Especially in the Reduction of Quebec. By Andrew Eliot. *8vo pamph., 43 p., fine copy; scarce.* *Boston*, 1759

1755 QUEBEC, PICTURE OF, with Historical Recollections. By Alfred Hawkins. *8vo, cl., uncut, illus., fine copy; scarce.* *Quebec*, 1834

1756 QUEEN'S CO., (N. Y.) DOCUMENTS AND LETTERS intended to Illustrate the Revolutionary Incidents in, with connecting Narratives, explanatory Notes, and additions. By Henry Onderdonk. *12mo, cl., rough edges. Scarce.* *N. Y.*, 1846

1757 QUINCY, Ill., HISTORY OF, and Lecture deliv. before the N. E. Society, Dec. 22, 1862. "Early Reminiscences of Quincy." By William Keyes. *8vo, uncut, 105 p. Very scarce.* *S. l., n. d.*

1758 QUINCY, Mass. A Poem, delivered in the Town of Quincy, May 25, 1840, the 200th Anniv. of the Incorp. of the Town. By C. P. Cranch. *8vo pamph., 26 p. Very scarce; fine copy.* *Boston*, 1840

1759 QUINCY, Mass. A Commemorative discourse pronounced at Quincy, May 25, 1840, on the Second Centen. Anniv., with an Appendix. By George Whitney. *8vo pamph., rough edges, fine copy, scarce; 71 p.* *Boston*, 1840.

1760 QUINCY, Mass., HISTORICAL SKETCH of the Old Church in. By Fredric A. Whitney. *8vo pamph.; scarce.* *Albany*, 1864 10

PAMPHLETS.

1761 Miscellaneous Pamphlets. *Fine lot.* [*Ten.*]

Queen's Answer, The. To the Letter from the King to his People. *Phila.*, 1821
Quincy, Josiah, Speech of, deliv., Jan. 5, 1813. *N. Y.*, 1813
——— Address, deliv., Jan. 3, 1829. *Boston.*
Quincy, Mass. Discourse on Bi-Centen. Anniv. By George Whitney. *Very scarce.* *Boston*, 1840
Quincy, Josiah Jr. Observations on Boston Port Bill. *Scarce.* *Boston*, 1774 8
——— Oration. Fiftieth Anniv. of Amer. Independence. *Boston*, 1826
——— Address of Taking Final Leave of Office of Mayor. *Boston*, 1829
——— Memory of James Grahame Vindicated. *Boston*, 1846
Quakers' Sermon. "Repent and be Converted." *Scarce.* *Phila.*, 1768
Quincy, Josiah. Address, Sept. 17, 1830. *Boston.*

R. H. R. Sketches in Verse. *8vo, bds, uncut.* *Philadelphia*, 1810

1763 RANTOUL, JR. ROBERT. April 19, 1775. Oration and Account of the Union Celebration at Concord, April 19, 1850. *8vo pamph., 135 p., scarce.* *Boston*, 1850

1764 RAYMOND, HENRY J. Political Lessons of the Revolution; address before Citizens of Livingston County, at Geneseo, N. Y., July 4, 1854. *8vo, paper.* *New York*, 1854

1765 READ, THOMAS BUCHANAN. The Wagoner of the Alleghanies. A Poem of the Days of Seventy-six. *8vo, cl.* *Phila.*, 1863

1766 READING, PA. THE DESCRIPTION OF THE BOROUGH OF, containing its Population, Institutions, Trade, Manufactures, with a Notice of its First Settlement, and many curious Historical Matters. By Major William Stahle. *12mo, bds., fine copy; extremely scarce.* *Reading*, 1841

1767 RED-JACKET; OR, SA-GO-YE-WAT-HA. The Life and Times of, being the sequel to the History of the Six Nations. Eng. title. By Wm. L. Stone. *Half dk. green lev. mor., gt. top, rough edges.* *New York*, 1841

1768 REDE, LEMAN THOMAS. The Art of Money Getting; showing the Means by which an individual may obtain and retain Health, Wealth and Happiness. *12mo, rough edges; Frontispiece.* *London*, 1828

1769 REED, JOSEPH. REMARKS ON A LATE PUBLICATION IN THE INDEPENDENT GAZETTEER; with a short address to the People of Penn., on the many Libels and Slanders which have lately appeared against the Author. *8vo pamphlet, perfect copy, in fine condition, excessively rare.* *Phila.*, 1783

1770 REED, JOSEPH. LIFE AND CORRESPONDENCE OF, Military Secretary of Washington, at Cambridge, etc. By his grandson, William J. Reed. *2 vols., roy. 8vo, cl. With portrait. Fine copy.* *Phila.*, 1847

1771 REED, WM. B. Address delivered before the Philomathean Society of the University of Penn., Nov. 1, 1838. *8vo pamph., important, 62 p.; scarce.* *Phila.*, 1838

1772 Reed, John. A Sermon preached before the Convention of the Congregational Ministers in Boston, May 27, 1807. *8vo*, 39 *p., good copy.* *Boston*, 1807

1773 Reed, Hon. Thomas B., of Miss. An Address to Cadets at West Point, June 20, 1827. *8vo, fine copy ; very scarce. Historical.* 40 *pages.* *New York*, 1827

1774 REHOBOTH, Mass. The History of, comprising a History of the present towns of Rehoboth, Seekonk, and Pawtucket, from their settlement to the present time, together with sketches of Attleborough, Cumberland and a part of Swansey and Barrington, to the time that they were severally separated from the original town. By Leonard Bliss, Jr. *Cl., 8vo. Scarce.* *Boston*, 1836

1775 REHOBOTH, Mass. An Historical Oration, delivered July 4, 1860. Also, an account of the proceedings in Seekonk, completing Two Hundred and Sixteen Years of its History. By S. C. Newman. *8vo pamph.*, 112 *p., with index. Scarce.* *Pawtucket*, 1860

1776 Rendell, Rev. E. D. The Antediluvian History and Narrative of the Flood, as set forth in the Early portions of the Book of Genesis. Critically examined and explained. *8vo, cl.* *Boston*, 1851

1777 Report of the Select Committee of the Society for Propagating the Gospel among the Indians and others in North America. Presented to the Sixty-seventh annual meeting, May 31, 1855. *8vo, cl.* *Boston*, 1856

1778 Report of the Joint Committee on the Conduct of the War. 3 vols. *8vo, cl.* *Washington*, 1863

1779 Reports of the Committee on the Conduct of the War. Fort Pillow Massacre. Returned prisoners. Report No. 65, 38th Cong., 1st Session. *8vo, cl.* 1864

1780 RHODE ISLAND Historical Society. Collections, Vol. I. Containing Roger Williams' Key to the Indian language. *8vo, paper cov., uncut.* *Providence*, 1827

1781 RHODE ISLAND. A Discourse, embracing the Civil and Religious History of, delivered April 4, 1838, at the close of the Second Century from the First Settlement of the Island. By Arthur A. Ross. *12mo, cl.* *Providence*, 1838

1782 RHODE ISLAND. An Historical Discourse on the Civil and Religious Affairs of. By John Callender, M. A., with a Memoir of the Author, Biographical Notices of some of his distinguished contemporaries ; and annotations and original documents illustrative of the History of Rhode Island and Providence plantations, from the First Settlement to the end of the first century. By Romeo Elton, D. D. 3d ed. *8vo, cl.* *Boston*, 1843

1783 RHODE ISLAND. An account of the Churches in, presented at an adjourned session of the Twenty-eight annual meeting of the Rhode Island Baptist State Convention, Providence, Nov. 8, 1853. By Henry Jackson. *8vo, cl., with plate.* *Providence, R. I.*, 1854

1784 RHODE ISLAND. Bibliography of. A Catalogue of Books

and other publications relating to the State of Rhode Island, with Notes, Historical, Biographical and Critical. By John R. Bartlett. *4to, half rox., 150 copies printed.* *Providence,* 1864

1785 RICHMOND, Va. The Calamity at, being a Narrative of the Affecting Circumstances attending the awful conflagration of the Theatre in the city of, Dec. 26, 1811, by which more than 70 of its valuable citizens lost their lives, etc., collected from Letters, Publications and Official Reports, accompanied with a preface. *8vo, 60 pages, good copy, very scarce.* *New York,* 1812

1786 RICHMOND in By-gone Days. By an Old Citizen. *8vo, cl.* *Richmond,* 1856

1787 RICHMOND. Prison Life in the Tobacco Warehouse. By a Ball's Bluff Prisoner, Lieut. Wm. C. Harris. *8vo, paper, uncut; plates.* *Phila.,* 1862

1788 RICHMOND: her glory and her graves. A Poem, in Two Parts. By Cornelia M. Jordan. *8vo pamph., 39 pages; scarce.* *Richmond,* 1867

1789 Riggs, Luther G. The Anarchiad: a New England Poem, written in concert by David Humphreys, Joel Barlow, John Trumbull, and Dr. Lemuel Hopkins, with Notes and Appendices. *16mo, cl.* *New Haven,* 1861

1790 RINDGE, N. H. Address by Rev. A. W. Burnham, at the Centennial Celebration, Sept. 13, 1865. *8vo, 12 p., pamph.* *n. d.*

1791 Rives, W. C. Discourse on the Uses and Importance of History. Illustrated by a comparison of the American and French Revolutions. Deliv. before the Alumni of Univ. of Va. *8vo, 57 p.; valuable.* *Richmond,* 1847

1792 Robbins, Archibald. Journal, comprising an account of the Loss of the Brig Commerce, upon the Western Coast of Africa, Aug. 28, 1815; also of the Slavery and Sufferings of the Author and Crew upon the Desert of Zahara, 1815, 1816, 1817; with an account of the Manners, Customs, and Habits of the Wandering Arabs; also, a brief Historical and Geographical view of Africa, Fifth edition. *12mo, sh.* *Hartford,* 1818

1793 ROBBINS, Rev. AMMI R., Journal of, Chaplain in the American Army, in the Northern Campaign in 1776. *8vo, bds.* *New Haven,* 1850

1794 Robbins, Chandler. A History of the Second Church, or Old North, in Boston. To which is added a History of the New Brick Church. With Engravings. *8vo, cl.* *Boston,* 1852

1795 ROBIN, ABBE. New Travels through North America: In a Series of Letters; Exhibiting the History of the Victorious Campaign of the Allied Armies, under his Excellency Gen. Washington, and the Count de Rochambeau, in the Year 1781. Interspersed with political and philosophical observations upon the genius, temper, and customs of the Americans. Also, Narrations of the capture of Gen. Burgoyne, and Lord Cornwallis with their Armies; and a variety of interesting particulars, which occurred in the course of the War In America. *8vo, old bdg.; very scarce.* *Boston, MDCCLXXXIV.*

1796 Robinson, Conway. An Account of Discoveries in the West until 1519, and of Voyages to and along the Atlantic Coast of North America, from 1520 to 1573. *8vo, cl.* *Richmond*, 1848

1797 ROCK CO., (Wisconsin,) History of, and transactions of the Rock County Agricultural Society and Mechanics' Institute. Edited and compiled by Orrin Guernsey and Josiah F. Willard. *8vo, cl.* *Janesville, Wis.*, 1856

1798 RODGERS, JOHN. A Sermon, preached in the American Revolution, New York, Dec. 11, 1783, Appointed by Congress as a day of Public Thanksgiving throughout the U. S. *12mo, unbd.* *New York: Samuel Loudon, MDCCLXXXIV.*

1799 ROGERS, Major ROBERT, Journal of, containing an Account of the several Excursions he made under the Generals who commanded upon the Continent of North America, during the late war, from which may be collected the most material circumstances of every campaign upon that Continent, from the Commencement to the Conclusion of the War. *8vo, cf.* *London: printed for the Author, MDCCLXV.*

1800 ROGERS, ROBERT, Maj. A Concise Account of North America: containing a description of the several British Colonies on that Continent, including the Islands of Newfoundland, Cape Breton, etc. To which is subjoined an account of the several Nations and Tribes of Indians residing in those Parts, etc. *8vo, cf., gt.; fine copy.* *London*, 1765

1801 ROGERS, ROBERT, Maj. A Concise Account of North America: containing a description of the several British Colonies on that Continent, including the Islands of Newfoundland, Cape Breton, etc. To which is subjoined an account of the several Nations and Tribes of Indians residing in those Parts. *12mo, cf.; very scarce.* *Dublin*, 1769

1802 ROGERS, Maj. ROBERT, Journals of, Containing an Account of the several Excursions he made under the Generals who commanded upon the Continent of *North America*, during the late War. *To which is added:* An Historical Account of the Expedition against the Ohio Indians in 1764, under the command of *Henry Bouquet, Esq.*, including his transactions with the Indians, relative to the delivery of the prisoners, and the preliminaries of peace. With an introductory account of the preceding campaign, and battle of *Bushy-Run.* *12mo, sh.; very scarce; with Bouquet's Expedition.* *Dublin, MDCCLXIX.*

1803 ROGERS, Maj. ROBT. Reminiscences of the French War; containing Rogers' expeditions with the New England Rangers. To which is added an account of the Life and Military Services of Maj. Gen. John Stark, with notices and anecdotes of other Officers distinguished in the French and Revolutionary War. With portrait of Stark. *8vo, boards, uncut; beautiful copy; very scarce.* *Concord*, 1831

1804 Rogers, Ammi, Memoirs of, a Clergyman of the Episcopal Church, persecuted in the State of Connecticut, on account of Religion and Politics, for almost twenty years; and finally, falsely accused and imprisoned in Norwich Jail, for two years, on the charge of Crimes said to have been committed in the Town of

Griswold, in the County of New London, when he was not within about One Hundred Miles of the place. Second Ed. *8vo, bds.; curious.* *Schenectady*, 1826

1805 Rogers. Memoranda of the experience, labors, and travels of a Universalist preacher. Replete with anecdotes of Western life and manners; also Historical and Biog. Sketches, etc. Written by *himself*. 12*mo, sh.* *Cincinnati, O.*, 1845

1806 Rogers, Rev. E. P. Historical Discourse on the Reformed Prot. Dutch Church of Albany. 8*vo, cl., plates.* *New York*, 1858

1807 Rolph, Thomas. A brief account, together with observations made during a visit in the West Indies, and a Tour through the United States of America, in parts of the years 1832–3, together with a Statistical account of Upper Canada. 8*vo, hf. dk. blue cr. lev. mor., gilt top, rough edges; bound by R. W. Smith.* *Dundas. U. C.*, 1836

1808 Romance of Matrimony. A Tale, founded on fact. 8*vo, cl., eng.* *Phila.*, 1865

1809 ROWLANDSON, Mrs. MARY. Narrative of the Captivity and Removes of Mrs. Mary Rowlandson, who was taken by the Indians at the Destruction of Lancaster, in 1676. 12*mo, bds.; scarce.* *Lancaster*, 1828

1810 ROWLEY, (Mass.), History of, anciently including Bradford, Boxford and Georgetown. From the year 1630 to the Present Time. By Thos. Gage. With an Address, deliv. Sept. 5, 1839, at the Bi-Centen. Anniv. of its settlement. By James Bradford. 8*vo, cl. Frontis. Very scarce; fine copy.* *Boston*, 1840

1811 ROXBURY, (Mass.), Sketch of the History of the Grammar School in the Easterly part of. By R. G. Parker. 8*vo, uncut, pamph.; rare.* *Boston*, 1826

1812 ROXBURIE, (Mass.), History of the Grammar School, or "The Free Schools of 1645," in. With Biographical Sketches of the Ministers of the First Church, and others. By C. K. Dillaway. 8*vo, cl.* *Boston*, 1860

1813 ROXBURY, (Mass.) An Address delivered on the 8th of October, 1830. The Second Centennial Anniv. of the Settlement of Roxbury. By H. A. S. Dearborn. Also, Change: a Poem, pronounced at Roxbury, Oct. 8, 1830, in commem. of the First Settlement of the Town. By Thomas Gray, Jr. 8*vo, paper cov.*, 40 *p. and* 25 *p., fine copy; very scarce.* *Roxbury*, 1830

1814 ROXBURY. The History of Roxbury Town. By Chas. M. Ellis. 8*vo pamph.*, 146 *p., fine copy; scarce.* *Boston*, 1847

1815 RUTLAND, (Mass.), History of, from its Earliest Settlement, with a Biography of its First Settlers. By Jonas Reed. *Extremely scarce.* 12*mo, cl. Plan.* *Worcester*, 1836

This little work contains Biog. Sketches of Persons, Incidents and Facts connected with the Revolutionary War, many of which are verbatim from the original authors. We believe there is no town of this name in the State at present.

REBELLION & SLAVERY PAMPHLETS.

1816 Rebellion and Slavery Pamphlets. [*Sixteen.*]

American Tract Soc. The Suppressed Tract and the Rejected Tract. *N. Y.*, 1858

Adams, Charles F. What makes Slavery a Question of National Concern? Lecture. *Boston*, 1855

Adams, F. Colburn. The Story of a Trooper. *N. Y.*, 1864

Adams, Henry W. Oration. The Past, Present and Future of America. *N. Y.*, 1865

Adams, John Q. Corresp. concerning the Charge of a Design to Dissolve the Union. *Washington*, 1829

—— Speech of, upon the Right of the People, Men and Women, to Petition, &c. *Wash.*, 1838

—— Speech on War with Grt. Britain and Mexico.

Bowdoin, Col., (Me.), in the War. Roll of Honor, May, 1867.

Boston. Oration, by Timothy Bigelow. *Boston*, 1853

—— Oration, by George Sumner, July 4, 1859.

—— Oration, by George Sumner. 3rd Ed. July 4, 1859.

—— Oration, by George T. Curtis, July 4, 1862.

—— Oration, by Oliver W. Holmes, July 4, 1863.

—— Oration, by J. M. Manning, July 4, 1865.

—— Oration, by S. K. Lothrop, July 4, 1866.

—— Oration, by Ellis W. Morton, July 4, 1869.

1817 Rebellion and Slavery Pamphlets. [*Ten.*]

Act to Provide a National Currency, secured by a Pledge of U. S. Bonds. *Wash.*, 1863

Act to Provide a National Currency, secured by a Pledge of U. S. Bonds. *Wash.*, 1864

Act to Provide for the more efficient Govt. of the Rebel States. *Wash.*, 1867

Agnew, J. H. Citizenship Sovereignty, by J. S. Wright, assist. by. *Chicago*, 1863

Army of the Cumberland. Defence of the. *Phila.*, 1864

Argument on the Consti. and Construc. of the "Riot Act" of 1855. *N. Y.*, 1864

Anti-Slavery Hist. of the John Brown Year. *N. Y.*, 1861

Address to People of the U. S., with the Proc. and Resolutions of the Pro-Slavery Conven. at Lexington, 1855. *St. Louis*, 1855

Anamnesis. The Civil War in America: its Causes and Objects.

Assoc. Brewers' Soc. Memorial to Hugh McCullough. *N. Y.*, 1867

1818 Anti-Slavery Society Pamphlets. [*Twenty-five.*]

New Eng. Anti-Slavery Soc. Const. of. *Boston*, 1832

New Eng. Anti.Slavery Soc. First Rep., Jan. 9, 1833.

New Eng. Anti-Slavery Soc. Second Rep. 1834.

New Eng. Anti-Slavery Con. Proc. of, May, 1836.
Boston Female Anti-Slavery Soc. Rep. of. 1835.
Boston Female Anti-Slavery Soc. Annual Rep. of. 1836.
Boston Female Anti-Slavery Soc. Annual Rep. of. 1837.
Evangel. Un. Anti-Slav. Soc. Address of, April, 1839.
Penn. Anti-Slav. Soc. Address by W. H. Furness, Dec. 19, 1849.
Aberdeen Anti-Slav. Soc. First Rep. of. 1825.
Church Anti-Slav. Soc. Proc. of Convention. *Worcester*, 1859
N. Y. City Anti-Slav. Soc. Address of. *N. Y.*, 1833
N. Y. Anti-Slav. Soc. Oration by D. P. Brown, July 4, 1834.
N. Y. Anti-Slav. Soc. Address by J. Parker, May 12, 1854.
Norwich Anti-Slav. Soc. Sermon by J. T. Dickinson, July 4, 1834.
Norwich Anti-Slav. Soc. Sermon by J. T. Dickinson, July 4, 1834. *Rochester Ed.*
Amer. and For. Anti-Slav. Soc. 9th Annual Rep. of. *N. Y.*, 1849
——— 10th Annual Rep. of. *N. Y.*, 1850
——— Debate at Lane Sem., Cinn. *Boston*, 1834
——— Review of 1st Annual Rep., by Dr. Reese. *N. Y.*, 1834
——— Declar. of Sentiments and Const. *Phila.*, 1861
African Abol. Freehold Soc. of Boston. Address by Wm Lloyd Garrison, July 16, 1832.
Conn. Soc. for Promotion of Freedom. Disc. by Jas. Dana on the African Slave Trade. *Scarce.* *New Haven*, 1791
——— Sermon by Jno. Edwards on the Injustice and Impolicy of Slave Trade. *Prov.*, 1792
N. Y. Soc. for Manumis. of Slaves. Disc. by Samuel Miller, Apr. 12, 1797. *N. Y.*

1819 Rebellion and Slavery Pamphlets. [*Twenty-two.*]
Agnew, Daniel. Our National Constitution: its Adaptation to a State of War or Insurrection. *Phila.*, 1863
Address on Slavery and against Immediate Emancipation. *N. Y.*, 1834
——— of Congre. Union in Scotland on subject of American Slavery. *N. Y.*, 1840
——— to Non-Slaveholders of the South on the Social and Political Evils of Slavery. *N. Y.* 1843
——— of Com. appointed for purpose of considering the recent case of Kidnapping from our Soil, &c. *Boston*, 1846
——— to Christians throughout the World. *Phila.*, 1863
Africa. A Poem, by Ann Evans. *Andover*, 1826
African Servitude. When, Why and by Whom Instituted. *N. Y.*, 1860

Andrew, John A. Addresses by Hon. Edward Everett, B. F. Thomas and Robert C. Winthrop. *Boston*, 1862
——— Corresp. between, and Maj.-Gen. Butler. *Boston*, 1862
——— Address. Dedica. of Monument to Ladd and Whitney. *Boston*, 1865
——— Eulogy on, by Edwin P. Whipple. *Boston*, 1867
"Alabama." Correspond. respecting the; also, the Bark "Maury." 1862
——— The "Loil" Legislature of. *Montgomery*, 1868
Albany. Proc. of the Democratic State Convention in. *Albany*, 1861
——— Discourse Commem. of Heroes, by Rufus W. Clark. *Albany*, 1864
Americanus, Junius. Review of Disc. on Death of Daniel Webster. *Boston*, 1853
American Soc. for promoting National Unity. *N. Y.*, 1861
American Soldier. A Pocket Manual for Recruits and Vol. *N. Y.*, 1861
Americus. Thoughts for the Times. *London*, 1862
American Tract Soc. Unanimous Remonstrance of Fourth Congre. Ch., Hartford, against the Policy of the. *Hartford*, 1855
——— Letter reviewing the report of Com. on the relation of the, to the Subject of Slavery. *Boston.*

1820 Rebellion and Slavery Pamphlets. [*Twenty.*]

Appeal to the Ministers and Members of the Meth. Epis. Ch. against the Schism of Anti-Abolition. *N. Y.*, 1838
Appeal to the Women of the Nominally Free States, by an Anti-Slavery Convention of American Women. *Boston*, 1838
Allen, Mr. Report of a Declaration of Sentiments on Slavery. *Worcester*, 1838
American Slavery as it is. Testimony of a Thousand Witnesses. *N. Y.*, 1839
Apology for Abolitionists, addressed by the Anti-Slavery Soc. of Meriden, Conn., to their Fellow-Citizens. 2nd Ed. *Middletown*, 1837
Adirondack. The National Finances and the Public Faith.
Atlee, Edwin P. Address on subject of Slavery. *Phila.*, 1833
Administration. The Conduct of the. *Boston*, 1832
Anti-Slavery Memorials. Report of Com. on. *Boston*, 1845
Appleton, Nathan. Corresp. between, and John G. Palfrey. *Boston*, 1846
Allen, Rev. Geo. Report on American Slavery. *Boston*, 1847
Alger, W. R. The Genius and Posture of America. Oration. *Boston*, 1857
Austro-Borealis. Platform for all Parties. *Baltimore*, 1860
Archer, Richard T. Speech in Answer to a Challenge from Messrs. B. G. Humphreys, Sr., and others. *Port Gibson*, 1860
Aikman, Wm. The Future of the Colored Race in America. *N. Y.*, 1862

Ashley, Hon. J. M. Speech on the Consti. Amendment for the Abolition of Slavery. *N. Y.*, 1865

Ariel. The Negro: what is his Ethnological Status? *Cincinnati*, 1867

Atkinson Edward. On the Collection of Revenue. *Boston*, 1867

Adamic Race. Reply to "Ariel." Drs. Young and Blackie on the Negro, by M. S. *N. Y.*, 1868

Agnew, J. H. Reply to Prof. Tayler Lewis' Review of Rev. Henry J. Van Dykes' Sermon on Biblical Slavery. *N. Y.*, 1861

1821 Rebellion and Slavery Pamphlets. [*Eleven.*]

Becker, A. R. Prize Essay on Gun-shot Wounds. *Boston*, 1865

Birdseye, George W. Women and the War. Poem. *N. Y.*, 1865

Bingham, John A. Argument of. *Washington*, 1865

Barrett, Joseph O. Hist. of "Old Abe," the Live War Eagle. *Scarce.* *Chicago*, 1865

Burnett, Judge Advocate H. L. Reply of, in Case of U. S. *vs.* Charles Walsh and others, charged with conspiring to release the Rebel Prisoners at Camp Douglas, Chicago, and to lay waste and destroy the City. *Cincin.*, 1865

Broom, W. W. Great and Grave Questions for American Politicians, with a Topic for America's Statesmen. *N. Y.*, 1865

Banks, Maj. Gen. Letter to Sen. Lane. *N. Y.*, 1865

Boynton, Rev. C. B. Thanksgiving Sermon. *Alexandria, Va.*, 1866

Bow, J. D. B. De. Address to People of Tenn.

Barton, Samuel. Letter to Com. of Ways and Means. *N. Y.*, 1867

Butts, Isaac. Brief Reasons for Repudiation, applicable to the War Debts of all Countries. *Rochester*, 1869

1822 Rebellion and Slavery Pamphlets. [*Fifteen.*]

Bishop, Levi. Mission on the Democracy. Address before Democratic Lit. Assoc., Cin., Feb. 4, 1864.

Bishop, Albert W. Oration deliv. at Fayetteville, Arkansas, July 4, 1865.

Bellows, Henry. Sermon. April 21, 1869. *N. Y.*

——— Disc. 2nd Unitarian Soc. Phila., Feb. 17, 1861.

——— Unconditional Loyalty. *N. Y.*, 1863

——— The War to End only when the Rebellion Ceases. April 30, 1863. *N. Y.*

Beecher, Charles. Sermon on the Fugitive Slave Law. *Newark*, 1851

Beecher, Henry Ward. War and Emancipation, a Thanksgiving Sermon. Brooklyn, N. Y., Nov. 21, 1861.

——— England and America. Speech. *Boston*, Oct., 1863

Burleigh, Wm. H. The Republican Pistol. No I. *New York*, 1860

Burleigh, Wm. H. The Republican Pistol. No. II. *New York*, 1860

Barnard, J. G. The Dangers and Defences of N. Y. 1859
——— The Peninsular Campaign and its Antecedents. *Washington*, 1864
Bassett, Wm. Letter to a Member of the Society of Friends against joining Anti-Slavery Soc. *Boston*, 1837
Bassett, J. M. Union Men and their Sufferings in N. W. Missouri. *N. Y.*, 1864

1823 Rebellion and Slavery Pamphlets. [*Thirteen.*]

Bacon, Benj. C. Statistics of the Colored People of Phila. 2d Ed. 1859
Bacon, Leonard. A Plea for Africa. New Haven, July 4, 1825.
——— Discourse deliv. in New Haven, Dec. 30, 1860.
Brooks, Preston S. Speech. *Boston*, 1856
Brooks, James. Defence of President Fillmore. *N. Y.*, May 30, 1856
——— Speech of, on the President's Message in the House of Representatives. Dec., 1864.
Brooks, Philips. Our Mercies of Re-occupation. Thanksgiving Sermon. Phila., Nov. 26, 1863.
Butler, Geo. B. The Currency Question. *N. Y.*, 1864
Butler, B. F. Character and Results of War. Speech. *Phila.*, 1863
——— A Review of Judge Pierrepont on Gen. Butler's defense in relation to the N. O. Gold. *N. Y.*, 1865
——— A Chaplain's Campg. with Gen. Butler. *N. Y.*, 1865
——— Speech upon the Campaign before Richmond. 1864. *Boston*, 1865
Bishop, John Prentiss. Thoughts For the Times. *Boston*, 1863

1824 Rebellion and Slavery Pamphlets. [*Eleven.*]

Brown, John. Address on a plan for the Instruction and Emancipation of Slaves. *Newburyport*, 1836
Brown, James. American Slavery in its Moral and Political Aspects. *Oswego*, 1840
Brown, A. G. Speech of, on the Slavery Question. *Washington*, 1856
Brown, S. D. Sermon on National Thanksgiving. *N. Y.*, Dec. 7, 1865
Brown, Solyman. Union and Extremes. Disc. on Liberty and Slavery. *N. Y.*
Blair, Montgomery. Speech of. Rockville, Maryland, Oct. 3, 1863.
——— Comments on the Policy inaugurated by the President. *N. Y.*, 1863
——— "The Munroe Doctrine." Speech delivered at Hagerstown, Md., July 12, 1865.
Bemis, George. Precedents of American Neutrality, in reply to the Speech of Roundell Palmer. Boston, May 13, 1864.

Bemis, G. American Neutrality, its Honorable Past, its Expedient Future. *Boston*, 1866

—— Hasty Recognition of Rebel Belligerency, and our right to complain of it. *Boston*, 1865

1825 Rebellion and Slavery Pamphlets. [*Thirteen.*]

Bell, John (Tenn.) Speech of, on Slavery in the U. S. *Washington*, 1850

Bell, Marcus A. Southside view of "Cotton is King," and the Philosophy of African Slavery. *Atlanta*, 1860

Book of the Prophet Stephen, Son of Douglass. Book Second. *N. Y.*, 1864

Book of the Prophet Stephen, Son of Douglass. Book First. *N. Y.*, 1864

Benjamin, St. The new Gospel of Peace according to. *N. Y.*, 1863

—— The new Gospel of Peace according to. Book Second. *N. Y.*, 1863

—— The new Gospel of Peace according to. Book Third. *N. Y.*, 1863

—— Revelations; a companion to the "New Gospel of Peace," according to Abraham. *N. Y.*, 1863

Bouse, Sir Lyon. Adventures of. By St. Benjamin. *N. Y.*, 1867

Bushnell, Horace. Disc. on the Slavery Question. 2d Ed. *Hartford*, Jan., 1839

—— Disc. on the Slavery Question. 1st Ed. *Hartford*, Jan., 1839

Birney, James G. Correspondence between, and several persons of the Soc. of Friends. *Scarce.* *Haverhill*, 1835

—— Sketches of the Life and Writings of. By Beriah Green. *Utica*, 1844

1826 Rebellion and Slavery Pamphlets. [*Nineteen.*]

British Slaves. The Rights of.

Boreas. Slave Representation. 1812

Burden, Dr. J. R. Remarks on the Abolition Question. *Phila.*, 1838

Bourne, Rev. George. Man-Stealing and Slavery denounced by the Presbyterian and Meth. Churches. *Boston*, 1834

Barber, J. W. History of the Amistad Captives. *Scarce.* *New Haven*, 1840

Bachman, John. Doctrine of the Unity of the Human Race. Examination on Principles of Science. *Charleston*, 1850

Brewster, Francis E. Slavery and the Constitution. Both Sides of the Question. *Phila.*, 1850

Black, Leonard. Life of—Pastor of the Bap. Ch., Brooklyn, Formerly a Slave. *Brooklyn*, 1851

Baird, Robert. Progress and Prospects of Christianity in the U. S. *London*, 1851

Boutwell, Geo. S. Address to People of Berlin on the Provisions of the New Constitution. *Boston*, 1853

Byrne, Oliver. Lectures on Art and Science of War. *Boston*, 1853

Barstow, Benj. Speech of, on the Abolition Propensities of Caleb Cushing. *Boston*, 1853

Burns, Anthony. Boston Slave Riot, Trial of. *Scarce.* *Boston*, 1854

Balkam, Rev. U. Sermon. The Harper's Ferry Outbreak and its Lesson. *Lewiston*, 1859

Buchanan, James. His Doctrines and Policy.

Boyden, E. The Epidemic of the Nineteenth Century. *Richmond*, 1860

Barnett, T. J. Speech—Our Union Ticket. *Wash.*, 1860

Breckinridge, Robt. J. The Civil War. Its Nature and End. *Cincinnati*, 1861

Betts, Samuel R. The Blockade. Opinion of, in the Cases of Hiawatha and other Vessels captured as Prize. *N. Y.*, 1861

1827 Rebellion and Slavery Pamphlets. [*Twenty-three.*]

Boston. Consecration of the Flag of the Union, by the Old South Soc. in. *Boston*, 1861

Baugher, H. L. The Christian Patriot. Discourse. *Gettysburg*, 1861

Baker, Edward D. Addresses on the Death of. *Washington*, 1862

Berry, J. R. Christian Patriotism. Sermon. *Albany*, 1861

Booth, Rev. Robert R. The Nation's Crisis and the Christian's Duty. Sermon. *N. Y.*, 1861

Beadle's Dime Union Song Book. *N. Y.*, 1861

Bermuda and Cargo. Arguments and Documents. *Phila.*, 1862

Bradford, A. W. Inaug. Address. *Annapolis*, 1862

British Aristocratic Plot. Present Attempt to Dissolve the Union, by B. *N. Y.*, 1862

Bates, Attorney-General. Opinion on Citizenship. *Washington*, 1862

Bastiles of the North, by Reverdy Johnson. *Baltimore*, 1863

Burr, C. Chauncey. Hist. of the Union and of the Consti. *N. Y.*, 1863

Bokum, Hermann. Testimony of a Refugee from East Tenn. *Very scarce.* *Phila.*, 1863

Ball, Major L. C. Speech on the War. *Washington*, 1863

Barrows, Rev. Wm. The War and Slavery; and their Relations to each other. *Boston*, 1863

Bowditch, Henry J. Brief Plea for an Ambulance System for the Army of the U. S. *Boston*, 1863

Brainerd, Rev. Thomas. Patriotism Aiding Piety. Sermon. *Phila.*, 1863

Boot on the other Leg, or Loyalty above Party. *Phila.*, 1863

Bonnefoux, L. The Constitution. *N. Y.*, 1864

Boker, Geo. H. Washington and Jackson on Negro Soldiers; Gen. Banks on the Bravery of Negro Troops, &c. *Phila.*

Brownlow, Miss Martha. Heroine of Tenn. *Scarce.* *Phila.*, 1864
Benedict, E. C. The War. Speech of. *Albany*, 1864
Blodget, Lorin. Commercial and Financial Strength of U. S. *Phila.*, 1864

20 1828 Rebellion and Slavery Pamphlets. [*Nineteen.*]

Baldwin E. Observations on the Physical, Intellectual, and Moral Qual. of our Col. Population. *New Haven*, 1834
Buffum, Arnold. Lecture, showing the necessity for a Liberal Party. *Cincin.*, 1844
Bull Run. Ballad. The Modern Gilpin. *N. Y.*, 1866
Butler, Gen. Official Doc. relating to a Chaplain's Campaign, (not) with, etc. By J. I. Davenport. *Lowell*, 1865
Conn. Rept. of Adjt. Gen., Apl. 1, 1863.
——— 1st Heavy Artillery : Report of movements and operations, to March 1, 1865.
——— Message of Gov. Buckingham, 1865.
Celebration of July 4th, 1862, by Common Council of New York. Oration of Gen. Walbridge. 4*to*, 16 *pages*
The American Flag. By J. Rodman Drake. Illust. by Darley. Illuminated cover. 4*to*, 14 *pages*. *N. Y.*, 1861
Ballads of the War. By A. J. H. Duganne. Splendidly illus. 4*to*, 36 *p*. *N. Y.*, 1862
The Duty of the Hour. The Great Issue, or the Rebellion against Democracy. Being 9 Nos. of the "*Iron Platform.*" *N. Y.*, 1863–'64.

22½ 1829 Colonization Society Pamphlets. [*Eleven.*]

Gurley, Ralph R. Disc. deliv. in Washington, July 4, 1825.
Carey, M. Reflections on the causes that led to the formation of the Col. Soc. *Phila.*, 1832
Garrison, Wm. Lloyd. Thoughts on African Col. *Boston*, 1832
Carey, M. Letters on the Col. Soc. *Phila.*, May 29, 1832
——— Letters on the Col. Soc., *Phila.*, March 20, 1835
Speeches deliv. Anti-Col. Soc. meeting, *London*, July 13, 1833
Wright, Elizur. The Sin of Slavery and its Remedy. *N. Y.*, 1833
Birney, James G. Letter on Col., addressed to T. J. Mills. *Boston*, 1834
Hist. Notes on Slavery and Colonization. *Elizabethtown*, 1842
Amer. Col. Soc. Report of Naval Com. *Washington*, 1850
Remarks on Col. of Western Coast of Africa, and Suppression of Slave Trade. *N. Y.*, 1850

20 1830 Rebellion and Slavery Pamphlets. [*Ten.*]

Cheap Cotton, by Free Labor. By a Cotton Manufacturer. *Boston*, 1861
Celebration of the 74th Anniv. of the signing of the Constitution of the U. S. of America. *Phila.*, Sept. 17, 1861

Civis, G. W. Songs for the great Campaign of 1860. Words and Music. *N. Y.*, 1860

Calicot, Theophilus. Speech against the Personal Liberty Bill, March 14, 1860. *Albany*

Chestnut, James. Speech, April 9, 1860. *Washington*

Clarigny, C., Mons. The Election of Mr. Lincoln. *London*, 1860

Charlton, Dimmock. Narrative of, Enslaved while a prisoner of War, and retained forty-five years in Bondage. Nov. 27, 1858.

Canfield, Sherman B. Disc. deliv. on day of Nat. Thanksgiving, Nov. 30, 1854. *Syracuse*

Controversy between N. Y. Tribune and Gerrit Smith. *N. Y.*, 1855

Carolinian. Slavery in the Southern States. *Cambridge*, 1852

1831 Rebellion and Slavery. [*Ten.*]

Calhoun, John C. Speeches of, and Daniel Webster, on the Subject of Slavery. *N. Y.*, 1850

Colton, Calvin. The rights of Labor. *N. Y.*, 1847

Condensed Anti-Slavery, Bible Argument. By a Citizen of Virginia. *New York*, 1845

Clapp, Theodore. Slavery, a Sermon deliv. in N. O., April 15, 1838. *Scarce.* *New Orleans*, 1838

Cincinnatus. Freedom's Defence, or a Candid Exam. of Mr. Calhoun's Report on the Freedom of the Press. *Worcester*, 1836

Constitutionalist. Bigotry exposed, or a calm discussion of the Abolition Question. *N. Y.*, 1835

Considerations on Slavery in the Southern States. *Baltimore*, 1835

Clough, Simon. Candid Appeal to the Citizens of the U. S. on the subject of Emancipation. *New York*, 1834

Continuation of the Appendix to the Second Report of the Committee on African Instruction. *London*, 1824

Considerations on Abolition of Slavery and the Slave Trade. *Oxford*, 1789

1832 Rebellion and Slavery Pamphlets. [*Thirteen.*]

Colyer, Vincent. Brief Rep. of the Services Rendered by the Freed People to the United States Army in North Carolina, 1862.

Church, M. C. C. The American Republic. Address delivered in Parkersburg, July 4, 1867.

Constitution, Alleged Atheism of. *Newark*, 1867

Craven, T. T., Record of the Testimony in the Trial of. Nov. 1865.

Cheshire, Conn. Dedication of the Soldiers' Monument. *N. Y.*, 1866

Chanler, John W., Speech of. *Washington*, 1866

Clason, A. W. The American Conflict. *N. Y.*, 1866

Conkling, Roscoe. Congress and the President. Speech, September 13, 1866.
Centz, P. C. Davis and Lee. *N. Y.*, 1866
Chipman, N. P., Argument by, in the Trial of Edmund E. Paulding, June, 1866. *Washington.*
Cowdin, Elliot C. The Tax on Cotton. Remarks, December 20, 1866.
Coddington, David S. Address, New York, November 1, 1864.
Crosby Howard. Sermon, National Thanksgiving. New York, September 11, 1864.

22½ 1833 Rebellion and Slavery Pamphlets. [*Thirteen.*]

Couto D. Jose Ferrer De. The Question of Slavery Conclusively and Satisfactorily solved as regards humanity at large. *New York*, 1864
Chapman Treason Case. Charges to the Jury by Judge Field and Hoffman. *San Francisco*, 1863
Cairnes on the Slave Power. Third Edition. *N. Y.*, 1863
Cleaveland, John, Opinion of, on State Taxation on Loans to the United States, April 29, 1863.
Copperheads, Ye Book of. *Phila.*, 1863
Crisis, The. *N. Y.*, 1863
Congdon, Charles T. The Warning of War: A Poem. New York, July 30, 1862.
Congress, the Rightful Power of, to Confiscate and Emancipate. *Boston*, June, 1862
Cline, A. J. Secession Unmasked; or, An Appeal from the Madness of Disunion to the Sobriety of Constitution. *Washington*, 1861
Clingman, Thomas L. Speech. Washington, February 4, 1861
Crummell, Alexander. The Relations and Duties of Free Colored Men in America to Africa. *Hartford*, 1861
Carpenter, H. S. Relations of Religion to the War. *N. Y.*, 1861
Civil War—Its Causes, Its Consequences, Its Crimes, and Its Compromises. *N. Y.*, 1861

22½ 1834 Colonization Society Pamphlets. [*Twenty-five.*]

American Colonization Society, Sixth Annual Report of. *Washington*, 1823
——— Extracts from an Article in North American Review. *Princeton Press*, 1824
——— Sermon by Wm. T. Hamilton. *Newark*, 1825
——— Proc. of, together with Addresses by Captain Stockton and Others. *N. Y.*, 1829
——— Sermon by John Newland Maffitt. *Boston*, 1830
——— Thirteenth Annual Report of. *Washington*, 1830
——— Address. *Washington*, 1832
——— British Opinions of. *Boston*, 1833
——— Thirty-eighth Annual Report. *Washington*, January 16, 1855
——— Fortieth Annual Report. *Washington*, Jan. 20, 1857

Kentucky Colonization Society, Annual Report of. January 25, 1853.
Vermont Colonization Society. Discourse. By J. K. Converse. *Burlington*, 1832
——— Sermon. By Joseph Tracy. *Windsor*, 1833
New York Colonization Society. Address. John H. B. Latrobe. Baltimore May 13, 1852.
——— Twenty-third Annual Report. New York. May, 1855
——— Twenty-fifth Annual Report. New York, 1857.
Pennsylvania Colonization Society. Discourse. By J. R. Tyson. Phila., Oct. 24, 1834.
——— Address. By R. R. Gurley. Phila., Nov. 11, 1839
——— Address. By Wm Petett and J. O'Durbin. *Phila.*, 1852
——— Discourse. By Alex. T. McGill. *Phila.*, 1862
Massachusetts Colonization Society. Oration. By Caleb Cushing. Boston July 4, 1833,
——— Fifth Annual Report. Boston, May 27, 1846.
Hampden Colonization Society. Address. By Wm. B. O. Peabody. *Springfield*, 1828
Harper, General, Letter from, to Elias B. Caldwell. *Baltimore*, 1818
Bacon, E., Abstract of a Journal of, and also one of J. B. Cates. *Phila.*, 1821

1835 Rebellion and Slavery Pamphlets. [*Twenty-seven.*]
Campbell, J. Unionists vs. Traitors, &c. *Phila.*, 1861
——— M. Is the Cotton Tax Constitutional? *N. Y.*, 1866
Cossham, H. The American War, &c. *N. Y.*, 1865
——— Friends of America in England. *Washington*, 1865
Cox, S. S, Puritanism in Politics. January 13, 1863. Speech.
——— The Nation's Hope in the Democracy. Speech, May 4, 1864.
——— Speeches of, during the Campaign of 1868.
Cummings, G. D. Sermon, Thanks., November 29, 1860. *Baltimore*
——— Sermon, Fast—The African a Trust From God, &c. January 4, 1861. *Balto.*
Colfax, R. H. Evidence against the Vices of the Abolitionists. &c. *N. Y.*, 1833
——— Schuyler. The Laws of Kansas. June 21, 1856.
Carey, M, Addresses to the Southern States against the Destructive Doctrine of Separation of the Union, &c. *Phila.*, 1835
Carrey, E. Grandeur, &c., of the United States. *Paris*, 1863
Carey, H. C. Two Letters to a Cotton Planter of Tennessee. *N. Y.*, 1852
——— On the Slave Trade. 1854
——— The French and American Tariffs Compared. *Phila.*, 1861
——— Financial Crisis, *Phila.*, 1864
——— Reconstruction, &c. *Phila.*, 1867
——— Shall We Have Peace? *Phila.*, 1869

Clarke, Lewis and Milton, Narratives of the Sufferings of, among Slaveholders of Kentucky. *Scarce.* *Boston*, 1846
——— R.W. Review of Moses Stuart's Pamphlet on Slavery. *Boston*, 1850
——— G. J. The Enemies of the Const, &c. Speech. *Lockport*, 1863
——— Col. I. E. Oration at the River House, July 4, 1867
——— J. F. Discourse on the Rendition of Burns. 1854
——— —— Discourse on the Aspects of the War. 1863
——— F. G. Sermon on Thankfulness, &c. *N. Y.*, 1861
——— —— Sermon, on our National Position. *N. Y.*, 1862

1836 Rebellion and Slavery Pamphlets. [*Twenty-five.*]
Channing, W. E. Remarks on Slavery. *Boston*, 1835
——— do do *Charleston*, 1836
——— Rev. of do do *Boston*, 1836
——— Extracts from Remarks, &c. *Boston*, 1836
——— Strictures on Annexation of Texas. *Hoboken*, 1837
——— Letter to Henry Clay. *Boston*, 1837
——— Last Address, at Lenox, August 1, 1842. *Boston* Edition,
——— Address at Lenox, Aug. 1, 1842. *Lenox* Ed.
Clay, M. C. Review of Wickliffe's Speech on Negro Law. *Lexington*, 1840
——— Speech of, University of Albany. *N. Y.*, 1863
——— Henry, Letter of Gerrit Smith to. *N. Y.*, 1839
——— Minstrel. *Boston*, 1844
——— Henry, Life and Public Services of. By E. Sargent. 1848
——— —— Speech of. *N. Y.*, 1850
Clarkson, Thomas. Essay on the Slavery and Commerce of the Human Species, &c. *Very rare.* *Phila.*, 1786
——— Thoughts on the Improvement of the Slaves in the British Colonies. *N. Y.*, 1823
——— Letters to, by Gov. Hammond. *Charleston Edition.*
——— Eulogium by Alex. Crummell, and a Poem by Chas. L. Reason. *N. Y.*, 1847
Child, L. M. The Evils and Cure of Slavery. 1836
——— do do 2d Ed. 1839
——— Anti-Slavery Catechism. 2d Ed. 1839
——— The Right Way and the Safe Way. *N. Y.*, 1860
——— D. L. The Despotism of Freedom. *Boston*, 1834
——— —— Oration on the Universal Emancipation. Aug. 1, 1834.
——— Rights and Duties of the United States, &c. *Boston*, 1861

1837 Rebellion and Slavery Pamphlets. [*Nineteen.*]
Clarke, F. G. The Church and Civil Government. *New York*, 1865
Chase, S. P. Presentation of Testimonial by Colored People of Cincinnati. 1845
——— Speech against Repeal of Miss. Comp. Feb. 3, 1854

Chase, S. P. How to Organize a Nat'l. Bank. *Phila.*, 1863
——— Speech on "Going Home to Vote." *Wash.*, 1863
Cairnes, J. E. The Slave Power. *N. Y.*, 1862
——— On the Slave Power. *N. Y.*, 1863
Coles, Ab. The Unity of the Origin of Mankind. *Scarce.* *Phila.*, 1857
——— Critique on Gliddon's Ethnological Works. *Scarce.* 1857
Curtis, B. R. Executive Power. *Camb.*, 1862
——— Answer to Executive Power. By G. P. Lowrey. *Scarce.* 1863
Curtis, Gen'l. Sam'l Ryan. In Memoriam. *Very scarce.* *Keokuk, Ia.*, 1866
Cheever, Geo. B. "The Fire and Hammer of God's Word against the Sin of Slavery." *N. Y.*, 1858
——— The same. Abol. Soc. Ed. 1858.
——— Immediate Emancipation, the Salvation of the Country, &c. *N. Y.*, 1861
Cooper, Jacob. Loyalty Demanded by the Present Crisis. *Phila.*, 1864
Cooper, Peter. Letters on Protection to American Labor. *N. Y.*, 1866
Cook, J. P. Speech on the Kansas Bill. *Wash.*, 1854
Cooke, Jay. How our Nat. Debt can be paid. *Phila.*, 1865

1838 Rebellion and Slavery Pamphlets. [*Sixteen.*]
Davenport, Rufus. The Right Aim. *Boston*, 1829
Duncan, Rev. James. The Slaveholder's Prayer. *Indiana*
Denny, J. F. Essay on the Political Grade of the Free Colored People under the Constitution of U. S., and the Consti. of Penn. *Chambersburg*, 1836
Dewey, Orville. Disc. on Slav. and the Annex. of Texas. *N. Y.*, 1844
Drake, J. R. The American Flag. *N. Y.*, 1861
Doggett, Thomas. Sermon, Fast Day. *Haverhill*, 1861
Duffield, Geo. Secession : its Cause and Cure. *Detroit*, 1861
Daly, Chas. P. Letter to Hon. Ira Harris. *N. Y.*, 1862
Denslow, Van Buren. Fremont and McClellan, their Political and Military Careers reviewed. *Yonkers*, 1862
Diary of the Great Rebellion. *Wash.*, 1862
Delphine. Solon, or the Rebellion of '61. Domestic and Polit. Tragedy. *Chicago*, 1862
Duganne, A. J. H. Ballads of the War. *N. Y.*, 1862
Dresser, H. E. Battle Record of the American Rebellion. *N. Y.*, 1863
Delorme, E. N. Les Etats-Unis et L'Europe. *Paris*, 1863
Duryea, J. T. Sermon, National Thanksgiving. *N. Y.*, 1863
Davenport, J. Chapter in the Hist. of Abol. at Syracuse, Oct. 26, 1839. *Scarce.*

1839 Rebellion and Slavery Pamphlets. [*Sixteen.*]
Davies, H. E. Opinion of, on Legal Tender. *Albany*, 1863

Davis, H. W. Speech on the Expulsion of Mr. Long. *Washington*, 1864
Davis, Jeff. Speeches of. *Baltimore*, 1859
——— Reply of, to Speech of Sen. Douglas. *Wash.*, 1860
Dorr, J. A. Objections to Fugitive Slave Law, Answered in a Letter to Hon. W. Hunt. *N. Y.*, 1850
——— Address. Justice to the South! *N. Y.*, 1856
Dexter, H. M. Sermon. April 23, 1865. *Boston*, 1865
Dexter, T. C. A. Case of. Arguments before Pres. by B. F. Butler and C. A. Peabody. *N. Y.*, 1866
——— Case of. Report of Maj.-Gen. Holt. *N. Y.*, 1867
Dodge, W. E. Influence of the War on our National Prosperity. Lecture. *N. Y.*, 1865
——— Speech on Reconstruction. *Wash.*, 1867
Dix, Maj.-Gen. Communication from—relative to Arrest of Hawley D. Clapp. *Albany*, 1864
——— Address of—at Seventh Regiment Reception. *N. Y.*, 1866
Demarest, James. The Present Duty of American Christians. Sermon. *N. Y.*, 1861
——— Sermon. Thanksgiving. *Hackensack*, 1861
Doolittle, Jas. R. Letter to—on the Public Debt. *N. Y.*, 1866

20 1840 Rebellion and Slavery Pamphlets. [*Twenty-One.*]
Delmar, Alex. Great Paper Bubble, or the Coming Financial Explosion. *N. Y.*, 1864
Dye, John S. The Adder's Den, or Secrets of the Great Conspiracy. *N. Y.*, 1864
Dawson, H. B. "Current Fictions tested by Uncurrent Facts." *N. Y.*, 1864
Doolittle, T. S. Thanksgiving Disc. *Schenectady*, 1866
Dickinson, D. S. Testimonial of Respect of Bar of N. Y. to the Memory of. *N. Y.*, 1866
Davidson, John. Oration, "Our Sleeping Heroes." *Trenton*, 1866
Derby, E. H. Position and Prospects of the U. S. with respect to Finance, &c., of Mass. *Boston*, 1868
Dwight, T. W. Trial by Impeachment. 1867
Democracy and People of Arkansas.
Democratic Party, the Record of. 1860–1865.
Democracy. The Great Issue, or Rebellion against. *N. Y.*, 1863
Democrats. A Word of Warning to. *Phila.*, 1863
Democratic Platform. People's Resolutions, &c. *N. Y.*, 1865
Democratic Documents for the Campaign, and Facts for the People. *Frankfort, Ky.*, 1868
Douglas, Stephen A. To.
——— Speech of, on Nebraska and Kansas. *Wash.*, 1854
——— Observations on—Views of Popular Sovereignty. *Washington*, 1859
——— The Dividing Line between Federal and Local Authority. *N. Y.*, 1859

Douglas, S. A. The Dividing Line between Federal and Local Authority. *N. Y.*, 1860

——— Disc. on Life and Character of. By John Keynton. *N. Y.*, 1861

Davies, Rev. Wm. Extracts from the Journal of. *Scarce.* *Llanidloes*, 1835

1841 Rebellion and Slavery Pamphlets. [*Twelve.*]

Extracts from the Writings of Friends on the Subject of Slavery. *Phila.*, 1839

England, Bp. Letters of, to John Forsyth on the subject of Domestic Slavery. *Baltimore*, 1844

Evarts, Wm. M. Speeches of the Republican Campaign of 1856.

England and America. From Princeton Review of Jan., 1862.

English Neutrality. Is the Alabama a British Private? *N. Y.*, 1863

Elliott, E. B. On the Military Statistics of the U. S. 4*to.* *Berlin*, 1863

Elder, Wm. Debt and Resources of the U. S. *Phila.*, 1863

Edge, Frederick Milnes. President Lincoln's Successor. *London*, 1864

Edson, Tracy R. Opinions of Daniel Lord and others in relation to the Patent Green Tint. *N. Y.*, 1864

Ellis, George E. Disc. deliv. in Charlestown, Nov. 13, 1864.

Eve, Paul F. Whisky and Tobacco, their effects upon Soldiers and others. *Nashville, Tenn.*, 1866

Egleston, N. H. Disc., in Stockbridge, Mass. Thanksgiving. Nov. 21, 1861.

1842 Rebellion and Slavery Pamphlets. [*Twelve.*]

Evans, Thomas W. Ambulance and Sanitary Material. *Paris*, 1867

Everett, Edward. Oration, July 4, 1861, and an Address by Joseph Holt, July 13, 1861.

——— Oration, July, 4, 1861. *New York.*

——— Oration, deliv. at inauguration of the Union Club, Boston, April 9, 1863.

——— Oration deliv. on the Battle-field of Gettysburgh, Nov. 10, 1863. *N. Y.*

Edwards, John. Injustice and Impolicy of the Slave Trade, etc., in a Sermon, Sept. 15, 1791. *Boston.*

Edwards, John. Injustice and Impolicy of the Slave Trade, etc., in a Sermon, Sept. 15, 1834. *Newburyport.*

Ewer, F. C. Disc. on the Nat. Crisis, New York, May 12, 1861.

Ewer, F. C. Rector's Reply to request for a Polit. Sermon. *N. Y.*, 1864

Edgar, Cornelius H. Germs and Growth, in a Sermon, deliv. N. Y., Nov. 28, 1861.

Edgar, Cornelius H. The Curse of Canaan rightly interpreted in Kindred Topics. Three Lectures. *N. Y.*, 1862

Edgar, Cornelius H. Sermon, on Thanksgiving day, Nov. 24, 1864. *N. Y.*

1843 Rebellion and Slavery Pamphlets. [*Twelve.*]

Facts for the People. The Address adopted by the Democratic State Convention, held in Indianapolis, March 15, 1866.

Forward or Backward. *N. Y.*, 1863

Franklin, Wm. B. Reply to the Report of the Joint Committee of Congress, on the conduct of the War, given to the Public. *Scarce.* *N. Y.*, 1863

Franklin, Wm. B. Reply of, to the Joint Committee of Congress on the conduct of the War, on the first battle of Fredericksburg. 2nd ed. *Scarce.* *N. Y.*, 1867

Fish, Henry Clay. The Valley of Achor, a Door of Hope, or the grand issues of the War. Disc., N. Y., Nov. 26, 1863.

Fish, Wm. S. Defence of, Submitted by his Counsel, Milton Whitney, Esq., Washington, April 11, 1864.

Fremont, John C. Life of. *N. Y.*, 1856

Fremont, John C., and the injustice done him by Politicians and envious military men. By W. Brotherhead. *Phila.*, 1862

Fremont, Jesse Benton. The Story of the Guard, a chronicle of the War. *Boston*, 1863

Foote, C. C. Amer. Women Responsible for the existence of Amer. Slavery. 3rd ed. *Rochester*, 1846

Foot, John. Memorial of, late Captain of Second Regiment of Minnesota Volunteers. *Port. Scarce.* *N. Y.*, 1862

Freedman's Savings and Trust Company. *New York*, 1865

1844 Rebellion and Slavery Pamphlets. [*Eleven.*]

Fitch, Charles. Slaveholding weighed in the balance of Truth and its Guilt illustrated. *Boston*, 1837

Farmer, Southern. Bondage a moral institution, sanctioned by the Old and New Testament. *Macon*, 1837

Fitzgerald, W. P. N. A Scriptural view of Slavery and Abolition. *New Haven*, 1839

Featherstonhaugh, G. W. Excursion through the Slave States. *N. Y.*, 1844

Free Soil Songs for the People. *Boston*, 1848

Fessenden, W. P. (Me.) Speech against the Repeal of the Missouri Prohibition North of 36° 30'. Washington, March 3, 1854.

Fillmore, Millard. Executive Acts of, with reasons for his election and Memoir of his Life and Administration. Port. *N. Y.*, 1856

Frothingham, O. B. Sermon, Jersey City, June 1, 1856. *New York.*

Free Negro Question in Maryland. *Baltimore*, 1859

For Whom will you Vote? For Whom ought you to Vote?

Faulkener's Hist. of the Revolution in the Southern States. *N. Y.*, 1861

1845 Rebellion and Slavery Pamphlets. [*Eleven.*]

Field, Richard S. "The Constitution not a Compact between Sovereign States," an Oration, deliv. in Princeton, N. J., July 4, 1861.

Free Negroism; or, results of Emancipation in the North and West India Islands. *N. Y.*, 1862

Fabeus, Joseph W. Facts about Santo Domingo applicable to the present Crisis, an Address, deliv. N. Y. City, April 3, 1862.

Fullerton, Alex. Coercion a Failure, necessarily and actually. *Phila.*, 1863

FISHER, J. FRANCIS. The Degradation of our Representative System, and its Reform. *Phila.*, 1863

Free Military School for Applicants and Commands of Colored Troops, by John H. Taggart. *Phila.*, 1863

Facts concerning the Freedmen. *Boston*, 1863

France Le Mexique et les Etats Confederes. *Paris*, 1863

Free-Trade Doctrine, Fallacy of. *Brooklyn*, 1864

Financial Situation. To Abraham Lincoln, etc. *N. Y.*, 1865

Farragut Testimonial. *New York*, 1865

1846 Rebellion and Slavery Pamphlet. [*Eighteen.*]

Amer. Assoc. Its Const. *Washington*, 1866

Penn Relief Assoc. for East Tenn. Rep. to the Contrib. *Phila.*, 1864

Univ. Franchise Assoc., Speech of J. K. H. Wilcox, July 19, 1867. *Wash.*

Freedmen's Bureau. Report of, Board of Educa., for 1864. *N. O.*

Freedman's Bureau. 3rd Semi-Annual Report on Schools for Freed., Jan. 1, 1867.

Freedman's Bureau. 4th Semi Annual Report on Schools for Freed., July 1, 1867.

Amer. Freedman's Union Com. The Amer. Freedmen, Vol. II, No 8 *N. Y.*, 1867

American Freedman's Union Com. Speeches, etc. *N. Y.*, 1865

Freedmen's Com. Convention at Annapolis, July, 1864.

Amer. Freedmen's Inquiry Com. Report, June 30, 1863.

Freedmen of Louisiana, Final Report of, by T. W. Conway. *N. O.*, 1865

Freedmen's Bureau. Prest. Johnson's Veto Message, 1866.

Assoc. for Colored Orphans, 10th and 18th Reports. *N. Y.*, 1846 and 1854

Report of Gen'l. Sup't. of Freedmen's Dept. of Tenn. and Ark., for 1864. *Memphis, Tenn.*, 1865

First Annual Report of Eductl. Com. for Freedmen, May 1863.

Address of Drs. Hague and Kirk, Eductl. Com. for Freedmen, May 28, 1863.

Catalogue of Eagle's Wood Mil. Acad., for 1864–5. *N. J.*

Third Annual Report of the Balto. Asso. for the Education of Colored people.

20 1847 Rebellion and Slavery Pamphlets. [*Twenty-Six.*]

Grant, U. S. Report of 1864–'65. *With his Autograph.*
—— The same. *Port.* *N. Y.*, 1865.
—— Nomination of. Mass Meeting, Cooper Institute. *N. Y.*, 1867
—— Life and Campaigns of. By James G. Wilson.
—— Campaign Text-Book. *N. Y.*, 1868
—— Lively Life of. Etc. *N. Y.*, 1868
—— Pierrepont's Speech, on the Elect. of. Oct. 21, 1868
Grant, and Colfax. German Camp. Doc.
—— Buckingham. Camp. Doc. *Norwich*, 1868
Grant U. S. His services, etc. Address, by H. C. Van Vorst. Oct., 1868. *N. Y.*
—— And the Jews, by Ph. Von Bort. *N. Y.*
Gallatin, A. The Oregon Question. *N. Y.*, 1846
—— James. Gov't Finances and the Currency. *N. Y.*, 1862
—— National Finances and the Currency. *N. Y.*, 1862
—— Proposed U. S. Banking System. *N. Y.*, 1863
—— Geo. B. McClellan, as a Patriot Warrior, etc.
—— The National Debt, Taxation, etc. *N. Y.*, 1864
—— The Financial Economy of the U. S. *N. Y.*, 1868
Greeley H. Decently Dissected, by A. Oakey Hall. *N. Y.*, 1862
—— History of the Struggle for Slavery Extension, etc. *N. Y.*, 1856
Green, Thomas J. Reply of, to Sam. Houston, Aug. 1, 1854.
—— J. D. Narrative of the Life of, a Runaway Slave. *Scarce.* 1864
—— Lieut. Gov. of R. I, on the Const. Amendment. *Prov.*, 1867
Garrison, Wm. Lloyd. Sketch of the Character etc., of. *N. Y.*, 1833
—— Trial of, for an alleged Libel on Francis Todd of Newburyport. *Very scarce.* *Boston*, 1834
Goodell, C. L. Sermon, New Britain, Conn., Thanksgiving, Nov. 26, 1863.

20 1848 Rebellion and Slavery Pamphlets. [*Twenty-Seven.*]

Griffin, E. D. A Plea for Africa. Sermon, New York, Oct. 26, 1817.
Graham, Wm. Bible and Abolitionism. *Cincinnati*, 1844
Goodell, Wm. Views of Amer. Const. Law. *Utica*, 1845
Goodloe, D. R. "Negro Slavery No Evil," etc. *Boston*, 1855
Ganse, H. D. "Bible Slaveholding not Sinful." *N. Y.*, 1856
Gaff, Wm. The American Union, Containing Orations, etc., on Rebellion.
Governing Race. A Book for the Time. *Washington*, 1860
"Geeup, Jehu." What is Slavery? 1861
Grattan, T. C. England and the Disrupted States of America.
Gordon, W. R. The Peril of our Ship of State. *N. Y.*, 1861

Guion, T. T. Sermon on National Fast Day, Jan. 4, 1861. *N. Y.*
Green, Buck. To his Country Friends. N. Y., 1862
Gardner, Daniel. On the Law of the American Rebellion. N. Y., 1862
Goldsmith, M. Report on Hospital Gangrene, etc. *Louisville*, 1863
Gierlow, J. A discourse on the Times, Aug. 6, 1863. *Augusta, Me.*
"Gray, Iron." The Gospel of Slavery, etc. N. Y.
"Gettysburg." Our Campaign, around, etc., a Memoir of the 23d N. Y. Reg't, 1864.
Garfield, J. A. Free Commerce, Speech on, March 24, 1864.
Grenard, Leo. Shots from the Monitor, etc. N. Y., 1864
Gillette, Charles. Histor. Records of the Church during the Rebellion in Texas. N. Y., 1865
Gorman, J. C. Lee's Last Campaign, with an accurate History of Stonewall Jackson's Last Wound. *Very scarce. Raleigh, N. C.*, 1866
Geary, J. W. Sketch of the Life and Mil. Services of. 1866
Gold. Highest and Lowest Prices of, for four years. N. Y.
Gayerre, Charles. Lecture on Oaths and Amnesties. *New Orleans*, 1866
Gholson, W. Y. On the Payment of Public Debt. *Cincinnati*, 1868
Grant, U. S. The Life of, New York, 1864, by Stansfield.
——— The same, New York, 1865, by Beadle.

1849 Rebellion and Slavery Pamphlets. [*Thirteen.*]

Henry, C. S. Patriotism and the Slaveholders' Rebellion, Oration. *N. Y.*, 1861
Heyrick, E. Immediate not Gradual Abolition. *Phila.*, 1837
——— Immediate not Gradual Abolition, or an inquiry into the getting rid of West India Slavery. *Boston*, 1838
Howard, F. K. Fourteen Months in Amer. Bastiles. *Baltimore*, 1863
——— Percy. The Barbarities of the Rebels. *Prov.*, 1863 20
Hitchcock, Boswell D. Sermon. Our Nat. Sin. *N. Y.*, 1861
——— Chronological Record of the Amer. Civil War. *New York*, 1866
Johnson, Reverdy. Speech of, in Support of the Resolution to Amend the Constitution so far as to Abolish Slavery. *Washington*, 1864
——— Andrew. Life and Speeches of. By G. W. Bacon. *London.*
——— Message to the Two Houses of Congress, at Commencement of First Session of Thirty-Ninth Congress. *Washington*, 1865
——— Moses; or, The Man who Supposes Himself to be Moses, no Moses at All. *N. Y.*, *1866*
——— Impeachment of, 40th Cong., House of Rep. Rep. Com. No. 7. *Washington*, 1867

Indianian. Is Slavery as it exists in the Southern States, Morally Wrong? *Brownstown, Ind.*, 1865

1850 Rebellion and Slavery Pamphlets. [*Ten.*]

Hancock, John. Letter to Samuel A. Eliot. *Boston*, 1851

——— Essays on the Elective Franchise; or, Who has a Right to Vote? *Phila.*, 1866

Hammond, Gov. Letters on Southern Slavery, addressed to Thomas Clarkson, S. C., Jan. 28, 1845.

——— Broderick and Wilson. Are Working men Slaves? The question discussed, March 4, 1858.

——— James M. Speech of, on the admission of Kansas under the Lecompton Constitution. *Wash.*, 1858

——— William A. Statement of the causes which led to the dismissal of, from the Army, Sept., 1864.

How, Dr. Answer to Slaveholding not Sinful. *New Brunswick*, 1856

——— Samuel B. The same. *N. Y.*, 1855

——— The same. 2d Ed. *New Brunswick*, 1856

Howe, S. G. Letter on the Sanitary condition of the Troops in the Neighborhood of Boston. *Washington*, 1861

1851 Rebellion and Slavery Pamphlets. [*Eleven.*]

Howe, M. A. De Wolfe. Loyalty in the Amer. Republic. Disc. on Nat. Thanksgiving. *Phila.*, 1863

Habeas Corpus. Opinion of Judge N. K. Hall on, in the case of Judson D. Benedict. *N. Y.*, 1862

——— The same. *Buffalo*, 1862

——— The same. *Buffalo*, 1863

Hall, W. W. Soldier-Health. 5th Ed. *N. Y.*, 1863

——— Nath'l. Sermon, deliv. Dorchester, Jan. 4, 1863. *Boston.*

Hunt, Washington. Speech of, at the Union Meeting in New York, Dec. 19, 1859.

——— E. B. Union Foundations. A study of Amer. Nat. *New York*, 1863

——— G. D. Sermon at Lexington, by Dr. Campbell, at the Interment of. *Cincinnati*, 1864

——— J. D. The Union Restored by Legal Authority. *New York*, 1865

Henry, C. S. Plain Reasons for the Great Republican Movement. *Geneva*, 1856

1852 Rebellion and Slavery Pamphlets. [*Ten.*]

Humanitas. New and interesting view of Slavery. *Baltimore*, 1820

Humphrey, Heman. Address deliv. at Amherst College, July 4, 1828.

Hints on a cheap mode of purchasing the Liberty of a Slave Population. *N. Y.*, 1838

Hamlet, James. The Fugitive Slave Law: its Hist. and Un-constitutionality, with an account of the seizure and enslavement of. *Scarce.* *N. Y.*, 1850

Hagadon, Wm. Comparison of American and British Slavery. *New York*, 1851

Higher Law, tried by Reason and Authority. *N. Y.*, 1851

Hughes Charles. Nebraska and Kansas. Speech. *Washington*, 1854

Higginson, Thos. W. Sermon, Worcester, June, 4, 1854. *Boston*

Hurd, John C. Topics of Jurisprudence connected with the conditions of Freedom and Bondage. *N. Y.*, 1856

Holly, Jas. T. Vindication of the capacity of the Negro Race for Self-Government and Civilized Progress, as demonstrated in the Haytian Revolution. *Port.* *New Haven*, 1857

1853 Rebellion and Slavery Pamphlets. [*Thirteen.*]

Hebberd, Wm. W. The right of Freedom. *Boston*, 1857

Hatch, I. T. Speech on subject of the Admission of Kansas as a State, March 30, 1858.

Hyatt, Thaddeus. Argument on behalf of, by John A. Andrew.

Hoit, T. W. Right of American Slavery. *St. Louis*, 1860

Haskell, T. N. Soldiers' Mission. *Boston*, 1861

Hartt, H. A. The British Mission of the Church of the Puritans. *N. Y.*, 1861

Hovey, Horace. Sermon, "The National Fast," deliv. at Coldwater, Mich., Jan. 4, 1861.

Holmes, John M'Lellan. Sermon. N. Y., Oct. 19, 1862.

Hare, J. I Clark. Opinions of, upon the Constitutionality of the Acts of Congress, Feb. 5, 1862.

Hurlbert, Wm. H. The Army of the Potomac: its Organization, its Commander and its Campaign. *N. Y.*, 1862

Halleck's, Gen. H. W., Report, Reviewed in the Light of Facts. *N. Y.*, 1862

Hawkins, Rush. C. Testimonial to Ninth Regiment N. Y. V., Hawkins' Zouaves. *N. Y.*, 1863

Halleck. Report of Gen.-in-Chief. *Washington*, 1863

1854 Rebellion and Slavery Pamphlets. [*Twelve.*]

Bible View of Slavery. *Burlington, Vt.*

Hamilton, Gail. Tracts for the Times. "Courage." Jan. 27, 1862.

Hamilton, A. J. Speech on the condition of the South under Rebel Rule, Oct. 3, 1862.

—— Speech, April 18, 1863. *Boston*

Hamilton, J. C. Coercion compiled; or, Treason triumphant. Remarks. N. Y., Sept., 1864.

Holt, Joseph. Address deliv. Louisville, July 13, 1861. *N. Y.*

—— Letter from, on the Policy of the General Government. *Washington*, 1861

—— Treason and its treatment. Remarks by, at Charleston, April 14, 1865.

—— Report of case of Thos. C. A. Dexter. *N. Y.*, 1867

Hamilton, A. J. Address on Suffrage and Reconstruction, Dec. 3, 1866. *Boston*
Hedge, F. H. Disc., Sept. 26, 1861. *Boston*
——— Sermon for the time. *Boston*, 1863

1855 Rebellion and Slavery Pamphlets. [*Twelve.*]

Hutchings, Robert C. Speech on the Gov. Annual Message, Albany, Feb. 26, 1863.
Harwood, Edwin. Sermon. New Haven, Oct. 25, 1863.
Haller, Granville O. Dismissal of, by order of the Secretary of War; also, a brief Memoir of his Military Services. Paterson, July 25, 1863.
Hubbell, Wm. Wheeler. The Way to secure Peace and Establish Unity as one Nation. *Phila.*, 1863
Hosford, E. N. The Army Ration. *New York*, 1864
Hist. of the N. W. Soldiers' Fair held in Chicago, 1864.
Haco, Dion. Perdita, the Demon Refugee's Daughter. *N. Y.*, 1865
Harris, Benj. G. Speech. Maryland, June 14, 1866.
Hist. of the Amer. Civil War, by Emma Willard. Troy, May, 1867.
House that Jeff Built.. *N. Y.*, 1868
Hist. of the War: its causes and results. 1868.
Hopkins, John H. Lecture deliv. before Young Men's Assoc. of Buffalo and Lockport. 1851.

1856 Rebellion and Slavery Pamphlets. [*Nine.*]

Inexorable Logic. Congressional Sovereignty *vs.* Democratic Faith. *St. Louis*, 1860
Jay, Wm. Letter to Com. chosen by Amer. Tract Soc. to inquire into the Proc. of its Exec. Com. in relation to Slavery. 1857
Joinville, Prince De. The Army of the Potomac: its Organization, &c. *N. Y.*, 1862
Johnstone, Wm. Address on the Aspect of National Affairs and the Right of Secession. *Cincinnati*, 1861
Johnson, W. C. Speech of, on the subj. of the Rejec. of Petitions for the Abol. of Slavery. *Wash.*, 1840
Judges. The Book of.
Journal of the Proc. of the National Repub. Conven. at Worcester. *Boston*, 1832
Johnson, Reverdy. The Dangerous Condition of the Country – the Causes which have led to it and the Duty of the People. *Baltimore*, 1867
James, Horace. "The Two Great Wars of America." Oration deliv. at Newbern before the 25th Regt., Mass. Vol., July 4, 1862.

1857 Rebellion and Slavery Pamphlets. [*Seventeen.*]

Jackson, Andrew. Lecture on Secession. Mrs. Cora L. Hatch. *N. Y.*, 1861
——— Proclamation and Farewell Address of. *Harrisburg*, 1864

Jackson, Francis. Testimonials to the Life and Character of. *Boston*, 1861

Jackson, William A., Memoir of, Member of the Albany Bar, and Col. of the 18th Regiment, N. Y. Vol. *Scarce.* *Albany: Munsell*, 1862

Jackson, Tatlow. Authorities Cited antagonistic to Horace Binney's Conclusions on Writ of Habeas Corpus. *Phila.*, 1862

Jay, John. Thoughts on the Duty of the Epis. Ch., in relation to Slavery. *N. Y.*, 1839

Jay, William. Reply to Remarks of Rev. Moses Stuart, on Hon. John Jay. *N. Y.*, 1850

Jay, John. America Free, or America Slave. Address on the State of the Country. *Bedford, Westchester Co., N. Y.*, 1856

——— Address, July 4, 1861. Mt. Kisco. *N. Y.*, 1861

——— ——— The Great Conspiracy and England's Neutrality. *N. Y.*, 1861

——— ——— to Citizens of Westchester Co., on the approaching State Election. *N. Y.*, 1862

——— ——— The Great Issue. Union Campaign Club. *N. Y.*, 1864

——— Second Letter on Dawson's Introduction to the Federalist. *N. Y.*, 1864

Jenkins, John J. Ho! Our Country, to the Rescue!! *N. Y.*, 1859

Jenkins, Howard M. Our Democratic Republic, Its Form, Its Faults, Its Strength, Its Need. Three Articles on the Suffrage Question. *Wilmington*, 1868

Johnson, S. M. The Dual Revolutions, Anti-Slavery and Pro-Slavery. *Baltimore*, 1863

Johnson, Reverdy. Reply to Review of Judge Advocate Gen. Holt, in Case of Maj. Gen. Fitz John Porter. Vindication of that Officer. *Baltimore*, 1863

1858 Rebellion and Slavery Pamphlets. [*Sixteen.*]

Jones, Absalom. Thanksgiving Sermon—Abolition of Slave-Trade *Very scarce.* *Phila.*, 1808

Irish Liberator, Address of, to the Irish Repeal Assoc. of Cincinnati, with the Pope's Bull on Slavery and the Slave-Trade. *N. Y.*, 1843

Junius Tracts, The. *N. Y.*, 1844

Juge, M. A. The American Planter, or the Bound Labor Interest in U. S. *N. Y.*, 1854

Jervis, J. B. Letters to Friends of Freedom and the Union. *N. Y.*, 1855

Jones, Uncle Tom, Life and Adventures of, for Forty Years a Slave. *Scarce.* *Boston.*

Justinian. Sovereign Rights of the States. *Washington.*

Jagger, Wm. Information with respect to Institution of Slavery. *N. Y.*, 1856

Jacobs, Col. Curtis. Speech on the Free Colored Population of Maryland. *Annapolis*, 1860

James, Henry. Oration—The Social Significance of Our Institutions. *Boston*, 1861

Ingersoll, Charles. Letter to a Friend in a Slave State. *Phila.*, 1862

Jones, Henry W. F. Sermon, Funeral Capt. Simeon A. Mellick. *Scarce.* *Bergen Point, N. J.*, 1862

Instructions to Mustering Officers and others of Kindred Duties. *Washington*, 1863

Income Record. List giving the Taxable Income of every resident of N. Y. *N. Y.*, 1865

Junkin, Rev, Geo. Integrity of our National Union vs. Abolitionism. Argument from the Bible. *Cincinnati*, 1843

——— Review of his Synodical Speech, in Defence of American Slavery. *Cincinnati*, 1844

1859 Rebellion and Slavery Pamphlets. [*Fourteen.*]

Kansas, Report of Congressional Investig. Com. of. July 1, 1856.

——— Memorial of Senators and Representatives, and the Constitution of State of. *Washington*, 1856

——— Subduing Freedom in. Report of Congres. Com., July 1, 1856.

Kelly, E. Appeal to the Colored People of U. S. *Phila.*, 1855

Kelly, George F. Eight Months in Washington, or Scenes behind the Curtain. Corruption in High Places, etc., 1863.

Kelley, Wm. D. Remarks in Support of his Proposed Amendment to the Bill, "To Guaranty to Certain States, whose Govts. have been usurped or Overthrown, a Repub. Form of Govt. *Washington*, 1865

——— Speech of. U. S. vs. William Smith. Piracy.

Keith, George B. An Offering to the Republican Democracy, in Support of U. S. Constitution. *Dedham*, 1863

Kettell, Thomas P. Southern Wealth and Northern Profits, as exhibited in Statistical Facts and Official Figures. *N. Y.*, 1861

Ketchum, Hiram. Gen. McClellan's Peninsular Campaign. *N. Y.*, 1864

Kirkland, Charles P. Letter to Hon. Benj. R. Curtis, in review of his late pamphlet on the "Emancipation Proclamation" of President. *N. Y.*, 1862

——— Liabilities of Govt. of Grt. Britain for Depredations of Rebel Privateers on Commerce of U. S., considered. *N. Y.*, 1863

——— The Destiny of our Country. *N. Y.*, 1864

——— Letter to Peter Cooper, on "The Treatment to be Extended to the Rebels Individ. *N. Y.*, 1865

1860 Rebellion and Slavery Pamphlets. [*Thirteen.*]

Krebs, John M. Discourse on the Nature and Extent of our Religious Subjection to the Govt. under which we live. *N. Y.*, 1851

Kroeger, A. E. Our Form of Govt., and the Problems of the Future.

Kugler, Rev. John B. Our National Sins. Sermon, Dec. 30, 1860. *Strasburg, Pa.*

Kennedy, John P. Mr. Ambrose's Letters on the Rebellion. 246 p. *N. Y.*, 1865

Kennedy, John H. Discourse. Sympathy, its foundation and legitimate exercise considered, in special relation to Africa. *Phila.*, 1828

Kirkland, Charles P. Letter to Hon. Benj. R. Curtis, in review of his late pamphlet on Emancipation Proclamation of the President. 2nd Edition. *N. Y.*, 1863

——— Address. Subject, The Destiny of our Country. *N. Y.*, 1864

Kempshall, Rev. Everard. Thanksgiving Sermon. *N. Y.*, 1863

Kimball, Rev. Joseph. Thanksgiving Sermon. *N. Y.*, 1864

Kelley, Daniel G. What I Saw and Suffered in Rebel Prisons. *Scarce.* *Buffalo*, 1868

Kansas Contested Election. Majority Report. 34th Cong., H. of Rep. Report No. 3, March, 1856.

Kettell, Thomas P. Southern Wealth and Northern Profits, as exhib. in Statistical Facts and Official Figures. *N. Y.*, 1860

Kansas and Nebraska. Disc. by R. H. Richardson. *Chicago*, 1851

1861 Rebellion and Slavery Pamphlets. [*Eighteen.*]

Leach, George. Psalms of Freedom for the American Christian Patriot. *N. Y.*, 1861

Lincoln, Abraham. Arbitrary Arrests. The Acts which the Baltimore Platform Approves.

Lovejoy, E. P. Memorial of the Martyred. Disc. by David Root. *Very scarce.* *Dover, N. H.*

Little, Mrs. L. J. A Mother's Peace Offering to American Houses; or the Martyr of the Nineteenth Century. *N. Y.*, 1861

Lieber, Francis. Two Lectures on the Constitution of the U. S. *N. Y.*, 1861

——— Guerrilla Parties considered with reference to the Law and Usages of War. *N. Y.*, 1862

Lowrey, G. P. The Commander-in-Chief, a Defence of the Proclamation of Emancipation. *N. Y.*, 1862

Lord, Eleazar. Six Letters on the Necessity and Practicability of a National Currency. *N. Y.*, 1862

Letter to an English Friend, on the Rebellion in the U. S., and on British Policy. *Boston*, 1862

Lyrics of the War. *Phila.*

Laws relating to Pensions, Military and Naval Bounty, and Back Pay and Bounty Lands. *Washington*, 1862

Laws relating to the Direct and Excise Taxes, passed during the First and Sec. Sessions of the Thirty-Seventh Congress. *Washington*, 1862

Leaves of the Year 1863.

Lossing, Benson J. The League of the States. *N. Y.*, 1863

Lewis, Charlton T. Sermon. National Fast. *Cincinnati*, 1863

Laboulaye, Edouard. Why the North cannot accept of Separation. *N. Y.*, 1863

Laboulaye, M. Edouard. Upon Whom rests the Guilt of the War? Separation: War without End. *N. Y.*, 1863

Low, Hon. Henry R. The Governor's Message Reviewed *Albany*, 1863

20 1862 Rebellion and Slavery Pamphlets. [*Nineteen.*]

Lieber, Francis. Address. No Party Now, but All for our Country. *Phila.*, 1863

Leavitt, Joshua. The Monroe Doctrine. *N. Y.*, 1863

Letter to an English Friend, on the American War. *N. Y.*, 1863

Loyalist's Ammunition. *Phila.*, 1863

Leavitt, Judge. Decision of, in Vallandigham Habeas Corpus Case. *Phila.*, 1863

Loyer, R. F., to E M. Stanton, in Self-Defence against the Aspersions of the Senate Com. *Phila.*, 1863

Loyal Reprints, No. 3. Grt. Mass Meeting of Loyal Citizens, Cooper Institute, March 6. *N. Y.*, 1863

Loring, Cha's G. Neutral Relations of England and U. S. *N. Y.*, 1863

——— England's Liability for Indemnity. Remarks on the Letter of "Historicus." *Boston*, 1864

Letter to President of U. S., by a Refugee. *Phila.*, 1863

Lang, Geo. S. Money. *Phila.*, 1868

Lincoln, Abraham. Assassination of, *Cincinnati*, 1865

——— Address, Union League of Phila., in Favor of the Re-election of. *Phila.*, 1864

——— Address to People of U. S., recom. the Re-election of. *N. Y.*, 1864

La Tourette, Rev. James, A. M. Sermon, Fast Day. *Potsdam*, 1864

Leavitt, Rev. W. S. Sermon, Sunday after the Capture of Richmond, April 9, 1865. *Hudson*, 1865

Lewis, Prof. Tayler. State Rights: a Photograph from Ruins of Ancient Greece. *Albany*, 1865

Lander, Mrs. F. W. Biograph. Sketch of, *Phila.*, 1867

Lincoln, Mrs., and Mrs. Davis. Behind the Seams. by a Nigger Woman who took in work. *N. Y.*, 1868

1863 Rebellion and Slavery Pamphlets. [*Nineteen.*]

"Liberty." The Image and Superscription on every Coin issued by the U. S. of America. 1837

——— The image and Superscription on every Coin issued by the U. S. of America. 1839

Lovejoy, Rev. E. P. Discourse in Commem. of the Martyrdom of, by Beriah Greene. *Very scarce.* *N. Y.*, 1838

——— The Martyr of Freedom : Discourse by Thomas T. Stone. *Scarce.* *Boston*, 1838

Lee, Jarena. Life and Religious Experience of, *Cincinnati*, 1839

Lincoln, Mr. Speech of, on the resolution to censure the Hon. John Q. Adams. *Washington*, 1837

Longfellow, Henry W. Poems on Slavery. *Cambridge*, 1842

Lawrence, Abbott. Letters from, to Hon. W. C. Rives. *Boston*, 1846

Lugenbeel, J. W. Sketches of Liberia. *Washington*, 1853

Liberia. Message of the Pres. of Republic of, *Monrovia*, 1858

Liberia's Offering. Addresses, Sermons, &c., by Rev. E. W. Blyden. *N. Y.*, 1862

Letters on the Necessity of a Prompt Extinction of British Colonial Slavery. *London*, 1826

——— Present State and Probable Results of Theological Speculations in Conn., by an Edwardean. 1832

Leavitt, Rev. W. S. Sermon : Thanksgiving Day. *Hudson*, 1862

Lord, Nathan. Second Letter to Ministers of the Gospel, on Slavery. *Boston*, 1855

——— Eleazar. Theories of Currency. *N. Y.*, 1864

Lincoln, Abraham. Political Debates between, and Hon. Stephen A. Douglas, in Campaign of 1858, in Illinois. *Columbus*, 1860

Lemmon Slave Case. Report of, N. Y. Court of Appeals. *N. Y.*, 1860

Letters of Hon. Joseph Holt, Hon. Edward Everett, and Com. Charles Stewart on the Present Crisis. *Phila.*, 1861

1864 Rebellion and Slavery Pamphlets. [*Twenty-five.*]

Lowrey, G. P. English Neutrality. *N. Y.*, 1863

Loyal Legion. Mil. Order of. *Phila.*, 1867

Letter from Secretary of War (Stanton) on Reconstruction. 1867

Maryland. Scheme of Expatriation Exam. *Boston*, 1834

May, Rev. Samuel J. Letter to Editor of Christian Examiner. *Boston*, 1835

Matlack, R. C. Loyalty of the Epis. Ch. Disc. Nov. 5, 1865. *Phila.*

New York. Men furnished and Pub. Funds Expended. *N. Y.*, 1865

New Jersey. Message of Theo. Runyon, Jan. 5, 1864. *Newark.*
——— Volunteers. Register of Com. Officers in Service. 1862
——— Volunteers. Campaign of 14th Regt., by Sergt. Terrill. 1866
Notes on Colored Troops and Mil. Colonies. *N. Y.*, 1863
New York. Hards and Softs: which is the True Democ.? 1856
National Debt and the Monroe Doctrine. *N. Y.*, 1866
Niles, Capt. Albert H. Funeral Discourse, by Rob't Turnbull. *Hartford*, 1863
Old Continental and the New Greenback Dollar.
O'Rielly, H. The great questions of the Times. *N. Y.*, 1862
Ohio Boys in Dixie. The Adventures of Twenty-two Scouts sent by Gen. O. M. Mitchell to destroy a Railroad, and Judge Holt's Rept. *N. Y.*, 1863
Our Resources. *N. Y.*, 1864
Opdyke, George, vs. Thurlow Weed. The Gt. Libel Case. *N. Y.*, 1865
"Oceanus." Trip of the Steamer, to Fort Sumter and Charleston. *Brooklyn*, 1865
O'Conor, Charles. Opinion of, on the Treasury Agent System of Cotton Seizure in the South. *N. Y.*, 1866
Our National Finances. Review of late Report of Sec. of Treasury. *N. Y.*, 1867
Pennsylvania. Rep't of Adj't Gen., for 1862.
——— Message of Gov. Curtin, for 1862.
——— Inaugural Address of Gov. Geary, 1867.

20 1865 Rebellion and Slavery Pamphlets. [*Thirteen.*]

Meade, Maj. Gen. The Life and Services of. *Phila. Ed.*
Massachusetts. Rep't of Surg. Gen. Dale, Dec. 1863.
——— Rep't of Surg. Gen. Dale, Dec., 1864.
——— Address of Gov. Banks, Jan. 6, 1860.
——— Inaug Ad. of Gov. Andrew, 1862.
——— Inaug. Ad. of Gov. Andrew, Jan. 9, 1863.
——— Inaug. Ad. of Gov. Andrew, Nov. 11, 1863.
——— Inaug. Ad. of Gov. Andrew, Jan. 6, 1865.
——— Address of Gov. Bullock, in the Case of E. W. Green, 1866.
——— Special Message of Gov. Andrew, Jan. 3, 1866.
——— Valed. Address of Gov. Andrew, Jan. 4, 1866.
——— Address of Gov. Bullock, Jan. 4, 1867.
Mason, J. K. Sermon. Hampden, Maine, April 28, 1861.

50 1866 Confederate Pamphlets.

Matthews, Jas. M. The Statutes at large, of the Confederate States of America, passed at 3d Sess. of First Cong., 1863. (*To be continued annually.*) *Richmond*, 1863
——— Private Laws of, in same vol.

1867 Rebellion and Slavery Pamphlets. [*Twenty-four.*]

Moody, Loring. Plain Statement to all Honest Democrats. *Boston*, 1868

——— History of the Mexican War. *Boston*, 1848

Maryland. Doc. accompanying the Governor's Message. *Annapolis*, 1864

Murphy, D. F. Proc. of National Union Conven. in Baltimore. *N. Y.*, 1864

McKaye, James. The Emancipated Slave face to face with his old Master. *N. Y.*, 1864

Maduff, Rev. J. R. The Soldier's Text-Book. *N. Y.*, 1864

Metropolitan Record. Articles from the. *N. Y.*, 1863

McLeod, Rev. Alex. Negro Slavery Unjustifiable. Discourse. *N. Y.*, 1863

Municipalist. Addenda to the.

Morse, Sidney E. Geog. Statis. and Ethical View of Amer. Slaveholders' Rebellion. *N. Y.*, 1863

McDowell, Maj. Gen. Irvin. Statement of, in review of the evidence before the Court of Inquiry. *Washington*, 1863

Morrison, Col. W. R. Speech, Oct. 13, 1863. *St. Louis*, 1863

McKeon, Hon. John. Speech : Peace and Union ; War and Disunion. *N. Y.*, 1863

Mediator between North and South, or the Seven Pointers of the North Star. *Baltimore*, 1863

Magie, David. Discourse : Thanksgiving, to commemorate the Signal Victories of the Federal Arms. *N. Y.*, 1863

McClellan, from Ball's Bluff to Antietam. By Geo. Wilkes. *Scarce.* *N. Y.*, 1863

McDougall, J. A. Speech, Feb. 3, 1863. *Baltimore*, 1863

Memorial of Wiard to Senate and H. of Rep. *N. Y.*, 1863

Meade, Edwin R. Argument, in case of George W. Jones against Wm. H. Seward. *N. Y.*, 1863

May, Henry. Speeches of, Ho. of Rep. *Baltimore*, 1863

Moore, George H. Hist. Notes on the Employment of Negroes in Amer. Army of Revolution. *N. Y.*, 1862

Miller, Samuel. Prayer for our Country. Three Sermons. *Phila.*, 1862

Mongrelites, or the Radicals—so-called. Satirical Poem. *N. Y.*, 1866

Meyer, Albert. The National Problem solved. *San Francisco*, 1867

1868 Rebellion and Slavery Pamphlets. [*Nineteen.*]

Moore, G. H. Historical Notes on the Employment of Negroes in the American Army of the Revolution. *N. Y.*, 1862

Memorial to the Gov't. of U. S. from Citizens of Chicago. *Chicago*, 1861

McClellan, Gen. The Harrison's Bar Letter of. 1862

——— and Fremont ; a Reply to "Fremont and McClellan ; their Political and Military Careers Reviewed." By Antietam. *N. Y.*, 1862

Martin, Edward W. The New Administration; containing complete and Authentic Biographies of Grant and his Cabinet. *N. Y.*, 1869

McDougall, Rev. James. God's Blessing of Peace. Disc. Thanksgiving. *Brooklyn*, 1866

Morrill, Mr. On Unmanufac. Cotton. Ho. of Rep. April 25, 1866.

Miscegenation Indorsed by the Republican Party.

McClellan, Gen. West Point Oration.

Marshall, Hon. Humphrey, and Hon. B. F. Hallett. Speeches of.

McCulloch, Hugh, and the Sec. of the Treasury. *Wash.*, 1865

Money by Steam. *N. Y.*, 1864

Miscegenation: Theory of the blending of the races, applied to the American White Man and Negro.

Mass. Governor's Address, 1864, in relation to National Cemetery at Gettysburg.

Miles, T. J. Conspiracy of leading men of the Repub. Party to Destroy the American Union. *N. Y.*, 1864

McClenthen, C. S. Narrative of Fall and Winter Campaign. Descrip. of Battle of Fredericksburg. *Syracuse*, 1863

Millard, Rev. Nelson. Discourse. Thanksgiving Day. *N. Y.*, 1863

Moody, Loring. Destruction of Democratic Republicanism the Object of the Rebellion. 2d Ed. *Boston*, 1863

——— Destruc. of Dem. Repub. the Object of the Rebellion. 3d. Ed. *Boston*, 1863

1869 Rebellion and Slavery Pamphlets. [*Twenty-four.*]

McClellan's Campaign. *N. Y.*, 1862

McClellan, Maj.-Gen. Geo. B. From Aug. 1, 1861, to Aug. 1, 1862. *N. Y.*

McKnight, Hon. Robt. Speech of. Ho. of Rep., June 3, 1862

Mill, John S. The Contest in America. *Boston*, 1862

Motley, John L. Causes of the American Civil War. *N. Y.*, 1861

Mercer, Alex. G. Sermon, National Fast. *Boston*, 1861

Mandeville, C. Henry. My Country, Disc. *Newburgh*, *N. Y.*, 1861

Motley, J. L. Pulpit and Rostrum. Causes of American Civil War. *N. Y.*, 1861

Morgan, Edwin D. Message of. *Albany*, 1861

McGill, Alex. T. Sermon, National Fast. *N. Y.*, 1861

Munson, M. The Gordian Knot United. Series of Letters to Hon. Ben Graham. *Geneseo*, 1861

Morton, James St. C. Memoir on American Fortification. *Washington*, 1859

McCarter, Rev. J. M. Border Methodism and Border Slavery. *Phila.*, 1858

Mattison, H. The Impending Crisis—of 1860. *N. Y.*, 1858

Miner, Charles. The Olive Branch, or the Evil and the Remedy. *Phila.*, 1856

Montgomery, Cora. The King of Rivers. *N. Y.*, 1850

Mott, Lucretia. Sermon to the Medical Students. *Phila.*, 1849

Mann, Horace ; Speech of, on the Right of Congress to Legislate for the Territories of U. S. *Boston*, 1848

Maryland, Slavery in. An Anti-Slavery Review. *Baltimore*, 1846

Morris, Rev. R. D. Slavery, its Nature, Evils and Remedy. Sermon. *Phila.*, 1845

McCaine, Alex. Slavery Defended from Scripture against Attacks of Abolitionists. *Baltimore*, 1842

Marcus. Examination of the Expediency and Consti. of Prohib. Slavery in Missouri. *N. Y.*, 1819

Miller, Samuel. Sermon, Synod of N. J., for benefit of the African School. *Trenton*, 1823

Minnesota. Message of Gov. Marshall. *St. Paul*, 1867

1870 Rebellion and Slavery Pamphlets. [*Twenty-two.*]

Negro's Memorial, or Abolitionist's Catechism. *Bristol*, 1830

Negro Emancipation, Essay. S. Pye. Also, Essay on the Phenomena of Dreams. *Curious.* *Brooklyn*, 1832

Nott, John C. Two Lectures on the Connection between the Biblical and Physical History of Man. *N. Y.*, 1849

Nelson, J. Discourse on the Proposed Repeal of the Missouri Compromise, April 6, 1854. *Worcester*, 1854

Nott, Samuel. Slavery and the Remedy. *Boston*, 1859

Nebraska Question. History of Missouri Compromise. *Chicago*, 1854

National Union, The. Vol. I., Nos. 1 and 2. Nashville, July 21, 1860.

Newhall, Rev. F. H. Discourse, National Fast. Boston, Jan. 4, 1861.

Nason, Elias. Record of Events in Exeter in 1861. *Exeter*, 1862

——— Record of Events in Exeter in 1862. *Exeter*, 1863

——— Discourse on the War. *Exeter*, 1861

Newberry, Dr. J. S. Letter. A Visit to Fort Donelson for the Relief of the Wounded of Feb. 15, 1862.

Nordhoff, Charles. The Freedmen of South Carolina. Account of their Appearance, Character, Condition and Peculiar Customs. *N. Y.*, 1863

Nation, The Book for the—and the Times. *Phila.*, 1864

Northrop, George ; Eighth Joint Debate between—and Hon. Wm. D. Kelley. *Phila.*, 1864

Navy Register of the United States for 1865. *Wash.*, 1865

Nordhoff, Charles. America for Free Working Men. *N. Y.*, 1865

New Jersey, History of Ninth Regiment of Volunteers of, Infantry. By Herman Everts. *Newark*, 1865

Negroleum, formerly known as Petroleum. By Horrible Greasy. *N. Y.*

New Orleans Riot. Its Official History. *Washington*, 1866

National Banks. System Unmasked. Greenbacks Forever. 1869

Nicholas, S. S. Conservative Essays, Legal and Political. *Louisville*, 1869

20 1871 Rebellion and Slavery Pamphlets. [*Eighteen.*]

New York and The Five Cotton States, or Remarks on the Social and Economical Aspects of the Southern Political Crisis. *N. Y.*, 1861

New York, Memorial in Behalf of—in respect to Adapting its Canals to the Defence of the Lakes. *Wash.*, 1862

——— Proc. at the Mass Meeting of Royal Citizens. *N. Y.*, 1862

——— Loyal Meeting of the People of—to Support the Gov't, Prosecute the War, and Maintain the Union. *N. Y.*, 1863

——— Presentation of Regimental Colors to the Legislature. *N. Y.*, 1863

——— Presentation of Trophy Flags to the Legislature. *Albany*, 1864

——— National Celebration of Union Victories. *N. Y.*, 1865

——— Report of the Special Com. of the Chamber of Commerce on Testimonials to Captain, Officers, and Crew of U. S. Sloop of War, Kearsarge. *N. Y.*, 1865

——— The State Military Record, devoted to the Interests of Soldiers of. *N. Y.*, 1866

——— National Union Celebration, Sept. 17, 1866.

——— Military Assoc. of. Proceedings of, Annual Meeting. *N. Y.*, 1866

——— Mass Meeting of Citizens of—to Approve the Principles announced in Message of Andrew Johnson. *N. Y.*, 1866

——— Eighth Annual Report of Board of Management of the Veterans of the National Guard. *N. Y.*, 1867

——— Annual Message of the Governor of. *Albany*, 1867

——— Is the Government of the State, a Republic or a Despotism?

——— National Celebration of Union Victories, Mar. 4, 1865.

——— Account of Reception by Citizens of—to the Survivors of the Officers and Crews of the U. S. Frigates, Cumberland and Congress. *N. Y.*, 1862

National Problem Solved. *San Francisco*, 1867

20 1872 Rebellion and Slavery Pamphlets. [*Sixteen.*]

Observations on Rev. Dr. Gannett's Sermon, entitled "Relation of the North to Slavery." *Boston*, 1854

O'Connell, Daniel. The Pope's Bull and the Words of. *N. Y.*, 1856

Ohio State Christian Anti-Slavery Convention, Proc. of. *Columbus*, 1859

O'Conor, Charles; Speech of. "Negro Slavery not Unjust." *N. Y.*, 1859

Otey, James H. Two Discourses. Trust in God, the Only Safety of Nations, and Constitutional Gov't founded upon the Recognition of God's Sovereignty. *N. Y.*, 1860

O'Conor, Charles; Letters to. The Destruction of the Union is Emancipation.

——— The Status of Slavery.

——— The Rights of the States and Territories. By Nath'l Macon. *Montgomery*, 1860

Oakey, Rev. P. D. Sermon. The War: Its Origin, Purpose, and our Duty respecting it. *N. Y.*, 1861

O'Rielly, Henry. Origin and Objects of the Slaveholder's Conspiracy against Democratic Principles. *N. Y.*, 1862

Olds, Hon. Edson B.; Speech of—for which he was Arrested, and his Reception Speeches on his return from the Bastile. (1862)

O'Rielly, Henry B.; Brief Memento of—who fell in Battle of Williamsburg, May 5, 1862.

Osbon, B. S. Cruise of U. Flag-Ship, Hartford, 1862–'63. *N. Y.*, 1863

Owen, Robert Dale. The Future of the North-West in connection with the Scheme of Reconstruction without New England. *Phila.*, 1863

Opinions deliv. by Judges of the Court of Appeals on the Contitutionality of the Act of Congress declaring Treasury Notes a Legal Tender for Payment of Debts. *Albany*, 1863

Owen, Robert Dale. Three Letters. The Policy of Emancipation. *Phila.*, 1863

1873 Rebellion and Slavery Pamphlets. [*Eleven.*]

Porter, Wm. D. State Sovereignty and the Doctrine of Coercion.

Paper, containing a statement of certain Political Opinions. *Chestnut Hill, Phila.*, 1862

Palfrey, John G. Papers on the Slave Power, first published in the Boston Whig.

Park, John W. Address on African Slavery. Atlanta, Georgia, July 14, 1857.

Porter, Fitz-John. Court Martial. Letter from the Secretary of War transmitting copy of Proc. of. Feb. 18, 1863.

Perry, N.; Speech of—on the Constitution. *N. J.*, 1862

Plain Words to Plain People by a Plain Man. Union League Ed. 1863.

Plain Words to Plain People by a Plain Man. Union League Ed. *Phila.*, 1863

Pierrpont, Judge; Speech of—at Cooper Inst., N. Y., Oct. 21, 1868.

Pierrpont, Edwards; Speech of—at Cooper Inst., N. Y., Nov. 1, 1864.

Post, T. M. Our National Union. Disc. Nov. 20, 1860. *St. Louis*

1874 Rebellion and Slavery Pamphlets. [*Twenty-one.*]

Prentiss, Geo. L. The Political Situation. *N. Y.*, 1866

Plumley, Rev. G. S. Thanksgiving Discourse, Dec. 7, 1865. *N. Y.*, 1866

Porter, Hon. W. D., Argument of. The Constitutionality of the Lawyers' Test Oath. *Charleston*, 1866

Pike, James S. The Financial Crisis—Its Evils and their Remedy. *N. Y.*, 1867

Platt, Isaac L. The Currency, the Standard of Value and the Circulating Medium, Financially Considered. *N. Y.*, 1867

Prince, L. Bradford, E Pluribus Unum ; or, American Nationality. The Articles of Confederation vs. The Constitution. *N. Y.*, 1867

Pike, James S. The Restoration of the Currency. *N. Y.*, 1868

Patriot. The Future of the Country.

Peckham, Robert. Historical Poem: Dedication of Soldiers' Monument, Westminster. *Fitchburg*, 1868

Pierrepont, Judge, Speech of. Meeting of War Democrats, Cooper Institute, Oct. 21, 1868.

Philadelphia, Union League of. Essays on Political Organization. *Phila.*, 1868

Pierce, Edward L. Speech, Milton, October 31, 1868. *Boston*, 1868

Protestant Episcopal Church. Proc. of Seventy-eighth Annual Convention. *Charleston*, 1868

Political Manuals for 1866 and 1868. By E. McPherson. *Washington*, 1866 and '68

——— Pamphlet. By E. A. Pollard. Vol. I., No. 1, Aug. 29, 1868.

——— Pamphlet. By E. A. Pollard. Vol. I., No. 2, Sept. 12, 1868.

——— Pamphlet. By E. A. Pollard. Vol. I., No. 3, Sept. 19, 1868.

Parker, Joel. The Domestic and Foreign Relations of United States. *Cambridge*, 1862

——— Habeas Corpus and Martial Law. *Cambridge*, 1861

——— The Right of Secession. *Cambridge*, 1861

——— Revolution and Reconstruction. Two Lectures. *N. Y.*, 1866

1875 Rebellion and Slavery Pamphlets. [*Nineteen.*]

Peterhoff, the British Steamship. Report of the Seizure by United States Cruiser Vanderbilt, and Proceedings in U. S. Prize Court before Hon. Judge Betts. *N. Y.*, 1863

Pilsen, Lieut.-Col., Reply of, to Emil Schalk's Criticisms of the Campaign in the Mountain Department under Maj.-General J. C. Fremont. *N. Y.*, 1863

Porter, Charles S. Sermon. National Fast. *Phila.*, 1863

Pope, Maj.-Gen. John. Campaign in Virginia of July and August, 1862. *Milwaukee*, 1863

Proc. of the Meeting in relation to Establishment of a Large National Bank. *N. Y.*, 1863
Paul, Henry St. Our Home and Foreign Policy. 1863
Potts, Rev. Wm. D. Campaign Songs for Christian Patriots and True Democrats. *N. Y.*, 1864
——— Freemen's Guide to the Polls and a Solemn Appeal to American Patriots. *N. Y.*, 1864
Paddock, Rev. Wilbur F. Thanksgiving Discourse, Nov. 26, 1863. *Phila.*, 1864
Patriot. Our National Finances. Serious Comedy. *N. Y.*, 1864
——— do do No. 11. " 1865
——— do do " 1868
Pierrepont, Judge, Review by, of Gen. Butler's Defense before the House of Representatives in relation to the N. Orleans Gold. *N. Y.*, 1865
Pauline, the Female Spy. By Lieutenant-Col. ——. Illustrated. *N. Y.*, 1865
Plumb, David. The Slaveholders' Rebellion. *N. Y.*, 1865
Parker, Cortlandt. Oration, Bloomfield, July 4, 1865. *Newark*, 1865
Patterson, James W. Speech, May 19, 1866. *Washington*, 1866
Philadelphia, Why Colored People in, are Excluded from the Street Cars. *Phila.*, 1866
Protestant Episcopal Freedman's Commission. Occasional Paper. *Boston*, 1866

1876 Rebellion and Slavery Pamphlets. [*Twenty.*]

Patten, Wm. Sermon on the Slave Trade. *Providence*, 1793
Pacificus, Philo. A Solemn Review of the Custom of War. *Cambridge*, 1816
Porter, Jacob. The Well-Spent Sou ; or, Bibles for the Poor Negroes. *New Haven*, 1830
Pierce, Willard. Discourse, December 3, 1835. *Dedham*, 1836
Pratt, Mr. Humanity ; or, the Rights of Nature. 1838
Philanthropist. The Guardian Genius of the Federal Union. *N. Y.*, 1839
Pillsbury, Parker. The Church as It Is ; or, the Forlorn Hope of Slavery. *Boston*, 1847
Porter, Rev. Elbert S. Thanksgiving Sermon. *Williamsburg*, 1850
Phillips, Wendell. Review of Webster's Speech on Slavery. *Boston*, 1850
Philadelphia, proceedings of Great Union Meeting in. *Phila.*, 1850
Past, the—the Present, and the Future. 1851
Phillips, Wendell, Speech of. Boston January 27, 1853.
Proceedings of the Convention of Radical political Abolitionists. *N. Y.*, 1856

Parker, Theodore. Sermon—The New Crime Against Humanity. *Boston*, 1854

——— Joel. Address—Non-Extension of Slavery and Constitutional Representation. *Cambridge*, 1856

——— Theo. Penn. Yearly Meeting of Progressive Friends, Proc. of, including Four Sermons. *N. Y.*, 1858

Pryor, Hon. Roger A., Speech of, on principles and policy of the Black Republican Party. *Washington*, 1859

Pantheon, the New; or, the Age of Black. *Rollo*, *N. Y.*, 1860

Proceedings of an Union Meeting held in New York. An Appeal to the South. *N. Y.*, 1860

Poem, Comprising a few Thoughts suggested by the Assault on Our Glorious Flag. *N. Y.*, 1861

1877 Rebellion and Slavery Pamphlets. [*Seventeen.*]

Prentiss, George L. Address, Assoc. of Alumni of Bowdoin College, August 8, 1861. *N. Y.*, 1861

Potter, Elisha R., Speech of, on the Resolution in Support of the Union. *Providence*, 1861

Peace! Peace! But there is no Peace. 1861

Palmer, Rev. B. M. Thanksgiving Sermon, December 29, 1860. *N. Y.*, 1861

Petersen, Fred. A. Military Review of the Campaign in Virginia and Maryland. *N. Y.*, 1862

——— Military Review of the Campaign in Virginia and Maryland; part II. *N. Y.*, 1862

Prentiss, George L. Address, the National Crisis. *N. Y.*, 1862

Pope's Campaign in Virginia. Its Policy and Results. The Relations of the Army of the Potomac to the Campaign Exposed. 1862

Palmer, Sir Roundell. Speech—The North American Blockade. *London*, 1862

Porter, John K. Speech at Union Ratification Meeting, Glens Falls, October 21. *Albany*, 1862

Pulpit and Rostrum. Sermons, Orat's, Lect's, &c. *N. Y.*, 1862

Philadelphia Malignants Typographed. By Tartan. *Phila.*, 1863

Potomac, Army of. History of its Campaigns. *N. Y.*, 1863

Porter, Maj.-Gen. Fitz John, Review by Judge Advocate Gen. of proceedings, findings, and sentences of a General Court-Martial for the Trial of. *Scarce.* *Washington*, 1863

Potter, Elisha R., Speech of, on present National Difficulties. *Providence*, 1863

Porter, John K., Argument of, in Court of Appeals in Case of the Metropolitan Bank and others, Respondents, against Henry H. Van Dyck, Superintendent of Bank Department, Appellant. *Albany*, 1863

Patriot Orphan Home, Report of, May 1, 1866. *N. Y.*

1878 Rebellion and Slavery Pamphlets. [*One Hundred and two.*]

Papers from the Society for the Diffusion of Political Knowledge. Nine Numbers. *N. Y.*

Loyal National League New York. Opinions of Loyalists. The Sumter Anniversary, 1863.

——— Opinions of prominent Men. Sumter Anniversary. N. Y., 1863.

——— Proc., &c., March 20, 1863.

——— Speech of Montgomery Blair, April 11, 1863.

Loyal Publication Society. 78 Numbers. *N. Y.*, 1863–'65

——— Eight pamphlets.

——— Of Ohio. No. 7.

National Equal Suffrage Association. Address by S. M. Booth *Washington*, 1866

Democ. Anti-Abolition State Right Association of New York, 1863.

1879 Rebellion and Slavery Pamphlets. (*Twenty-four.*)

Townsend, S. P. Our National Finances. N. Y., 1868

Trial by Impeachment. By Theo. S. Dwight.

Tracy, Jos. Historical Examination of Society in Western Africa. *Boston*, 1845

——— The True and the False. Oration, Yale College, July 30, 1862.

Trumbull, R. J. Observations on State Sov. N. Y., 1850

Tanner, B. T. Sermon, Baltimore, November 29, 1866. Thanksgiving.

Thompson, J. P. The Psalter and the Sword. Sermon, November 27, 1862. N. Y.

Van Evrie, J. H. Negroes and Negro Slavery. 1853

Van Dyke, John. Slaveholding not Sinful : A Reply to the Argument of Dr. How. *New Brunswick*, 1856

Virginia, Horrid Massacre in (Nat. Turner) by the Blacks. *Very scarce.* N. Y., 1831

——— The State of, to the People of Great Britain. 1866

——— Physical Survey of, preliminary Report, by M. F. Maury. *Richmond*, 1868

Vinton, Francis. Christian Idea of Civil Government. N. Y., 1861

——— Alex. H. The Mistakes of the Rebellion. Sermon, National Thanksgiving. N. Y., 1863

——— Cause for Thanksgiving. Sermon Second. National Thanksgiving. N. Y., 1864

——— Duties of Peace. The Nation's Third Thanksgiving. N. Y., 1865

West Virginia. Message of Gov. Boreman, and Adjutant-General's Report. 1864

——— do do do 1867

Willard, Major Sidney, Tribute to the Memory of. December 21, 1862. By C. A. Bartol.

Yates, Wm. Rights of Colored Men to Suffrage, Citizenship and Trial by Jury. *Phila.*, 1838

Yale College. Oration by Charles Tracy. Poem by Rev. C. D. Helmer. Phi Beta Kappa Society of. *New Haven*, 1862

Ye Sneak, Yclepid Copperhead. Satirical poem. *Phila.*, 1863

Yeaman, G. H. Observations on International Prize Law, &c. *Copenhagen*, 1867

Zabriskie, Rev. F. N. God's Battle. Sermon, June 30. *Albany*, 1861

——— Funeral Discourse in Memory of Captain Lansing Hollister. *Coxsackie*, N. Y., 1863.

1880 Rebellion and Slavery Pamphlets. [*Eleven.*]

Quashy; or, the Coal-Black Maid. A Tale, by Capt. T. Morris. *Very scarce.* *London*, 1796

Querist, The. An Humble Imitation of a work under a similar title, published by the celebrated Berkley, Bishop of Cloyne. *Phila.*, 1839

Quincy, Josiah. Address—Nature and Power of the Slave States and the Duties of the Free States. *Boston*, 1856

Report of Chief Signal Officer, Army of Potomac, Previous to and during the Campaign on Penin., Va. *Wash.*, 1864

Report of Com. to Recruit the Ninth Army Corps. *N. Y.*, 1866

Report and Resolves on the Subject of Slavery, Ho. of Rep., Jan. 16, 1836.

Report of Mr. Wilson on Military Affairs, Feb. 14, 1863.

Report of Com. on Commerce on the Reciprocity Treaty with Grt. Britain, &c. *Washington*, 1862

Report of Message from Pres. of U. S., July 19, 1867.

Report of Message from Pres. of U. S., Jan. 20, 1841.

Reflections on the Inconsistency of Man. *N. Y.*, 1796

1881 Rebellion and Slavery Pamphlets. [*Twenty-four.*]

Rebuke of Secession Doctrines, by a Southern Statesman. *Phila.*, 1863

Redpath's Books for the Camp-fires. Hospital Sketches, by L. M. Alcott. *Boston*, 1863

Rules for keeping the principal Record Books used at Depart. and Gen. Headquarters and Adjut. Gen Office. *Wash.*, 1864

Rip Van Winkle Club. Political Transac. of. *Tarrytown*, 1864

Ruggles, Samuel B. Address—Metropolitan Fair. *N. Y.*, 1864

Reminisco, Don Pedro Quærendo. Life in the Union Army. *N. Y.*, 1864

Results of Emancipation in U. S. of America. *N. Y.*, 1864

Rubek, Sennoia. The Burden of the South; or, Poems on Slavery. *N. Y.*, 1864

Republican Campaign Songster for 1864. *Cincinnati*, 1864

Russell, W. H. The Civil War in America. *Boston*, 1861

Rightful Power of Congress to Confiscate and Emancipate. *Boston*, 1862

R. I. Communication from James Y. Smith transmitting the Report of Col. Charles E. Bailey touching the Quota of. *Providence*, 1865

Rules and Regulations concerning Commercial Intercourse with Insurrectionary States. *Wash.*, 1865

Reilly *vs.* Huber. Case of. Disfranchisement of Deserters. *Phila.*, 1865

Remarks on the Existing Rebellion. *St. Louis*, 1865

Reconstruction in America, by a Member of N. Y. Bar. *N. Y.*, 1865

Rebellion, The Slaveholders', by David Plumb. *N. Y.*, 1865

Rebel Brag and British Bluster, by Owls Glass. *N. Y.*, 1865

Reconstruction on "My Policy;" or, its Author at the Confessional, by Zedekiah Comitatus. *Skaggaddahunk*, 1866

Real Questions before the Country. *N. Y.*, 1866

Rebel States. The President and Congress. *N. Y.*, 1866

Reconstruc. Letter from Peter Cooper to Pres. Johnson.

Rooney, Alderman, at the Cable Banquet. *Funny.* *N. Y.*, 1867

Radical Reconstruction on the Basis of One Sovereign Republic. *Sacramento*, 1867

1882 Rebellion and Slavery Pamphlets. [*Seventeen.*]

Roll of Honor. Names of Soldiers who Died in Defence of the American Union. *Washington*, 1868

Register, Official Army, for 1866. *Washington*, 1866

——— Official Army, for Sept. 1861. *Washington*, 1861

Rice, Rev. David. Speech—Slavery Inconsist. with Justice and Good Policy. *N. Y.*, 1812

Rice, N. L. Ten Letters on Slavery. *St. Louis*, 1856

Remarks on a Plan for Total Abolition of Slavery. *N. Y.*

Review of the Slave Question, by a Virginian. *Richmond*, 1833

Ruggles, Samuel B. Review of Address of Hon. Mr. Banks, with the Reply and Rejoinder. *N. Y.*, 1856

Remarks on Popular Sovereignty as Maintained and Denied respectively by Judge Douglas and Attor.-Gen Black. *Baltimore*, 1859

Review of the Opinion of Charles O'Conor, Esq. *Washington*, 1866

Report, Annual, of the Missionary to the Negroes in Liberty Co., Ga. *Charleston*, 1834

Report of Arguments of Council in Case of Prudence Crandall *vs.* State of Conn. *Boston*, 1834

Report of Corresp. with Southern Eccles. Bodies on Slavery to Gen. Assoc. of Mass. *Salem*, 1844

Report upon an Individual of the Bushman Tribe of Hottentots brought from the Cape of Good Hope, by Mr. Chase.. *N. Y.*, 1848

Report of the Com. on Slavery to Convention of Congress. Ministers. *Boston*, 1849

Report of Majority and Minority of Com. on Slavery at Gen. Conference of Meth. Epis. Ch. *Buffalo*, 1860

Report of Com. of Merchants for Relief of Colored People Suffering from the Late Riots. *N. Y.*, 1863

1883 Rebellion and Slavery Pamphlets. [*Twenty-one.*]

Ross Slaves. Brief History of. *N. Y.*, 1848

Robertson, Rev. D. F. National Destiny and Our Country. Discourse. *N. Y.*, 1851

Ruggles, Samuel B. Speech. Defence of the Right and Duty of the American Union to Improve its Navigable Waters. *N. Y.*, 1852

Reflections and Suggestions on the Present State of Parties. *Nashville*, 1856

Reddington, D. Speech on the Political Issues of Campaign of 1856. *Keokuk*, 1856

Rogers, Rev. E. P. Repeal of the Missouri Comprom. Considered. *Newark*, 1856

Republican Documents. Proc. of Meeting, N. Y. April 29, 1856.

Ross, Dr. F. A. Position of the Southern Ch. in rela. to Slavery. *N. Y.*, 1857

Ruggles, Samuel B. Speech, on the Proposed Court of Appeals. *N. Y.*, 1859

Ryerson's Patent. Brief Acct. of Submarine Machines, and of. *N. Y.*, 1860

"Reign of Terror." The New, in Slaveholding States. *N. Y.*, 1860

Rendition of Fugitive Slaves. Acts of 1793 and 1850, and the Decisions of Supreme Court sustaining them. *N. Y.*, 1860

Raphall, M. J. Discourse—Bible View of Slavery. *N. Y.*, 1861

Rejected Stone; or, Insurrection *vs.* Resurrection. *Boston*, 1861

Reynolds, Lieut.-Col. John G. Proc. of a Marine Gen. Court Martial for Trial of. *Very scarce and valuable.* *Wash.*, 1862

Rush, B. Letter on the Rebellion. *Phila.*, 1862

Right of Recognition. Sketch of Present Policy of the Confed. States. *London*, 1862

Read, John M. Opinions of, in Favor of the Consti. of the Act of Cong. of March 3, 1863. *Phila.*, 1864

Reconstruction of the Union. Suggestions to People of the North, on a. By a Citizen of Iowa. *N. Y.*, 1863

Rosecrans, Gen. Letters from, to Democ. of Indiana. *Phila.*, 1863

Revere, Brig.-Gen. Joseph W. Statement of the Case of. *N. Y.*, 1863

1884 Rebellion and Slavery Pamphlets. [*Sixteen.*]

Rebellion Record. Diary of Amer. Events, by Frank Moore. Nos. 1 to 4. Parts 60, 61, 62, 64, 65, 66, 68, 71, 72.

——— Gen. McClellan's Report.

Rebellion and War for the Union. Nos. 1 to 16 incl. in 4 Parts. *N. Y.*, 1861

Report of Bureau of Ordinance, Navy Dept., Oct. 20, 1863.

Report of Sec'y of Treas. on Banking Assoc. 1861–2.

——— (Chase.) 1862.

Report of Treasury Investigation. The suppressed Documents on the Printing of Public Money. *Rich and racy.*

Report of Sec'y of Treas. (McCullough.) 1867.

Rhode Island Soldiers. Mrs. Dailey's Report. *Prov.,* 1863

Report of Cong. Com. on Operations of Army of Potomac. 1863.

1885 Rebellion and Slavery Pamphlets. [*Twelve.*]

Smith, Goldwin. Welcome to, by the Citizens of N. Y., Nov. 12, 1864.

Smith, Edw. Dunlap. Our Country ; its Constitution and Laws. Disc. *N. Y.,* 1851

Smith, Philip Anstie. Seizure of Southern Commissioners with reference to International Law, and the Question of War or Peace. *London,* 1862

Seward, Wm. H. and Lewis Cass. Speeches. N. J., March, 1850.

Seward, Wm. H. True Basis of Amer. Ind. Lecture. *N. Y.,* 1853

——— Speech for immediate admission of Kansas into the Union, Washington, Apr. 9, 1856.

——— Speech for Immediate admission of Kansas into the Union, N. Y., Apr. 9, 1856.

——— Closing Speech of, Apr. 30, 1858. *Washington.*

——— The Irrepressible Conflict. Speech deliv. at Rochester, Oct. 25, 1858.

——— The Nat. Divergence and Returns. Speech, Sept. 4, 1860. *Detroit.*

——— Freedom and the Union. Speech, Washington, Feb. 29, 1860.

——— The State of the Country. Speech, N. Y., Feb. 29, 1860.

1886 Rebellion and Slavery Pamphlets. [*Eleven.*]

Smith, E. Delafield. Argument of, in Case of the Prize Steamer "Peterhoff," New York July 10, 1863.

——— Brief Appeals for the Loyal Cause. *N. Y.,* 1863

——— Non-Inter. with Insurrect. Districts. *N. Y.,* 1865

——— Speech for Grant and the Republican Cause, deliv. at Cooper Inst., N. Y., Oct., 1868.

——— Retractions of Reflections contained in a Cong. Rep. in the case prosecuted by. *N. Y.,* 1867

Smith, Truman. Speech of, on the Nebraska Question, Washington, Feb. 10, 11, 1854.

Smith, M. B. Sermon deliv. at Passaic, N. J., Apr. 21, 1861.

——— Sermon on the day of Nat. Thanksgiving for Victory. New York, Aug. 6, 1863.

Smith, Gerritt. Substance of the Speech made by, in the Capitol of the State of N. Y., March 11, 12, 1850.

——— Speech of, at Cooper Inst., N. Y., June, 1865.

Smith, Goldwin. Letter to a Whig Member of the Southern Independence Assoc. *Boston,* 1864

1887 Rebellion and Slavery Pamphlets. [*Eleven.*]

Sickles, Daniel E. Speech on Mr. Colfax's Postal Service Suspension Act, Washington, Feb. 5, 1861.

——— Speech of, on the State of the Union, Washington, Jan. 16, 1861.

Stearns, Wm. A. Sermon, Fast Day, April 6, 1854. *Cambridge.*

Stearns, Edw. J. Sermon, Sword of the Lord, Sept. 26, 1861. *Baltimore.*

Stearns, Adjutant. Memorial of. Port. *Boston,* 1862

Stearns, Geo. L. Few Facts pertaining to Currency and Banking. *Washington,* 1864

——— The equality of all men before the Law. *Boston,* 1865

Spring, Gardiner. Sermon—"State Thanksgiving during the Rebellion," N. Y., Nov. 26, 1861.

Spring, Lindley. "Peace :" a Lecture deliv. at Cooper Inst., Aug. 4, 1864. *N. Y.*

Skinner, Thos. H. Address, Fast Day, N. Y., Sept. 20, 1861.

——— "Light in Darkness." Disc. *Stapleton, S. I.,* 1862

1888 Rebellion and Slavery Pamphlets. [*Twenty-two.*]

Stephens, A. H. Speech on the Kansas Election, Feb. 19, 1856.

——— Speech on the Kansas Election, March 11, 1856.

Stringfellow, Thornton. Script. Test. on Slavery : an Essay. *Richmond,* 1841

——— Slavery : its Origin, Nature, and History. *Alexandria,* 1860

Specie Payments. How to Resume without Contraction. *N. Y.,* 1865

——— Plan Looking to an Early Resumption. *N. Y.,* 1867

——— Resumption of, by A. H. Simonin. *N. Y.,* 1868

Spooner, L. Rewiew of Essay on Uncon. of Slavery. *Boston,* 1847

——— New System of Paper Currency. *Boston,* 1861

——— No Treason. Nos. I. and II. *Boston,* 1867

Stone, A. L. The War, and the Patriot's Duty. Disc., April 21, 1861.

——— Praise for Victory. Disc., Feb. 23, 1862.

——— National Godliness. Fast Day Sermon, April 7, 1864.

Statement of Disposition of some of the Bodies of Union Soldiers in National Cemeteries. Vols. II. and III. *Washington,* 1868

Stillé, C. J. How a Free People Conduct a Long War. *Phila.,* 1862

——— How a Free People Conduct a Long War. *N. Y.,* 1863

——— How a Free People Conduct a Long War. *Phila.,* 1863

——— How a Free People Conduct a Long War. *Phila.,* 1863

——— Northern Interests and Southern Indep. *Phila.,* 1863

Scott, Dred. Report of Decis. of Sup. Court of U S., by B. C. Howard. 1857.

——— Report of Decis. of Sup. Court of U. S., by B. C. Howard. N. Y. ed.

——— Examination of the Case of, by Samuel A. Foot. *N. Y.*, 1859

1889 Rebellion and Slavery Pamphlets. [*Ten.*]

Schenck, Rob't. C., U. S. A., of Vols., Life of. *Ohio*, 1862

Schenck, N. H. Thanksgiving Sermon, Balto., Nov. 26, 1863.

Schenck, N. H. "Epochs of Transition." Oration in New Jersey College, June 26, 1866. *Phila.*

Sprague, W. B. Disc. on the Annual Thanksgiving in N. Y., Nov. 28, 1861. *Albany.*

Sprague, J. N. Sermon, May 19, 1861. *Newark, N. J.*

Sprague, J. N. Sermon, on day of Nat. Thanksgiving, Aug. 6, 1863. *Newark, N. J.*

Sprague, Judge. Opinions of, in the Revere and Amy Warwick Prize Cases.

Smith, James. Slavery.

Smith, Mellville C. The divine ordeal of the Amer. Republic. Speech, July, 1864. *Minnesota.*

Smith, Franklin W. Prosecution of, by the U. S. Navy department. *Boston*, 1865

1890 Rebellion and Slavery Pamphlets. [*Ten.*]

Storrs, George. Mob under pretence of Law, or the arrest, and trial of. *Scarce.* *Northfield, N. H.* and *Concord*, 1835

Stanton, Henry B. Remarks of, on subject of Slavery. 5th ed. *Boston*, 1837

Sawyer, Leceister A. A dissertation on Servitude. *New Haven*, 1837

Sydney's Letters to Wm. E. Channing on the annexation of Texas to U. S. *Charleston*, 1837

Sibbald, Charles F. Documents in evidence of a claim submitted by. *Phila.*, 1837

Sleigh, W. W. Abolitionism exposed. *Phila.*, 1838

Spencer, Ichabod. The religious duty of obedience to Law, a Sermon. *N. Y.*, 1850

Selections from the Speeches and Writings of Prominent men in U. S. *N. Y.*, 1851

Stowe, Mrs. Patent Key to Uncle Tom's Cabin. *N. Y.*, 1853

Slavery Domestic. Address before the Pro-Slavery Conven. *St. Louis*, 1855

1891 Rebellion and Slavery Pamphlets. [*Twelve.*]

Subgenation, the theory of the Normal Relation of the Races, an answer to Miscegenation. *N. Y.*, 1864

Sahler, D. Dubois. America viewed Physically, Politically and Religiously, Disc., Nov. 24, 1864. *N. Y.*

Sherman, Maj. Gen. Reports. *N. Y.*, 1864

Sanderson, Jas. M. My Record in Rebeldom, as written by Friend and Foe. *N. Y.*, 1865

Syle, E. W. Sermon, on Nat. Thanksgiving, Dec. 7, 1865. *N. Y.*

Sabine, Wm. T. Thanksgiving Sermon, deliv. Dec. 7, 1865. *Phila.*

Sunderland, Byron. Sermon, deliv. Feb. 25, 1866. *Washington.*

Stillwell, Silas M. Nat. Finances, Phil. Exam. of Credit. *N. Y.*, 1866

Swann, Thos. Record of the Proc. of the investigation before, for official misconduct. *Baltimore*, 1866

Schieffelin, Samuel B. The Pres. and Congress. A Hint to the South. A Warning to the North. *N. Y.*, 1867

State of the Country. From the Princeton Review, Jan. 1861.

Slavery and Domes. Slave Trade in the U. S. *Phila.*, 1841

1892 Rebellion and Slavery Pamphlets. [*Eleven.*]

South, Voice from. Comprising letters from Georgia to Mass. and to the Southern States. *Balto.*, 1847

Slavery in the U. S., its Evils, Alleviations and Remedies. *Boston*, 1851

Southern Platform ; or, Manual of Southern sentiment on the subject of Slavery, by D. R. Goodloe. *Boston*, 1858

Southern Notes for Nat. Circulation. *Boston*, 1860

Southern Slavery considered on general principles, by a North Carolinian. *N. Y.*, 1861

Southern Envoys. Case of the seizure of. *London*, 1861

Southern Hatred of the Amer. Gov., and people of the North, and Free Institutions. *Boston*, 1862

Stewart, Wm. B. Sermon, Thanksgiving day, Phila., Nov. 27, 1862.

South. Letter from a friend in the North, on the effects of disunion upon Slavery. *Phila.*, 1856

Statesman. What says the Constitution? or, Congress and the Pres. Judicially revealed. *N. Y.*, 1868

South, Spirit of ; or, Persecution in name of Law, also, its effect upon the nation and its Genl. Government. *Washington*, 1869

1893 Rebellion and Slavery Pamphlets. [*Ten.*]

South. Letter from a friend in the North to a friend in the South. *Phila.*, 1856

Syracuse. Proc. and address of Democ. State Conven., Jan. 10–11, 1856. *Albany.*

Shepherd, J. R. Hist. of the Oberlin Wellington Rescue. *Boston*, 1859

Samford, Wm. F. Letter of, to Gov. Wise, Ala., March 16, 1859.

Sanders, John. Memoirs of Life and Services of, by J. C. Morton. *Pittsburgh*, 1861

Seelye, E. E. Sermon, "Nat. Crisis," Schenectady, April, 1861.

Stringfellow. Slavery ; its Origin, Nature and Hist. *N. Y.*, 1861

Secession. Effect of, upon Commercial Relations between North and South. *N. Y.*, 1861

Seymour, Horatio. Speech, Albany, Sept. 10, 1862.

Sanborn, F. B. Supreme Judicial Court in the matter of, on Habeas Corpus. Brief of Council for Silas Carleton. *Boston*, 1862

1894 Rebellion and Slavery Pamphlets. [*Twelve.*]

Spalding, E. G. Speech on the Finances, Jan. 28, 1862. *Washington.*

Sherwood, Lorenzo. The great Question of the Times, involved in the Slave-holders' Rebellion, as set forth in speech of. *N. Y.*, 1862

Story, Wm. W. The American Question. *London*, 1862

Santvoord, Geo. Van. Oration deliv. on anniv. of Amer. Ind. at Hudson, N. Y., July 4, 1862.

Stanton, Edwin M. A System of Target Practice. *Washington*, 1862

Sterry, D. C. Sermon, in memory of the Heroic Dead, who have fallen in the battles of Freedom, June, 1862. *Minnesota.*

Seward, Mr. The Diplomatic Year, being a review of For. Corres. of 1862, by a Northern Man. *Phila.*, 1863

Secrets of the Amer. Bastile. *Phila.*, 1863

Savoury Dish for Loyal men. *Phila.*, 1863

Schenck, B. S. The burning of Chambersburg, (Penn.,) with Corroborative statements. *Scarce.* *Phila.*, 1864

Sargent, F. W. England, the U. S. and Southern Confederacy. *London*, 1864

Southgate, Horatio. Prayer and Thanksgiving for the Nation, Sept. 11, 1864. *N. Y.*

1895 Rebellion and Slavery Pamphlets. [*Nine.*]

Sumner Charles. The Rebellion. Its Origin, etc., N. Y., Nov. 27, 1861.

——— Letter to, on Secession, Concession, etc. *Boston*, 1861

——— Our Foreign Relations, Cooper Inst., Sept. 10, 1863.

——— A Bridge from Slavery to Freedom. Speech, June 13, 1864.

——— Slavery and the Rebellion etc. Cooper Inst., Nov. 5, 1864.

——— Our Foreign Relations. *N. Y.*, 1863

——— The Case of the Florida. *N. Y.*, 1864

——— Letter from E. Stanley, Milit. Gov., among Abolit., 1865.

——— The one man Power, *vs.* Congress. *Boston*,1866

1896 Rebellion and Slavery Pamphlets. [*Eleven.*]

Scott, Dred. Opinion of Judge Taney, and an Essay on the Natural Hist. of the Prognathous Race, etc., by Dr. Cartwright.

Scott, Dred. Decision, etc,
Sumner, Charles. The True Grandeur of Nations. Oration, July 4, 1845. *Boston.*
——— The True Grandeur of Nations. Oration, July 4, 1845. *Phila.*
——— Freedom National, etc. Speech. *Washington*, 1852
——— Freedom National, etc. Speech. *Boston*, 1852
——— Lect. on the Anti-Slavery Enterprise. *N. Y.*, 1855
——— The Crime against Kansas. Speech, May 19, 1856.
——— The Barbarism of Slavery. Speech, June 4, 1860. *Boston.*
——— The Barbarism of Slavery. Speech. *Washington*, 1860
——— The Repub. Party, Its origin, etc., July 11, 1860. *N. Y.*

1897 Rebellion and Slavery Pamphlets. [*Seventeen.*]
Spear, Samuel T. The Law-Abiding Conscience, and the Higher Law Conscience, Brooklyn, Dec. 12, 1850.
——— Obedience to the Civil Authority, and Const. Gov. against Treason. *N. Y.*, 1861
——— The Nat. Blessing in Trial. Sermon, Nov. 27, 1862 *Brooklyn.*
——— Radicalism and the Nat. Crisis. Sermon, Brooklyn, Oct. 19, 1862.
——— The Duty of the Hour. *N. Y.*, 1863
——— Punishment of Treason. Disc., April 23, 1865. *Brooklyn.*
Stiles, Joseph C. Speech on the Slavery Resolutions, Detroit, May, 1850.
——— The Nat. Controversy ; or, Voice of the Fathers. *N. Y.*, 1861
Sickles, Daniel E. Speech on the state of the Union. *Washington*, 1860
Sedgwick, Theo. Thoughts on the proposed Annexation of Texas to U. S. *N. Y.*, 1844
Sumner, Charles. Les Relations Extérieures des États-Unis. *Paris*, 1863
Speeches delivered at the Republican Union Festival in commem. of Birth of Washington. *N. Y.*, 1862
Sherman, W. T. General and Field Orders. Campaign of the Armies of the Tenn., Ohio, and Cumberland, 1864–'5. *St. Louis.*
Strong, Theo. Address deliv. by Howard Crosby, at the funeral of, March 3. *New Brunswick.*
Seward, Wm. H. Lewis Cass. Speeches of, *N. Y.*, 1850
Scott, John W. Baccalaureate Sermon, Washington Col., Aug. 31, 1862.
Sights and Notes by a looker on in Vienna. *Wash.*, 1864

1898 Rebellion and Slavery Pamphlets. [*Twenty-Two.*]
N. Y. Soc. for Manumis. of Slaves. Disc. by E. H. Smith. New York, April 11, 1798.

Wilberforce Phil. Assoc. Oration on Abolition of Slave Trade. By Joseph Sidney, New York, Jan. 2, 1809.
Full Statement of the Reasons offered to the Legisl. of Mass., respecting Abolitionists and Anti-Slav. Soc. *Boston*, 1836
Fourth Annual Rep. Female Soc. of N. Y., for the support of Schools in Africa, Feb. 1838.
Disc. By Walter Clarke, on Amer. Anti-Slav. Soc., at War with the Church, in Canterbury, Conn. June, 30, 1844.
Seward Wm. H. Review of, diplomacy, by a Northern Man, 1862.
——— Speech of. *Auburn*, Oct. 20, 1865
——— The same. " " 31, 1868
Stewart, Charles. The West India Question. *New Haven*, 1833
——— Immediate Emancipation, an outline for it, and remarks on Compensation. *Newburyport*, 1838
——— Alvan. Legal Argument before the Supreme Court of New Jersey, for deliv. of 4000 persons from bondage. *N. Y.*, 1845
——— M. Remarks on the Speech of Daniel Webster. *Boston*, 1850
Soldiers' and Sailors' Half-Dime Tales of the late Rebellion. Vol. I., Nos. 1–15 inclusive. *N. Y.*, 1868
The Christian Disciple. No. 4, April 1818.
Quarterly Anti-Slavery Mag., by E. Wright, Jr. *New York*, July, 1836
Baptist Anti-Slavery Correspondent. Vol. I., No. 1. *Worcester*, Feb., 1841
African Repository. Nos. 2, 11, 12. *Washington*, Feb., 1847
——— Vol. XXVI. *Washington*, 1850
Congregational Record, Sept. and Oct. Vol. V., Nos. 9 and 10. *Kansas City, Mo.*, 1863
The Alarm Bell. No. 1. N. Y. 1863
Brownson's Quarterly Review. No. 4. *N. Y.*, Oct., 1864
Military Measures of the U. S. Congress, 1861–'65. By Henry Wilson.

1899 Rebellion and Slavery Pamphlets. [*Twenty-Eight.*] 18
Train, Geo. Francis. Union Speeches during the War.
——— The Downfall of Eng., etc.
——— Great Speeches in Eng. on Slavery, etc.
——— on T. C Grattan. *Boston*, 1862
——— and the Pennsylvanians. *N. Y.*, 1864
Thayer, T. The State. Oration, Brown Univ. *Prov.* 1862
——— Russell. Reply to Ingersoll. *Phila.*, 1862
——— Address. Phila., July 4, 1865. The Great Victory.
Tyng, D. A. Our Country's Troubles, Sermon, June 29, 1856
——— S. H. Victory and Re-union, Sermon, April 20, 1865
Thompson, Joseph P. The Fugitive Slave Law. N. Y., 1850
——— No Slavery in Nebraska. N. Y., 1854
——— The President's Fast. N. Y., 1861
——— A. C. Mil. Success from God. *Boston*, 1862
——— J. P. The Psalter and the Sword. N. Y., 1863
——— Christianity and Emancipation. N. Y., 1863

Texas. The War in.
——— Wharton and Austins' Address, in Louisville, 1836.
——— The War in, a Crusade against Mexico, etc. *Philadelphia*, 1837
——— The Question Reviewed. N. Y., 1844
——— Appeal to Mass. *Boston*, 1844
——— Thoughts on Annexation, by Theo. Sedgwick. N. Y., 1844
——— Protest against the Rebellion, 1845.
——— Proc. of Conv. on Annexation of, etc. *Boston*, 1845
Tremain, Lyman. Speech, Syracuse, 1862.
——— Fred. L. Memorial of, Killed at Hatchers Run, Feb. 6, 1865, late Lieut. Col., 10th N. Y. Caval. By his Father. *Portrait.*
Thornwell, J. H. The Rights and Duties of Masters. *Charleston, S. C.*, 1850
——— Hear the South! N. Y., 1861

1900 Rebellion and Slavery Pamphlets. [*Twenty-Five.*]

Taylor, Miles (La.) Speech of, on the Brooks' Assault, 1856.
——— J. W. "Alleghania," Geog. and Statis. Memoir. *Very important.* *St. Paul*, 1862
Terrell, W. H. H. Communication from, Adjt. Gen'l. of Ind. 1867.
Tucker, Col. J. M. 2d Reg't, N. J. Vols. In Memoriam. Oration, by J. F. Foster. Sermon, by E. R. Craven. *Newark*, 1862
——— G. J. Speech, Oct. 19, 1866. N. Y.
Taney, Chief Justice. Decision in the Merryman Case. *Phila.*, 1862
——— The Unjust Judge. N. Y., 1865
Treatise on the Patriarchal System, as it exists in America, 1834.
Thoughts on Slavery, and another Pamphlet. *Lowell*, 1848
Twenty Millions thrown away, and Slavery Perpetuated. *London.*
Trial of Castner Hanway and others for Treason. *Phila.*, 1851
Thrasher, J. S. Prelim. Essay on Purchase of Cuba.
Talmage, G. Admonitions for the Times. N. Y., 1861
Treadwell, F. C. Secession an Absurdity. N. Y., 1861
Thurston, Mrs. J. P. Appeal to my Countrymen. *Portland*, 1861
Thomas, B. F. Remarks of, Ho. of Rep., on the Seceded States. *Boston*, 1862
Thoughts on the Times. *Baltimore*, 1863
Treason and Rebellion, being the Legisl. of Cong. and State of Cal., together with charge of Judge Field. *San Francisco*, 1863
Tharin, R. S. Arbitrary Arrests in the South, or Scenes from the Experience of an Alabama Unionist. N. Y., 1863
Tyson, Bryan. (of N. C.) The Institution of Slavery. *Washington*, 1863

Thoughts on Labor, etc. *Baltimore*, 1864
Taxation. The Question of. The State and Nat'l Banks. *Albany*, 1864
Tobey, E. S. The Industry of the South. *Boston*, 1865
Tousey, Sinclair. Business man's views of Public Matters. N. Y., 1865
Thoughts on the Currency. *Lowell*, 1866

1901 Rebellion and Slavery Pamphlets. [*Eleven.*]

Union Com. Room. Circular. N. Y., 1860
Union, (The.) Sermon by J. House Taylor, New York, Jan. 4, 1861.
——— As it Was, And as it Is. New York, Dec., 1862
——— The Constitution and Slavery. New York, 1864.
——— Victories. Nat'l Celebration of, New York, March 6, 1865.
——— Home and School, 4th Annual Report. N. Y., 1866
——— The same, 5th " " 1867
Union League Club. Vincent Colyer's Report to, N. Y., 1865
U. S. *vs.* E. A. Smith., Gen. Ct. Martial. *Cincinnati*, 1863
Union League Club. Address by J. P. Thompson, March 15, 1864. N. Y.
U. S. Christ. Com., Second Annual Report for 1863.

1902 Rebellion and Slavery Pamphlets. [*Nineteen.*]

United States Party. The U. S. Democracy. N. Y., 1866
——— District Court of, for So. Dist. of New York.
——— *vs.* the Steamship Meteor, her Tackle, etc. N. Y., 1866
——— The Financial Condition and Resources. By J. F. D. Lanier. N. Y., 1865
——— *vs.* Steamer "Peterhoff," and her Cargo ; with Appendix, Containing the Opinions of Judge Marvin, in Cases of the Dolphin and Pearl. N. Y., 1864
——— Narrative of Privation and Suffering of Officers and Soldiers of, while Prisoners of War. *Boston*, 1864
——— Narrative of Privation and Suffering of Officers and Soldiers of, while Prisoners of War. *Phila.*, 1864
——— Regulations for the Recruiting Service of the Army of the. *Washington*, 1863
——— Allotment System, Report to the Pres. of the Commis. for the State of New York. N. Y., 1862
——— Consti. of, Acts of Cong. Relating to Slavery, Nebraska and Kansas Bill. *Rochester*, 1854
——— Proc. of Senate on the Fugitive Slave Bill. Abolition of the Slave Trade in the Dist. of Colum., etc. *Washington*, 1850
Undelivered Speech on Executive Arrests, by Charles Ingersoll. *Phila.*, 1862
Upfold, George. Sermon, National Fast. N. Y., 1863
Upshur, Abel P. Brief Enquiry into the Nature and Character of our Federal Govt. *Phila.*, 1863

Uncle Samuel's Whistle, and What it Costs. 1864
Unification of North America. N. Y., 1837
Union, (The) being a Condemnation of Mr. Helper's Scheme. N. Y.
——— Meeting. Proceedings of, and Washington's Farewell Address. N. Y., 1850
——— Meeting. New York, Dec. 19, 1859, Official Report of.

1903 Rebellion and Slavery Pamphlets. [*Eighteen.*]

U. S. Navy. Brief sketch of some of the Blunders in Engineering Practice. *N. Y.*, 1868
Union League, Phila. Second Annual Report of Bd. of Directors. *Phila.*, 1864
——— Phila. Proc. of. Oration of Charles Gibbons, July 4. *Phila.*, 1865
——— Phila. Charge by Hon. Peleg Sprague to Grand Jury. *Salem*, 1863
——— Club, N. Y. Address by Joseph P. Thompson. *N. Y.*, 1864
——— Report of Special Com. on Emigration. *N. Y.*, 1864
——— Com. on providing a Thanksgiving Dinner for the Soldiers and Sailors. *N. Y.*, 1865
——— Spec. Com. on passage of the Const. Amendment for Abol. of Slavery. *N. Y.*, 1865
——— Exec. Com., Treasurer's Rep., Charter and By-Laws, etc. *N. Y.*, 1866
——— Address of President. *N. Y.*, 1866
——— Report of Exec. Com., Treasurer's Rep., Charter and By-Laws, etc. *N. Y.*, 1867
——— Proc. of the Conference at Richmond, 1867. *N. Y.*, 1867
——— Proc. in reference to Death of John A. King. *N. Y.*, 1867
——— Proc. in reference to Death of John A. Andrew. *N. Y.*, 1867
United States, Civil Service of. *Boston*, 1867
——— in Acct. with the Rebellion.
——— Laws and Information relating to Claims Against the Govt. of the. *Washington*, 1867
——— Courts, Opinions of, for the Eastern District of Missouri, and Southern Dist. of Illinois, on the Non-Intercourse and Captured Property Acts, etc. *Washington*, 1866

1904 Rebellion and Slavery Pamphlets. [*Fifty-Nine.*]

Campaign Doc., Loy. Repr., Anti-Abolition. 11 Pamphlets.
Anti-Slavery Exam., Nos. 5, 6, 7, 8, 11, 13. 6 Pamphlets,
Sanit. Com. Bulletins, Nos. 4, 8, 9, 30, 35, 36. 6 Pamphlets.
——— Bulletin, Reports of, Nos. 39, 41, 59, 64, 87. 6 Pamphlets.
——— Bulletin. Reports of Dr. Steiner. *N. Y.*, 1862

U. S. Sanit. Com. Speech of Dr. Bellows, Feb. 24, 1863. *Phila.*
——— Catalogue of Paintings presented to Metropolitan Fair. *N. Y.*, 1864
——— List of Officers, etc., in Phila., Jan. 1, 1864.
——— Rep. of Gen'l Sup. of Phila. Branch, Jan. 1, 1866.
——— Rep. of Penns. Branch, April 1, 1864.
——— Catalogue of Flags, Trophies, and Relics, exhibited at Metrop. Fair Exhib. *N. Y.*, 1864.
——— Boston Branch. Rep. No. 1. 1864.
——— Rep. of Treas. of Metrop. Fair, Aug. 1, 1864.
——— "Cinderella," Dramatized by Fitz Hugh Ludlow.
——— "The Spirit of the Fair." 17 Nos. Complete. *Uncut; very scarce.*
——— Ages of U. S. Soldiery. *N. Y.*, 1866
Western Sanit. Com. Rep. on the Hospitals of St. Louis, Aug. 1, 1862.
——— Sketch of its Origin, Hist., etc. *St. Louis*, 1864

1905 Rebellion and Slavery Pamphlets. [*Sixteen.*]
United States of America, Correspondence between Gt. Britain and, On the Present Relations. *Boston*, 1862
Union League Club. Report of Com. of Volunteering. *N. Y.*, 1864
——— Charter, By-Laws and List of Members. *N. Y.*, 1865
——— Report of Exec. Com. and Treasurer. *N. Y.*, 1865
Universal Suffrage. Female Suffrage, by a Republican. *Phila.*, 1867 /8
View of the Present State of the African Slave-Trade. *Phila.*, 1824
Vigornius, and others. Essays on Slavery. *Scarce.* *Amherst, Mass.*, 1826
Van Evrie, J. H. Negroes and Negro "Slavery;" The First an Inferior race, the Latter its Normal condition. *N. Y.*, 1853
Van Rensselaer, C. Address, Dec. 31, 1856, opening of the Ashmun Institute. *Phila.*, 1859
Van Horn, Burt. Liberty and the Union. Speech in Assembly, Jan. 18, 1860.
Vallandigham, C. S., Biographical Memoir of, by his Brother. *N. Y.*, 1864
Voice From Rebel Prisons. Horrors of the Stockades at Andersonville, Milan and other Prisons, by a returned Prisoner of War. *Very scarce.* *Boston*, 1865
Van Dyke, H. J. Sermon, The Character and Influence of Abolitionism. *N. Y.*, 1860
——— Sermon, Character and Influence of Abolitionism, Dec. 9, 1860. *N. Y.*, 1860
——— Review of, discourse on the Character and Influence of Abolitionism, by Rev. J. R. W. Sloane. *N. Y.*, 1861
——— Antidote to his Pro-Slavery Disc., by Rev. W. H. Boole. *N. Y.*, 1861

20 1906 Rebellion and Slavery Pamphlets. [*Twenty-Five.*]

Webster, Dan'l. "The Const. not a Compact," etc., Jan., 1833. *N. Y.*, 1866

——— on Slavery. Extracts from Speeches of, etc. *Boston*, 1861

West, Byrd. Revelations of a Slave Smuggler; being the Autobiography of Rich. Drake. *N. Y.*, 1860

West, N. Sermon, Nov. 28, 1861, Nat'l Thanks. *Brooklyn.*

——— Hist. of Satterlee. U. S. A. Gen. Hosp., 1863.

Wikoff, H. Letter to Vis. Palmerston, on Amer. Slavery. *N. Y.*, 1861

——— Letter to Vis. Palmerston, on Secession and its Causes. *N. Y.*, 1861

Williams, Jas. Narrative of Events, since Aug. 1, 1834, in Jamaica.

——— Patent Bullet. Rept. of Experiments. *N. Y.*, 1862

Williams, Thos., Speech of, on Reconstruction. *Washington*, 1866

Williams, Wm. R. Disc., on Nat'l Changes, etc., May 29, 1862. *N. Y.*

——— on Nat'l Renovation. *N. Y.*, 1863

Williams, Peter (a Descendant of Africa). An Oration, on the Abolition of the Slave-Trade. *Very scarce. N. Y.*, Jan. 1, 1808

——— Circular Letter to the Clerical and Lay Delegates, etc., 1819.

Weston, S. H., Sermon by, Chaplain 7th Regt., N. Y. *Washington*, April 28, 1861

——— "The March of the Seventh Regt." Sermon, June 9, 1861.

Walker's Appeal to the Colored Citizens, etc. *Boston*, 1830

Walker, Geo. Consid. touching the suppression of Nat'l Banks.

Walker, R. J. In favor of Re-election of Lincoln, 1864.

——— Letter of, on Nat'l Finances.

Wiard, Norman. Facts about Ordnance.

——— Manufacture of Small Arms, etc. *N. Y.*, 1863

——— Great Guns, and the Method of Constructing them.

Wilkes, Geo. McClellan from Ball's Bluff to Antietam. *N. Y.*, 1863

Wilkes, Chas., Defence of, before Gen'l Court Martial. 1864.

20 1907 Rebellion and Slavery Pamphlets. [*Twenty-Two.*]

Ward's Father. Letter to Prof. Stuart, Aug., 1837.

What has the North to do with Slavery?

What is Abolition?

Weaver, Amos. Address to People of N. C., on Slavery. *Greensboro, N. C.*, 1830

Wilberforce. Eulogium, by David P. Brown. *Phila.*, 1834

Weller, J. B., Addresses at Dinner to, Jan. 22, 1857. *Washington.*
Webb, J. W. Mass Meeting at Tippecanoe Battle Ground.
Waterbury, J. B. Friendly Counsels for Freedmen. *N. Y.*
Watson, Benj. The Prayer of Asa. *Phila.*, 1861
War, in its Financial Aspects. *N. Y.*, 1861
——— and its End; or its Cause and Cure. *N. Y.*, 1861
Willard, S. D. Regimental Surgeons in the Rebellion from N. Y., 1861–3.
Wedgewood, W. B. Flag of the Democratic Empire.
War Songs of the American Union. *Boston*, 1861
War and Slavery; or victory only through Emancipation. *Boston*, 1861
Wortman, Denis, Jr. Living for Principles. *N. Y.*, 1862
War, and Why it is. *Boston*, 1862
Walbridge, Gen'l Hiram. 4th July Celeb., Cooper Inst., 1862.
Ward, Thos., War Lyrics by. *N. Y.*
Weiss, John. Causes for Thanksgiving. *Boston*, 1862
Washington, Geo. Speeches at Birthday Festival, Feby. 22, 1862.
Winter Campaigns the Test of Generalship. *N. Y.*, 1862

1908 Rebellion and Slavery Pamphlets. [*Twelve.*]
Wheeler, E. P. The Char. and Conduct of the War. *N. Y.*, 1863
War Songs for Freemen. *Boston*, 1863
Wells, David A. Our Burden and our Strength. *Troy*, 1864
West Point. Battle Monument, Oration of Gen. McClellan, 1864.
Wakeman, A. Speech, Greenfield Hill, Conn., Nov. 3, 1864.
Wainwright, J. H. Gold Currency and Funded Debt. *N. Y.*, 1864
"Wilfred;" or the First Year of the War. A Poem. *Pontiac, Wis.*, 1865
Woodbury, Augustus. The President and Congress. *Providence*, 1866
White, A. D. Address at Yale College, July 25, 1866.
Willich, Maj. Gen'l August., The Army, an Essay by. *Cincinnati*, 1866
Woodford, S. L. Loyal Reconstruction, Oct. 22, 1868.
Winfield, C. H., on the Constit. Amendment, Feb. 19, 1868. *Jersey City.*

1909 Rebellion and Slavery Pamphlets. [*Twenty-Eight.*]
Winthrop, R. C. Speech, New London, October 18, 1860.
West India Emancipation, Address on, by Jas. R. Willson. *Phila.*, 1838
Wilson, Jas. Grant. Biog. Sketches of Illinois Officers. *Chicago*, 1862
Wilson, W. D. Letter to Sam'l A. Foot, on Attainder of Treason. *Albany*, 1863
Wilson, H. Mil. Measures of the U. S. Cong., 1861–1865. *N. Y.*

Wall, Jas. W. Address on the Const., Burlington, Feb. 20, 1862.
——— ——— at Newark. July 4, 1863.
Wood, Benj. Speech on the State of the Union, May 16, 1862.
——— ——— on Peace, Feb. 27, 1863.
Wood, Fern. Speech on Govt. Finances, April 19, 1864.
——— ——— Confiscation, Jan. 26, 1864.
Whiting, Wm. The War Powers of the Pres't. *Boston*, 1862
The same. 4th Ed. *Boston*, 1863
The same. 7th Ed. *Boston*, 1863
Wright, Elizur. Perforations in the "Latter Day Pamphlets." *Boston*, 1850
Wright, Wm. A Simple Remedy for a Sore Evil. *Paterson*, 1864
Wright, J. S. Citizenship Sovereignty. *Chicago*, 1863
——— State Sovereignty. *Chicago*, 1864
——— Reply to Chas. G. Loring. *Chicago*, 1867
Webster, Noah. Effects of Slavery on Morals and Industry. *Uncut; very scarce.* *Hartford*, 1793
Webster, Warren. The Army Medical Staff, Address, Feb. 22, 1865. *Worcester.*
Webster, Sidney. "Duties of Neutrality," U. S. vs. Steamship "Meteor," Closing Argument. *N. Y.*, 1866
Webster, Dan'l. Speech on the War with Mexico, March 23, 1848.
——— and Haynes' Speeches. *Phila.*
——— Speech to Young Men of Albany, May 28, 1851.
——— " on Slavery, Remarks on, by M. Stuart.
——— " on Mr. Clay's Resol. *Washington*, 1850
——— " on Slavery, Remarks on, by Wendell Phillips.

1910 Rebellion and Slavery Pamphlets. [*Sixteen.*]

Western Sanitary Com. Report on the White Refugees of the South. *St. Louis*, 1864
U. S. Rev. Com., Rep. of, Jan., 1866.
U. S. Christ. Com. 1st Annual Rep., Work and Incidents. *Phila.*, 1863
——— 2nd Annual Rep. *Phila.*, 1864
——— A Delegate's Story, by H. Q. Butterfield.
——— Maj. Gen. Howard's Address. *Phila.*, 1864
——— Record of the Fed. Dead. *Phila.*, 1865
——— Rep. of V. Collier. *N. Y.*, 1862
——— Third Annual Rep. of the Army Com. *Boston*, 1864
——— Selections of Sketches of Work of, 1865.
New England Soldiers' Relief Assoc., Report of the Sup.
——— Minutes of, the Organiz. and Proc. of. *N. Y.*, 1862
——— Final Rep. of. *N. Y.*, 1866
N. Y. Nat. Freed. Assoc., Sketches of its Hist. *N. Y.*, 1866
——— Officers, etc. *N. Y.*, 1864
——— The Nat. Freed. Journal, Vol. I., No. I. *N. Y.*, 1865

1911 Railroad Pamphlets. [*Ten.*]

Essay on Railroads.

Sketch of the Geographical Route of a Great Railway to connect the Canals and Navigable Waters of New-York, Penn'a, &c., and Western States. *N. Y.*, 1829

——— Route of a Great Railway to connect the Canals and Navigable Waters of New York, Penn'a, &c., and the Western States. 2d Ed. *N. Y.*, 1830

Report of Examinations and Surveys for a Railroad from Canajoharie to Village of Catskill. *Catskill*, 1831

Reply to a Pamphlet entitled "A Statement of Facts in relation to the Origin, Progress and Prospects of N. Y. and Harlem R. R. Co. *N. Y.*, 1833

Report of Joint Special Committee relative to N. Y. and Albany Railroad. Doc. No. 10. July 24, 1840.

——— relative to Penn. Railroad.

Wharton, Thomas I. Letter to Robert Toland and Isaac Elliott, on Right and Power of Phila. to Subscribe for Stock in Penn. Railroad Co. *Phila.*, 1846

Binney, Horace. Opinion of, on the Right of City Councils to Subscribe for Stock in Penn. R. R. Co. *Phila.*, 1846

Report of President and Managers of Phila. and Reading R. R. Co. to Stockholders. *Phila.*, 1849

1912 Miscellaneous. *Ten.*]

Rutgers College. Address deliv. before the Peithesophian and Philaclean Soc., by Wm. Wirt. 1830

——— Address deliv. before the Peithesophian and Philaclean Soc., by Theo. Frelinghuysen. 1831

——— Address deliv. before the Peithesophian, &c., by Alex. H. Everett. 1838

——— Address deliv. before Peithesophian, &c., by Robert Strange. 1840

——— Address deliv. before the Peithesophian, &c., by R. S. Cope. 1844

——— Oration before, on "The Christian Patriot," by C. C. Vanansdalen. July 18, 1837

——— A Baccalaureate Disc. on "The Choice of a Profession," by J. Proudfit. 1841

——— Address, "The Manly, Independent Thinker," by David D. Demarest. 1855

——— Disc. on Popular Education, by Charles F. Mercer, Sept. 26, 1826

——— Address, by J. H. Livingstone, " 25, 1810

1913 Miscellaneous. *Fine lot.* [*Fifteen.*]

Randolph, Hon. John. Speech, on the retrenchment resolutions, Feb. 1, 1828. *Boston*, 1828

——— Observations on the speech of, by the author of War in Disguise.
London, printed; New York, reprinted, 1806

——— Vindication of Mr. Randolph's resignation. *Phila.*, 1795

Rantoul, Robert, Jr. Oration before the inhabitants of South Reading, Fourth of July, 1832. *Salem*, 1832

——— Oration before the Gloucester Mechanics' Assoc., Fourth of July, 1833. *Salem*, 1833

——— Remarks on the ten million bank question. *Boston*, 1836

——— Oration before the Democrats and Anti-Masons, at Scituate, Fourth of July, 1836. *Boston*, 1836

——— Introd. Disc. delivered before the Amer. Inst. of Instruction, 1839. *Boston*, 1840

——— Speech at the late Anti-Bank meeting in Salem. *Boston*, 1834

——— Remarks on Education.

Reese, David M. The "extinguisher" extinguished! or D. M. R. "used up," by D. Ruggles, a colored man. *New York*, 1834

Review of the late negociation and arrangement with the British Government, respecting the West India trade. *Phila.*

Review of "The New divinity tried;" or, an examination of Rev. Mr. Rand's strictures on a sermon by Rev. C. G. Finney. *Boston*, 1832

Rhees, M. J. The Good Samaritan: an Oration, May 22, 1796. *Phila.*, 1796

Rhode Island and Providence plantations. Sermon on the conclusion of the second century of the settlement, by T. Williams. *Providence*, 1837

20 1914 Miscellaneous. [*Fifteen.*]

Richards, James. A Disc. on John VI. 44. *Newark*, 1816

——— Sermon, Dec. 12, 1822, [on] Thanksgiving. *Newark*, 1823

Richards, Wm. Disc. concerning Baptism. *Lynn*, 1793

Ritchie, Andrew. Oration, July 4, 1808. *Boston*, 1808

Robbins, Chandler. Sermon, Nov. 6, 1836. *Boston*, 1836

Robbins, Philemon. Sermon at the ordination of Mr. Chandler Robbins, Jan. 30, 1760. *Boston*, 1760

Rogers, Wm. M. Sermon, occasioned by the loss of the Harold and the Lexington, Jan. 26, 1840. 2d ed. *Boston*, 1840

Romaine, Benj. Observations, etc., on the Yellow Fever. *New York*, 1823

Rome. A voice from, answered by an American citizen. *Phila.*, 1844

Romeyn, John B. Two sermons, del. in the Presbyterian church, Albany, Sept. 8, 1808 [on fast day.] *Albany*, 1808

——— Disc., occasioned by the death of, Feb. 27, 1825. *New York*, 1825

Root, David. A Thanksgiving sermon, Nov. 26, 1835, in Dover, N. H. *Dover*, 1835

Roscoe, Wm. Considerations on the present war. *Phila.*, 1808

——— Letter to, containing strictures on, "Considerations, [etc.]" *Liverpool, printed; New York, reprinted*, 1808

Ross, Mr. and Morris. Speeches, in the Senate, 24th Feb., 1803. *Phila.*, 1803

1915 Miscellaneous. *Valuable.* [*Twenty.*]

Rensselaer, Stephen Van. Funeral Disc. on Death of, by Thomas E. Vermilye. *Albany*, 1839

——— Sermon after Death of, by Wm. B. Sprague. *Albany*, 1839

——— on Life, Services and Character of, by Daniel D. Barnard. *Very scarce and valuable.* *Albany*, 1839

Republican, The. No. I. London, March 1, 1817.

Representatives, House of. Report, No. 596. Steam Commun. with China and the Sandwich Islands. May 4, 1848

——— House of. Report No. 26. Railroad across Isthmus of Panama, Jan. 16, 1849.

Report of Committee of Senate appointed to inquire into Extent and Causes of Present General Distress. *Penn.*, 1819

——— of Committee of Senate appointed pursuant to Communi. of Hon. Jasper Ward. *Albany*, 1826

——— of Commissioners to Indian Stream. Nov., 1836

——— of Joint Special Committee on Fire in New st. 1845

——— of Exploring Expedition,to Rocky Moun. By Brev. Capt. J. C. Fremont. *Very scarce.* *Washington*, 1846

——— of an Expedition down the Zuni and Colorado Rivers, by Capt. L. Sitgreaves. *Important.* *Washington*, 1853

——— of Explorations for a Railroad Route from Miss. River to Pacific Ocean. By Lieut. A. W. Whipple. *Scarce.* *Washington*, 1854

Rhode Island. Rights and Wrongs of, by Wm. Goodell. *New York*, 1842

——— Address on Civ. Gov't of, by Wm. G. Goddard. *Scarce.* *Providence*, 1843

——— Oration and Poem before the "Sons of R. I.," on First Anniv., by Rev. Francis Vinton, and Geo. W. Curtis. *N. Y.*, 1863

——— Society. Transactions of, for Encouragement of Domestic Industry. *Providence*, 1869

Rogers, Rev. Wm. Circular Letter on Doctrine of Justification. *London*, 1786

——— Sermon on Death of Rev. Oliver Hart. *Phila.*, 1796

——— John. The Executioner. Account of the Man who Burnt John Rogers. By James Rogers. *Phila.*.

1916 Miscellaneous. [*Nineteen.*]

Rutland Marble Co., West Rutland, Vt. By-Laws. *N. Y.*, 1864

Rodgers, Ravaud K. Thanksgiving Sermon, Nov. 28, 1861. *N. Brunswick*, 1861

Royal Request.

Review of Dr. Scott's Bible and Politics. By Rev. W. C. Anderson and Fletcher M. Haight. *San Francisco*, 1859

Rutgers Medical College. Introductory Lecture to Course of Anatomy and Physiology, in. By John D. Godman. *N. Y.*, 1826
—— Introductory Lecture to Course of Anatomy and Physiology, in. By John D. Godman. *N. Y.*
—— Address before Peithessophian and Philoclean Societies of. By Alex. H. Everett. *N. Y.*, 1838
—— Address at Inauguration of Hon. Abraham B. Hasbrouck, as President of. *N. Y.*, 1840
—— Address before Peithessophian and Philoclean Societies of. By Stacy G. Potts. *N. Y.*, 1850
—— Address before Peithessophian and Philoclean Societies of—at their Anniv. By George W. Brown. *N. Y.*, 1851
Review of Decision of Court of Appeals on the Manor Question. *Albany*, 1859
Richards, George. Farewell Discourse. *Boston*, 1859
Reynolds, Rev. Grindall. Sermon at Instal. of. By Chandler Robbins. *Boston*, 1858
Raymond, Henry J. Address before Rochester University Literary Societies. *N. Y.*, 1854
Reply to Messrs. G. and C. Merriam's Attack on Character of Dr. Worcester and his Dictionaries. *Boston*, 1854
Rock River Valley Union R. R. Co. Letter to Hon. John Letcher in relation to. *Milwaukee*, 1854
Rock Island and its Surroundings in 1853. *Davenport*, 1854
Reviewer Reviewed, or Answer to Attack made by Rev. J. L. Hodge on Rev. Lebbeus Armstrong's New Work, entitled an "Allegorical Dialogue on John's Baptism." *N. Y.*, 1851
Ross, Edward C.; Tribute to Memory of. By John M. Macauley. *N. Y.*, 1851

1917 Miscellaneous. [*Twenty-six.*]
Rochester Knockings. Discovery and Explanations of. *Buffalo*, 1851
Regnault, Ch. New Theory of Music. *N. Y.*, 1850
Rayner, John. Cod-Liver Oil: Its Uses, &c. (4th Amer. Ed.) *N. Y.*, 1850
Revolutions in Europe, and Memoir of Louis Phillipe. By R. O. Old. *N. Y.*, 1848
Rushtaboo. By Sundown. *N. Y.*, 1848
Remsen Abraham and A. Remsen Schenk. Memorial of. By A. Hamilton Bishop. *Astoria, L. I.*, 1849
Report, Thirteenth Annual, of Exec. Com. of Benevolent Fraternity of Churches. *Boston*, 1847
Russell, Philemon R.; Primary Scriptural Manual by. *Exeter, N. H.*, 1844
Roy, Wm. L. Specimen of Work on Revelation.
Radical, The. Contin. of the Working Man's Advocate. No. 2, Vol. I. 1841.
Riddle, D. H. Discourse on National Fast. *Pittsburgh*, 1841
Richardsiana, or Hits at the Style of Popular American Authors. *N. Y.*, 1841

Rafinesque, C. S. Amenities of Nature, or Annals of Hist. and Natural Sciences. Good Book. No. I. *Scarce.* *Phila.*, 1840
Riell, Henry E. Appeal to Citizens of U. S. on Elective Franchise. *N. Y.*, 1840
Rubeta," "The Vision of. Critical Exami. of Poem entitled. *N. Y.*, 1839
Rice, Henry L. Sermon at Close of Session of the Classical Institution of German Ref. Church. *Chambersburg*, 1836
Root, J. Address, Calling upon Christians to use the Plain Word of God.
Rudd, J. C. The Temple Destroyed, or the Parish in Affliction. Sermon. *Auburn*, 1832
Regeneration. By H. U. O. 1832
Rush, Hon. Richard. Two Letters on Free Masonry and the New Berlin Trial. *Utica*, 1831
Review of Mr. Whitman's Letters to Prof. Stuart on Religious Liberty. *Boston*, 1831
Repplogel, George. New System for Preservation of Bees. *Greensburgh, Pa.*, 1830
Right of Free Discussion. *N. Y.*, 1829
Railway. Single Rail. *Boston*, 1827
Review of Pamphlet on the Trust Deed of Hanover Church. *Boston*, 1828
Redivivus, Quevedo. The Vision of Judgment. *London*, 1824

1918 Miscellaneous. *Fine lot.* [*Fourteen.*]

Rush, Benjamin. Inquiry into Effects of Ardent Spirits on the Human Body and Mind. *Boston*, 1823
Romeyn, John B. Sermon on Danger and Duty of Young People. *N. Y.*, 1810
Rhode Island Politics and Journalism. Letter from Thomas Davis to Hon. Henry B. Anthony. *Providence*, 1866
Robert the Hermit of Mass. Life and Adventures of. *Uncut and scarce.* *Providence*, 1829
Richmond, Calamity at; being a Narrative of Awful Conflagration of the Theatre, Dec. 26, 1811. *Very scarce.* *N. Y.*, 1812
Rhode Island, Annals of, and Providence Plantations, and a Rhyme of.
——— and the Times, by Geo. Wm. Curtis. *N. Y.*, 1863
——— Mr Goddard's Address on Civil Government. *Providence*, 1843
——— and Providence Plantations. Centennial Ser. By Thos. Williams. *Providence*, 1837
——— Indian names of places, by Usher Parsons. *Providence*, 1861
Rio Grande Valley. By John A. Stevens. *N. Y.*, 1864
Rock Island and its Surroundings in 1853. *Davenport*, 1854
Russell, John. The Nature of the Gospel Delineated, Sermon, preached in Kilmarnock, Aug. 18th, 1796. *Ayr*, 1796
Russia, The Resources of, in the Event of a War with France. *Boston*, 1812

1919 Miscellaneous. *Valuable.* [*Twenty-two.*]

Reformers of Great Britain, To the. R. Carlisle. *Dorchester*, 1821

Richmond, Duke of. The Bill for Universal Suffrage and Annual Parliaments. *London*, 1817

Rowson, Susanna ; Spelling Dictionary, (2d Ed.) *Portland*, 1815

Rolliad. Criticisms on the Poem. *London*, 1784

Remarks on Dr. Lowth's Letter to Bishop of Gloucester. *London*, 1786

Ramsay, Allan ; Familiar Epistles between Lieut. Wm. Hamilton and. *Belfast*, 1757

Reed, Joseph. Historical Essay. By George Bancroft. *N. Y.*, 1867

Reed, Pres., in Reply to Mr. Geo. Bancroft and others. *N. Y.*, 1867

Reed, Wm. B., Expert in Art of Exhumation of Dead. By Benj. Rush. *London*, 1867

——— Criticism of Aspersions of, on Character of Benj. Rush. *Phila.*, 1867

Report of the Kanzas Congressional Investigating Committee, July 1st, 1856.

Report, Official, of Col. L. C. Baker to S. P. Chase, Secretary of Treasury, in the Case of Stuart Gwynn and S. M. Clarke, June, 1864. *N. Y.*

Report of Case of Russell Jarvis, May 16, 1828.

Report from the Commissioner of Patents, showing the operations of Patent Office for 1842. Feb. 1, 1843.

Report of Secretary of War. Feb. 4, 1848.

Rodger, Alex. Scotch Poetry ; consisting of Song, Odes, &c. *London*, 1821

Rann, Jack ; Life of, who was executed Nov. 30, 1774. *London*

Repository, Monthly. No. LXIII. March, 1832

——— ——— No. LXIV. April, 1832

Report, House of Refuge. *N. Y.*, 1824

—— of Third Spa-Fields Meeting. *Spa-Fields*, 1817

Raymond, Wm. Biograp. Sketches of Dis. Men of Columbia Co. *Scarce.* *Albany*, 1851

1920 Revolutionary Pamphlets. *Valuable.* [*Four.*]

Gray, John, of Mt. Vernon, Last Soldier of the Revolution. *Very scarce.* *Washington*, 1868

Smith, J. H. Revolutionary Claims, House of Reps. Doc. No. 1028. *Washington*, 1842

Report of Convention in Independence Hall. *Phila.*, 1852

Battle of Trenton. By Henry K. How. *Very scarce.* *N. Brunswick*, 1856

1921 Revolutionary Pamphlets. *Exceedingly Valuable.* [*Fourteen.*]

Speech of Joseph Galloway in answer to John Dickinson. *London*, 1765

Considerations of Imposing Taxes in the British Colonies. *N. Y.*, 1765

Grievances of the American Colonies. *London*, 1766
Thanksgiving Discourse by John Lathrop. *Boston*, 1774
Whitney's Disc. on the Public Fast, July 14. *Boston*, 1774
Extracts from Votes and Proceedings of American Continental Congress. *Boston*, 1774
Considerations on the British Colonies in America. *Hartford*, 1774
Friendly Address to all Reasonable Americans. *N. Y.*, 1774
Strictures on a Pamphlet, entitled Friendly Address. *Boston*, 1775
Thanksgiving Discourse by Rev. Wm. Gordon. *Boston*, 1775
Sermon on American Affairs by Wm. Smith. *Phila.*, 1775
Observations on the Nature of Civil Liberty by Richard Price. *London*, 1776
Sermon, preached at Lexington April 20, 1778, by Jacob Cushing. *Boston*, 1778
Anticipation. His M——y's most Gracious Speech to both H——s of P——L——t. 4th Ed. *London*, 1778

1922 Revolutionary Pamphlets. *Exceedingly Valuable.* [*Fourteen.*]

Oration, delivered July 4, 1803, by Lewis M. Ogden. *Newark*, 1803
Address, delivered at Union Celebration of Indepen. at Sutton, by L. Hoadley. *Worcester*, 1824
Sketch of the Olden Time, by an Antiquary. *N. Y.*, 1829
History of the Fight at Concord, April 19, 1775, by Rev. Ezra Ripley. 2d Ed. *Concord*, 1832
Treason of Benedict Arnold, by Winthrop Atwill. *Northampton*, 1837
Gen. Woodhull and his Monument, by Luther R. Marsh. *N. Y.*, 1848
Leicester in the Revolution, Address commem. of; by E. Washburn. *Boston*, 1849
Oration on Battle of Lexington, by Robert Rantoul, Jr. April 19. *Boston*, 1850
Ethan Allen's Narrative of Capture of Ticonderoga. 5th Ed. With Notes. *Burlington*, 1854
Martyrs to the Revolution in the Prison Ships in Wallabout Bay. *N. Y.*, 1855
The American Spy. By J. R. Simms. *Albany*, 1857
Reminiscences of Military Life and Sufferings of Col. Timothy Bigelow, by Charles Hersey. *Worcester*, 1860
Patriots of the Revolution of '76. Sketches of the Survivors. *Boston*, 1864
Champe's Adventure, by Gen. Henry Lee. *N. Y.*, 1864

1923 Pre-Revolution and Revolutionary Pamphlets. *Very Valuable.* [*Four.*]

A Dissertation on the Polit. Union and Constitution of the Thirteen U. S. of N. A. Which is necessary to their Preservation and Happiness. Humbly offered to the Public. By a Citizen of Phila. *Very scarce.* *Re-Printed, Hartford*, 1783

PRICE, RICHARD. OBSERVATIONS on the Importance of the Amer. Revolution, and the Means of Making it a Benefit to the World. *Very scarce.*
London: Printed. N. Haven: Re-printed, 1785

OBSERVATIONS ON THE CASE OF THE WHIG MERCHANTS indebted to Great Britain at the Commencement of the late War. By a Citizen. *Extremely scarce.* *N. Y.*, 1785

HERRING, ELBERT. AN ORATION on the Anniv. of the Battle of Lexington, deliv. at request of the "United Whig Club." *Very scarce.* *N. Y.*, 1809

1924 PRE-REVOLUTION AND REVOLUTIONARY PAMPHLETS. *Very Valuable and Rare.* [*Five.*]

THE INTEREST OF GREAT BRITAIN considered with regard to her Colonies. 2d Ed. *London*, 1761

CONSIDERATIONS ON THE PROPRIETY OF IMPOSING TAXES in the British Colonies. *Very rare edition.*
North America: Printed by a North American. N. Y.: Reprinted by John Holt, 1765

REMARKS ON THE REVIEW OF THE CONTROVERSY BETWEEN GR. BRITAIN AND HER COLONIES, in which the Errors of its Author are Exposed, and the Claims of the Colonies Vindicated, upon the Evidence of Historical Facts and Authentic Records. To which is subjoined, A Proposal for Terminating the Present Unhappy Dispute with the Colonies; Recovering their Commerce; Reconciliating their Affections; Securing their Rights; and Establishing their Dependence on a just and permanent Basis, Humbly submitted to the Consideration of the British Legislature. By Edward Bancroft. *Very rare edition.*
London: Printed in the year 1769. *New London in N. E.: Reprinted and Sold by T. Green*, 1771

THE REVOLUTION OF AMERICA. By the Abbé Raynal. *Very scarce Ed.* *Salem*, 1782

CONSIDERATIONS ON THE MEASURES carrying on with respect to the British Colonies in N. A. *Very scarce Ed.*
London: Printed. Hartford: Reprinted and Sold by Eben Watson, near the Great Bridge, 1774

1925 PRE-REVOLUTION AND REVOLUTIONARY PAMPHLETS. *Extremely Rare lot.* [*Seven.*]

SMITH, WM. Sermon on the Present Situation of Amer. Affairs, preached in Christ Church, June 23, 1775, at the Request of the Officers of the Third Battallion of the City of Phila. and District of Southwark. *Rare.*
Phila.: Printed and Sold by James Humphreys, 1775

TOULMIN, JOSHUA. "The American War Lamented." A Sermon deliv. at Taunton, Feb. 18 and 25. *Very rare.*
London, 1776

"PEACE AND UNITY RECOMMENDED." A Sermon deliv. at Stockland, Dorset, before the Friendly Soc., May 22, 1777. By a Country Clergyman. *Exeter*

PRICE, RICHARD. Observations on the Nature of Civil Liberty, &c. 7th Ed. *London*, 1776

——— Additional Observations on the Nature of Civil Liberty, &c. 2d Ed. *London*, 1777

——— Observations on the Nature of Civil Liberty, &c. *London: Printed*, 1776. *Phila.: Reprinted and Sold by John Dunlap*, 1776

AMERICAN REVOLUTION, OBSERVATIONS ON. Published according to a resolution of Congress, by their Committee, for the Consideration of those who are desirous of comparing the Conduct of the opposed Parties and the several Consequences which have followed from it. *Excessively scarce.* *Philadelphia*, 1779

SABINE, L. Notes on Duels and Duelling. Alphabetically arranged, with a preliminary Historical Essay. *8vo, cl.* *Boston*, 1855

1927 SABRE, Lieut. G. E. Nineteen Months a Prisoner of War. His Experience in the War prisons and Stockades of Morton, Mobile, Atlanta, Libby, Belle Island, Andersonville, Macon, Charleston, and Columbia, and his Escape to the Union Line. To which is appended a List of Officers Confined at Columbia during the Winter of 1864, '65. *12mo, paper, with plate.* *New York*, 1866

1928 SACO and BIDDEFORD, Me., HISTORY OF, with Notices of other Early Settlements and of the Proprietary Governments in Maine, including the Provinces of New Somersetshire and Lygonia. By George Folsom. *8vo, boards, uncut. Frontis., extremely scarce in this condition, probably unique; beautiful copy.* *Saco*, 1830

Rev. Joseph B. Felt's copy with Autograph.

1929 SAFFELL, W. T. R. RECORDS OF THE REVOLUTIONARY WAR. Containing the Military and Financial Correspondence of Distinguished Officers: General orders of Washington, Lee, and Greene at Germantown and Valley Forge; with a list of Distinguished Prisoners of War, the Time of their Capture and Exchange. *8vo, cl.* *New York*, 1858

1930 SALEM, Mass. A DISCOURSE Pronounced at the request of the Essex Historical Society on the 18th of September, 1828, in Commemoration of the First Settlement of Salem. By Joseph Story. *Paper cov., 90 p., uncut; fine copy, scarce.* *Boston*, 1828

1931 SALEM, Mass. A Memorial of the Old and New Tabernacle, 1854–'55. By Samuel M. Worcester. *Cloth, 12mo.* *Boston*, 1855

1932 SALEM, Mass. An Account of the Newspapers and other Periodicals published in Salem, 1768 to 1856. By Gilbert L. Streeter. *8vo pamph., 32 p.* *Scarce.* *Salem*, 1856

1933 SALEM, Mass. HISTORY OF the Salem and Danvers Aqueduct. By C. M. Endicott. *8vo pamph., 16 p.* *Salem*, 1860

1934 SALEM BELLE. A Tale of 1692. *8vo, cl.* *Boston*, 1842

From a manuscript which contains all the material circumstance of a remarkable legend, founded on the witchcraft delusion of 1692.

1935 SALEM WITCHCRAFT, RECORDS OF, copied from the Original Documents. 2 volumes. *Small 4to, half mor., gilt top, uncut.* *Privately printed for W. E. Woodward, Roxbury*, 1864.

Only 200 copies. No. 163. Woodward Historical Series, No. 1.

1936 SALEM, Vt., ANNALS OF. By Pliny H. White. *8vo, 4 p., dble. cols. Scarce.* *n. d.*

1937 SALEM, WEST JERSEY, AN HISTORICAL ACCOUNT OF THE FIRST SETTLEMENT OF. By John Fenwick, Esq., Chief Proprietor of the same ; with many of the Important Events that have occurred, down to the present Generation, embracing a period of One Hundred and Fifty Years. By R. G. Johnson. *12mo, cl. Very scarce.* *Phila.*, 1839

1938 SALISBURY, Vt., HISTORY OF. By John M. Weeks, with a Memoir of the Author. *12mo, cl. ; with portrait.* *Middlebury*, 1860

1939 SAMPSON, DEBORAH. THE FEMALE REVIEW ; OR, MEMOIRS OF AN AMERICAN YOUNG LADY, whose life and character are peculiarly distinguished, being a Continental Soldier, for nearly Three Years in the late American War. During which time she performed the duties of every department into which she was called, with punctual exactness, fidelity, and honor, and preserved her chastity inviolate, by the most artful concealment of her sex. With an Appendix. By a Citizen of Mass. Dedham, 1797. Reprinted with an Introduction and Notes by John Adams Vinton. *Boston*, 1866

Large paper, 35 copies. No. 27.

1940 SAMUEL, THE FIRST AND SECOND BOOKS OF, and the First Book of Kings, translated into the Choctaw Language. *16mo, unb.* *New York*, 1852

1941 SANDERSON, JOHN P. Republican Landmarks. The Views and Opinions of American Statesmen on Foreign Immigration. Being a Collection of Statistics of Population, Pauperism, Crime, Etc. *8vo, cl.* *Phila.*, 1856

1942 SANDERSON, JOHN. BIOGRAPHY OF THE SIGNERS TO THE DECLARATION OF INDEPENDENCE. Revised and Edited by Robert T. Conrad. Illustrated with Sixty Engravings from Original Drawings of the Residences of the Signers, &c., on India paper, mounted : an Historical Account of the Residences not previously printed. Collected and prepared by William Brotherhead. *160 copies Printed. 4to, paper uncut.* *Phila.*, 1865

1943 ST. AUGUSTINE, Fla., SKETCHES OF, with a View of its History and Advantages as a Resort for Invalids. By R. K. Sewall. *Cloth. 12mo, plates.* *New York*, 1848

1944 ST. AUGUSTINE, Fla. HISTORY AND ANTIQUITIES OF the City of St. Augustine, founded 1565. Comprising some of the most interesting portions of the Early History of Florida. By Geo. R. Fairbanks. *8vo, cl. Plates and maps.* *New York*, 1858

1945 ST. PAUL, HENRY. Our Home and Foreign Policy, *12mo, paper.* *s. l.*, 1863

1946 ST. ANTHONY and MINNEAPOLIS, [Minnesota Ter.,] Sketch of. *12mo, pamphlet, illustrated*, 30 *pages. Scarce.* *St. Anthony*, 1857

1947 ST. LOUIS, Mo., SKETCH-BOOK OF. Containing a Series of Sketches of the Early Settlement, &c. By Taylor and Crooks. *12mo. cl. With plates.* *St. Louis, Mo.*, 1858

1948 SAN FRANCISCO. THE ANNALS OF, containing a summary of the History of the first discovery, settlement, progress and present condition of California, and a Complete History of all the important events connected with its great city, to which are added biographical memoirs of some prominent citizens. By Frank Soule, John H. Gihon and James Nisbet. Illustrated with one hundred and fifty engravings. *8vo, cl., scarce.* *New York*, 1855

1949 SANTAREM, VISCOUNT. RESEARCHES RESPECTING AMERICUS VESPUCIUS and His voyage. Translated by E. V. Childe. *12mo, cl., uncut.* *Boston*, 1850

1950 SARGENT, LUCIUS M. Hubert and Helen, with other Poems. *8vo, bds. uncut.* *Boston*, 1813

1951 SARGENT, L. M. DEALINGS WITH THE DEAD. By a Sexton of the Old School. 2 *vols. in sheets, folded, 8vo, front. Scarce in this style.* *Boston*, 1856

1952 SARGENT, WINTHROP. THE LOYALIST POETRY OF THE REVOLUTION. *Half rox., rough edges*, 100 *copies. No.* 49, *with the canceled leaf.* *Philadelphia*, 1857

1953 "SCANK, PHILEMON." A few Chapters to Brother Jonathan, concerning "Infallibility, etc," or, Strictures on Nathan L. Rice's "Defence of Protestantism," etc. *12mo, bds.* *Bardstown, Ky.*, 1835

1954 SCITUATE, MASS. HISTORY OF, from its settlement to 1831. By Samuel Deane. *8vo, cl., uncut, very scarce ; beautiful copy,* *Boston*, 1831

1955 SCHOOLCRAFT, HENRY R. NARRATIVE JOURNAL OF Travels through the Northwestern regions of the United States, extending from Detroit through the great chain of American Lakes, to the sources of the Mississippi River. Performed as a Member of the Expedition under Gov. Cass in 1820. Embellished with a map and eight copper engravings. *8vo, bds., uncut, beautiful copy.* *Albany*, 1821

1656 SCHOOLCRAFT, H. R. ALGIC RESEARCHES, comprising inquiries respecting the mental characteristics of the North American Indians. First Series, Indian Tales and Legends. In two volumes. *8vo, half crim. lev. mor., gt. ; bound by R. W. Smith.* *New York*, 1839

1957 SCHOOLCRAFT, HENRY R. NOTES ON THE IROQUOIS ; or, contributions to American History, Antiquities and General Ethnology. *8vo, cl., colored plates.* *Albany*, 1847

1958 SCHOOLCRAFT, HENRY R. SUMMARY NARRATIVE of an exploratory Expedition to the Sources of the Mississippi River in 1820, resumed and completed, by the Discovery of its origin in Itasca Lake in 1832. By Authority of the United States. With Appendices, comprising the Original Report on the Copper mines of Lake Superior and observations on the Geology of the Lake basins, and the summit of the Mississippi; together with all the Official reports and Scientific Papers of both Expeditions. 8*vo, cl., with maps.* *Phila.*, 1855

1959 SCOTT, WINFIELD, LIEUT-GEN. MEMOIRS OF. Written by Himself. With portraits. *Roy* 8*vo, cl., uncut.* *New York*, 1864

1960 SCOTT, B. "THE PILGRIM FATHERS, NEITHER PURITANS NOR PERSECUTORS." *Very interesting and important document.* 8*vo, uncut, fine copy, scarce.* *London*, 1866

1961 SCOTT, SIR WALTER. Demonology and Witchcraft. Illustrated with six full-page steel engravings by Geo. Cruikshank. 16*mo, cl., uncut.* *London; Wm. Tegg*, 1868

1962 SEARS, REUBEN. A Poem on the Mineral Waters of Ballston and Saratoga, with Notes illustrating the History of the Springs and adjacent Country. 16*mo, half sh., very scarce.* *Ballston Spa, N. Y.*, 1819

1963 SEARS, EDMUND H. PICTURES OF THE OLDEN TIME, as shown in the Fortunes of a Family of the Pilgrims. With a Genealogy. Private edition. 12*mo, cl.*

IN SAME VOLUME, Genealogies and Biographical Sketches of the Ancestry and Descendants of Richard Sears, the Pilgrim. *Portrait.* *Boston*, 1857

1964 SELBORNE, Eng. The Natural History of Selborne. By Gilbert White, A. M. With Additions by Sir William Jardine. 12*mo, cl.* *Phila.*, 1832

1965 SERGEANT, JOHN. A Lecture, delivered before the Mercantile Library Co. of Phila., Nov. 1, 1839. On "Mercantile Character." 8*vo*, 36 *pages, fine copy, valuable.* *Phila.*, 1839

1966 SEWELL, MRS. "Our Father's Care," A Ballad. 12*mo, paper. Confederate.* *Richmond*, 1864

1967 SHAKERS. REPORT of the Examination of the Shakers of Canterbury and Enfield, before the New Hampshire Legislature, 1848; including the testimony at length, several extracts from Shaker publications, &c. 8*vo pamph.*, 100 *p. Very interesting.* *Concord*, 1849

1968 SHAKESPEARE'S DRAMATIC WORKS, POEMS, DOUBTFUL PLAYS, and BIOGRAPHY; also, Mrs. COWDEN CLARKE'S CONCORDANCE, CHARLES KNIGHT'S ORIGINAL PICTORIAL EDITION, with the remarkably brilliant impression of the many hundred beautiful engravings on wood, of Views, Costumes, Old Buildings, Antiquities, Etc. Together, *Nine Vols., royal* 8*vo, bound from the Original Numbers, with the covers by Matthews, in gr. lev. mor., wide corners and backs, gilt top, edges uncut. Very scarce, beautiful copy.* *Charles Knight & Co., London*, 1839, *etc.*

1969 SHAKESPEARE, WILLIAM. The Official Programme; or, the Tercentenary of the Birth of. To be held at Stratford-upon-Avon, commencing Saturday, April 23, 1864. Also, an account of what is known of the Poet's Life: a Guide to the Town and Neighborhood of Stratford-upon-Avon, &c. With portrait. 8*vo.* *London*, 1864

1970 SHAPLEIGH, Me., A History of. By Rev. Amasa Loring. 8*vo*, *paper cover*, 40 *pages*. *Fine copy, scarce.* *Portland*, 1854
"What the Fathers have told us, we will not hide from the children."
Autograph of Pliny H. White of Vermont.

1971 SHARP, GRANVILLE. The Just Limitation of Slavery in the Laws of God compared with the unbounded Claims of the African Traders and British American Slaveholders. With a copious Appendix. 8*vo*, *boards, uncut.* *Scarce and early document on slavery.* *London*, 1776

1972 SHAW, Doctor JOHN, Poems by. To which is prefixed a Biographical Sketch of the Author. 12*mo*, *boards, uncut.* *Phila.*, 1810

1973 SHAW, SAMUEL, Maj., THE JOURNALS OF. The First Amer. Consul at Canton. With a Life of the Author. By Josiah Quincy. 8*vo*, *cloth.* *Portraits.* *Boston*, 1867

1974 SHEDD, W. G. T., Inaugural Discourse by, on "The Nature and Influence of the Historic Spirit." 8*vo*, *original cover*, 52 *p.* *Andover*, 1854

1975 SHERBURNE, Mass., HISTORY OF, from its Incorporation, 1674, to the end of the year 1830, including that of Framingham and Hollister, so far as they were constituent parts of the Town. By William Biglow. 8*vo pamphlet, uncut*, 80 *p.* *Very scarce, beautiful copy.* *Milford, Mass.*, 1830

1976 SHERIDAN, PHILIP H., Major-General, ILLUSTRATED LIFE, Campaigns and Public Services of. By C. W. Denison. With a full History of his Life, Battles, and Campaigns. Portrait, plates, &c. 8*vo*, *paper.* *Phila.*, 1865

1977 SHREWSBURY, Mass., A HISTORY OF THE TOWN OF. Furnished for the Worcester Magazine and Historical Journal. By Andrew H. Ward. 8*vo pamphlet, uncut*, 36 *p.* *Scarce, fine copy.* *Worcester*, 1826

1978 SHREWSBURY, Mass., HISTORY OF, from its Settlement in 1717, to 1829, with other matters relating thereto not before published, including an extensive Family Register. By Andrew H. Ward. Portrait of General Ward. *Cloth*, 8*vo.* *Scarce.* *Boston*, 1847

1979 SHOREHAM, Vt. HISTORY OF THE TOWN OF, from the date of its Charter, October 8, 1761, to the present time. By Josiah F. Goodhue. Together with a Statistical and Historical account of the County of Addison, By Samuel Swift. 8*vo*, *illustrated*, 198 *pages.* *Fine copy.* *Middlebury*, 1861

1980 SHIPTON, C. E., A SKETCH OF THE EARLY SETTLEMENT AND HISTORY OF. By Edw. Cleveland. 12*mo pamphlet*, 78 *p.* *Canada East*, 1858

1981 Sigourney, Mrs. L. H. Traits of the Aborigines of America: A Poem. *12mo, boards, uncut.* *Cambridge, Mass.*, 1822

1982 ——— The same. *Half mor.*

1983 Sigourney, L. H. Pocahontas, and other Poems. *8vo, cl. With plates.* *New York*, 1841

1984 SIMCOE, J. G., Lieut.-Col. Military Journal. A History of the Operations of the Partisan Corps, called the Queen's Rangers, during the War of the American Revolution. Illustrated by ten engraved Plans of Actions, &c. Now First Published, with a Memoir of the Author. *8vo, boards, rough edges; very scarce, fine copy.* *New York*, 1844

1985 Simms, William Gilmore. Southern Passages and Pictures. *12mo, cl.* *New York*, 1839

1986 Simms, W. Gilmore. Areytos; or, Songs of the South. *8vo, paper.* *Charleston*, 1846

1987 SIMMS, JEPHTHA R. Trappers of New York; or, a Biography of Nicholas Stoner and Nathanael Foster; together with anecdotes of other celebrated Hunters, and some account of Sir William Johnson, and his Style of living. Illustrated. 2d Edition. *8vo, half crim., lev. mor., gilt. Bound by R. W. Smith.* *Albany: Munsell*, 1851

1988 Simon, Mrs. B. A. Evangelical Review of Modern Genius; or, Truth and Error Contrasted, *12mo, bds., uncut.* *New York*, 1823

1989 SIMON, BARBARA ANNE, The Hope of Israel; presumptive evidence that the Aborigines of the Western Hemisphere are descended from the Ten Missing Tribes of Israel. *8vo, bds., uncut.* *London*, 1829

1990 SIMON, Mrs. B. E. The Ten Tribes of Israel Historically Identified with the Aborigines of the Western Hemisphere. *8vo cloth, uncut.* *London*, 1836,

1991 SIMPSON, THOMAS. Narrative of the Discoveries on the North Coast of America; effected by the Officers of the Hudson's Bay Company, during the years 1836–'39. *8vo, cloth, uncut; with map.* *London*, 1843

1992 Simpson, Sir George. An Overland Journey Round the World during the years 1841–'42. *8vo, cloth. In two parts.* *Phila., Pa.*, 1847

1993 SIMPSON, JAMES H. Journal of a Military Reconnoissance from Santa Fe, New Mexico, to the Navajo Country, made with the Troops under the command of Brevet Lieutenant-Colonel John M. Washington, Governor of New Mexico, in 1849. *8vo, cloth. Colored plates.* *Phila.*, 1852

1994 SIMSBURY, GRANBY and CANTON, Conn. From 1642 to 1845. By Noah A. Phelps. *8vo, paper.* *Hartford*, 1845

1995 SIMSBURY, Now East Granby. A History of Newgate of Connecticut, its Insurrections and Massacrees; the Imprisonment of the Tories in the Revolution, and the working of its Mines. Also, some account of the State prison at Wethersfield. By Richard H. Phelps. *Sm. 4to, sheets folded. Port.* *Albany*, 1860

1996 Skinner, Joseph B. Sketch of the Life and Character of. By H. Skinner. *8vo, sheets folded.* *N. Y.*, 1853

1997 SLAVE TRADE. Letter from, in London, to his Friend in America, on the subject of. 8*vo, unbound, very early tract on the slave question.* *New York*, 1784

1998 Smalley, John. A Sermon delivered in the College Chapel in New Haven, on Morning after Commencement. 8*vo pamph., scarce.* *New Haven*, 1787

1999 SMITH, CAPT. JOHN. The True Travels, Adventures and Observations of, in Europe, Asia, Africke and America; beginning about the yeere 1593, and continued to this present 1629. From the London edition of 1629. 2 *vols.*, 8*vo. With portraits, maps, half mor., gt. top, rough edges, now scarce. Richmond: Re-published at the Franklin Press*, 1819.

2000 SMITH, CAPT. JOHN. Advertisements for the Unexperienced Planters of New England, or anywhere; or, the Pathway to erect a Plantation. With a fac-similie of Smith's map of New England, with additions and corrections as published in 1635. *Sm.* 4*to, cl., uncut. Reprinted from the London edition of* 1616. *William Veuzie, Boston*, 1865

Only 250 copies printed.

2001 SMITH, CAPT. JOHN. A Description of New England; or, Observations and Discoveries in the North of America in the year of our Lord, 1614. With the success of six ships that went the next year, 1615. With a Fac-similie of the Original Map. *Sm.* 4*to, cl, uncut. Reprinted from the London edition of* 1631. *William Veazie, Boston*, 1865

Only 250 copies printed.

2002 SMITH, CAPTAINE JOHN. A True Relation of such occurrences and accidents of noate as hath hapned in Virginia since the first planting of that Collony, which is now resident in the South part thereof, till the last returne from thence. Virginia Series, No. 1. 4*to.* *Printed, London*, 1608.
Re-printed: Boston, 1866. *With an introduction and notes by Charles Deane. Thirty-five copies, roy.* 4*to.* *No.* 35.

2003 SMITH, M. Geographical View of the British Possessions in North America, comprising Nova Scotia, New Brunswick, New Britain, Lower and Upper Canada. With an Appendix, containing a concise History of the War in Canada to 1814. 12*mo sh., scarce.* *Baltimore*, 1814

2004 SMITH, ETHAN. View of the Hebrews, exhibiting the Destruction of Jerusalem, etc. *Bds., rough edges, scarce and interesting.* *Poultney, Vt.*, 1823

2005 Smith, Aaron. The Atrocities of the Pirates: being a faithful narrative of the unparalleled sufferings endured by the Author during his Captivity among the Pirates of the Island of Cuba, with an account of the excesses and Barbarities of those Inhuman Freebooters. 12*mo, bds., uncut.* *London*, 1824

2006 SMITH, JOSHUA TOULMIN. The Northmen in New England; or, America in the Tenth Century. 8*vo, cl., scarce, fine copy.* *Boston*, 1839

2007 Smith, James, Esq. The Winter of 1840 in St. Croix, with an Excursion to Tortola and St. Thomas. *Cl.*, 12*mo.* *New York*, 1840

2008 Smith, Seba. Powhattan ; A Metrical Romance in Seven Cantos. 8*vo, cl.* *New York*, 1841

2009 SMITH, REV. THOMAS and REV. SAMUEL DEANE. Journals of, with Biographical Notices and a Summary History of Portland. By Wm. Willis. *L.* 8*vo, bds., uncut, plates, very scarce.* *Portland*, 1849

The great fire of 1864 destroyed a great many copies of this work, and the work in this style is now *rarely* met with.

2010 SMITH, ELBERT H. Ma-ka-tai-me-she-kia-kiak, or Black Hawk and Scenes in the West. A National Poem, in six cantos. 8*vo, cl., plates.* *New York*, 1849

2011 SMITH, JOSEPH. Old Redstone ; or, Historical Sketches of Western Presbyterianism, its early Ministers, its Perilous Times and its First Records. 8*vo, cl., ports.* *Phila.*, 1854

2012 Smith, Edmond Reuel. The Araucanians ; or, notes of a tour among the Indian tribes of Southern Chili. 12*mo, cl., plates.* *New York*, 1855

2013 SMITH, T. MARSHALL. Legends of the War of Independence, and of the earlier settlements in the West. 8*vo, cl., very scarce. Slightly water stained, but can be cleansed with slight expense.* *Louisville, Ky.*, 1855

2014 "Snapping Turtle, Simon," Esq., The Paradise of Fools ; or, the wonderful adventures of Beelzebub Bubble. A Satire on somebody. By Nathan Nobody. With a Critique. 8*vo pamph.* *Baltimore*, 1841

2015 Soliloquy of a Fallen Women, or the Lament over Virtue Lost. 12*mo, cl.* *New York*, 1868

2016 Soran, Charles. Patapsco, and other poems *Cl.*, 8*vo*, *Baltimore*, 1841

2017 SOUTHAMPTON, L. I. Early History of, with Genealogies. By Geo. Rogers Howell. 8*vo, cl.* *N. Y.*, 1866

"We congratulate the good people of Southampton, who have so generously subscribed to the work, and more especially as within a short time there will not be a copy to be had at *any* price."—Pub. Pref. *Not stereotyped.*

2018 SOUTH AMERICA. Voyages and Discoveries in. The First, up the River Amazons to Quito in Peru, etc. By Christopher D'Acugua. The Second, up the River Plata, and to the Mines of Potosi. By Mons. Acarete. The Third, from Cayenne into Guiana in search of the Lake of Parmia, &c. By M. Grillet and Bechamel. Illustrated with maps, etc. *Full pol. cf., gt. By R. M. Smith. Beautiful copy.* *London*, 1698

2019 SOUTH BOSTON, Mass. History of, formerly Dorchester Neck, now Ward XII., of the City of Boston. By Thos. C. Simonds. 12*mo, cl. ; portraits.* *Boston*, 1857

2020 SOUTH CAROLINA. History of, from its First Settlement in 1670, to 1808. In two volumes. By David Ramsay, M. D. *Bds., uncut, map ; beautiful copy ; very scarce.* *Charleston*, 1809

2021 SOUTH CAROLINA. Geography of. By Wm. Gilmore Simms. 12*mo cl.* *Charleston*, 1843

2022 SOUTH CAROLINA. Manual Pereira; or, the Sovereign Rule of. With views of Southern Laws, Life and Hospitality. By F. C. Adams. 8*vo, paper, uncut.* *Washington, D. C.*, 1853

2023 SOUTH CAROLINA in the Revolutionary War: being a reply to certain misrepresentations and mistakes of recent writers in relation to the course and conduct of this State. By a Southron (Wm. Gilmore Simms). 8*vo, cl.* *Scarce.* *Charleston*, 1853

2024 SOUTH CAROLINA. Collections of the Historical Society of. Vol. I. 8*vo, cl.* *Scarce.* *Charleston, S. C.*, 1857

2025 SOUTH CAROLINA. Address of the People of, to the People of the Slaveholding States of the U. S. 8*vo, paper.* *Charleston*, 1860

2026 SOUTH CAROLINA. Correspondence between the Commissioners of, and the President of U. S. 8*vo, paper.* *Charleston*, 1861

2027 Southern States. Three Months in. By Lieut.-Col. Freemantle, Coldstream Guards. With portrait. 12*mo, cl.* *New York*, 1864

2028 SPENCER, Mass. History of, from its earliest settlement to the year 1841; including a brief sketch of Leicester to the year 1753. By James Draper. 8*vo, paper cov.; first edition; very scarce;* 159 *pages; fine copy; rough edges.* *Worcester*, 1841

2029 SPENCER, Mass. History of, from its Earliest Settlement to the Year 1860. Including a brief sketch of Leicester to the Year 1753. By James Draper. *Second Edition.* 8*vo, sheets folded; illustrated* *Worcester*, (*n. d.*)

2030 SPRAGUE, CHARLES. Writings of. Now first collected. 8*vo, cl.* *New York*, 1841

2031 STAMFORD, Conn. Historical Address, delivered at the Celebration of the Second Centennial Anniversary of the First Settlement of the Town, Dec. 22, 1841. By J. W. Alvord. 8*vo pamphlet,* 40 *p.; fine copy; very scarce.* *New York*, 1842

2032 STARK, JOHN, GENERAL. Memoir and Official Correspondence of, with notices of several other Officers of the Revolution. Also, a Biography of Capt. Phinehas Stevens and of Col. Robert Rogers, with an account of his services in America during the "Seven Years' War. By Caleb Stark. *Royal* 8*vo, hf. cr. lev. mor., gilt top, rough edges.* *Concord*, 1860

2033 STAMFORD, Conn. Soldiers' Memorial. By Rev. E B. Huntington. *Cl.* 8*vo.* *Stamford, Conn.*, 1869

2034 Stansbury, P. A Pedestrian Tour in North America to the Lakes, The Canadas, and the New England States, performed in 1821. *Illustrated.* 8*vo, bds., uncut.* *New York*, 1822

"This is too bad."

2035 Stedman, Edmund C. The Prince's Ball: a Brochure from "Vanity Fair." 12*mo, cl.* *New York*, 1860

2036 Stevens, Alex. H. Lectures on Lithotomy, December, 1837. 8*vo,* 93 *p.,* 4 *plates; fine copy.* *New York*, 1838

2037 STEVENS, HENRY. HISTORICAL NUGGETS, BIBLIOTHECA AMERICANA; or, a descriptive account of my rare collection of Books relating to America. 12*mo, cl., uncut; 2 vols.; beautiful copy.* *London*, 1862

2038 STEVENS, REV. A. W. "Temptation." Sermon preached at Cambridge, Mar. 24, 1867. *Small 8vo., orig. cov.*, 14 *pages.* *Cambridge (privately printed)*, 1867

2039 STEVENSON, JOHN HALL. CRAZY TALES. 4*to, unbound.* *London*, 1762

2040 STEPHENSON, MARMADUKE—WM. ROBINSON, AND MARY DYER. A CALL FROM DEATH TO LIFE: being an Account of the Sufferings of, in New England in the year 1659. *Sm.* 4*to, unb.* *Printed by Friends in London*, 1660. *Privately re-printed.* *Providence, R. I.*, 1865

Only 100 copies printed.

2041 STEVENSON, WILLIAM G. Thirteen Months in the Rebel Army: being a Narrative of personal Adventures in the Infantry, Ordnance, Cavalry, Courier and Hospital Services. By an Impressed New Yorker. 16*mo, cl., plate.* *New York*, 1862

2042 STREET, ALFRED B. THE BURNING OF SCHENECTADY and other Poems. 8*vo, cl.* *Albany*, 1842

2043 STREET, ALFRED B. Poems of. *Cl.*, 12*mo.* *New York*, 1845

2044 STREET, ALFRED B. FRONTENAC, a Poem. 8*vo, cl.; rough edges.* *London*, 1849

2045 STREETER, SEBASTIAN F. THE FIRST COMMANDER OF KENT ISLAND. Maryland; Historical Tract concerning Geo. Evelin. 8*vo, uncut*, 44 *p.; scarce.* *Baltimore*, 1868

2046 STYLES, EZRA. A HISTORY OF THREE OF THE JUDGES OF KING CHARLES I., Maj.-Gen. Whalley, Goffe, and Col. Dixwell: Who, at the Restoration, 1660, Fled to America; and were secreted and concealed, in Massachusetts and Connecticut, for near Thirty Years. With an account of Mr. Theophilus Whale, of Narragansett, Supposed to have been also one of the Judges. 12*mo, sh., portrait and plates; fine copy. Extremely scarce.* *Hartford*, 1794

2047 STOBO, MAJ. ROBERT. MEMOIRS OF, Of the Virginia Regiment. 12*mo, full red Turkey, gt. Bound by R. W. Smith.* *Pittsburgh*, 1854

2048 STOCKBRIDGE, Mass. PAST AND PRESENT; or, Records of an Old Mission Station. By Miss Electa Jones. 8*vo, cl.* *Springfield*, 1854

2049 STODDARD, SOLOMON. "THE DANGER OF SPEEDY DEGENERACY." A Sermon preached at the Lecture in Boston, 5th of July, 1705. 16*mo*, 28 *pages.* *Boston; Printed by B. Green*, 1705

2050 STONE, WILLIAM L. UNCAS AND MIANTONOMAH, a Historical Discourse Delivered at Norwich, Conn., on the Fourth day of July, 1842, on the occasion of the erection of a monument to the Memory of Uncas, the White Man's Friend, and First Chief of the Mohegans. 12*mo, cl.* *N. Y.*, 1848

2051 STONE, EDWIN MARTIN. THE INVASION OF CANADA IN 1775, including the Journal of Capt. Simeon Thayer, describing the Perils and Sufferings of the Army under Benedict Arnold, in its March through the Wilderness to Quebec. With Notes and Appendix. Paper. *8vo, uncut.* *Providence*, 1867

2052 STONEHAM, MASS. A BRIEF HISTORY OF THE TOWN OF, from its first settlement, to the present time, with an account of the Murder of Jacob Gould, Nov. 25, 1819. By Silas Dean. *Sm. 8vo, 36 pages, fine copy ; in original covers. Very scarce.* *Boston*, 1843

2053 STORY, JOSEPH. COMMENTARIES ON THE CONSTITUTION OF THE UNITED STATES ; with a preliminary review of the constitutional History of the Colonies and States, before the adoption of the Constitution. 3 vols. *Royal 8vo, bds., uncut.* *Boston*, 1833

2054 STRYKER, Rev. PETER. A Historical Discourse, delivered at the last service held in the Reformed Protestant Dutch Church, New York City, April 15, 1860. *12mo, cl. ; Frontispiece.* *N. Y.*, 1860

2055 STUART, CARLOS D. Ianthe and other Poems. *12mo, sh.* *New York*, 1843

2056 STURBRIDGE, Mass. AN HISTORICAL SKETCH OF, from its Settlement to the Present Time. By Joseph S. Clark. *8vo, paper cover, 48 p., fine copy ; scarce.* *Brookfield*, 1838

2057 STURBRIDGE AND SOUTHBRIDGE, Mass. HISTORICAL SKETCH OF. By George Davis. *8vo, cl. ; scarce.* *West Brookfield*, 1856

2058 SUFFOLK SURNAMES. *L. 8vo, cl. 2nd ed. enlarged.* By N. J. Bowditch. *Boston*, 1858

2059 SUMMERFIELD, JOHN. A Sermon, preached in the Ref. Dutch Church, in Nassau Street, New York, in behalf of the New York Inst. for the Deaf and Dumb ; with an Appendix, giving information relative to the Institution. *8vo, 16 p. ; scarce.* N. Y., 1822

2060 SUTCLIFF. ROBERT. Travels in some parts of North America, in the years 1804, '5 and '6. *12mo, bds., uncut ; with plate.* *Phila.*, 1812

PAMPHLETS.

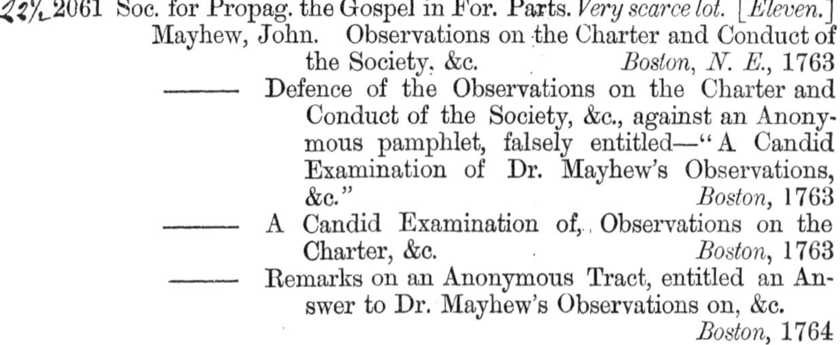

2061 Soc. for Propag. the Gospel in For. Parts. *Very scarce lot.* [*Eleven.*]

Mayhew, John. Observations on the Charter and Conduct of the Society, &c. *Boston, N. E.*, 1763

——— Defence of the Observations on the Charter and Conduct of the Society, &c., against an Anonymous pamphlet, falsely entitled—"A Candid Examination of Dr. Mayhew's Observations, &c." *Boston*, 1763

——— A Candid Examination of, Observations on the Charter, &c. *Boston*, 1763

——— Remarks on an Anonymous Tract, entitled an Answer to Dr. Mayhew's Observations on, &c. *Boston*, 1764

Frazer, Alex. Sermon—The Prophecies of the New Testament concerning the Man of Sin considered and applied, June 3, 1784, *Edinburgh.*

Apthorp, East. Missionary at Cambridge. Considerations on the Institutions and Conduct of the Society, &c. *Boston, N. E.,* 1763

Lord, John. Sermon before the Society, &c., Feb. 18, 1785. *London.*

Snodgrass, John. Sermon before the Society, &c. The Leading Doctrines of the Gospel Stated and Defended, May 29, 1794. *Edinburgh.*

Peet, Edward W. Sermon—The True Glory of the Church, on 150th Anniv. *N. Y.,* 1851

Response from the Diocese of New York, on the Third Semi-Centennial Jubilee. *N. Y.,* 1851

Reception of the Delegates from the Society, &c., by the Board of Missions. New York, October 6, 7, 10, 1854.

2063 Schools, &c. [*Eighteen.*]

School Houses, Report of the Secretary on the subject of, supplementary to his First Annual Report. *Boston,* 1838

——— High. Annual Catalogues of Teachers and Students, January, 1845. *St. Louis.*

——— Public. Appeal to the Legislatures of the United States in Relation to. By C. Brooks. *Medford,* 1869

——— ——— Some Reasons for the immediate establishment of a National System of Education for United States. By C. Brooks.

——— Sunday, the Beneficial Effects of. Address by John Henry Hobart, December 31, 1817. *N. Y.*

——— ——— Union. Sermon delivered July 29, 1830, 4th Anniversary, by C. Burroughs. *N. Y*

Sunday-school Teacher. Sermon by G. W. Doane. *Boston,* 1831

School, Mason St. Sabbath, Report of Superintendent of, 1835 and 1836.

State Sabbath Convention, Proceedings of, at Harrisburg, May 30, 31, 1844. *Phila.*

Sunday-school Union, Episcopal. Two Letters of Bishop Meade to the Board of Managers and Executive Committee of. *Baltimore,* 1847

Sabbath-school Society, Mass., brief History of. *Boston,* 1850

——— National Convention of United States, 1869. *Phila.*

——— and Publishing Society, 37th Annual Report of the Congregational, May 27, 1869.

Sacred Circle. Nos. 1 and 2. November, 1856, December, 1856. *N. Y.*

Swedenborg. Professor Bush's Reply to Mr. Emerson.

Sense Interior, in the Divine Word, with the Law of its Eduction.

Swedenborg, Emanuel, Posthumous Tracts, translated from, by J. J. G. Wilkinson. *London*, 1847

——— Sketch of Life, Character, etc., by B. F. Barret. *Cin.*, 1851

2064 Scientific Pamphlets. *Valuable.* [*Eleven.*]

Instructions at Large, for the Use of Hadley's Quadrant; wherein are contained the Principles on which that most ingeniously contrived and useful instrument is constructed; together with a Description and Use of Vernier's, erroneously called Nonne's Divisions. *London*, 1766

The Nature and Use of Hadley's Quadrant. *London*, 1766

Imison, John. A Treatise on the Mechanical Powers. 2d edition. *London*, 1794

Busby, C. A. Essay on the Propulsion of Navigable Bodies. *N. Y.*, 1818

Bull, Marcus. A Defence of the Experiments to Determine the Comparative Value of the Principle Varieties of Fuel. *London*, 1828

Herschel, John, Great Astronomical Discoveries lately made by, at the Cape of Good Hope. *N. Y.*, 1835

Scientific Tracts. Granite Rock, by Samuel Fish. *Boston*, 1836

Poyen, Charles. A Letter to Col. Wm. L. Stone, on Animal Magnetism. *Boston*, 1837

Griglietta, C. Electro-Magnetism. *Phila.*, 1838

New York Assembly Document No. 161, Botanical Report of Dr. John Torrey; Zoological Report of Dr. James E. De Kay; Mineralogical Report of Dr. Lewis C. Beck; Geological Report of Dr. Mather; Geological Report of Emmons; Geological Report of Conrad; Geological Report of Vanuxem. February 10, 1837.

Teschemacher, J. E. Address delivered at the Annual Meeting of the Boston Natural History Society, May 5, 1841

2065 Scientific. [*Eleven.*]

Lyell, Charles. Eight Lectures on Geology. *New York*, 1842

Lardner, Dionysius, Course of Lectures delivered by, on the Sun, Comets, Fixed Stars, Electricity, &c. *N. Y.*, 1842

Hare, Robert. Objections to the Theories severally of Franklin, Dufay, and Ampere. 1845

Sumner, Thomas J. Analysis of the Cotton-Plant and Seed, with suggestions as to manures, &c. *Charleston*, 1848

Senate Document No. 224. Report of Mr. Mason on behalf of the Hartford Argillo Manufacturing Company, February 8, 1849.

Report on the Lands of the East Tennessee Mining Company. *Providence*, 1850

Johnson, Walter R. Comparison of Experiments on American and Foreign Building Stones to determine their Relative Strength and Durability. *N. Haven*, 1850

Mathiot, George. The Electrotyping Operations of the United States Coast Survey, Nov. 29, 1851.

Smelting and Refining in New York. Report of the Committee, N. Y., Aug. 28, 1851.

Deck, Isaiah. Report on certain Mineral Lands Visited and Explored by him in the Island of Jamaica, May 20, 1854.

Thomson, Thomas. Records of General Science on Calico Printing, March and May, 1835.

2066 Sermons. *Very scarce.* [*Six.*]

Lambe, Charles. Sermon Preached in the Cathedral Church of Rochester, before the Hon. Mr. Justice Tracy, Judge of Assize, on March 27, 1716. The Common People's Reasons for their Disaffection to the Government Examined. Viz. : First.—The Pretender's Right. Secondly.—Their Affection for the Late Duke of Ormond. Thirdly.—The Dishonor of Changing Sides and Leaving Old Friends. *London*, 1716

Gibbons, Thomas. Sermon preached at Haberdasher's Hall, November 30, on Occasion of the Tremendous Earthquake at Lisbon, Nov. 1, 1755. *London*, 1755

Henderson, John. The Legal Temper Displayed in its Nature and Tendency. Three Sermons by. *Edinburgh*, 1779

Robinson, Robert. The Christian Doctrine of Ceremonies. Sermon Preached at Rev. Dr. Fordyce's Meeting in Monkwell St., London, December 25, 1780, to the Society *London*, 1781

Johnstone, Rev. John. Importance of a Proper Choice of Company. Sermon preached in the Tron Church of Edinburgh, May 22, 1781.

Birch, Thomas L. The Obligations upon Christians and Especially Ministers to be Exemplary in their Lives. Sermon preached before the Very Reverend the General Synod of Ulster, at Lurgan, June 26, 1793. *Belfast*, 1794

2067 Sermons. *Very scarce.* [*Ten.*]

Colman, Benjamin. Sermon—On a Day of Prayer kept by the North Church in Boston, on Tuesday, Jan. 25, 1732. *Boston*, 1732

Prince, Thomas. Sermon, to the North Church in Boston, January 25, 1731, '32. Being a Day of Prayer for the Divine Direction, in their Choice of Another Colleague Pastor to succeed the Rev. Dr. Cotton Mather. *Boston*, 1732

Ashley Jonathan. Sermon—The Great Duty of Charity. Preached at the Church in Brattle St., Boston, November 28, 1742.

Caldwell, John. Sermon preached at the French Meeting-House, in Boston, July 11, 1742.

Hooper, William. The Apostles neither Impostors nor Enthusiasts. A Sermon preached at the West Church in Boston, Sept., 1742.

Hancock, John. Discourse upon the Good Work, Pembroke, Sept. 7, 1742. *Boston*, 1743

Colman, Benjamin. The Case of Satan's Fiery Darts in Blasphemous Suggestions and Hellish Annoyances. Considered in several Sermons. *Boston*, 1744

Discourse on Government and Religion. By an Independent. *Boston*, 1750

Mayhew, Jonathan. Discourse concerning Unlimited Submission and Non-Resistance to the Higher Powers. *Boston*, 1750

Pierson, John. Sermon, Newark, N. J., May 8, 1751. Before the New York Presbytery in Session there. *Boston*, 1751

2068 Sermons. *Scarce lot.* [*Seventeen.*]

Moore, Thos L. Sermon—Trinity Ch. and St. Paul's, N.Y.. Oct. 4, 1792.

Priestly, Joseph. Sermon—Gravel Pit Meeting, in Hackney, March 30. *London*, 1794

——— Sermon—Gravel Pit Meeting, in Hackney, Feb. 28. *London*, 1794

Popkin, John S. Sermon—Attempt to Recommend Justice, Charity and Unanimity in Matters of Religion. *Newburyport*, 1805

——— Sermon, on an Afflictive Occasion. *Newburyport*, 1814

——— Sermon, on the Seasons, Time and Eternity, Dec. 12, 1813. *Newburyport*, 1814

Pierpont, John. Sermon—Newburyport, Oct. 26, 1823. *Cambridge*, 1823

——— Sermon—Hollis St. Ch., Dec. 8, 1833. *Boston*, 1834

——— Sermon—Hollis St. Ch., April 16, 1837. *Boston*, 1837

Pusey, Rev. E. B. Sermon, preached before the University, in Cathedral Church of Christ, in Oxford. *Phila.*, 1843

——— Sermon, preached before University, in Cathedral Church of Christ, in Oxford, Fourth Sunday after Easter. *N. Y.*, 1843

Sessions, Alexander J. Sermon—Haverhill, Dec. 17, 1837. *Boston*, 1838

Spring, Gardiner. Something Must be Done: a New-Year's Sermon. *Newburyport*, 1816

——— Dissertation on Native Depravity. *N. Y.*, 1833

Smalley, John. Two Discourses on John VI. 44. *Very scarce.* *Hartford*, 1769

——— Sermon—Wallingford—with special reference to the Murryan Controversy. *Hartford*, 1785

——— Sermon—Wallingford—with a view to the Universalists. *Hartford*, 1786

2069 Sermons. [*Thirteen.*]

Mason, Erskine. The Subject and Spirit of the Ministry. Sermon, Oct. 16, 1838. *N. Y.*, 1838

Hooker, Edward W. Address—Theological Institute, East Windsor Hill, Conn.. Aug. 5, 1839. *Hartford*, 1839

Upfold, George. Discourse—Trinity Church, May 14, 1841. *Pittsburgh*, 1841

Farley, Frederick A. Sermon—Sec. Unitarian Church, Brooklyn, Aug. 8 1841.

Lafon, Rev. Thomas. The Great Obstruction to Conversion of Souls at Home and Abroad. *N. Y.*, 1843

Manning, Henry E. Penitents and Saints. Sermon in behalf of Magdalen Hospital at St. George-in-the-Fields, May 8, 1844. *London*, 1844

Blain, Rev. Wilson. Psalms of David; every Way suitable to Christian Worship. Discourse. *Rossville*, 1844

Paddock, Rev. S. B. Sermon, preached in Christ Church, Norwich, Sept. 8, 1844: Resignation of Rectorship. *Norwich*, 1844

Gannett, Ezra S. Peace not War—Sermon, Federal St. Meeting-House. *Boston*, 1845

Dana, Daniel. Discourse—Fiftieth Anniv. of Ordination, Nov. 19, 1844. *Newburyport*, 1845

Bedell, Rev. G. T. The Present Profit of Godliness. Sermon. Church of the Ascension. *N. Y.*, 1852

Hopper, Rev. Edward. Sermon—Presb. Ch., Sag Harbor. *N. Y.*, 1855

Muhlenberg, William A. Sermon—Re-opening of the Church of Augustus, Trappe, Montgomery Co., Pa., Sept. 5, 1860. *N. Y.*, 1861

2070 Sermons. [*Eighteen.*]

Bancroft, Aaron. The Nature and Worth of Christian Liberty. Sermon, Sec. Cong. Ch. *Worcester*, 1816

——— Discourse—Duties enjoined by the Fourth Commandment. *Worcester*, 1817

——— Discourse on Conversion. *Worcester*, 1818

——— Sermon—Keene, Aug. 15, 1819. *Worcester*, 1821

——— Discourse—Sec. Congre. Soc. *Worcester*, 1827

Bronson A. The Errors of "Concord" Refuted, and the Truth of God Vindicated, on the subject of Christian Baptism. Address. *Providence*, 1834

——— Lecture on subject of Bible Translations. *Fall River*, 1836

Belknap, Jeremy. Sermon: Jesus Christ the only Foundation. *Boston*, 1792

——— Two Sermons on the Institution and Observation of the Sabbath. *Boston*, 1801

Baldwin, Thomas. The Dangerous Influence of Vicious Example. Sermon. *Boston*, 1809

——— Discourse: The Supreme Deity of Christ, illustrated. *Boston*, 1812

Bacon, Leonard. Sermon: Duties connected with the Present Commercial Distress. *New Haven*, 1837
——— Sermon: Foreign Evangelical Soc. *New Haven*, 1845
Chauncy, Charles. Sermon: Enthusiasm described and cautioned against. *Boston*, 1742
——— Sermon: Various Gifts of Ministers. *Boston*, 1742
Channing, Wm. E. Sermon, Boston, Sept. 18, 1814.
——— Sermon, Easter Sunday, 1834. *Boston*, 1835
——— Discourse: Anniv. Benev. Fraternity of Churches. *Boston*, 1835

2071 Sermons. [*Eighteen.*]

Channing, Wm. E. Sermon on War, Jan. 25. *Boston*, 1835
Dewey, Orville. Two Discourses on Nature and Province of Natural, Revealed and Experimental Religion. *N. Y.*, 1841
——— Sermon: The Character and Claims of Seafaring Men. *N. Y.*, 1845
Frothingham, N. L. Plea against Religious Controversy. *Boston*, 1829
——— Sermon, First Church, Feb. 21. *Boston*, 1836
——— Sermon: Duties of Hard Times. *Boston*, 1837
——— Sermon, Brattle Sq. Ch., June 17. *Boston*, 1838
Griffin, Edward D. Farewell Sermon, May 28, 1809, at Newark, N. J. *Newburyport*, 1809
——— Sermon: Living to God. June 16. *N. Y.* 1816
Johnson, Wm. L. Discourse on Nature, Use and Lawfulness of Oaths. *Trenton*, 1824
Johnson, John B. Farewell Sermon, Sept. 26, North Dutch Church. *Albany*, 1802
Knox, John. Two Discourses: Parental Responsibility and Parental Solicitude. *N. Y.*, 1834
——— Discourse: The Church Glorious. *N. Y.*, 1839
Lathrop, Joseph. Two Discourses: Christ's Warning to the Churches to Beware of False Prophets who come as Wolves in Sheep's Clothing, and the Marks by which they are known. 3rd Ed. *Springfield*, 1792
——— Sermons on the Mode and Subjects of Christian Baptism. *Boston*, 1793
——— Sermon, Second Church in Boston, May 10, 1812.
——— Two Sermons, First Parish, W. Springfield, Aug. 25. *Springfield*, 1816
Moore, Benjamin. Doctrine of Regeneration asserted and explained. *N. Y.*, 1791

2072 Sermons. [*Fourteen.*]

Sellon, Rev. J. Series of Sermons on the Doctrine of Everlasting Punishment. *Canandaigu*, 1828
Brown, Solyman. Sermons illustrating the Method of Interpreting the Sacred Scriptures in their Spiritual Sense. *N. Y.*, 1829

Sprague, Wm. B. Causes of an Unsuccessful Ministry. Two Sermons. *Albany*, 1829

Barnes, Albert. Discourse on Sovereignty of God. Morristown, June 21, 1829.

Bush, George. Attempted Explication of the Vision of the Liv ing Creatures and Wheels contained in the First and Tenth Chap. of Ezekiel. *Cincinnati*, 1829

Parkman, Francis. Sermon, occas. by Recent Revolutions in France. *Boston*, 1830

Gill, John. Infant Baptism a Part and Pillar of Popery ; being a Vindication of a paragraph in a preface to a reply to Mr. Clarke's defence on Infant Baptism. *N. Y.*, 1831

Truair, John. Two Discourses. *Northampton*, 1831

Toplady, Augustus M. Free-will and Merit fairly examined. *N. Y.*, 1832

Grosvenor, Cyrus P. Discourse. Salem, Jan. 13, 1833.

Weight, George. First and Last Sermons deliv. in Surrey Chapel by Rev. Rowland Hill, to which is added the History of Surrey Chapel, by *London*, 1833

Clarke, Joseph. Sorrows and Advantages of Affliction. Sermon. *N. Y.*, 1833

Putnam, George. Sermon, preached March 6, 1836. *Boston*, 1836

Kellogg, Rev. E. B. Sermon on Forms of Prayer. *N. Y.*, 1838

2073 Sermons. [*Fourteen.*]

The Unity of God. Sermon deliv. in America, Sept., 1816 (3d Ed.) *N. Y.*, 1820

Wilson, James R. Sermon—The Subjection of Kings and Nations to Messiah. Sept. 6, 1819. *N. Y.*, 1820

Bascom, Ezekiel L. Farewell Disc. deliv. at Phillipston, Dec. 31, 1820. *Worcester*, 1821

Powers, Rev. H. P. The Angel's Salutation to the Shepherds. Christmas Sermon. *Newark*, 1822

Grear, Ezekiel G. Sermon for Benefit of the Greeks. Ithaca, Jan. 18, 1824.

Fitz, Henry. The Non-personality, Origin and End of that Old Serpent called the Devil and Satan, which deceiveth the whole World. Discourse. N. Y., March 13, 1825.

Maffitt, John M. Prayers and Sermons. *Phila.*, 1825

Cuming, Rev. F. H. Sermon—The Church Perfect and Entire. *Canandaigua*, 1825

Potts, John. Prayer and Sermon. *Phila.*, 1825

Woods, Leonard. Sermon on the Nature and Influence of Faith. *Andover*, 1826

Wenham, Rev. John. Sermon preached before the Bishop of Quebec and Clergy of Upper Canada, Aug. 30, 1826. *Brockville*, 1826

Wardlaw, Ralph. Two Sermons, occasioned by a passage in Inaugural Disc. of Henry Brougham. *N. Y.*, 1826

Christmas, Joseph S. Discourse on the Nature of that Inability which prevents sinners from embracing the Gospel. *Montreal*, 1827

Smith, Rev. James. Sermon deliv. in Light St. Ch., Baltimore, June 12, 1825. *Phila.*, 1827

2074 Sermons. [*Fifteen.*]

Gardiner, John S. J. Sermon—Divinity of Jesus Christ, Trinity Church, Dec. 25, 1810. *Boston*, 1811

Miller, Samuel. Sermon on Burning of Theatre in Richmond, Jan. 19, 1812. *N. Y.*, 1812

Boston, Thomas. Sermon—The Everlasting Espousals. *Troy*, 1812

Osgood, David. Solemn Protest against the late Declaration of War. *Exeter*, 1812

Morss, James. Sermon preached at St. Paul's Church, Newburyport, Dec. 25, 1812. *Exeter*, 1813

Bradford, John M. Sermon on the Present Struggle of the Dutch for Emancipation. Albany, Feb. 18, 1814.

Stanford, John. Discourse—The Utility of Learning, to a Young Minister. *N. Y.*, 1814

Cary, Samuel. Ignorance of the True meaning of the Scriptures, and the Causes of it. *Boston*, 1814

Judson, Adoniram. Sermon preached in the Lal Bazar Chapel, Calcutta, Sept. 27, 1812. *Boston*, 1817

Norton, Andrews. Discourse on Religious Education. *Boston*, 1818

Merwin, Rev. Samuel. Sermon on Opening the Methodist Ch. in John St., N. Y., Jan. 4, 1818.

Bangs, Rev. Nathan. Sermon on Opening Methodist Ch. in John St., N. Y., Jan. 4, 1818.

Capen, Lemuel. Farewell Address, Sterling, Jan. 21, 1819. *Boston*, 1819

Sumner, Joseph. Sermon, Semi-Centen. Anniv. of his Induction into the Pastoral Office, deliv. at Shrewsbury, June 23, 1812. *Worcester*, 1819

Milnor, Rev. James. Sermon—The Widow and her Mites. *N. Y.*, 1819

2075 Sermons. [*Sixteen.*]

Huntington, William. Advocates for Devils Refuted and their Hope for the Damned Demolished. *Phila.*, 1796

Lewis, Isaac. Sermon preached at Stamford, Oct. 11, 1796, before the Consociation of the Western District in Fairfield Co. *N. Haven*, 1796

Hall, Robert. Modern Infidelity Considered with respect to its Influence on Society. Sermon. *Charlestown*, 1801

Mason, John M. Living Faith. Sermon. *N. Y.*, 1802

M'Leod, Alexander. Messiah Governor of the Nations of the Earth. Discourse. *N. Y.*, 1803

Kippis, Andrew. Sermon on the Lord's Supper. *Newburyport*, 1803

Ware, Henry. Sermon deliv. at Scituate, Oct. 31, 1804. *Boston*, 1804

Cooley, Timothy M. Sermon, Granville, May 1, 1805. *Hartford*, 1805

Nott, Eliphalet. Sermon preached before General Assembly of Presb. Church, May 19, 1806. *Phila.*, 1806

Romeyn, John B. Introd. Sermon deliv. in New Presb. Ch., Nov. 13, 1808. *N. Y.*, 1808

Carnahan, James. Christianity Defended against the Cavils of Infidels and the Weakness of Enthusiasts. Sermon. May 15, 1808. *Utica*, 1808

Austin, Samuel. Sermon on Incomparable Excellency of Religion as the Life of Man. *Catskill*, 1808

Clowes, Rev. J. Sermon on the Sacred Doctrine of the Divine Trinity. *Manchester*, 1809

Neill, Rev. Wm. Farewell Sermon to Congre. in Cooperstown, Sept. 3, 1809.

Smith, Samuel S. Discourse on Resurrection of the Body. *Washington*, 1809

Paley, Wm. Sermon, July 15, 1777, at Visitation of Rt. Rev. Edmund, Lord Bishop of Carlisle. *Cambridge*, 1809

2076 Sermons. *Scarce and valuable.* [*Fourteen.*]

Inglis, Charles. Essay on Infant Baptism, in which the Right of Infants to Sacrament of Baptism is proved from Scripture. *N. Y.*, 1768

Hooker, Nathanael. Six Discourses on different subjects. *Hartford*, 1771

Casy, Thomas. Sermons on Importance of Salvation, &c. *Boston*, 1773

Tappan, David. The character and best exercises of unregenerate sinners set in a Scriptural light. *Newburyport*, 1782

Gordon, William. The Doctrine of Final Universal Salvation examined, and shewn to be Unscriptural, in Answer to a Pamphlet entitled, Salvation for all Men, illustrated and vindicated as a Scripture Doctrine. *Boston*, 1783

Edwards, Jonathan. The Necessity of Atonement. Three Sermons. *N. Haven*, 1785

Murray, John. (The Pioneer of Universalism in this country.) The Origin of Evil. Sermon. *Newburyport*, May 23, 1784

Tucker, John. Sermon deliv. at Newburyport, Aug. 14, 1788.

Reese, Thomas. Essay on the Influence of Religion in Civil Society. *Scarce.* *Charleston*, 1788

Rice, David. Essay on Baptism. *Baltimore*, 1789

Linn, William. Sermon. Character of Simon the Sorcerer. *N. Y.*, 1793

Davies, Samuel. The Method of Salvation through Jesus Christ. Sermon. *Providence*, 1793

Dwight, T. Discourse on the Genuineness and Authenticity of New Testament. *N. Y.*, 1794

Maxcy, Jonathan. Sermon. Aug. 9, 1795. *Providence*

2077 Sermons. [*Twenty.*]

Sprague, W. B. Sermon—"The Tribute of a Mourning Husband." July 1, 1821. *N. Y.*

Spring, Gardiner. Sermon, "Something must be done," deliv. Dec. 31, 1815, by. *N. Y.*, 1821
——— Appeal to the Citizens of New York in behalf of the Christian Sabbath. *N. Y.*, 1823
——— Sermon, "The Discriminating Preacher," deliv. Dec. 1, 1824, at installation of C. Wilcox. *Hartford*
——— Sermon, "The Doctrine of Election," and a reply to the same by Henry Fitz. *N. Y.*, 1826
——— Sermon preached Aug. 3, 1832. *N. Y.*, 1832
——— "Hints to Parents." Sermon. *N. Y.*, 1833
——— Dissertation on Native Depravity. *N. Y.*, 1833
——— " " the Rule of Faith. *N. Y.*, 1844
Smith, William. Sermon—A Guide and Encouragement to Charity. April 23, 1790.
Smith, J. A. Disc. "on Sense of Touch." *N. Y.*, 1837
Smyth, T. Two Disc. on the Great Fire in Charleston. 1838
Smith, James. Man with his Ability through the Atonement, &c. 1841
Smith, C. B. M. Address deliv. before Wirt Institute, Jan. 4, 1841. *Pittsburgh*
Smith, Drs., and Anthon. A Statement of Facts in relation to the recent ordination in N. Y. 1843
Smith, Sidney. Letters on American Debt. *N. Y.*, 1844
Smith, Whitefoord. Sermon, "God the Refuge of His People," deliv. before the General Assembly of S. C., Dec. 6, 1850.
Smith, E. D. Disc. "Our Country and its Constitution and Laws." Dec. 12, 1850. *New York*
Smith, Truman, of Conn.; Speech of. Feb. 17, 1853.
Smith, Mary Ann; The Abduction of, by the Roman Catholics, and Imprisonment in a Nunnery. By Rev. H. Mattison. *Jersey City*, 1868

℣ 2078 Sermons. [*Twenty-seven.*]

Sprague, Wm. B. Sermon at interment of Mrs. Elizabeth Lathrop, May 15, 1821. *Springfield.*
——— Sermon, "The Danger of Evil Company," March 20, 1823.
——— Two Sermons. Second Pres. Con. in Albany, Aug. 30, 1829.
Sprague, Mary L., Tribute to the memory of. *Albany*, 1837
Sprague, Wm. B. Sermon on Death of his wife, March 4, 1838. *Albany.*
——— Address before Young Men's Assoc. for Mutual Improvement. *Albany*, 1838
——— Disc. Commem. of Rev. Samuel Miller. *Albany*, 1850
Scott, I. War Inconsistent with Doctrine and Example of Jesus Christ. *Phila.*, 1804
Scott, Job, Letter to Luke Howard in which the Character of, in Vindicated, 1826.
Scott, Sir Walter, Life of, by Robert Chambers. (First Amer. Ed.) N. Y., 1832

Scott, Gen. Winfield, Life of.
Saurin, Rev. James. Sermon on Repentance of the Unchaste Woman. *Boston*, 1823
Sectarianism, Spirit of, with observations on Duty and Means of Destroying Prejudice. *London*, 1833
So. Carolina, Internal Improvement of, by Robert Mills. *Columbia*, 1822
——— Oration on Absolute Necessity of Union, and the Folly and Madness of Disunion, by Thomas S. Grimke. *Charleston*, 1829
——— Report of Com., and Progress of Agricultural Survey, by Edmund Ruffin. *Very scarce.* *Columbia*, 1843
Southgate, Rev. Horatio. Letter from Missionaries at Constantinople. *Boston*, 1844
——— Letter to Mem. of Prot. Epis. Church from. N. Y., 1844
Stone, Wm. L. Maria Monk and the Nunnery of Hotel Dieu. N. Y., 1836
Stone, John S. Sermon before N. Y. Auxil. to Prot. Epis. Soc. N. Y., 1849
Shakspeare, The Home of, by W. F. Fairholt. N. Y., 1848
——— Stratford as Connected with. *Stratford-upon-Avon*, 1851
Strong, Nathan. Sermon on Fast. *Hartford*, 1812
Strong, Titus. " at the Institution of Rev. James B. Howe. *Windsor*, 1819
Strong, Paschal N. Sermon after the Cessation of Yellow Fever. N. Y., 1822
Stansbury, A. O. Considerations on Lawfulness of Lotteries. N. Y., 1813

2079 Sermons. *Scarce.* [*Seventeen.*]

Searle, Rev. Roger. Discourse on Anniv. of St. John the Evangelist. *Hartford*, 1814
Searle, John. Funeral Sermon on Death of Rev. Jno. Parsons, July 19, 1776. *Newburyport*, 1778
Strong, Gov. Answer to the Questions: Why are you a Federalist? and Why shall you Vote for Gov. Strong? 1805
Strong, Paschal N. Sermon after Cessation of Yellow Fever. N. Y., 1823
Strong, Nathan. Sermon at Funeral of Rev. James Cogswell. *Hartford*, 1807
Strong, Wm. Sermon at Interment of Mrs. Lydia Ellsworth. *Hartford*, 1806
Strong, Nathan. " at Consecra. of New Brick Ch. in Hartford. *Hartford*, 1808
Sprague, Wm. B. " after Intelligence of Death of Hon. Jno. Cilley, who was shot in a duel with Hon. Wm. J. Graves. *Albany*, 1838
Sargent, Gov., Papers in relation to Official Conduct of. *Boston*, 1801

Sargent, John O. Lecture on Late Improvements in Steam Navigation, and Arts of Naval Warfare. *N. Y.*, 1844

Smith, Samuel S. Discourse on Subjects of National Gratitude. *Phila.*, 1795

——— Discourse on Nature and Reasonableness of Fasting. *Phila.*, 1795

——— Discourse on Nature, the Proper Subjects, and the Benefits of Baptism. *Phila.*, 1808

Smalley, John. Second Sermon at Wallingford, with a View to the Universalists. *Hartford*, 1786

——— Sermon at Wallingford, with Special Reference to the Murrean Controversy. *Hartford*, 1785

——— Sermon deliv. in College Chapel. *New Haven*, 1787

Smith, John. Narrative of Shipwreck and Sufferings of Crew and Passengers of English Brig "Neptune." *N. Y.*, 1830

2080 Sermons. [*Twenty-two.*]

Smith, Jonathan B. Oration deliv. before Assoc. of Democratic Young Men in Phila., March 4, 1813.

Smyth, Rev. Thomas. The Theatre, a School of Religion, Manners and Morals. Two Disc. *Charleston*, 1838

——— Two Disc. on occasion of Great Fire in Charleston, 1838.

Stiles, Ezra. Discourse at Instal. of Rev. Samuel Hopkins. *Scarce.* *Newport*, 1770

Starkweather, John. Object and Importance of a Church Covenant. Sermon by. *Providence*, 1833

Sharp, Daniel. Disc. at Inter. of Rev. Stephen Gano. *Boston*, 1828

Seabury, Samuel. Disc. before Triennial Conven. of Prot. Epis. Ch. *N. Y.*, 1792

Stockton, Capt., Address of, to People of New Jersey. *Trenton*, 1840

Sullivan, J. L. Descrip. of Sub-Marine Aqueduct. *N. Y.*, 1830

Sullivan, Wm. Oration, July 4, 1803. *Boston*, 1803

——— Address to Members of Bar of Suffolk. *Boston*, 1825

Sullivan, James. Observations on the Govt. of U. S. A. *Boston*, 1791

Sullivan, J. L. Exposition of Errors in Calculation of Board of Water Commissioners. *N. Y.*, 1835

Stanford, John. Directory to Holy Scriptures.

Schools. County Lyceums designed to promote Manual Labor Schools. *Savannah*, 1833

Sunday School Union Soc. Eleventh Annual Report. *N. Y.*, 1827

Schools, Common. Remarks on the School Law. *Phila.*, 1826

Serious Facts. Voice of Warning to Religious Republicans. 1800

Society for Propogation of Gospel in Foreign Parts. Sermon at Anniv. Meeting, Feb. 20, 1767, by John, Lord Bp. of Landaff. *N. Y.*, 1768

State Substitute for a General Bankrupt Law, etc. *N. Y.*, 1840

Sketch of Geographical Route of a Great Railway. *N. Y.*, 1830

Spurzheim, Gaspar, Funeral Oration at Burial of, by Charles Follen. *Boston*, 1832

2081 Historical. *Valuable.* [*Nine.*]

Salem, Mass. Dedication of Plummer Hall, Mr. Hoppin's Address, and Judge White's Memoir of Plummer Family, Oct. 6, 1857,

Salem, Vermont, Annals of, by Pliny H. White.

Schoharie Cave, Account of. *N. Y.*, 1853

Schenectady. Semi-Centen. Discourse on Union College, by A. Potter, 1854.

Saco. Centennial Anniv. of First Church, Address by Edward S. Dwight, 1862. 25

South Carolina Society for Advancement of Learning, Anniversary Oration, by Hon. Wm. Harper, Dec. 9, 1835. *Columbia*, 1836

—— Literary and Philosophical Soc., Address of. *Charleston*, 1834

—— Exhortation to the Inhabitants of, by Sophia Hume. *Very scarce.* *Bristol*, 1750

Stamford, Conn. Hist. Address at Second Centen. Anniv., by Rev. J. W. Alvord. *N. Y.*, 1842

2082 St. Nicholas Society. *Scarce.* [*Four.*]

Memorial Dis. on the Life, etc., of Gen. Jer. Johnson, 1854.

Anniv. Disc., The Pioneers of New York, by C. F. Hoffman, 1847. 22½

—— The causes of the prosperity of N. Y., by Wm. Betts, Dec. 3, 1850. 1851

N. Y. as it was during latter part of the last Century, W. A. Duer, 1849.

2083 Miscellaneous. [*Twenty-one.*]

Smith, Albert. Inaugural Address at Annual Commencement of Marshall College. *Chambersburg*, 1838

Smith, Dr. John A., Exposition of Conduct and Character of, by James R. Manley. *N. Y.*, 1841

Smith, Nathan, Eulogium on, by J. Knight. *New Haven*, 1829 10

Smith, Samuel B., Renunciation of Popery, by. *Phila.*, 1833

Smyth, Rev. Thomas. Reflections on Loss of Steamboat "Home." *Charleston*, 1837

—— Oration on Forty-eighth Anniv. of the Orphan House. *Charleston*, 1837

Sprague, Charles. Oration, July 4, 1825. *Boston*, 1825

Sprague, Wm. B. Sermon on Death of Rev. Edward D. Allen. *Albany*, 1843

Spring, Samuel. Discourse, Feb. 6, 1785. *Newburyport*, 1785

Stanford, John. Discourse on Death of Mrs. Sarah Hoffman. *N. Y.*, 1821

——— Discourse on "Urim and Thummim," deliv. before the Hiram Lodge, No. 72. *N. Y.*, 1820

——— Discourse on Death of Elijah Hunter. *N. Y.*, 1817

——— Discourse on Death of George Vanderpool. *N. Y.*, 1821

——— Discourse deliv. to Lunatics in the Asylum. *N. Y.*, 1821

——— Discourse deliv. at Funeral of Mrs. Rachel Lewis. *N. Y.*, 1820

——— Discourse deliv. at Funeral of Mrs. Rachel Roome. *N. Y.*, 1820

Stebbins, Rufus P. Address on Subject of Peace, on Anniv. of Bowdoin St. Young Men's Peace Soc., by. *Boston*, 1836

Sterling, Hon. Micah, Letter to, on Expediency of adopting a Uniform System of Bankruptcy in U. S. *N. Y*, 1822

Stetson, Caleb. Discourse on Duty of Sustaining the Laws. *Boston*, 1834

Stone, William L. Letter to Dr. A. Brigham on Animal Magnetism. *N. Y.*, 1837

Story, Joseph. Disc. before Phi Beta Kappa Soc. at Anniv. Celeb. *Boston*, 1826

2084 Miscellaneous. [*Twenty-three.*]

Sampson, I. P. C. Valedictory deliv. at the Forum. *N. Y.*, 1817

Scholefield, Rev. James. Second Letter to Rt. Hon. Earl of Liverpool, in Reply to that from Rev. H. H. Norris, by. *N. Y.*, 1823

Scott, Sir Walter, Life of, by Robert Chambers. N. Y., 1832

Scott, Rev. W. A. Disc. on Duty of Praying for our Rulers. *New Orleans*, 1843

Sheriff's Office, Roberts' Second Ed. of Secret "Customs" and Revenue of the. *Phila.*, 1820

Sheys, James B., Oration at Paterson, July 4, 1825, by. *Newark*, 1826

Sidney, Algernon. Address to People of N. England. *Albany*, 1809

Seybert, Adam. Oration, May 19, 1809. *Phila.*, 1809

Sullivan, Wm. Discourse before Boston Mercantile Assoc. *Boston*, 1832

Stevens, John H., Duty of Union in a Just War, Discourse by. *N. Y.*, 1813

Sense, Plain, or National Industry. Addr. to People of U. S. *N. Y.*, 1820

Stephens' Incidents of Travel in Egypt, Arabia Petræa and Holy Land, Remarks on. *Scarce.* *Cambridge*, 1839

Sandwich Islands, Narrative of Five Youths from. *N. Y.*, 1816

Southern Excitement against the American System. *Poughkeepsie*, 1829

Shakers, Declar. of the Soc. of People commonly called. *Albany*, 1815

Sega, James, Essay on Practice of Duelling, by. *Phila.*, 1830

Southard, Samuel L. Address before American Whig and Cliosophic Soc. of N. J. College, Sept. 26, 1837. *Princeton*, 1837

Sinclair, Hannah. Letter on Principles of Christian Faith. *Phila.*, 1819

Sewall, Henry D. Reply to Rev. Henry J. Feltus. N. Y., 1820

Spence, William. Britain Indepen. of Commerce. *Phila.*, 1808

Schroeder, Rev. Dr., Brief Statement touching Last Publication of, Entitled, Doc. Concern. Recent Measures of Vestry of Trinity Church. N. Y., 1839

Stranger. A Literary Paper. *Albany*, 1814

Slavery, Remarks on, Occas. by attempts made to Circulate Improper Publications in South. States. *Phila.*, 1835

2085 Miscellaneous. [*Nineteen.*]

Sweetzer, Wm. Dissertation on Intemperance by. *Boston*, 1829

Sprague, Charles. Ode, at Centen. Celebra. of Settle. of Boston, by. *Boston*, 1830

Sabine, James. Sermon before Assoc. Congre. Ministers of Salem and Vicinity. *Charlestown*, 1819

Savage, Edward. Tribute to Memory of. Disc., by Rev. Thomas C. Reed. *Schenectady*, 1840

Sanderson, John. Remarks on Plan for College. *Phila.*, 1826

South America. Strictures on a Voyage to. *Baltimore*, 1820

Stuart, M. Sermon at dedication of Church in Hanover St., Boston. *Andover*, 1826

Stephens, Rev. Daniel. The Character of a Faithful and Evangelical Ministry. Sermon, by. *Baltimore*, 1818

Sparks, Jared. Sermon at Ordi. of, by Wm. E. Channing. *Baltimore*, 1819

Stone, Rev. John S. Address deliv. before Boston Childrens' Friend Soc., at Fourth Annual Meeting. *Boston*, 1838

Spring, Samuel. Sermon at Ordi. of Rev. Benjamin Bell, by. *Newburyport*, 1784

Staughton, Rev. Wm. Discourse, occasioned by death of three young persons by drowning. *Phila.*, 1797

Shamrock Friendly Assoc. Oration by Stephen P. Lemoine. *N. Y.*, 1819

Sandford, John. Death of Euphemia M——. Letter by. *Hammersmith*, 1784

Stebbins, Samuel. Policy of the Devil to hinder the success of the Gospel. Sermon, by. *Hartford*, 1806

Sunday School Jubilee. Address at Celebration of. Address by Thomas S. Grimke. *Phila.*, 1832

Sprague, Wm. B. Sermon at Annual Election. *Boston*, 1825

Soule, Joshua. Discourse, Jan. 4, 1818, by. *N. Y.*, 1818

Stiles, Ezra. Funeral Sermon at Inter. of Mr. Chauncey Whittelsey. *N. Haven*, 1787

6 2086 Miscellaneous. *Valuable.* [*Sixteen.*]

Silliman, Benjamin. Address, on Life and Services of, by Theodore D. Woolsey. *N. Haven*, 1865

Saltonstall, Leverett. Disc., on Life and Char. of, by John Brazer. *Scarce.* *Salem*, 1845

Sukey. A Poem. *Very scarce.* *Baltimore*, 1821

Smith, Horace W. Nuts for Future Historians to Crack. *Phila.*, 1856

Stuart, Isaac W. Inaugural Discourse in So. Carolina. *Columbia*, 1836

"Sparrow-Hawk." Loss of the, in 1826. "Ye Ancient Wrecke." 2d ed. *Boston*, 1865

"Sparrow-Hawk." Loss of the, in 1826. "Ye Ancient Wrecke." *Scarce.* *Boston*, 1865

Schuyler, Gen. Philip. Remarks on Character of, by George S. Schuyler. *N. Y.*, 1867

Stephens, Mrs. Ellen. The Cabin Boy Wife, Adventures of. *N. Y.*, 1840

Spiritualism shown as it is. *Boston*, 1859

Spring, Gardiner. Dissertation on Native Depravity. *N. Y.*, 1833

Secretary of State. Letters from, to Messrs. Monroe and Pinckney. Part III. *Wash.*, 1808

Stevens, Thaddeus. Speech of, in favor of a bill to establish a School of Arts. *Harrisburg*, 1838

Suworow. Life of. *London.*

Stearne, Samuel. The Mystery of Animal Magnetism revealed to the World. *London*, 1791

Spring, Gardiner. Discourse on Death of the Pres. *New York*, 1814

7 2087 Miscellaneous. [*Sixteen.*]

Stansbury, Arthur J. Sermon on Fast. *Goshen, N. Y.*, 1813

Stevens, John L. Memoir of Eventful Expe. in Central America. *N. Y.*, 1850

Stevens, Byron, *vs.* Rutland and Burlington Rail R. Co. Opinion of Chan. *Burlington*, 1851

Stewart, David. Anniv. Oration before Philokusean Soc. *Baltimore*, 1822

Stuart, M. Scriptural View of Wine Question. Letter to Rev. Dr. Nott. *N. Y.*, 1848

Sullivan, James. Observations upon the Government of the U. S. of Amer. *Boston*, 1791

Smithsonian Institution. Account of, by Wm. J. Rees. *Wash.*, 1857

Smooth Ephraim. The Child of Nature A Poem. *London*, 1825

Southey, Rob't. Wat Tyler, a dramatic Poem in three acts. *London.*

Schroeder, J. F. Disc., Nov. 24, 1825. *N. Y.*

Slape, Albert H. Stultorum. Poem. *Carlisle, Pa.*, 1864

Wayland, Francis. Address, Baptist Meeting House, Baldwin Place, Boston, June 29, 1834.

Wayland, Francis. Discourse, Opening of the Providence Athenæum, July 11, 1838.

Wayland, Francis. Discourse, First Baptist Church, May 22, 2d ed. *Providence*, 1842

Wayland, Francis. Discourse, First Baptist Church, Providence, May 22, 1842. *Boston*, 1842

Wayland, Francis. Discourse, the claims of whalemen on Christian Benevolence. *New Bedford*, 1843

2088 Miscellaneous. *Valuable lot.* [*Twenty-five.*]

Secretary of the Navy. Letter from, account of capture of British Sloop "Epervier," by U. S. Sl. "Peacock." *Washington*, 1814

——— Letter from, Acct. of Cap. of Brit. Sloop "Reindeer," by U. S. Sloop "Wasp." *Washington*, 1814

——— War. Letter from, observations on appro. for Military Service of U. S. for 1817 and 1818. *Washington*, 1818

——— State. Letter from, to Chairman of Com. on Commerce. *Washington*, 1820

——— State. Letter from, July 26, 1833. French Govt. and St. Domingo. *Washington*, 1833

——— Treasury. Letter from, Dec. 12, 1837, on affairs of Gen'l Land Office. *Washington*, 1837

——— Treasury. Report of, Dec. 16, 1844, on affairs of Gen'l Land Office. *Washington*, 1844

——— Treasury. Report of, May 24, 1844. Result of experiment of using Gas instead of Oil in Lighthouse. *Washington*, 1845

——— Treasury. Report of, Dec. 14, 1848. Report of Commis. of Genl. Land Office. *Washington*, 1848

——— Treasury. Letter from, Dec. 31, 1849. Report of Coast Survey. *Washington*, 1850

——— Interior, Dec. 9, 1850. Report of Commis. of Gen'l Land Office. *Washington*, 1850

Stearns, John. Philosophy of Mind. *N. Y.*, 1840

Stearns, Oliver. Farewell Sermon to third Congre. Ch. Hingham. *Boston*, 1856

Sinclair, John. Great Britain and America. Sermon, by, *N. Y.*, 1853

Shaw, W. Enquiry into the Authenticity of Poems ascribed to Ossian. *London*, 1781

Shaw, Elijah. Narrative of his 21 yrs. service in the American Navy. 3d ed. *Rochester*, 1845

Seaman, Henry J. Speech of, on the Tariff. *Washington*, 1846

Seaman, Henry J. Speech of, on appro. for Fortification at Narrows on Staten Island. *Washington*, 1846

Sommers, Lord. The Judgment of Whole Kingdoms and Nations. 12th ed. *Newport*, 1774

Somers Mutiny, Case of. Defence of Alexander S. Mackenzie. *N. Y.*, 1843

Swett, Wm. G. Five Sermons of. *Boston*, 1843

Swett, S. History of Bunker Hill Battle, by. 3rd ed. *Boston*, 1827

Swett, S. Who was the Commander at Bunker Hill? *Boston*, 1850

Swett, S. Original Planning and Construc. of Bunker Hill Mon. *Albany*, 1864

Sinclair, Hannah. Letter on Principles of Christian Faith. *Phila.*, 1819

2089 Miscellaneous. *Good lot.* [*Twenty-seven.*]

Sanderson, Mary. The Mistake on Both Sides, a Petite Comedy. *N. Y.*, 1852

Skinner, Thomas H. Love of Country. Discourse, by. *N. Y.*, 1851

Scherpf, George A. Appeal to the Public; or, a Story without Fiction. *N. Y.*, 1851

Sparrow, Wm. Sermon before Prot. Epis. Society. *N. Y.*, 1851

Sterling, John. The Onyx Ring, with Sketch of his Life. *N. Y.*, 1850

Sizer, Nelson. Cupid's Eyes Opened, and Mirror of Matrimony. *Hartford*, 1848

Spencer, John C. Review of Pamphlet, by. *N. Y.*, 1845

Sawyer, Lemuel, Biography of John Randolph. *N. Y.*, 1844

Sibthorp, Richard W. The True Path for the True Churchman. *N. Y.*, 1843

Schoolcraft, Henry R. The Rise of the West, or Prospect of the Missis. Valley. *With autog. letter of Mrs. Schoolcraft. Very scarce.* *N. Y.*, 1841

Sutherland, Th. Jefferson. Letter to Her Majesty, the British Queen. *Albany*, 1841

Sullivan, John L. Considerations of States' National Bank. *New Haven*, 1838

Spolasco, Baron. Narrative of Wreck of Steamer Killarney. 2d ed. *Cork*, 1838

Schiller, Fredrick. The Song of the Bell, Poem, by. *Phila.*

Short, C. W. Sketch of Progress of Botany in West. America. *Scarce.* *Lexington, Ky.*, 1836

Southard, Samuel L. Anniv. Address before Columbian Insti. *Wash.*, 1828

Sanborn, Reuben. Freemasonry, a Covenant with Death. *Bath, N. Y.*, 1828

Schroeder, Rev. John F. Disc. in Trinity Church. *N. Y.*, 1825

Sharp, Daniel. Sermon, at Funeral of Wm. Eustis. *Boston*, 1825

Singleton, Arthur. Letters from the South and West. *Boston*, 1824

Stanford, John. Disc., on Death of George Vanderpool. *N. Y.*, 1821

Sukey. A Poem. *Baltimore*, 1821

Sherwin's Weekly Political Register, No. 16. Vol. V. London, Aug. 21, 1819.

Sloan, Mr. Speech on Fifth Embargo Bill. *Salem*, 1809

Schlegel, J. F. W. Neutral Rights. *Phila.*, 1801

Stonington Association. Sentiments and Plan of. *Stonington*, 1787

Stebbing, Henry. Letter to Dean of Bristol. *London*, 1759

2089*Miscellaneous. *Scarce lot.* [*Nineteen*]

Salisbury, J. H. Microscopic Examination of Blood. *N. Y.*, 1868

Sheffield, Amos. In Memoriam. *Hartford*, 1868

Spain, The Arabs of. Poetry of, by G. J. Adler. *N. Y.*, 1867

"Sparrow-Hawk." Loss of, in 1626. *Boston*, 1865

Sullivan Benjamin, Sen. Address Commem. of Life and Services of, by Theodore D. Woolsey. *New Haven*, 1865

Sunnyside. Sketches of Distin. American Authors represented in Darley's New National Picture, entitled "Washington Irving and his Literary Friends." *N. Y.*, 1863

St. Stephen's College. Sermon in Chapel of, by Robert B. Fairbairn. *Albany*, 1863

Shea, George. Speeches of, for Defence, on Trial of State of N. J. *vs.* Orrin Van Derhoven. *Paterson*, 1862

Sing Sing Female Seminary. Catalogue of Teachers and Pupils of, by Rev. S. N. Howell. *Sing Sing*, 1861

Schetky, George P. Valedictory Sermon on Fifteenth Sunday after Trinity. *Phila.*, 1860

Schenck, Rev. Noah H. Valedictory Discourse on Christmas Night. *Chicago*, 1859

Stratton, Joseph B. Sermon before General Assembly of Presb. Ch. on behalf of Board of Publication. *Phila.*, 1857

Spaggiari, John. Latin-English Bimensal Periodical. No. I., Jan. and Feb., 1856.

Sandford, Edward. Argument of, in matter of Extending Albany St. to Broadway. *N. Y.*, 1854

Spalding, M. J. Address on Intolerant Spirit of Times. *Louisville*, 1854

Shakers. Fifteen Years in the Senior Order of, by Harvy Elkins. *Hanover*, 1853

St. Lawrence River. View of, from Niagara Falls to Quebec. *N. Y.*

Soule, Mr. Speech of, on Colonization of America and the Political Condition of Cuba, Jan. 25, 1853.

Sunderland, Rev. Byron. Memories of the Metropolis. *Washington*, 1853

/0 2090 Miscellaneous. [*Fourteen.*]

Strong, Hon. Caleb. Biography of, by Alden Bradford. *Boston*, 1820

Schools. Plan for General Establishment of, by Robert Coram. *Wilmington*, 1791

——— Public. Rules of School Com. and Regulations of. *Boston*, 1839

——— Report of Sch. Com. of Shrewsbury. *Worcester*, 1839

——— Address upon Education and Common, by James Henry, Jr. *Albany*, 1843

Sunday School Union. Fifth Report of American. *Phila.*, 1829

——— Soc. of Newburyport. Address at Third Anniv., by R. C. Waterson *Boston*, 1835

Swett, S. Abstract of Baron De Rogniat's Considerations on the Art of War, by. *Boston*, 1817

Schenck, Abraham H. Reply of, in Vindic. of his Character against Slanderous Charge, by Churchill C. Camberleng. *N. Y.*, 1828

Secretary of Treasury. Communication from, to Chairman of Com. appointed to Investigate the State of Treasury. *Washington*, 1802

Sleigh, W. W. Unmasked. The Veil Removed. *N. Y.*, 1836

Stone, Wm. L. Maria Monk and Nunnery of Hotel Dieu. Account of Visit to Convents of Montreal. *N. Y.*, 1836

Smith, Samuel S. Sermon on Love of Praise. *N. Brunswick*, 1810

Smith and Anthon, Drs. Statement of Facts in relation to Recent Ordination in St. Stephen's Ch. *N. Y.*, 1843

ALES OF THE NORTHWEST; or, Sketches of Indian Life and Character. By a Resident beyond the Frontier. 12*mo, cl., uncut; very scarce.* *Boston*, 1830

2092 TANNER, JOHN. A NARRATIVE OF THE CAPTIVITY AND ADVENTURES OF, during thirty years' residence among the Indians in N. A. By Edwin James, M. D. *8vo, bds., uncut. With portraits.* *New York*, 1830

2093 TARLETON, LIEUT.-COL. A HISTORY OF THE CAMPAIGNS OF 1780 and 1781, in the Southern Provinces of North America. By Lieutenant-Colonel Tarleton, Commandant of the British Legion. *Royal 8vo, bds., uncut. With maps. Beautiful copy.* *London: printed for T. Cadell, in the Strand.* MDCCLXXXVII.

2094 TARRYTOWN, N. Y. A HISTORICAL DISCOURSE delivered in the First Prot. Dutch Church. By Abel T. Stewart. *8vo. Plates.* *New York*, 1866

2095 TAUNTON, MASS. MINISTRY OF, with Incidental Notices of other Professions. By Samuel Hopkins Emery. With an Introductory Notice by Hon. Francis Baylies. 2 *vols. 8vo, cl.; portrait.* *Boston*, 1853

2096 TAZEWELL, L. W. DISCOURSE on the Life and Character of, June 29, 1860. By Hugh Blair Grigsby. *8vo, cl.*, 124 *p.; fine copy; rare.* *Norfolk*, 1860

2097 TE-HO-RA-GWA-NE-GEN. THE LIFE OF (*alias* Thos. Williams), a Chief of the Caughnawaga Tribe of Indians in Canada. By Eleazer Williams. *Imp. 8vo, hf. cr. lev. mor., gt. top; rough edges.* *Albany: Munsell*, 1859

200 copies. No. 67.

2098 TEMPLE, N. H. THE HISTORY OF. By Henry Ames Blood. *8vo, cl.* 28 *Illustra.* *Boston*, 1860

2099 TEMPLETON, MASS. A Sermon preached Sept. 1, 1811, on leaving the Old and First House of Worship built in Templeton. By Charles Wellington. *8vo pamphlet, uncut*, 25 *p.; rare.* *Brookfield*, 1812

2100 TEXAS. Narrative of the Texan Sante Fé Expedition: comprising a description of a Tour through Texas and across the great South-Western Prairies, the Camanche and Caygüa Hunting-Grounds; with an Account of the sufferings from want of food, losses from hostile Indians, and final Capture of the Texans, and their march as prisoners to the City of Mexico. With Illustrations and a Map. By Geo. Wilkins Kendall. In two volumes. *6th ed.* *8vo, cl.* *N. Y.*, 1850

2101 TEXAS. Notes Taken During the Expedition Commanded by Capt. R. B. Marcy, U. S. A., through Unexplored Texas in the Summer and Fall of 1854. *12mo., bds.* *Philadelphia*, 1856

2102 TEXAS. History of, from its First Settlement in 1685 to its Annexation to the United States in 1846. By H. Yoakum, Esq. In two volumes. With an extended appendix and engravings. *8vo, cl.; scarce.* *N. Y.*, 1856

2103 THACHER, JAMES. An Essay on Demonology, Ghosts and Apparitions and Popular Superstitions. Also, an account of the Witchcraft Delusion at Salem in 1692. *8vo, full red turkey, gt. top, uncut, by R. W. Smith; scarce.* *Boston*, 1831

2104 Thatcher, B. B. Indian Biography; or, an Historical Account of those Individuals who have been distinguished among the North American Natives as Orators, Warriors, Statesmen and other Remarkable Characters. In two volumes. *12mo, cl.* *New York*, 1834

2105 Thatcher, B. B. Indian Traits: being Sketches of the Manners, Customs and Character of the North American Natives. In 2 vols. *16mo, cl.* *New York*, 1865

2106 THAYER, ELISHA. Family Memorial. Part I.: Genealogy of fourteen families of the Early Settlers of New England, of the names of Alden, Adams, Arnold, Bass, Billings, Capen, Copeland, French, Hobart, Jackson, Paine, Thayer, Wales and White, from their first settlement in this country to about the middle of the last century. With occasional notes and references, biographical sketches, memoirs of some distinguished individuals, epitaphs, &c. Collected from ancient records, manuscripts and printed works. All these families are more or less connected by marriage, and most of them of late generations, the descendants of John Alden. Part II.: Genealogy of Ephraim and Sarah Thayer, with their fourteen children, from the time of their marriage to 1835, with notes of reference, &c., as in part first. *8vo, cl.; scarce.* *Hingham*, 1835

2107 Thomas, John. The Origin and Course of Intemperance, a Poem in Five Cantos. *12mo, bds.* N. Y., 1832

2108 THOMASTON, Rockland, and So. Thomaston, Me. History of, from their first exploration A. D. 1605; with Family Genealogies. By Cyrus Eaton. 2 vols. *8vo, cl.* *Hallowell*, 1865

2109 THOMPSON, THOMAS. An Account of Two Missionary Voyages. By the Appointment of the Society for the Propagation of the Gospel in Foreign Parts. The one to New Jersey in North America, and the other from America to the Coast of Guiney. *8vo, hf. cf.; scarce.* *London*, 1758

2110 THOMPSON, Rev. WM. Memoirs of the Rev. Samuel Munson, and the Rev. Henry Lyman, late Missionaries to the Indian Archipelago, with the Journal of their Exploring Tour. *8vo, cl.* N. Y., 1839

2111 THORNTON, J. W. Lives of Isaac Heath, and John Bowles, and of Rev. John Eliot, Jr. (For private distribution.) Fifty copies printed. *8vo, cl.* *MDCCCL.*

2112 THURSTON, CHARLES MYRICK, AND RACHEL HALL PITMAN, (his wife.) Genealogy of, formerly of Newport, R. I. After Dec., 1840, of New York. With an Appendix of the names of Edward Thurston and Henry Pitman. By Charles Myrick Thurston. *8vo, scarce.* N. Y., 1865

2113 TOLLAND, Conn. EARLY HISTORY OF. An Address delivered before the Tolland County Historical Society. By Loren P. Waldo. *8vo, cl.* *Hartford*, 1861

2114 "TOMO-CHI-CHI," MICO OF THE YAMACRAWS. By Charles C. Jones, Jr. *8vo, bds., uncut; rubric title.* *Albany, Joel Munsell*, 1868

2115 TOMPKINS, ISAAC. A CENTURY SERMON delivered in Middleborough, Mass., Sept. 10, 1818, at the residence of Mr. John Alden, the day he completed his hundreth year. *8vo pamph., uncut, 16 p.; scarce.* *Haverhill*, 1818

2116 TOPSFIELD, Mass. An Address delivered, Aug. 28, 1850: the Two Hundredth Anniv. of the Incorporation of the Town. By Nehemiah Cleveland. With portrait of John Endicott, and Appendix of 39 pages; with port's of Simon Bradstreet, Mrs. Huntington and Neh. Cleveland. *8vo, paper covers, 74 p.; good copy.* N. Y., 1851

2117 TOUCHSTONE, GEOFFERY. "THE HOUSE OF WISDOM IN A BUSTLE." A Poem, descriptive of the noted Battle lately fought in C-ng-ss, 1798. *8vo pamph., fine copy; very rare.* N. Y., 1798

For an account of "the noted battle, between Roger Griswold and Mathew Lyons," see the Hist. Mag., for Jan. 1864.

2118 TOWNSEND, JOHN K. A Narrative of a Journey across the Rocky Mountains, to the Columbia River, and a Visit to the Sandwich Islands, Chili, etc.; with a Scientific Appendix. *8vo, cl.* *Phila.*, 1839

2119 TRAITS OF AMERICAN INDIAN LIFE and Character. By a Fur Trader. *8vo, cl., uncut.* *London*, 1853

2120 TRENTON, N. J. HISTORY OF the Presbyterian Church in, from the First Settlement of the Town. By John Hall. *12mo, cl.* N. Y., 1859

2121 TRENTON FALLS, N. Y. PICTURESQUE AND DESCRIPTIVE. By N. Parker Willis. Embracing the Original Essay of John Sherman, the First Proprietor and Resident. Engravings. *12mo.* N. Y., 1862

2122 TRIAL OF WILLIAM WEMMS, JAMES HARTEGAN, WM. M'CAULEY, HUGH WHITE, MATTHEW KILLROY, WM. WARREN, JOHN CARROL, AND HUGH MONTGOMERY, Soldiers in His Majesty's 29th Regiment of Foot, for the Murder of Crispus Attucks, Samuel Gray, Samuel Maverick, James Caldwell and Patrick Carr, on

Monday evening the 5th of March, 1770. Held at Boston, the 27th day of Nov., 1770. Taken in Short-Hand by John Hodgson. *8vo, hf. cf., fine copy ; very scarce.*
Boston, Printed ; London, Re-printed. (1770)

2123 TRIAL OF THE BRITISH SOLDIERS for the Murder of Crispus Attucks, Samuel Gray, Samuel Maverick, etc., March 5, 1770. *8vo, bds.* *Boston,* 1824

2124 TRIAL OF THE BRITISH SOLDIERS, etc. *8vo, paper covers ; scarce.* *Boston,* 1807

2125 TRIAL OF WILLIAM BLOUNT. REPORT OF THE COMMITTEE of the House of Representatives of the United States, on Articles of Impeachment, of High Crimes, and Misdemeanors. *8vo paper, uncut ; very scarce.*
Phila. Printed by John Fenno, 1797

2126 TRIALS OF SMITH, WM. G. and SAM'L G. OGDEN. For misdemeanours, had in the Circuit Court of the United States for the New York District, in July, 1806. Also, account of the Proceedings against Smith and Ogden in the April Term. By Thomas Lloyd. *8vo, sh.* N. Y., 1807

2127 TRIAL OF COL. AARON BURR. On an Indictment for Treason, held in Richmond, Virginia, May Term, 1807. Including the Argument and Decisions. By T. Carpenter. 2 vols. *Bds. uncut ; very scarce.* *Washington City,* 1808

2128 TRIAL OF PRESCOTT, JAMES, Judge. Report of the Trial by Impeachment of, for Misconduct and Maladministration in Office, before the Senate of Mass. in 1821. With an Appendix, containing an account of former impeachments in the same State. By Octavius Pickering, and Gardiner. *8vo, bds., uncut. Autograph of Dan. Webster on Title.* *Boston,* 1821

2129 TRIAL OF LIEUT. JOEL ABBOT by the General Naval Court-Martial, Holden on Board the United States Ship Independence, at the Navy Yard, Charlestown, Mass., on Allegations made against him by Captain David Porter ; to which is added an Appendix. *8vo, bds., uncut.* *Boston,* 1822

2130 TRIALS, CONFESSIONS and BIOGRAPHICAL SKETCHES of the most cold-blooded Murderers who have been Executed in this Country from its First Settlement to the Present Time ; containing also, accounts of various other Daring Outrages committed in other Countries. Engravings. *8vo, sh. Anderson's plates.* *Boston,* 1840

2131 TRIAL OF WILLIAM PALMER, Report of, for Poisoning John Darson Cook, at Rugely. Illustrated and Unabridged Edition of the Times. *Cloth,* 16*mo, uncut.* *London,* 1856.

2132 TRIAL OF THE OFFICERS AND CREW of the Privateer Savannah on the Charge of Piracy in the United States Circuit Court of New York. *Large 8vo, sheets folded.* *N. Y.,* 1862

2133 TRIAL OF CHARLES M. JEFFERDS for Murder at New York, Dec., 1861. Charles E. Wilbur, Reporter. *Cloth, 8vo.*
New York, 1863

2134 TRIAL OF JOSHUA HETT SMITH, for Alleged Complicity in the Treason of Benedict Arnold, 1780. Edited by H'y B. Dawson.

Fifty copies printed, numbered and signed. No. 30. 8*vo, orig. cover, uncut.* *Morrisania, N. Y.*, 1866

2135 TROLLOPE, FRANCES. Domestic Manners of the Americans. 5th Edition; with portrait. 12*mo, bds.* *London, Eng.*, 1839

2136 TROY, N. H., HISTORICAL SKETCH OF, and her Inhabitants from the First Settlement of the Town in 1764, to 1855. By A. M. Caverly. 8*vo, cloth. Portraits ; scarce.* *Keene*, 1859

2137 TRUMBULL, BENJ. AN APPEAL to the Public, especially to the Learned, with Respect to the Un-Lawfulness of Divorces, in all cases, excepting those of Incontinency. 8*vo pamph.; very scarce.* *New Haven*, 1788

2138 TRUMBULL, JOHN. THE POETICAL WORKS OF. Containing McFingal, a Modern Epic Poem. The Progress of Dullness, and a Collection of Poems on Various Subjects, written before and during the Revolutionary War. In two volumes, illustrated. 8*vo, bds., uncut,* *Hartford*, 1820

2139 TRYON COUNTY, N. Y. ANNALS OF; or, the Border Warfare of New York, During the Revolution. By Wm. W. Campbell. 8*vo, cl. Map and plate. Very scarce, fine copy.* *N. Y.*, 1831

2140 TUCKERMAN, H. T. A Sheaf of Verse bound for the Fair. 8*vo, paper.* *N. Y.*, 1864

2141 TUDOR, WILLIAM. Letters on the Eastern States. 8*vo, boards, uncut, L. P.* *Boston*, 1821

2142 TURNER, O. HISTORY OF THE PIONEER SETTLEMENT OF PHELPS' AND GORHAM'S PURCHASE and Morris' Reserve, to which is added the Pioneer History of Monroe County; some Account of Border Wars of the Revolution; Early Difficulties with the Indians; with a Glance at the Iroquois. 8*vo, sheets stitched; very scarce in this condition.* *Rochester*, 1851

2143 TYSON, JOB R. Discourse on The Integrity of the Legal Character, delivered before the Law Academy of Philadelphia. 8*vo. Fine copy,* 36 *pages; very scarce. Valuable notes.* *Phila.*, 1839

PAMPHLETS.

TRIALS.—*Very scarce and valuable collection.*

2144 SHEPHERD, SAMUEL. Sermon delivered at Lenox, Mass., February 20, 1806. Being the day of the Execution of Ephraim Wheeler, pursuant to his sentence, for a Rape committed on his Daughter, Betsey Wheeler. *Very scarce.* *Stockbridge: Printed by H. Willard, March*, 1806.

2145 BOORN, STEPHEN AND JESSE. Mystery Developed; or, Russell Colvin, supposed to be murdered, in Full Life, and his convicted murderers, rescued from Ignominious Death by Wonderful Discoveries. Containing: I.—A Narrative of the whole Transaction, by Rev. Lemuel Haynes. II.—Rev. Mr. Haynes' Sermon. III.—A Succinct Account of the Indictment, Trial, and Conviction of Stephen and Jesse Boorn. Second Edition. *Scarce.* *Hartford*, 1820

2146 Bullions, Dr., Case of, Fairly Stated by an Observer. *N. Y.*, 1835

—— Rev. Alexander, History of the Trial of, before the Associate Presbytery of Cambridge on a Libel exhibited against him by that Reverend Body in May, 1829. *N. Y.*, 1831

2147 Court of General Sessions. The People vs. John H. Cooper, Kennith Defries and Others, for combination and conspiracy to raise their wages, &c. *Hudson*, 1836

2148 Supreme Court of U. S. A., James Carver *vs.* James Jackson. *Albany*, 1829

2149 Young, John, Conversation and Conduct of, who was Executed for Murder of Robert Barwick, from time of Receiving Sentence of Death, to his Execution, by Christopher Flanagan. *Scarce.* *N. Y.*, 1797

2150 Report of Proc. under a Writ of Enquiry of Damages. Lord Boringdon, Plaintiff, Sir Arthur Paget Defendant. By Mr. Gurney. *London*, 1808

Impeachment and Correction of Errors. Pres., Directors and Co. of Union Turnpike Road adsm. Thomas Jenkins. *Hudson*, 1804

Proceedings of Com. appointed to Inquire into Official Conduct of Wm. W. Van Ness. *Scarce.* *N. Y.*, 1820

Medad M'Cay, for Murder of his Wife ; by M. T. C. Gould. *Albany*, 1821

2151 Joseph Mason, for Murder of William Farrel ; by M. T. Gould. *Onondaga*, 1820

Case of Divorce, of Andrew Ure, M.D. vs. Catharine Ure. Refutation of Certain Calumnies published in a pamphlet entitled Correspondence between Mr. Granville Sharp Pattison, and Dr. Nathaniel Chapman ; by Granville S. Pattison. *Very interesting and scarce.* *Baltimore*, 1820

Pigott, Charles, Case of. *London*, 1793

Daniel I. Eaton, for Selling a Letter, "Addressed to the Addressers," by Thomas Paine. *Scarce.* *London*, 1793

2152 Daniel I. Eaton, for Selling a Supposed Libel entitled Politics for the People ; or, Hog's Wash. *London*, 1794

Daniel I. Eaton, for Selling a Supposed Libel, " The Second Part of the Rights of Man, combining Principle and Practice,' by Thomas Paine. *London*, 1793

Report of, on Indictment for Libel, in The American Lancet. Containing the whole Evidence. Dr. J. B. Beck and others against Dr. J. G. Vought. *N. Y.*, 1831

Muller, Dr. A. A., Statement of Facts and Circumstances of Trial of, Late Rector of Trinity Church, Clarksville, Tenn. *Nashville, T.*, 1841

2153 Jenkins, Elisha, vs. Solomon Van Rensellaer. *Very scarce.* *N. Y.*, 1808

King vs. Rev. Robert Taylor, for Blasphemous Discourse. *N. Y.*, 1827

Brown, George, Confession of, Late Mate of schooner Retrieve, for Mutiny and Murder of Capt. John Lewis. *N. Y.*, 1819

2154 Trial of Amistad Captives. Report by John W. Barber. *N. Haven*, 1840

——— John Taylor vs. Edward C. Delavan, for Libel. *Albany*, 1840

Case of James Maurice against Samuel Judd. Is a Whale a Fish? Reported by Wm. Sampson. *N. Y.*, 1819

2155 Trial for Sedition, of Thomas Muir. *N. Y.*, 1794

Trial of Wilson, Bruce, and Hutchinson, relative to the escape of the Convict Lavalette. *Paris*, April 23.

Account of Arguments and Counsel, Pleaded by James Foy, on Indictment for Procuring, Stirring, and Provoking Andrew Creagh and Others to Slee and Murder Patrick Randal, McDonnell, and Charles Hipson. *Dublin*, 1786

2156 Nicholas Fernandez, Dying Declaration of, who, with Nine Others, were executed in Cadiz Harbor for Piracy and Murder, Dec. 29, 1829; by Ferdinand Bayer. 1830

Report of Proceedings on Criminal Information against Abraham Lemon and Others for Conspiracy and Riot at Theatre Royal. *Liverpool*, 1810

2157 Report of Trial on Action for Damages brought by Rev. Charles Massy against Marquis of Headfort for Criminal Conversation with Plaintiff's Wife. *Scarce.* *Phila.*, 1804

Sketch of Life of R. P. Robinson, the alleged Murderer of Helen Jewett. *New York*, 1836

Opinion of Supreme Court of United States in Case of Gibbons vs. Ogden. Delivered by Chief Justice Marshal. *Albany*, 1824

2158 Wm. Gross, the Last Words and Dying Confession of, who was Executed February 7, 1823, for murder of Kesiah Stow. *Scarce.* *Phila.*, 1823

Somer's Mutiny. Defence of Alexander S. Mackenzie. *N. Y.*, 1843

2159 Trapnell, Rev. Joseph, Jr. Report of Trial of. *Baltimore*, 1847

Hagerman, Henry B. Trial of, on an Indictment for an Assault and Battery with Intent to Murder, Committed on Wm. Coleman. By David Bacon. *N. Y.*, 1818

Report in Chancery. George Codwise Jr. and others *vs.* Comfort Sands, Henry Sands, Lewis Sands and others. *Albany*, 1808

Commissioners of the Alms-House *vs.* Alexander Whistelo, a Black Man, Remarkable case of Bastardy. *Extremely scarce.* *N. Y.*, 1808

2160 Report of the Case, Nicholds, etc., against Wells, being that of a Treasury Warrant, opposed to a County Court Pre-emption. *Scarce.* *Frankfort.* Ky., 1803

Interesting Extracts. Historical and Fictitious, Embracing Adventures of Soldiers, Robbers, Pirates, etc. *N. Y.*, 1833

Channing, Henry. A Sermon preached at New London, Dec. 20, 1786. Occasioned by the Execution of Hannah Ocuish, a Mulatto Girl, Aged 12 Years and 9 Months. For the Murder of Eunice Bolles, Aged 6 Years and 6 Months. *Very scarce.* *New London. Printed by T. Green*, 1786

FOBES, PERES. A SERMON. The Substance of which was delivered at Taunton, Nov. 11, 1784, Upon the Day of the Execution of John Dixon, for Burglary, Aetat 24. With an Appendix, on the Nature and Enormity of Burglary, and a Sketch of Dixon's Life. *Very scarce.* *Providence. Printed by Bennett Wheeler*, 1784

2161 LEVI WEEKS, for the supposed Murder of Julianna Elmore Sands. By James Hardie. 2d Ed. *Scarce.* *N. Y.*, 1800

Court of Oyer and Terminer, etc. The People *vs.* Richard D. Croucher. *N. Y.*, 1800

JOHN FRIES, for Treason. Two Trials. *Very scarce.* *Phila.*, 1800

Maurice Margarot, for Seditious Practice. By Mr. Ramsey. *N. Y.*, 1794

Barthelemy, P., and L. De Bullion, for Conspiracy and Libel against Rev. A. Verren, *vs.* the People. *N. Y.*, 1841

ROBINSON, PETER, for Murder of Abraham Suydam. By Wm. H. Attee. *N. Y.*, 1841

2162 Barry Case. The People ex-relatione John A. Barry *vs.* Thomas R. Mercein. By John A. Barry. *N. Y.*, 1839

Robertson, James, for Perjury. By N. B. Blunt. *N. Y.*, 1824

Despard, Col., and his Associates, for High Treason and Conspiracy. *N. Y.*, 1803

MAFFIT, JOHN N., before Council of Ministers of M. Epis. Ch. *Boston*, 1823

McRae, Alexander, Plaintiff; Thomas Morton, Defendant. *N. Y.*, 1823

Merritt, Henry W. Trial of. *N. Y.*, 1840

2163 HUTTON, PERREGRINE. Confession of, who with Morris N. B. Hull, was Executed in Baltimore, July 14, 1820, for Robbing the Mail, and Murdering the Driver. *Scarce.* *Phila.*, 1820

SMITH, RICHARD, and ANN CARSON, *alias* Ann Smith, for Murder of Capt. John Carson. *Very scarce.* *Phila.*, 1816

BOORN, STEPHEN and JESSE, for Murder of Russell Colvin. 2d Ed. *Very scarce ed.* *Rutland*, 1819

MRS. CARSON'S LAST ADVENTURE. Trial of Ann Carson, Sarah Maland, Sarah Willis alias Kelly, Wm. Butler and Dr. Loring, for passing Counterfeit Notes. *Phila.*, 1823

CRAIG, JOHN H. Life and Execution of, for Murder. *Chester*, 1818

LECHLER, JOHN. Confession and Dying Words of, Tried and Executed for Murder. *Lancaster*, 1822

2164 African Captives. Prisoners of the Amistad. *N. Y.*, 1839

Achilli *vs.* Newman, for Seduction and Adultery. *N. Y.*, *n. d.*

BANKS, JOHN. Life and Death of, for Murder of his Wife. *Very scarce.* *N. Y.*, 1806

Boyle, Humphrey, to which is attached the trial of Joseph Rhodes, for Blasphemous and Seditious Libel. *London*, 1822

Burdett, Sir Francis. Political Offence. *London*, 1820

Beall, John Y., as a Spy and Guerrillero. *N. Y.*, 1865

2165 Beale, Stephen Y., Dr., for Immorality. *Phila.*, 1855
Burch. Divorce Case. Cont'g Mrs. Burch's Confession of Adultery. *N. Y.*
Beardsley, Divorce Case, for Adultery. *Uncut*, 1860. *N. Y.*
Baldwin, Charles N., for a Libel. *Uncut, scarce.* *N. Y.*, 1818
BOOTH, JOHN WILKES. Trial and Execution of. *Uncut.* *N. Y.*
Burns, Anthony. Boston Slave Riot. *Uncut.* *Boston*, 1854

2166 Carlile, Mary Ann. Defence of. *London*, 1821
——— Report of the Trial, for Publishing New Year's Add. *London*, 1821
Colt, John C. Life and Letters, for Murder of Sam'l Adams. *N. Y.*, 1842
Crim "Con." Remarkable Trials for. *Uncut.* *N. Y.*, 1842
Clason *vs.* Shotwell. Court of Impeachment, or Cor. of Errors. *Albany*, 1814
Chase, David, John W. Fellows, and Jireh Bull, for Perjury. *N. Y.*, 1829
Campion, William, and others, for Selling Anti-Christian Publications. *London*, 1824
Clough, Joel, for Murder of Mary Hamilton. *Uncut.* *N. Y.*, 1838

2167 Doane, Bp. Proceedings of Court of Bishops. *N. Y.*, 1852
Denny, George. Confession of, for Murder. *Very scarce.* *N. Y.*, 1844
Daley, Dominic, and James Halligan, for Murder of M. Lyon. *Northampton*, 1806
D'Hauteville *vs.* Sears. Report of. Phila., 1840. *Uncut. Scarce.*

2168 Fairchild, Joy H. Statement and Review, for Adultery. *Boston*, 1845
Forrest Divorce Case, Containing Remarkable Disclosures. *N. Y.*, 1852
Forrest Divorce Case. Report of. *Uncut.* *N. Y.*, 1852

2169 Fox, JOHN, for the Murder of John Henry. *New Brunswick, N. J.*, 1856
Goodwin, Robert M. Charged with Killing James Stoughton, Esq. *Uncut.* N. Y., 1821
Green, Henry G. Trial of, for Murder of his wife. *Uncut.* *Troy*, 1845
——— Confession of. *Uncut.* *Troy*, 1845
Garretson, Rev. Garret J., for Immorality, etc. N. Y., 1853
Hunt, John, *vs.* The King, for Libel on House of Commons. *London*, 1821
Hicks, Albert W. The Pirate and Murderer. *Uncut.* N. Y., 1860
Hughes, Dr. John W., for Murder. *Cleveland*, 1866
Harden, Jacob S., for the Murder of his Wife. *Uncut.* *Hackettstown, N. J.*, 1860

2170 Hone, William. 1st Trial of, for Pub. Parody on the Litany. *London*, 1818
——— 2d Trial of, for Pub. Parody on the Athanasian Creed. *London*, 1818
——— 3d Trial of, for Three Parodies. *London*, 1818

Holmes, William Vanplew, for Sedition and Blasphemy. *Uncut.* *London*, 1824

Impeachment Trials. Robinson, *vs.* Lorillard. N. Y., 1829

——— Dale, Fulton, and als *vs.* Hugh Williamson's Exec. *Scarce.* N. Y., 1823

——— Lawrence et. als. *vs.* Watts Orphan House. N. Y., 1844

——— of Oliver Cromwell. *Uncut, rare.* *London*, 1649

——— and Trial of Andrew Johnson. *Phila.*, 1868

2171 Jerolomon, Antoine. Murder of Two Women. N. Y., 1841

Jewett, Miss Ellen, Sketch of the Life, Murdered in New York. *Scarce.* N. Y., 1836

Jarvis, Mrs. Sarah M. Petition for Divorce, from Samuel F. Jarvis. *Hartford*, 1839

KENNAN, LIEUT. BEVERLY. Message from President Monroe. *Washington*, 1834

Lawrence *vs.* Norton and others. Fullerton's arg't. *L. P.* *Uncut.* N. Y., 1866

Lynn, David. Prince Kein and others, for Murder. *Uncut.* *Augusta, Me.*, 1809

Littlejohn, Libel Suit, against Horace Greeley. N. Y., 1861

Lee, Pamela. Private Hist. and Confession of, for Murder of her Husband. *Uncut.* *Pittsburgh, Pa.*, 1852

2172 Methodist Church Property Case. Bascom vs. Lane. *N. Y.*, 1851

——— E. Church, Centenary. The Case of. *N. Y.*, 1848

Miranda's Expedition. Gen'l acc't of, including Trial and Exec. *Uncut.* *N. Y.*, 1808

Mexico. Marine Corps. Conclusive Exculpation, by Maj.-Gen. Reynolds. *N. Y.*, 1853

Matthias, The Prophet. Memoir of. Full Exposure. *N. Y.* 1835

——— The Prophet. For swindling. *N. Y.*, 1834

MOREHOUSE, A. The First Trial of, for Forgery. Written by Himself. *Uncut; very scarce.* *N. Y.* 1789

2173 Myers, Mrs. Virginia, and D. M. Hoyt. Letters and Corress. *Phila.*, 1847

MAFFITT, REV. JOHN N. Narrative of his First Marriage, &c. *N. Y.*, 1850

McLeod, Alex., for murder of Amos Durfee. *N. Y.*, 1841

New York Court of Appeals. "B'k of the Commonwealth." *N. Y.*, 1862

ONDERDONK, Bp. Benj. T. *N. Y.*, 1845

Parish Will Case. Opinion of Hon. Samuel L. Selden. *Albany*, 1861

——— Argument of Mr. Evarts. *Albany*, 1861

2174 Pierrepont, Hon. Edwards. Charge to the Jury, in case of ship *Achorn.* *N. Y.*, 1859

Probst, Anton. Trial of, for Murder. *Phila.*, 1866

Palma, Thomas Fyshe, for Sedition. *Perth*, 1793

Parshall, Rev. Revilo F., for Licentiousness, &c. *N. Y.*, 1860
PORTER, MAJ.-GEN. FITZ JOHN. Rev. of the Judge Adv. Gen'l. *Washington*, 1863
Porter, David, Com. Gen. Court Martial. *Uncut.* *Washington*, 1825
Robinson, Richard P., for murder of Ellen Jewett. *Scarce.* *N. Y.*, 1836

2175 Rachel, Mme. Life and Trial of. Cosmetics, to make Women Lovely. *London*, 1868
"Riot Act" of 1855. Argument on the Const. and Construction of. *N. Y.*, 1864
Robbins, Jonathan. Letters on the case of, and on the recent captures of Am. Vessels by British Cruisers; on the right of expatriation. By Cha's Pinckney. *Uncut; scarce.* *Phila.*, 1799
Ross, James, for cruelty to Jane Marie. *Uncut; scarce.* *Penn.*, 1808
Robinson, R. P. Sketch of the Life of, Murderer of Ellen Jewett. *N. Y.*, 1836
Restell, Madame, alias Ann Lohman, for Abortion. *N. Y.*, 1848
Robinson, Peter, for Murder of Abr. Suydam. *Scarce.* *N. Y.*, 1841

2176 SMITH, JOSEPH AND HYRUM (Mormons). Correct acc't of the Murder of. *Very scarce.* *Nauvoo*, 1845
SMITH, Jos. Trial of Persons for Murder of, Carthage Jail. *Nauvoo, Ill.*, 1844
Smith, Miss Madeline. Poisoning her Lover. *London*, 1857
"Strong" divorce case. Argument of E. T. Gerry for Mrs. Strong. *N. Y.*, 1865
Sharp, Sarah, and Charles Edwards, victims of crime. *Cincinnati*, 1853
STRANG, JESSE, AND MRS. WHIPPLE *Very scarce.* *N. Y.*, 1827
Somers Mutiny. Case of. Defence of Alex. Slidell Mackenzie. *N. Y.*, 1843

2177 SICKELS, DANIEL E. Opening Speech of John Graham. *N. Y.*, 1859
"Senator" Case. Argument of Wm. Curtis Noyes. *N. Y.*, 1863
Thayers, Trial of the three, for Murder. *Very scarce.* *Buffalo*, 1825
Thistlewood, Arthur, Gent., and others, for High Treason. *Uncut.* *London*, 1817
Taylor, Rev. Robert, for Blasphemy. *Uncut.* *N. Y.*, 1827
TALLMADGE, HON. FREDERICK A. Argument of Wm. Curtis Noyes. *N. Y.*, 1858
——— (Gen'l Sup't of Metrop. Police.) *N. Y.*, 1858

2178 Tirrell, Albert J., for Murder of Mrs. Bickford. *Boston*, 1850
Tocker, Mary Ann, for an alleged libel on Mr. R. Gurney, Jr. *London*, 1818

Wright, Mrs. Susanna, for Publishing Carlisle's Corress. *Uncut.* *London*, 1822

Wakefield, Mr. Edward Gibbon, &c., for Abduction. *Very interesting.* *Liverpool*, 1827

Wright, Mrs. Susanna. Speech before the Court of the King's Bench. *London*, 1822

Whittlesey, Rev. John, for Immorality. *N. Y.*, 1845

Wirz, Capt. Henry, the Demon of Andersonville. *Phila.*, 1866

2179 Webster, Prof. John W. Reported for the Boston Journal. *Uncut.* *Boston*, 1850

——— Prof. John W. *N. Y.*, 1850

——— Prof. John W. Reported for the Boston Herald. *Uncut.* *Boston*, 1850

Opdyke vs. Weed. The Great Libel Case. N. Y., 1865

Opdyke "versus" Weed. *N. Y.*, 1865

Trial of Archibald Hamilton Rowan, for Libel. *Frontispiece.* *N. Y.*, 1794

Marine Seizures, or Right of Jury Trial in Federal Courts, in Cases of Seizures on Tide Waters. *N. Y.*, 1832

2180 John Quay vs. the Eagle Fire Company of N. Y.

John D. White and Winslow Curtis, for murder on the High Seas. *Boston*, 1827

Henry Fauntleroy, for Forgery. *Scarce.* *N. Y.*, 1825

George G. Barnard vs. John J. Gaul, and Mary H., his wife, for breach of promise. *Very scarce.* July, 1835.

Davis, M. L. Speech of—for conspiracy—on his trial.

2181 Impeachments. James Jackson and Caleb Hate. *N. Y.*, 1825

Alex. Addison, on an impeachment. *Lancaster, Pa.*, 1803

Ensign Rob't Dillon, for Mutiny. *Scarce.* *N. Y.*, 1809

Jenkins vs. Van Rensselaer. Assault and Battery. *Scarce.* 1808

James Cheatam, for libelling Madame Bonneville, in his life of Thomas Paine. Speech of Counsellor Sampson. *Very scarce.* *N. Y.*, 1810

2182 The Commissioners of the Alms-House vs. Alexander Whistelo, a Black Man; being a remarkable case of Bastardy. *Extremely scarce and interesting.* *N. Y.*, 1808

Report of the Arguments of the Attorney of the Commonwealth, at trial of Abner Kneeland, for Blasphemy, Jan. to May, 1834. *Boston*

J. F. Knapp, for Murder of Joseph White, Esq. (*Famous speech of Webster in this.*) *Salem*, 1830

Avery, Ephraim K. Arguments of Counsel at close of trial of, for murder of Sarah M. Cornell, May 6—June 2, 1833. Also, a literal report of the Medical Testimony of Professor Walter Channing and Dr. Wm. Turner. *Boston*, June, 1833

Action on Case brought by Silvanus Miller against Mordecai M. Noah, for Alleged Libel. By L. H. Clarke. *Scarce.* *New York*, 1833

2183 Ephraim K. Avery. Vindication of the result of the trial of: to which is prefixed his statement of facts relative to the circumstances by which he became involved in the prosecution. With a Map. *Scarce.* *Bost*

Wm. Parkinson, for assault and battery upon Mrs. Eliza Wintringham. *Excessively scarce; almost impossible to be found.* *N. Y.*, 1811

Of the Murderers of Richard Jennings, with arguments of Counsel. *Newburgh*, April, 1819

Case of James Maurice against Samuel Judd, by Wm. Sampson. *New York*, 1819

Henry B. Hageman, for assault and battery, with intent to murder, upon Wm. Coleman. *N. Y.*, 1818

Account of the trial of Thomas Cooper, for charge of Libel, by T. Cooper. *Phila.*, 1800

Report of, Pedro Gibert, Bernardo de Soto and others, for Piracy. *Boston*, 1834

2184 Maurice Margarot, for seditious practices, by Mr. Ramsey. *N. Y.*, Jan., 1794

Col. Despard and his associates, for High Treason and a Conspiracy, &c., &c. *N. Y.*, 1803

Mr. Hardy. Mr. Erskine's speech in defence of, for High Treason, Nov., 1794. *Dublin*

James Johnson, for Murder of Lewis Robinson; also of John Sinclair, for Murder of David Hill. *Scarce.* *N. Y.*, 1811

Rev. Ephraim K. Avery, for Murder of Sarah M. Cornell; by Richard Hildreth. *Scarce,* *Boston*, 1833

For Seduction. Nancy Van Haun vs. Silas E. Burrows. *N. Y.*, 1833

Short History of Persecutions of John Bamber, Sen., and Jas. Bamber; with Account of their Surrender, by Gov. Marcy, to British Gov't.

2185 Brick, Joseph W.; Estate of. Opinion of Chas. P. Daly. *New York*, 1863

Webster, J. W. Statement of Reasons showing the Illegality of that Verdict.

McMillan, Rev. John; for Defaming Thomas Leslie Birch. *Uncut.* *Washington*, 1806

Strang, Jesse; for Murder. *Uncut.* *Albany*, 1827

Hendrickson, John, Jr.; for Murder of his Wife by Poison. *Albany*, 1853

Jenkins, Jacob. The Murderer's Cave. By Wm. Wadsworth. *Boston*, 1818

Selfridge and Austin, Statement of Controversy between. *Uncut.* *Charlestown*, 1807

Selfridge, "Thos. O.;" Trial of, for Killing Chas. Austin. *Boston*, 1806

2186 Stow vs. Converse, for Libel. *Uncut.* *New Haven*, 1822

Strang, Jesse; Confession of, for Murder of John Whipple. *Uncut.* *N. Y.*, 1826

Sey, Rev. John; Trial for Alleged Immorality. *N. Y.*, 1847

Daniels, Thomas H.; Particulars of the Life of. *Boston*, 1819

Thomas, Francis. Statement. *Maryland*, 1845

Wilhelms, Cornelius; One of the Braganza Pirates. *N. Y.*, 1839

WEBSTER, JOHN W.; for Murder. *Uncut.* *N. Y.*, 1850
FREMONT, LIEUT.-COL. JOHN C. Court Martial. *Scarce.* *N. Y.*, 1848

2187 Lathrop, Geo.; Dark and Terrible Deeds; for the Murder of his Father. *New Orleans*, 1848
Machie, Wm., et als., vs. Dan Lord, et als.; Trial of Impeachments. *Uncut.* *N. Y.*, 1825
Hipper, John, vs. United German Lutheran Church of N. Y. 1824
Colt, J. C.; Life and Letters of. Extra Tattler, Oct. 21, 1842. *N. Y.*
Hone, Wm.; Trial by Jury and Liberty of the Press. *London*, 1818
Trials, Criminal; by R. R. Howison. *Richmond, Va.*, 1851

2188 Fletcher, John, of Boston. Remarks on the Case and Trial of T. O. Selfridge, for Shooting C. Austin. *Uncut; very scarce.* *Boston*, 1807
McDaniel and Joseph Brown, account of, parties in the Murder of Chavis on "The Santa-Fe Trace." *St. Louis*, 1844
Rhind, Lieut. A. C. Before a Naval Court Martial in Pacific Ocean. *Very scarce.* *N. Y.*, 1855
McKinley, Andrew; for Administering Unlawful Oaths. *Edinburgh*, 1818
Thurtell, John, and Joseph Hunt, for Murder of Mr. Wm. Weare. *London*
Hunter, Edward; for Murder of Elizabeth Hunter. *N. Y.*, 1865

2189 LUNG, PETER; Charged with the Crime of Murder. Vindication of the Calling of the Special Superior Court. By Zephaniah Swift. *Very scarce.* *Windham*, 1816
The King vs. Thomas Williams, for publishing the Age of Reason. Speeches of Hon. Thomas Erskine. June 28, 1797. *Phila.*, 1797
LAMBERT AND PERRY, also trial of William Cobbett for Libelling his present majesty, George III. *N. Y.*, 1810
Josef Perez, for Piracy, on board schooner "Bee." Sept. 9, 1823. *N. Y.*
Inquiry into the Somers Mutiny. Account of Execution of Spencer, Cromwell and Small. *N. Y.*, 1843
Trial of Indictment against Thomas Walker, Samuel Jackson, James Cheetham, Oliver Pearsal, Benjamin Booth, and Joseph Collier, for a Conspiracy to Overthrow the Constitution and Government. By Joseph Gurney. *Phila.*, 1794

2190 Tammany Soc. Pamphlets. *Rare lot.* [*Fourteen.*]
Linn, Wm. "The Blessings of America," a Sermon deliv. July 4, 1791. *N. Y.*
Eacker, George I.; 25th Anniv. of. Oration deliv. July 4, 1801. *N. Y.*
Clinton, Geo. Oration, July 4, 1798. *N. Y.*
Davis, M. L. Oration, 24th Anniv. of American Ind., July 4, 1800. *N. Y.*

Tam. Soc. Celebration, July 4th, Tammany Hall. 1865
——— " " " 1866
——— " " " 1862
——— " " " 1863
——— " " Laying the Corner Stone of New Hall. 1867
——— Oration, by W. L. Marcy, on the Life of the Indian Chief Tammany. *Very scarce.* *Troy, N. Y.*, 1809
——— Oration by Samuel B. Romaine, July 4, 1812. *N. Y.*
——— Address of, to its Absent Members. *N. Y.*, 1819
——— Oration, July 4, 1806, by P. H. Wendover. *N. Y.*
——— Sermon, July 4, 1794, by Rev. Joseph Pilmore. *N. Y.*, 1794

2191 Thanksgiving Sermons. *Fine lot.* [*Ten.*]

White, Wm. Sermon on the Celebration of the Festival appointed as a Thanksgiving. Oct. 29, 1786. *Scarce.*
McKnight, John. "The Divine Goodness to the U. S. of America." *N. Y.*, 1795
Linn, Wm. Disc. deliv. Nov. 26, 1795. *N. Y.*
Bicheno, J. "An Estimate of the Peace," discourse deliv. at Newbury. London, June 1, 1802.
Hobart, John Henry. Sermon—"The Security of a Nation." New York, April 13, 1815.
Beecher, Lyman. Sermon—"The Means of Nat. Prosperity." Hartford, Dec. 2, 1819.
Sabine, James. Sermon—"Solemn Feasts, Solemn News." Boston, Dec. 5, 1822.
Crosby, Daniel. Disc.—"Who Troubles Israel." Amherst, Nov. 29, 1832.
Macdill, D. A Disc.—"Three Nat'l Blessings." Rossville, Dec. 2, 1841.
Hart, Oliver. "America's Remembrances," &c. Sermon deliv. in Hopewell, N. J., Nov. 26, 1789. *Scarce.* *Phila.*, 1791

2192 Thanksgiving Disc. *Valuable.* [*Fourteen.*]

Wayland, Francis. Disc. deliv. in Providence, R. I., July 21, 1842.
Hart. Oliver. Sermon deliv. in Hopewell, N. J., Nov. 26, 1789.
Popkin, John S. Disc. deliv. in Newbury, Mass., April 13, 1815.
——— Sermon deliv. in Newbury, Mass., Nov. 25, 1813.
Parish, Elijah. Disc. deliv. in Byfield, Mass., Nov. 29, 1804.
Andrews, John. Sermon deliv. in Newburyport, Mass., Feb. 19, 1795.
Haslitt, Wm. Disc. deliv. in Hallowell, Me., Dec. 15, 1785. *Rare.*
Osgood, D. Sermon—"Reflections on the goodness of God in supporting the People of the U. S. through the late war

and giving them so advantageous and honorable a peace." *Scarce.* *Boston,* Dec. 11, 1783

Patten, Wm. Sermon—"Directions with regard to the improvement of temporal blessings." *New London,* Dec. 2, 1784

Noble, Mason. Sermon deliv. Nov. 22, 1832, at Washington.

Petigru, Chas. Oration prepared for delivery on the occasion of laying the corner stone of a monument erected to the memory of Kosciuszko at West Point, by a Corps of Cadets, July 4, 1828.

McKnight, John. "The Divine Goodness to the U. S. of America." Feb. 19, 1795. *Scarce.* *N. Y.*

Cutler, B. C. Disc. deliv. in Brooklyn, Dec. 17, 1840 *N. Y.*

Smith, S. S. "The Divine Goodness to the U. S. of America." Disc. Feb. 19, 1795. *Scarce.* *Phila.*

2193 Temperance Pamphlets. [*Thirteen.*]

Kirkland, John T. Sermon deliv. before Mass. Soc. for the suppression of intemperance, May 27. 1814

Sprague, Charles. Address before Mass. Soc. for suppression of intemperance. Boston, May 31. 1827

Flint, Joshua B. Address before Mass. Soc. for suppression of intemperance. Boston, May 29. 1828

Lothrop, Samuel K. Address before Mass. Soc. for suppression of intemperance. Boston, May 31. 1835

Channing, Walter. Annual Address deliv. before Mass. Temperance Soc., with the Annual Report of the Society. 3rd Ed. May 29. 1836

Mass. Temp. Soc. 24th Annual Report of. May 27. 1836

Clark, T. M. Annual Address deliv. before Mass. Temp. Soc. Boston, May 27. 1838

Twenty-Sixth Report of the Council of the Mass. Temp. Soc. Boston, June 1. 1838

Proceedings of the Annual Meeting of the Young Men's Temp. Soc. of Albany. 1836

Stetson, Caleb. Letter on the State of the Temp. Reform. *Boston,* 1836

Temp. Manual of Amer. Temp. Soc. for Young Men. *Boston,* 1836

Young, T. G. Constitution of Ballston Spa Young Men's Temp Assoc. Dec. 22, 1841. *Ballston Spa*

Marsh, Abram. Disc.—Reasons for Law with special reference to the traffic in Intoxicating Drinks. *Hartford,* 1846

2194 Miscellaneous. [*Ten.*]

Trumbull, Benjamin. Sermon at Ordina. of Rev. Aaron Woodward. *N. Haven,* 1794

Thomson, John. Enquiry concerning the Liberty and Licentiousness of the Press, etc. *Very scarce and important.* *N. Y.,* 1801

Treaty of Amity, Commerce, and Navigation between His Britannic Majesty and the U. S. of America. 2d Ed. *Phila.,* 1795

Trumbull, Gov. Biographical Sketch of Character of. *Scarce.*
Taunton Lyceum. Address before Members of. By Francis Baylies. *Boston*, 1831
Trollope, Nicodemus. Scribes of Gotham. Poem. *N. Y.*, 1833
Thorburn, Grant. Sketches from Note Book of Laurie Todd. Hints to Young Merchants and their Clerks. *New York*, 1847
Thorburn, Grant. Sketches from Note Book of Laurie Todd. Hints to Married Men and Bachelors. *N. Y.*, 1847
Thrush, Thomas. Letter add. to the King. *Cambridge*, 1825
Trinity College (Conn.) Catalogue of Officers and Students. *Hartford*, 1845

2195 Miscellaneous, [*Eighteen.*]
Trinity. Church of the Holy. Discourse on its Completion, by Rev. T. Stafford Drowne. *N. Y.*, 1868
Trinity Church. Remonstrance of Corporation of. *N. Y.*, 1846
Trinity Church Cemetery. Rules and Regula. of the Vestry concern. *N. Y.*, 1852
Trinity Churchyard. Argument of Peter Y. Cutler, in matter of Extending Albany St. to Broadway through. *N. Y.*, 1854
Trinity Church. Facts against Fancy, or a True and just View of, by Rev. Wm. Berrian. *N. Y.*, 1855
Trinity Church. Report on State of Parish of, by Wm. Berrian. *N. Y.*, 1856
Trinity Church Title. Exposure of Miller's Letters. *Albany*, 1856
Trinity Church. Argument of the Counsel of, before Senate Com. *Albany*, 1857
Trinity Church Bill. Argument of Daniel E. Sickels on the. *Albany*, 1857
Trinity Church Bill. Debates on, by Douglas A Levien. *Albany*, 1857
Trinity Church. Report concerning the Finances.
Trinity Church. Report, Committee on condition of Finances, by John H. Hopkins.
Trinity School. One Hundred and Fiftieth Anniv. of. *N. Y.*, 1859
Town, Ithiel. Account and Descrip. of Improvement in construction of Bridges. *N. Y.*, 1831
Town, Ithiel. Outline of plan for establish. an Academy and Institution of Fine Arts. *N. Y.*, 1835
Town, Ithiel. Descrip. of Improve. in Principle, Construc., etc., of Bridges for Roads, Railroads and Aqueducts. *N. Y.*, 1839
Thompson, Col. Alex. R. "Preparation for Death." Sermon on Death of, by Rev. J. Knox, Feb. 11, 1838. *N. Y.*
Thatcher, Peter Oxenbridge. A charge to the Grand Jury of Co. of Suffolk, by. *Boston*, 1834
Tories. Foul Charges of the, against Editor of the Aurora. 1798

2196 Miscellaneous. [*Twenty-eight.*]

Tyng, Stephen H., Jr. Letters to Rt. Rev. Horatio Potter. *Washington*, 1868

Trenck, Frederick, Baron. Life, Adventures and Uncom. Escapes of. *N. Y.*, 1826

Trenck, Frederick, Baron. Life and Adventures. *Albany*, 1853

Thomas, Rev. Abel C. Triangle. The Catholic Question consid. *Phila.*, 1851

Thomas, John A. Constitutional Law; argument of. *London*, 1854

Taylor, J. R. Report of Great Public Meeting. 4th ed *London*, 1857

Taylor, Robt. Who is the Devil? *N. Y.*, 1859

Turner, Samuel H. Intro. Disc., at opening of Theological Seminary of Prot. Epis. Ch. *Hartford*, 1820

Turner, Samuel H. Remarks on Editorial Article in the Churchman. *N. Y.*, 1845

Tuel, John. Facts for the People. *N. Y.*

Tappan, David. Two Friendly Letters to Rev. Samuel Spring. *Newburyport*, 1785

Tappan, David. Sermon before Annual Conven. of Congre. Ministers. *Boston*, 1797

Tappan, Lewis. Statement of Controversey between Edward E. Dunbar, and. *N. Y.*, 1846

Tappan, Henry P. Discourse on Education. *N. Y.*, 1846

Thomson, George. Essay on Christ's Mediatory Kingdom. *Glasgow*, 1795

Thomson, Charles. Holy Bible, containing Old and New Covenant. *Phila.*, 1808

Thompson, Otis. Sermon, at Ordination of Rev. Josephus Wheaton. *Providence*, 1816

Thompson, Otis. Sermon, at Ordi. of Rev. Stetson Raymond. *Prov.*, 1817

Thompson, Otis. Sermon, at Ordi. of Rev. Silas Shores. *Taunton*, 1822

Thomson, John. Vindication of Thomsonian System of Medcine. *Albany*, 1825

Thompson, Rev. John S. Reformed Christian Guide. *N. Y.*, 1831

Thompson, J. Autographical Counterfeit Detector. *N. Y.*, 1849

Thompson. Joseph P. Sermon, at Ordi. of Luther H. Gulick. *N. Y.*, 1851

Thorburn, Grant. Sketches from Note Book of Laurie Todd. *N. Y.*, 1847

Thorburn, Grant. Laurie Todd's Notes on Virginia. *N. Y.*, 1848

Texian, A. Remarks on Dr. Channing's Letter to Henry Clay. *Boston*, 1837

Texas. Prariedom, Rambles and Scrambles in, by a Southron. *N. Y.*, 1845

Texas. Teachers' State Convention, Proceedings of. *Louisville, Ky.*, 1866

2197 Miscellaneous. [*Twenty-seven.*]

Thorndike, Herbert. Just Weights and Measures. *London*, 1662

Toll, Mr. Letter to Rt. Rev. Dr. Warburton. *London*. 1760

Turnbull, Benjamin. Plea, in Vindication of the Conn. Title. *Rare and valuable.* *New Haven*, 1774

Thrum, Tam. Look before ye Loup. *Phila.*, 1798

Tythingman, A. Remarks on Observation of the Lord's day. *Cambridge*, 1816

Tompkins, Daniel D. Letter to. *Albany*, 1820

Teackle, Mr. Report of, on Citizens Praying the Estab. of a States' Bank. *Annapolis*, 1831

Temperance. Proc. and Speeches at Meeting for promotion of. *Washington*, 1833

Troy Lyceum. Essay before. *Troy*, 1834

Townson. N. Correspondence, etc. *Washington*, 1835

Thoughts on Causes of Present Distresses. *Albany*, 1837

Thebes. Description of Great Temple of Karnak and City of, by F. Catherwood. *N. Y.*, 1839

Tallmadge, N. P. Speech of, on Finances of the Gov't. *N. Y.*, 1839

Toplady, Augustus M. Free will and Merit Fairly Examed. 5th ed. *Manchester*, 1754

Talbot, James B. Miseries of Prostitution. *London*, 1844

Taylor, Zachary. Anecdotes of, by Tom Owen. *N. Y.*, 1848

Towell, Rev. T. Chesnut Grove Collegiate School. *N. Y.*, 1849

Timony, Patrick. American Fistiana. *N. Y.*, 1849

Turkey and the Turks, by Dr. Jerome V. C. Smith. *Boston*, 1852

Troy and Rutland Railroad. 1852

Tounghoo Women. *N. Y.*, 1860

T. J. E. Publishers' Festival, or Parnassus "Served Up." *N. Y.*, 1855

Tribune Club. Proceedings of, Presentation, etc., *N. Y.*, 1855

Thayer, Christopher T. Valedictory Disc. *Boston*, 1858

Train, George Francis. Report of Banquet given by. *Liverpool*, 1860

Travellers' Steamboat and Railroad Guide. *N. Y.*, 1866

Thackery, Miss. Jack the Giant Killer. *Boston*, 1866

2198 Miscellaneous. [*Twenty-five.*]

Triangle. Dedication to John Doe and Richard Roe, by Investigator. *N Y.*, 1816

Triangle. By Investigator. *N. Y.*, 1816

Triangle. By Investigator, upon Three Theological Points. *N. Y.*, 1816

Theology. Views in. No. XV., Vol. IV., Nov. 1834. *N. Y.*, 1834

Taylor, Rev Dr. Remarks on Letter to Dr. Hawes, by Bennet Tyler. *Boston*, 1832

Tyng, Stephen H. Thanksgiving Sermon, by. *N. Y.*, 1850

Taylor. Review of Diegesis. *Boston*, 1832

Tilghman, Wm. Eulogium in Com. of Dr. Caspar Wistar. *Phila.*, 1818

Toulmin, Joshua. Sermon on death of Samuel Morgan. *London*, 1794

Trinity Church. Letter to Members of, by Rev. J. F. Schroeder. *N. Y.*, 1839

Thoughts on the Moral Influence on Paris, and Continent in General, by English Residents and Visitors. *London*, 1836

Tyler, Bennet. Review of Pres. Day's Treatise on the Will. *Hartford*, 1838

Townsend, Peter S. Dissertation on the Influence of the Passions. *N. Y.*, 1816

Thacher, Peter. Oration on Thirty-first Anniv. of Ind. of U. S. 2d ed. *Boston*, 1807

Theophrastus. Moral Characters of. *Andover*, 1826

Trumbull, Jno. Disc. on Death of, by Timothy Dwight. *New Haven*, 1809

Temperance. Order of Sons of. *N. Y.*, 1847

Tallmadge, James. Speech on Subject of Caucus. *Albany*, 1824

Turnbull, Benjamin. Sermon at Ordi. of Nehemiah Prudden. *Very scarce.* *Springfield*, 1783

Tyler, Edward R. Sermon, by. *New Haven*, 1829

Tucker, Mark. Sermon, Annual Fast. *Providence*, 1838

Tariff. No. 1. Its Injustice on Prin. of Revenue. *N. Y.*, 1843

Treat, Capt. Joseph W. Vindication of. *Phila.*, 1815

Townsend, Alexander. Oration, July 4, 1810. *Boston*, 1810

Trumbull, Benjamin. Discourse at Anniv. Meeting of Freemen of N. Haven, April 12, 1773. *Rare.* *N. Haven*, 1773

UNDERHILL, JOHN. NEWS FROM AMERICA ; or, a new and experimentall Discoverie of New England, containing a true Relation of their War-like proceedings these two years last past. By Captaine John Underhill, a Commander in the Warres there. *8vo, half mor., uncut.* *London*, 1638. *Reprint*

2200 UNION, ME. A HISTORY OF THE TOWN OF, to the middle of the Nineteenth century, with a family register of the settlers before the year 1800, and of their Descendants. By J. Langdon Sibley. *8vo, cl. ; port.* *Boston*, 1851

2201 UNITED BRETHREN ; OR, UNITAS FRATRUM. The Ancient and Modern History of, or a Succinct Narrative of the Protestant Church of, in the remoter ages, and particularly in the present century. Written in German by David Cranz. Now Translated into English, with Notes. By Benjamin Latrobe. *8vo, old cf. binding, scarce.* *London*, 1780

2202 UNITED STATES. THE HISTORICAL REGISTER. Edited by T. H. Palmer. *2d edition, 4 vols., bds.* *Phila.*, 1814

2203 UNITED STATES OF AMERICA. A STATISTICAL VIEW of the commerce of, in connection with Agriculture and Manufactures, with a brief review of the Trade, etc., previous to their Independence. By Timothy Pitkin. *8vo, bds, uncut ; very fine copy ;* *Hartford*, 1816

2204 UNITED STATES. HISTORY OF, from their First Settlement as Colonies, to the cession of Florida, comprising every important Political event ; with a progressive view of the Aborigines, etc., and Copious Alphabetical Index. Third edition. By Wm. Grimshaw. *12mo, sh.* *Phila.*, 1822

2205 UNITED STATES ANTI-MASONIC CONVENTION. The Address of, Phila., Sept. 11, 1830, to the People of U. S. *8vo, 22 p., fine cond. ; scarce..* *Phila.*, 1830

2206 UNITED STATES. HISTORY OF, from the Plantation of the British Colonies, till their Revolt and Declaration of Independence. By James Grahame. In four volumes. *8vo, cl., uncut.* *London : Smith, Elder, & Co.*, 1836

2207 UNITED STATES OF NORTH AMERICA, History of, from the Plantation of the British Colonies till their assumption of National Independence. In four volumes. By James Grahame, L.L. D. *8vo, cl., rough edges.* *Phila.*, 1845

2208 United States, A General View of. Comprising, also, a description of each State and Territory in the Union, etc. By S. A. Mitchell. *8vo, bds., map.* *Phila.*, 1846

2209 UNITED STATES, History of, from the Discovery of the American Continent. By Geo. Bancroft. 8 *Vols. Imp. 8vo, cl., uncut. With Portraits on India paper.* *Boston : Little, Brown and Company*, 1861

Large paper. Only 50 copies printed, 3 of which were destroyed by the fire at C. B. Richardson's store, in New York, Sept., 1864.

2210 UNITED STATES SANITARY COMMISSION. A Sketch of its Purposes and its Work, compiled from Documents and Private Papers. *8vo.* *Boston*, 1863

2211 UNITED STATES SANITARY COMMISSION. A Sketch of its Purposes and its Work, compiled from Documents and Private Papers. By K. G. Wormely. *8vo, bds., uncut.* *Boston*, 1863

2212 United States Service Magazine. Vols. I., II., III., complete. Extra Vol. IV., Nos, 1, 2, 4, 6 ; Vol. I., Nos. 3, 4, 5, 6 ; Vol. II., No. 10 ; Vol. V., Nos. 1, 4, 6. *New York*, 1864 and 1865

2213 U. S. SANITARY COMMISSION, Phila. Memorial of the Great Central Fair, June, 1864. By Chas. J. Stillé. *4to, cl. Photographs, gt. top, rough edges, rubric title.* *Phila.*, 1864

2214 UNITED STATES CAVALRY, History of, from the Formation of the Federal Government to the 1st of June, 1863. To which is added a list of all the Cavalry Regiments, with the Names of their Commanders, which have been in the United States Service since the breaking out of the Rebellion. By Albert G. Brackett. *8vo, sheets stitched, frontis.* *N. Y.*, 1865

2215 UNITED STATES, THE, During the War. By Auguste Laugel. *8vo, cl., uncut.* *New York, etc.*, 1866

2216 United States, Pictorial History of, from the Earliest Period to the Present time. By Benson J. Lossing. *Illustrated.* 3 *Nos.*, 1, 2, 3, *uncut.* *Hartford*, 1867

2217 Untaught Bard, The. An Original Work. *12mo, sh.* *New York*, 1804

2218 Upham, Thomas C. American Sketches. *12mo, bds., uncut.* *N. Y.*, 1819

2219 UPHAM, CHAS. W. Lectures on Witchcraft, comprising a History of the Delusion in Salem, in 1692. *Full red Turkey, 8vo, gilt top, edges uncut. By R. W. Smith.* *Boston*, 1831

2220 UPHAM, CHARLES W. Salem Witchcraft, with an account of Salem Village and a History of Opinions on Witchcraft and kindred subjects. *In Two Volumes. Engravings, 8vo, cl., uncut.* *Boston*, 1867

2221 The Same. *L. P.* 50 *copies only.*

PAMPHLETS.

2222 Unitarian Association Pamphlets. [*Twenty-Three.*]

Uni. Assoc., First Annual Report of. *Boston*, 1827
——— Proc. of 2nd Annual Meeting. *Boston*, 1839
——— Proc. of 12th Annual Meeting. *Boston*, 1849
——— Proc. of 13th Annual Meeting. *Boston*, 1850
——— Proc. of 14th Annual Meeting. *Boston*, 1851
——— Tests of True Religion. *Boston*, 1828
——— 11th Semi-Annual Report. *Boston*, 1833
——— 13th Report. *Boston*, 1838
——— 20th Report, May 27, 1845.
——— Sketch of the Hist. of the Doctrine of Atonement, by James Freeman Clark. *Boston.*
——— Rec. of a Sermon, by F. P. Greenwood. 1845
——— 23d Report, May 30, 1848. *Boston.*
——— Romanism, by S. G. Bulfinch. *Boston*, 1849
——— Gospel of Luke, the Apostles' Creed, by Austin Craig.
——— 25th Report of, May 28, 1850. *Boston*, June, 1850
——— 26th Report of, May 27, 1851. *Boston*, May 27, 1851

Kelley, John. Solemn and important reasons against becoming a Universalist. *Haverhill*, 1815

Belsham, Thos., Amer. Unitarianism ; or a brief Hist. of the Progress and Present State of the Unitarian Churches in Amer. 5th Ed. *Boston*, 1815
——— The same. 1st Ed. *Boston*, 1815

Woods, Leonard. Letters to Unitarians, occasioned by the Sermon of Wm. E. Channing, at ordination of J. Sparks. *Andover*, 1820

Little, Robt. "Religious Liberty and Unitarianism Vindicated." Sermon. *Washington*, Apr. 28, 1822

Mason, Dr., An Appeal from the Denunciations of. *N. Y.*, 1822

Warning against Unitarian and Hopkinsian Errors, deliv. Associate Ch. of N. A. 2nd Ed. *Albany*, 1826

2223 Miscellaneous. [*Seventeen.*]

Union College. Address before, July, 1838, by Tayler Lewis. *Albany.*

United States. Sketch of the internal condition of. *Baltimore*, 1826
——— Instructions to the Envoys Extraordinary and Ministers Plenipotentiary of. *Phila.*, 1798
——— Desultory reflections of the new Political aspects of Public Affairs in. *N. Y.*, 1799
——— Plain Sense on National Industry, addressed to the People of the U. S. *N. Y.*, 1820
——— Appeal to the people of. *Boston*, 1831
——— Translation of a note from the Minister of the French Republic to Sec. of State of the U. S. *N. Y.*, 1796

Union College. Disc. on the Privileges and Duties of Man as a Progressive Being. Deliv. July 23, 1833, by B. F. Joslin. *Schenectady.*

——— Address deliv. before Library Soc. of, July, 1837, by George W. Bethune. *Phila.*

——— Disc. deliv. July 26, 1836, by G. C. Verplanck. *N. Y.*

——— The Documentary Evidence relative to the controversy. *Schenectady*, 1823

Upham, Chas. W. Disc. on Prophecy as an Evidence of Christianity. *Salem*, 1835

Unitas Fratrum. A concise hist. account of the present constitution of, by B. La Trobe. *Scarce.* *London.*

Unitarian's Answer.

Unterwalden. The Wrongs of, by Th. Jefferson, Oct. 27, 1807

Union College. Disc. deliv. July 19, 1846, by Wm. B. Sprague. *Albany.*

United States. Remarks on the Bank of, April, 1830.

2224 Miscellaneous. [*Twenty-five*]

Univ. of N. C. Address by Chas Manly. *Raleigh*, 1838

——— Maryland. Lecture by Wm. R. Fisher. *Phila.*, 1837

——— Penn. Address by Geo. Potts, Nov. 15, 1852.

——— Penn. Address by R. F. Conrad, Jan. 25, 1842.

——— Vermont. Address by H. J. Raymond, Aug. 6, 1850.

——— Alabama. Address by Alva Woods, Dec. 17, 1836.

U. S. Declaration of Independence and Constitution of. *N. Y.*, 1796

Union College. Nott, Eliphalet. Address at the commencement, July 29, 1807.

——— Address at the Commencement, July 30, 1806.

Mitchell, S. L. Disc. before Phi Beta Kappa. *Albany*, 1821

——— Clinton De Witt. Disc. before Phi Beta Kappa. *Albany*, 1823

——— Lewis, Tayler. Address before Phi Beta Kappa. *Albany*, 1838

——— Videns, Fabricus. The Spy-Glass, for July, 1840.

——— Kent, William. Address before Phi Beta Kappa Soc., N. Y., July 27, 1841.

——— Catalogue of the Officers and Students in. *Troy*, 1841

——— Butler, Benj. F. Address, July 26, 1841.

——— First Semi-Centen. Anniv. of, July 22, 1845.

——— Sumner, Charles. "The Law of Human Progress:" an Oration before, July 25, 1848.

——— Address at the anniversary commencement, May 1st, 1805, by Eliphalet Nott. *Albany*, 1805

Union College. The advantages and the dangers of the American scholar. A discourse by G. C. Verplanck. *New York*, 1836

——— Catalogue of the Officers and Students, 1837–8. *Schenectady*, 1837

——— Representative Democracy in the U. S. Address by B. F. Butler. *Albany*, 1841

——— Address before the Phi Beta Kappa Society, by W. Kent. *New York*, 1841

——— The American Citizen: a discourse, by T. Sedgwick. *New York*, 1847

——— Modern Benevolence: a Satire, by E. Phelps. *New York*, 1860

2225 Miscellaneous. [*Seventeen.*]

Union Theological Seminary, New York. Charge and inaugural address on the Induction of H. B. Smith. *New York*, 1855

——— Addresses to the graduating classes, by W. Adams and T. H. Skinner, May, 1868. *New York.*, 1868

Universal Life Insurance Co. Hand-book for Agents of. *N. Y.*, 1868

United States. Case decided in Supreme Court of. *Phila.*, 1793

——— Acts passed at First Session of Sixth Congress. *Phila.*, 1799

——— Constitution of, and New Jersey. *Newark*, 1798

Ullmann, Daniel. Civil and Religious Liberty. Disc. at Wilmington, deliv. July 4, 1855. *New York*, 1855

Umbrellas and their History, by Clyde and Black. *Riverside Press, Cambr.*, 1864

Union Safety Committee, Rules and Bye-laws. *New York*, 1850

Unitarianism. The Unity of God: a Disc. by R. Eddowes. *Phila.*, 1813

——— The sufferings of Unitarians in former times: a Disc. at Essex St. Chapel, by Thomas Belsham. *London*, 1813

——— Remarks on Unitarianism and Mahometanism, in reply to H. D. Sewall. By H. I. Feltus. *New York*, 1820

——— Letter from a gentleman in Boston to a Unitarian Clergyman. Second ed. *Boston*, 1828

——— Cudworth defended, and Unitarianism delineated. *Salem*, 1833

Upfold, George. The Last Hundred Years: a Lecture. *Pittsburgh*, 1845

——— Practical Charity: a Sermon. *Pittsburgh*, 1849

Upham, Charles W. A Disc. on the Decease of Hon. Timothy Pickering. *Very scarce.* *Salem* 1829

2226 Miscellaneous. [*Sixteen.*]

United States. Charter of the United States Inebriate Asylum. *New York*, 1855

U. S. Senatorial Qnestion. Speeches in the Assembly of N. Y., Feb., 1855. *Albany*, 1855

U. S. Guano Manufacturing Company, N. Y. *New York*, 1857

The U. S. and France, by E. Laboulaye. *Boston*, 1862

The commercial conduct of the U. S. considered. *Very scarce.* *New York*, 1786

Review of the administration of the government of the U. S. since the year ninety-three. *Boston*, 1797

Address by the Members of the House on the War with Great Britain. *Baltimore*, 1812

Exposition of the Causes and Character of the late War. *Middlebury, Vt.*, 1815

Tide-tables for the principal Seaports of the U. S., by A. D. Bache. *New York*, 1855

Important and interesting events in the history of the U. S., by H. Tuttle. 16th ed. *Buffalo*, 1854

United States Review, Jan. 1853. Vol. I., No. I. *New York*, 1853

Disturnell's U. S. National Register for 1852. *New York*, 1852

Sketch of the U. S. Dry Docks at Phila., etc. Plates. *New York*, 1849

American Citizen's Manual of Reference, compiled by W. H. Hadley. *New York*, 1840

United States Telegraph Extra, Oct. 8, 1832. *Washington*, 1832

View of the U. S., by John Hayward. *New York*, 1832

AN BUREN, Martin. Biography of, with an Appendix containing selections from his Writings; among which will be found the late Letter of Colonel Thomas H. Benton, to the Convention of the State of Mississippi. By William Emmons. *2nd Ed. 8vo, bds.* *Washington,* 1835

2228 VANE SIR HENRY, Kt. Tryal of, at the King's Bench, June 2nd and 6th, 1662, with what he intended to have Spoken the Day of his Sentence. With Occasional Speeches, &c. Also, his Speech and Prayer on the Scaffold. *Sm. 4to, hf. mor.* *London: printed in the year* 1662

2229 VARNUM. Col. JOSEPH B. An Address deliv. to the Third Division of Massachusetts Militia at a Review on the Plains of Concord, Aug. 27, 1800. *8vo, 26 p. rough edges; scarce.* *Cambridge* 1800

2230 Vaux, Roberts. Memoirs of the Lives of Benjamin Lay and Ralph Sandiford, two of the Earliest Public Advocates for the Emancipation of the Enslaved Africans. *8vo, bds., uncut. Plate.* *Phila.,* 1815

2231 VERMONT. The Natural and Civil History of. By Samuel Williams. In two volumes. The second edition. Corrected and much enlarged. *2 vols, 8vo, sheep. With map.* *Burlington,* 1809

2232 VERMONT State Papers: being a Collection of Records and Documents; together with the Journal of the Council of Safety, the First Constitution, the Early Journals of the General Assembly, and the Laws from 1779 to 1786 inclusive. To which are added the Proceedings of the First and Second Council of Censors. Compiled by W. Slade, Jr. *8vo, bds., uncut.* *Middlebury,* 1823

2233 VERMONT. The History of, with Descriptions Physical and Topographical. By Rev. Hosea Beckley, A. M. *12mo, hf. mor.; very scarce.* *Brattleboro, Vt.,* 1846

2234 VERMONT. Catalogue of the Principal Officers of, as connected with its Political History from 1778 to 1851, with some Biographical Notices, &c. By Leonard Deming. *8vo, bds.* *Middlebury,* 1851

2235 VERMONT QUARTERLY GAZETTEER. A HISTORICAL MAGAZINE, embracing a Digest of the History of each Town. Edited by Abby Maria Hemmenway. 6 parts complete. Nos. 1, 2, 3, 4, 5, 6. *8vo, uncut, paper. With portraits.* *Ludlow, Vt.*, 1860

2236 VERMONT HISTORICAL GAZETTEER. A MAGAZINE embracing a Digest of the History of Each Town, Civil, Educational, Religious, Geological and Literary. By A. M. Hemenway. In one volume. Por. plates. Nos. 7, 8, 9, 10, 11. Chittenden and Essex Counties. *Paper, uncut.* *Burlington*, 1867

"A work of Great Value, replete with facts and rich in personal details, Specimens and Sketches so arranged alphabetically by Counties and Townships as to be of easy reference."

2237 VESPUCIUS, AMERICUS, LIFE AND VOYAGES OF, with Illustrations concerning the Navigator, and the Discovery of the New World. By C. E. Lester and A. Foster. *8vo, cl. Portrait and plates.* *New York*, 1846

2238 VERMONT, HISTORY OF THE STATE OF. By Zadock Thompson. *18mo, Boards.* *Burlington*, 1858

Comprising Addison, Bennington, Caledonia, and Chittenden Counties.

2239 VIDE, V. V., American Tableaux. Sketches of Aboriginal Life. *Cloth, 12mo.* *New York*, 1846

2240 VINCENNES, Ind., COL. HISTORY OF, from its First Settlement down to the Administration of Gen. Harrison. Address by Judge Law before the Vincennes Historical Antiquarian Soc. February 22, 1839. With additional Notes and Illustrations. *8vo, cloth; scarce.* *Vincennes*, 1858

2241 VIRGINIA. THE HISTORY OF THE BRITISH PLANTATIONS IN AMERICA. With a Chronological Account of the most Remarkable things which happened to the First Adventurers in their several Discoveries in that New World. Part I. Containing the History of Virginia; with remarks on the trade and commerce of that Colony. By Sir William Keith. Engraved title and Map. *4to, half mor., gt. top, uncut. Very rare.* *London, MDCCXXXVIII.*

2242 VIRGINIA, NOTES ON THE STATE OF. With an Appendix. By Thomas Jefferson. 3d American edition, with map and portrait. *8vo, sheep; fine copy.* *New York*, 1801

2243 VIRGINIA, HISTORY OF. From its First Settlement to the Present Day. By John Burk. 3 *volumes, 8vo, sheep.* *Petersburg, Va.*, 1804–'5

2244 VIRGINIA, A HISTORY OF. From its Discovery till the Year 1781. With Biographical Sketches of all the Most Distinguished Characters that occur in the Colonial, Revolutionary or Subsequent Period of our History. By J. W. Campbell. *8vo, sh.* *Phila.*, 1813

2245 VIRGINIA AND THE DISTRICT OF COLUMBIA. A New and Comprehensive Gazetteer of, containing a Copious Collection of Geographical, Statistical, and Political Information, &c. By Joseph Martin. To which is added a History of Virginia from its First Settlement, to the year 1754, with an Abstract of the principal events from that period to the Independence of Virginia, written expressly for the Work. By a Citizen of Virginia. *8vo, Boards.* *Charlottesville*, 1835

2246 VIRGINIA, Historical Collections of. Containing a Collection of the most Interesting Facts, Traditions, Biographical Sketches, Anecdotes, &c., relating to its History and Antiquity, together with Geographical and Statistical Descriptions; to which is appended an Historical and descriptive sketch of the District of Columbia. Illustrated by over 100 engravings, giving views of the principal Towns, Seats of Eminent Men, Public Buildings, Relics of Antiquity, Historic Localities, Natural Scenery, &c. By Henry Howe. *8vo, sheep, spr. edges. Maps, plates.* *Charleston*, 1852

2247 VIRGINIA, Sketches of. Historical and Biographical. By the Rev. Wm. Henry Foote, D.D. 2d Series. *8vo, cloth.* *Phila.*, 1856

2248 VOYAGES from Montreal through the Continent of North America, to the Frozen and Pacific Oceans in 1789 and 1793. With an account of the rise and progress of the Fur Trade of that Country. In two volumes. Illustrated with portraits and maps. By Alexander Mackenzie. *8vo, sheep.* *London*, 1802

2249 VIRGINIA, History of. In Four Parts.

I.—The History of the First Settlement of Virginia, and the Government thereof, to the year 1706. II.—The Natural Productions and Conveniences of the Country suited to Trade and Improvement. III.—The Native Indians: Their Religion, Laws, and Customs, in War and Peace. IV.—The Present State of the Country, as to the Polity of the Government, and the Improvements of the Land, the 10th of June, 1720. By a Native and Inhabitant of the Place. (Richard Beverly.) The Second Edition revised and enlarged by the author. *8vo half mor., gilt top. With plates; beautiful copy, scarce.* *London*, 1722

PAMPHLETS.

2250 Miscellaneous, [*Eighteen.*]

Veritas. Remarks on the Letter of Domesticus containing the Doctrine of Incest Stated. *New York*, 1827

Virginia, Presbyterian Church of. Remarks on the act of the General Assembly of 1837. *Richmond.*

Vermilye, T. E. Discourse—"The Defense of the Gospel." Delivered December 16, 1841, on Inauguration of S. A. Van Vranken.

Van Buren, Governor, Message of, on Subject of Banks, Jan. 26, 1829.

Vlierden, Peter Van. Sermon delivered at Catskill, July 30, 1812. *Albany*

Villager, the : a Literary Paper. Nos. 1, 2, 3, 4, 5—1819. *Albany.*

Vechten, P. Van. Oration, 37th Anniversary of American Independence. *Very scarce.* *Albany,* July 12, 1813

Vermilye, Thomas E. Introductory Address to a Course of Lectures before Young Men's Association, Albany, delivered December 19, 1837.

Virginia Address to the Episcopalians in. *Very rare.* *New York,* 1771

——— Voice of, on approaching Election.

Vermont Classical Sem., Castleton. Discourse by W. B Sprague. *Albany,* May 27, 1830

Visions. Remarkable Visions. From the German. *Boston,* 1844

Vital Truth and Deadly Error. *Cin.,* 1853

Voltaire. Lord Chesterfield's Ears ; a true story. *London,* 1826

Vermont, Historical Discourse on Semi-Centennial Anniversary of University of, by Rev. John Wheeler. *Burlington,* 1854

——— before the Phi Sigma Nu Society, by C. S. Henry. 1836

Virginia, the Case of the Planters of Tobbaco in. *Rare.* *London,* 1733

——— Company of London. Extracts from Manuscript Transactions. By Edward D. Neill. *Washington,* 1868

2251 Miscellaneous. [*Fourteen.*]

Van Buren, Martin. Review of the Political Life of, by a Harrison Democrat. 3d edition. *Washington,* 1840

Van Dyke, J. The Spirituality and Independence of the Church : a Speech. *New York,* 1864

Vancouver, G., and Broughton. Journal of a Voyage of Discovery to the North Pacific Ocean, 1791–1795. *London,* 1802

Vans, William, a true Statement of the Demand of, against the Heirs of J. Codman. 1804

Vermilye, T. E. Discourse in the Reformed Dutch Church, New Brunswick, Dec. 16, 1841, on the Inaug. of S. A. Van Vranken. *New York,* 1842

Vermont Letter on the Nebraska Bill.

Vinton, Rev. Francis. Farewell Disc. to Trinity Church, Newport, R. I., July 7th, 1844. *Providence,* 1844

Vinton, Alexander H. Farewell Sermon preached at St. Paul's Church, Boston, Oct. 3, 1858. *Boston*, 1858

——— Sermon, on Thanksgiving Day, Nov. 27, 1862. *New York*, 1862

Virginia. Public Defaulters brought to Light. Letters by a Native of Virginia. *N. Y.*, 1822

——— Letters on the Richmond Party, by a Virginian. *Washington*, 1823

——— Observations on the Mineral Waters of Virginia. *Scarce.* *Phila.*, 1834

——— Trip to the Virginia Springs; or, the Belles and Beaux of 1835. By a Lady. *Scarce.* *Lexington, Va.*, 1843

——— My Ride to the Barbecue; or, Revolutionary Reminiscences of the Old Dominion. *New York*, 1860

WAIT, BENJAMIN. Letters from Van Dieman's Land, written during Four years Imprisonment for Political offences committed in Upper Canada. 8*vo, full cf., front.* *Buffalo,* 1843

2254 WAKELEY, Rev. J. B. Lost chapters recovered from the Early History of American Methodism. 8*vo, cl.; with portrait, fac-similes, and plates.* *New York,* 1858

2255 WALES, Mass. An Address, delivered in, Oct. 5, 1862, being the Centennial Anniversary of Organization of the Town; to which is annexed a "Roll of Honor," being a Catalogue of the Names, etc., of Soldiers from this Town, who Served in the late Civil War. By Absalom Gardiner. 8*vo pamph.,* 44 *p.* *Springfield,* 1866

"That undiscovered country, from whose bourn, no traveller returns."

2256 WALLACK, JAMES WILLIAM, SEN. Actor and Manager, Sketch of the Life of. *L.* 8*vo, uncut.* *N. Y., T. H. Morrell,* 1865

Only 250 copies printed.

2257 WALTON, Mr. IZAAK. THE UNIVERSAL ANGLER, Made so, by Three BOOKS of FISHING. The First Written by Mr. Izaak Walton; The Second by Charles Cotton, Esq.; The Third by Col. Robert Venable. 12*mo. mor.* *London. Printed for Richard Marriott, and sold by most Booksellers. MDCLXXVI.*

2258 WALTON, IZAAK. THE COMPLEAT ANGLER; or, The Contemplative Man's Recreation. Being a Discourse of Fish and Fishing, Not unworthy the perusal of most Anglers. *Sq.* 12*mo, cf.* *London, Printed by T. Maxey, for Richard Marriot,* 1653. *Reprinted exactly from the very rare first ed., with col'd plates.*

2259 WALTON AND COTTON. THE COMPLETE ANGLER; or, Contemplative Man's Recreations, being a discourse on Rivers, Fish-Ponds, Fish, and Fishing. In Two Parts: The First Written by Mr. Izaak Walton; The Second by Charles Cotton, Esq. With the Lives of the Authors, and Notes, Supplementary, Historical, and Explanatory. By Sir John Hawkins, Knt., and the present Editor. With Portraits and Illustrations.

Bagster's 2d ed., being the eighth of this work. *Roy.* 8*vo, hf. mor., gt. top, rough edges. London; Printed for Samuel Bagster, in the Strand.* *MDCCCXV.*

2260 WALTON and COTTON. The Complete Angler; or, The Contemplative Man's Recreation; being a discourse of Rivers, Fish-Ponds, Fish, and Fishing; Written by Izaak Walton; and instructions how to Angle for a Trout or Grayling in a clear Stream, by Charles Cotton. With Original Memoirs, and Notes by Sir Harris Nicolas. Portraits, Views and Plates of Fish. Rubricated Titles. 2 vols. *Imp.* 8*vo, hf. green mor., rough edges.* *London, Wm. Pickering,* 1836

2261 Wansey, Henry, F. A. S. The Journal of an Excursion to the United States of North America, in the Summer of 1794. Embellished with the Profile of Gen. Washington, and an Aqua-tinta view of the State House, at Philadelphia. 8*vo, bds., uncut.* *Salisbury,* 1796

2262 WAR, THE. Being a faithful Record of the Transactions of the War between the United States of America and their Territories, and the United Kingdom of Great Britain and Ireland, and the dependencies thereof, declared on the Eighteenth Day of June, 1812. Vols. I., II. *Fol., bds.* 2 *vols. in one, uncut.* *New York,* 1813–'14

2263 Ward, Rev. Nath'l. The Simple Cobler of Aggawam in America, willing to help Mend his Native Country, etc. By Theodore de la Guard. 8*vo, hf. crim. cr. lev. mor., gt. top; uncut. Bound by R. W. Smith. London,* 1647. *Reprint, Boston,* 1843

2264 Wardlaw, Rev. Ralph. Lectures on Magdalenism: its Nature, Extent, Effects, Guilt, Causes, and Remedy. 12*mo, cl.* *New York,* 1843

2265 Ware, William. Sermon, preached on the Sunday succeeding the Great Fire in New York, Dec. 16, 1835. 8*vo, orig. cov.,* 18 *p.; uncut.* *New York,* 1835

2266 WARE, Mass. An Address delivered at the Opening of the New Town Hall, March 31, 1847. Containing Sketches of the early History of that Town, and its First Settlers. By Wm. Hyde. 8*vo pamph.,* 56 *p.; scarce.* *Brookfield,* 1847

2267 Warner, Col. Seth. Memoir of, by Daniel Chipman. To which is added, the Life of Col. Ethan Allen, by Jared Sparks. 16*mo, cl.* *Middlebury, Vt.,* 1848

2268 WARREN, (R. I.) History of, from the Earliest Times, with particular notices of Massasoit and his Family. By G. M. Fessenden. *Providence,* 1845. In the same Vol., Justin, Josiah P. Discourse delivered at the New Edifice of the Baptist Church, May 8, 1845. 12*mo, cl., rough edges; scarce.* *Providence,* 1845

2269 WARREN, Me. Annals of Town of, with the Early History of St. George's, Broad Bay, and the Neighboring Settlements on the Waldo Patent. By Cyrus Eaton. 12*mo, cl.; Map.* *Hallowell,* 1851

2270 WARREN, Gen. JOSEPH. Biographical Sketch of, Embracing the prominent events of his Life, and his Boston Orations of 1772 and 1775 ; together with the celebrated Eulogy pronounced by Perez Morton, M. M., on the Re-interment of the Remains by the Masonic Order, at King's Chapel, in 1776. *Boston*, 1857

In same volume.

CARROLL, ANNA ELLA. The Union of the States, and a Review of Pierce's Administration, showing its only popular measures to have originated with the executive of Millard Fillmore. *8vo, cl. ; Port. of Warren.* *Boston*, 1856

2272 WARREN, Gen. JOSEPH. INAUGURATION of the Statue of, by the Bunker Hill Monument Association, June 17, 1857. *8vo, cl.* *Boston*, 1858

WASHINGTON EULOGIES.

2273 ALDEN, TIMOTHY. A Sermon delivered at the South Church, at Portsmouth, on the Vth January, MDCCC., occasioned by the Sudden and Universally Lamented Death of George Washington, etc. First Edition. *8vo, pp.* 24. *Extremely rare.* *Printed Feb.*, 1800

2274 ALEXANDER, CALEB. A Sermon occasioned by the Death of His Excellency, George Washington ; delivered at Mendon, Mass. Contains a Valuable Historical and Biographical Appendix, of five pages. *Rare, 8vo, pp.* 23. *Boston*, 1800

"This sermon was composed and delivered before any official intelligence was received of the death of Washington."

2275 ALSOP, RICHARD. A Poem : Sacred to the Memory of George Washington, late President of the United States, and Commander-in-Chief of the Armies of the United States ; adapted to the 22d of Feb., 1800. *8vo, pp.* 23, *clean. Fine copy, very scarce.* *Hartford*, 1800

2276 AMES, FISHER. ORATION on the Sublime Virtues of General Geo. Washington, pronounced at the Old South Meeting House, in Boston, before his Honor the Lieutenant Governor. Published by the State of Mass. *8vo, pp.* 51. *Boston*, 1800

2277 AMES, FISHER. An Oration on the Sublime Virtues of Gen. Geo. Washington, etc. *8vo, pp.* 31, *uncut ; scarce.* *Boston*, 1800

2278 AMES, FISHER. Oration on the Sublime Virtues of Gen'l George Washington, pronounced at the Old South Meeting House, in Boston. *8vo, fine copy, very scarce.* *New York*, 1800

Not in Woodward's Catalogue.

2279 BALDWIN, THOMAS, A.M. A Sermon delivered to the Second Baptist Society in Boston, on Lord's Day, Dec. 29, 1799, occasioned by the Death of General George Washington, etc. *8vo, pp.* 28, *clean.* *Boston*, 1800

2280 BANCROFT, AARON. An Eulogy on the Character of the late Gen. George Washington, delivered before the Inhabitants of the Town of Worcester, Commonwealth of Mass., on Saturday, the 22d of Feb., 1800. *8vo, pp.* 21, *clean copy. Scarce.* *Worcester*, 1800

2281 Bradford, Alden. An Eulogy in Commemoration of the Sublime Virtues of Gen. George Washington, late President of the United States, who died Dec. 14, 1799. Pronounced in Wiscasset, Feb. 22d, 1800, etc. *8vo, pp.* 16. *Rare.* *Wiscasset,* 1800

2282 Braman, Isaac. An Eulogy on the late Gen. George Washington, who died Saturday, 14th Dec., 1799. Delivered at Rowley, Second Parish, February 22d, 1800. *8vo, pp.* 24. *Rare.* *Haverhill,* 1800

2283 Bigelow, Timothy. An Eulogy on the Life, Character and Services of Brother George Washington, Deceased, pronounced before the Fraternity of Free and Accepted Masons, by Request of the Grand Lodge, at the Old South Meeting House, Boston, on Tuesday, Feb. 11, 1800, etc. *8vo, pp.* 26. *Very scarce.* *Boston,* 1800

2284 Blake, George B. A Masonic Eulogy on the Life of the Illustrious Brother George Washington, pronounced before the Brethren of St. John's Lodge, on the Evening of the 4th Feb., 5800, etc. *8vo, pp.* 23, *Rare.* *Boston,* 1800

See Woodward's Catalogue, 5812.

2285 CALDWELL, CHARLES. An Elegiac Poem, on the Death of Gen. Washington, etc. *8vo, half mor.; bound by Bradstreet. Extremely rare.* *Phila.,* 1800

Not in Woodward's Catalogue.

2286 Carroll, Bishop. A Discourse on Gen'l Washington, delivered in the Catholic Church of St. Peter, Feb. 22, 1800. *8vo, pp.* 24. *Half cf.* *Baltimore,* 1800

Portrait of Carroll and the very rare portrait of Washington, by Savage, inserted.

2287 CHARLESTOWN, Mass; Proceedings of the Town of—in respectful testimony of the late Geo. Washington. Containing a Prayer and Sermon, with a Sketch of his Life. By Jedediah Morse. Dec. 31, 1799. To which is prefixed an account of the Proceedings, written by Josiah Bartlett, and the "Valedictory Address" of the Deceased to his Fellow Citizens. *8vo, calf, beautiful copy; rare.* *January,* MDCCC.

2288 Chaudron, Simon. Oraison Funèbre du Frère George Washington, le premier Janvier, 1800, dans la Loge Française "L'Amenité." *8vo, pp.* 35. *A Philadelphie,* 1801

2289 Coffin, Ebenezer, Rev. A Sermon delivered Feb. 22d, 1800, the day of National Mourning recommended by the Government of the United States, for the Death of General George Washington. *8vo, pp.* 16. *Very rare.* *Portland,* 1800

See Woodward's Catalogue, 5838.

2290 Cummings, Henry. An Eulogy on the late Patriot, Washington, addressed to the People of Billerica, Jan. 10, 1800. *8vo, pp.* 16, *fine copy, very scarce.* *Amherst, N. H.,* 1800

2291 Dana, Daniel. A Discourse on the Character and Virtues of Gen. George Washington, delivered on the Twenty-second of February, 1800, the day of National Mourning for his death. *8vo, pp.* 31, *fine copy; scarce.* *Newburyport,* 1800

2292 Davis, John. An Eulogy on General George Washington, pronounced at Boston, on Wednesday, February xix., mdccc., before the American Academy of Arts and Sciences, by their appointment, and published at their request. *4to, pp.* 24; *very rare; uncut.* *Boston*, mdccc.

Davis, John. The same. *Uncut.* *Reprinted: Boston*, 1859

2293 Dunham, Josiah, A.M. A Funeral Oration on George Washington, late General of the Armies of the United States, pronounced at Oxford, Massachusetts, etc. *8vo, pp.* 20. *Rare.* *Boston*, 1800

2294 Dwight, Timothy. Discourse on Death of, etc., etc. *8vo, fine copy; rare.* *New Haven*, 1800

Not in Woodward's Catalogue.

2295 Fiske, Thadeus. A Sermon delivered Dec. 29, 1799, at the Second Parish in Cambridge, being the Lord's Day immediately following the Melancholy Intelligence of the Death of Gen. Geo. Washington, late President of the United States of America. *8vo, pp.* 21. *Scarce.* *Boston*, 1800

2296 Forbes, Eli. An Eulogy Moralized on the Illustrious Character of the late General George Washington, who died on Saturday, the 14th day of December, 1799. Delivered at Gloucester, on the 22d of February, 1800, etc. To which is added, Washington's Address, etc. *8vo, pp.* 40; *very fine copy; rare.* *Newburyport*, 1800

2297 Frisbie, Levi, A.M. An Eulogy on the Illustrious Character of the late General George Washington, etc., delivered at Ipswich, on the 7th day of January, 1800. To which is added, Gen'l Washington's Paternal and Affectionate Address to his Country. *8vo, pp.* 61, *rare.* *Newburyport*, 1800

2298 Guirey, William. A Funeral Sermon on the Death of General George Washington, who died at Mount Vernon, Dec. 14, 1799, aged 68. Delivered, by request, before the Methodist Episcopal Church at Lynn, January 7, 1800, etc. *8vo, pp.* 22. *Rare.* *Printed at Salem*, 1800

2299 Harris, Thaddeus Mason. A Discourse delivered at Dorchester, Dec. 29, 1799, being the Lord's day after hearing the Distressing Intelligence of the death of General George Washington, etc. *8vo, pp.* 16. *Charlestown*, mdccc.

2300 Holcombe, Henry. A Sermon, occasioned by the Death of Lieutenant-General George Washington, late President of the United States of America. *4to, pp* 18, *uncut; fine copy; full cr. crim. lev. mor.; by R. W. Smith.* *Savannah*, 1800

2301 Huntington, Asahel. A Sermon delivered at Topsfield, January 5, 1800, occasioned by the Death of George Washington, Commander-in-Chief of the American Armies, and late President of the United States. *8vo, pp.* 32, *uncut. Includes an historical sketch. Very rare.* *Salem*, 1800

See Woodward's Catalogue, No. 5898.

2302 Jackson, Major William. Eulogium on the Character of Gen'l Washington, late President of the United States, pronounced before the Pennsylvania Society of the Cincinnati, on the

Twenty-second day of February, Eighteen hundred, at the German Reformed Church, in the City of Philadelphia. *8vo, pp.* 44. *Phila.*, 1800

2303 Johnson, John B. Eulogy on General George Washington, a Sermon delivered February 22d, 1800, in the North Dutch Church, Albany, before the Legislature of the State of New York, at their request. *8vo, pp.* 22. *Scarce.* *Albany*, 1800

2304 Kirkland, John Thornton. A Discourse occasioned by the Death of General George Washington, delivered Dec. 29, 1799. To which is added the Valedictory Address of the late President, to the People of the United States. *8vo, pp.* 22 ; *very fine copy. Scarce.* *Boston*, 1800

2305 LEDYARD, ISAAC. Oration at Newtown, L. I., etc. *8vo, fine copy ; excessively rare.* *Brooklyn*, 1800

Not in Woodward's Catalogue, nor any other that has come under the owner's personal inspection for the past ten years.

2306 Lee, Major-General Henry, Funeral Oration on the Death of General Washington, Delivered at the Request of Congress by, Member of Congress from Virginia. *8vo*, 15 *p., clean.* *Boston*, (1800)

The Boston Edition of Lee's Oration is scarce.

2307 Lee, Major-General Henry. A Funeral Oration on the Death of George Washington, late President and Commander-in-Chief of the Armies of the United States of America, who departed this Life at Mount Vernon, in Virginia, on the 14th of Dec., 1799, in the 68th year of his age. Delivered at the Request of Congress. To which is subjoined an Eulogy, by Judge Minot. *8vo*, 28 *p. ; scarce.* *London*, 1800

2308 Lee, Maj.-Gen. Henry. Funeral Oration on the Death of Gen. Washington. Delivered at the Request of Congress, Dec. 26, 1799. *8vo, fine copy ; rare.* *Phila.*, 1800

Not in Woodward's Catalogue.

"As a Composition, it has only to be read to be admired for the purity and elegance of its language and the powerful appeal it makes to the hearts of its readers ; and we will venture to affirm, that it will rank among the most celebrated performances of those highly distinguished men, who mounted the rostrum on that imposing occasion of National Mourning."—Custis' Recoll. of Washington, N. Y., 1860, p. 360.

2309 Linn, William. A Funeral Eulogy, occasioned by the Death of General Washington, Delivered February 22d, 1800, before the New York State Society of the Cincinnati. *8vo*, 44 *p. ; very scarce.* *New York*, 1800

2310 Literary Society, An Oration in Memory of the Virtues of Gen. George Washington, Delivered at Lovett's Hotel, on the Evening of the 22d February, 1800, and Published by their Order. By a Member. *8vo*, 23 *p. ; very rare.* *New York*, 1800

2311 Magaw, Samuel. Oration on Death of George Washington, etc. *8vo, fine copy ; rare.* *Phila.*, 1800

Not in Woodward's Catalogue.

2312 Marsh, Ebenezer Grant. An Oration delivered at Wethersfield, February 22, 1800, on the Death of General George Washington, who died December 14, 1799. *8vo, 16 p., uncut; very scarce.* *Hartford*, 1800

2313 Mason, John M. Funeral Oration, deliv. Feb. 22, 1800, in New York. 2d Ed. *N. Y.*, 1800

2314 Minot, George Richards. An Eulogy on George Washington, Late Commander-in-Chief of the Armies of the United States of America, who died December 14th, 1799. Delivered before the Inhabitants of the Town of Boston, at the Request of their Committee. *8vo, 24 p., clean.* *Boston*, (1800)

2315 Minot, George Richards. An Eulogy on Geo Washington, who Died Dec. 14, 1799. Delivered before the Inhabitants of the Town of Boston. *2nd Ed.* *8vo, fine copy; very scarce.* *Boston*, 1800

Not in Woodward's Catalogue.

2316 Miller, Samuel. A Sermon Delivered December 29, 1799, Occasioned by the Death of General George Washington, Late President of the United States and Commander-in-Chief of the American Armies. *8vo, 39 p., uncut.* *New York*, 1800

2317 Morris, Gouverneur. An Oration upon the Death of General Washington, Delivered at the request of the City of New York, 31st Dec., 1799. *8vo, 24 p., fine copy; very scarce.* *New York*, 1800

2318 Morse, Jedidiah. Prayer and Sermon deliv. at Charlestown, Dec. 31, 1799, with Sketch of his Life, etc. Prefixed, the Proc. of the Town. *8vo, uncut; very scarce.* *London*, 1800

2319 Mycall, John. A Funeral Address on the Death of the late Gen. Geo. Washington, interspersed with Sketches of, and Observations on his Life and Character. Delivered in Harvard, Feb. 22, 1800. *8vo, 27 p., fine copy; rare.* *Boston*, 1800

2320 Niles, Samuel. Sermon delivered at Abington, (Mass.), Feb. 22, 1800, etc. *8vo, fine copy; very rare.* *Boston*, 1800

Not in Woodward's Catalogue.

2321 Ogden, Uzal. Two Discourses occasioned by the death of General George Washington, at Mount Vernon, December 14, 1799. *8vo, 46 p.; rare.* *Newark, MDCCC.*

2322 Osgood, David, D.D. A Discourse delivered December 29, 1799, the Lord's Day immediately following the melancholy tidings of the loss sustained by the Nation in the Death of its most Eminent Citizen, George Washington, etc. *8vo, 19 p., fine copy; scarce.* *Boston*, 1800

2323 Paine, Thos. An Eulogy on the Life of George Washington, written at the request of the Citizens of Newburyport, and delivered at the first Presbyterian Meeting-House in that town, January 2, 1800. *8vo, 22 p.* *Newburyport*, 1800

2324 Payson, Rev. Phillips. A Sermon Delivered at Chelsea, on the Death of George Washington. *8vo, 15 p., clean; rare.* *Charlestown*, 1800

2325 Pennsylvania State Society of the Cincinnati, with the Original

Institution of the Order, etc., to which is annexed the Testimonial to the Memory of Gen'l Washington. *Hf. cf.; rare.* *Phila.*, 1801

2326 PIERCE, JOHN. An Eulogy on George Washington, the Great and the Good. Delivered on the Anniversary of his Birth, at Brookline, and published at the request of its inhabitants. *8vo, 24 p.; scarce.* *Boston*, 1800

2327 PORTER, ELIPHALET. An Eulogy on George Washington, late Commander of the Armies, and the First President of the United States of America, who died on the 14th of December, 1799, Ætatis 68. Delivered Jan. 14, 1800, before the Inhabitants of the Town of Roxbury, at the Request of their Committee, and Published in Compliance with their wishes. *8vo, 22 p.* *With the Farewell Address in 22 additional pages.* *Boston*, 1800

2328 RAMSAY, DAVID. An Oration on the Death of Lieutenant-General George Washington, late President of the United States, who died Dec. 14, 1799. Delivered in St. Michael's Church, January 15, 1800, at the request of the inhabitants of Charleston, South Carolina, and published by their desire. *8vo, pp. 30.* *Charleston*, 1800

2329 SACRED DIRGES, HYMNS AND ANTHEMS, COMMEMORATIVE OF THE DEATH OF GEORGE WASHINGTON. An original Composition. By a Citizen of Mass. *4to, uncut; beautiful copy; extremely rare; possibly unique.* *Boston: I. Thomas and T. Andrews.* 1800

Not in Woodward's Catalogue.

2330 SEWALL, JONATHAN M. Eulogy on the late General Washington, pronounced at St. John's Church, in Portsmouth, New Hampshire, on Tuesday, 31st December, 1799, at the request of the inhabitants. *4to, pp. 28; very rare.* *Printed at Portsmouth, N. H.* 1800

See Woodworth's Catalogue, 6003.

2331 SMITH, SAMUEL STANHOPE.. AN ORATION upon the Death of General George Washington, delivered in the State House at Trenton, on the 14th of January, 1800. *8vo, pp. 46.* *Trenton*, 1800

2332 SMITH, SAMUEL STANHOPE. AN ORATION upon the Death of Washington, delivered in Trenton, Jan. 14, 1800, by Rev. Samuel Stanhope Smith. *8vo; port. of Smith; half mor., pp. 46; very scarce.* *Trenton: G. Craft.* 1800

2333 SMITH, SAMUEL I. An Oration, delivered at Trenton, Jan. 14, 1800. Third Ed. 92 *pp.* *Trenton*, 1817

2334 Spring, Samuel. A Discourse on the Death of General George Washington, delivered at the North Congregational Church in Newburyport, December 29, 1799. *8vo, 28 pp.; clean; scarce.* *Newburyport*, 1800

2335 STONE, ELIAB, A. M. A Discourse delivered at Reading, Feb. 22, 1800, the day recommended by Congress to the observance of the people of the United States, by their assembling in such manner as might be convenient, and publicly testifying their grief for the death, and their respect for the memory of Gen. George Washington. *8vo, pp.* 23 ; *clean ; very scarce* *Boston,* 1800

Contains a Hymn prepared for the occasion. See Woodward's Catalogue, 6019.

2336 Story, Isaac. An Eulogy on the glorious virtues of the illustri ous General George Washington, who died at Mount Vernon, December 14th, 1799, in the 68th year of his age, ripe in honor and full of glory. Written at the request of the inhabitants of Sterling, and delivered before them on Saturday, the 22d of February, 1800. *8vo, pp.* 23 ; *scarce.* *Worcester: printed by Isaiah Thomas, Jr., April,* 1800

2337 SUMNER, CHA'S PINCKNEY. Eulogy on the illustrious George Washington. Pronounced at Milton (Mass.), Feb. 22, 1800. *8vo, pp.* 24 ; *first edition ; very scarce.* *Dedham,* 1800

2338 TAGGART, Rev. SAMUEL. A Discourse delivered at Colrain, Feb. 22, 1800 ; being the day recommended by Congress and the Legislature of Massachusetts for the public testifying of our respect to the memory of that late illustrious statesman, and singular benefactor to his country, General George Washington, who died December 14, 1799. *8vo, pp.* 32 ; *rare.* *Greenfield,* 1800

2339 THACHER, PETER. A SERMON occasioned by the death of General George Washington, and preached Feb. 22, 1800, by their direction, before his Honor Moses Gill, Esq., Commander-in-Chief, the Honorable Council, the Honorable Senate and House of Representatives of the Commonwealth of Massachusetts. *8vo, pp.* 21 ; *uncut ; rare.* *Boston,* 1800

2340 THACHER, THOMAS CUSHING. An Eulogy on the memory of Gen. George Washington, who died December 14, 1799, aged 68. Pronounced at the request of the citizens of Lynn, Jan. 13, 1800, and published by the desire of the Committee of Arrangements. *8vo, pp.* 12 ; *rare.* *Boston,* 1800

2341 TRUMBULL, BENJAMIN. A Funeral Discourse delivered at North Haven, December 29, 1799, on the death of General George Washington, who died December 14, 1799. *8vo, pp.* 31 ; *fine copy ; scarce.* *New Haven,* 1800

2342 VINING, JOHN. An Eulogium delivered to a large concourse of respectable citizens, at the State House in the town of Dover, on the 22d of February, 1800, in commemoration of the death of General George Washington. *Half cf.*, *8vo, pp* 20 ; *scarce.* *Phila.,* 1800

2343 WADSWORTH, BENJAMIN. An Eulogy on the excellent character of George Washington, late Commander-in-Chief of the American Armies, and the first President under the Federal Constitution, who departed this life December the 14th, 1799, in the 68th year of his age. Pronounced February 22, 1800 ; being the anniversary of his birth, and the day recommended by Congress to testify the national grief for his death. *8vo, pp.* 32 ; *scarce.* *Salem,* 1800

2344 WEST, SAMUEL. A Sermon occasioned by the death of George Washington, late Commander-in-Chief of the Armies, and first

President of the United States of America, who died December 14, 1799, aged 68. *8vo*, 17 *pp., with* 23 *additional pages of "Farewell Address."* *Boston*, 1800

2345 Willard and Tappan. An Address, in Latin. by Joseph Willard, LL.D., President; and a Discourse, in English, by David Tappan, Hollis Professor of Divinity, delivered before the University in Cambridge, Feb. 21, 1800, in solemn commemoration of Gen. George Washington. *4to, pp.* 31, *large paper; scarce.* *Boston*, 1800

2346 Worcester, Leonard. An Oration pronounced at Peacham, in commemoration of the death of the late General George Washington, February 22d, 1800. *8vo, pp.* 20; *very rare.* *Peacham, Vt.*, 1800

Woodward's Catalogue, 6096.

2347 Dwight, Jasper. A Letter to George Washington, President of the United States, containing Strictures on his Address on the Seventeenth of September, 1796, Notifying his Relinquishment of the Presidential Office. *8vo*, 48 *p.; rare.* *Philadelphia*, 1796

2348 Buckminster, Joseph. Discourse deliv. at Portsmouth, N. H., Nov. 1, 1789, on the occasion of the President's Visit to that Capital. *Fine copy; rare.* *Portsmouth*, 1789

2449 BUCKMINSTER, JOSEPH. A Discourse delivered in Portsmouth, Dec. 14, 1800, on the Anniversary of the Death of Geo. Washington. 21 *p. 8vo; beautiful copy; uncut; very rare.* *Portsmouth*, 1800

2350 WASHINGTON, GEORGE. The Life of, First President of the United States. To which is prefixed an Introduction containing a compendious view of the Colonies Planted by the English on the Continent of North America, from their Settlement to the Commencement of that War which terminated in their Independence. By John Marshall. 5 *vols., bds., uncut. With portrait; fine copy.* *Philadelphia, Pa.*, 1804

2351 WASHINGTON, GEORGE. The Life of. Compiled by the Hon. Bushrod Washington from Original Papers bequeathed to him by his deceased Relative. By John Marshall. *8vo, uncut. Second Ed.* 2 *vols., cl.; por.; fine copy.* *Phila.*, 1832

2352 WASHINGTON, GEORGE. An Essay on the Life of. By Aaron Bancroft. *Cl., 8vo, bds., uncut; with portrait by Edwin. Exceedingly scarce.* *Worcester*, 1807

This edition is very rarely met with, and the condition of this copy gives it an additional value.

2353 WASHINGTON, GEORGE. The Life of. By Aaron Bancroft. *8vo, bds. uncut.* *London*, 1808

2354 WASHINGTON, GEORGE. The Life of. By Aaron Bancroft. In two volumes. *Sheep, 12mo.* *Boston*, 1826

2355 WASHINGTON, GEORGE. The Life of, including the Declaration of Independence and the Constitution of the United

States. By John Corry. *First American Edition.* *8vo, sh.; portrait by Scoles; beautiful copy.* *N. Y.*, 1807

This edition is extremely scarce.

2356 WASHINGTON, GEORGE. Life of, interspersed with Biographical Anecdotes of the most Eminent Men who effected the American Revolution. By John Corry. *8vo, sh.; portrait by Scoles; fine copy; rare.* *N. Y.*, 1809

2357 WASHINGTON, GEN. GEORGE. Biographical Memoirs of. *12mo, bds.; port. and eng'd title; very rare; beautiful copy.* *New Haven: from Sidney's Press*, 1810

2358 WASHINGTON, GEN. GEORGE. Memoirs of, Late President of the United States of America. Fifth ed. *12mo, bds.* *Phila.*, 1811

2359 WASHINGTON GEORGE. Biographical Memoirs of. *12mo, sh; portrait; very scarce; fine copy.* *Barnard, Vt.*, 1813

Contains the rare portrait of Washington, "Pro Patria," crowned.

2360 WASHINGTON, GEORGE. Biographical Memoirs of, containing a History of the principal events of his Life, with extracts from his Journals, Speeches to Congress and Public Addresses; also, a sketch of his Private Life. *8vo, sh.; fine copy; scarce.* *Brattleborough*, 1814

2361 WASHINGTON GEORGE. Life of. *24mo, cf.; very rare; portrait of Washington, "Pro Patria."* *Boston*, 1815

2362 Washington, George. The Life of. *Eng'd title; good copy; 12mo, hf. cf.; illustrated.* *Phila.*, 1832

2363 WASHINGTON, GEORGE. Life of. Tales, Sketches and Anecdotes. With engravings. *8vo, bds.* *Philadelphia*, 1836

2364 WASHINGTON, GEORGE. The Life of, and History of the American Revolution; together with his Farewell Address, Declaration of Independence, and Constitution of the U. S. *12mo, bds.; plates.* *N. Y., n. d.*

2365 WASHINGTON, GEORGE. Pictorial Life of, embracing Anecdotes illustrative of his Character, and embellished with engravings. *Sq. 12mo.* *Philadelphia*, 1847

2366 Washington. Entertaining Anecdotes of, exhibiting his Patriotism, Courage, Benevolence and Piety. *Sm. 4to, cl.; illust.* *Boston*, 1848

2367 WASHINGTON. The Memory of, with Biographical Sketches of his Mother and Wife, Relations of Lafayette to Washington, with Incidents and Anecdotes in the lives of the two patriots. *8vo, cl.; frontis.; fine copy.* *Boston*, 1852

2368 WASHINGTON. Recollections and Private Memoirs of, by his Adopted Son, Geo. W. Parke Custis, with a Memoir of the Author by his Daughter; and Illustrative and Explanatory Notes by Benson J. Lossing. With Illustrations. *8vo, cl.; fine copy; very scarce; portraits of Custis, Washington, Mrs. E. P. Lewis and Martha Washington, and Fac-similes.* *New York*, 1860

2369 WASHINGTON, GEN. GEORGE. The Life of. By John Kingston. *24mo, sh.; scarce; lacks portrait.* *Baltimore*, 1813

2370 WASHINGTON, GEORGE. THE LIFE OF. By David Ramsay. *8vo, bds., uncut; eleg. portrait by Heath, after Stuart; fine copy; scarce.* *London*, 1807

2371 WASHINGTON, GEORGE. THE LIFE OF. By David Ramsay. *8vo, bds., uncut; fine copy. Port. by Leney.* *New York*, 1807

2372 WASHINGTON, GEORGE. THE LIFE OE. By David Ramsay. 2d ed. *8vo, sh.; portrait, wood-cut. Fine copy.* *Boston*, 1811

2373 WASHINGTON GEORGE. THE LIFE OF. By David Ramsay. Fourth edition. With six engravings. *8vo, sh.; fine copy.* *Baltimore*, 1815

FRONTIS.—" Firm as the Surge-repelling Rock.

2374 WASHINGTON, GEORGE. THE LIFE OF. Sixth Edition with Six Engravings. By David Ramsay. *8vo, sh.; curious frontis., " Firm as a Rock," etc.* *Baltimore*, 1825

2375 WASHINGTON, JORGE. LA VIDA DE COMANDANTE en Gefe de los Egercitos de los Estados Unidos de America, en La Guerra que Establecis su Independencia; y Su Primer Presidente. Escrita en Ingles por David Ramsay; y Traducida al Espanal por Eduardo Barry. *8vo, hf. cf.* *Filadelfia*, 1826

2376 WASHINGTON, GEORGE. THE LIFE OF. By David Ramsay. With notes and Biographical Sketch of the Author. *8vo, sh., with portrait.* *Ithaca, N. Y.*, 1840

2377 WASHINGTON, GEORGE. THE LIFE OF, with curious Anecdotes. Seventh Edition. By M. L. Weems. *8vo, bds., portrait; scarce.* *Phila.*, 1808

2378 WASHINGTON, GEORGE. LIFE OF, with curious anecdotes. Ninth ed., greatly improved. Embellished with seven engravings. By M. L. Weems. *12mo, sh., frontis.* *Phila.*, 1809

2379 WASHINGTON, GEORGE. THE LIFE OF, with curious anecdotes equally honorable to himself and exemplary to his young countrymen. Tenth ed., greatly improved, embellished with seven engravings. By M. L. Weems. *8vo, sh., scarce; good copy.* *Phila.*, 1810

2380 WASHINGTON, GEORGE. THE LIFE OF, with curious anecdotes, etc. Fifteenth ed. Illust. with eight engravings. By M. L. Weems. *8vo, sh.* *Phila.*, 1816

2381 WASHINGTON, GEORGE. THE LIFE OF, with curious anecdotes, equally honorable to himself, and exemplary to his young countrymen. Twenty-first edition. Greatly improved, embellished with eight engravings. By M. L. Weems. *12mo, sh.* *Phila.: M. Carey & Son.* 1818

2382 WASHINGTON, GEORGE. THE LIFE OF, with curious anecdotes, etc. Twenty-second ed. Embellished with eight engravings and map. By M. L. Weems. *8vo, sh., fine copy.* *Phila.*, 1819

2383 WASHINGTON, GEORGE. THE LIFE OF, with curious anecdotes, etc. By M. L. Weems. Embellished with six engravings. *8vo, sh. Port.* *Phila.*, 1832

2384 WASHINGTON, GEORGE. THE LIFE OF, with curious anecdotes, equally honourable to himself, and exemplary to his young countrymen. Embellished with six engravings. By M. L. Weems. *8vo, sh., port.* *Phila.*, 1844

2385 WASHINGTON, GEORGE. The Life of, with curious anecdotes. Illust. with six engs. By M. L. Weems. *8vo, sh., port.* *Phila.*, 1847

2386 WASHINGTON, GEORGE. The Life of, with curious anecdotes, equally honorable to himself, and exemplary to his young companions. Embellished with six engravings. By M. L. Weems. *8vo, cl., port.* *Phila.*, 1858

2387 WASHINGTON, GEORGE. The Life and Times of, By Cyrus R. Edmonds. 12*mo, cl., uncut,* 2 *vols., fine copy ; Frontis.* *London*, 1835

2388 WASHINGTON, GEORGE. A Life of. By James K. Paulding. 12*mo,* 2 *vols., cl., uncut ; Plates and Engraved Titles. Scarce.* *New York*, 1835

2389 WASHINGTON. Life of. By James K. Paulding. *In* 2 *vols.,* 12*mo, cl., uncut. Portrait and Eng. Title.* *New York*, 1840

2390 WASHINGTON, GEORGE. The Writings of, being his Correspondence, Addresses, Messages and other Papers, Official and Private, selected and published from Original Manuscripts. With a Life of the Author, Notes and 34 illustrations. By Jared Sparks. 12 *vols., L. P., bds., uncut.* *Boston*, 1837

2391 Washington, George. Life of. By Jared Sparks. 2 *vols., cl.,* 12*mo.* *Boston*, 1822

2392 WASHINGTON, GEORGE. Life of, in Latin Prose. By Francis Glass, A. M. *Cl.,* 12*mo ; Frontispiece.* *New York*, 1834

2393 WASHINGTON, GEORGE. A Life of, in Latin Prose. By Francis Glass of Ohio. Edited by J. N. Reynolds. *8vo, cl. ; medallion port. by Ormsby.* *New York*, 1835

2394 Washington, George. A Life of, in Latin Prose. By Francis Glass. Edited by J. N. Reynolds. Third edition. *8vo, cl., medallion port. of Washington, eng. by Ormsby.* *New York*, 1836

2395 WASHINGTON, GEORGE. By Monsieur Guizot. Translated by Henry Reeve. *8vo, cl., uncut ; fine copy, port. inserted, eng. by Read.* *London : John Murray*, 1840

2396 Washington. By Monsieur Guizot. Translated by Henry Reeve. 12*mo, half cf., gt. top, uncut, scarce. Port., eng. by Storms, after Houdon.* *Paris*, 1840

2397 WASHINGTON, GEORGE. Essay on the Character and Influence of, in the Revolution of the United States of America. Second edition. Translated from the French. By M. Guizot. *8vo, cl., portrait ; clean, nice copy.* *Boston*, 1851

2398 WASHINGTON, GEORGE. Vie de, pris de L'Anglais, et dédié a la Jennesse Americaine. By Prof. A. N. Girault. 12*mo, cl.,* 24*th ed., plates.* *Phila.*, 1850

2399 WASHINGTON, GEORGE. The Life of, in the form of an Autobiography, the narrative being, to a great extent conducted by Himself, in extracts and selections from his own writings.

With Portraits and other engravings. By Charles W. Upham. *In two vols., 8vo, cl. First and only Amer. Ed. Very scarce.* *Boston*, 1840

No portraits or engravings were published for this work, the edition having been suppressed by the author.

2400 WASHINGTON, GEN. THE LIFE OF, First President of the United States, written by himself, comprising his memoirs and correspondence, as prepared by him for publication, including several original letters, now first printed. Ed. by Rev. C. W. Upham. *2 vols., 8vo, cl. With port.* *London*, 1851

2401 WASHINGTON, GEORGE. LIFE OF, written by himself, comprising his Memoirs and Correspondence, as prepared by him for Publication, including several original letters, now first printed. Edited by the Rev. C. W. Upham. *In two vols., 8vo, cl. Portraits and Eng. Titles.* *London*, 1852

2402 WASHINGTON, GEORGE. LIFE OF. By Edward Everett. *12mo, cl.* *New York*, 1860

2403 WASHINGTON, GEO. A DISCOURSE delivered in New Market, N. H., at the particular request of a Respectable Musical Choir, to a numerous Assembly, convened for Celebrating the Birthday of the Illustrious Washington. By James Miltimore. *8vo, uncut, 24 pages. Very scarce.* *Printed at Exeter*, 1794

2404 WASHINGTON SOCIETY of Alexandria, Va. An Oration delivered February 22, 1815, by Col. John Eager Howard. *8vo, uncut, fine copy ; 16 pages. Very rare.* *Alexandria: Printed by Allen and Hill, n. d.*

2405 WASHINGTON, GEO., THE COUNSEL OF. Recommended in a Discourse delivered at Cambridge, Feb. 22, 1800, by Abiel Holmes. *8vo ; fine copy. Very scarce, 23 pages.* *Boston*, 1800

2406 WASHINGTON, GEO., A SELECTION OF ORATIONS AND EULOGIES pronounced in different parts of the United States, in commemoration of the Life, Virtues, and Pre-eminent Services of, Who died at Mount Vernon, December 14, 1799, in the 68th year of his age. *8vo, sheep. Woodcut on title ; excessively rare. Fine copy.* *Amherst*, 1800

Brought in Woodward's sale, $45.

2407 WASHINGTON, GEO. THE WASHINGTONIANA. Containing a Biographical Sketch of. With various outlines of his Character, and an Account of the various Funeral Honors devoted to his Memory ; to which are annexed his Will and Schedule of his Property. Embellished with a good Likeness. *8vo, sh. Port. after Savage.* *Baltimore*, 1800

Good Copy of this Rare book.

2408 WASHINGTON, GEO., EULOGIES AND ORATIONS on the Life and Death of. "The Mournful Tribute of a Nation's Love." Beautiful Copy of this rare book. *8vo, sh.* *Boston*, 1800

2409 WASHINGTON'S POLITICAL LEGACIES ; to which is annexed an Appendix containing an account of his Illness, Death, and the

Nat. Tribute of Respect paid to his Memory, with a Biographical outline of his Life and Character. *8vo, sheep; beautiful copy. Very scarce.* *Boston*, 1800

Rufus Choate's copy, with Autograph.

2410 WASHINGTON, Gen. GEO, THE COLUMBIAN PHENIX and Boston Review. Containing a great variety of matter instructing and Curious. Also the following Orations and Eulogies, delivered at the Death of General Washington as follows: General Henry Lee, G. R. Minot, Fisher Ames, and Louis Fontaines. *8vo, bds., uncut. Rare.* *Boston*, 1800

2411 WASHINGTON, GEO. THE WASHINGTONIANA. Containing a Sketch of the Life and Death of, with a collection of elegant Eulogies, Orations, Poems, &c., Sacred to his Memory; also, an Appendix comprising all his most valuable Public Papers and his Last Will and Testament. *8vo, sheep; beautiful copy and fine portrait, by Edwin. Very rare.* *Lancaster*, 1802

Newspaper cuttings 1789, *inserted.*

2412 WASHINGTON, GEO. POLITICAL LEGACIES. To which is annexed an Appendix containing an account of his Illness, Death, and the National Tributes of Respect paid to his Memory, with a Biographical Sketch of his Life and Character, his Will, and Dr. Tappan's Discourse before the University of Cambridge. *8vo, sheep; beautiful copy, very rare.* *N. Y.*, 1800

2413 WASHINGTON, GEO. MONUMENTS OF PATRIOTISM. Being a collection of the most Interesting Documents connected with the Military Command and Civil Administration of the American Hero and Patriot. To which is annexed an Eulogium on the Character of General Washington. By Major William Jackson. *8vo, sheep. Fine copy, with the very rare portrait by Savage, and the engraving of Washington's Resignation by Barrelet.* *Phila.*, 1800

2414 WASHINGTON'S MONUMENTS OF PATRIOTISM. Being a collection of the most Interesting Documents connected with the Military Command and Civil Administration of the American Hero and Patriot: to which is annexed an Eulogium on the Character of Gen. Washington. Selected and arranged by two Gentlemen, eminent for their Literary and Political Information. *8vo, half calf. Rare, good copy.* *Phila.*, 1802

Contains Eulogy deliv. at Woodbury, N. J., by John Croes; usually missing. Phil. 1800.

2415 WASHINGTON, GEO. OFFICIAL LETTERS TO THE HONORABLE AMERICAN CONGRESS, written during the War between the United Colonies and Great Britain, by His Excellency, Commander-in-Chief of the Continental Forces, now President of the United States. In two volumes. *8vo, sheep. Fine copy, scarce.* *Boston*, 1795

2416 WASHINGTON, GEO. OFFICIAL LETTERS TO THE HONORABLE AMERICAN CONGRESS, written during the War between the Uni-

ted Colonies and Great Britain. Second Boston Edition. In two volumes. 8vo, *unbound. With the excessively scarce Portrait engraved by S. Hill. Rarely found in any copies*
Boston, 1796

It has been doubted whether there ever was any Portrait engraved for this edition, but this copy sets that doubt aside.

2417 WASHINGTON, GEO. OFFICIAL LETTERS to the Honorable American Congress. Written during the War. 2 volumes. *Boards, uncut.* *London*, 1795

2418 WASHINGTON, GEO. EPISTLES, DOMESTIC, CONFIDENTIAL AND OFFICIAL, written about the Commencement of the American Contest. With an Interesting Series of his Letters to the British Admirals, General Sir Henry Clinton, Lord Cornwallis, Count de Grasse, &c., respecting an attack of New York. None of which have been printed in the two volumes of Official Letters. 8vo, *paper covers, uncut, very rare. Fine copy.* *N. Y.*, 1796

2419 WASHINGTON, GEO. Epistles, Domestic, Confidential, &c. *Half morocco, marbled edges.* *London*, 1796

2420 WASHINGTON, GEO. AN AUTHENTIC ACCOUNT of the Proceedings with regard to laying the Corner Stone of the Monument in the City of Baltimore. With an Engraving of the Monument; also, an Address from the Citizens of Baltimore to the Man who was "First in war, first in peace, and first in the hearts of his countrymen." Together with his Answer. Also, Fac-similes of the engraved plate deposited under the Cornerstone, and a Biographical Sketch of General Washington. 8*vo, bds. Very rare, fine copy.* *Baltimore*, 1815

2421 WASHINGTON, GEO., THE TOMB OF, at Mount Vernon, embracing a full and accurate description of Mount Vernon, as well as of the Birthplace, Genealogy, Character, Marriage, and Last Illness of Washington, together with incidents pertaining to the Burial, Removal from the old Family Vault, and his being placed in the New Tomb in a Marble Sarcophagus. By J. A. Winneberger. *L. P.*, 8*vo, cl., illustrated; good copy.*
Washington, 1858

2422 WASHINGTON, GEO., THE HOME OF, AT MOUNT VERNON. Embracing a full and accurate description as well as of the Birthplace, Genealogy, Character, Marriage, and last Illness of Washington, together with Incidents pertaining to the Burial of, Removal from the Old Family Vault, and his being placed in the new Tomb in a Marble Sarcophagus. By J. A. Winneberger. 8*vo, cl. Port. after Stuart, and Illustrated.*
Washington, 1858

2423 WASHINGTON, NATIONAL MONUMENT to. Oration Pronounced by the Hon. Robert C. Winthrop, July 4, 1848, on the Occasion of laying the Corner Stone, Etc. 8*vo pamph.*, 23 *pages.*
Washington, 1848

2424 WASHINGTON, THE HOME OF, AND ITS ASSOCIATIONS, HISTORICAL, BIOGRAPHICAL AND PICTORIAL. New edition, revised, with additions. By Benson J. Lossing. Illustrated by numerous engravings, chiefly from Original Drawings by the Author. *Roy. 8vo, cl. uncut.* 100 *copies printed.* *New York*, 1865

2425 WASHINGTON'S FAREWELL ADDRESS to the People of the United States. Published for the Washington Benevolent Soc. Second edition. 12*mo, half mor. Portrait, very rare.* *N. Y.*, 1809

This book is particularly valuable on account of the small number struck for the private use of the members of the Society only. Each copy contained the Certificate of Membership of the member to whom it was issued. This copy has the certificate of Rufus Greene, dated July 3, 1809, with remarkably fine signatures of Isaac Lebring, President, and Hon. Gulian C. Verplanck, Secretary of the Washington Benevolent Society of New York.

2426 WASHINGTON'S FAREWELL ADDRESS to the People of the United States. Rare Portrait of Washington. *Boards,* 12*mo. In fine condition.* *Brookfield, Mass.*, 1812

Published for the Brookfield Washington Benevolent Society.

2427 WASHINGTON, GEORGE. FAREWELL ADDRESS to the People of the United States. 16*mo, bds. Fine condition.* *Springfield*, 1812

2428 WASHINGTON, GEO. Farewell Address to the People of the United States. Rare Portrait by Reed. 8*vo, bds. Fine copy.* *Windsor*, 1812

Very rare with the Portrait and Certificate of Membership.

2429 WASHINGTON, GEO. VALEDICTORY ADDRESS OF, to the People of the United States. 24*mo, unbound ; scarce.* *Boston*, 1812

2430 WASHINGTON, GEO. AN INQUIRY into the formation of Washington's Farewell Address. By Horace Binney. *L.* 8*vo, cl., elegant portraits of Washington, Binney, Madison, and Hamilton, inserted.* *Phila.*, 1859

Fine Copy, Containing numerous Newspaper Cuttings, Hor. Binney's Essay on Washington, Oct. 14, 1859 ; Autog. Letter of, Dec. 2, 1826, to E. Chauncey, Esq., and Advertisements from old Papers, etc., 1799 ; Notices, Anecdotes, etc., relative to Washington.

2431 WASHINGTON BENEV. Soc., of Newburyport. "The Portrait." A Poem. Delivered, Oct. 27, 1812. By John Pierpont. 8*vo, uncut, fine copy ;* 36 *p., scarce, first ed.* *Boston*, 1812

2432 WASHINGTON, GEO. THE TEXT-BOOK OF THE WASHINGTON BENE. Soc. Containing a Biography, and Character of his Farewell Address to the People of the United States, and the Federal Constitution, with the Amendments. 3d Ed. 12*mo, bds., rare portrait ; fine copy.* *Concord*, 1814

2433 "WASHINGTON BENEVOLENTS." The Fourth Book of, otherwise called, the Book of Knaves. *S.* 8*vo,* 24 *p., uncut. Rude Wood Cut, Portrait on Title. Printed by N. Coverly, Milk St.* *Boston*, 1814

"Verily their folly exceedeth the comprehension of man ; and they shall be laughed to scorn."

The War of 1812, written in Scripture Style ; very curious dedication.

2434 WASHINGTON SOCIETY. An Historical View of the Public Celebrations of, and those of the Young Republicans, from 1805 to 1822. 12*mo, bds., portrait,* *Boston,* 1823

2435 WASHINGTON, GEO. The Diary of, from 1789 to 1791, embracing the opening of the First Congress, and his Tours through New England, Long Island, etc., together with his Journal of a Tour to the Ohio, in 1753. Edited by Benson J. Lossing. 8*vo, cl.,* 248 *pages ; fine copy. Very scarce.* *Richmond,* 1861

Published by the Va. Hist. Soc.

2436 WASHINGTON, GEO. The Diary of, from 1789 to 1791 ; embracing the opening of the First Congress, and his Tours through New England, Long Island, and the Southern States. Together with his Journal of a Tour to the Ohio, in 1753. By Benson J. Lossing. 12*mo, cl. ; with portrait.* *New York,* 1860

2437 WASHINGTON, GEO. Reprint of the Original Letters from, to Joseph Reed, during the American Revolution, referred to in the Pamphlets of Lord Mahon and Mr. Sparks. By Wm. B. Reed. 8*vo, paper covers,* 155 *pages.* *Phila.,* 1852

2438 Washington, Geo. Remarks on a "Reprint of the Original Letters from, to Joseph Reed, during the American Revolution, referred to in the Pamphlets of Lord Mahon and Mr. Sparks." By Jared Sparks. 8*vo, cl.* *Boston,* 1853

Presentation copy from the Author.

2439 WASHINGTON, GEO. Reply to the Strictures of Lord Mahon and others, on the mode of editing the Writings of. By Jared Sparks. 8*vo, cl.* *Cambridge,* 1852

2440 WASHINGTON, GEO. Letter to Lord Mahon, being an answer to his letter addressed to the Editor of Washington's Writings. By Jared Sparks. 8*vo, cl.* *Boston,* 1852

2441 WASHINGTON, GEO. A Letter to, on Affairs, Public and Private. By Thomas Paine, *Phila.,* 1796. In the same volume, A Letter to the Infamous Tom Paine, in answer to his brutal attack on the Federal Constitution, and on the conduct and character of General Washington. 8*vo, hf. mor. Bound by Pawson & Nicholson. Fine copy.* *Phila.,* 1796

2442 WASHINGTON, GEO. An Answer to Paine's Letter to, including some Pages of Gratuitous Counsel to Mr. Erskine. By P. Kennedy. 8*vo, uncut, scarce, fine copy,* 42 *pages.* *Phila.,* 1798

2443 WASHINGTON, GEO. An Answer to Mr. Paine's Letter to, or Mad Tom convicted of the blackest Ingratitude, etc. By P. Kennedy. 8*vo,* 55 *pages, scarce ; good copy.* *London,* 1797

2444 WASHINGTON, GEO. Expostulatory Letter to, of Mount Vernon in Virginia, on his continuing to be a Proprietor of Slaves. By Edward Rushton. 8*vo,* 24 *p., uncut ; very rare.* *Liverpool. Printed,* 1797

The Preface opens as follows:—"In July last, 1796, the following letter was transmitted to the person to whom it is addressed, and a few weeks ago it was returned under cover, without a syllable in reply, etc." What follows is yet more interesting.

2445 WASHINGTON, Gen. GEO. THE WILL OF, to which is Annexed a Schedule of his property, directed to be sold; also, the Oration by Maj.-Gen. Lee. *8vo, fine copy, very rare*, 42 *p.* *London*. 1800

2446 WASHINGTON, GEO. LETTERS TO ARTHUR YOUNG, containing an account of his Husbandry, with a Map of his Farm, his opinions on various questions in Agriculture, and many particulars of the Rural Economy of the United States. *8vo, paper, uncut.* *London*, 1801

2447 WASHINGTON, GEO. LIBERTY RESTORED. A Poem, in Ten Books. By Thomas Northmore. *8vo, bds., uncut, beautiful copy. Very scarce.* *Baltimore*, 1809

2448 WASHINGTONIAN SONGSTER. The Cold Water Melodies. 4th Ed. *Boston*, 1842

2449 WASHINGTON, and other Poems, by a Graduate of the New York Institution for the Blind—Cynthia Bullock. *12mo, cl.* *New York*, 1847

2450 WASHINGTON, GEO. CROWNED BY "EQUALITY, FRATERNITY, AND LIBERTY." A Democratic Poem. By George Rogers. *8vo, cl.; portrait by Roberts.* *N. Y.*, 1849

2451 WASHINGTON, GEO. The Religious opinions and Character of. By E. C. M'Guire. *8vo, cl., fine copy; scarce.* *N. Y.*, 1836

2452 WASHINGTON, GENERAL, REVOLUTIONARY ORDERS OF, issued during the Years 1778–'80–'81 and 82, selected from the MSS. of John Whiting, and Edited by his son Henry Whiting. *8vo, cl.* *New York*, 1844

2453 WASHINGTON AND JOHN ADAMS, Memoirs of the Administrations of, from the papers of Oliver Wolcott, Sec. of Treas. By George Gibbs. *8vo, cl. In two vols. Portrait.* *N. Y.*, 1846

2454 WASHINGTON, GEORGE, MEMOIRS OF THE MOTHER AND WIFE OF. By Margaret C. Conkling. *Second edition, enlarged. Portrait of Martha Washington.* *8vo, cl., fine cond.* *Auburn*, 1850

2455 WASHINGTON and the Principles of the Revolution. Oration, July 4, 1850. By Edwin P. Whipple. *12mo, cl.* *Boston*, 1850

2456 WASHINGTON. REPUBLICAN COURT, or American Society in the days of Washington. With Twenty-one Portraits of Distinguished Women, of the time of Washington. By Rufus Wilmot Griswold. *In 12 Nos., Large 8vo, as originally issued.* *New York*, 1856

2457 WASHINGTON, GEORGE, IN DOMESTIC LIFE. From Original Letters and Manuscripts. By Richard Rush. *8vo, cl., uncut.* *Phila.*, 1857

WASHINGTON PAMPHLETS.

2458 WASHINGTON. [*Ten.*]

Declaration of Independence, etc. Farewell Address. *N. Y.*, 1854

Celebration of the Birthday of, and the victories of the Union armies, 1865. *Trenton, N. J.*, 1865

Memory of, an oration, Feb. 22, 1861, by Rev. N. H. Schenck. *Baltimore*, 1861

Letters from, to his friends, June and July, 1776. *Rare.* *Phila.*, 1795

Address in Galveston, 22d Feb., 1848, by A. Smith. *Galveston*, 1848

Oration before the Legislature of Mass., Feb. 22, 1832, by F. C. Gray. *Boston*, 1832

Oration at Rosse Chapel at the celebration of the birthday of, by W. P. Browne. *Gambier, Ohio*, 1864

Celebration of Washington's Birthday at N. Y. *N. Y.*, 1851

Exhibition of Leutze's picture of Washington crossing the Deleware. *N. Y.*

Welch's Portrait of. Circular.

2459 Washington. *Scarce and valuable.* [*Ten.*]

Farewell Address, with Ger. Trans. by F. W. Bogen. *Boston*, 1852

Oration on the laying of the Corner Stone of Monument to the Memory of Washington, July 4, 1848, by Robt. C. Winthrop. *Washington*, 1848

Address in aid of fund for Ball's Equestrian Statue of Washington, May 13, 1859, by Robt. C. Winthrop. *Boston*, 1859 /0

Letter to, on Public and Private Affairs, by T. Paine. *Phila.*, 1796

Washington, Conduct of, compared with that of the Pres. Admin. *Boston*, 1813

——— Vindication of, from the Stigma of adherence to secret societies, by Joseph Ritner. *Scarce.* *Boston*, 1841

Oration deliv. on the Centennial Anniv. of Birth of, Feb. 22, 1832, by John Pitman. *Providence*, 1832

Portrait of, by Stuart, descrip. of.

Oration on centen. anniv. of birthday of, in Albany, Feb. 22, 1832, by Orang G. Otis. *Very scarce.* *Albany.*

Testimony of, in favor of the special providence of God. *Prov.*, 1836

2460 Washington. *Rare lot.* [*Eleven.*]

Answer to Mr. Paine's Letter to, or Mad Tom, by P. Kennedy, 1797.

Cent. Anniv. at Washington, 1832.

To Joseph Reed. Remarks on reprint of original letters, by Jared Sparks. *Boston*, 1853 /0

Reply to Strictures of Lord Mahon and others. By J. Sparks. *Cambridge*, 1852

Crossing the Delaware, by E. Lutze, 1852.

Oration. Bp. Doane. *Burlington, N. J.*, 1859

Memorials. *Boston*, 1861

Speeches at the Rep. Un. Fest., Feb. 22, 1862.

Receiving his Mother's last Blessing, by W. H. Powell.

Oration by H. Maynard. *N. Y.*, Feb. 22, 1861,

Disc., by C. A. Smith. *Easton, Pa.*, Feb. 22, 1852,

2461 Washington. *Scarce lot.* [*Nine.*]

Letter to Lord Mahon ; answer to his letter to the editor of Washington's writings. *Boston,* 1852

Letters from W. to Arthur Young, and Sir John Sinclair. *Alexandria,* 1803

Resignation of.

Washington, Preliminary Investigation of the Alleged Ancestry of, by J. L. Chester. *Boston,* 1866

Pres. Washington, Message of, Relative to France and G. B. *Phila.,* 1793

Description of Mr. Huntington's painting of the Republican Court ; or Lady Washington's reception day. *N. Y.*

New doctrine of intervention tried by the teachings of, address, by H. A. Boardman. *Phila.,* 1852

Washington, Address on birth of, by Robt. L. Harper. Feb., 1810. *Scarce.*

——— Address deliv. before the Washington Benev. Soc., July 5, 1813. *Phila.*

2462 WASHINGTON. *Very scarce and valuable.* [*Seventeen.*]

BATES, ISAAC C. ORATION, Hampshire Co., Feb. 22, 1812. *Uncut.* *Northampton: printed* 1812

SULLIVAN, WILLIAM. ORATION. Boston, April 30, 1812. *Uncut.*

FOSTER, FESTUS. Oration. Northfield, N. H., July 5, 1813. *Uncut.* *Printed, Brattleborough,* 1813

HARRIS, T. M. Address. Dorchester, Feb. 22, 1813. *Uncut.*

——— Address. Brimfield, (Mass.), Feb. 22, 1813.

QUINCY, JOSIAH. Oration. Boston, April 30, 1813. *Uncut.*

PRENTISS, CHAS. "New England Freedom," a Poem deliv. at Brimfield, (Mass.), Feb. 22, 1813, with Notes. *Very scarce.* *Brookfield,* 1813

PRENTISS, CHAS. A Poem, deliv. at Brookfield, July 5, 1813. *With Notes.*

COOKE, PHINEHAS. Oration. Keene, (N. H.), July, 5, 1813. *Uncut.*

BURNSIDE, SAM'L M. Oration. Worcester, April 30, 1813. *Uncut.*

BIGELOW, HON. TIM. Address. Boston, April 30, 1814. *Uncut.*

DUNHAM, JOSIAH. Oration. Hanover, (N. H.), July 5, 1814. *Uncut.*

STANLEY, GEO. W. Oration. Wallingford, (Ct.), Feb. 22, 1815. *Uncut.*

BIGELOW, AND. Oration. Cambridge, July 5, 1815. *Uncut.*

ANDREWS, E. W. Address. Poem. Newburyport, Feb. 22, 1816. *Uncut. Beautiful copy. This pamphlet is very rare.*

DWIGHT, WM. T. Oration. Phila., Feb. 22, 1827. *Uncut.*

DIRECTORY of Names and Places of Bus. of Members of Wash. Benev. Soc. of Mass. 63 *p.* *Boston,* 1813

2463 Washington. *Very valuable.* [*Seven.*]

Holroyd, John. Oration before Mt. Vernon Lodge, Providence, Feb. 22, A. L. 5811. *Uncut, fine copy,* 16 *p.*

Knapp, Sam'l L. Oration deliv. before "The Associated Disciples of Washington," Feb. 22, 1812. 23 *p.* *Newburyport,* 1812

Motley, Jos. Address, occasioned by the Peace between America and Grt. Britain, Feb. 17, 1815, deliv. at Lynnfield on the Birthday of Washington. *Uncut,* 12 *p.*

Waterman, Jotham. Discourse deliv. at Plymouth, N. C., Feb. 22, 1818, and at Ipswich, Feb. 22, 1819. *Uncut,* 18 *p., fine copy.* *Boston Ed.,* 1819

Washington, Geo., Speeches at Celeb. of Centen. Anniv. of, and his Farewell Address. *Uncut,* 32 *p.* 1832

Hale, Salma. Oration at Keene, N. H., Feb. 22, 1832. 28 *p., scarce.*

Fox, Thos. B. Oration before Wash. Light Inf., in Newburyport, Feb, 22, 1832. *Fine copy, uncut,* 22 *p.*

2464 Washington. *Very scarce lot.* [*Nine.*]

Burns' Painting of Washington, Explanation of. *N. Y.,* 1850

Proceedings of House of Rep. of U. S., on Presentation of Sword of Washington and the Staff of Franklin, Feb. 7, 1843. *Uncut,* 15 *p.* *Washington,* 1843

Washington and Napoleon. A Fragment Poem, by F. Lieber. 200 copies for the Metro. Fair. *N. Y.,* 1864

The President's Address to the People of the United States, announcing his design of retiring from Public Life, etc., deliv. Sept. 17, 1796. 16 *p., fine copy.* *Phila., Sept.* 20, 1796

The Legacy of the Father of his Country. Address of Geo. Washington, etc. *Scarce,* 26 *p.* *Stockbridge,* 1796

Valedictory Address, Harrisburg, 1834. 14 *p.*

Valedictory Address. Will from Irving's L. P. Life. 52 *p.*

Farewell Address. 24 *p.* *N. Y.,* 1861

Farewell Address. The Procl. of Jackson against Nullification, and the Decl. of Indep. *Washington,* 1862

2465 Washington. *Valuable lot.* [*Seven.*]

Washington Almanac. Bailey's, for 1823. *Port.* *Phila.*

Washington, Geo. and Benj. Franklin; Imaginary Debate between the Departed Spirits of, on the Question, "Can a Man fall violently in Love with a Damsel rationally at first sight?" *Curious and licentious.* *Uncut.* 1838

——— A Word to Federalists and to those who Love the Memory of. *Uncut.*

"——— and the Principles of the Revolution." Oration, by E. P. Whipple, at Boston, July 4, 1850. 30 *pages.*

Hunt, Benj. Faneuil. Oration, Washington Soc. of Charleston, July 4, 1839. *Uncut.* 45 *pages.* 1839

Nott, Sam'l. Lessons of Piety and Patriotism from Harrison and Washington. *8vo*, 48 *pages.* *Boston*, 1841

Boston. Account of the Erection of the Equestrian Statue of Washington. 12 *pages.* 1869

35 2466 Washington. *Valuable lot.* [*Fifteen.*]

Lincoln, Sol. Oration at Plymouth, Feb. 22, 1832. *Uncut, fine copy;* 24 *p.*

Pitman, John. Oration at Providence, Feb. 22, 1832. *Uncut, fine copy;* 36 *p.*

Burroughs, Chas. Oration on the Moral Grandeur of Geo. Washington, deliv. Feb. 22, 1832, at Portsmouth, N. H. *Uncut, fine copy;* 59 *p.*

Wilson, W. D. Discourse on Slavery, before the Anti-Slavery Soc., in Littleton, N. H., Feb. 22, 1839. 51 *pages.* *Concord*, 1839

Ullmann, Dan'l. Address before the Tippecanoe and other Harrison Assoc. of N. Y., Feb. 22, 1841. 44 *p.*

Lincoln, F. W. Address before Mech. App. Lib. Assoc. of Boston, Feb. 22, 1844; also Anniv. Poem, by George Coolidge.

Sprague, Wm. B. Address, February 22, 1847, before Y. M. Assoc. of Albany. 51 *p.*

Ely, Alfred B. Oration, Feb. 22, 1850. 40 *p.* *N. Y.*

Tator, H. H. Oration, Feb. 22, 1851. *Uncut.* *Francisville, N. Y.*

Rush. "The 22d of February, 1851." For Private Circulation. 13 *p.* *Phila.*

Washington's Birth Day. Cong. Banquet. 1852. 37 *p.*

Boardman, H. A. "Kossuth, or Washington." 2d Ed. *Phila.*, 1852

Whitney, Thos. R. Oration, Feb. 22, 1855. 32 *p.* *N. Y.*

Ellis, Geo. E. "Commemoration of Washington." Disc., Feb. 22, 1837. *Charlestown*

Hunter, R. M. T. Opening Ode and Oration, at Inaug. of Crawford's Equest. Statue of Washington, Richmond, Feb. 22, 1858.

20 2467 Washington. [*Eleven.*]

Jay, Peter Augustus. Oration delivered before the Washington Benev. Soc. in the City of New York, Feb. 22. 1810

Hitchcock, David. Address, "The Bond of Friendship," April 22, 1812

Pierpont, John. A Poem, "The Portrait," Boston, Oct. 27, 1812

Dwight, Wm. P. Oration before the Wash. Benev. Soc. of Penn. Phila., Feb. 22, 1827

Speeches and other Proceedings at the Public Dinner in Honor of the Centennial Anniv. of Washington. 1832

Whipple, Edwin P. Oration—"Washington and Principles of the Revolution." Boston, July 4, 1850

Sparks, Jared. Reply to the Strictures of Lord Mahon and others on the Mode of Editing the Writings of Washington. *London*, 1852

Sullivan, W. Oration before Washington Benevolent Society of Massachusetts. *Boston*, 1812

Quincy, J. Oration before Washington Benev. Society. *Boston*, 1813

Verplanck, G. C. Oration by the Washington Benev. Soc. of the City of New York. *New York*, 1809

Grimké, T. S. Oration on the Duties of Americans, Washington Society, and other Citizens of Charleston. With Address of W. Drayton. *Charleston*, 1833

2468 Washington. [*Nine.*]

Doane, Geo. W. "One World; One Washington." Feb. 22, 1859

Botts, J. M.; Speech of. N. Y., Feb. 22, 1859.

Inaug. of the Mills Statue, Feb. 22, 1860.

Pennsylvania, Proc. of the Legisl. of. Feb. 22, 1861. 29 *pages*.

De Costa, B. F. The 18th Mass. Reg't. Discourse deliv. at Falls' Church, Va., Feb. 23, 1862. 15 *p*.

Briggs, Geo. W. Address in Salem, Feb. 22, 1862. 24 *p*.

Winthrop, R. C.; Oration by, on July 4, 1848, on the Laying of the Corner-Stone of the National Monument to the Memory of Washington. *Wash.*, 1848

Speeches at the Eighteenth Ward Republican Festival, Feb. 22, 1860. *N. Y.*, 1860

Hobart College, Poem before the Students of, and the Citizens of Geneva, Feb. 22, 1862. *Geneva, N. Y.*, 1862

2469 Washington *Very Valuable.* [*Eight.*]

Washington, George; A Word to Federalists and to those who Love the Memory of.

——— Farewell Address to the People of the U. S. of America, Sept., 1796. *Harrisburg*

——— Oration on the Birth of. By Robert G. Harper. Feb. 22, 1810. *Scarce.* *Alexandria*

——— The N. E. Patriot, being a candid comparison of the principles and conduct of the Washington and Jefferson Administrations. *Boston*, 1819

——— The Masonic Character and Correspondence of. *Uncut*, 18 *p.*, *scarce.* *Boston*, 1830

——— An Exemplification of Free Masonry. An Oration by S. H. Tyng. 31 *p*. *N. Y.*, 1852

——— An Oration deliv. on the Centen. Anniv. of the Initiation of, among the Freemasons, in Newport, Nov. 4, 1852. By K. J. Stewart. 17 *p*.

——— Celebration of the One Hundredth Anniv. of the Initiation of, into the Order of Free Masonry, at Peterboro, N. H.; with Address by Justice Spalding. 1854. *Scarce.* 18 *p*.

2470 WASHINGTON in 1835. Picture of Plan of the City, 1822. *Folded Map; 16mo, mor.* *s. l. s. a.*

2471 WASHINGTON. A SKETCH OF the Events which preceded the Capture of, by the British on the Twenty-fourth of August, 1814. By E. D. Ingraham *8vo, half mor.; map.* *Phila.*, 1849

Portrait of Ingraham inserted.

Bound in same Volume, "Slavery in the United States, &c." *Boston*, 1851

2472 WASHINGTON. HISTORY OF THE INVASION AND CAPTURE OF. The Events which preceded and followed. By John S. Williams. *8vo, cl.* *New York*, 1857

2473 WASHINGTON Sketch Book. By Viator. *16mo, cl.; rough edges. Plate.* *New York*, 1864

2474 WATERBURY, CONN.; THE HISTORY OF. The Original Township, embracing present Watertown and Plymouth, and parts of Oxford, Wolcott, Middlebury, Prospect and Naugatuck. With an Appendix of Biography, Genealogy and Statistics. By Henry Bronson. *8vo, sheets, folded; very scarce in this condition.* *Waterbury*, 1858

2475 WATERTOWN, Mass.; An Historical Sketch of—from the first settlement of the Town to the close of its second Century. By Convers Francis. *8vo, paper cov.; 151 pages; rough edges; beautiful copy; very scarce.* *Cambridge*, 1830

"Rev. Mr. Felt, with the respects of C. Francis."

2476 WATERTOWN, MASS. FAMILY MEMORIALS. Genealogies of the Families and Descendants of the Early Settlers of—including Waltham and Weston; to which is appended the Early History of the Town. With Illustrations, Maps and Notes. By Henry Bond, M.D. *2 vols., 8vo, half mor., gilt top, uncut; beautiful copy, and scarce in this condition.* *Boston*, 1855

2477 WATSON, JOHN F. HISTORIC TALES OF OLDEN TIME, concerning the Early Settlement and Progress of Philadelphia and Pennsylvania. Illustrated. *8vo, sh.* *Phila.*, 1833

2478 WATSON, WINSLOW C. PIONEER HISTORY OF THE CHAMPLAIN VALLEY; being an account of the Settlement of the Town of Willsborough, by William Gilliland; together with his Journal and other papers, and a Memoir, and Historical and Illustrative Notes. *Sm. paper.* *Albany*, 1863

2479 WATSON, ELKANAH; MEMOIRS OF. MEN AND TIMES OF THE REVOLUTION; including Journals of Travels in Europe and America, from the year 1777 to 1842, and Reminiscences and Incidents of the American Revolution. Edited by his Son, Winslow C. Watson. 2d Ed. With Portrait. *8vo, cl.* *N. Y.*, 1857

2480 WATTS, I. Dr. Watts's Imitation of the Psalms of David. Corrected and Enlarged, by Joel Barlow; to which is added a Collection of Hymns; the whole applied to the State of the Christian Church in General. The Fourth Edition. *12mo, sheep.* *Hartford: Printed by Nathaniel Patten*, 1785

2481 WATTS, I. The Psalms of David, Imitated in the Language of the New Testament; with an Index. *12mo, full mor., gilt top, uncut.* *Boston: Printed by Thomas and John Fleet,* 1787

2482 Watts, Isaac. Hymns and Spiritual Songs. In Three Books. *12mo, full mor., gilt top, uncut.* *Boston. Printed by Thomas and John Fleet,* 1787

2483 Wau-bun. The "Early Day" in the North-West. By Mrs. John H. Kinzie. With Illustrations. *8vo, cl.* *N. Y.,* 1856

2484 WAYLEN, Rev. EDWARD. Ecclesiastical Reminiscences of the United States. *8vo, cl., rough edges; plates; very scarce.* *London,* 1846

2486 WAYNE, ANTHONY, Gen. Life and Services of. Founded on Documentary and other Evidence furnished by his son, Col. Isaac Wayne. By H. N. Moore. With Engravings. *12mo, cl.* *Phila.,* 1845

2487 WEBBER, C. W. Historical and Revolutionary Incidents of the early settlers of the United States, with Biographical sketches of the lives of Allen, Boone, Kenton, and other celebrated Pioneers. Illustrated. *8vo, half crim. lev. mor., gilt top; bound by R. W. Smith.* *Phila.,* 1861

2488 WEEMS, M. L. (*formerly Rector of Mt. Vernon Parish.*) God's Revenge against Gambling exemplified in the miserable Lives and Untimely deaths of a number of Persons of both Sexes: with curious anecdotes of Miss Fanny Braddock, sister of Gen. Braddock, who, from gambling, hung herself; of Jack Gilmore, of Va.; of T. Alston (N. C.), and Marie Antoinette, who, for gambling, was brought to the guillotine, &c. *2d Ed. 8vo, fine copy; 51 pages; very scarce; frontis.; curious.* *Phila.,* 1812

2489 The same. *3d Ed. Uncut; 47 pages.* *Phila.,* 1816

2490 WEEMS, M. L. God's Revenge against Drunkenness; or, The new Drunkard's Looking-Glass, &c. *First Ed. 8vo, curious frontis.; 62 pages; very scarce.* *Phila.,* 1812

2491 The same. *3d Ed. Uncut; frontis.; 57 pages.* *Phila.,* 1814

2492 WEISS, M. CHARLES. History of the French Protestant Refugees, from the Revocation of the Edict of Nantes to our own days. Translated by H. W. Herbert. With an American Appendix, by a Descendant of the Huguenots. *2 vols. 8vo, cl.; frontispieces; scarce; fine copy.* *N. Y.,* 1854

2493 WENHAM (Mass.), History of, from its settlement, in 1639, to 1860. By Myron O. Allen. *8vo, cl.; scarce.* *Boston,* 1860

2494 WESLEY, JOHN. The Experience of Several Eminent Methodist Preachers; with an account of their Call to, and Success in the Ministry. In a Series of Letters, written by themselves, to. *8vo, half mor.; very rare; fine copy.* *Chambersburg,* 1812

2495 Wesley, John. Memoirs of Mr. Wesley's Missionaries to America, compiled from authentic sources. By P. P. Sandford. *12mo, sh., mbld. edges; scarce.* *N. Y.,* 1843

2496 West, John. A Journal of a Mission to the Indians of the British Provinces of New Brunswick and Nova Scotia, and the Mohawks on the Ouse or Grand river, Upper Canada. *12mo; map; bds., uncut.* *London,* 1827

2497 WEST, J., Bishop of Montreal. Journal of, during a Visit to the Church Missionary Society's North-West America Mission. To which is prefixed, by the Secretaries, an introduction, giving an account of the formation of the Mission, and its Progress to August, 1848. *2d Ed.. 8vo, cl.; rough edges.* *London*, 1849

2498 WEST, J. Notes of the Flood at the Red River, 1852, by the Bishop of Rupert's-Land. *12mo, cl., rough edges* *London*, 1852

2499 WEST CAMBRIDGE, ON THE NINETEENTH OF APRIL, 1775. An Address delivered in behalf of the Ladies' Soldiers' Aid Society, by Samuel A. Smith. *Cl., 12mo.* *Boston*, 1864

2500 WESTCHESTER COUNTY (N. Y.) A HISTORY OF, from its First Settlement to the Present Time. By Robert Bolton, Jr. *2 vols., 8vo cl. With maps, plates, &c.* *New York*, 1848

2501 WESTCHESTER CO. (N. Y.) HISTORY OF THE PROTESTANT EPISCOPAL CHURCH, from its Foundation, A.D. 1693, to A.D. 1853. By Robert Bolton, A. M. *8vo, cl. With portrait and plates.* *New York*, 1855

2502 WESTERN VIRGINIA. HISTORY OF THE EARLY SETTLEMENT AND INDIAN WARS OF. Embracing an account of the various Expeditions in the West, previous to 1795. Also, Biographical Sketches of Zane, McCulloch, Wetzel, Lewis, Brodhead, Brady, Crawford, and other distinguished actors in our Border Wars. By Willis De Haas. *8vo, cl.; illustrated by numerous engravings.* *Wheeling*, 1851

2503 WESTFIELD, Mass. A HISTORICAL SKETCH OF. By Emerson Davis. *8vo pamphlet; 36 pages; rare; good copy.* *Westfield*, 1826

2504 WESTMINSTER, Mass. A HISTORY OF THE TOWN OF, from its First Settlement to the Present Time. By Charles Hudson. *8vo, paper cov.; uncut; 42 pages; beautiful copy; very scarce.* *Mendon, Mass*, 1832

2505 WESTMINSTER, Mass. Celebration of the One Hundredth Anniversary of the Incorporation of, containing an Address by Charles Hudson, and Poem by W. S. Heywood, &c. *8vo, uncut; 127 pp.* *Boston*, 1859

2506 WESTON, Mass. A Sermon delivered at, Jan. 12, 1813, on the Termination of a Century since the Incorporation of the Town. By Samuel Kendal. *8vo, paper cov.; uncut; 60 pp.; fine copy; extremely scarce.* *Cambridge*, 1813

2507 WEST POINT. SKETCH OF THE HISTORY AND TOPOGRAPHY OF, and the U. S. Military Academy. By Roswell Park. *12mo, cl.; scarce; good copy.* *Phila.*, 1840

2508 WEST POINT. Guide Book to, and Vicinity; containing sketches of the U. S. Military Academy, and of other objects of interest. *12mo, cl.; map.* *New York*, 1844

2509 WHATELY, Mass. EARLY ECCLESIASTICAL HISTORY OF, being the substance of a Discourse del. Jan. 7, 1849. By J. Howard Temple. With an Appendix, containing Family Records. *8vo, scarce.* *Northampton*, 1849

2510 WHEATON, HENRY. History of the Northmen, or Danes and Normans, from the Earliest Times to the Conquest of England by William of Normandy. *8vo, bds., uncut.* *London*, 1831

2511 WHEATLEY, PHILLIS, Negro Servant to Mr. John Wheatley of Boston. in New England. Poems, on various subjects, Religious and Moral. *16mo, cf.; port.* *London: A Bell*, 1773

2512 Wheeler, Alfred. The Age: a Satire. Valedic. Poem, before the New York Soc. of Lit., Jan. 23, 1845. *8vo, 24 p.; good copy.* *New York*, 1845

2513 WRENTHAM, Mass. A Sermon, delivered Oct. 26, 1773, on completing the first century since the Town was incorporated. By Joseph Bean. *8vo pamph., uncut, 36 p.; very scarce.* *Boston*, 1774

Printed at the earnest desire of the hearers, for the Preservation of Ancient things to future posterity.

2514 White, Dan'l. A. An Address delivered at Ipswich, before the Essex County Lyceum, at their First Annual Meeting, May 5, 1830. *8vo pamph., uncut, 60 p.; scarce.* *Salem*, 1830

"What is man,
If his chief good and market of his time,
Be but to sleep and feed? A beast, no more.
Sure he, that made us with such large discourse,
Looking before, and after, gave us not
That capability and God-like reason,
To rest in us unused."

2515 WHITEFIELD, Rev. GEORGE. A Sermon on the Death of. Delivered at the Thursday Lecture at Boston, in America, October 11, 1770. By Ebenezer Pemberton, D. D. To which is added an Elegiac Poem on his Death, by Phillis, a Negro Girl of Seventeen years of age, belonging to Mr. J. Wheatley of Boston. *8vo pamphlet; scarce.* *London*, 1771

2516 Whitefield, George. A Funeral Sermon on the death of, who died suddenly of a fit of the Asthma, at Newbury Port, at six of the Clock, Lord's Day morning, Sept. 30, 1770. The Sermon preached the same Day, Afternoon, by Jonathan Parsons, A. M., and Minister of the Presbyterian Church there. To which are added, an account of his interment; the speech over his grave, by the Rev. Mr. Jewet; and some Verses to his Memory, by the Rev. Tho. Gibbons, D. D. *London*, 1771

2517 WHITFIELD, HENRY. The *Light* appearing more and more towards the perfect *Day*, | or, | A farther *Discovery* of the present state | of the Indians | in | New England, | *Concerning* the *Progresse* of the *Gospel* | amongst them. | Manifested by *Letters* from such as preach | to them there. Published by *Henry Whitfeld*, late *Pastor* to the | *Church* of *Christ* at *Gilford* in *New England*, who | came late thence. | *Sm. 4to, unbound, 46 p.*

London: *Printed by T. R. & E. M. for John Bartlet, and are to be | sold at the Gilt Cup, neer S. Austins gate in Pauls | Church-yard.* 1651

2518 WHITE MOUNTAINS. History of, from the First settlement of Upper Coos and Pequaket. By Lucy, wife of Ethan Allen Crawford. 12*mo, Cl., very scarce.* *White Hills*, 1846

2519 WILBRAHAM, Mass. Historical Address, delivered at the Centennial Celebration of the incorporation of the Town of, June 15, 1863. With an appendix. By Rufus P. Stevens. 8*vo, plates, gr. cl., gt. top, rubricated title.* *Boston*, 1864

2520 Wilbur, Homer. The Bigelow Papers. Edited, with an introduction, notes, glossary and copious Index. 8*vo, cl., rough edges.* *Cambridge*, 1848

2521 WILLARD, JOSEPH. An Address to the Members of the Bar of Worcester County, Mass., Octo. 2, 1829. 8*vo, rough edges; fine copy; scarce;* 144 *p.* *Lancaster*, 1830

2522 WILLARD, S. D. Historical Address, delivered before the Medical Society of the County of Albany, Nov. 11, 1856. 8*vo pamph.,* 28 *p.; port.* *Albany*, 1857

2523 WILLIAMS, ROGER. Memoir of, The Founder of the State of Rhode Island. By James D. Knowles. 8*vo, cl. with Facsimile of his handwriting.* *Boston*, 1834

2524 Williams, Roger. The Spirit of, with a portrait of one of his Descendants. By Lorenzo D. Johnson. 16*mo, cl.* *Boston*, 1839

2525 Williams, Roger, of Providence, in New England. Experiments of Spiritual Life and Health, and their Preservatives. In which the weakest child of God may get assurance of his Spiritual Life and Blessedness, and the Strongest may finde proportionable Discoveries of his Christian Growth, and the means of it. *Sm.* 4*to, bds.*
London: Printed in the Second Month, 1652. *Reprinted by S. S. Rider, Providence,* 1863

2526 WILLIAMS, CATHARINE R. Biography of Revolutionary Heroes; containing the Life of Brig. Gen. William Barton, and also of Capt. Stephen Olney. *Frontis.,* 8*vo, hf. gr. cr. lev. mor., gt., bound by R. W. Smith.* *Providence*, 1839

2527 WILLIAMS, MRS. C. R. The Neutral French; or, the Exiles of Nova Scotia. *Two vols. in one. Second edition.* 8*vo, cl.* *Providence*, 1841

2528 Williams, Edwin. Book of the Constitution, containing the Constitution of the United States, a synopsis of the several State Constitutions, with various other important Documents and useful information. 12*mo, bds.; port.* *New York*, 1833

2529 WILLIAMS, THOMAS, (Ye-ho-ra-gwa-ne-gan,) Life of, a Chief of the Caughnawaga Tribe of Indians in Canada. By Rev. Eleazer Williams, reputed Son of Thomas Williams, and by many believed to be Louis XVII., son of the last reigning Monarch of France previous to the Revolution of 1789. 8*vo, cl.* 200 *copies only.* *Albany, N. Y.*, 1859

2530 WILLIAMS, REV. JOHN. A Biographical Memoir of, with a Slight Sketch of Ancient Deerfield, and an account of the Indian wars in that place and vicinity. With an appendix, containing the Journal of the Rev. Dr. Stephen Williams of Longmeadow, during his captivity, and other papers relating to the

Early Indian wars in Deerfield. By Stephen U. Williams, A. M. *8vo, cl., very scarce; fine copy.* *Greenfield, Mass.*, 1837

2531 WILLIAMS FAMILY. The Genealogy and History of, in America, more particularly of the Descendants of Robert Williams of Roxbury. By Stephen W. Williams. *8vo, cl. Portraits and Fac-similes of Autographs, Coat of Arms, etc., very scarce; fine copy.* *Greenfield*, 1847

2532 Williams College Necrological Annals, 1867–'68. Compiled by Calvin Durfee. *8vo pamphlet, 19 p.* *Pittsfield*, 1868

2533 WILLIAMSBURGH VILLAGE, N. Y. The Charter of, and the Several Acts relating thereto, with the By-Laws and Ordinances. With Appendix. Also, Amendments to the Village Charter, 1848. *8vo, pamphlet.* *Williamsburgh*, 1844

2534 Williamson, Thomas S. (Missionary). Extracts from Genesis and the Psalms, the 3rd chap. of Proverbs and 3rd chap. of Daniel, in the Dacota language. *12mo, cl.* *Cincinnati*, 1839

2535 WILLETT, Col. MARINUS. A Narrative of the Military Actions of, taken chiefly from his own Manuscript. Prepared by his son, William M. Willet. Portrait and plate. *Roy. 8vo, full crushed crim. lev. mor., gt. top, uncut; splendid copy.* *New York: Carvill*, 1831

2536 WILLEY, Rev. B. G. Incidents in White Mountain History: containing facts relating to the Discovery and Settlement of the Mountains, Indian History and Traditions, a minute and authentic account of the destruction of the Willey Family, Geology and Temperature of the Mountains, together with Anecdotes illustrating Life in the Back Woods. *12mo, cl.; plates.* *Boston, etc.*, 1856

2537 Willis, N. P. Poem delivered before the Society of United Brothers, at Brown University, on the day preceding commencement, Sept. 6, 1831. With other Poems. *8vo, cl.* *N. Y.*, 1831

2538 WILMINGTON, N. C. Historical Notices of St. James' Parish. By Rev. R. B. Drane. *12mo, paper; scarce.* *Philadelphia*, 1843

2539 WILTON, N. H. An Address delivered at the Centennial Celebration, Sept. 25, 1839. By Ephraim Peabody. With an Appendix. *8vo, paper cov., 103 pages; scarce; fine copy.* *Boston*, 1839

2540 WINDHAM, Conn. A View of Ecclesiastical Proceedings in the County of, in which the original Association of that county and a few members of the First Church were concerned; containing public documents relating to the subject: to which are annexed the result of council and addresses to the society, &c. By John Sherman, A. B. *8vo, cl., uncut.* *Utica, N. Y.*, 1806

2541 WINDHAM, Me. An Historical Address, delivered July 4, 1839, at the Centennial Anniversary. By Thos. L. Smith. *8vo, uncut pamphlet, 32 p.; very scarce; fine copy.* *Portland*, 1840

2542 WINDSOR, Conn. The History of, including East Windsor, South Windsor and Ellington, prior to 1768, the Date of their Separation from the Old Town, and Windsor Bloomfield and Windsor Locks to the Present Time. Also, the Gene-alogies and Genealogical Notes of those Families which Sett[illegible] within the Limits of Ancient Windsor prior to 1800. W[illegible] a Supplement to the History and Genealogies, containing [illegible] rections and additions. By Henry R. Stiles. 8vo, *she[illegible]; folded; frontis.; scarce.* *Albany: J. Munsell,* 1[illegible]8

2543 WINKFIELD, UNCA ELIZA. THE FEMALE AMERICAN; [illegible]'s the Extraordinary Adventures of, &c. Compiled by Hers[illegible] to *Full cr. crim. lev. mor., gt. top, uncut,* 8*vo.* *R. W. Smith.* In-
Newburyport (n. d.), (1795 [illegible]

2544 WINTHROP, ME. A BRIEF HISTORY OF, from 1764 to Oct. 4 1855. By David Thurston. 8*vo, cl.* *Portland,* 1855

2545 WISE, JOHN. THE CHURCHES QUARREL ESPOUSED; or, a Reply in Satyre, &c., &c. 8*vo, full pol. calf, gt.* *By R. W. Smith.* *Boston,* 1772

2546 WISE, JOHN. A VINDICATION OF THE GOVERNMENT OF NEW ENGLAND CHURCHES, &c. 8*vo, full polished cf.* *By R. W Smith.* *Boston,* 1772

2547 WISCONSIN TERRITORY. NOTES ON, with map. By Lieutenant Albert M. Lea. 12*mo, bds.; rare.* *Philadelphia,* 1836

2548 WISCONSIN. CARVER'S TRAVELS IN. From the third London edition. 8*vo, unbound, portrait and plates.* N. Y., 1838

2549 WISCONSIN TERRITORY. A GEOGRAPHICAL AND TOPOGRAPHICAL DESCRIPTION OF, with brief sketches of its history, geology, mineralogy, natural history, &c. By J. A. Lapham. 12*mo, cl., with map.* *Milwaukie, Wis.,* 1844

2550 WISCONSIN. THE HISTORY OF, in Three Parts: Historical, Documentary and Descriptive. By William R. Smith. 8*vo, cl.; 2 vols.* *Madison, Wis.,* 1854

2551 WISCONSIN STATE HISTORICAL SOCIETY. Collections of, First, Second, Third, Fourth Reports. 4 *vols.,* 8*vo.* *Vols.* 1 *and* 2, *paper covers; vols.* 3 *and* 4, *cloth.* *Madison,* 1855–59

2552 WISNER, BENJ. B. The History of the Old South Church, in four Sermons: being the First and Second Sabbaths after the Completion of a Century from the first occupancy of the present Meeting-House. 8*vo, uncut,* 122 *p.; valuable notes; beautiful copy.* *Boston,* 1830

2553 WOBURN, MASS. THE HISTORY OF, from the Grant of its Territory to Charlestown in 1640 to the year 1860. By Samuel Sewall. Port. of Samuel Sewall. 8*vo, sheets folded.* With a Memorial Sketch of the Author, by Rev. C. C. Sewall.
Boston: Wiggin & Lunt, 1868

2554 WOOD, WILLIAM. NEW ENGLAND'S PROSPECT: A true, lively and experimentall description of that part of America commonly called New England; discovering the state of that Countrie, both as it stands to our new-come English Planters, and to the old Native Inhabitants. Laying downe that which may both enrich the knowledge of the mind, travelling Reader, or benefit the future Voyager. By William Wood.
Printed at London, 1634; *re-printed at Boston,* 1865
Publications of the Prince Society. 150 copies printed. No. 133.

2555 WOODBURY, LEVI. An Oration delivered at Hanover, N. H., August 27, 1812, before the Handel and Central Musical Societies. 8*vo*, 18 *pages; good copy; very scarce and interesting.* *Amherst, N. H.*, 1812

2556 WOODBURY, Conn. HISTORY OF ANCIENT WOODBURY, from the first Indian Deed in 1659 to 1854, including the present Towns of Washington, Southbury, Bethlem, Roxbury and a part of Oxford and Middlebury. By William Cothren. 8*vo, port. and plates; cl.; fine copy; very scarce.* *Waterbury*, 1854

This history is divided into the following sections: Physical, Indian, Revolutionary, Ecclesiastical, Civil, Biographical, Genealogical and Statistical. The Genealogical Section embraces the History of Eighty-eight Families, arranged in Alphabetical Order. Very important. Embellished with Coats of Arms, &c.

2557 WORCESTER COUNTY, MASS., HISTORY OF, with a Particular Account of every Town, from its First Settlement to the Present Time, including its Ecclesiastical State; together with a Geographical Description of the same. To which is prefixed a Map of the County at large, from Actual Survey. By Peter Whitney. 8*vo, hf. mor., gilt top, rough edges; fine copy; scarce.*
Printed at Worcester, Mass., by Isaiah Thomas, 1793

2558 WORCESTER MAGAZINE, AND HISTORICAL JOURNAL, Containing articles original and selected, miscellaneous, historical, biographical, descriptive of remarkable places and scenery, relating to the arts, scientific, poetical, and amusing. 2 vols. Vol. 1., from Oct. 1825, to April, 1826. Vol. 2., from May, 1826, to Oct., 1826. By Wm. Lincoln & C. C. Baldwin, Editors. 8*vo. In the original numbers, as issued, uncut; very scarce.* *Worcester*, 1826

2559 WORCESTER, Mass. HISTORY OF, from its Earliest Settlement, to Sept., 1836; with various notices, relating to the History of Worcester County. By Wm. Lincoln. *Portraits.* 8*vo, sheets, scarce.* *Worcester*, 1862

2560 WORTHINGTON, Mass. SECULAR AND ECCLESIASTICAL HISTORY OF THE TOWN OF, from its First Settlement, to the present Time. 8*vo pamph.*, 72 *pages.* *Albany*, 1853

2561 WYMAN, SETH. Life and Adventures of, embodying the Principal Events of a Life spent in Robbery, Theft, Gambling, passing Counterfeit Money, etc. Written by Himself. 12*mo, cl.* *Manchester, N. H.*, 1843

2562 WYOMING, Pa. SKETCH OF THE HISTORY OF. By Isaac A. Chapman. To which is added an Appendix, containing a Statistical Account of the Valley, and Adjacent Country. By a Gentleman of Wilkesbarre. 8*vo, cl.; scarce.* *Wilkesbarre, Pa.*, 1830

2563 WYOMING, Penn. THE POETRY AND HISTORY OF, containing Campbell's Gertrude, with a Biographical Sketch of the Author, by W. Irving, and the History of Wyoming, from its Discovery, to the beginning of the present Century, by W. L. Stone. 12*mo, cl.; with plates.* *N. Y.*, 1841

2564 WYOMING, Pa. HISTORY OF, In a Series of Letters from Chas. Miner to his Son, Wm. P. Miner. *8vo, hf. cl., sprinkled edges, fine copy; map, etc.* *Phila.*, 184

2465 WYOMING, Pa. ITS HISTORY, STIRRING INCIDENTS AND ROMANT ADVENTURES. By George Peck, D.D. Illustrated. *8vo, cl scarce.* *N. Y.*, 18

2566 WYOMING. THE POETRY AND HISTORY OF, containing Campbel Gertrude, and the History of Wyoming, from its Discovery the Beginning of the Present Century. 3d Ed., with an dex. By Wm. L. Stone. *8vo, paper covers, uncut, rub titles.* *Albany, Munsell*, 186

PAMPHLETS.

2567 Webster Pamphlets. [*Twenty-one.*]

Webster, Daniel. Disc. in commemoration of Adams and Jefferson. *Boston*, 1826

——— Speech, on the President's Veto of the Bank Bill, July 11, 1832.

——— Speech, at the National Republican Convention, Worcester, Oct. 12, 1832. *Boston*, 1832

——— Speech, on the President's Protest. *Washington*, 1834

——— Speech, at Niblo's Saloon, New York, March 15, 1837. *N. Y.*, 1837

——— Speech, in answer to Mr. Calhoun, March 22, 1838.

——— Address, at the Completion of the Bunker Hill Monument. *Boston*, 1843

——— Speech, on Mr. Clay's Resolution, March 7, 1850. *Washington*, 1850

——— Correspondence between Mr. Hulsemann and W. *Washington*, 1851

——— Speeches, at Buffalo, Syracuse, and Albany, May 1851. *N. Y.*

——— Great Orations and Senatorial Speech of. *Rochester*, 1853

——— Dinner to, by the Citizens of Philadelphia, Dec. 2, 1846. *Phila.*, 1847

——— Seventy-second Anniversary of the Birthday of, Celebrated at the Astor House. *N. Y.*, 1854

——— Seventy-fourth Anniversary of the Birthday of, Celebrated at the Revere House. *Boston*, 1856

——— Discourse occasioned by the Death of. By T. Parker. *Boston*, 1853

——— Discourse occasioned by the Death of. By G. Richards. *Boston*, 1852

——— Discourse occasioned by the Death of. By J. Weiss. *Boston*, 1853

——— Remarks on the Life and Writings of. *Phila.*, 1831

Webster, Noah. The Critic Criticised; a Reply to a Review of Webster's System. By E. Sargent. *Springfield*, 1856

——— John. Review of the Webster Case. *Very scarce.* *N. Y.*, 1850

——— Gen. Hayne, in Reply to Mr. Webster. *Charleston*, 1830

2568 Webster Pamphlets. [*Seventeen.*]

Webster's Speech, on the Greek Revolution. *Boston*, 1824

——— Daniel. Disc. in Commemoration of the Lives and Services of John Adams and T. Jefferson. *Boston*, 1826

——— Second Speech of, delivered in the Senate of the United States. *Boston*, 1830

——— Speech of, in Reply to Mr. Hayne of S. C. *N. Y.*, 1830

——— Speech of, on the Subject of The Public Lands, Jan. 20, 1830.

——— Remarks on the Life and Writings of. *Phila.*, 1831 /0

——— Speech of, in the Senate of the U. S., July 11, 1832. *Boston.*

——— The same. *Boston.*

——— Speech of, in Reply to Mr. Calhoun's Speech, delivered *Washington*, Feb. 16, 1833

——— Speech, deliv. at Dinner given to, by the Merchants of Balt. *N. Y.*, May 18, 1843

——— Speech of, in Defence of the Christian Ministry and in Favor of the Religious Instruction of the Young. *Washington*, Feb. 10, 1844

——— Speech of, delivered at Festival of the Sons of New Hampshire, in Boston, Nov. 7, 1849.

——— Address at the Laying of the Corner Stone of the Addition to the Capitol, *Washington*, July 4, 1851

——— Speech of, on Mr. Clay's Resolutions, Washington, March 7, 1850.

——— Speech of, to the Young Men of Albany, May 28, 1851.

——— Correspondence between Mr. Hulsemann and. *Washington*, 1851

——— Disc. deliv. before the Faculty, Students, and Alumni of Dartmouth College, Commemorative of. By Rufus Choate *Boston*, 1853.

2569 Webster Pamphlets. [*Twenty.*]

Speech on Greek Revolution. *Wash.*, 1824

Adams and Jefferson. *Boston*, 1826 12½

Speech National Repub. Conv. " 1832

——— In Senate of United States on the Bank Bill. *Boston*, 1832

——— In Reply to Calhoun. *Wash.*, 1833

Speech. On Sub. Treas. Bill, March 12th. *Wash.*, 1838
——— do do and in answer to Calhoun. *Wash.*, 1838
——— At Andover, Nov. 9, 1843. *Boston*, 1843
——— On Mr. Clay's Resolutions, March 7, 1850 *Wash.*, 1850
——— At Corner Stone of Capitol, July 4, 1851. *Wash.*, 1851
——— At Reformed Convention of Maryland, March 25. *Wash.*, 1851

The Austro-Hungarian Question. " 1851

Speech to Young Men of Albany, May 28, 1851. *Albany*, 1851

Discourse on Death of Daniel Webster, by W. P. Lunt. *Boston*, 1852

Proceedings and Address of Friends of Daniel Webster. *Boston*, 1852

Discourse on Death of Daniel Webster, by Rufus Choate, Dart. Col., 1853.

Proceedings of South Carolina Legislature on the Death of, 1853.

Discourse on Death of Webster, by John Weiss, November 14, 1852.

Proceedings on Deaths of Clay and Webster, by, South Car., Nov., 1852.

Daniel Webster as a Jurist. Address by Joel Parker. *Cambridge*, 1853

2570 Miscellaneous. [*Eighteen.*]

Wabash College, Ia. Address before the Society of Inquiry, July 22, 1845, by John P. Cleaveland. *Cincinnati*, 1845

Waddell, J. H. A Fair Epistle from a Little Poet to a Great Player. *N. Y.*, 1818

——— Waddell to Coleman. Facts and Fancy. *Scarce.* *N. Y.*, 1819

Wainwright, J. M. Plea for Unity. Sermon before the Convention of the Diocese of New York. *N. Y.*, 1850

Wakely, Joseph B. The Ethics of Funerals: Vindication of the Methodist Episcopal Church and J. B. W., with regard to the Funeral of W. Poole. *N. Y.*, 1855

Warburton, Maj. Geo. The Conquest of Canada. *London*, 1857

Warden, D. B. History of the Silk Bill. Letter from Peter S. Du Ponceau, to D. B. W. *Phila.*, 1837

Walker, James. Discourse in Harvard Church, Charlestown, on taking leave of his Society. *Cambridge*, 1839

Wall, Hon. James W. Speeches for the Times. *New York*, 1864

Wallace, W. Alban the Pirate. *New York*, 1848

Wallis, S. T. Leisure: Its Moral and Political Economy. A Lecture before the M. L. A., of Baltimore. *Baltimore*, 1859

Walsh, Michael, Sketches of, including his Poems and Correspondence. *Scarce.* *New York*, 1843
Walton, W. C. Narrative of a Revival in the Third Presbyterian Church in Baltimore. *Northampton*, 1826
War. Considerations respecting the Lawfulness of. *New York*, 1848
Ware, Henry. Sermon at the Dedication of the Second Congregational Church in Northampton. *Northampton*, 1825
Ware, William. Sermon on the Sunday succeeding the great fire, December, 1835. *New York*, 1835
Warner, Col. Seth, Life of. By D. Chipman. *Burlington*, 1858
Warning Voice From a Watery Grave. *New York*, 1840

2571 Miscellaneous. *Valuable.* [*Eighteen.*]

Waterland, Daniel. Regeneration ; a Discourse. *London, Reprinted, New York*, 1793
Watson, Bishop. Strictures on (his) Apology for the Bible. *New York*, 1796
Waters, George Van. Poetical Geography. *Louisville*, 1850
Watts, Talbot. The Drunkard's Children, the Sequel to "The Bottle." By H. P. Grattan. *New York*, 1849
Wayland, Francis. Discourse at Dedication Manning Hall Brown University, Feb. 4, 1835. *Providence*, 1835
Watts, Isaac. Divine Songs in easy language for the Use of Children. *Boston.*
Wilde, John. Sermon delivered January 11, 1835, at Interment of Hannah R. Batcheller, January 9, 1835. *Worcester.*
Whitteley's, Samuel, Sermon Preached at Ordination of S. Whittcley, Jr. *Scarce.* *Boston*, 1739
Weems, M. L. God's Revenge against Gambling exemplified in the Miserable Lives and Untimely Deaths, &c., with Anecdotes of Miss Fanny Braddock, Sister of General Braddock, Jack Gilmore, Maria Antoniette, and others. *Phila.*, 1812
Webster, Daniel, Speech of, January 20, 1830. *Washington.*
——— Remarks of, May 9, 1828. *Boston.*
——— R. F. Hayne, Speech of, Delivered Jan. 21–26, 1830 *Boston.*
——— Eulogy on, by C. Van Rensselaer. *Scarce.* *Burlington, N. J.*, 1852
Whitney, Eli, Memoir of, by D. Olmsted. *New Haven*, 1846
Whitney, Geo. Sermon, preached 24th September 1837. *Boston*, 1837
Whittington, Rev. Wm. R. Sermon, Aug. 3, 1832, the Day

of Public Fast. *New York*, 1832

Wesleyan Methodist Missionary Society. Report for 1828. *London*, 1829

Wesleyan University, Middletown, Conn. The Duty of the American Scholar. Oration by G. W. Curtis. *New York*, 1856

2572 Miscellaneous. [*Sixteen.*]

Waterman, Simon. Sermon at Funeral of John Trumbull, delivered in Watertown December 14, 1787. *Scarce.* *Hartford.*

Walker, James, Sermon delivered on the day of General Election, May 28, 1828. *Boston.*

——— Discourse delivered in Groton, Mass., at Installation of Charles Robinson, November 1, 1826. *Boston.*

Worcester, Thos., Discourse by. *Boston*, 1810

Walker, James. Sermon in Brooklyn, Conn., at Installation of Samuel Joseph May, November 5, 1823. *Boston*, 1824

West, Stephen. Sermon on the Mosaic Account of the Creation, etc. *Very scarce and important.* *Stockbridge*, 1809

——— Sermon at the Ordination of Amasa Jerome, Aug. 18, 1802. *Hartford.*

White, Wm. Sermon delivered at Consecration to the Episcopacy of William Meade, Philadelphia, August 19, 1829. *N. Y.*

Wistar, Caspar, Tribute to the Memory of, by D. Hosack. *Scarce.* *N. Y.*, 1818

Wetmore, Robert G. Extensive Charity in a Small Compass. *Ga.*, 1802

Woodbridge, Wm. Sermon on Doctrine of Absolute Predestination. *Middletown*, 1805

White, Wm. Ser. on the Duties, etc., of the Gospel Ministry, delivered Sept. 14, 1804, at Consecration of Bishop Parker. *N. Y.*, 1804

Weeks, Holland. Funeral Sermon on Death of P. Lewis, at Salem, Conn., April 30, 1804. *New Haven.*

Wolcott, Oliver. Address, April 19, 1802. *Hartford.*

Waddell, Thomas. Letters to the Editor of the Catholic Miscellany. *N. Y.*, 1830

Wylie, S. B. Two Sons of Oil ; or, The Faithful Witness. *N. Y.*, 1832

2573 Miscellaneous. [*Sixteen.*]

Wedderburn, Rev. R. Address to the Court of King's Bench at Westminster, on appearing to receive Judgment for Blasphemy, May 9, 1820. *London*, 1820

Wells, Daniel. Examination of the Message of the Governor Returning the Bill for Regulating the Militia. *Cambridge*, 1833

——— John. Oration, 4th of July, 1798, at St. Paul's Church before the Young Men of the City of New York. *Rare.* *New York*, 1798

Wendell, Judge. Remarks in Relation to the Extension of Albany Street through Trinity Church Yard. *New York*, 1854

West, Benjamin. Description of West's Picture of Christ Healing the Sick. By J. Robinson. *Phila.*, 1818

West Point United States Military Academy. Graduates. *N. Y.*, 1847

——— United States Military Academy. Exposé of Facts concerning Recent transactions, relating to the Corps of Cadets of. *Scarce.* *Newburgh*, 1819

Westchester County, N. Y. Proceedings of the Board of Supervisors of, 1863. *Peekskill*, 1864

——— Homœopathic Medical Society. Constitution and By-Laws. 1865

Western Baptist Educational Association. A Voice from the West. Rev. B. Jacobs' Report of his Tour, 1833. *Relates to Indian Instruction, &c.* *Boston*, 1833

Western Country, Appeal in behalf of.

Western Waters. Conclin's New River Guide; or, Gazetteer of All the Towns of. *Cincinnati*, 1850

Western University of Pennsylvania. Address before the Philomathean Literary Institute of, by D. Ritchie. *Pittsburgh*, 1844

Westfield, Mass., Historical Sketch of. By E. Davis. *Very scarce.* *Westfield*, 1826

Westminster Election, Proceedings, with the Speech of G. Jones *Lond.*, 1818

Weston the Pedestrian. Adventures on his Walk from Boston to Washington. *New York*, 1862

2574 Miscellaneous. [*Fifteen.*]

Whately, Richard. The Kingdom of Christ delineated, in two Essays. *Phila.*, 1843

Wheeler, E. P. The Supreme Court as a Co-ordinate Branch of the U. S. Government. *N. Y.*, 1860

Whewell, Rev. Dr. William. Inaug. Lecture on the Results of the Exhibition. *London*, 1851

Whipple, Hon. John. Free Trade in Money, or Note-Shaving. An Answer to Jeremy Bentham. *Boston*, 1856

——— Speech, at the Whig Meeting at the Town House, Providence, Aug. 28, 1837.

Whitaker, Nathanael. Two Sermons on the Doctrine of Reconciliation, in Answer to a Dialogue by the Rev. Wm. Hart. *Very scarce.* *Salem*, 1770

White, Charles E. The Dream of Alla-ad-deen. From the Romance of "Anastasia." *N. Y.*, 1838

White, G. S. The Christian Memorial; containing God's Abundant Grace [etc.] to the Author. *London*, 1809

White, Hon. Hugh L. Reply of B. F. Currey, to Charges against him, by H. L. White. *Washington*, 1836

Whitlock, William, Capt. of the Ship Hunter. Fourth Memorial of J. W. Brackett and S. Leggett, in the Case of the Ship Hunter. *N. Y.*, 1823

——— Supplementary Memorial. *N. Y.*, 1823

Whitman, Bernard. Two Letters to the Rev. M. Stuart, on Religious Liberty. *Boston*, 1830

——— Same. 2d Ed. *Boston*, 1831

Whitmore, W. H. The Cavalier Dismounted: an Essay on the Origin of the Founders of the Thirteen Colonies. *Scarce.* *Salem*, 1864

——— Reasons for the Regulation of the Use of Coat-Armor in the U. S. *Boston*, 1868

$5 2575 Miscellaneous. [*Eighteen.*]

"Wickedest Man," The, in New York. *N. Y.*, 1868

Wilberforce, Archdeacon. Strictures on [his] Doctrine of the Incarnation. *N. Y.*, 1851

Wilkes, Chas. Western America, including California and Oregon; with maps. *Scarce.* *Phila.*, 1849

Wilkes, Geo. Mysteries of the Tombs. *Very scarce.* *N. Y.*, 1844

Willard, Emma. Address to the Public, Proposing a Plan for Improving Female Education. *Middlebury*, 1819

——— Series of Maps to an Abridgement of the History of the U. S. *N. Y.*, 1831

Willard, Joseph. Address to the Members of the Bar of Worcester County, Mass. Oct. 2, 1829. *Valuable and important.* *Lancaster*, 1830

Williams College. Sermon at the Ordination of E. Fitch, President of. By E. Judson. *Very scarce.* *Stockbridge*, 1796

——— Address before the Adelphic Union Soc. of, Aug. 20, 1850. By H. B. Stanton. *N. Y.*, 1850

Williamsburgh Ferry Companies, New and Old. *N. Y.*, 1848

——— Williamsburgh Ferries. *N. Y.*, 1848

Williamstown Missionary Monument. Proceedings at the Dedication of, July 28, 1867. *Boston*, 1867

Willson, Marcius. Report on American Histories. *N. Y.*, 1847

——— Reply to Mrs. Willard's "Appeal." *N. Y.*, 1847

Willison, John. The Young Communicant's Catechism. First American Ed. *Phila.*, 1803

Wilmer, Simon. Sermon, in Burlington, at the Convention of the Prot. Episc. Church in N. J. *Very scarce.* *Burlington*, 1811

Wilson, Amos. The Pennsylvania Hermit. Narrative of the Life of. *Uncut.* *N. Y.*, 1838

Wilson, James. The Doctrine of the Self-existent Father, [etc.] considered. *Providence*, 1835

2576 Miscellaneous. *Valuable lot.* [*Eighteen.*]

Williams, Wm. R. Disc. Oct. 26, 1834. *Boston*

Witherspoon, John. Sermon on Religious Education of Children. *Elizabeth-Town*, 1789

Williston, Seth. Sermon, Oct. 6, 1802, at Installation of David Higgins. *Owego*

Wilson, J. Lyde. The Code of Honor. *Charleston*, 1838

Williams, Samuel. Sermon at Ordination of T. Barnard. *Salem*, Jan. 13, 1773

Welles, Noah. Disc. deliv. at Funeral of Noah Hobart, Dec. 6, 1773. *N. Y.*

Wells, John. Oration deliv. July 4, 1798, at N. Y.

Williams College. Address before. Semi-Centen. Anniv., Aug. 16, 1845. By Mark Hopkins. *Boston*

Weld, T. D. Annual Report of Soc. for Promoting Manual Labor, Jan. 23, 1838. *N. Y.*

Warren Assoc.; Minutes of. Held at Sturbridge, 1788. *Boston*

Wainwright, J. M. Sermon deliv. Jan. 7, 1835. *Boston*

Webster, Noah; Sketches of. *Very scarce.* *Hartford*, 1785

Wayland, Francis. Two Disc. April 7, 1825. *Boston*

Ware, William. Sermon. Dec. 16, 1835. *N. Y.*

War in Disguise. Answer to. By Isaac Riley. Feb., 1806.

——— Or, Frauds of the Neutral Flags. By I. Riley. *London*, Jan., 1806

Williams, Thos. Disc. for Month of April, 1816. *Providence*

White, Henry. Sermon deliv. on Death of John Nitchie. *N. Y.*, 1838

2577 Miscellaneous. [*Seventeen.*]

Wine Question. Reply to Prof. Stuart and Pres. Nott, on the Wine Question, by Rev. James Lillie. *Phila.*, 1848

Wines, E. C. A Peep at China, in Mr. Dunn's Chinese Collection. *Phila.*, 1839

Wing, Halsey R. Essay on the Moral and Intellectual Effects of Studying the Mathematical and Physical Sciences. *Albany*, 1834

Winslow, Miron. Sermon at the Old South, Boston, June 7, 1819, the evening previous to the Sailing of the Missionaries to Ceylon. *Andover*, 1819

Winterton. Narrative of the Loss of. Aug. 20, 1792. By the Third Mate. *London*

Winthrop, Robert C. Address at the Opening of the Grand Musical Festival, at the Music Hall. *Boston*, 1857

Winthrop, Theodore. A Companion to the Heart of the Andes. *N. Y.*, 1859

Wirt, William. Disc. on the Life of. By J. P. Kennedy. *Very scarce.* *Baltimore*, 1834

Wirt Institute. The Votaries of Twilight. A Poem. Jan. 6, 1840. By E. G. Nicholson. 1840

——— Address before. By A. H. Miller. *Pittsburgh*, 1840

Wisconsin. The Two Women : a Ballad, written for the Ladies of W. *Milwaukee*, 1868

——— The Emigrant's Hand Book and Guide to. *Milwaukee*, 1851

Washington, Martha. Case in the Circuit Court for Ohio.

Washington Art Association. Address before. By J. R. Tyson. *Phila.*, 1858

Washington College. Remarks on. *Hartford*, 1825

——— ——— Terms of Admission, etc. *Hartford*, 1826

——— ——— Extracts from the Journal of the Convention of the Diocese of Conn., containing Documents relating to. *Middletown*, 1835

2578 Miscellaneous. [*Eleven.*]

Wood, Benjamin. Speech on the State of the Union. *Wash.*, 1862

Wood, Fernando. Address at the Funeral Ceremonies of Maj.-Gen. W. J. Worth. *N. Y.*, 1857

——— Biography of F. W. No. 1.

Woodbridge, Sylvester. Histor. Disc., Nov. 29, 1840, at the Dedication of "Christ's First Church" Chapel, in Raynor, South Hempstead, L. I. *Scarce.* *N. Y.*, 1840

Woods, Leonard. Theology of the Puritans. *Boston*, 1851

Worcester, Noah, D.D. Tribute to the Memory of. Disc. by W. E. Channing. *Boston*, 1837

Wreath, The. *New Orleans*, 1862

Wrentham Jubilee. Sermon, June 12, 1849, by E. Fisk. *Boston*, 1850

Wyche, Wm. Essay on the Theory and Practice of Fines. *N. Y.*, 1794

Wyckoff, I. N. Christian Example; a Sermon, occasioned by the Death of Christian Miller. *Albany*, 1844

Wyvill, Rev. Christopher. Summary Explanation of the Principles of Mr. Pitt's intended Bill for Amending the Representation of the People. *London*, 1785

2579 Miscellaneous. [*Fourteen.*]

Thompson, Joseph H. Oration deliv. before the Associate Alumni of Washington College. *Hartford*, Aug. 5, 1840

Coxe, A. Cleveland. "Athanasion," an Ode before the Associate Alumni of Washington College. *Hartford*, 1840

Blair, David. Anniv. Address before the Washington Literary Soc. *Pa.*, Feb. 22, 1836

Snodgrass, Wm. D. Address before the Alumni Assoc. of Washington College, Pa. *N. Y.*, Sept. 23, 1845

Cowan, Edgar. Address before the Literary Soc. of Wash. Coll., Pa., Sept. 24, 1846.

Chandler, Joseph R. Address before the Literary Soc. of Wash. Coll., Pa., Sept. 29, 1847.

Gow, John Loudon. Introductory Lecture on Municipal Law, in Washington College, Pa. *Wash.*, *Pa.*, Dec. 16, 1848

King, James. Introductory address deliv. to the Students of Wash. College, May 14, 1850. *Washington, Pa.*
Black, Samuel W. The Past and Future of the Nineteenth Century. Address, the Union and Washington Soc., Sept. 25, 1850. *Pittsburg.*
Elliott, David. Introductory address deliv. at Inauguration of James Clark, as President of Washington College, Penn. Sept. 24, 1850.
Western Theological Sem., Pa. Address by David Elliott. *Pittsburg,* 1842
——— Address by Alex. T. M. Gill. *Pittsburg,* 1843
Western Univ., Pa. Address by George Upfold. *Pittsburg,* 1842
Washington, Mount, Collegiate Institute. Catalogue. *New York,* 1858–9

ALE COLLEGE, Annals of, from its Foundation, to 1831, with an Appendix, containing Statistical Tables, and Exhibiting the Present Condition of the Institution. By Ebenezer Baldwin. *8vo, bds., uncut; scarce.* *New Haven,* 1831

2581 YALE COLLEGE. Philosophic Solitude, or the Choice of a Rural Life. A Poem. By a Gentleman Educated at Yale College. *8vo pamphlet; very scarce.* *Boston,* 1762

PAMPHLETS.

2582 Yale College. [*Seventeen.*]

Smalley, John. Sermon deliv. on morning after Commencement. *New Haven,* 1787
New Testament, Disc. on the genuineness and authenticity of, deliv. New Haven, Sept. 10, 1793.
Stebbins, Joseph. Address, after Exam. of Senior Class. *New Haven,* July 20, 1796
Dwight, Timothy. The Nature and Danger of Infidel Philosophy, in two disc. *New Haven,* Sept. 9, 1797
Marsh, Ebenezer Grant. Oration at New Haven, on Public Commencement, Sept., 1798.
Dutton, Warren, Poem deliv. at Public Comm. of, Sept. 10, 1800.
Bishop, Abraham. Oration deliv. in New Haven, Sept., 1800.
Spring, Gardiner, Oration before Alumni of, in Commem. of Timothy Dwight. *N. Y.,* Feb. 5, 1817
Fitch, Ezra T. Disc. deliv. in, on Day of Thanks. *New Haven,* Nov. 29, 1827
Taylor, Nath'l W. Sermon, Sept. 10. *New Haven,* 1828
Silliman, Prof. Introductory Lecture in Laboratory of. *New Haven,* Oct., 1828

Reports on the Course of Instruction in, and the Academical Faculty. *New Haven*, 1830

Johnston, Frank. A Poem, and a Valedictory Oration by Joseph Fenton, July 1, 1835.

Smith, Eli. Address before Soc. of Inquiry in the Theol. Sem. in New Haven, April 1, 1840.

Robinson, Wm. Erigena. Valedictory Oration. *New Haven*, July 6, 1841

Andrews, Wm. W. Oration before Linonian Soc., Aug. 17, 1841.

Bushnell, Horace. Discourse before Soc. of Alumni in. *New Haven*, Aug. 16, 1843

5 2583 Miscellaneous. [*Nineteen.*]

Yale College. Catalogus senatus academici. *Novi Portus*, 1811

——— Catalogue of the Officers and Students, 1836–37, 1838–39. *New Haven*, 1836–39

——— Reports on the Course of Instruction. *New Haven*, 1830

——— Annual Address to the Candidates for Degrees and Licences, in the Medical Institution of, Feb. 26, 1839. *New Haven*, 1839

——— Address before the Phi Beta Kappa Soc., Aug. 20, 1833. *New Haven*, 1833

——— Address before the Phi Beta Kappa Soc., Sept. 13, 1831. *New Haven*, 1831

——— Oration before the Phi Beta Kappa Soc., Aug. 15, 1837. *New Haven*, 1837

——— Brief Memoirs of the Members of the Class of 1802. By D. D. Field. *New Haven*, 1863

——— Commemorative Celebration, held at Yale College, July 26, 1865. *New Haven*, 1866

——— Discourse before the Alumni of, Aug. 16, 1843, by H. Bushnell. *New York*, 1843

——— Laws of. *New Haven*, 1837

Yang-Pih-We-Wing-Tzonga-Foh; or, Musings over a cup of Tea. *New York*, 1868

Yellott, Coleman. Oration, at the Celebration at St. Timothy's Hall, Baltimore County, Maryland, July 5, 1852. *Baltimore*, 1852

Yonkers, Charter of the Village of, Apr. 17, 1857. *Yonkers*, 1857

——— Charter of the Village of, June 28, 1860. *Yonkers*, 1860

——— Circulating Library Association. Catalogue, etc. *New York*, 1860

——— Horticultural Society, Report of the Board of Management, with list of premiums, etc. *New York*, 1860

Young Men's Association of Utica. The Passion for Riches, a Lecture before, by J. W. Williams. *Utica*, 1838

Young, Alexander. Discourse on the Life and Character of Hon. N. Bowditch, March 25, 1838. *Scarce.* *Boston,* 1838

2584 Yale College. [*Twelve.*]

Adams, Wm. Address before the Alumni of Yale College. *New Haven,* Sept. 18, 1847

Finch, Francis M., Poem by, and Valedictory Oration by Horace Hollister. *New Haven,* July 3, 1849

Woolsey, Theodore, Hist. Disc. before Graduates of, Aug. 14, 1850.

Marsh, Ebenezer G. Oration before Phi Beta Kappa Soc. *New Haven,* Dec. 5, 1797

Jarvis, Samuel F. Oration before Phi Beta Kappa Soc., on anniv. of that Soc. *New Haven,* Dec. 5, 1806

Catalogue of the Members of the Conn. Alpha of. *New Haven,* April, 1808

Hillhouse, James A. Oration pronounced at New Haven before Soc. of Phi Beta Kappa, Sept. 12, 1826.

Gould, James. Oration at New Haven before Conn. Alpha of the Phi Beta Kappa Soc. *New Haven,* Sept. 13, 1825

Percival, James G. Poem before the Conn. Alpha of the Phi Beta Kappa Soc. *Boston,* Sept. 13, 1825

Olmstead, Denison. Oration deliv. at New Haven before the Conn. Alpha of the Phi Beta Kappa Soc. *New Haven,* Sept. 11, 1827

Everett, Edward. Address deliv. before the Phi Beta Soc. of Yale College. *Scarce.* *New Haven,* Aug. 20, 1833

Hall, Willis. Address before Soc. of Phi Beta Kappa in Yale College. *New Haven,* 1844

2585 Miscellaneous. [*Twenty.*]

York Baptist Assoc., Minutes of, June 12–13, 1833. *Portland.*

Temp. Soc. of New Haven. Address by Rev. John S. Stone, Dec. 20, 1830.

Y. M. Soc. of Pittsfield. Lecture by J. Todd, Sept. 13, 1842.

——— Boston. Lecture by B. F. Butler, Dec. 29, 1841.

——— Richmond, Va. Disc. on Genius, by J. H. Nichols, Nov. 26, 1832.

Y. M. Assoc. of Albany. Address by D. D. Barnard, Jan. 7, 1834.

——— Sixth Annual Report of, Feb. 4, 1839.

——— Geneva. Lecture by Benj. Hale, Nov. 8, 1837.

Y. M. Merc. Lib. Assoc. of Cinn. Address by James Hall, Apr. 18, 1846.

——— Address by Robt. Dale Owen, Feb. 1, 1848.

Young, Samuel. Lecture on Civilization, before the Young Men's Assoc. of Saratoga Springs, Mar. 8, 1841. *Saratoga Springs,* 1841

——— Suggestions on the best mode of Promoting Civilization and Inprovement. A Lecture. *Albany,* 1837

Young, Sam'l. Discourse at Schenectady, July 25, 1826, before the New York Alpha of the Phi Beta Kappa. *Ballston Spa*, 1826

Young, Alexander. Discourse on Twentieth Anniv. of his Ordination. *Boston*, 1845

——— Discourse on Life of Hon. Nathaniel Bowditch. *Scarce.* *Boston*, 1838

Yale College in 1868. Statements regarding the Condition.

——— Catalogus Collegii Yalensis. *New Haven*, 1823

——— Catalogus Collegii Yalensis. *New Haven*, 1841

——— Address before Phi Beta Kappa Soc., by James Kent. *New Haven*, 1831

——— Semi-Centen. Address to Alumni of, by S. B. Ruggles. *N. Y.*, 1864

ZEISBERGER, Rev. DAVID. The History of our Lord and Saviour Jesus Christ, comprehending all that the Four Evangelists have recorded concerning him. By The Rev. Samuel Lieberkuhn. Translated into the *Delaware Indian* Language. 12*mo, unbound.* *N. Y.*, 1821

SUPPLEMENT.

SUPPLEMENT.

 MANUAL OF RELIGIOUS LIBERTY. By an Author, as yet, unknown. The Second Edition. *12mo, hf. dk. Rox., gilt edges. Printed for* Mr. RIVINGTON, in New York ; Mr. Flexney, in London, &c. MDCCLXVII.

" Where reason calls, my duty I declare,
And hold my zeal unprostituted there."

2588 AMERICAN ANTIQUARIAN SOCIETY (Archæologia Americana). Transactions and Collections of. Published by direction of the Society.

Vol. I.	Worcester,	MDCCCXX.
II.	Cambridge,	1836
III.	"	1857
IV.	Boston,	1860

In four volumes, 8vo, hf. dk. Rox., gilt top, uncut ; fine copy ; scarce. v. l. 1820–1860

These volumes contain matter of the highest importance and value, particularly of the Aboriginal Monuments and Vestiges of the West; Father Hennepin's account of the discovery of the Mississippi, etc.

2589 AMERICAN ANTIQUARIAN SOCIETY. A CATALOGUE of Books in the Library of, in Worcester, Mass. *Roy. 8vo, hf. dk. Rox., gilt top, rough edges.* *Worcester,* 1837

2590 APPLETON, NATH'L. "*Gospel Ministers must be fitted for The Master's Use, and Prepared to every Good Work, if they would be Vessels unto Honor.*" Illustrated in a Sermon Preached at Deerfield, Aug. 31, 1735, at the Ordination of Mr. John Sargent To the Evangelical Ministry, with a special Reference to the Indians of Houssatonnoc, who have lately manifested their desires to receive the Gospel. *8vo, pp. XIV., 33 ; fine copy ; very scarce. Boston : S. Kneeland and T. Green.* MDCCXXXV.

" With a long historical preface."

2591 APOSTLE JOHN. THE THREE EPISTLES OF. Translated into Delaware Indian, by C. F. Dencke. *12mo, full crushed crimson levant, beautiful tooling on sides, inside border, full gilt ; bound by R. W. Smith; very scarce ; 42 pages.* *New York,* 1818

2592 ARMSTRONG, JOHN. NOTICES OF THE WAR OF 1812. In Two Volumes. *8vo, cloth ; fine copy ; very scarce. New York,* 1840

2593 ATWATER, CALEB. REMARKS ON A TOUR TO PRAIRIE DU CHIEN · thence to Washington City, in 1829. *8vo, half maroon mor., gilt top, rough edges ; beautiful copy ; scarce.* *Columbus, O.*, 1831

2594 BALDWIN, J. G. PARTY LEADERS. Sketches of Thomas Jefferson, Alex. Hamilton, Andrew Jackson, Henry Clay, John Randolph, of Roanoke ; including notices of many other distinguished statesmen. *8vo, cloth, 369 pages.* *New York*, 1855

2595 BALTIMORE. A NARRATIVE OF EVENTS which occurred in Baltimore Town during the Revolutionary War. To which are appended various Documents and Letters, the greater part of which have never been heretofore published. By Robert Purviance. *8vo, cloth, good copy.* *Baltimore*, 1849

2596 BARTON, B. S. OBSERVATIONS ON SOME PARTS OF NATURAL HISTORY : to which is prefixed an Account of several Remarkable Vestiges of an Ancient date, which have been discovered in different parts of North America. Part I. *8vo, unbound; very scarce ; fine copy.* *London*, 1787

"A prefixed advertisement to this work informs us that it is the production of a very young man, written chiefly as a recreation from the laborious studies of medicine. It is, however, a curious tract. We have here only the first part ; the other three, which will complete the work, are to be published in a few months."—*Monthly Review.*

"This part, the only one ever published, relates entirely to antiquities, giving an account of the Indian ruins in the Muskingum, and remarks on the first peopling of America." &c.—*Sabins' Bib. Amer., Vol. I., p.* 507.

2597 BARTON, B. S. NEW VIEWS OF THE ORIGIN OF THE TRIBES AND NATIONS OF AMERICA. Second Edition. *8vo, unbound ; fine copy ; very scarce.* *Philadelphia*, 1798

"This edition has an Appendix, containing Notes and Illustrations. It is the first philosophical treatise on American Philology by an American author."—*Sabins' Bib. Amer., p.* 507, *Vol. I.*

2598 BOCCACCIO, GIOVANNI. THE DECAMERON ; or, Ten Days' Entertainment of. Translated from the Italian. To which are prefixed Remarks on the Life and Writings of Boccaccio ; and an Advertisement. *Large 8vo, full crimson crushed levant mor., gilt edges, panelled sides, beautifully tooled, inside borders; a superb copy; with Portrait of Boccaccio, after Van Dalen, inserted.* *London*, 1845

2599 BOCCACCIO, GIOVANNI. SELECTIONS FROM THE DECAMERON OF, including all the passages hitherto suppressed. Translated from the Italian. *8vo, full crushed crimson levant mor., gilt edges; bound to match the Decameron.* *London*, 1865

This copy contains, at the end, list of "The Rare Copies of Boccaccio's works now extant."

2600 BOSTON. ORATION DELIVERED AT THE REQUEST OF THE INHABITANTS OF THE TOWN OF, to commemorate the evening of the Fifth of March, 1770, when a number of Citizens were killed by a party of British Troops quartered among them in a time of Peace. Second Edition. *8vo, half Turkey mor, gilt tops, edges rough ; fine copy.* *Boston*, 1807

2601 BOSTON (EAST). A HISTORY OF, with Biographical Sketches of its Early Proprietors, and an Appendix. By Wm. H. Sumner. *8vo, half red Rox., gilt tops, rough edges; Portraits and Engravings.* *Boston*, 1858

2602 BRADBURY, JOHN. TRAVELS IN THE INTERIOR OF AMERICA, in the years 1809, 1810, and 1811; including a description of Upper Louisiana, together with the States of Ohio, Kentucky, Indiana, and Tennessee; with the Illinois and Western Territories, and containing Remarks and Observations useful to Persons emigrating to these Countries. *L. 8vo, half crimson levant mor, gilt top, rough edges; beautiful copy; scarce.* *Liverpool*, 1817

2603 BRISSOT, J. P. The Commerce of America with Europe, particularly with France and Great Britain; showing the importance of the American Revolution to the interests of France, and pointing out the actual situation of the U. S. of America in regard to Trade, Manufactures, and Population. *8vo, bds., uncut; Portrait.* *London*, 1793

2604 BURTON, ROBERT. THE ANATOMY OF MELANCHOLY. What it is, with all the kinds, causes, symptoms, prognostics, and several cures of it. In Three Partitions. With their several Sections, Members, and Subsections, Philosophically, Medically, Historically opened and cut up. By Democritus, Junior. With a Satirical Preface, conducing to the following Discourse. A new Edition. In Three Volumes. *8vo, half dk. blue crushed levant, gilt top, edges rough, rubric title and coat-of-arms in blue and gold.* *Cambridge: Riverside Press*, 1861

75 copies printed; large paper.

2605 CHAPPELL, Lieut. EDWARD. VOYAGE to NEWFOUNDLAND AND THE SOUTHERN COAST OF LABRADOR. Of which countries no account has been published by any British Traveller since the Reign of Queen Elizabeth. *8vo, half crimson levant morocco, gilt top, rough edges. Fine copy, Illustrated.* *London*, 1818

2606 CHASTELLUX, MARQUIS de. TRAVELS IN NORTH AMERICA, in the years 1780, '81, '82. Translated from the French, with Notes. Also, a Biographical Sketch of the Author. Letters from Gen. Washington, and Notes and Corrections by the American Editor. *Large 8vo, half crimson levant mor., gilt top, rough edges. Fine copy.* *New York*, 1827

2607 COLMAN, GEORGE, *The Younger*. BROAD GRINS. COMPRISING, with New Additional Tales in Verse, those formerly published under the title of "My Night Gown and Slippers." The Fifth Edition. Illustrated. *12mo, half crushed crimson levant, gilt top, rough edges.* *London*, 1811

The engravings in this volume are on wood, by Nesbitt, and the character and style of the poetry is very free.

2608 CUMING, HOOPER. A Sermon delivered at Schoharie before the Grand Lodge, at the Installation of Hicks' Lodge, No. 305, July 4, 1818. *8vo pamph., 16 p. Fine copy; scarce.*
Schoharie: Printed by D. Van Veghten. 1818

2609 DEDHAM, MASS., HISTORY OF. From the Beginning of its Settlement in September, 1635, to May, 1827. By Erastus Worthington. *8vo, half red Roxburghe, gilt top, rough edges. Beautiful copy, very scarce.* *Boston*, 1827

2610 DIBDIN, Rev. T. F. THE **Library Companion**; or, The Young Man's Guide, and the Old Man's Comfort, in the Choice of a Library. In two vols. *Large 8vo, full crushed levant, gilt edges, paneled sides, elegant tooling, inside borders. Superb copy.* *London*, 1824

At end of the Second Volume is bound in the Index to whole work, which was published separately, and is most always wanting.

2611 FIELD, T. W. THE MINSTREL PILGRIM. *Sm. 4to, cloth gilt, 50 p.*
New York, 1848

2612 FLORIDA: ITS CLIMATE, SOIL, AND PRODUCTIONS, with a Sketch of its History, Natural Features, and Social Condition. *8vo, 151 p.* *Jacksonville*, 1869

2613 FREMONT, Capt. J. C. REPORT OF THE EXPLORING EXPEDITION to the Rocky Mountains in the year 1842, and to Oregon and North California in the years 1843–'44. *8vo, cloth, maps and plates, 693 p. Good copy; scarce* *Washington*, 1845

2614 FRENCH WAR, REMINISCENCES OF. Containing Rogers' Expeditions with the New England Rangers under his command, with Notes and Illustrations. To which is added an account of the Life and Military Services of Major-General John Stark, with notices and anecdotes of other officers distinguished in the French and Revolutionary Wars. *8vo, half red Rox., gilt top rough edges. Fine copy; scarce; with portrait of Gen. John Stark.* *Concord*, 1831

2615 GARDEN, ALEX. ANECDOTES OF THE REVOLUTIONARY WAR IN AMERICA. With Sketches of Character of Persons most distinguished in the Southern States, for Civil and Military Services. *Imperial 8vo, half red Rox., gilt top, rough edges. Beautiful copy; very scarce.* *Charleston*, 1822

2616 GRANT, Mrs. MEMOIRS OF AN AMERICAN LADY. With sketches of Manners and Scenery in America, as they existed previous to the Revolution. *8vo, half dark Rox., gilt top, uncut. Beautiful copy.* *New York*, 1809

2617 GUIREY, WM. THE HISTORY OF EPISCOPACY. In four parts; from its Rise to the Present Day, among the Methodists in America. *8vo, full dark blue calf, gilt edges, 385 p. Very scarce; fine copy.* *s. l. s. a.*

The preface to this work ends as follows: "As this work was principally intended for the information of the Inhabitants of the Backwoods of Ga;" and it is probable that the book was printed in some of the Southern States, and most likely North Carolina, about 18(?)0.

2618 HARDIE, JAMES. THE AMERICAN REMEMBRANCER and Universal Tablet of Memory. The whole being intended to form a

Comprehensive abridgement of History and Chronology, particularly of that part which relates to America. *8vo, half red turkey, gilt edges.* *Phila., MDCCXCV.*

2619 HEAD, SIR FRANCIS B. The Emigrant. *half Rox., gilt top, rough edges.* *John Murray, London,* 1847

2620 HENRY, ALEXANDER. TRAVELS AND ADVENTURES IN CANADA AND THE INDIAN TERRITORIES, between the years 1760 and 1766. In two parts. Portrait of Henry. *Large 8vo, half crimson levant morocco, gilt top, rough edges. Beautiful copy ; very scarce.* *New York,* 1809

These transactions range themselves under these heads : First, the Author's Personal Incidents and Adventures. Second, Natural History and Geography of the Countries Visited. And third, the Views of Society and Manners among the Indians with whom he was brought in contact.

2621 HOLDEN, HORACE. A NARRATIVE OF THE SHIPWRECK, CAPTIVITY, AND SUFFERINGS OF Horace Holden and Benj. H. Nute : who were cast away in the American ship " Mentor," on the Pelew Islands, in the year 1832, and for two years afterwards were subjected to unheard of sufferings among the Barbarous Inhabitants of Lord North's Island. *12mo, plates. 4th edition, half Rox., gilt.* *Boston,* 1836

Dedicated to John Pickering, Esq., who makes frequent reference to this narrative in his " Memoirs of Lord North's Island." See No. —

2622 HOLMES, ABIEL. AMERICAN ANNALS, or, a Chronological History of America, from its Discovery in MCCCCXCII to MDCCCVI. With additions and corrections by the Author. In two volumes, with map. *8vo, half dark Rox., gilt top, rough edges. Very scarce.*
Cambridge, printed ; London Reprinted, 1808

2623 HOWLAND, JOHN, a Revolutionary Soldier, the Life and Recollections of. Late President of the Rhode Island Historical Society. By Edwin M. Stone. *8vo, half Roxburghe, gilt top, rough edges. Portrait and plate.* *Providence,* 1857

"His varied experience and minute observation while in the Continental Service, his intimate acquaintance with the leading men of Rhode Island, and his personal knowledge of Washington, Greene, Lee, Gates, Sullivan, Arnold, Paul Jones, and other distinguished officers of the Revolution, impart to these Recollections an unusual historic value.

2624 HOYT, E. ANTIQUARIAN RESEARCHES. Comprising a History of the Indian Wars in the Country bordering on Connecticut River and parts adjacent, and other interesting events, from the First Landing of the Pilgrims, to the Conquest of Canada by the English in 1760 ; with notices of Indian depredations in the neighboring country, and of the first planting and progress of settlements in New England, New York and Canada. *8vo, half red Rox., gilt top, rough edges. Beautiful copy, eng. frontispiece and plates. Very scarce.* *Greenfield,* 1824

2625 HUDSON, HENRY, AN HISTORICAL INQUIRY CONCERNING. His friends, relatives and Early life, his connection with the Muscovy Company and Discovery of Delaware Bay. By John

Meredith Read, Jr. *Royal 8vo, half red Rox., gilt top, rough edges, rubric title. Arms of Muscovy Co. as Frontispiece.*
Joel Munsell, Albany, 1866

2626 INDIAN TREATIES, and Laws and Regulations relating to Indian Affairs ; to which is added an Appendix. *Large 8vo, hf. dark Rox., gilt top, rough edges. Fine copy.*
Washington City, 1826

2627 IRVING, WASHINGTON, A Discourse on the Life, Character and Genius of, delivered before the New York Historical Society, April 3d, 1860. By William Cullen Bryant. *8vo, cloth, 46 pages, tinted paper.* *New York,* 1860

2628 IRVING, WASHINGTON, The Life and Letters of. By Pierre M. Irving. In 4 vols. *Small 4to. half crim. cr. lev. mor., gilt top, rough edges ; portraits.* *New York,* 1862–'64.

See pamphlet lot No. 1084, *for a Rare document on Irving's "Wife."*

2629 JEFFERSON, THOMAS. A Manual of Parliamentary Practice. For the Use of the Senate of the United States. 12*mo, sheep. Good copy ; scarce.* *Washington City, MDCCC.*

2630 JEMISON, MARY, Life of. By James E. Seaver. *Fourth edition, 8vo, cloth. Frontispiece, with explanatory notes and Indian Vocabulary.* *N. Y.,* 1856

2631 JERSEY PRISON SHIP, Recollections of. From the Original Manuscripts of Captain Thomas Dring, one of the Prisoners. By Albert G. Greene. Edited by Henry B. Dawson. *Large 8vo, half crushed crimson levant morocco, gilt top, rough edges.* 100 *copies printed, No.* 61. *Morrisania,* 1865

2632 KEITH. GEORGE The Fundamental Truths of Christianity, briefly hinted at by way of Question and Answer. To which is added a Treatise of Prayer, in the same method. 16*mo, full dark blue levant.*
LONDON: Printed in the year MDCLXXXVIII.

2633 KINGSLEY, CHARLES. Sir Walter Raleigh and his Time, with other papers. *8vo., cloth ; fine copy.* *Boston,* 1859

2634 LINCOLN, ABRAHAM (Late President of U. S. A.) The Assassination of, and the attempted Assassination of William H. Seward, Secretary of State, and Frederick W. Seward, Assistant Secretary, on the evening of the 14th of April, 1865. Expressions of Condolence and Sympathy inspired by these Events. *Royal 8vo, half dark blue crushed levant, gilt top, rough edges ; fine copy, now scarce,* 717 *pages.* *Washington,* 1866

2635 MA-KA-TAI-ME-SHE-KIA-KIAK ; or, Black Hawk, Life of. Embracing the Tradition of his Nation ; Indian wars in which he has been engaged ; cause of Joining the British in their late war with America, and its History ; Description of the Rock River Village, Manners and Customs, &c. ; with an Account of the Cause and General History of the late War ; his Surrender and Confinement and Travels through the United States. Dictated by Himself. *8vo, half crimson levant, gilt edges. India proof Portrait of Black Hawk inserted.*
Boston, 1834

2636 MASSACHUSETTS BAY, Continuation of the History of the Province of, from the year 1748. With an Introductory sketch of events from its Original Settlement. In two vols.: Volume I.—From 1748. Volume II.—From 1748 to 1765. By George Richards Minot. *8vo, half red Rox., gilt top, rough edges; fine copy, very scarce.* *Boston*, 1798–1803

2637 MATHER, COTTON—PSALTERIUM Americanum. The Book of | PSALMS. | In a Translation Exactly conformed | unto the Originals; | but all in | Blank Verse, | Fitted unto the Tunes commonly used in our Churches. Which Pure | Offering is accompanied with | Illustrations, digging for *Hidden* | *Treasures* in it; And Rules to | Employ it upon the Glorious and | Various Intentions of it, | Whereto are added, | Some other Portions of the Sacred | Scripture, to Enrich the | Cantional. |

12mo, full maroon crushed levant morocco, elegant tooling on backs and sides, inside borders richly tooled, gilt; beautiful copy, extremely rare. Bound by R. W. Smith.

BOSTON: in N.E. | *Printed by* S. Kneeland, *for* B. Eliot, | S. Gerrish, D. Henchman, *and* | J. Edwards, *and sold at their Shops* | 1718.

2638 Methodist Epis. Church, the Doctrines and Disciplines of, in America. With explanatory Notes by Thomas Coke and Francis Asbury. *12mo, sheep, 169 pages, good copy.* *Phila.*, 1798

In same volume. Four Discourses on the duties of the Gospel Ministry by Thomas Coke. Philadelphia 1798. 109 pages.

2639 MUNSELL'S HISTORICAL SERIES.

Vol. I.—Expedition Against Ticonderoga and Crown Point. 1759.
Vol. II.—King Philip's Indian War. 1675.
Vol. III.—Orderly Book of the Northern Army. 1776–1777.
Vol. IV.—Diary of the Siege of Detroit.
Vol. V.—Obstructions to the Navigation of Hudson's River.
Vol. VI.—The Loyal Verses of Stansbury and Odell.
Vol. VII.—Burgoyne's Orderly Book. 1777.
Vol. VIII.—Early Voyages up and Down the Mississippi.
Vol. IX.—Indian Treaties.—1.
Vol. X.—Indian Treaties.—2.

Ten volumes. *Half red Rox., gilt tops, rough edges. Contents lettered on back as above. Beautiful Library copy; covers bound in.* *Albany, J. Munsell*, 1857–'61

2640 NATIONAL ACADEMY OF DESIGN, Historic Annals of, with occasional Dottings by the Wayside, from 1825 to the Present Time. By Thomas S. Cummings. *8vo, cloth; fine copy.* *Phila.*, 1865

2641 NEW AMSTERDAM, Affairs and Men of, in the Time of Gov. Peter Stuyvesant. Compiled from Dutch Manuscript Records. By J. Paulding. *8vo, cloth; fine copy.* *New York*, 1843

2642 NEW PLYMOUTH, An Historical Memoir of the Colony of, from the Flight of the Pilgrims into Holland in the year 1608, to the Union of that Colony with Massachusetts, 1692. By Francis Baylies. With some Corrections, Additions, and a Copious Index. By Samuel G. Drake. In two volumes. *Imperial 8vo, half red Rox., gilt top, rough edges; fine copy.* *Boston*, 1830: *Wiggin and Lunt*, 1866

2643 O'Connell James F. A Residence of Eleven Years in New Holland and the Caroline Islands. Being the Adventures of ——. Edited from his verbal narration. 12*mo, half red Rox., gilt, eng.* *Boston*, 1836

"All of which I saw, and part of which I was."

2644 PAUL, MOSES. A Sermon Preached at the Execution of Moses Paul, an Indian, who was executed at New Haven, on the 2d of September, 1772, for the Murder of Mr. Moses Cook, late of Waterbury, on the 7th of December, 1771. Preached at the desire of said Paul. By Samson Occom. 8*vo, full dk. blue levant,* 21 *pages. Cleaned, mended, extended and put in perfect order. Very scarce edition.* *Exeter, N. H.*, 1819

Contains also 1 page of Biog. Sketch of Paul, and a Hymn.

2645 PENHALLOW, SAMUEL. The History of the Wars of New England, with the Eastern Indians; or, a Narrative of their Continued Perfidy and Cruelty, from the 10th of August, 1703, to the Peace of July 13, 1713, &c. 138 *p. In same volume:* Lieft Lion Gardner. His Relation of the Present Warres, from the original MS., with interesting letters of W. T. Williams in relation to Lion Gardener, &c., never before published. 35 *pages,* 4*to, half crim. crushed lev., gilt top, rough edges.* *Cinn.*, 1859

2646 PHELPS AND GORHAM'S PURCHASE, and Morris Reserve, History of the Pioneer Settlement of. Embracing the counties of Monroe, Ontario, Livingston, Yates, Steuben, most of Wayne and Allegany, and parts of Orleans, Genesee, and Wyoming. To which is added a Supplement, or extension of the Pioneer History of Monroe County. The whole preceded by some account of French and English Dominion; Border Wars of the Revolution; Indian Councils and Land Cessions; Early Difficulties with the Indians; Our immediate Predecessors the Senecas, with "a glance at the Iroquois." By O. Turner. *Royal 8vo, half crimson crushed levant, gilt top. rough edges. Very scarce in this condition.* *Rochester*, 1851

2647 PICKERING, JOHN. An Essay on a Uniform Orthography for the Indian Languages of North America. 4*to, half Rox., gilt top, edges uncut. Very scarce.* *Cambridge*, 1820

2648 PITTSBURGH, Pa., The History of, with a brief notice of its facilities of communication and other advantages for commercial and mauufacturing Purposes, with two maps. By Neville B. Craig, Esq. 8*vo, hf. dk. blue levant, gt. top. With inserted plate of Braddock's Defeat. Very fine copy.* *Pittsburgh*, 1851

Presentation copy to Charles Cist, Esq., of Cinn.

2649 PRESCOTT, WM. H. HISTORY OF THE CONQUEST OF MEXICO. With a preliminary view of the Ancient Mexican Civilization, and the Life of the Conqueror Hernando Cortes. In three volumes. *8vo, cloth. Fine copy of the now scarce first ed.* *New York*, 1844

2650 PRINCE, THOMAS, M.A. A | CHRONOLOGICAL HISTORY | of | NEW ENGLAND, | In the Form of | ANNALS: | BEING A summary and exact *Account* of the most material *Transactions* and *Occurrences* relating to THIS COUNTRY, in the Order of Time wherein they happened, from the *Discovery* by Capt. GOSNOLD in 1602, to the *Arrival* of Governor BELCHER in 1730, &c., &c. Volume I., Parts 1 and 2. *12mo, full dk. blue lev. mor., gt. edges, elegant tooling on back and sides, inside borders. Bound by R. W. Smith. Beautiful copy; extremely scarce.*
BOSTON, N. E.
Printed by KNEELAND and GREEN, *for* S. GERRISH. MDCCXXXVI.

2651 RITTER, ABRAHAM. HISTORY OF THE MORAVIAN CHURCH IN PHILADELPHIA. From its Foundation in 1742, to the present time. Comprising Notices, defensive of its Founder and Patron, Count Nicholas Ludwig Von Zinzendorff. Together with an Appendix. *8vo, cl. Portraits.* *Phila.*, 1857

2652 ROGERS, HENRY. ESSAYS Selected from Contributions to the Edinburgh Review. In two volumes—
Vol. I.—Biographical and Critical.
Vol. II.—Theological and Political.
8vo, cloth, uncut. Scarce. *London*, 1850

2653 ROGERS, HENRY. ESSAYS Selected from Contributions to the Edinburgh Review. Volume III. *8vo, cloth, uncut.* *London*, 1855

This volume of Essays is supplementary to the two former volumes, and is composed of Philosophical Treatises, and a History of the English Language.

2654 SCHOOLCRAFT, HENRY R. ALGIC RESEARCHES. Comprising inquiries respecting the mental characteristics of the North American Indians. First Series Indian Tales and Legends. In two volumes. *8vo, hf. tky., gilt edges. In fine condition; scarce.* *New York*, 1839

2655 SEMINOLE WAR, SKETCH OF, and Sketches during a Campaign, By a Lieutenant of the Left Wing. *8vo, half dark green lev., gilt top, uncut. Bound by R. W. Smith.* *Charleston*, 1836

2656 SHEPPARD, THOMAS. *Late pastor in the Church in Cambridge in New England.* Subjection | to | Christ | in all his | Ordinances, | and | Appointments, | The best means to preserve our | Liberty. |
8vo, full dk. blue calf, gilt edges.
LONDON,—*Printed by S. G., for John Rothwell at the Fountain in Cheapside,* 1657.

2657 SHEPPARD, THOMAS, THESES SABBATICÆ ; or, the Doctrine of the SABBATH.

Wherein the Sabbath's { *I.—Morality.* *II.—Change.* *III.—Beginning.* *IV.—Sanctification.* } are clearly discussed.

Which were first handled more largely in Sundry SERMONS in *Cambridge* in *New England.* *8vo, full calf*
London, Printed by S. G., for *John Rothwel, &c.,* 1655
In same Volume,—
CERTAIN SELECT CASES RESOLVED. *Rough edges.*
London, 1655

2658 SIGOURNEY, LYDIA H. TRAITS OF THE ABORIGINES OF AMERICA. A Poem. *8vo, half crushed crimson lev. morocco, gilt top, rough edges. Beautiful clean copy.* *Cambridge,* 1822

With Appendix of 100 pages of valuable notes of Indian history, customs, etc.

2659 SOUTHAMPTON, L. I. A DISCOURSE delivered on the 22d of November, 1804, being the Anniversary Thanksgiving in the Presbyterian Church. By David S. Bogart. *8vo, 24 pages. Fine copy, scarce.*
Sag Harbor: Printed by Alden Spooner, 1805

2660 SMITH, CHARLOTTE. ELEGIAC SONNETS and other Poems. The first Worcester Edition. *12mo, hf. dark blue levant, gilt top, rough edges. Illustrated by five plates engraved by Seymour.*
Printed at Worcester by ISAIAH THOMAS, 1795

"The Editor, I. Thomas, doubts not but a proper allowance will be made for work engraved by an artist who obtained his knowledge in this country." Also, "The making of the particular kind of paper on which these Sonnets are printed, is a new business in America ; it is the first manufactured by the Editor."

2661 SPRAGUE, JOHN T. THE ORIGIN, PROGRESS, AND CONCLUSION OF THE FLORIDA WAR. To which is Appended a record of Officers, Non-commissioned Officers, Musicians and Privates of the U. S. Army, Navy, and Marine Corps, who were killed in Battle, or died of disease. Together with the order for collecting the remains of the dead in Florida, and the ceremony of interment at St. Augustine, August 14, 1842. *Royal 8vo, hf. red Rox., gilt top, rough edges, maps and plates.*
New York, 1848

2662 STAMFORD, Conn., HISTORY OF, From its settlement in 1641, to the present time, including Darien, which was one of its Parishes until 1620. By E. B. Huntington, A.M. *8vo, hf. red Rox., gilt top, rough edges. Illus.* *Stamford,* 1868.

One of Five copies only which were saved uncut.

2663 ST. CLAIR, ARTHUR, Maj.-Gen. A NARRATIVE of the Manner in which the Campaign against the Indians in 1791 was conducted, etc., and the Reports of the Committees appointed to inquire into the causes of the failure thereof. *8vo, half red Rox., gilt top, rough edges. Fine copy, very scarce.*
Phila., 1812

2664 THE COMPANION: being a Selection of the Beauties of the most celebrated authors in the English Language. In Prose and Verse. *Sq. 12mo, dk. blue levant, gilt top, rough edges; in fine condition.* PRINTED BY NATHANIEL AND BENJAMIN HEATON FOR JOSEPH J. TODD, PROVIDENCE. MDCCXCIX.

Contains, among various other matter, "The Fashionable Songs for 1798," "Adams and Liberty," "The Federal Constitution and Washington for Ever," &c., &c.

2665 THE WEAL-REAF. A RECORD OF THE ESSEX INSTITUTE FAIR, held at Salem, Sept. 4, 5, 6, 7, 8, with Two Supplementary Numbers. Complete. *4to, half crim. crushed lev. mor., gilt top, rough edges.* (*Salem,*) 1860

G. W. Curtis, Nathaniel Hawthorne, Rev. C. T. Brooks and other eminent writers contributed matter of an interesting local character to this publication.

2666 THOMPSON, DANIEL P. THE RANGERS; OR, THE TORY'S DAUGHTER. A Tale illustrative of the Revolutionary History of Vermont and the Northern Campaign of 1777. In Two Volumes. 4th Ed. *8vo, half dk. Rox., gilt edges. Boston,* 1851

A very entertaining Historical Romance. See Hall's Eastern Vt., vol. II., p. 584.

2667 TONGA ISLANDS. An Account of the Natives of, in the South Pacific Ocean, compiled and arranged from the extensive Communications of Mr. William Mariner, several years resident in those Islands. By John Martin, M.D. *8vo, half red turkey mor., gilt edges. Portrait of Mariner. First Amer. Edition. Boston,* 1820

2668 TRIAL OF JOSEPH GERRALD, Delegate from the London Corresponding Society, to the British Convention, for Sedition. *8vo, half dk. blue levant morocco, gilt top, rough edges; fine copy. Portrait of Gerrald. New York: Samuel Campbell,* 1794

2669 TRUEMAN, JOHN AND RICHARD ATKINS. The Lives of; to which is added a short account of Atkins' sister. Also, the Life of William Baker, and a Sermon at his Funeral. *8vo, half dk. blue crushed levant, gilt edges.*

2670 TRUMBULL, JOHN. (A Whig of 1776.) MCFINGAL: a Modern Epic Poem. In four Cantos. With explanatory notes. *12mo, bds., uncut. Scarce ed. Albany,* 1813

2671 TRUMBULL, JOHN. THE POETICAL WORKS OF, containing McFingal: a Modern Epic Poem, revised and corrected, with copious explanatory Notes; the Progress of Dullness; and a Collection of Poems on various subjects, written before and during the Revolutionary War. In Two Volumes. Portrait and Plates. *L. 8vo, half crimson levant mor., gilt top, rough edges; scarce; fine copy. Hartford,* 1820

2672 TRUMBULL, HENRY. HISTORY OF THE DISCOVERY OF AMERICA; of the landing of our Forefathers at Plymouth, and of their most remarkable engagements with the Indians in New England, from their first landing in 1620 until the subjugation of the Natives in 1679. To which is annexed, the particulars of almost every important engagement with the Savages at the westward to the present day, including the defeat of Generals Braddock, Harmer and St. Clair, the Creek and Seminole War, &c. *8vo, half crimson crushed levant, gilt top, rough edges; beautiful copy; very scarce in this condition.* *Boston*, 1828

2673 TURNER, G. Traits of Indian Character, as generally applicable to the Aborigines of North America; drawn from various sources; partly from observation of the Writer. In Two Volumes. *8vo, half red Rox., gilt edges.* *Phila.*, 1836

2674 TUTHILL, JOHN. A Family Meeting of the Descendants of, one of the original settlers of the Town of Southold, N. Y., with Genealogy. *8vo, pamphlet, 60 pages. Scarce.* *Sag-Harbor*, 1867

2675 UNITED STATES. Remarks during a Tour through the U. S. of America in the years 1817, 1818, 1819. In a series of Letters to Friends in England. By Wm. Tell Harris. *8vo, half dk. Rox., gilt top, rough edges.* *London*, 1821

2676 Vans, William. A Short History of the Life of, written by himself, who was appointed Consul in France by Geo. Washington in 1794. *12mo, bds. Curious.* *Boston*, 1825

2677 VERMONT. The Natural and Political History of the State of. To which is added an Appendix, containing answers to sundry queries addressed to the Author. By Ira Allen, Esquire. *8vo, half dk. Rox., gilt top, rough edges; map; fine copy; scarce.* *London*, 1798

2678 VERMONT, EASTERN. History of, from its earliest settlement to the close of the Eighteenth Century. With a Biographical Chapter and Appendices. By Benjamin H. Hall. *In Two Volumes. Half crushed crimson levant morocco, wide backs and corners, gilt top, rough edges.* Large Paper Copy. *Only Fifty Printed.* No. 15. *Albany: J. Munsell*, 1865

2679 WARREN, JOSEPH. Life and Times of. By Richard Frothingham. *Roy. 8vo, half dk. blue levant mor., gilt top, rough edges.* *Boston*, 1865

2680 WHEATLEY, PHILLIS, *Negro Servant to Mr. John Wheatley of Boston, in New England.* Poems on Various Subjects, Religious and Moral. *8vo, full crushed crimson levant morocco, paneled sides, inside borders; magnificent copy. Portrait.* *London: Printed for A. Bell, &c.*, MDCCLXXIII.

2681 WILLIAMS, REV. JOHN. A Biographical Memoir of, First Minister of Deerfield, Mass. With a slight sketch of Ancient Deerfield, and an Account of the Indian Wars in that place and vicinity. With an Appendix, containing the Journal of the Rev. Doct. Stephen Williams of Longmeadow, during his Captivity, and other papers relating to the early Indian Wars in Deerfield. By Stephen W. Williams. *8vo, half Rox., gilt edges; fine copy; scarce.* *Greenfield, Mass.*, 1837

2682 WILLIAMSBURG (N. Y.) A History of the City of, containing a succinct account of its early Settlement, rapid growth and prosperous condition, with many other important and interesting facts connected with the same. By Samuel Reynolds. *8vo, half crushed crim. levant, gilt top, rough edges; beautiful copy; very scarce.* *Williamsburgh,* 1852

2683 WOOD, SILAS. A SKETCH OF THE FIRST SETTLEMENT of the several Towns on Long Island; with their political condition, to the end of the American Revolution. A new Edition. *8vo, half dk. Rox., gilt top, rough edges; fine large copy; scarce.* *Brooklyn,* 1828

PAMPHLETS.

2684 Miscellaneous. [*Three.*]

Letters to Rev. W. E. Channing, by M. Stuart. *Andover,* 1819
Sermon. Ordination of Missionaries, by M. Stuart. *Salem,* 1819
Letters to Unitarians, by L. Woods. *Andover,* 1820

2685 Miscellaneous. [*Eleven.*]

Constitution, By-Laws and Regulations of the Philharmonic Soc. of New York. *N. Y.,* 1824
Transactions of the Apollo Assoc. for the year 1843. *N. Y.*
Maryland Academy of Science and Literature.
Proceedings of Franklin Inst. of Penn. relative to the establishment of a School of Design for Women. *Phil.,* 1851
Charter and By-Laws of Society for Promotion of Useful Arts. *Albany,* 1815
Charter and By-Laws of Phil. Athenæum, with List of Books Maps, Medals, &c., which have been presented; also, Catalogue of Maps, Medals, &c., belonging to the Inst. 80 *p. Scarce.* *Phil.,* 1820
Fourth Annual Exhib. of Columbian Soc. of Artists and Penn Academy. 32 *p. Scarce.* *Phil.,* 1814
New York Athenæum.
Constitution and By-Laws of N. Y. Athenæum. *N. Y.,* 1825
Disc. deliv. in Columbia College before National Academy of Design, by S. F. B. Morse. *N. Y.,* 1827
Constitution and By-Laws of National Academy of Design. *N. Y.,* 1843

2686 Miscellaneous. [*Five.*]

1st Rep. of Bost. Pris. Disc. Soc., June 2, 1826.
2d " " June 1, 1827.
3d " " *Boston,* 1828
5th " " *Boston,* 1830
9th " " May 27, 1834.

2687 Railroad Co. Pamphlets. *No duplicates.* (20.)
2688 Reports Blind Asylum. (20.)
2689 Temperance Soc. Reports and Addresses. *No dup. Fine lot.* (20.)
2690 Bank Reports. *Early Southern Imprints. No dup.* (18.)

2691 Miscellaneous Pamphlets. (19.)
2692 " " (19.)
2693 " " (18.)
2694 " " (16.)
2695 " " (16.)
2696 Sermons. (16.)
2697 " (16.)
2698 Political Pamphlets. (22.)
2699 Miscellaneous Pamphlets, Reports, &c. (14.)
2700 Pamphlets—Speeches by Senators of the U. S., 1820–1826. Archer on Tariff Bill. (14.)
2701 Small Pamphlets, various dates, 1765, &c. *Some rare.* (26.)
2702 Sermons, various years. (24.)
2703 Political Pamphlets. *Good lot.* (14.)
2704 Episcopal Convention Sermons and General Theol. Seminary Pamphlets. (23.)
2705 Sermons, Speeches, Addresses, &c., from 1806. *A good collection.* (24.)
2706 Speeches, Bankrupt Laws, Documents, Letters, &c. (14.)
2707 Miscellaneous Pamphlets, Reports, &c. (21.)
2708 Sermons—Miscellaneous. (21.)
2709 Ordination, Installation and Fast Sermons. *Good lot.* (20.)
2710 " " " *Very fine lot.* (20.)
2711 Pastoral Letters of Bp.Bowen, White (in 1808), B. T. Onderdonk, Hobart. (12.)
2712 Sermons, Reports, Addresses, &c., by Meade, Dewey, McIlvaine, Hook, Onderdonk of N. Y., Cornelius, Bp. Hopkins, Sparrow, Moore (in 1806), Sampson Reed, Ashbel Green, Spring, W. Ingraham Kip, &c. (40.)

2713 Reports, Sermons, &c. [*Twenty-one.*]

Sermons before various Religious Societies, 1792–1857.
Sermons before Peace Society, Windham, Conn., Feb. 4, 1830.
21st Report, Baptist Society for Promoting Gospel in Ireland. *Lond.*, 1835
25th Report American Soc. for Melior. Cond. of the Jews, with Sermon by Nathan Lord. *N. Y.*, 1848
Francis Wayland's Address, Amer. Inst. of Instruction. *Bost.*, 1830
Catholicism Compatible with Repub. Govt., by Fenelon. 1844
Reports of N. Y. Fem. Benev. Soc., 1837 ; Mercantile Lib. Assoc., 1841 ; N. Y. Deaf and Dumb, 1832 ; Address by J. F. Schroeder, 1830 ; Arcade Ladies' Inst., Prov., R. I., 1834.
Result of an Ex-parte Council. *Prov.*, 1832
Proc. of Amer. Lyceum, May 4, 1831. *Boston.*
Address to the Working-men of N. E., by Seth Luther. *N. Y.*, 1833
Declar. of Objects and Measures of Working-men. *N. Y.*, 1831

2714 Educational, &c. *Very scarce.* [*Twelve.*]

An Address upon Education and Common Schools, delivered at Cooperstown, Otsego Co., N. Y., Sept. 21, 1843, by James Henry, Albany, 1843. 58 *p.*

A Discourse on Education, by Jacob Brodhead, N. Y., 1831. *Valuable.* 38 *pages.*
Some account of the Jacotot System of Universal Instruction, with a Reference to the Systems of Lancaster, &c., before the Albany Institute. 33 *pages.* *N. Y.*, 1831
Discourse on Popular Education, by Charles Fenton Mercer, delivered Sept. 26, 1826, Princeton, N. J. 86 *pages.* *With valuable Appendix.* 41 *pages.*
Thoughts on the Annexation of Texas, by Theo. Sedgwick, N. Y. 1844. 55 *pages.*
An Article on the Debts of the States, Cambridge, 1844. 48 *pages.*
Biog. Sketch of Rembrandt Peale.
Oration, July 4, 1838, by Edwin Forrest, N. Y., 1838. 21 *p.*
Description of Napoleon's Costly and Curious Military Carriage, taken on the evening of the Battle of Waterloo, with the circumstances of the Capture, by Maj. Von Keller, by whom it was taken. (Illustration of the Capture.) 20 *pages, uncut.* *London*, 1816
The History of the Inquisition of Spain. 1843. 208 *pages.*
Public Defaulters brought to Light, by a Native of Va. N. Y., 1822. 54 *pages ; fine copy ; scarce.*
Official Corresp. between Don Luis de Onis and John Quincy Adams in relation to the Floridas and the Boundaries of La., with other matters. *Very scarce.* *London*, 1818

2715 Miscellaneous. [*Eleven.*]

The Crisis of the Country, by Junius, and Sequel to. *Uncut.*
The Monthly Chronicle. Vol. I. Mar.–June, 1838. *London.*
The Monthly Lecturer. Vol. I. Nos. 1, 2. 1841.
The Monthly Anthology for Sept., 1809. *Uncut.*
Museum of Foreign Lit., Science and Art. Mar., 1831.
The Evangelical Intelligencer. (New Series.) Vol. II. No. 9. 1808.
The Spirit of Missions. Vol. VII. No. 9. 1842.
Cyclopædia of Biblical Literature.
Address deliv. at First Anniversary of N. Y. Temperance Soc., by David Hosack, May 11, 1830.
The Parthenon ; or, Literary and Scientific Museum, edited by S. Woodworth, N. Y., Oct. 10, 1827.
The Montreal Pilot. (Extra.) Speeches and Papers relating to Rebellion Losses, Montreal, Feb. 26, 1849.

2716 Miscellaneous. [*Eleven.*]

First Report of Phil. Bible Society. *Phil.*, 1809
Third Rep. of N. Y. Bible Society. *N. Y.*, 1812
Sixth Rep. of Augusta Bible Society, Mar. 3, 1824.
Eighth Rep. of N. Y. Bible Society. *N. Y.*, 1824
Fourteenth Rep. of N. Y. Bible Society. *N. Y.*, 1829
Address deliv. before N. Y. Bible Society, by Bp. Hobart. *N. Y.*, 1816

Address deliv. before Columbia Co. Bib. Soc., by Thos. Warner. *N. Y.*, 1817

Address deliv. before Phila. Bib. Soc. *Phil.*, 1810

Letter on the subject of British and Foreign Bible Soc., by James Scholefield. 67 *p.* *Scarce.* *N. Y.*, 1823

Appeal to Friends of the Bible, by Amer. and For. Bib. Soc. in 1845. *N. Y.*, 1845

Ninth Rep. of L. I. Bib. Soc., Flushing, Sept. 15, 1824. *Scarce.*

2717 Miscellaneous. [*Eleven.*]

Annual Report of Managers of N. Y. State Lunatic Asylum. Jan. 18, 1844.

First Report of Provident Soc. for Employment of the Poor. Phil., Jan. 11, 1825

Fifth Report of Soc. for Prevention of Pauperism in N. Y., 1821.

Address and Const. of N. Y. Female Assoc. to aid indigent Deaf and Dumb. *N. Y.*, 1830

An Act to Incorporate Members of N. Y. Inst. for Deaf and Dumb. *N. Y.*, 1819

Statement of Committee of Eye and Ear Infirmary. *Boston*, 1828

Sermon preached for benefit of Portsmouth Female Asylum, by Edwd. D. Griffin *Bost.*, 1812

Explanation of Views of Soc. for Employing Female Poor. *Bost.*, 1826

Plan of Ladies' Charity School of St. Sepulchre, London.

Disc. on Opening of New Building in House of Refuge in New York, by John Stanford. *N. Y.*, 1826

Fourth Annual Rept. of Surgeons of Eye and Ear Infirmary. *Bost.*, 1828

2718 Miscellaneous. *Very scarce lot.* [*Sixteen.*]

Report of Sec. of Treasury (Alex. Hamilton, in 1790) on National Bank, Jan. 27, 1810.

Argument of Sec. of Treasury (Alex. Hamilton, in 1790) on Constitutionality of National Bank.

Memorial of Stockholders of the Bank of U. S., Dec. 18, 1810.

Letter from Sec. of Treasury (Albert Gallatin) on Bank of U. S., Feb. 5, 1811.

Report of Sec. of Treasury on Manufactures, 1791. *Wash.*, 1809

Letter from Sec. of Treasury on Amer. Manufactures. In part. Apr. 19, 1810.

Report of Sec. of Treasury on Public Roads and Canals, Apr. 12, 1808.

Speech of Mr. Pope on the Bank Bill, Feb. 22, 1811. 22 *p.*

Speech of Mr. Fiske on the Bank Bill, Jan. 18, 1811. 13 p. *Dble. col.*

Speech of Mr. P. B. Porter on the Bank Bill, Jan. 18, 1811. 15 *p.* *Dble. col.*

Speech of Mr. R. M. Johnson on the Bank Bill, Jan. 22, 1811. 14 *p.*

Speech of Mr. Nicholson on the Bank Bill, Jan. 23, 1811. 13 *p.* *Dble. col.*

Speech of Mr. Ramsay on the Treasury Bill. 7 *p.* *Dble. col.*

Speech of Henry Clay on the American System, Feb. 1832. 43 *p.*

Hints on Banking, in a letter to a gentleman in Albany. N. Y., 1827. 43 *p.*

The War on the Bank of the U. S., Phil., 1834. 155 *p.*

2719 Miscellaneous. [*Eleven.*]

Letters of Fabius to William Pitt on proposed Abolition of the Test. With Appendix contain. Mr. Pitt's Speech in 1790. *London*, 1801 6

Letters to Daniel D. Tompkins, late Gov. of N. Y. *Albany*, 1820

Cursory Remarks on Various Topics in Meteorology. With map.

The British Treaty of Mr. Jay, 1794. 86 *p.*

The Anti-Gallican Sentinel, by Don Antonio Campany. *N. Y.*, 1809

The Anti-Gallican Sentinel, by Don Antonio Campany. Part II. *Phil.*, 1810

Lecture on the Antecedent Causes of the Irish Famine in 1847, by Bp. Hughes. *N. Y.*, 1847

Association Discussed ; or, the Socialism of the Tribune examined, by H. Greeley and H. J. Raymond. 1847.

Introduction to the Study of Natural History, by Prof. Agassiz. N. Y., 1847. Illustrated with numerous engrav.

The Amer. Electro Mag. Telegraph, by Alfred Vail. Phil., 1845. Illustrated by eighty-one wood engrav.

Descrip. of Amer. Electro Mag. Telegraph, in operation bet. Baltimore and Washington, by Alfred Vail. Illustrated by fourteen wood engravings.

2720 Medical. *Very valuable lot.* [*Eighteen.*]

Dissert. on the Medical Properties and Injurious Effects of the Habitual Use of Tobacco, by A. McAllister. 1832. 36. *p.*

An Essay on Alcoholic and Narcotic Substances, by Edward Hitchcock. Amherst, 1830. 48 *p.* 15

Prospetto Della Clinica Chirurgica, esercitata dal primo Germajo, 1832, a tutto Dicembre, 1833. Nell' imp., E. R. Arcispedale e. Firenze, 1834. 62 *p.*

Inaug. disc. on Medical Eclecticism, by J. C. Cross. Cincinn., 1835. 20 *p.*

The Affiliation of the Natural and Physical Sciences, by R. Harlan. Phila., 1837. 31 *p.*

Homœopathy Vindicated, in a letter to J. V. C. Smith, by Dr. Lillie.

The Reformation of Medical Science, by William Channing. N. Y., 1839. 58 *p.*

Letters on Medical Education, by Arch. Hall. Montreal, 1842, 30 *p.*

Discourse on the Power of Small Doses and attenuated Medicines, including a Theory of Potentization, by B. F. Joslin. N. Y., 1847. 18 *p.*

The Field and the Work of the Medical Prof. Address before Castleton Medical College, June 18, 1845, by Horace Eaton. 31 *p.*

Sketch of the Progress of Physical Science, by Thomson, and Lardner's Lectures. 96 *p.*

Intro. Address by C. R. Gilman, College of Phys. and Surg., N. Y., 1840, on Obstetrics, &c. 24 *p.*

Univ. of N. Y. Valed. Lect. by Prof. Draper. N. Y., 1842. *Very scarce.* 14 p.

Valedict. Add. by Gunning S. Bedford, N. Y. Univ. 1845. *Important.*

Address by G. S. Bedford on Medical Science and Education in this Country, N. Y. Univ., Nov. 15, 1835. *Scarce and valuable.* 32 *pages.*

Intro. Lect. by David M. Reese, Albany Med. Col., Oct. 1, 1839, 22 *p.*

Dr. Sewall's Drawings of the Human Stomach. Documents in relation to.

Trans. of N. Y. State Medical Society. Annual Address by Samuel White, Feb. 7, 1844. Vol. VI. 150 *pages.*

20 2721 Miscellaneous. *Valuable.* [*Twenty.*]

Cause of and Cure for Hard Times, N. Y., 1818. *Scarce.* 78 *pages.*

Address to the Bapt. Denom. *N. Y.*, 1843

Reports of Debates of Gen'l Con. of M. Epis. Ch., 1844. N. Y. 240 *p.*

Sermons by Onderdonk, &c. 1840.

Catalogue—Bartlett and Welford—American History, &c.

The People's Rights Reclaimed. By Thos. Hortell. N.Y., 1826. *Scarce.*

Interest made Equity. *N. Y.*, 1826

Survey of the Lottery System. *Phila.*, 1833

Lecture on the Christmas Festival, by T. T. Waterman. *Prov.*, 1835

Rep. from Commiss. to Revise Statute Laws of N. Y. 1826

The Catholic Doctrine of the Blessed Eucharist. A Sermon delivered in Newton, L. I., by Richard Bulger, Roman Catholic. N. Y., 1822. *Scarce.*

Remarks on the Projected Revis. of Laws of N. Y. 1825.

Smooth Preaching (by a Smooth Preacher). N. Y., 1823. *Curious.* 12 *p.*

Sermon on Human Depravity, by E. Q. Sewell, Unit. *Amherst, N. H.*, 1825

Reply to Rev. of Dr. Beecher's Sermon, by Dr. Beecher. 1825. 59 *p.*

Sermon before Church Schol. Soc., Middletown, Conn., by Sam. Farmar Jarvis. 1835.
Walter King's Farewell Disc., with Appendix, giving an account of Ground of Difficulty between Pastor and Soc. *Norwich, Conn.*, 1811

2722 Miscellaneous. *Very valuable lot.* [*Eleven.*]

Consti. and Canons of Prot. Epis. Church in N. Y. 1812. *Scarce.*
Canons for the Govt. of Prot. Epis. Ch. in U. S. N. Y., 1808. *Scarce.*
Sermon before Con. of Prot. Epis. Ch. in N. Y., by Isaac Wilkins. 1804.
Statement of Facts in Defence of Cong'l Church, Fall River, against certain Charges of Unchristian Conduct of A. Bronson. *Prov.*, 1835
Catalogue of Rare, Curious and Valuable Books, by Bangs, Richards and Pratt. *N. Y.*
Essay on the Origin and Antiquity of the Scots and Irish Nations, with an Oration before the Caledonian Soc., by D. Fraser. New York, 1800. *Very scarce.*
The Lives of Eminent British Statesmen, by T. B. Macaulay. N. Y., 1835. 125 *pages. Dble. col.*
Description of the Croton Aqueduct, by John B. Jervis. *Fine copy.* (With scarce Woodcut of Fountain in the Park and of Harlem Bridge.) N. Y., 1842. 31 *p. Scarce.*
View of the Civil Admin. and Polit. Char. of Napol. Bonaparte. N. Y., 1821. 31 *pages.*
Descrip. of Rome. *N. Y.*, 1840
Wealth and Wealthy Citizens of N. Y. 1842. *Scarce.*

2723 Miscellaneous. [*Thirteen.*]

Nat'l Preachers. Various yrs. 1826-1834 incl.
Liberal Preacher. Nos. 1, 2, 4, 5, 6, 7. Vol. II. 1828.
The Amer. Pulpit. Vol. II. No. 3. 1846.

2724 Miscellaneous. [*Eight.*]

Walker's Hibernian Magazine for Oct., 1801.
Mechanics' " " 1834. Vol. 4. No. 4.
American Quart. Temp. Magazine for May, 1833. No. 2.
" " " for Nov., 1834. No. 4.
Monthly Magazine for Mar., 1818. 2 of Vol. 45. No. 309. Engraving of the "Scoliophis Atlanticus," the Great Serpent of the North American Seas.
Knickerbocker Magazine for Sept., 1851. Vol. 38. No. 3.
" " for Mar., 1852. Vol. 39. No. 3.
Hopkinsian Magazine for year 1824. Vol. I. 12 Nos.

2725 Miscellaneous. [*Ten.*]

Monthly Repository for June, July, Oct., 1830. Vol. I.
" " " 1831. Vol. II.

Monthly Monitor for Sept., 1835. Vol. III. No. 3.
Cheap Magazine for yrs. 1813–14. Vols. I. and II. Nos. 6 and 12.
"Moral Reformer." Dr. Alcott. Vol. II. *Boston*, 1836
Journal Inutile. New York, Nov. 13, 1824. Vol I. No. 1.

2726 Moses Stuart. [*Twelve.*]

Is the Mode of Christ. Baptism prescribed in the New Testament? By M. Stuart. *Andover*, 1833
Two Disc. on the Atonement, by M. Stuart. *Andover*, 1824
Letters on the Eternal Generation of the Son of God, by M. Stuart. 1822.
Two Letters to M. Stuart on Relig. Lib., by Bernard Whitman. *Bost.*, 1830
A Reply to the Review of Whitman's Letters to Prof. Stuart, by Bernard Whitman. *Bost.* 1831
Views in Theology. Vol. IV. Nov. 1833 to May 1835.
" " " No. XVI. May, 1835. *N. Y.*, 1835
Study of the Orig. Languages of the Bible, by M. Stuart. *Andover*, 1827
Letters addressed to Trinitarians and Calvinists, by Henry Ware. *Cam.*, 1820
Letters on Theological Speculations in Conn. 1832.
A Sermon by Edward R. Tyler. *New Haven*, 1831
The "Spirit of the Pilgrims." Vol. IV. No. 3. Mar., 1831

2727 Miscellaneous. *Choice Lot.* [*Thirteen.*]

Essays on Money, Exchanges and Political Economy: shewing the Cause of the Fluctuation in Prices and of the Depreciation in the Value of Property of late Years. By Henry James. No. I. 41 *pages.* *London*, 1820
Essays on Money, &c. No. II. 216 *pages.* *London*, 1820
Religion and Politics, by Robert Dick. Glasgow, 1837. 72 *p.*
Literary Beauty of the Bible. By Robt. Jones. *Staines* (Eng.), 1837. 35 *p.*
Education based on Scriptural Principles, &c., by R. Weaver. Lond. 1838. 44 *p.*
The Causes of Deism and Atheism, by Geo. Harris. Lond. 1823. 87 *p.*
Socialism in its moral tendencies compared with Christianity (as propounded by Robt. Owen), by John E. Giles. Lond. 1839. 95 *pages.*

Improvements in Education as it respects the Industrious Classes. By Joseph Lancaster. Lond., 1803. *Very scarce.* 66 *p.*

Mr. Blores' Statement of Corresp. with Rich. Phillips respecting "The Antiquary's Magazine. Stamford (Eng.), 1808. 31 *pages.*

A Letter from the King to His People. Lond. 1821. *Scarce*

Essays on Government, Jurisprudence, Liberty of the Press and Law of Nations, by Jas. Mill. *Not for sale.* 33 *pages.*

Hints on Banking, in a Letter to a Gentleman in Albany, by a New Yorker. New York, 1827. 43 *pages.*

Considerations on the Accumulation of Capital and its Effects on Profits. *London,* 1822

2728 Miscellaneous. [*Twenty-three.*]

Account of the Life of John Wickliffe and of Hugh Latimer. — Practical Disc. on the Communion. — Life and Martyrdom of Cranmer and of John Hooper. — Loyalty, Episcopacy, and Confirmation. — Parochial Minister Affect. Expostul. — Guide to the Church. — Preparation for Death. — Sunday Evening Recollections. — Explanation of Church Catechism. — Short reasons for Communion. — Two Dial. between Tho's Steady and William Candid. — Doctrine and Discipline Ch. of Eng'd. — Churchman's reasons for Baptism. (2.) Hints on Public Worship. — The Sum of the Whole Scripture. — Life and Martyrdom of Tho's Bilney and of Jas. Bainham. — First Homily of the United Church of England.

2729 Miscellaneous. [*Thirty.*]

Memoirs of John Woolman. Phila., 1822. — On Divine Grace. Phila., 1818. — Thoughts on Importance of Religion. Phila., 1819. — Truth and Divine Origin of Christ. Rev. Phila., 1826. — The Anc. Christ. Principle. Phila., 1818. — Christian Instruction. — Extracts from Dr. Rush's Essay on Ardent Spirits. — A Christian Memento. — Anecdotes of Gambling. By M. L. Weems. — Religious Duties. — Nature and Efficiency of Cross of Christ. — Memoir of H. G. — Influence of the Holy Spirit. — Biog. Notices of Emlen, Pemberton, &c. — On Education of Children. — Swear not at all. — Life and Death of Job Scott. — Observations on Theatrical Amusements. — Christianity and Infidelity Contrasted. — Memoirs of Caroline E. Smelt. — On Worship, Ministry and Prayer. — Comfort and Counsel.

— Comfort and Counsel. — What shall we do to be Saved? — On the Holy Scr iptures. — Thoughts on Reason and Revelation. — On Detracti on. — The True Christian Faith. — Faith in Jesus Christ. — Some Account of J—— S——. — Instances of Early Piety.

5 2730 Miscellaneous Tracts. [*Thirty.*]

Const. of N. E. Tract Society.	1829
The Happy Negro.	1815
The Dairyman's Daughter.	1825
The Shepherd of Salisbury Plain.	1821
Prayer for Revival of Relig.	1820
Reflections on the seven days.	1820
Sixteen Short Sermons.	1818
The Hermit.	
Account of Abigail Hutchinson. By Jon'n Edwards.	
The Seaman's Compass.	1818
Conversion of a Mahometan.	1820
A Sermon on War. Channing.	1819
Short Address to Sick Persons.	1822
Word to a Minister.	1825
The Dairyman.	1821
Two Pious Letters.	1822
Account of Charles Grafton.	1821
Address to a Sabbath School Child.	1821

The New Birth.
Advice from a Master to his Apprentice.
The Happy Waterman.
Little Henry.
Important Questions.
Way to Convert a Cottage into a Palace.
Conversion of Mrs. Eleanor Emerson.
Life of Col. Jas. Gardiner.
Conversion of the World.
Corresp. between Member of Col. and Minister.
Memoir of Tho's Hogg.
Death-bed of a Free Thinker.
Hints on Relig. Education.
Disc. on Divine Truth, by J. H. Church.
The Village in the Mountains.
Memoir of Mrs. Harriet Newell.
Joy in Heaven.

5 2731 Miscellaneous. [*Twenty-three.*]

Speech of Mr. King, of Georgia, March 18, 1840.	*Washington.*
" " Dunn. of Ind., May 14, 1838.	"
" " Rives, of Va., Feb. 6, 1838	"
" " Carroll, of N. Y., July 1, 1840.	"

Speech of Mr. Hudson, of Mass., April 10, 1844.
" " Crittenden, of Ky,, April 16, 1846.
" " Sergeant, of Pa., June 24, 1840
" " Dix, of N. Y., Feb. 18, 1846.
" " Stewart, of Pa., Dec. 9, 1845.
" " Evans, of Me., March 17, 1842.
" " Slade, of Vt., Dec. 23, 1835
" " White, of Tenn., Feb. 16, 1835.
" " Nicoll, of N. Y., Feb. 15, 1848.
" " Giddings, of Ohio, June 30, 1848.
" " Duer, of N. Y., Feb. 14, 1848.
" " Seaman, of N. Y., July 23, 1846.
" " Marsh, of Vt., April 22, 1846.
" " Miller, of N. Y., July 1, 1846.
" " Campbell, of N. Y., April 8, 1846.
" " Rives, of Va., Aug. 17, 1842.
Letter of H. Van Rensselaer to his Const., Aug., 1842.
Speech of Mr. Tallmadge, of N. Y., May 22, 1840.
" " Ketchum, in Senate of N. Y., 1841.

2732 Miscellaneous. [*Thirty-one.*]

Speech of Albert Constable, of Md., March 11, 1846. *Wash.*
" Mr. Berrien, of Ga. April 9, 1844- "
" " Morrison, of N. Y. *Albany*, 1845
" " Barnard, of N. Y., Feb. 13, 1844. *Washington.*
" " Potter, of R. I., March, 1844. "
" " Proffitt, of Ind., Feb. 13, 1840. "
Report of " McKeon, of N. Y., Feb. 2, 1837. "
Letter of " B. W. Leigh to Gen. Assem., Va., Mar. 2, 1836.
Speech of Mr. Hardin, of Ky., Jan. 28, 1836.
Remarks of Mr. Webster, of Mass., Dec., 1840.
Speech of Mr. Morris, of Pa., April 24, 1844.
" " Tallmadge, of N. Y., June 17, 1836.
" " McKeon, of N. Y., Jan. 17, 1837.
" " Adams, Mass., Jan. 22, 1836.
" " Phillips, Mass., Feb. 16, 1836.
" " Walker, of Miss., Jan. 28, 1837.
" " Maison, on Power of Expulsion.
" " Robbins, of R. I., Feb. 18, 1836.
" " Evans, of Maine, Jan. 28, 1836.
" " Duer, of N. Y., July 29, 1848.
" " Bernard, of N. Y., March 25, 1840.
" " Adams, of N. Y., Sept. 4, 1841.
" " Campbell, of N. Y., Jan. 27, 1846.
Letter of Hugh L. White, of Tenn., 1840.
Speech of Mr. Clay, Jan. 20, 1840.
" " Ogle, of Pa., on Life and Char. of W. H. Harrison, April 16, 1840.
Speech of Mr. Waddy Thompson, March 24, 1840.
" " Winthrop, of Mass., Dec. 30, 1841.
" " Clay, of Ky., Aug. 19, 1841.
" " McKeon, of N. Y., July 5, 1842.
" " Sergeant, of Pa., June 24, 1840.

5 2733 Miscellaneous. [*Eight.*]

Tracts on Several Important Topics of Religion. By George Weller. *Phila.*, 1830
Disc. on the Inventions of men in Worship of God. By Wm. King. *Phila.*, 1828
The Doctrine of the Sacraments. By Barrow. " 1829
Regeneration. By Dr. Waterland. " 1829
Short and Easy Method with the Deists. By Charles Leslie. *Phila.*, 1830
Two Letters to Bishop Hoadley in defence of Episcop. By Wm. Law.
Third do do do

10 2734 Miscellaneous. *Small valuable lot.* [*Seventeen.*]

Full Length Port. of Calvinism. By an Old-Fashioned Churchman. (Rev. Dr. Bowden.) N. Y., 1809. 55 pages.
Sermon, St. Peter's. *Albany*, 1816
Declaration of Faith, 3d Baptist Ch. *Boston*, 1818
Const. of Prayer-Book Assoc.
Address Mass. Society for Suppression of Intemperance. By Charles Sprague, May 31, 1827. *Scarce.* *Boston.*
Reasons for Change of Sentiment and Practice on the Subject of Baptism. By J. A. Haldane. *Edinburgh*, 1809
Catiline : His Conspiracy. A Tragedy. By Ben Jonson. *Rub. titles*, 107 *p.* *Fine copy.* *Lond.*, 1739
Private Thoughts upon the Relics of Antiquity. 72 *p.* *Phila.*, 1826
Narrative of a Voyage from Dublin to Quebec, in N. A. By Jas. Wilson. 36 *p.* *Dublin*, 1822
Hand Book of Information for Emigrants to New Brunswick. By M. A. Perley. Map and plates. *St. Johns*, 1854
The Union of the States. By Anna Carroll. *Boston*, 1856
The Emigrant's Manual—America. 133 pages.
Remarks upon pamphlet entitled—"Inquiry into the Validity of Methodist Episcopacy." *Uncut, scarce.* *Balto.*, 1808
Character of a Methodist. *Uncut.* *N. Y.*, 1808
The Experience of Wm. Keith. *Scarce, uncut.* *Utica*, 1806
A Compendium of Logic. *Uncut.* *Balto.*, 1808
Leslie's Short and Easy Method with the Deists. *Baltimore*, 18—

5 2735 Miscellaneous. [*Twelve.*]

Annual Report, Bank Commerce. *N. Y.*, 1840
Reports of Commissioners of Bank, State of Alabama. *Tuscaloosa*, 1840
——— ——— of Branch Bank of Alabama at Huntsville. *Tuscaloosa*, 1840
——— President and Cashier, Bank of Ala. at Huntsville, 1840
——— Commiss. Br. Bank of Alabama, at Mobile, 1840
——— President do do "
——— Commiss. do at Decatur, "
——— do Planters' Bank, at Mobile, "

Assembly, N. Y. Doc. No. 2, 1841.
Correspondence between Governor of New York and Virginia. 1839.
Assembly, New York, Doc. No. 5, 1841
do do No. 13, 1841.

2736 Miscellaneous. [*Twelve.*]

The Bible and Its Literature. By E. Robinson, *N. Y.*, 1841
Claims of Civil and Ecclesiastical Hist. By Geo. W. Eaton. *Utica*, 1841
The Duty and Rewards of Original Thinking. By Geo. W. Eaton. *Hamilton*, 1842
Voluntary Associations. Discourse by D. D. Pratt. *Nashua*, 1841
The Finances of the Canal Fund of New York, in a letter to the Hon. Stephen Allen and G. B. Throop, from Geo. Tibbits. *Albany*, 1829 5
Report of the Canal Commissioners of Pa. *Harrisburg*, 1831
Ninth Report of Bank of Savings in New York. 1828
Constitution and By-Laws of New York Athenæum. *N. Y.*, 1825
Discourse By Rich. Fuller, of S. C., on "The Cross." *Phila.*, 1841
The Moral Law of Accumulation. By F. Wayland. *Prov.*, 1837
Discourse at Opening the Prov. Athenæum, July 11, 1838, by F. Wayland.
The Necessity of Religion. By James Griffin, with Biographical Sketch of R. S. McAll. *Lond.*, 1839

2737 Miscellaneous. [*Seven*].

George Washington's Message to Congress relative to France and Great Britain. *Scarce.* *Phila.*, 1795 5
Letters of Secretary of State to Mr. Monroe, March 23, 1808. Part II.
Letter of Secretary of State to Mr. Monroe. Part III.
Letters from Mr. Monroe to Secretary of State. Part IV.
Papers on French Affairs—Armstrong to Monroe. 1808.
Letter from Mr. Erskine to Secretary of State. 1808.
Letter from M. Champigny to General Armstrong. 1808

2738 Miscellaneous. [*Fifteen.*]

Letter from Secretary Treasury, March 3, 1809
——— do January 6, 1810
Report of Com. on Coins, December 27, 1810
Letter from Secretary of Treasury, December 31, 1810 5
Message President, February 23, 1810
——— January 12, 1810
Document on the Approp. Bill, January 30, 1810
Message President United States, January 15, 1811

Report Secretary Treasury, Feb. 4, 1811
Letter do " 7, "
Message, President, " 5, "
——— ——— " 11, "
Letter, Secretary Treasury, " 7, "
Report of Com. of Com. and Manuf., February 25, 1811
Letter of Secretary of Treasury, February 6, 1811

2739 Congressional Documents. 1838–1840. 2 volumes. *Valuable lot.*

2740 Miscellaneous. [*Eleven.*]

Tract Upon Conversion, by James Kemp. *Balto.*, 1807
Duplicity Exposed.
Relig. Education. Sermon by James Montgomery. *Phila.*, 1826
J. F. Schroeder's Sermon, Eleventh Anniversary New York Protestant Episcopal Sunday School Society, 1828
Pastoral Advice to Young Persons. *Lond.*, 1821
Bishop Hobart's Address on Confirmation. *Phila.*, 1828
Pastor's Address to Young People.
Answer to "Why are you a Churchman?" 1829
Regeneration Stated and Explained, by Dr. Waterland. 1829
Tracts on Important Topics of Religion. By Geo. Weller. 1830
Answer to "Why are you a Churchman?" 1829

2741 Miscellaneous. [*Fourteen.*]

Declar. of Principles of True Believer's—Infidel.
Human Nature ; or, the Moral Science of Man.
Conjectures on Theology.
The Right of Free Discussion. *N. Y.*, 1829
The Third Gen'l Epistle of Peter. *Balto.*, 1832
The Memoir of Light. Proc. of Infidel Conv. in N. Y., 1845
Vale's "Citizen of the World. No. 3 *N. Y.*, 1850
——— ——— " 28 " 1851
——— ——— " 31 " "
——— ——— " 1, Vol. II. " "
The Independent Beacon.
Essay on the Astronomy and Worship of the Ancients.
Paley Refuted in his own Words, by G. J. Holyoake. *Lond.*
Cometarium ; or the Astronomy of Comets, by G. Vale. *N. Y.* 1832

2742 Miscellaneous. [*Ten.*]

Constitution of New York, November 10, 1821, Adopted.
Address to Legislature of New York.
Fifth Report New York Institution for Deaf and Dumb, 1824
Constitution of New York, November 10, 1821, Adopted.
Channing's Sermon, Ordin. of Jared Sparks. *Balto.*, 1819
Army Reports, 1822
Letter to Arch. McIntyre, Comp. N. Y., 1819

Letters of Philo-Cato to De Witt Clinton, on Aaron Burr. *Rare.*
Topographical and Statistical Manual of New York, 1822
Proclamation by the President, James Monroe.

2743 Miscellaneous. [*Twenty-three.*]
First, Second, and Fourth Annual Reports Prot. Epis. Ch. Missionary Society, 1845, '6, '8, *N. Y.*
Sermon before P. E. Missionary Society of New York, by Alexander H. Vinton. 1848
Fifth, Sixth, and Seventh Annual Reports P. E. Missionary Soc. of N. Y., 1849, '50, '51.
Const. of Educ. and Miss. Soc. of N. Y., 1832.
Sixth, Seventh, and Eighth Report Educ. and Miss. Society of N. Y., 1839, '40, '41.
Report of St. Luke's Home. *N. Y.*, 1852
Fourth, Fifth and Sixth Annual Reports of St. Luke's Home, 1855, '56, '57.
Const. of the Orphan's Home in N. Y., 1852, '54.
Annual Reports of Orphan's Home in N. Y., 2d, 3d, and 4th
Second Annual Report of Church Char. Foundation.
Rules of the Society for the Relief of Widows, &c. *Charleston, S. C.*, 1819
Jubilee Tract. *Lond.*, 1849

2744 Miscellaneous. (*Seven.*)
W. E. Channing's Sermon at Ord. of J. Sparks. *Balto.*, 1819
——— Letter to Rev. S. C. Thacher. *Boston*, 1815
Samuel Worcesters' Letter to Rev. W. E. Channing. " "
——— Second Letter to Rev. W. E. Channing. " "
——— Third do do " "
W. E. Channing's Remarks on Dr. Worcester's Second Letter. *Boston*, 1815
Review of the Unit. Controv.

2745 Miscellaneous. (*Thirteen.*)
Personality and Work of the Holy Spirit, by Alex. McCaul. *Lond.*, 1837
Two Letters : First—Between a Papist and a Jew. Second—Protestant and Jew. *Lond.*, 1819
Account of Conversion of Theo. John, a Jew. *Lond.*, 1819
Popular Objection—Prom. Christ. among the Jews. *Lond.*, 1821
Address both to Christians and Jews, by E. Bichersteth. *Lond.*, 1838
Mosaism, Rabbinism, and Christ., by Alex. McCaul. " 1834
Letter from a Christian to a Jew. " 1832
Account of the Death of a Jewish Girl.
The True Israelite. *Lond.*, 1829
A Minister's Address to his Flock. " 1839
The Prophecies Concerning the Messiah. " 1827
Solemn and Affecting Address to the Children of Abraham. *Lond.*, 1824
Proofs that the Messiah must have Come. " 1841

*2746 Miscellaneous. [*Nineteen.*]

Outline of the Testimony of Scripture, by H. Ware. *Boston*, 1832
Samuel Eddy's Reasons for Withdrawing from the Baptist Church in Prov. *Boston*, 1841
The Worship of the Father. By W. E. Channing. 1838
On the Exclusive System. By Jas. Walker. *Boston*, 1832
The Philos. of Man's Spiritual Nature. By James Walker. *Boston*, 1834
The Law of Spiritual Life. By Jas. Walker. " 1835
The Doct. of Two Natures in Jesus Christ. By Alvan Lamson. *Boston*, 1828
The Apostle Paul a Unitarian. " 1828
Scriptural Arguments for the Unitarian Faith. " 1833
Explanation of Isaiah 9 : 6, and John 1 : 1. By Geo. R. Noyes. *Boston*, 1833
The Doctrines of the Trinity. " 1833
Virtue the End of Man's Creation. By James D. Green. *Boston*, 1837
Christ as a Purely Internal Principle. By Convers Francis. *Boston*, 1836
On the Atonement. By E. B. Hall. " 1839
Piety and Morality. By George Whitney. " 1835
Reason and Revelation. By A. A. Livermore. " 1838
The Doctrine of Pronouns Applied to Christ's Testimony of Himself. By Noah Worcester. *Boston*, 1827
On the Original Text of the New Testament. " 1829
The New Test. Conformed to Griesbach's Text. " 1829

*2747 Miscellaneous. [*Twenty-two.*]

Speech of S. M. Hopkins. *Albany*, 1822
Correspondence between J. Q. Adams, etc. *Boston*, 1829
Report of Committee on Banks, &c. *Albany*, 1829
Speech of Mr. Holmes on Removals from Office.
House of Representatives. Document No. 82. Free Trade
Governor Throop's (N. Y.) Message, January 3, 1852
Jackson's Veto Message Bank Bill.
——. Message, December 3, 1833.
Webster's Speech, February 16, 1833.
Clay's Speech, December 26, 1833.
—— do do
House of Representatives. Document No. 312 and 313. Removal of Public Department.
McDuffie's Speech on the Removal of Public Department.
Webster's Speech, May 7, 1834.
Inquiry into the Causes of the Public Distress. *N. Y.*, 1834
Proofs that Credit, as Money, Preferable to Coin, &c.
Gouge's History of Paper Money, &c. *N. Y.*, 1835
Proceedings of Meeting of Whig Young Men in N. Y., 1834
Post-Office Department Report, 1834
Seward's Speech on Marcy's Six Million Mortgage.
Starr's Address to Whig Convention. *Utica*, 1824

2748 Miscellaneous. [*Eleven.*]

First Annual Report of American Temperance Society. *Andover*, 1827

First Report of American Home Missionary Society. *N. Y.*, 1827

Second Report of Amer. Home Miss. Soc. *N. Y.*, 1828

Third Report of Amer. Home Miss. Soc. *N. Y.*, 1829

Fifth Report of Amer. S. S. Union. *Phila.*, 1829

First Report of Amer. Tract Soc. *N. Y.*, 1826

Fourth Report of Amer. Tract Soc. " 1829

Thirteenth Report of Amer. Bible Soc. " 1829

Second Report of Prison Discip Soc. *Boston*, 1827

Third Report of Prison Discip. Soc. " 1828

Sixteenth Report of Receipts and Expenditures of Boston, May 1, 1828. *Scarce.*

2749 Miscellaneous. [*Eleven.*]

James Abercrombie's Sermon, May 9, 1798, Philadelphia. (National Fast.) *Scarce.*

——— Sermon on Death Alex. Hamilton, July 22, 1804, Philadelphia. *Scarce.*

——— Sermon, June 15, 1808, Philadelphia.

——— Lectures on the Catechism. *Phila.*, 1807

——— Charge to Senior Class, Philadelphia Academy, July 27, 1804.

——— —— do do July 31, 1805

——— —— do do July 31, 1806

——— —— do do July 30, 1807

——— —— do do July 30, 1808

——— —— do do July 27, 1809

James P. Morris, Val. Oration, Senior Class, Philadelphia Academy July 27, 1809.

2750 Miscellaneous. [*Thirteen.*]

Catal. of General Theological Seminary, New York, 1836–'37, 1837–'38, 1838–'39, 1839–'40, 1840–'41, 1841–'42, 1845–'46.

Publication of the Assoc. Alumni, New York, 1840, 1857.

Minutes of the Assoc. Alumni, New York, 1841

The Constitution and By-Laws, Protestant Episcopal Church in New York, 1832.

Catalogue of Theological Seminary in Diocese of Virginia. *Washington*, 1840–'41

City Mission Society. *N. Y.*, 1838

2751 Miscellaneous. *Good lot.* [*Twelve.*]

The New York State Register for 1844. By O. L. Holley. *Uncut, scarce.*

The Fatal Effects of Ardent Spirits. Sermon by Eben Porter. *Hartford*, 1811

Desilver's U. S. Register and Almanac for 1837. *Frontis.*, 48 *p.*, *fine copy.*

Two Discourses on the Atonement. By Moses Stuart. *Andover*, 1824

Report of the School Com. Recommending Various Improvements in the System of Instruction in Grammar Schools. *Fine copy.* *Boston*, 1828

Regulations of the School Com. of Boston, 1827

Report of School Com. of Boston, 1826

Porter's Health Almanac, 1832. 80 *p. uncut.* *Phila.*

Remarks on Judge Hertell's Argument on Right of Property to Married Women, 1839

The Advantages and Disadvantages of the Married State. By John Johnson. *Boston*, 1809

The Marriage Question. By Parsons Cooke. " 1842

Speech of Dr. Matthews on the "Lawfulness of Marrying a Deceased Wife's Sister." *N. Y.*, 1843

2752 Miscellaneous. [*Seven.*]

Report of Com. &c., on Correspondence of Madison and Monroe. *Wash.*, 1808

Letters from Secretary of State to Monroe, &c. " "

——— do do " 1806

——— Monroe to Secretary of State. " 1808

Papers Relating to Fr Affairs. " "

Letter from British Minister to Secretary of State. " "

——— Champagny to General Armstrong. " "

2753 Miscellaneous. [*Nine.*]

Webster. Speech on the Removal of the Deposits. 1834

——— ——— May 7, 1834

Clay's Speech, December 26, 1833

Report of Com. of Ways and Means, March 4, 1834

Message of President, May 2, 1834—Naval Affairs.

Letter from Secretary of Treasury, Dec. 17, 1833.

——— ——— Navy, Jan. 27, 1835.

Report of Secretary of War, Nov 29, 1833.

House of Representatives. Doc. No. 295. Equalize Pay—Army and Navy, 1833.

2754 Miscellaneous. *Splendid lot.* [*Eighteen.*].

Part the First of an Address to the Public, from the Soc. for the Suppression of Vice. 106 *p.* *Lond.*, 1803

Harmony between the Teachings of Nature and of Christianity. By R. E. B. Maclellan. *Edinb.*, 1839

Sketches from the Note-Book of Laurie Todd. By Grant Thorburn. *Port.* 32 *p.* *Scarce.* *N. Y.*, 1847

Lectures on the Catechism, on Confirmation, etc. By James Abercrombie. 238 *p.* *Phila.*, 1811

Memorandum of a visit to Hospitals, Prisons, etc., in France, Scotland, and England. *Phila.*, 1840

Am. Copyright Club. Address to the U. S., Oct. 18, 1843. *N. Y.*

Speech of Mr. Frelinghuysen on Sabbath Mails. *Washington*, 1830

Explanation of views of Soc. for Employing Female Poor. *Camb.*, 1825

Answer to Rev. of "Episcopacy tested by Scripture." *Phila.*, 1834

Corresp. respecting Russia, between R. G. Harper and Robert Walsh. *Fine copy*, 140 *p.* *Scarce.* *Phila.*, 1813

Memorial of Henry D. Gilpin, John T. Sullivan and others, Directors of the U. S. Bank. 55 *p.* 1833

Can there be a Church without a Bishop? *N. Y.*, 1844

Lecture on the Importance of a Christian Basis for the Science of Polit. Economy. By Bp. Hughes. *Scarce.* *N. Y.*, 1844

Lecture on the Mixture of the Civil and Ecclesiastical Power in the Governments of the Middle Ages, Dec. 18, 1843. By Bp. Hughes.

Persecutions of Popery. Historical Narratives of. By Fred. Shobert. 183 *p.* *N. Y.*, 1844

Lectures on Geology. By Charles Lyell. To which is added a Lecture on the different Races of Men. By J. A. Smith. Frontis.; Rept. by H. J. Raymond. *Scarce.* *N. Y.*, 1843

A Memoir on Ireland, Native and Saxon. By Daniel O'Connell.

The Constitution of Man Considered in relation to External Objects. By George Combe. 60 *p.*, *dble. col.* *Scarce.* *N. Y.*, 1835

2755 Miscellaneous. *Good lot.* [*Ten.*]

Letters to Lord Hawkesbury, on the Treaty of Amiens. By Wm. Cobbett. 111 *p.* *Lond.*, 1802

The Tri-Color; Devoted to Political Literature, etc. By Robert Greenhow. *Nos.* 1 *to* 4, *incl.* *N. Y.*, 1830

The Unitarian Chronicle, April, 1832. *No.* 3. English.

Substance of the Speech of Sir Wm. Scott, relative to the Non-residence of the Clergy. 58 *p.* *Lond.*, 1802

Reports of the Leading Decisions of High Court of Admiralty in Cases of vessels sailing under British Licences. By Thomas Edwards. 55 *p.* *Scarce.* *Lond.*, 1802

The Pastor's New Year's Gift. *Manchester, Eng.*, 1787

Addresses by Wm. Wirt, Frelinghuysen, and David P. Brown, at Rutgers College, 1830. *Scarce.*

Lecture. "The Study of Science favorable to Religion." By Samuel Luke. *Chester, Eng.*, 1838

2756 Miscellaneous. [*Twelve.*]

Dissertation on the Nature of Christian Faith. By John Erskine. 67 *p.* *Edinb.*, 1804

Defence of Public Education. By Wm. Vincent. 48 *p.* *Lond.*, 1802

Consider. on the Gen'l Conditions of the Christ. Covenant. By Joseph Holden Pott. 126 *p.* *Lond.*, 1805

Considerations Affording Consolation to the Afflicted. By Rev. James Hervey. 20 *p.* *Scarce.* *Phila.*, 1793

A Few plain reasons why we should believe in Christ. By Richard Cumberland. 46 *p.* *Lond.*, 1801

A Few remarks on an Address to the Roman Catholics of the United States of America. *Worcester, Eng.*

An Essay on the Law of Celibacy imposed on the Clergy of the Roman Catholic Church. By Rev. J. Hawkins. 195 *p.* *Worcester, Eng.*

Disquisitions on Several Subjects. By Soame Jenyns. *Phila.*, 1790

Two Letters from a late Dissenting Teacher, proving that the Doctrines, Discipline and Government of the Church of England, are truly Primitive, and Apostolical. By Tho's Foster. 180 *p.* *Scarce.* *Lond.*, 1764

Discourse from a New Eng. Pastor, to his Flock, March 26, 1826.

Wellington Banquet at Dover, Aug. 30, 1839.

Speech of Mr. Rives of Virginia, on the Public Revenue. 1837.

2757 Miscellaneous. [*Thirteen.*]

By-Laws of New York Prot. Epis. Pub. School, etc., 1841.

Geneva Coll. Catal., 1837.

——— Regist., 1840–'41–'43.

Hobart Free Coll. Geneva, N. Y., 1852 and '54.

Account of Grammar School of St. Paul's Col., N. Y., 1842.

St. Paul's Col., Flushing, L. I., 1847.

Rev. of Jubilee Col., Ill., 1843.

Opening of St. James' Hall, Hagerstown, Md., 1842.

Studies, Discip., etc., of St. James' Hall.

Prospectus of St. Timothy's Hall, Md., 1846.

Prog. of Exam. and Exhib., at St. Timothy's Hall, 1847, '48, '49.

7th and 8th Ann. Rept. of Patapsco Fem. Inst., Md. 1847, '48.

2758 Miscellaneous. [*Seventeen.*]

Message, Prest. U. S., Jan. 17, 1809.

Doc. accomp. Message, May 23, 1809.

Message, Pres't U. S., June 16, 1809.

Doc. accomp. Mess., Nov. 29, 1809.

Message, Prest. U. S., Dec. 18, 1809. — Feb. 1, 1810. — Feb. 19, 1810.

——— April 2, 1810. — May 1, 1810. — Dec. 31, 1810.

——— Jan. 12, 1811. — Jan. 14, 1811. — Jan. 31, 1811.

——— Nov. 6, 1811. — Nov. 8, 1811. — Nov. 6, 1811. — Feb, 19, 1811.

2759 Miscellaneous. [*Seven.*]

Annual Rev. of Bus. of Chicago, for 1852.
The Rail Roads, History and Commerce of Chicago, 1853.
The same, for 1854–5–6–7.
J. L. Scripp's Lect., on the Undeveloped Northern Portion of the American Continent. *Chicago*, 1856

2760 Miscellaneous, Tracts, Etc. [*Sixteen.*]

2761 Miscellaneous. [*Fifteen.*]

Sermon, preached in Christ Church, Phila., May 9, 1798, by James Abercrombie.
——— on Death of Alex. Hamilton, by James Abercrombie. *Phila.*, 1804
——— on Liturgy of Prot. Epis. Ch. *Phila.*, 1808
Charge, Phila. Acad., July 27, 1804, by James Abercrombie.
——— ——— " 31, 1806, " " "
——— ——— " 30, 1807, " " "
——— ——— " 30, 1808, " " "
——— ——— " 27, 1809, " " "
Valed. Oration, Phila. Acad., July 27, 1809, by Jas. P. Morris.
Charge Phila. Acad., July 26, 1810, by Jas. Abercrombie.
Documents relative to the Celebration of a late Marriage. *Scarce.* *Phila.*, 1809
Discrip. of the Yellow Springs in Pa.
Lectures on the Catechism, by James Abercrombie. 1811
Two Sermons. Fast. By James Abercrombie. *Phila.*, 1812
Funeral Sermon, by James Abercrombie. " 1814

2762 Miscellaneous. *Scarce lot.* [*Ten.*]

Money; its Use and Abuse by Christians. *Lond.*, 1837
Efficiency of Primitive Missions. By Baron Stow. *Boston*, 1838
Delineation of the Charac. Features of a Revival of Religion in Troy, in 1826–'27. By J. Brockway. 64 *p.*
Melody; The Soul of Music. An Essay toward the improvement of the Musical Art; with an Appendix, containing an Account of an Invention. 82 *p.* (*Curious.*) *Glasgow*, 1798
Truth in Pursuit of Wardle; being a Letter to Col. G. L. Wardle, on his scheme for introducing Frenchmen into the Militia. Written by J. Farquharson. *Lond.*, 1808
An Examination and Complete Refutation of the observations contained in Col. Wardle's Letter to Lord Ellenborough. By Erinaceus. *Lond.*, 1809
Remarks on the New Edition of Bellendenus, with some Observations on the Extraordinary Preface. *Lond.*, 1787
An Exposition of the Causes and Character of the Late War with Great Britain. By James Madison. 101 *p.* *Lond.*, 1815

Letter to the Hon. Thomas Erskine. 180 *p.*
An Address to the People of Great Britain. By R. Watson. *Lond.*, 1798

2763 Miscellaneous. *Valuable.* [*Twenty-two.*]

Sermons by Burgess, 1841; Bp. Johns, 1838; Bp. Henshaw, 1823; T. E. Vermilye, 1841.

6th Rept. N. Y. Female Benev. Soc., 1838.

The "Preaching and Procedure," of Rev. Samuel Nott. (For distribution among the People at Wareham, Mass.) 1839

Rept. of the N. Y. Maternal Assoc., for 1837 and 1839.

"The Messiah;" a Sacred Oratorio, by Handel. *With notes.* *N. Y.*, 1834

On the Management of Children in Sickness and in Health. By Dr. G. Ackerly. *N. Y.*, 1836

Letter to the Rev. Noah Porter, in reference to Dr. Bellamy's doctrines.

23d Report of Soc. for Promot. Permanent and Univ. Peace. *Lond.*, 1839

Baptism by Affusion and Sprinkling.

Performance of Sacred Music, in Allen Street Church. *N. Y.*, 1839

The Venereal Disease, its primary cause explained, and the possibility of its being fully prevented described. By James Glenn. 1857

Quarterly Register of the Amer. Educ. Soc., Feb. 1831. Vol. III. No. 3.

Lives and Opinions of Butler and Jesse Hoyt. By Wm. L. Mackenzie. 152 *p.* *Very scarce.* *Boston,* 1845

The Life of Beau Brummell. By Capt. Jesse. Two vols. in one. 164 *p.* 1844

Change for the American Notes. 88 *p.* *N. Y.*, 1843

American Notes for General Circulation. By Cha's Dickens. *N. Y.*, 1842

Welcome to Charles Dickens; The Boz Ball, Jan. 26. *Scarce.* 1842

Bubbles from the Brunnens of Nassau, by an Old Man. 89 *p.* *Curious.* *N. Y.*, 1836

2764 Political. [*Eight.*]

Clay, Henry. Speech of, on Removal of the Deposits, Dec. 30, 1833. *Uncut.*

Who Shall be Governor? Strong or Sullivan? or the Sham Patriot unmasked. 1806. *8vo, uncut,* 30 *pages.*

Grimke, T. S. Letter to J. C. Calhoun, R. Y. Hayne, Geo. McDuffie and others. *8vo,* 17 *pages.* Phila., 1832.

Bates, Benjn. Memorial and Petition of the Religious Society of Friends to the Legist. of Va., 1812. *8vo,* 14 *pages.*

Sargent, Ezra. A Book. 24 *pages.* *N. Y.*, 1807.

The Martling Man. Says I to myself, How is this? 5 Nos., 23 *pages, curious. Tammany Hall doc. about* 1810.
Cheves, Langdon. Speech of, Jan. 18, 1812, on the Navy. 11 *pages.*
Remarks on the Auction System, etc. 8*vo*, 20 *pages.* *N. Y.*, 1831

2765 Political. [*Thirteen.*]
Baylies, Francis. Speech before the Whigs of Taunton, Sept. 13, 1837. 8*vo*, 16 *pages, scarce.*
Barton, Cyrus. Defence of, against the attacks of Isaac Hill, Sept. 7, 1840. 8*vo*, 16 *pages, uncut.*
Melish, John. Letters to Jas. Monroe, on the state of the Country. 8*vo*, 32 *pages.* *Phila.*, 1820
Webster, Dan'l. Speech of, at Richmond, Octo. 5, 1840. 8*vo*, 24 *pages.*
Strictures on Nullification. 8*vo, uncut*, 73 *pages. Boston*, 1832
Cushing, Caleb. Speech, Octo. 27 and 31, 1857. 8*vo*, 48 *pages.*
Quincy, Josiah. Speech of, Jan. 14, 1811, on admitting the Orleans Territory. 8*vo, dbl. cols.*, 11 *p., scarce.*
Eppes. Speech, Feb. 9, 1811, Concerning Commercial Intercourse
Porter, P. B. Speech on Internal Improvements, Feb. 8, 1810. 8*vo*, 18 *p.*
"Numa." Letter to John Randolph. 8*vo*, 38 *pages.*
Woodward, John. "Plain Sense," on National Industry. 8*vo*, 51 *pages.* *N. Y.*, 1820
Message from Prest. of U. S., July 10, 1832, with Biog. Sketch of Van Buren. 12*mo*, 48 *pages.*
Blodget, L. Commercial and Financial Strength of the U. S. as shown in the Balances of Foreign Trade, etc. 8*vo*, 39 *pages.* *Phila.*, 1864

2766 Harvard College. [*Fourteen.*]
Channing, W. E. Dudleian Lecture, March 14, 1821. 36 *pages.*
Dewey, Orville. Dudleian Lecture, May 14, 1836. Discourse on Miracles. 23 *pages.*
Report of Com. of Overseers, Jan. 6, 1825. 225 *pages.*
Report of Com. of Overseers, May 4, 1824. 11 *pages.*
Remarks on Report of Com., May 4, 1824. 12 *pages.*
Remarks on Pamphlet, by Prof. and Tutors. By an Alumnus. 58 *pages.*
A Letter to John Lowell, etc., 1824. 102 *pages.*
Further Remarks on the Memorial, etc., 1824. By an Alumnus. 36 *pages.*
Letter to Gov. Lincoln, from F. C. Gray. 63 *pages.*
The Annual Report of the President, 1825–6.
Remarks on Changes lately proposed or adopted in Harvard University, by Geo. Ticknor.
Speech, before Overseers of H. U., Feb. 3, 1825, by Andrew Norton. 34 *pages.*
Report of Com. of Overseers, Jan. 6, 1825.
Memorial of Prof. and Tutors., March, 1824.

2767 Rhode Island, etc. [*Nine.*]

The close of the late Rebellion in Rhode Island, by a Mass. Man. 1842. *8vo*, 16 *pages*, *scarce.*

The Affairs of Rhode Island. Discourse, May 22, 1842, by Francis Wayland. *8vo*, 32 *pages.*

Considerations on the Adoption of a Const. and extension of Suffrage in R. I., by Elisha R. Potter, 1842. *8vo*, 64 *pages. uncut.*

An Address to the People of R. I., May 3, 1843, on occasion of change in the Civil Govt. of R. I., by Wm. G. Goddard. *8vo*, 80 *p.*, *fine copy*; *scarce.*

Cape Cod Assoc. Const. of, with an account of the Celeb. of its First Anniv., at Boston, Nov. 11, 1854. *8vo*, 80 *pages.*

Calvert, Geo. H. Oration, on Fortieth Anniv. of Battle of Lake Erie, Sept. 10, 1853. 40 *pages*, *8vo*, *fine copy*, *scarce.*

An Account of proc. of Battle of Lake Erie Monument Assoc. and Celeb. of 45th Anniv. at Put-in Bay Island, Sept. 10, 1858. *8vo*, 49 *pages.* *Sandusky*, 1858

Inauguration of Perry Statue at Cleveland, Sept. 10, 1860, with sketch of Wm. Walcutt, the Sculptor. *8vo*, *cl.*, *frontis.*, 128 *pages.*

Documents relating to Com. O. H. Perry and Capt J. D. Elliott. *8vo*, *uncut*, 22 *pages*, *scarce.* *Washington*, 1821

2768 Rail Road. [*Six.*]

Remarks on establishing a Rail Road from Boston to Conn. River. *8vo*, *uncut*, 71 *pages.* *Boston*, 1827

Report on practicability of Rail Road from Boston to Hudson River and to Providence. Annexed Reports of Engineers, with plans and profiles of the Routes. *8vo*, *uncut*, 119 *pages.* *Boston*, 1829

Lecture on Rail Roads, deliv. Jan. 12, 1829, before Mass. Mech. Assoc., by Wm. Jackson. *12mo*, 36 *p.*, *scarce.* *Boston*, 1829

N. Y. and Erie Rail Road Co. Address, Oct. 1844.

Twenty Years war against the Rail Roads. Ross Winans *vs.* N. Y. Central.

Letter of John D. Perry, Prest. of U. P. R. R., and Reports of Engineer and Geologist, Jan. 1868. *Maps*, 28 *pages.*

2769 Canal. *Very scarce lot.* [*Five.*]

Observations on Canal Navigation, 1811. *8vo*, 15 *pages*, *with plan.*

Report of Com. to Explore the route of an inland Navig., from Hudson's River to Lake Ontario and Lake Erie. *Autog. of P. B. Porter.* *8vo*, *uncut*, 35 *pages*, *scarce.* *Albany*, 1811

Report of Com., for the consideration of all matters relating to Inland Navigation. *8vo*, 40 *pages.* *Albany*, 1812

Vindication of the claim of Elkanah Watson, to the Merit of projecting the Lake Canal Policy, and also a Vindication of the claim of the late General Schuyler. by Robert Troup. *Autog.: "Presented to R. T. by his friend, E. Watson."* *8vo*, 38 *pages*; *very scarce*, *beautiful copy.* *Geneva*, 1821

A Letter to Hon. Brockholst Livingston, on the Lake Canal Policy, with Supplement, by Robert Troup. *8vo, uncut, fine copy,* 112 *pages.* *Albany,* 1822

2770 Miscellaneous. [*Seven.*]

PARKER, THEODORE. Sermons of the Moral and Spiritual Condition of Boston. Feb. 11, 1849. *8vo, uncut,* 74 *pp.*

——— Two Sermons on the 14th and 21st of Nov., 1852. Historical. *8vo,* 59 *pages.*

——— Sermon on the Dangers which threaten the Rights of Man in America. July 2, 1854. *8vo,* 56 *pages.*

——— "The New Crime against Humanity," the rendition of Burns, June 4, 1854. *8vo,* 76 *pages.*

——— Sermon of Old age, Jan. 29, 1854. *8vo,* 32 *pages.*

——— The Nebraska Question. Some thoughts on the new assault upon Freedom in America, and of the general state of the Country, Feb. 12, 1854. *8vo,* 72 *pages.*

——— Sermon, on the dangerous classes in Society, Jan. 31, 1847. *8vo,* 48 *pages.*

2771 Boston Schools. [*Seventeen.*]

Dedication of Lincoln Grammar School House, Sept. 17, 1859. 24 *pages.*

Course of Study for Grammar Schools, 1868.

Report on the Public Schools, 1867.

Report of Special Com. on Physical Training in the Public Schools, 1860.

Annual Reports of Supt. of Public Schools for 1852-3-5-6 and 1860.

Quarterly Reports for 1857-9.

Semi-Annual Reports for 1860-1-2-5-6 and '7.

2772 Boston. [*Nine.*]

List of Persons, Copartnerships, etc., Taxed on Ten Thousand Dollars and upwards, for the years 1857, '59, '60, '63 and '64.

Young Men's Christ. Assoc. Address, May 25, 1852. 1st anniv., by Chas. Theo. Russell.

Assoc. of Franklin Medal Scholars, 1858.

Young Men's Christ. Assoc. Address, by Robt C. Winthrop, 1859. 64 *pages.*

Discourse before Bost. Merc. Assoc., by William Sullivan, Feb. 7, 1832. *Uncut, scarce.*

2773 Boston. [*Seventeen.*]

List of Persons of the Town of Boston doomed, valued, assessed, taxed, for 1821. 206 *pages, uncut.*

Ordinances of the City and Acts of Legislature for 1865.

Description of City Hospital, 1865. 129 *pages.*

Report of Com. on Back Bay Streets, 1863.

Ordinance in relation to Mount Hope Cemetery.

Address to the Citizens of Boston on Rural Cem.

Tabular Representation on the Cond. of Boston.

Report of Com. in relation to Public Garden, 1850.

Report of Com. on Annexation of Roxbury, 1867.
Third Annual Report of City Hospital, 1865.
Index to City Documents, 1834 to 1865.
Report of Com. on Charles River Bridge, 1853.
Second Report, on Truancy and Compulsory Education, 1863.
Report of Supt. Chambers Street Chapel, 1863.
Report of the Com. on the Eastern Avenue, 1861.
Truancy and Compulsory Educ. in Boston, 1862.
Rules and Regulations, 2d Church, 1851.

2774 Boston. [*Twelve.*]

Considerations on Annexation of Charlestown and Boston, by Josiah Quincy.
Letter to Abbot Lawrence and Robt. G. Shaw, on cond. and growth of Boston, 1853.
Reasons against a New Bridge from Charlestown to Boston, 1825. *Uncut* 32 *pages.*
15th Annual Report of Receipts and Expenditures for 1827. 47 *pages.*
Report of the Cholera in Boston, 1849.
Boston Railways, their condition and Prospects.
Remarks on Organization and Powers of City Council, by Josiah Quincy, 1851.
Annual Report of New Eng. Hosp., 1858.
Political Reminiscences, by J. B. Derby, 1835.
Complimentary Banquet to Admiral Lessoffsky, June 7, 1864.
Reception of Prest. of the U. S., 1867.
Descrip. of Boston Water Works, etc., 1848. 12*mo, scarce.*

2774* Boston. *Valuable.* [*Nine.*]

Miscellaneous Remarks on the Police of Boston, Feb., 1814. *Uncut, very scarce,* 42 *pages.*
Historical Sketch of Boston, containing a brief account of its Settlement, rise and progress, 1861. 8*vo,* 96 *pages.*
Proceedings at dedication of City Hall, Sept. 18, 1865.
Sketch of the Origin, Object and Character of the Franklin Fund, for the benefit of young maimed Mechanics, 1866.
Inaugural Address of Mayor Lincoln, 1866.
Inaugural Address of Mayor Wightman, 1861.
Address, at opening the Eastern Rail Road, August 27, 1838, by Geo. Peabody. 8*vo, uncut,* 19 *p., scarce.*
The "Bostoniad," by Jas. T. S. Lidstone, 1853.
Boston. A Commercial Metropolis in 1850, her growth, population and wealth, by E. H. Derby.

2775 Historical. *Scarce.* [*Five.*]

WRENTHAM, Mass. Anniv. Sermon, deliv. June 14, 1846, by E. Fisk. 8*vo,* 25 *p.*
WRENTHAM. Sermon by Rev. E. Fisk, 50th anniv. of his ordination, June 12, 1849. 8*vo,* 64 *p. A vast accumulation of facts and dates of local and of general interest.*
SACO, Me. One Hundredth Anniv. of the First Church. Address by E. S. Dwight. 8*vo, uncut;* 27 *p.*

Saco. Discourse, 20th anniv. of his ordination, April 12, 1863, by J. T. G. Nichols. *8vo, 19 p.*

Hopkinton, Mass. A Century Sermon, Dec. 24, 1815, by Nath'l Howe. *2nd ed. 8vo, 31 p.; very scarce.*

"This is an original production, a diamond of the first water. It was very favorably noticed on its first appearance by the N. Amer. Rev. and by the newspapers generally. It has passed through several editions and has been translated into foreign languages. Perhaps no sermon ever published in New England is more generally known.

2776 Historical. [*Three*].

Leonard, Bacon. Commemorative Discourse, Theol. Seminary at Andover, 1858. 46 *p.*, *8vo.*

Dr. Sprague's Sermon, 25th Anniv. of his Installation at Albany, 1854. 40 *p.*, *8vo.*

S. F. Clarke's Centennial Discourse, in Athol, Mass., with an appendix. *Scarce, 8vo, 95 p.*

2777 Historical. *Very scarce.* [*Three*].

Thos. Snell. Sermon, June 27, 1848. 50th Anniv. of his Ordination, North Brookfield. *8vo, 56 p.*

Micah Stone. An Octogenarian's Birthday Memorial. Discourse, in Brookfield, 1850. *8vo, uncut, 26 p.*

Micah Stone. Reminiscences of a half century Pastorate, in Brookfield, 1851. *8vo, 72 p.*

2778 Historical. *Fine lot.* [*Five*].

Columbia, Conn. 150th Anniv. of Organization of Church, Octo. 24, 1866. Historical papers, etc. *Moor's Indian School, etc. 8vo, 96 p.*

Concord, N. H. Two Sermons, Nov. 21, 1830. Commemoration of the organizing 1st Church and Settlement of 1st minister, Nov. 18, 1730, by Nath'l Bouton. *8vo, uncut, map, scarce; 102 p.*

Cambridge, Mass. Commem. of 25th Anniv. of Settlement of J. A. Albro. *8vo, 76 p.*

Chelsea, Mass. Historical Discourse, 25th Anniv. of Winnisimmet Cong. Church, Sept. 20, 1866, by Isaac P. Langworthy. *8vo, 47 p.*

Charlestown, Mass. A Disc., on the 25th Anniv. of his Ordination, with an Historical note, 1865, by Geo. E. Ellis. *8vo, 43 p.*

2779 Historical. [*Nine*].

Brown Univ., R. I., Under the Presidency of Asa Messer. *8vo, 23 p.*

Essex Institute, Salem. Report of Com. on the First Church of the Pilgrims, June 19, 1865. *8vo, 8 p.*

Lawrence Academy, Groton, Mass. The Jubilee of July 12, 1854. *8vo, Illust. 108 p.*

Loring Hall, Hingham, Mass. Address at Dedica., Octo. 14, 1852, by Oliver Stearns. *8vo, 36 p.*

Leicester Academy, Mass. Brief Sketch of the History of, by Emory Washburn. *8vo, 158 p., scarce.*

Hamilton College. Historical Discourse, by Samuel W. Fisher, July 16, 1862. *8vo, 43 p.*

Baltimore. Address, at Laying of Corner stone of City Hall, Octo. 18, 1867, by J. H. B. Latrobe. *8vo, 22 p.*

Table Rock Album. Niagara Falls. Sketches of, and Scenery. 120 *p.* *Buffalo,* 1848

Quincy, Mass. Poem, May 25, 1840. 200th Anniv. of Incorp. of the Town, by C. P. Cranch. *8vo, 26 p.; scarce.*

2780 Historical. *Valuable.* [*Eight*].

Boston. A Discourse in Two Parts, preached at Commencement of 19th Century, by John Lathrop. *8vo, uncut, 40p.; scarce.*

Boston. Discourse, Public Lectures, March 16, 1797, by John Lathrop, with an appendix, containing an account of several daring attempts to set Fire to the Town and rob the Inhabitants. *8vo, uncut, scarce;* 30 *p.*

Boston. Two Sermons, before Second Church, on Occasion of Taking down their Ancient place of worship, March 10, 1844, by Chandler Robbins. *8vo,* 76 *p.; very scarce.*

Boston. Sermon, before New North Church, May 2, 1804, upon completion of House of Worship, by John Eliot. *8vo, uncut,* 31 *p.; scarce.*

Boston. Discourse, at Dedication of Church in Arlington Street, Dec. 11, 1861, by Ezra S. Gannett. *8vo,* 83 *p., valuable appendix.*

Boston. Sermon, Bowdoin St. Cong. Soc., on closing their church, May 4, 1862, by Nehemiah Adams.

Boston. Sermon, Dedication of 1st Presb. Church, Jan. 31, 1828, by James Sabine.

Boston. Farewell Disc., Purchase St. Cong., April 30, 1848, by J. I. T. Coolidge.

2780* Historical. *Very scarce.* [*Four*].

Dedham, Mass. A History of the First Church, Nov. 18, 1838, on the completion of the Second Century since the gathering of the Church, by Alvan Lamson. *8vo, uncut scarce.* 104 *p.*

Dedham, Mass. Sermon, 40th Anniv. of his Ordi., by Alvan Lamson. *8vo,* 63 *p.; scarce.*

Dedham. A Historical Discourse, at closing of the Old Episcopal Church, Nov. 30, 1845, by S. B. Babcock. *8vo, uncut; scarce,* 23 *p.*

Dedham. Sermon, 225th Anniv. of 1st Church, Nov, 8, 1863, by Jonathan Edwards. *8vo,* 16 *p.*

2781 Historical. [*Nine*].

Worcester, Mass. A Historical Dis., in Old South Meeting House, Sept. 22, 1863, the Hundredth Anniv. of its Erection, by Leonard Bacon. *8vo,* 106 *p.*

Worcester. A Sermon, Jan. 31, 1836, 50 yrs. ministry, by Aaron Bancroft. *8vo,* 44 *p.; scarce.*

WORCESTER. Disc., 25th Anniv. of his Ordi., March 28, 1852, by Alonzo Hill. *8vo*, 46 *p.*

WORCESTER. Hist. Disc., 50th Anniv. of First Baptist church, Dec. 9, 1862, by Isaac Davis. *8vo*, 52 *p. ; valuable.*

JACKSONVILLE, Ill. Twelfth Annual Disc., Oct. 28, 1860, by L. M. Glover. *8vo*, 22 *p.*

WENHAM, Mass. Two Sermons, Second Centennial Anniv. of First Church, by Daniel Mansfield. *8vo*, 72 *p.*

LANESBOROUGH, Mass. A Centennial Sermon, St. Luke's Church, Oct. 6, 1867, by S. B. Shaw. *8vo*, 22 *p.*

HAVERHILL, Mass. Centennial Discourse of Celebration of Baptist Church, May 9, 1865, by A. S. Train. With Historical Notes. *8vo*, 96 *p., valuable.*

LITCHFIELD, Ct. Proceedings of the North and South Consociations of Litchfield Co., to Commemorate the Centennial Anniv., July, 1852. *8vo*, 154 *p. ; valuable.*

2782 Historical. [*Nine.*]

UPTON, (Mass.) Sermon June 1, 1846, 50 years Completion of his Ministry, by Benj. Wood. *8vo*, 32 *p.*

NEWARK, (N. J.) The 50th Anniv. of 2d Presb. Ch., Sept. 29, 1861, by J. Few. Smith. 12*mo*, 75 *p.*

FARMINGTON, (Ct.) Half-Century Disc. of Ordin. of Noah Porter, Nov. 12, 1856. *8vo*, 54 *p.* ; *valuable.*

JAMAICA PLAIN, (Mass.) Half-Century Sermon, April 24, 1842, by Thos. Gray. *8vo*, 44 *p.*

JAMESTOWN, (N. Y.) The Fiftieth Anniv. of First Cong. Ch. Sermon, Historical Sketch, etc. *8vo*, 72 *p., uncut ; scarce and valuable.*

PETERSHAM, (Mass.) Sermon, Jan. 17, 1802, by Festus Foster. *8vo*, 16 *p.*

SAYBROOK, (Ct.) Valed. Add., Jan. 7, 1838, 55th year of Pastoral Service, by F. W. Hotchkiss. *8vo*, 16 *p.*

HARRISBURGH, (Pa.) "The Memories of the Past." Sermon by W. R. DeWitt, 70th anniv. of his Birthday. *8vo*, 30 *p.*

SAN FRANCISCO. Decade Sermons. Two Historical Disc., March, 1859, by S. H. Willey. *8vo*, 46 *p.*

2783 Historical. [*Nine.*]

LEOMINISTER, (Mass.) A Centennial Disc. 1st Cong. Church, Sept. 24, 1843, with appendix, by Rufus P. Stebbins. *8vo*, 112 *p. ; scarce.*

POMFRET, (Ct.) The 150th Anniv. of the First Church, Oct. 26, 1865. Sermon, Historical Papers, etc. *8vo, uncut*, 96 *p.* ; *important.*

PUTNAM, (Ohio.) A Sermon, Presb. Ch., Jan. 1, 1860. "Memorial of Former Days," by A. Kingsbury. *8vo*, 30 *p.*

GRAFTON, (Mass.) A Sermon, July 18, 1863, 25th Anniv. of Ordin., by Thos. C. Biscoe. *8vo*, 26 *p.*

WOBURN, (Mass.) A Sermon, Jan. 4, 1846, 25th Anniv. of Ordin., by Joseph Bennett. *8vo*, 22 *p.*

UXBRIDGE, (Mass.) Twenty-Fifth Anniv. Sermon, Jan. 10, 1858, by Saml. Clarke. *8vo*, 20 *p*.

NEWTON, (Mass.) A Farewell Disc., March 21, 1869, by E. J. Young. *8vo*, 21 *p*.

HOLDEN, (Mass.) Thirtieth Anniv. Sermon, Oct. 25, 1863, by Wm. P. Paine. *8vo*, 27 *p*.

GEORGETOWN, (Mass.) A Semi-Centennial Discourse, June 7, 1847, 50th Anniv. of his Ordin., by Isaac Braman. *8vo*, 39 *p.*; *valuable.*

2784 Historical. [*Five.*]

HADLEY, (Mass.) An Half-Century Discourse, March 3, 1803, by Saml. Hopkins. *8vo, uncut, orig. cov.*; *very scarce*, 32 *p*. *Northampton*, 1805

HADLEY. Half-Century Sermon, Two Disc., June 24, 1860, on 50th Anniv. of Ordin., by John Woodbridge. *8vo*, 35 *p*.

PROVIDENCE, (R. I.) A Discourse on the Conclusion of the Second Century, from the settlement of the State, by Thos. Williams, June, 1836. *8vo*, 32 *p.*; *scarce.*

PROVIDENCE. Historical Discourse deliv. May 28, 1865, 90 years after Dedication of First Baptist Ch., by S. L. Caldwell. *8vo*, 22 *p*.

PROVIDENCE. A Centennial Discourse, March 22, 1866, by D. Patten. *8vo*, 29 *p*.

2785 Historical. [*Nine.*]

GLOVER, (Vt.) Disc. Semi-Centennial Celebration First Cong. Church, Jan. 12, 1867, by S. K. B. Perkins. *8vo*, 8 *p.*, *dble. col.*

LISBON, (Vt.) A Half-Century Sermon, deliv. Dec. 5, 1854, by Levi Nelson. *8vo*, 23 *p.*; *scarce.*

EAST HAMPTON, (Mass.) A Half-Century Sermon, Aug. 18. 1839, by Payson Williston. *8vo*, 24 *p.*; *scarce.*

HINGHAM, (Mass.) Sermon, June 28, 1856, 50th Anniv. of his Ministry, by Jos. Richardson. *8vo*, 48 *p*.

PRINCETON Theol. Seminary. Discourse on Completion of Half Century, April 30, 1862, by Wm. B. Sprague. *8vo*, 72 *p*.

STOW, (Mass.) An Aged Minister's Review of Fifty Years, Sermon, Oct. 11, 1824, by Jon. Newell. *8vo, uncut*, 20 *p*.

BERKSHIRE Association, Proc. at Centennial Commem. of, Oct. 28, 1863. Historical Disc. by Prof. A. Hopkins. *8vo*, 56 *p.*; *important.*

WESTMINSTER, (Vt.) Sermon, June 11, 1867, One Hundredth Anniv. of Cong. Church, by Pliny H. White. Historical Paper, by Alfred Stevens. *8vo*, 48 *p.*; *valuable.*

2786 Historical. [*Three.*]

IPSWICH, (Mass.) A Centennial Disc., Aug. 10, 1834, by D. T. Kimball. *8vo*, 32 *p.*; *scarce.*

IPSWICH. Thirtieth Anniv. Disc., June 29, 1856, by Dan'l Fitz. *8vo*, 23 *p*.

IPSWICH. Disc., Oct. 8, 1856, 50th Anniv. of his Ordin., by D. T. Kimball. *8vo*, 96 *p*. *Port.*

2787 Miscellaneous. *Rare and Interesting.* [*Three.*]

Emmons, Nath'l. A Discourse addressed to the Cong. in Franklin, 1809.

Chalmers, Thos. A Series of Discourses on the Christian Revelation, in Connexion with Modern Astronomy, N. Y., 1817. *8vo*, 275 *p.*

M'Leod. Alex. A Scriptural View of the Character, Causes, and Ends of the Present War. N. Y., 1815. *8vo*, 224 *p.*

2788 Sermons. Historical. [*Thirteen.*]

Mann, Sam'l. A Sermon preached in Wrentham, Jan. 1, 1701, and now published at the request of several of his descendants. *8vo*, *uncut*, 24 *p.* *Dedham*, 1801

Ingersoll, Geo. G. A Farewell Address, June 2, 1844.

Tappan, David. A Discourse delivered in Newbury, occasion of his removal to Univ. at Cambridge. *8vo*, *uncut*, 35 *p.* *Portsmouth*, 1793

Snell, Thos. Discourse delivered in Brookfield, before the Female Bible Cent. Society, Aug. 4, 1815. *8vo*, 23 *p.*

Allerton, Isaac. Sermon, addressed particularly to the Baptist Denomination, on the Communion of All Saints. *Mount Pleasant, N. Y.*, 1822

Romeyn, J. B. A Sermon delivered in Phila., May 23, 1808, on Missions.

Osgood, David. A Sermon on the day of Annual Thanksgiving, Nov. 20, 1794. *8vo*, *uncut*, 29 *p.*

Smith, Ethan. Farewell Sermon, deliv. at Haverhill, N. H., June 30, 1799. *8vo*, 27 *p.*, *uncut*; *very scarce.* *Peacham, Vt.*, 1800

Hopkins, A. T. "The Evils and Remedy of Lewdness." *Utica*, 1834

Chapin, Calvin. Sermon before the "Conn. Soc. for Promoting Good Morals," Hartford, May 18, 1814. 34 *p.*

Johnson, J. B. A Farewell Sermon, Sept. 26, 1802, in Albany. 96 *p.*; *scarce.*

Kirk, E. N. "Our Duty in Perilous Times," Sermon, June 1, 1856, in Boston.

Barstow, Z. S. Sermon at Installation of J. M. Putnam, Dunbarton, N. H., July 8, 1830.

2789 Historical. [*Seven.*]

Beverly, (Mass.) Lecture, comprising the History of the Second Parish, July 6, 1834, by Edwin M. Stone. *8vo*, *uncut*, 35 *p.*; *very scarce.*

Beverly, (Mass.) A Valedictory Discourse, July 4, 1858, in First Church, by C. T. Thayer. *8vo*, 52 *p.*

Ipswich, (Mass.) A Sketch of the Ecclesiastical History of, 1823, by David T. Kimball. *8vo*, *uncut* 44 *p.*; *very scarce.*

Ipswich. The Last Sermon Preached in the Ancient Church of First Parish, Feb. 22, 1846, by David T. Kimball. *8vo*, 32 *p.*; *scarce.*

SALEM. The Claims of the Tabernacle Church to be the Church of 1735. *8vo*, 56 *p.* *Salem*, 1847

SALEM. Candid Review of Correspondence in relation to Tabernacle Church.

SALEM. Correspondence between the First Church and Tabernacle Church. *8vo, uncut*, 176 *p.* *Salem*, 1832

2790 Historical. [*Ten.*]

HOMER, (N. Y.) Sketch of the History of the Cong. Church, by J. C. Holbrook. *8vo*, 9 *p.*, *dble. col.*

NEW BRUNSWICK, (N. J.) A Record of Christ Church, by Alfred Stubbs. *8vo.* 76 *p.* ; *valuable.*

NEWBURYPORT, (Mass.) Sermons by Mr. Cary and Andrews, on leaving the Old Church, and Dedication of new one, Sept. 27, 1801. *8vo*, 56 *p.* ; *scarce.*

ORLEANS, (Mass.) Discourse, Barnstable Conference, Dec. 19, 1855, Illustrating the rise, growth, decline, etc., by Jos. S. Clark. *8vo*, 36 *p.*; *very interesting.*

POTTSVILLE, (Pa.) Historical Sketch of the Synod of N. J., by B. K. Rogers. *8vo*, 25 *p.*

QUINCY, (Ill.) Memorial of the Illinois Association, completing a Quarter of a Century of its History, and an Historical Appendix, by Wm. Carter, Oct. 26, 1869. *8vo*, 98 *p.*

SCITUATE, (Mass.) Historical Sketch of the First Cong. Church. *12mo*, 51 *p.*

SOMERVILLE. (Mass.) Address at laying of Corner Stone 1st Cong. Ch., Sept. 28, 1844, by R. M. Hodges. *8vo*, 19 *p.*

UPTON, (Mass.) Sermon, on leaving the Old Meeting-House, Dec. 31, 1848. Also, Sermon at Dedication of New Cong. Church, Jan. 3, 1849 both. By Benj. Wood. Sermon at Funeral of Rev. Benj. Wood, April, 1849, by H. A. Tracy. *8vo*, 60 *p.*

WEST LEXINGTON, (Ky.) A Sketch of the Immigrant Church, Sept. 1, 1858, by J. D. Shane. *8vo*, 27 *p.* ; *valuable.*

2791 Historical. *Valuable.* [*Ten.*]

WESTON, (Mass.) Address deliv. July 4, 1853, by Asa D. Smith. *8vo*, 45 *p.*

WOODSTOCK, (Conn.) History of the First Cong. Church, by L. Grosvenor. *8vo*, 28 *p.* ; *valuable.*

RICHMONDVILLE, (N. Y.) The Early History of the Lutheran Church in New York, by G. A. Lintner. *8vo, uncut*, 24 *p.* ; *valuable.*

PORTSMOUTH, (N. H.) Four Sermons, connected with the Re-opening of Church of South Parish, Dec., 1858, and Jan., 1859, by G. P. Peabody. *12mo*, 112 *p.* ; *scarce.*

PORTSMOUTH. "Its Advantages and Needs." Sermon, Nov. 30, 1854, by Wm. Lamson. *8vo*, 23 *p.*

PORTSMOUTH. Sermon at Closing Sunday School Room in Court Street, Feb. 15, 1857, by A. P. Peabody. *8vo*, 24 *p.*

SALEM, (Mass.) "Principles of the Reformation." Sermon at

Dedication of First Cong. Ch., Nov. 16, 1826, by Chas. W. Upham. *8vo, uncut, 62 p ; scarce and valuable ; fine copy.*

Salem. Sermon at Installation of Rev. Geo. W. Briggs, Jan. 6, 1853, with notices of the First Church and its Ministers. *8vo, 62 p.*

Salem. Two Discourses on taking leave of the Old Church in Salem, Dec. 28, 1845, by James Flint. *8vo, 48 p.*

Salem. Sermon, on Anniv. of Ordination North Church, Nov. 19, 1837, by John Brazer. *8vo, uncut, 22 p.*

2792 Historical. *Valuable.* [*Seven.*]

J. Abbott's Sermon on the 15th Anniv. of his Ordination at Beverly, 1848. *8vo, 22 p.*

R. S. Storr's Disc., July 3, 1861, on the 50th Anniv. of his Ordination, Braintree. *8vo, 102 p. ; scarce.*

Jos. Vaill. A Memorial Sermon, Feb. 7, 1864, Commem. 50 yrs. settlement Brimfield, Mass. *8vo, 42 p.*

Jas. Thompson. Sermon on 37th Anniv. of Ordination, in Barre, Mass., Jan. 11, 1841. *8vo, 35 p.*

Jas. Thompson. Discourse, Jan. 11. 1854, End of Ministry of 50 yrs. in Barre. *8vo, 91 p.*

John Pierce. Reminiscences of Forty Years, March 19, 1837. Brookline, Mass. *8vo, 35 p., uncut ; very scarce.*

John Pierce. Brookline Jubilee Disc., March 15, 1847, 50 yrs. from his Ordination. *8vo, 72 p. ; scarce.*

2793 Historical. [*Seven.*]

Warren. Historical Disc. Centennial of Warren Assoc., Sept. 11, 1867, by S. L. Caldwell. *8vo, 19 p.*

Pepperell, (Mass.) A Centennial Disc., Jan. 29, 1847, with Historical Notices, by David Andrews. *8vo, 48 p.; scarce.*

Pepperell. A Centennial Discourse, being a plea in vindication of the Rights of Cong. Churches, Feb. 9, 1847, by Chas. Babbidge. *8vo, 44 p.*

Newburyport, (Mass.) A Discourse, Nov. 19, 1844, 50th Anniv. of his Ordin., by Dan'l Dana. *8vo, 32 p.*

Newburyport. A Historical Discourse, Commemorative of First Centennial of First Presb. Church, Jan. 7, 1846, by J. F. Stearns. *8vo, 64 p. Port. Scarce.*

Hartford, (Ct.) Historical Address, Trinity College, 25th Anniv., by E. E. Beardsley. *8vo, 31 p.*

Hartford, (Ct.) Twentieth Anniv. North Church, May 22, 1853, by Horace Bushnell. *8vo, 32 p.*

2794 Historical. *Very scarce.* [*Five.*]

Dover, N. H. A Bi-Centennial Sermon, Nov. 29, 1838. By David Root. *8vo, 31 pp. ; scarce.*

Dorchester, Mass. Memorials of the First Church, from its settlement in New England to the end of the Second Century. July 4, 1830. By Thaddeus Mason Harris. *8vo, uncut, 67 p. ; scarce ; fine copy.*

Deerfield, Mass. History of First Church. Sept. 22, 1857. By Samuel Willard. *8vo*, 42 *pp.*

Dover, Mass. Thirty Years' Ministry. Ry Ralph Sanger. Sept. 18, 1842. *8vo*, 24 *pp.; scarce.*

Dudley, Mass. An Anniv. Disc., March 20, 1853; with Topographical and Historical Notices of the Town. By Joshua Bates. *8vo*, 58 *pp.; scarce.*

2795 Historical. *Valuable.* [*Ten.*]

Amherst, Mass. Sermon: Dedication of College Chapel. Feb. 28, 1827. By Heman Humphrey.

Andover, Mass. Sermon: Completion of new College Edifice, Sept. 13, 1821. By Moses Stuart.

Brimfield, Mass. Annals of the Church in, with Appendix, showing the Origin of Churches in Holland, Wales, and Monson. Also, map, indicating residence of Early Settlers. 1856. *8vo*, 83 *pp.; scarce and valuable.*

Brookfield, Mass. Historical Sketch of the Baptist Church. 8 *pp.*

Brookline. Sermon on decease of Samuel Hammond, Oct. 13, 1816, by Jon. Homer. *8vo, uncut; valuable Appendix;* 26 *pp.*

Charlestown. "The duty of Commemorating the deeds of our Fathers." Sermon, June 18, 1865, by J. E. Rankin.

Dorchester, Mass. Memorial of the Proprietors of New South Church, &c. *8vo, uncut*, 48 *pp.*

Halifax, N. S. Origin and Formation of the Baptist Church, 1828

Hardwick, Mass. Address, at laying Corner-Stone of Calvinistic Society, Sept., 1828, by Parsons Cooke.

Hingham. "The Old Man's Calendar." Discourse, Aug. 26, 1781. Reprinted May, 1846. By Ebenezer Gay.

First printed by John Boyle, of Boston, in 1781; afterwards in England and Holland. It is now difficult to find copies of it. Jos. B. Felt's copy. Autog. of Solomon Lincoln.

2796 Historical. [*Eight.*]

Fuller, Arthur B. A Historical Disc. in New North Ch., Boston, 1854. *8vo*, 33 *pp.*

Ellis, Geo. E. A Commen. Disc. in New South Church, Boston, 1864. 50th Anniv. *8vo*, 46 *pp.*

Gannett, Ezra S. Sermon, 40th year of his Ministry, Boston, 1864. *8vo*, 22 *pp.*

Sharp, Daniel. Services at 40th Anniv. of his Installation, Boston, 1852. *8vo, cl.*, 68 *pp.*

Barrett, Samuel. Two Disc., 12th Cong. Ch., 25th year of his Ministry. Boston. *8vo.* 40 *pp.*

Young, Alex. Discourse on 20th Anniv. of his Ordination, Jan. 19, 1845. Boston. *8vo, uncut*, 32 *pp; scarce.*

Winchell, Jas. M. Two Disc., exhibiting an Historical Sketch of the First Baptist Church, in Boston, from 1655 to 1818. *8vo.* 47 *pp ; very scarce.*

Thacher, Peter. Sermon, Dec. 29, 1799, on the Completion of Century of Brattle Street Church, Boston. *8vo, uncut ; scarce ;* 18 *pp.*

2797 Historical. [*Seven.*]

New Haven. Discourse, Fifty Years' Ministry, Feb. 25, 1855, by Sam'l Merwin. *8vo,* 72 *pp.*

New Haven. Disc. Commemorative of History of Church of Christ, in Yale College, during the First Century of its existence. Nov. 22, 1857. With Notes and an Appendix. By Geo. P. Fisher. *8vo,* 98 *pp.*

Salem, Mass. Discourse, First Centennial Anniv. of Tabernacle Church, April 26, 1835. By Sam'l M. Worcester. *8vo,* 64 *pp., uncut.*

Salem. Sermon, 38th Anniv. of his Ordin., 1843. By Brown Emerson. *8vo,* 31 *pp.*

Salem. Historical Discourse, 50th Anniv. of First Baptist Church, Dec. 24, 1854. By Rob't C. Mills. *8vo,* 78 *pp.*

Salem. Discourse, 50th Anniv. of his Ordination, April 24, 1855. By Brown Emerson. *8vo,* 96 *pp.*

Salem. A Semi-Centennial Add., Aug. 24, 1859, in Universalist Ch.—50th Anniv. of Ordin. of Edw. Turner, and Ded. of Church. By Lemuel Willis. *8vo,* 84 *pp.*

2798 Historical. [*Eight.*]

Lowell, Cha's. Disc. in West Church, Boston, Aug. 3, 1845. *8vo,* 25 *pp.*

Ware, Henry. Two Disc., containing the History of the Old North and New Brick Churches, May 20, 1821—Complet. Century. Boston. *8vo, uncut,* 60 *pp. scarce.*

Robbins, Chandler. Sermon, Dec. 5, 1858—25th Anniv. of Ordination as Pastor 2d Church, Boston. *8vo,* 47 *pp.*

Frothingham, N. L. Two Hundred Years Ago. Sermon, Aug. 29, 1830. Boston. *8vo, uncut,* 20 *pp.*

——— Celebration of close of 2d Century of the Thursday Lecture. Boston, 1833. *8vo,* 16 *pp.*

——— Twentieth Anniv. of his Ordina., First Church. Boston, 1835. *8vo, uncut,* 16 *pp.*

Parkman, Francis. Sermon, Centennial of the New North Church, Boston, 1814. *8vo, uncut,* 25 *pp. ; scarce.*

——— Discourses in New North Church—Completion of 124th year of establishment of Church, 1839. *8vo,* 40 *pp., uncut.*

2799 Historical. [*Eleven.*]

Cambridge, Mass. Sermon on Re-opening of Christ Church, Nov. 22, 1857 ; with a Historical Notice of the Church. By Nicholas Hoppin. *8vo, illust.,* 79 *pp.*

Cambridge. Discourse on the Church-Gathering in 1636, by Wm. Newell. Feb. 22, 1846. *8vo, 65 pp., scarce and valuable.*

Dedham, Mass. Valedictory Discourse, Dec. 20, 1829, by Wm. Cogswell. *8vo, uncut.*

Boston, Mass. Chronicles of Old South Church. Sept. 1, 1861. 10 *pp.*

Boston. Reasons for the appointment of Com. to investigate the prudential affairs of Old South Church. Added, copies of Mrs. Norton's deeds. 1858.

Boston. "A Memorial of the Federal Street Meeting-House." Discourse by Ezra S. Gannett; with an Appendix and Illust. March 13, 1859. *8vo, 89 pp; valuable.*

Boston. Historical Account of Christ Church. By Rev. Mr. Eaton. 1824. *8vo, uncut; frontis.; 39 pp.; scarce.*

Boston. Discourse delivered at opening of new Meeting-House—Second Baptist Church—Jan., 1811, by Thomas Baldwin. *8vo, 35 pp; scarce.*

Boston. Historical Notices of the New North Church; with Anecdotes of Andrew and John Eliot. *8vo, 51 pp., uncut; very scarce.*

Boston. Discourse, Dedication of Church on Church Green, 1815; to which are added Notes and Illustration. By S. O. Thacher. *8vo, 43 pp.; scarce.*

Boston. Discourse, delivered in West Church, Dec. 31, 1820, by Cha's Lowell. *8vo, uncut, 44 pp.; valuable.*

2800 Historical. [*Ten.*]

Mass. Eye and Ear Infirmary. Address at Dedication of new Building, July 3, 1850, by E. Reynolds. *8vo, frontis.*, 40 *pp.*

Williams College. Poem, by S. E. Burrill, deliv. July 29, 1867. *8vo, uncut,* 14 *pp.*

N. Y. Univ. Valed. Lect., by Prof. Draper, Feb. 23, 1842. *8vo,* 11 *pp.*

Leicester Acad., Mass. Address, at Dedic., Oct. 26, 1853, by A. H. Washburn. *8vo,* 28 *pp.*

Charter Oak Hall, Hartford, (Ct.) Proceedings at Dedic. with Addresses of I. W. Stuart and others. May, 1856 *8vo.* 45 *pp. Plans, &c.*

Malden Town-Hall, Mass. Oration, Poem, Speeches, Chronicles, &c., at Dedic., Oct. 29, 1857. *8vo.,* 52 *pp.*

Cayuga Lake Academy. Celebration of, July 22, 1857. Ledyard, N. Y.. Address, by Salem Town. *8vo,* 22 *pp.*

Andover Theol. Sem. Poem, Sept. 22, 1829, by Richard H. Dana. *8vo, uncut; scarce; fine copy;* 15 *pp.*

Lancaster Soldiers' Memorial Hall, (Mass.) Address, June 17, 1868, by C. T. Thayer: and Ode, by H. F. Buswell. With an Historical Appendix. *8vo,* 70 *pp.; valuable.*

Plummer Hall, Salem, (Mass.) Proceedings on Dedica., Oct. 6, 1857: and Judge White's Memoir of the Plummer-Family. *8vo,* 97 *pp.*

2801 Miscellaneous. [*Eight.*]

WELLS, J. D. Sermon on death of Dr. E. Woodward. Containing a Biographical Sketch. Printed for Private Distribution. *One of* 8 *uncut copies.* 1869.

FROTHINGHAM, N. L. "The duties of Hard Times." Sermon, April 23, 1837. *Boston.*

FROTHINGHAM, N. L. "Gold." Sermon, Dec. 11, 1848. *Boston.*

ROBBINS, CHANDLER. Address at Laying Corner Stone of Second Church, May 30th, 1844. *Boston*

ROBBINS, CHANDLER. Sermon, Nov. 6, 1836.

ELLIS, GEO. E. "The Organ and Church Music." Two Discourses, Sept. 26, 1852, delivered in Charlestown.

ELLIS, GEO. E. "The Preacher and the Pastor." Two Discourses, March 15, 1840.

WALKER, JAMES. Discourse on taking leave of his Church in Charlestown, July 14, 1839.

2802 Miscellaneous. [*Twelve.*]

PERKINS, NATHAN. Conn. Election Sermon, May 12, 1808. *Scarce.*

FOSDICK, DAVID. Anniv. and Farewell Sermons, March 3, and Sept. 19, 1847. *Boston.*

WILDER, JOHN. An Address to the Members of Attleborough Soc. for Agriculture, &c., Feb. 22, 1805. *Contains Eulogy on Washington.*

WILDER, JOHN. Discourse, Feb. 3, 1805, in Attleborough. *Historical.*

GRIFFIN, E. D. Farewell Sermon, May 28, 1809, Newark, N. J. *8vo, uncut.* 16 *p.*

EATON, WM. Sermon at Fitchburg, Jan. 8, 18:3, at close of his ministry. *8vo, uncut.* 24 *pages.*

NASON, ELIAS. Sermon. Dedication of 1st. Cong. Church in Natick, Mass., Nov. 15, 1854.

TODD, JOHN. Sermon at Dedication in Groton, Mass., Jan 3, 1827.

SMITH, ASA D. Sermon before Synod of N. Y. and N. J., Oct. 18, 1848, in N. Y.

SALTMARSH, S. Sermon on the Election in Mass. delivered in Canton, Nov. 19, 1854.

HALL, NATH'L. Discourse, July 19, 1835, to 1st Church, Dorchester.

NEWELL, WM. Discourse, Jan 22, 1854, in Cambridge.

2803 Miscellaneous. *Valuable.* [*Seven.*]

Murray, Lindley. Extracts from the writings of divers authors, &c., representing the evils of Stage Plays. *8vo.* 24 *pages.* *Phila.*, 1799

Philadelphia. The Address and Petition of a number of Clergy to the Senate and H. of Rep. of the State of Pa.

in relation to the Prohibition of Theatrical Exhibitions. 8*vo*. 16 *pages*. *Phila*., 1793

Boston Acad. of Music. Address on the opening of the Odeon. By Samuel A Eliot. 8*vo*. 17 *pages*. *Boston*, 1835

GORHAM, Me. "*Dead on the Field of Honor*." Dedication of the Soldiers' Monument, Oct. 18, 1866, Addresses, Poems, &c. 8*vo*, 32 *pages*. *Valuable*. *Portland*, 1866

Mount Hope Cemetery—in Dorchester and West Roxbury. Exercises at Consecration. *Boston*, 1852

Williamstown, Mass. Dedication of the Missionary Monument. *Boston*, 1867

BRIGHTON, Mass. Oration at Dedication of Soldiers' Monument, July 26, 1866, by F. A. Whitney, with an Appendix containing Notices of the Deceased Soldiers. 8*vo*, 62 *pages*. *Boston*, 1866

30 2804 Miscellaneous. *Scarce lot*. [*Eleven*.]

Illinois. A Sketch of the Military Bounty Tract, by F. Taylor. 8*vo*. 12 *pages*. *Scarce*. *Phila*., 1839

Minnesota: its Advantages to Settlers. *St. Paul*, 1869

Lowell, Mass. Profits on Manufactures. A Letter from the Treas. of a Corp. (Thos. G. Cary), to J. S. Pendleton, Va. 8*vo*. 23 *pages*. *Boston*, 1845

Portsmouth, N. H. The Portsmouth Jubilee. Reception of the Sons of, July 4th, 1853. Poem by "Mrs. Partington." 8*vo*. 80 *pages*. *Portsmouth*, 1853

South Manchester (Conn.) and its Silk Manuf. 1868.

Bennett, James Gordon. The War of the Giants against, and other recent matters. 8*vo*, 19 *pages*. *Curious*. *N. Y*., 1840

Barstow, Z. S. Remarks on the "Preliminary Hist." of. Two Discourses by Aaron Bancroft. 8*vo*, *uncut*. 24 *pages*. *Bellows Falls*, 1821

A Polemic Essay in defence of the Doctrine of Election. 8*vo*. 42 *pages*. *Newark*, 1799

Lloyd, Thomas. Sermon, April 8, 1787. *London*

Miami, O. Manifesto and Declaration of the Free Assoc. Presbytery. *Xenia*, 1843

Assoc. Ref. Synod. Extracts from the Minutes of the Acts, &c., of, May 29, 1793 (?) 8*vo*. 56 *p*. *Scarce*. *N. Y*., 1793

5 2805 Miscellaneous [*Nine*.]

Woodlawn Cemetery—in Chelsea and Malden, Mass. Address at Consecration of, by Geo. E. Ellis. *Boston*, 1851

Edmonds, J. W. An Address on the Constitution and Code of Procedure and the Modifications of the Law. 8*vo*. 47 *pages*. *N. Y*., 1848

The Guilford Spring, Vermont.

Mass. State Prison. Laws of the Commonwealth for the Government of, &c. 8*vo*, *uncut*; *frontis*. 112 *p*. *Charlestown*, 1830

Case of Contempt; or, Proceedings of the House of Assembly

of N. Y., against Moses Jaques and Levi D. Slamm. *8vo.* 18 *pages.* *N. Y.*, 1837

The Constitutions of U. S. and New York, 1835. *Port. of Washington. 8vo, uncut.* 28 *pages.*

Report of the Evidence and Reasons of the Award bet. J. Orlandos and A. Luriottis, Greek Dep., and Le Roy, Bayard & Co., by the Arbitrators. *8vo.* 72 *pages.* *N. Y.*, 1826

West Boston Soc. Rep. of Com. on subject of Land in front of the Church, April, 1849.

McMaster, Gilbert. The Moral Character of Civil Government, &c. *8vo.* 72 *pages.* *Albany*, 1832

2806 Miscellaneous. *Valuable.* [*Eleven.*]

Pamphlet in the Armenian Language.
" " Russian "

New York City. Wealth and Biog. of the Wealthy Citizens of. 6th Ed. 34 *pages.* 1845.

Boston. "Our First Men." A Calendar of Wealth, Fashion, and Gentility, &c. *8vo.* 48 *p., uncut.* *Boston*, 1846

The "Hive." Vol. I. 12 Nos. Edited by Bloomfield. *8vo, uncut Curious.* *New York*, 1846

Something. Edited by Nemo Nobody, Esq. "*'Tis Something—Nothing.*" *No.* 15. *Vol. I.* *Uncut.* *Boston*, 1810

Royal American Magazine for October, 1774. *8vo, uncut.* *Boston*, 1774

Lawrence, Mass. An Authentic History of the Lawrence Calamity, embracing a description of the Pemberton Mill, &c. *8vo, uncut; fine copy.* *Boston*, 1860

——— Report of Treas'r of Com. of Relief for Sufferers of the Pemberton Mill. 8vo. 51 *pages.* *Lawrence*, 1860

Spencertown, N. Y. Proceedings of the Independence Jubilee, July 4, 1846. *8vo.* 48 *pages.* *Albany*, 1846

Junior Pioneer Association. Historical Collections. No. 1. Address by F. De W. Ward. *8vo.* 48 *pages.* *Rochester, N. Y.*, 1860

2807 Miscellaneous. *Valuable.* [*Eight.*]

Willlams, John. New Observations on the Diseases of the Eye and Ear; or, every Man his own Oculist. *8vo, uncut.* 108 *pages.* *N. Y.*, 1840

Fowler O. S. Fowler on Matrimony; or, Phrenology and Physiology applied to the selection of Companions for Life, including directions to the Married, &c. "*Natural Waists, or no Wives.*" *N. Y.*, 1842

——— A Disquisition on the Evils of Using Tobacco, and the necessity of immediate and entire reformation. *Uncut.* *Boston*, 1835

Union Bank of Fla. An Act to Incorporate, &c. *Uncut.* *Tallahassee*, 1834

Gurley, R. R. The Report of, to obtain information in respect to Liberia. 116 *pages.* *Illus.* *Washington*, 1850

Poughkeepsie Female Bible Soc. The First Annual Report, Oct. 6, 1815. 8*vo.* 20 *pages.* *Poughkeepsie*, 1815

EVERETT, ALEX. H. An Address in Salem, Mass., Jan. 8, 1836, in Commem. of the Victory of New Orleans. 8*vo.* *Fine copy.* 61 *pages.* *Scarce.* *Boston*, 1836

RIVES, W. C. Discourse on the Uses and Importance of History, illustrated by a Comparison of the American and French Revolutions. 8*vo ; orig. cov.* 57 *pages.* *Fine copy.* *Scarce.* *Richmond*, 1847

2808 Miscellaneous. *Valuable.* [*Twenty-one.*]

Pickering, John. A Lecture on the alleged uncertainty of the Law. 8*vo.* 28 *pages, uncut.* *Very valuable.* *Boston*, 1834

Thacher, Peter O. An Address pronounced before the Members of the Bar of Suffolk Co., Mass. 8*vo, uncut.* 28 *pages.* *Very scarce and important.* *Boston*, 1831

Association for Exhibition of the Industry of all Nations, 1858. *N. Y.*

Atlantic and Pacific Oceans. Subject of a communication between. *Georgetown*, 1836

Atlantic and Pacific R. R. Co. Extr. devel. by C. G. Peebles. 1854.

Gallatin, Albert. Peace with Mexico. *New York.*

Tochman, Maj. G. Lecture on the Social, Political and Literary Condition of Poland. *Balt.*, 1844

Stevens, John L. Memoir of an Eventful Expedition in Central Amer. *New York*, 1850

Memoirs of the Irish Union, by Messrs. Emmett, O'Connor and McNevin, with an exam. of these gentlemen. *London*, 1798

Voyages, Adventures and Situation of the French Emigrants, from the Year '89 to '99, by a Lady. *Very rare.* *Western imprint.* *Lexington*, 1800

Fraser D. Essay on the Origin, Antiquity, &c., of the Scots and Irish Nations. To which is added an Oration deliv. before Caledonian Soc. *N. Y.*, 1801

Hist. Sketch of the Origin, Progress and Present State of the College of Physicians and Surgeons of the Univ. of N. Y. 1813

Hist. of Origin and Progress of the late Revolution in Geneva. *Phil.*, 1791

Description, Statis. and Geog. of the Countries of Europe. *Hartford*, 1848

Examination of certain statements in Macaulay's Hist. of England in regard to the Church of Eng., attributed to James Craik and John M'Gill. *Louisville*, 1849

Smith, J. Toulmin. Parallels between the Constitution and Constitutional His. of Eng. and Hungary. *Boston*, 1850

Rickards, R. India ; or, Facts submitted to illustrate the Character and Condition of the Native Inhabitants. *London*, 1828

Davis, A. Antiq. of America., &c. *Buffalo*, 1849

Calvert, George. Review of Hon. John P. Kennedy's Disc. on Life and Character of. *Baltimore*, 1846

Le Livre Rouge ; or, Red Book. Being a List of Private Pensions, paid from the Public. Treasury of France. *New York*, 1794

Clery, M. A. Journal of Occurrences at the Temple during the confinement of Louis XVI., King of France. *Dublin*, 1798

2809 ALLEN, COL. ETHAN. MEMOIR OF, containing the most interesting incidents connected with his private and public career. By Hugh Moore. *8vo, half dk. green lev., gilt top, rough edges ; very scarce in this condition.* *Plattsburgh*, 1834

2810 ALSTEAD, N. H. A SERMON preached on the First Sabbath in January, 1826, with HISTORICAL SKETCHES OF THE TOWN. By Seth S. Arnold. *8vo.* 19 *pages Sermon and* 28 *pages Appendix, embracing Historical Sketches ; extremely scarce ; beautiful copy.* *Alstead, N. H.*, 1826

2811 ALSTEAD, N. H. CONTINUATION OF AN APPENDIX, embracing Historical Sketches of the Town from 1826 to 1836. *8vo,* 12 *pages ; extremely scarce.* *Keene, N. H.*, 1836

2812 AMERICAN WAR OF 1812. HISTORY OF, from the commencement until the final termination thereof on the 8th of Jan., 1815, at New Orleans. Embellished with a likeness of General Pike and six other Eng. *8vo, half tur. mor., red, gilt top ; fine copy ; with a cotemporary plate of the Battle of New Orleans inserted.* *Philadelphia*, 1816

2813 ANDRÉ, MAJOR JOHN. AN AUTHENTIC NARRATIVE OF THE CAUSES WHICH LED TO THE DEATH OF MAJOR JOHN ANDRÉ, Adjutant-General of His Majesty's Forces in North America. By Joshua Hett Smith. To which is added, A MONODY ON THE DEATH OF MAJOR ANDRÉ, by Miss Seward. 12*mo, full polished calf, gilt edges ; bound by Bedford ; with the very rare portrait of André, by Scoles.*
NEW YORK : *Printed for Evert Duyckinck.* 1809

2814 ANDRÉ, MAJ. JOHN. VINDICATION OF THE CAPTORS OF. By Egbert Benson. With Introduction and Appendix. *8vo, full crimson crushed levant, gilt top, rough edges.*
New York : Privately printed. 1865.

80 copies. For F. S. Hoffman.

2815 A. W. FARMER. A VIEW OF THE Controversy between Great Britain and her Colonies : including a mode of determining their Present Disputes, FINALLY and EFFECTUALLY ; and of Preventing All Future Contentions. *8vo,* 37 *pages ; fine copy ; very scarce.*
NEW YORK : Printed by JAMES RIVINGTON. MDCCLXXIV.

2816 A. W. FARMER. THE CONGRESS CANVASSED ; or, an Examination into the Conduct of the Delegates at their GRAND CON-

VENTION, held in Philadelphia, Sept. 1, 1774, addressed to the MERCHANTS of *New York*. 8*vo*, 28 *pages ; fine copy ; very scarce.*
PRINTED (*by Jas. Rivington*) IN THE YEAR MDCCLXXIV.

2817 ALEXANDER, JOHN H. Memoir of. By William Pinkney. Read before the Maryland Historical Society, Thurs. Even'g, May 2, 1867. 8*vo, uncut ;* 33 *pages ; on tinted paper. Baltimore*, 1867
Contains list of Dr. Alexander's Works, Published and in Manuscript.

2818 BENTON, JESSE (*Brother of Thomas Benton*). AN ADDRESS to the People of the United States on the Presidential Election. 12*mo*, 34 *pages ; fine copy ; very rare and valuable.*
Nashville, Tenn., 1824

2819 BISHOP OF ST. ASAPH. A SPEECH intended to have been spoken on the Bill for Altering the Charters of the Colony of Massachusetts Bay. 8*vo*, 24 *pages ; fine copy ; scarce.*
BOSTON, MDCCLXXIV.

2820 BREWSTER, WILLIAM, CHIEF OF THE PILGRIMS ; or, the Life and Time of—ruling Elder of the Pilgrim Colony that Founded New Plymouth, the Parent Colony of New England, in 1620. By Rev. Ashbel Steel. Illust. with Five Steel and Four other Eng. 8*vo, cl.*, 416 *pages ; fine copy.*
Philadelphia, 1857

2821 BROOKLINE, MASS. A DISCOURSE delivered 24 November, 1805, the Day which completed a Century from the Incorporation of the Town. By John Pierce, the Fifth Minister of Brookline. 8*vo, stiff cover*, 32 *pages ; beautiful copy of this exceedingly scarce Local History.* *Cambridge*, 1806
Your Fathers, where are they?

2822 CHAUNCY, CHARLES. "ALL Nations of the Earth, blessed in CHRIST, the Seed of ABRAHAM." SERMON PREACHED AT BOSTON at the ORDINATION of the Rev. JOSEPH BOWMAN to the WORK of the Gospel-Ministry, MORE ESPECIALLY among the *Mohawk Indians* on the Western Borders of NEW-ENGLAND, August 31, 1762. 8*vo*, 50 *pages ; fine copy ; rare.* *Boston*, 1762

2823 CANADA. UPPER AND LOWER A Tour through, Containing a View of the Present State of Religion, Learning, Commerce, Agriculture, Colonization, Customs and Manners among the English, French and Indian SETTLEMENTS. By a Citizen of the United States. 12*mo, old shp. bdg. ; fine copy ; very scarce imprint.* *Printed at Litchfield* (*Ct.*), 1799

2824 CITIZEN. THE OTHER SIDE OF THE QUESTION ; or a DEFENCE of the LIBERTIES of North America. In ANSWER to a late FRIENDLY ADDRESS to All Reasonable Americans on the subject of our POLITICAL CONFUSIONS. *By a* CITIZEN. 8*vo*, 31 *pages ; fine copy ; very scarce.*
NEW YORK : *Printed by* JAMES RIVINGTON. MDCCLXXIV.

2825 COGHLAN, MRS. MARGARET, MEMOIRS OF, written by Herself, and Dedicated to the British Nations ; being interspersed with ANECDOTES of the late AMERICAN and present FRENCH WAR ; with Remarks, Moral and Political. 8*vo, full dk. blue crushed levant, gilt top, rough edges ; beautiful copy ; with the very scarce Preface by the Editor of this edition.* *New York*, 1795

2826 CONGRESS. *What think ye of the* CONGRESS *now?* or, An Enquiry how far the AMERICANS are bound to abide by and execute the decisions of the late CONGRESS? *8vo,* 48 *pages; fine copy; very scarce.*
NEW YORK: Printed by JAMES RIVINGTON. MDCCLXXV.

2827 CONNECTICUT. ELECTION SERMON, May 8th, 1783. The UNITED STATES elevated to Glory and Honor. A Sermon preached before His Excellency JONATHAN TRUMBULL, Esq., LL.D., and the Honorable the GENERAL ASSEMBLY of The State of CONNECTICUT, Convened at Hartford, At the Anniversary ELECTION, May 8th, 1783. By EZRA STILES, D.D., President of Yale College. *8vo,* 99 *pages; beautiful copy of the very scarce First Edition; with half title.*
NEW HAVEN: *Printed by* THOMAS & SAMUEL GREEN.
MDCCLXXXIII.

This Sermon preached just after the close of the War embraces a large amount of Aboriginal, Revolutionary and Ecclesiastical History. Presentation Copy from Dr. Stiles.

2828 CONNECTICUT. ELECTION SERMON, MAY, 8th, 1777. *The Duty and Interest of a People to sanctify the Lord of Hosts.* A Sermon preached before the General Assembly of the State of Conn., at Hartford, on the Day of the Anniversary Election, May 8, 1777. By John Devotion, Pastor of the Third Church in Saybrook. *8vo,* 39 *pages, unb.; with half title; very fine copy.*
HARTFORD: *Printed by* EBEN WATSON near the GREAT BRIDGE.
MDCCLXXVII.

This sermon, preached during "the darkest days of the Revolution," abounds with historical allusions to the various defeats and disasters which attended our Army in the winter of '76, '77. There is also appended an "Independence" Anthem, composed by Mr. Devotion, of which we give a short extract:

Piano.
Sister States, heaven's care, Philadelphi. the centre:
Brotherly love, the bond of union, heaven cement them,
Rays divine dart effulgence on the CONGRESS;
Wisdom, firmness, moderation, virtue, still attend them.

Granda.
Live, Live, Live,
Beloved of the Lord, until he comes
Whose right it is to reign;
Call her FREE *and* INDEPENDENT *STATES of AMERICA!*
Hallelujah, Praise the Lord. AMEN.

2829 CONTROVERSY BETWEEN GREAT BRITAIN AND HER COLONIES REVIEWED; the Several Pleas of the Colonies in Support of their Right to all the Liberties and Privileges of British Subjects, &c., stated and considered, and the Nature of their connection with and Dependence on Great Britain, shown upon the Evidence of Historical Facts and Authentic Records. *8vo,* 100 *p.; good copy, rare.*
BOSTON: Printed by MEIN and FLEEMING, MDCCLXIX,

2830 COOPER, WILLIAM. THE DOCTRINE OF PREDESTINATION UNTO LIFE, Explained and Vindicated. In *Four* SERMONS, preached to the Church of Christ, meeting in *Brattle Street.* With a PREFACE by the *Senior Pastors* of the Town. *Sm. 8vo, full dk. blue lev., gt. edges. Beautiful copy.*

BOSTON : Printed by J. DRAPER for J. EDWARDS and H. FOSTER, in *Cornhil.* MDCCXL.

2831 CORYAT, THOMAS. CRUDITIES ; REPRINTED from the EDITION OF 1611. To which are now added, his LETTERS from INDIA, &c., and EXTRACTS RELATING TO HIM, from various Authors ; being a more particular Account of his TRAVELS (mostly on FOOT) in DIFFERENT PARTS of the GLOBE, than any hitherto published. Together with his ORATIONS, CHARACTER, DEATH, &c. With COPPER PLATES. IN THREE VOLUMES. *8vo full cr. crim. lev. mor., gt. edges, inside borders. Beautiful copy ; quite scarce. Engraved title.*

LONDON : *Printed for W. Cater, &c.* MDCCLXXVI.

2832 COTTON, JOHN. THE POWRING out of the Seven VIALS ; OR, an Exposition of the Sixteenth Chapter of the REVELATION, with an Application of it to our Times. Wherein is revealed God's powring out of the full vials of his fierce Wrath. Very fit and necessary for this present age. Preached in Sundry Sermons at *Boston* in *New-England*, By the Learned and Reverend JOHN COTTON. *Sm. 4to, full brown lev., gt. edges, by Matthews,* 156 *p.*

LONDON : Printed for *R. S.*, and are to be sold at *Henry Overton's* Shop in *Popes Head Alley*, 1645.

2833 COVERLY, SIR ROGER DE. A CURE FOR THE SPLEEN ; or, AMUSEMENT for a WINTER'S EVENING : being the substance of a Conversation on the Times, over A FRIENDLY TANKARD AND PIPE, between, SHARP, BUMPER, FILLPOT, GRAVEAIRS, TRIM, BRIM, AND PUFF. *8vo,* 32 *p. Fine copy ; scarce.*

AMERICA : Printed and sold in the year MDCCLXXV.

Tory Document—in the form of a Dialogue—in which the complaints of the Colonists are ridiculed, and the differences between Whig and Tory made to appear very light.

2834 CUSHING, THOMAS. A SERMON Occasioned By the Great and Publick Loss in the DEATH of the Hon. THOMAS CUSHING, Speaker of the *House of Representatives* of the Province of *Massachusetts-Bay, April* 11, 1746. Delivered at the *South Church* in BOSTON, by THOMAS PRINCE. *8vo,* 38 *p. Fine copy with half title.*

BOSTON : Printed for T. RAND, in Cornhil, 1746

"Nath'l Eell's. The gift of the sorrowfull widow, May 30, 1746."

2835 DEANE, SILAS. AN ADDRESS TO THE FREE AND INDEPENDENT CITIZENS OF THE UNITED STATES OF NORTH AMERICA. *Sm. 8vo,* 30 *p., unb. Fine copy. Exceedingly scarce.*

HARTFORD : *Printed by* HUDSON and GOODWIN, MDCCLXXXIV.

Charges of fraud and peculation in the management of the public moneys, and of engaging himself in the interest of the enemies of his Country, &c., led to the publication of this Address.

2837 ELIOT, REV. JOHN, The Life of, the First Missionary to the Indians in North America. By Cotton Mather. *12mo, full crim. cr. lev., gt. top, rough edges. Scarce ; beautiful copy.*
London, 1820

2838 ENGLAND. An Address to the People of, being the Protest of a Private Person against every Suspension of Law that is liable to injure or endanger Personal Security. *8vo*, 76 *p. Fine copy ; very scarce ; privately printed.*
LONDON : Printed in the Year MDCCLXXVIII.

Acts of the British Ministry condemned in suspending the writ of Habeas Corpus. Very cautiously written, and very little said on the subject of the war, but enough to show that the writer is bitterly opposed to it.

2839 FARMER REFUTED ; or, a more impartial and comprehensive View of the Dispute between Great Britain and the Colonies, in Answer to a Letter from *A. W.* Farmer, intitled "*A View of the Controversy,*" &c. *8vo*, 78 *p. Fine copy ; very scarce.*

"The Title promises Remedies, but the box itself contains Poisons."

New York : *Printed by* James Rivington, 1775

2840 FARMER. Free Thoughts on the Proceedings of the Continental Congress, held at Philadelphia, September 5, 1774 ; wherein their Errors are exhibited, the Reasonings Confuted, &c., in a Letter to the Farmers, and other Inhabitants of North America in General, and to those of the Province of *New York* in Particular. *By a* Farmer. *8vo*, 24 *p. Fine copy ; very scarce.*

Hear me, for I will speak.

Printed (*by James Rivington in the year*, MDCCLXXIV.

2841 FRIEND. A Few Remarks upon some of the Votes and Resolutions of the Continental Congress, held at Philadelphia in September, and the Provincial Congress held at Cambridge in November, 1774. By a Friend to Peace and Good Order. *8vo*, 20 *p. Fine copy ; scarce.*
Printed for the Purchasers in 1775

2842 DICKINSON, JONATHAN. Ongelukkige Schipbreuk en Yslyke. Reystogt, van etlyke Engelschen, in den Jaare 1696 vau Jamaika in *West-Indiën*, na PENSYLVANIA t'scheep gegaan, en in de Golf van *Florida* gestrand, &c. En daaruyt vertaald door. W. Sewel. *8vo*, 100 *p. and Index.*
Te Leyden. By Pieter van der Aa, Beokverkooper.
n. d.

Illustrated by Three engravings and map—in beautiful condition.

2843 GREAT BRITAIN. The Address of the People of, to the inhabitants of America. *8vo*, 60 *p., fine copy ; scarce.*
LONDON : MDCCLXXV.

2844 GREAT BRITAIN AND THE COLONIES. A Candid Examination of the Mutual Claims of, with a Plan of Accommodation on Constitutional principles. *8vo*, 62 *pages. Fine copy. Scarce.*
NEW YORK : Printed by James Rivington, MDCCLXXIV.

2844 HARRISON, WM. HENRY. DISCOURSE ON THE ABORIGINES OF THE VALLEY OF THE OHIO. In which the opinions of the conquest of that valley by the Iroquois, or Six Nations, in the Seventeenth Century, supported by Cadwallader Colden of N. Y., Gov. Pownal of Mass., Dr. Franklin, the Hon. De Witt Clinton of N. Y., and Judge Haywood of Tenn., are examined and contested. To which are prefixed some Remarks on the Study of History. *8vo, pamphlet. Excessively scarce.* *Cincinnati*, 1838

51 *pages. Beautiful copy; almost all the edges are rough.*

2846 HEATH, WILLIAM, MEMOIRS OF. CONTAINING ANECDOTES, DETAILS OF SKIRMISHES, BATTLES AND OTHER MILITARY EVENTS during the AMERICAN WAR. Written by himself. *8vo, full crushed crimson levant morocco, gilt edges; very tall, handsome copy. Bound by Bedford.* *Printed at Boston, by* I. THOMAS *and* E. T. ANDREWS. *August,* 1798.

2847 HERBERT, GEORGE, THE WORKS OF, in Prose and Verse. In two volumes. *Roy. 8vo, full dk. blue lev., gilt top, edges rough.* LONDON: WM. PICKERING, 1853

A beautiful specimen of Pickering's incomparable Typography.

2848 JOHNSTON, CHARLES (of Botetourt Co., Va.) A NARRATIVE OF THE INCIDENTS ATTENDING THE CAPTURE, DETENTION AND RANSOM OF, who was made Prisoner by the Indians, on the River Ohio, in the year 1790; together with an Interesting Account of the fate of his Companions, Five in number, one of whom suffered at the Stake. To which are added SKETCHES OF INDIAN CHARACTER AND MANNERS, WITH ILLUSTRATIVE ANECDOTES. *8vo, full crimson crushed levant mor., gilt top, rough edges; very clean copy.* *New York*, 1827

2849 KEHUKEE BAPTIST ASSOCIATION, A CONCISE HISTORY OF. From its Original Rise to the Present Time. Wherein are its first Constitution, Increase, Numbers, Principles, Form of Government, Decorum, Revolutions that Association has passed through, etc., etc., and all other useful articles relative to Church History. By Elders LEMUEL BURKITT and JESSE READ, *Ministers in North Carolina. 8vo, full dk. blue polished cf., gt. edges. Fine copy.* HALIFAX (N. C.) *Printed by A. Hodge*, 1803

This early Southern work, contains short Biog. sketches of the Pioneers of the Baptist denomination in North Carolina, a History of its Trials during the Revolution, and of its Churches throughout that State and Virginia. A List of Subscribers is also appended, which is of some importance.

2850 LIVINGSTON, WILLIAM. A LETTER TO the Right Reverend John, Lord Bishop of Landaff; occasioned by some passages in his Lordship's Sermon on the 20th of February,

1767, in which the American Colonies are loaded with great and undeserved reproach. 8*vo*, 25 *p*. *Fine copy, valuable and scarce.*

NEW YORK: Printed for the AUTHOR, and to be sold by GARRAT NOEL, near the *Coffee House*. MDCCLXVIII.

2851 LESLIE, CHARLES. *The* RELIGION *of* JESUS CHRIST *the only True* RELIGION; or, A Short and Easie METHOD WITH THE DEISTS, wherein the *CERTAINTY* of the Christian Religion is demonstrated by *Infallible Proof* from **Four Rules**, WHICH ARE incompatible to any *imposture* that ever yet has been, or that can *possibly be*. *In a* LETTER *to a* Friend. 12*mo, paper cov.*, 58 *p*. *Fine copy.*

BOSTON: Printed by **T. Fleet**, and are to be sold by **John Checkley**, at the Sign of the *Crown* and *Blue Gate*, over against the *West* End of the Town House, 1719.

This is the very rare First American Ed. for publishing which, Mr. John Checkley was tried, convicted. and sentenced in a penalty of £50 and costs. See No. 369, page 47, of this catalogue. H. B. Dawson, Esq., has reprinted the speech of John Checkley upon his Tryal at Boston, in 1724, and in his very valuable Historical Magazine for May, 1868, says: "Mr. John Checkley was a native of Boston, who was educated at Oxford; became a publisher and bookseller at the 'sign of the Crown and Blue Gate, over against the West End of the Town House in Boston;' and was soon out of favor with those in authority in that model republican locality. They accordingly arrested Checkley; and they tried him on a trumped up charge; they dare not face the music like men, just as those who have succeeded them in that department dare not face it to-day. He defended himself in a speech of great merit; but the magistrates and ministers carried too many guns. and Checkley was convicted," etc. One Hundred Copies of this speech were reprinted in elegant style on tinted laid paper for private circulation.

2852 LOVE, THE (OECONONY) (*sic*) OF LOVE. A Poetical Essay, *Insanire docet certa ratione modoque.* A new Edition, Revised and Corrected by the Author. 8*vo*, 45 *pages, fine copy, very free.*

London, MDCCLXXXI.

"This little *Juvenile* Performance was chiefly intended as a Parody upon some of the Didactic Poets; and that it might be still the more ludicrous, the Author in some places affected the stately language of Milton."

2853 MATHER, COTTON. THE WONDERS OF THE INVISIBLE WORLD: Being an Account of the TRYALS of **Several Witches**, Lately Executed in NEW ENGLAND: And of several Remarkable Curiosities therein Occurring. Published by Special Command of his EXCELLENCY the Governor of the Province of the *Massachusetts-Bay*, in *New England*. **The Second Edition.** 62 *pages, small 4to, full crimson crushed levant mor., gilt edges, remarkably large margins; with the very rare half-title; the whole book cleaned and put in beautiful condition.*

Printed first at *Boston*, in *New England*, and reprinted at *London*, for *John Dunton*, at the *Raven* in the *Poultrey*. 1693.

2854 MATHER, SAMUEL. AN | APOLOGY | For the Liberties of the Churches in | *New England:* | To which is prefixed, | A Discourse concerning | *Congregational Churches.* 8*vo, full dark brown mor., gilt edges. Bound by Matthews. Very scarce.*

BOSTON: Printed by T. Fleet, for DANIEL HENCHMAN, *over against the Brick Meeting House in Cornhill.* 1738.

2855 MODERN PROPENSITIES; or, an Essay on Strangulation, Steam Stimulus, Manuduction, &c.; including Anecdotes of Modern Characters. 8*vo*, 90 *pages, very scarce, free and licentious.* *London*, n. d. (1780 ?)

2856 MARYLAND HIST. SOC. 1.—Const. and By-Laws, 1867. 2.—Memoir of J. H. Alexander. By Wm. Pinkney. 3.—The First Commander of Kent Island. By Sebastian F. Streeter. [3 *pamphs.*]

The above should have been catalogued with No. 977, and belong to the set.

2857 NEW ENGLAND, A CHRONOLOGICAL HISTORY OF—in the Form of Annals. By Thomas Prince. THIRD EDITION: TO WHICH IS ADDED, A MEMOIR OF THE AUTHOR, an attempt towards a perfect Catalogue of his Writings, a Genealogy of his Family, and the names of the Subscribers to the original Edition. By Samuel G. Drake. *Imperial* 8*vo, full crushed crimson levant gilt top, rough edges, very scarce, only Thirty Copies.* *Boston*, 1852.

2858 NORTH AMERICAN COLONIES, CONSIDERATIONS RELATIVE TO. 8*vo*, 48 *pages, scarce, fine copy.* *LONDON*, MDCCLXV.

2859 OHIO. A TOPOGRAPHICAL DESCRIPTION OF THE STATE OF OHIO, INDIANA TERRITORY, AND LOUISIANA, comprehending the Ohio and Mississippi Rivers, the face of the Country, Soils, Waters, Towns, Villages, etc., and A CONCISE ACCOUNT OF THE INDIAN TRIBES west of the Mississippi. To which is added AN INTERESTING JOURNAL OF MR. CHARLES LE RAYE, while a captive of the Sioux nation. By a late Officer of the U. S. Army (Cutler). 8*vo, full crimson crushed levant mor., gilt edges, beautiful copy, frontis. and engravings, very scarce.* *Boston*, 1812

2860 PHILOPOLITIES. A FREE AND CALM CONSIDERATION of the Unhappy MISUNDERSTANDINGS and DEBATES, which have arisen, and yet subsist, between Great-Britain and these American Colonies, contained in Eight Letters, formerly printed in the *Essex Gazette.* Written by one, who was born in the Colony of the *Massachusetts-Bay*, before King WILLIAM III. and Queen MARY II. ascended the Throne. 8*vo*, 52 *pages, fine copy, very rare.* *SALEM:* Printed by S. and E. HALL, 1774.

2861 PILGRIM FATHERS, CHRONICLES OF THE, of the Colony of Plymouth, from 1602 to 1625. Now first collected from original Records and Contemporaneous printed Documents, and Illustrated with Notes. By Alexander Young. Second Edition. 8*vo, full crushed crimson levant mor., gilt top, rough edges, splendid copy, very scarce. Portrait.*

BOSTON: *Charles C. Little and James Brown*, MDCCCXLIV.

"The mother of us all."

2862 QUINCY, JOSIAH. OBSERVATIONS on the Act of Parliament called Boston Port-Bill; with Thoughts on Civil Society and Standing Armies. 8*vo*, 82 *pages, uncut, very scarce in this condition.*

BOSTON, N. E.: Printed for, and sold by EDES and GILL, in Queen Street. 1774.

2863 ROSS, ROBERT. (Pastor of the Church in *Stratfield*.) A SERMON, in which the UNION of the COLONIES is considered and recommended; and the bad Consequences of Divisions are represented. Delivered on the PUBLIC THANKSGIVING, November sixteenth, 1775. 8vo, 28 *pages, fine copy, very scarce.*
NEW YORK: Printed by JOHN HOLT, in WATER STREET, near the Coffee House. M,DCC,LXXVI.

2864 SHEPARD, THOMAS. (*Minister of the Gospel at Cambridge, in New England.*) THE CLEAR SUNSHINE OF THE GOSPEL, BREAKING FORTH UPON THE *INDIANS* IN NEW ENGLAND; Or, An Historicall Narration of God's Wonderfull Workings upon sundry of the Indians, both Chief Governors and Common-people, etc. *Sm. 4to, full smooth mor., gilt edges,* 38 *pages, large margins, fine copy, excessively scarce.*
London: Printed by R. Cotes for John Bellamy, at the *three golden Lions* in *Cornhill, near the Royall Exchange.* 1648.

2865 SHEPARD, THOMAS. THE SOUND BELEEVER. A Treatise of Evangelicall Conversion. 8vo, *full polished calf, blue, gilt edges, fine copy.* *LONDON: Printed in the Yeere* 1652.

2866 SHEPPARD, THOMAS. The | Sincere Convert: | DISCOVERING | the small number of true | BELEEVERS, | And the great difficulty of Saving | CONVERSION | etc. Whereto is now added the *Saint's Jewell;* and the *Soul's Invitation* unto *Jesus Christ.* 8vo, *full dark blue levant mor., gilt edges, fine copy.*
London: Printed by *E. Cotes,* for *John Sweeting,* at the Angel, in *Pope's-head Alley.* 1655.

2867 SHEPHARD, THOMAS. THE FIRST PRINCIPLES of the ORACLES of GOD. 8vo, *full polished calf, gilt edges, fine copy,* 17 *pages.*
LONDON: Printed for *John Rothwel.* 1655.

2868 SIMMS, J. R. THE AMERICAN SPY; or, Freedom's Early Sacrifice: a Tale of the Revolution, founded upon Fact. Frontis. Hale's Monument. *Large paper copy, only* 28 *copies, full crimson crushed levant mor., gilt top, rough edges.*
Albany: J. Munsell, 1857

2869 STILES, EZRA. A HISTORY OF THREE OF THE JUDGES OF KING CHARLES I. Major-General WHALLEY, Major-General GOFFE and Colonel DIXWELL: who, at the Restoration, 1660, fled to America; and were secreted and concealed, in Massachusetts and Connecticut, for near Thirty Years. WITH AN ACCOUNT OF MR. THEOPHILUS WHALE, of Narragansett, *supposed to have been also one of the Judges.* 8vo, *full polished calf, gilt edges. Bound by Bedford. With Portrait of Stiles, and all the Plates; beautiful copy; exceedingly scarce.*
HARTFORD: PRINTED BY ELISHA BABCOCK, 1794.

2870 STODDARD, SOLOMON. (*Pastor of the Church in Northampton.*) A GUIDE TO CHRIST; or, the Way of Directing Souls that are under the Work of Conversion. Compiled for the Help of Young Ministers. With an Epistle perfixed, (sic) by the Reverend Dr. *Increase Mather.* 12*mo, orig. b'dg., calf,* 85 *pages, good copy.*

BOSTON: Printed by *J. Draper,* for D. HENCHMAN, in *Cornhill,* MDCCXXXV.

2871 STRICTURES ON A PAMPHLET entitled a "Friendly Address to All Reasonable Americans on the subject of our Political Confusions," addressed to the PEOPLE of AMERICA. "Let's Canvas Him in his broad Cardinal's Hat." 8*vo,* 20 *pages, fine copy, scarce.*

AMERICA: BOSTON: Re-printed. M,DCC,LXX,V.

2872 STRONG, JA. *Batchelour, &c.* JOANEREIDOS, or Feminine Valour Eminently discovered in Westerne Women; as well by defying the mercilesse Enemy at the face abroad, as by fighting against them in Garrison Townes. *Sm.* 4*to;* 42 *pages; very curious;* 6 *pages of the Poem, and* 36 *pages Commendatory!*

Printed An. Dom., 1645.

2873 T. W. A LETTER TO A FRIEND, GIVING a concise, but just, representation of the hardships and sufferings the town of BOSTON is exposed to and must undergo, in consequence of the late ACT of the BRITISH PARLIAMENT; which, by shutting up its port, has put a fatal bar in the way of that commercial business on which it depended for its support. *By* T.W., *a* BOSTONIAN. 8*vo,* 35 *pages, fine copy; rare.*

BOSTON, N. E. MDCCLXXIV.

2874 VIRGINIAN, A LETTER from, to the Members of the Congress to be held at Philadelphia, on the first of September, 1774. 8*vo,* 31 *p., fine copy; extremely scarce.* BOSTON, 1774

2875 WALTON, ISAAC. THE COMPLETE ANGLER; OR, CONTEMPLATIVE MAN'S RECREATION; being a Discourse on Rivers, Fish-Ponds, Fish, and Fishing. In Two Parts;—The first written by Isaac Walton; the second by Charles Cotton, Esq. With the Lives of the Authors; and notes Historical, Critical, Supplementary, and Explanatory. By Sir John Hawkins, Knt. *Roy.* 8*vo, full crim. cr. lev. mor., gt. top, rough edges. Beautiful copy, and very scarce in this condition.* 7*th Ed.*

LONDON: *Printed for Samuel Bagster.* 1808

2876 WALTON ISAAC, AND CHARLES COTTON. THE COMPLETE ANGLER; OR, CONTEMPLATIVE MAN'S RECREATION; being a Discourse on RIVERS, FISH-PONDS, FISH AND FISHING. In Two Parts. With the Lives of the Authors; and Notes, Historical, Supplementary, and Explanatory. By Sir John Hawkins, and the Present Editor. Portrait of Walton, after Housemann; and Cotton, after Sir Peter Lely. *Roy.* 8*vo, full crimson crushed lev., mor., gilt top, rough edges; very fine copy; extremely scarce in this condition. Eighth Edition.*

LONDON: PRINTED FOR SAMUEL BAGSTER. MDCCCXV

2877 WASHINGTON, GEORGE, A FUNERAL ORATION ON. By John Miller Russell. 8*vo,* 22 *pp., uncut, and some of the pages unopened; beautiful copy, extremely rare.*

BOSTON: JOHN RUSSELL. 1800

See Woodward's Catalogue, No. 5997.

2878 WASHINGTON, GEORGE. An Address in Latin, by Joseph Willard, President, and a Discourse in English, by David Tappan, delivered before the University, in Cambridge, February 21, 1800, in Solemn Commemoration of General George Washington. *8vo, 44 pp., fine copy.*

(*Charlestown*). *E Typis* Samuel Etheridge. MDCCC.

2879 WASHINGTON, GEORGE. A History of the Life and Death, Virtues and Exploits of General George Washington; faithfully taken from Authentic Documents, and, now, in a Second Edition, improved, respectfully offered to the perusal of his countrymen; as also, all others who wish to see human nature in its most finished form.

A life, how glorious, to his country led!
Belov'd while living, as rever'd, now dead.
May his example, virtuous deeds inspire!
Let future ages read it—and admire!

By the Rev. M. L. Weems, of Lodge No. 50—Dumfries. *8vo, 82 pp. Port. in oval and square, with the name,* "G. Washington," *beneath; by Tanner. Very scarce, beautiful copy, rough edges. Dedicated to "Mrs Martha Washington."*

Philadelphia: Re-printed by John Bioren. (1800.)

2880 WASHINGTONIANA: Containing a Sketch of the Life and Death of the Late GEN. GEORGE WASHINGTON; with a collection of elegant Eulogies, Orations, Poems, &c., sacred to his Memory; also an Appendix, comprising all his most valuable papers, and his last Will and Testament. *8vo, full dk. blue levant; gilt edges; large, fine, clean copy. Portrait.*

Lancaster, 1802

2881 WASHINGTON'S Valedictory Address to the People of the United States. Published by the Washington Benevolent Society of Massachusetts. *24mo, unbound, 62 pp., beautiful copy.*

Boston: 1812

2882 WASHINGTON, GEN. GEORGE, Biographical Memoirs of the Illustrious,—late President of the United States of America, and *Commander-in-chief of their Armies during the Revolutionary War.* Dedicated to the Youth of America. *12mo, full crimson crushed levant mor., gilt edges, inside borders; by Matthews.* Portrait of Washington—"Pro Patria."

Barnard, Vt. Published by Joseph Dix, 1813

2883 WASHINGTONIANA; Containing a Biographical Sketch of the late Gen. George Washington; with various outlines of his Character, etc., and an Account of the various Funeral Honors devoted to his Memory. To which are annexed, his Will and Schedule of his Property. Embellished with a good Likeness. *Imp. 8vo, full dk. blue crushed levant, gilt top, rough edges, inside tooling. Baltimore:* 1800. *By E. Dexter & Son. New York,* 1855. Small paper. 100 copies. *Reprinted.*

2884 WYOMING, (PA.) A Sketch of the History of, By the late Isaac A. Chapman, Esq. To which is added an Appendix, containing a statistical account of the valley and adjacent country. By a Gentleman of Wilkesbarre. *8vo, hf. dk. gr. lev. mor., rough edges, gilt tops, fine copy, very scarce.* *Wilkesbarre*, 1830

2885 WASHINGTON. GENERAL GEORGE. A HISTORY OF THE LIFE AND DEATH, VIRTUES AND EXPLOITS OF, faithfully taken from authentic Documents, and now, in a Third Edition, improved. *8vo, unbound,* 61 *pp., fine copy, very scarce.*
Elizabeth-Town, N. J. n. d.

2886 WASHINGTON, GEORGE. ORATION IN COMMEMORATION OF THE BIRTHDAY OF. Delivered at Salem, Mass., February 22d, 1793. By William Bentley D. D. *8vo, in sheets, folded,* 27 *pp.*
Morrisania, N. Y., 1870

Printed for private circulation only, and the Edition numbers only Thirty Copies. The wide-spread reputation of Dr. Bentley, as well as the occasion which called forth this *Oration,* will serve to make it among the most highly-prized of the privately-printed tracts of the day; while collectors of Washingtoniana will search in vain for anything which is better entitled to their respect.—*Hist. Mag.*

HISTORICAL SOCIETY PAMPHLETS.

2887 AMERICAN HISTORICAL SOCIETY. Discourse at the Capitol. By Hon. Lewis Cass. 1836.

2888 AMERICAN GEOLOGISTS AND NATURALISTS' ASSOC. Address by Prof. Silliman. *N. Y.*, 1842

2889 —— —— —— Address by Prof. Hitchcock. April 5, 1841. *Phila.*

2890 —— GEOG. AND STATIS. SOC. Bulletin Vol. I., August, 1852.
—— —— " " I., Part III., 1855
—— —— " " I., " II., 1854.
—— —— "New York Harbor." By D. E. Wheeler. 1856.
—— —— "Syrian Exploration." *N. Y.*, 1857
—— —— "Arizona and Sonora." By S. Mowry. 1859.
—— —— Annual Report. 1857
—— —— By-Laws. 1855
—— —— Object and Plans. 1857
—— —— Catalogue of Library. 1857
—— —— Report of Chamber of Com. 1857
—— —— Statement of the Objects and Organization of, and Charter. 1857
—— —— "Denmark and its Relations." By J. Leavitt. *N. Y.*, 1864

2891 —— STATIS. ASSOC. Const. and By-Laws. 1840.
—— —— Collections. *Boston*, 1843

2892 —— ASSOC. FOR ADVANCEMENT OF SCIENCE. Address in Commemoration of S. C. Walker. By B. A. Gould, April 29, 1854.

2893 —— Assoc. Address by J. D. Dana, August, 1855.

2894 —— PHILOSOPHICAL SOC. Discourse on the Early History of Pennsylvania. By P. S. Du Ponceau. *Very scarce* 1821

2895 American Ethnological Society, Bulletin of—January, 1861.
——— ——— ——— Memoir on the European Colonization of America in Ante-Historic Times. By Dr. C. Adolph Zestermann. April, 1851. *Scarce.*

2896 American Antiquarian Society. Vol. III., Part I. Trans. and Collections of. 1850.
——— Proceedings at the Annual Meeting, Oct. 21, 1866.
——— " " " " " 22, 1860.
——— " at Semi-Annual Meeting, April 25, 1860.

2897 Buffalo Historical Soc. The Niagara Frontier, embracing Sketches of its Early History and Indian names. By Orasmus Marshall.

2898 Essex Historical Soc. (Salem, Mass.) Disc. by Joseph Story. Sept. 18, 1828.

2899 Iowa Historical Soc. Annals of Iowa. Vol. VII., No. I. Jan., 1869.

2900 Maine Historical Soc. Annual Discourse. By George Folsom. 1847.
——— ——— Remarks on the Popham Colony. By S. F. Haven. 1865.
——— ——— Address by R. C. Winthrop. Sept. 5, 1849.

2901 Maryland Historical Soc. Memoir of Benj. Banneker. 1845.
——— Discourse on Sir Walter Raleigh. 1846.
——— Memoir of Major Sam'l Ringgold. 1847.
——— Disc. at Dedication of Athenæum. 1848.
——— Origin and Growth of Civil Liberty in Maryland. 1850.
——— Tah-gah-jute and Capt. Cresap. 1851.
——— Disc. on the African Slave Trade in Jamaica. 1854.
——— Maryland Two Hundred Years Ago. 1852.
——— Martin Behaim. 1855.
——— Memoir of Baron De Kalb. 1858.
——— Memoir of John H. Alexander. 1867.
——— and Peabody Inst. 1866.
——— Hist. Possessions and Prospects. 1867.
——— Catalogue of Paintings. 1868.
——— First Commander at Kent Island. 1868.

2902 Massachusetts Historical Soc. Act of Incorporation, By-Laws, Catal. of Members and Circular Letters. *Boston*, 1813
——— ——— Addition to Wood's Continuation of Goldsmith's Hist. of England. *Boston*, 1815
——— ——— List of Portraits in the Hall. 1838
——— ——— The New Eng. Confederacy of 1642. By John Quincy Adams. 1847
——— ——— Memoir of Hon. Abbott Lawrence. 1856

2902 MASSACHUSETTS HISTORICAL SOC. Description of the Dowse Library. 1857

—— —— In Memory of W. H. Prescott. 1859.

—— —— Memoir of Thad. Mason Harris. 1859

—— —— Naturalization in the American Colonies. 1859

—— —— Memoir of Nathan Appleton. 1861

—— —— Remarks on the Narragansett Patent 1863

—— —— Journal de Castorland. 1864

—— —— Memoir of Josiah Quincy. 1867

—— —— Memoir of Joseph Story. 1868

—— —— Mass. and its Early History. 1869

2903 MECHANICS' SOC. (of New York). Progress of the City. A Lecture by Chas. King. 1852.

2904 MICHIGAN HIST. SOC. Annual Discourse by H. R. Schoolcraft. *Rare.* *Detroit*, 1830

2905 MINNESOTA HIST. SOC., Collections of—containing Voyage to the Falls of St. Anthony in 1817. By Maj. Long. *Phila.*, 1860

2906 MONTREAL HIST. SOC. Memoires et Documents. 1859.

2907 NEW YORK HIST. SOC. An Anniversary Discourse, deliv. Dec. 7, 1818, by G. C. Verplanck. *8vo, orig. covers, uncut,* 121 *pages, very scarce.* *N. Y.*, 1818

2908 NEW JERSEY HIST. SOC. "The Goodly Heritage of Jerseymen." Address by Bp. Doane, Jan. 15, 1846. *Burlington*

2909 OHIO HIST. SOC. "Facts and Conditions of Progress in the North West." Annual Disc., by T. W. Gallagher. *Cinn.*, 1850

2910 PENNSYLVANIA HIST. SOC. Disc. on the Colonial History of the Eastern and some of the Southern States. By Job R. Tyson. Feb'y 21, 1842. *8vo,* 64 *pages; fine copy; scarce.*

—— —— History of the Ordinance of 1787. By Edward Coles. *8vo, uncut,* 33 *pages.* *Press of the Soc.*, 1856

—— —— Resolutions of, on Death of A. Lincoln. *8vo,* 4 *pages.*

2911 SOUTH CAROLINA HIST. SOC. First and Second Reports of the Historical Com. Prepared by Benj. Elliott. *8vo,* 24 *pages.* *Charleston*, 1835

2912 VERMONT HIST. SOC. Address by D. P. Thompson. 1850.

—— Two Addresses by P. H. White and A. D. Hagar. 1858.

—— Proceedings at Special Meeting in Burlington. 1862.

—— Annual Address by J. W. De Peyster. 1864.

—— Addresses by Edmunds, White and Rankin. 1866.

—— Memorial Address on Hon. Jacob Collamore. By J. Barrett. *Woodstock*, 1868

2913 VIRGINIA HIST. REGISTER. Edited by Wm. Maxwell. Vol. VI. 1853.

2914 WISCONSIN HIST. SOC. "The Influence of Hist.," etc. By Paul R. Chadbourne. Jan. 30, 1868. *Madison*

2915 Miscellaneous. *Valuable.* [*Ten.*]

Report of Capt. Brewerton, connected with the Improvement of the Hudson River Navigation. 24 *pages.* *Albany,* 1839

GENET, EDMUND CHARLES. Memorial on the Alluvions or Obstructions at the head of the Navigation of the River Hudson. 8*vo*, 46 *pages, fine copy, very scarce.* *Albany,* 1818

Elmendorf, L. Facts and Observations on the Merits of the Memorial of the President and Directors of the first Great South-Western Turn-Pike Road Company, for relief. 15 *pages.* *Albany,* 1829

Act Incorporating the Proprietors of the Locks and Canals on the Merrimac River. *Boston,* 1792

By-Laws of the same. *Newburyport,* 1792

Jackson, Andrew. Life of. By Amos Kendall. No. 1. 48 *pages, uncut.* *N. Y.,* 1843

——— Official Record of the Court-Martial, which tried, and the orders of—for shooting the six militiamen. *Uncut,* 32 *pages, very scarce.* *Wash.,* 1828

——— Addresses on the presentation of the sword of—to the U. S. Feb. 26, 1855. 8*vo*, *cloth,* 40 *pages.* *Wash.,* 1855

——— Review of the Veto Message on the Bank of the U. S. *Uncut,* 24 *pages.*

Schuyler, Maj.-Gen. Philip. Correspondence and Remarks upon Bancroft's Hist. of the Northern Campaign of 1777. By Geo. L. Schuyler. *Uncut,* 47 *pages.* *N. Y.,* 1867

2916 Miscellaneous. [*Twelve*].

ORLEANS COUNTY, Vt. History of the Cong'l. Churches, with Biographical Notices of the Pastors and Native Ministers. By Pliny H. White. 8*vo, uncut,* 61 *p.* *Rutland,* 1868

WESTHAMPTON, Mass. Memorial of the Reunion of the Natives, Sept. 5, 1866. Contains Historical Address, by C. P. Judd and Otis Clapp. 8*vo,* 85 *p.; fine copy.*

> "Young folks are smart, but all ain't good thet's new;
> I guess the gran'thers they knowed sunthin, 'tu."

BATTLE OF THE FROGS at Windham, 1758, with various accounts and three of the most popular Ballads on the subject. By W. L. Weaver. 8*vo,* 31 *p.; scarce.* *Willimantic, Conn.,* 1857

Blake, Mortimer. "The Issues of the Rebellion," Sermon, before the Taunton and Raynham Volunteers, Col. D. N. Couch, June 2, 1861, Sabbath evening. 13 *p.; fine copy.* *Taunton,* 1861

Rensselaer County, N. Y. A Geological and Agricultural Survey of, to which is annexed a Geological Profile. Taken under the direction of the Hon. Stephen Van Rensselaer. By Amos Eaton. *8vo,* 70 *p. ; fine copy, very scarce.* *Albany,* 1822

Fall River, Mass. Extract from a Review. 6 *p.*

Yankee Farmer. Peace without Dishonor, War without Hope. Enquiry into the question of the Chesapeake. *8vo, uncut,* 43 *p. ; fine copy.* *Boston,* 1807

Channing, W. E. Sermon, Aug. 20, 1812, day of Fasting and Prayer, in consequence of Declaration of War. *Uncut,* 15 *p.* *Boston,* 1812

Perpetual War, the Policy of Mr. Madison. *8vo, uncut,* 119 *p. ; beautiful copy.* *Boston,* 1812

Morris, Gouverneur. Oration, deliv. June 29, 1814, on the recent deliverance of Europe from Mil. Despotism. *Uncut,* 16 *p. ; scarce.* *Salem,* 1814

North Amer. Rev. To the Editor of. By Patrick S. Casserly. 16 *p.*

Parker, Theo. The Nebraska Question. Some Thoughts on the new assault upon Freedom in America, and the General state of the country, in a Discourse, Feb. 12, 1854. *8vo,* 72 *p. ; scarce.* *Boston,* 1854

2917 Miscellaneous. [*Sixteen*].

Thoughts, in Answer to a Question respecting the Division of the States. By a Mass. Farmer. *8vo, uncut,* 24 *p.* 1813

Defense of the Legislature of Mass.; or, the Rights of New England Vindicated. *8vo, uncut ;* 28 *p.* *Boston,* 1804

Amendments of the Constitution of Mass., proposed by the Convention of Delegates, etc., assembled at Boston, Nov. 1820. *Uncut,* 32 *p.* *Boston,* 1821

Rules of the Bar of the County of Suffolk. *8vo, stiff cov.,* 28 *p.* *Boston,* 1827

Thatcher, Peter O. Address, before the Bar of Suffolk Co., March, 1831. *8vo, uncut,* 40 *p.* *Boston,* 1831

Thomas, Daniel. Oration in Bridgewater, Sept. 12, 1804. *Uncut,* 19 *p.* *Prov.,* 1804

Upham, Charles W. Remarks of, on the Institutions of Mass., and the Ordinance of 1787, delivered Feb. 27, 1855. *Wash.,* 1855

Grand National Peace Jubilee. Official Monthly Bulletin. No. I. Feb.

Mass. College of Pharmacy. Report of Com. on Spirituous Liquors. *Boston,* 1867

Harvard University. The Harvard Lyceum. Vol. I., No. 1, July 14, 1810. *Uncut,* 24 *p.*

——— Don Quixotes at College; or, a History of the Gallant Adventures lately achieved; interspersed with some facetious reasonings. By a Senior. *Uncut,* 20 *p. ; very scarce.* *Boston,* 1807

Harv. Univ. Re-Commencement, Commencement again, Commencement in earnest, Commencement indeed. Called also Censure, Scandal, Vague Report, or what you please. A Poem. By a Brother. *Uncut*, 11 *p*. *Boston*, 1811

——— Re-Re-Commencement ; a kind of a Poem ; calculated to be recited before an assemblage of N. England Divines. By a Friend of Everybody. *Uncut*, 8 *p*. *Salem*, 1812

——— Inaugural Discourse, Dec. 8, 1819. By E. T. Channing. *Uncut*, 31 *p*. *Cambridge*, 1819

Duane, W. J. Letters to the people of Pennsylvania, on the Internal Improvement of the State, by means of roads and canals. 8*vo*, 125 *p*. *Phila.*, 1811

Report of Comm. of the Senate of N. Y., to explore the route of an inland navigation ; from Hudson's River to Lakes Ontario and Erie. 35 *p*. *Albany*, 1811

2918 Miscellaneous, [*Thirteen*].

Thirteenth Annual Report of the Bd. of Publication of the Presb. Church. *Phila.*, 1851

Report of Joint Com. of Gen'l. Conv., 1841, on Standard Prayer Book. 40 *p*.

Report of Com. from "St. George's Church" in N. Y., Beekman St. *N. Y.*, 1849

Communication to the Rector, etc., of "St. George's Church." *N. Y.*, 1850

Sketches of Liberia, comprising a brief account of the Geography, Climate, Productions and Diseases. By J. W. Lugenbeel, 8*vo*, 43 *p*., *dbl. col.* *Wash.*, 1850

Information about going to Liberia. 16 *p*. *Wash.*, 1848

Appeal to the Managers of St. Luke's Hospital, etc. *N. Y.*, 1852

Muhlenberg, W. A. A Plea for a Church Hospital in N. Y. City. *N. Y.*, 1850

Report of Commissioners of Fisheries, Jan. 1, 1868. *Boston.*

Report of the Smithsonian Institution on the History of the Discovery of Neptune. By B. A Gould. 56 *p*. *Wash.*, 1850

Report of the Librarian of the State Library, Sept. 30, 1867. *Boston*

Report of the U. S. Revenue Com. on Petroleum. *Treas. Dept.*, 1866.

Sermon and other Exercises at the Ordination of Alex. McKenzie, Aug. 28, 1861. *Augusta, Me.*, 1861

2919 Miscellaneous. [*Eleven*].

Manning, J. M. Discourse, Dec. 13, 1863, in Old South Church, Boston.

Morris, Gouverneur. Oration, deliv. June 29, 1814, on the recent delivr. of Europe from MIlitary Despotism. *8vo, uncut*, 16 *p.* *Salem*, 1814

Names and Sketches of nearly two thousand of the Richest Men of Mass. 2nd ed., with additions. *8vo*, 224 *p., fine copy, very scarce.* *Boston*, 1852

Mass. House Doc. No. 150, in relation to the Hutchinson Papers, March 19, 1868.

Necrological Report of Middlebury College for 1867. 8 *p., dbl. col.*

Montgomery, N. Y. Historical Disc., regarding the Goodwill Presbyterian Church, 125th anniv. of its settlement. By D. M. Maclise. 32 *p.* *N. Y.*, 1865

Macintosh, Sir James. Discourse on the Study of the Law of Nature and of Nations. *8vo*, 103 *p.* *Boston*, 1843

Minutes of the General Conf. of Cong'l. Churches in Maine, 1863.

Mr. Dexter's Address to the Electors of Mass. *Boston*, 1814

Address to the Electors of Mass., 1814.

Quincy, Josiah. Remarks on some of the Provisions of the Laws of Mass. affecting Poverty, Vice and Crime. *Cambridge*, 1822.

2920 Miscellaneous. [*Eleven*].

Worcester, Samuel. Sermon July 23, 1812. Public Fast on account of the War. *8vo*, 24 *p.* *Salem*, 1812

Madison Univ. Speech of Mr. MacMaster, Oct. 4, 1844. *8vo*, 39 *p.* *Madison, Ind.*, 1844

Macdill, D. Sketch of the History of the Assoc. Ref. Church, deliv. in Oxford, O., March 2, 1843.

The New States; or, a Comparison of the Wealth, Strength and Population of the Northern and Southern States. *8vo*, 36 *p.* *Boston*, 1818

The Devil let Loose; or, a Wonderful Instance of the Goodness of God. *8vo*, 24 *p., autog. of Uzal Ogden.* *N. Y.*, 1805

Mellen, Granville. "The Rest of the Nations." A Poem. *8vo*, 28 *p.* *Portland*, 1826

Bradford, G. Address before the Mass. Temp. Soc., June, 1826. *8vo, uncut*, 24 *p.* *Boston*

Remarks on the Character and Writings of John Milton. *8vo*, 48 *p.* *Boston*, 1826

Sprague, Charles. Address before the Mass. Temp. Soc., May 31, 1827. *8vo*, 30 *p.; scarce.* *Boston*, 1827

Report and Resolves of the State of Maine Legist. respecting international Lit. Exchanges. *8vo*, 109 *p.* *Augusta*, 1847

Prospectus of the Union Ins. Co. *N. Y.*, 1818

2921 Miscellaneous. [*Twenty-nine*].

Newark College, N. J. Address, by Thos. E. Bond, Sept. 23, 1840.

Lindsly, Philip. Plea for the Theological Seminary at Princeton, N. J. *Trenton*, 1821

Prot. Epis. Miss. Soc. 4th Annual Report, 1820.
——— 5th Annual Report, 1821.
——— 10th Annual Report, 1826.
——— 11th Annual Report, 1827.
——— 13th Annual Report, 1829.
——— 15th Annual Report, 1831.
——— Address by Bp. Hobart, 1817.
——— ——— C. R. Duffie, 1826.
——— Sermon by J. M. Wainwright, 1828.
——— ——— Bp. Otey, 1838.
——— ——— J. Johns, 1838.
——— ——— J. S. Stone, 1839.
——— Letters by Bp. Onderdonk.
——— Spirit of Missions, July, 1850.
N. Y. Young Men's Miss. Soc. First and Fifth Annual Reports, 1820 and 1824. Two.
Foreign Miss. Soc. Sermon by Erskine Mason.
——— ——— Asa D. Smith.
——— ——— M. S. Hutton.
——— ——— S. T. Spear.
——— ——— R. W. Clarke.
Amer. Baptist Home Miss. Soc. Discourse by Stephen Chapin. *Balto.*, 1841
——— Discourse by W. R. Williams, Phila., June 7, 1836
Baptist Home Miss. Soc., London. Two Sermons, Semi-Centennial of its organization. 8*vo*, 83 *p.* *London*, 1842
Boston Baptist For. Miss. Soc. Sermon by F. Wayland.
American Bd. of Com. for For. Miss., 24th Annual Report.
——— Sermon by T. H. Skinner.

2922 Miscellaneous. [*Twelve.*]

Letters on the New Theatre.
Letter from the Secry. of State to Mr. Monroe, on the Subject of the Attack on the Chesapeake, March 23, 1808. 8*vo*, 88 *pages.* *City of Washington*, 1808
Letters from the Secry. of State to Mr. Monroe on the subject of Impressments, March 23, 1808. 8*vo*, 137 *pages.* *Washington City*, 1808
Memorial of Benj. Silliman. 9 *pages.*
Mass. Charitable Mech. Assoc. Tenth Exhibition, Sept., 1865. *Boston*, 1865
Maryland Hist. Soc. and the Peabody Institute Trustees. Report March 5, 1866. 15 *pages.*
Maryland Toleration; or, Sketches of the Early History of Md., to the year 1650. By Rev. Ethan Allen. 8*vo*, 64 *pages; very scarce; fine copy.* *Baltimore*, 1855
Historical Discourse deliv. at Worcester in the Old South Meeting-House, Sept. 22, 1863, the Hundredth Anniv. of its Erection. By Leonard Bacon. Intro. remarks by Ira M. Barton, and an appendix. *Frontis.* 8*vo*, 106 *pages; valuable; fine copy.* *Worcester*, 1863

Boston Grammar Schools. Course of Study.
——— Report on the Public Schools of N. Y., Phila., Balto. and Washington. *8vo*, 64 *pages*. *Boston*, 1867
——— Second Report on Truancy and Compulsory Educ. 55 *pages*.
——— Description of the City Hosp. *Illus.* *8vo*, 131 *pages*. *Boston*, 1865

2923 Miscellaneous. [*Twelve.*]

Missisquoi Springs and their Wonderful Cures.
Declaration of the County of Essex (Mass.), by its Delegates in Conv., respecting Embargo, July 21, 1812. *8vo, uncut; scarce.* 16 *pages*. *Salem*, 1812
Quincy, Josiah. Speech Jan. 5, 1813. *8vo, uncut.* 33 *pages*.
Mr. Madison's War, &c. By a New Eng. Farmer. *8vo*, 62 *pages*. *Boston*, 1812
Austin, Samuel. The Apology of Patriots ; or, the heresy of the friends of the Washington and peace policy defended. Sermon Augt. 20, 1812. *8vo, uncut.* *Worcester*, 1812
Mead, Samuel. Sermon on the War, Augt. 20, 1812. *Uncut.* *Newburyport*, 1812
Osgood, David. Solemn Protest against the Declaration of War. *Exeter, N. H.*, 1812
Morse, Jedidiah. Sermon, July 23, 1812, on day of Public Fast on account of the War. *Uncut*, 32 *pages*. *Charlestown*, 1812
Treaty of Peace signed at Ghent, 1814, and all others since 1783. *Uncut*, 24 *pages*. *Boston*, 1815
Features of Mr. Jay's Treaty. *Uncut.* *Phila.*, 1795
Harrison, Wm. H. Memorial of the National Bereavement, by H. N. Wilson. *Scarce.* *Sag-Harbor, L. I.*, 1841.
New Haven Col. Hist. Society. Papers of. Vol. I., 1865. 15 *pages*.

2924 Miscellaneous. [*Seventeen.*]

N. Y. Aux. Bible Society. Act. of Incorp. and By-Laws. *N. Y.*, 1818
——— Eleventh and Twelfth Annual Reports, 1827. (2.)
Bible Society of Central N. Y. Sermon by John C. Rudd, July 12, 1837.
N. Y. Bible Soc. Sermon by H. Wheaton, Sept. 25, 1844.
Washington Bible Soc. Tidings of Great Joy for all People. Sermon, Jan. 31, 1816, at Granville, N. Y. *8vo*, 32 *pages; scarce.* *Salem, N. Y.*, 1816
Scoharie Bible Soc. Sermon by John F. Schermerhorn, Jan., 1817. *8vo*, 20 *pages; scarce.* *Albany*, 1817
Park, E. A. Disc. before Convention of Cong'l Ministers. May 30, 1850. *8vo*, 44 *pages*. *Boston*
Princeton College, N. J. Sermon by Philip Lindsly. May 27, 1821. 23 *pages*.
College of New Jersey. Address by R. S. Coxe, Sept. 24,

College of New Jersey. Address by George M. Dallas, Sept. 27, 1831. 26 *pages.*
——— Address by John Sergeant, Sept. 25, 1833. 44 *p.*
——— Address by William Gaston, Sept. 29, 1835. 42 *pages.*
——— Address by S. J. Wilkin, Sept. 28, 1842.
——— Address by Samuel L. Southard, Sept. 26, 1832.
——— Catalogue, 1827.
Rutgers College. Address by William Wirt, July 20, 1830.

2925 Miscellaneous. [*Twenty-five.*]

Maine Miss. Soc. Sermon by Allen Greely, June 23, 1824.
Mass. Dom. Miss. Soc. 5th Ann. Report, 1823.
American Home Miss. Soc. Sermon by David H. Riddle, May, 1851. *N. Y.*
Female Miss. Soc. of N. Y. Disc., 1st Annual Meeting, by M. La Rue Perrine, May 12, 1817.
United Domestic Miss. Soc. Second Report, May 14, 1824.
Prot. Epis. Miss. Soc. 5th Annual Report, Oct. 6, 1836. *N. Y.*
Johnson, Evan M. Discourse, Feb. 24, 1839, "Missionary Fanaticism." *N. Y.*, 1839
Bushnell, Horace. Barbarism the First Danger. *N. Y.*, 1847
Letter from John Philip to the Society of Inq. on Missions, at Princeton, N. J., 1833.
Osborne, Michael. Sermon at First Meeting of Central Board of For. Missions. *8vo ; scarce ;* 40 *pages.* *Richmond*, 1843
Engles, W. M. The Patriot's Plea for Domestic Missions. Sermon, Oct. 31, 1833. *Phila.*
Amer. Temp. Soc. Sixth Report, 1833.
Smith, James. Man, through the Atonement, able to render himself acceptable to God. *Albany*, 1841
Hodges, E. An Essay on the Cultivation of Church Music. *N. Y.*, 1841
Stowe, C. E. Letter to R. D. Massey on the utter groundlessness of all the Millenial Arithmetic. *Cinn.*, 1843
Webster, Daniel. Speech of, on the Veto of the Bank Bill, July 11, 1832.
Stack Richard. Lectures on the Acts of the Apostles. *8vo, unbound*, 314 *p.* *Annapolis*, 1815
Smith, Robert. Address to the People of the U. S. *8vo, uncut*, 41 *p.* *Baltimore*, 1811
Percival, James G. Poem before the Phi Beta Kappa, Sept., 13, 1825, Yale College. *8vo*, 40 *p.* *Boston*, 1826
Fisk, Ezra. Oration before Alumni of Williams College, Sept. 7, 1825. *8vo*, 20 *pages* *New York*, 1825
Wright, Elizur. A Curiosity of Law, and what Came of It, &c. *8vo*, 96 *pages.* *Boston*, 1866
Parish, Elijah. Sermon before the Female Charitable Soc. of Newburyport, May 17, 1808. 5th Anniv. *8vo*, 28 *pages.*
Lexington, Ky. Memorial of Mechanics and Manuf. to Congress, Jan. 22, 1811. 14 *pages, uncut.*

Remarks on the Study of Languages, preparatory to admission into College. *Brunswick (Me.)*, 1826

Report of Com. of West Parish Assoc. on the State of Religion. *Boston*, 1825

2926 Miscellaneous. [*Nineteen.*]

Knowlton, Dr. C. Two Remarkable Lectures deliv. in Boston on the day of his leaving the Jail at East Cambridge, March 31, 1833, where he had been imprisoned for publishing an obscene book. 8*vo*, 24 *pages.* *Boston*, 1833

Wilmer, Simon. Sermon deliv. May 1, 1811, at Conv. of Prot. Epis. Ch. in N. J. 8*vo*, 35 *pages.* *Burlington*, 1811

Parkman, George. Proposals for Establishing a Retreat for the Insane. 8*vo*, 12 *pages.* *Boston*, 1814

Porter, Ebenezer. Sermon, Sept. 22, 1818, Dedication of Theological Seminary in Andover. 8*vo*, 30 *pages.* *Andover*, 1818

Pusey, E. B. Sermon on the "Holy Eucharist." *N. Y.*, 1843

"Puseyism no Popery. 8*vo*, 72 *pages.* *Boston*, 1843

Smith, Ethan. Two Sermons, August 3, 1818, at Bolton, N. Y. 8*vo*, 46 *pages.* *Ballston, Spa.*, 1818

Plymley, Peter. Letters on the subject of Catholics, to my Brother Abraham, who lives in the Country. 8*vo*, 83 *pages*, *fine copy.* *Baltimore*, 1809

Lyon, James. The Saint's Daily Assistant; or, Meditations Morning and Evening. 8*vo*, *uncut.* *Newburyport, n. d.*

Smith, Rev. Ethan. Sermon to Dr. Spring's Society, Nov. 30, 1809. 8*vo*, 23 *p.* *Newburyport*, 1809

Belsham, Thomas. Vindication of Certain Passages in a Discourse on the Death of Dr. Priestley; added, the Discourse on Death of, &c. 12*mo*, 118 *pages.* *Boston*, 1809

The Snow Storm, a Scottish Tale, and the Secret of Fortune-Telling. 12*mo*, 26 *pages.* *N. Y.*, 1834

To the Unfortunate Female. *London*

A Voice from the Church. 28 *pages.* *N. Y.*, 1834

Nature, Design and General Rules of the Meth. Soc., with John Wesley's Advice in regard to Dress. 24 *pages.* *N. Y.*, 1809

Institution of the Mass. Humane Soc., with the Rules and Methods of Treatment to be used with Persons apparently Dead. 12*mo*, *uncut*, 22 *p.*; *very scarce.* *Boston*, 1788

The Christian's Pocket Library. No. V., Vol. I., 48 *pages*, *uncut.*

Our Country: its Capabilities, its Perils and its Hope. 12*mo*, 60 *pages.* *N. Y.*, 1842

A Blow at the Root, &c. 12*mo*, 12 *pages.* *Elizabethtown, N. J.*, 1809

2927 Miscellaneous. [*Fifteen.*]

Grimke, Thos. S. Letter to J. C. Calhoun, R. Y. Hayne, &c. 8*vo*, 15 *p.* *Charleston*, 1832

Girard, Stephen. Bill in Chancery, filed in the Circuit Court of U. S. in behalf of the heirs of, to recover all the Real and Personal Estate, &c. *8vo*, 12 *p.* *Phila.* 1836

Green, Lewis W. Inaug. Address before the Synod of Pittsburgh, Oct., 1840. 8vo, 20 *p.* *Pittsburgh*, 1843

Spooner, W. J. Address deliv. before the Phi Beta Kappa at Cambridge, Aug. 29, 1822. *8vo*, 34 *p.* *Boston*, 1822

Story, Joseph. Discourse before the Phi Beta Kappa, Aug. 31, 1856, at Cambridge. *8vo*, 58 *p.* *Boston*, 1826

N. Y. Historical Soc. Memorial, 1827. 32 *p.*

Onderdonk, B. T. Voice of Truth. Number two. 48 *p.*

——— Pastoral Letter to the Clergy, &c. 19 *p.* *New York*, 1844

CONNECTICUT. Continuation of the Narrative of the Missions to the New Settlements in. *8vo*, 32 *p.* *New Haven*, 1794

CHEETHAM, JAMES. A Dissertation concerning Political Equality and the Corporation of N. Y. *8vo*, 50 *p.* *N. Y.*, 1800

West, Stephen. Animadversions on a Publication entitled "The Duty and Obligation of Christians to Marry only in the Lord." *8vo*, 15 *p.*; *very scarce.* *Fish-Kill: Sam. Loudon*, 1779

Witherspoon, Rev. John. Sermon on the Relig. Educ. of Children. *8vo*, *half mor.*, 23 *p.*; *fine copy.* *Elizabethtown*, 1789

Hughes, Rev. Dr. John. Lecture on the Mixture of Civil and Ecclesiastical Power in the Middle Ages. *8vo*, *uncut*, 24 *p.* *N. Y.*, 1843

Ingenac, B. The Rural Code of Haïti, literally translated, together with Letters from that Country concerning its Present Condition. *8vo*, 48 *p.* *Granville, N. J.*, 1837

Gage, Wm. L. Valedictory Sermon, April 4, 1858. *Manchester, N. H.*, 1858

2928 Miscellaneous. [*Thirteen.*]

Scott, John. The Fatal Consequences of Licentiousness: a Sermon preached March 18th, 1810, at Kingston, on occasion of the Trial of a Young Woman of that Town for the alleged Murder of her Illegitimate Child. 12*mo*, 43 *pp.*, *fine copy.* *Hull, England*, 1810

Saul—*an Apostle of Liberty.* The Rights of Conscience presumed upon the Principles of Genuine Christianity. Intended as a Refutation of Bigotry and Superstition, and a Defence of the Common Rights of Citizens against Church Coalitions. 12*mo*, 21 *pp.*, *very curious* *New York*, 1779

Totten, Joseph. A Short Account of Five Camp-meetings held in the New Jersey District, in 1808. 12*mo*, 22 *pages.* *New York*, 1808

Stevens, Calvin F. A List of the Post-offices in the U. S.; their Names, Counties, and States; distance from Washington; Rates of Postage, and distance from N. Y.; with Laws and Regulations. *Small 4to*, 92 *pages*, *uncut.* *New York*, 1808

McLeod, Allan. Lackington's Confession—rendered into Narrative: added, observations on the bad consequences of educating daughters at Boarding-schools. 12*mo*, 150 *pages*. *London*, 1804

Bowden, John. Letter from, to the Rev. Ezra Stiles, concerning Church Government. 12*mo*, 48 *pages* *Unadilla, N. Y.*, 1825

Randolph, John. Speech of, March 5th, 1806, upon non-Importation of British Goods. 12*mo*, *uncut*, 23 *pages*. *Salem, Mass.*, 1806

Hicks, Elias. An Examination of an Epistle issued by the Followers of, Relative to their Separation from the Society of Friends. 12*mo*, 54 *pages*. *Philadelphia*, 1827

Hillhouse. Propositions for Amending the Constitution of the U. S., April 12th, 1808. 12*mo*, *uncut*, 60 *pages*.

Grew, Henry. Narrative of Proceedings in the Bank Street Ch., relative to the Reception of an Adhering Freemason. With an Examination of Masonic Oaths, &c. 12*mo*, 36 *pages*. *Phila.*, 1836

Greene, Benj. Oration before the Members of Murray's Lodge, No. XVII., at Festival of St. John. 12*mo*, 15 *pages*. *Montreal*, 1817

Newman's Observations for the Use of the Pious. 12*mo*, 23 *pages*. *Otsego, N. Y.*, 1807

——— ——— Second Part. 12*mo*, 24 *pages*. *Otsego, N. Y.*, 1809

2930 Miscellaneous. [*Twenty-seven.*]

Locke, John. A Letter concerning Toleration. 12*mo*, 71 *pages*. *Dedicated to Governor Thos. Chittenden.* *Windsor, Vt.* *Printed by Alden Spooner*, MDCCLXXXVIII.

A very rare imprint.

Pope, Alexander. An Essay on Man; in Four Epistles. 12*mo*, 45 *pages*. *Brattleborough*, 1807

Randolph, John, Speech of, on non-Importation of British Goods, March 13, 1806.

Lathrop, Joseph. Sermon at the Ordination of Rev. Heman Ball, Feb. 1, 1797. 12*mo*, 34 *pages*. *Rutland*, (*Vt.*) 1797.

Wesley, John. Popery calmly considered. 12*mo*, 25 *pages* *London*, 1779.

Scott, Walter. Religious Discourses. By a Layman 12*mo*, 48 *pages*. *New York*, 1828

Huit, Monsieur. Letter to Mons. De le Grais, upon the Original of Romances. 12*mo*, 63 *pages*. *London*, MDCCXX

Williams, H. M. Letters from France containing many new anecdotes relative to the French Revolution. 12*mo*, *uncut*, 138 *pages*. *Boston*, 1792

Ruggles, S. B. Semi-Centennial Address at Yale College to the Graduates of 1814. July 27, 1864 45 *pages*. *New York*, 1864

Church of England Tracts, 1796 to 1800,—(*nine*),—*in one volume*.

Boston Grammar Schools. Course of Study for July, 1868.

A Dispassionate Inquiry into the Reasons alleged by Mr. Madison for Declaring an Offensive and Ruinous War against Great Britain. By a New-England Farmer. Second Edition. *8vo, uncut,* 63 *pages.* *Boston,* 1812

Boston Baptist For. Miss. Society. Sermon by F. Wayland, Jr. 4th edition. *Boston,* 1826

N. Y. Prot. Epis. Miss. Soc. Discourse, Jan. 15, 1826, by C. R. Duffie.

Genl. Prot. Epis. S. S. Union. Third Annual Report, June 25, 1829. *N. Y.*

——— of N. Y. Eleventh Annual Report,—1828.

Maryland Toleration; or, Sketches of the Early History of Maryland to the Year 1650. By Rev. Ethan Allen. *8vo,* 64 *pages, fine copy, scarce.* *Balto.,* 1855

Osgood, David. A Solemn Protest against the late Declaration of War. *8vo, uncut,* 20 *pages.* *Cambridge,* 1812

2931 Indian Pamphlets. *Valuable.* [*Six.*]

Speech of Mr. Storrs on the Seminole War. 18 *p.; scarce.* 1828

Speech of Mr. Vinton on the Emigration of Indians. 28 *p. Scarce.* *Wash.,* 1828

Priest, Josiah. Stories of Early Settlers in the Wilderness, embracing the Life of Mrs. Priest, and a Short Account of Brant and of the Massacre of Wyoming. *8vo,* 40 *p. Wants plate. Portrait of Brant and of an old Indian Battle inserted. Fine copy.* *Albany,* 1837

Cusick, David. History of the Six Nations. Published at Tuscarora Village, June 10, 1825. Wants Title. *Uncut,* 36 *p.* This edition is so very rare, that a gentleman, several years ago, took the trouble to visit the Tuscarora Village in order to find a copy, and offered $10, but did not succeed in securing one.

Hanson's, Williamson's and Smith's Captivities. Extracted from an Old Book of Indian Narratives. 109 *p.*

Rights of the Indians. Memorial to House of Representatives of United States, by Citizens of Massachusetts, February 22, 1830. 16 *p.*

2932 Miscellaneous. [*Thirteen.*]

Sturbridge (Mass.) Historical Sketches of the Baptist Ch., from 1740 to 1843. By Rev. Joel Kenney. *12mo,* 54 *p.* *N. Y.,* 1844

Channing, W. E. A Sermon on War, May 30, 1816. *8vo, uncut,* 40 *p.* *Boston,* 1812

Address to the Clergy of New England on their Opposition to the rulers of the United States. By a Layman. *8vo,* 28 *p.* *Concord,* 1814

HULL-GULL. THE WARS OF THE GULLS. An Historical Romance in Three Chapters. Chapter I.—Showing How and Why, and with Whom the Gulls went to War. II.—How the Gulls made the Deep to Boil like a Pot. III—Showing how a Certain Doughty General of the Gulls goes forth to Play the Game of Hull-Gull in Upper Canada:

" And from the pinnacle of glory,
Falls headlong into purgatory."

After having quieted himself with the sagacious reflection—

" That when a fight becomes a chase,
Those win the day that win the race."

8vo, uncut. Fine copy; scarce. 36 *pages* *New York*, 1812

Act for Regulating, Governing and Training the Militia of Massachusetts, passed March 6, 1810. *Boston*, 1810

Speech of Mr. Mallary of Vermont on the Tariff Bill. 34 *p.* *Wash.*, 1828

Burroughs, Stephen, Memoirs of. 12*mo, Vol. II. only.* 202 *p. Fine copy; very scarce Ed.* *Boston*, 1804

Webster, Noah. Observations on Language. Addressed to the New York Lyceum. Also on Commerce. 12*mo,* 39 *p.* *New Haven*, 1839

Scarce and Important.

Worcester, Noah. A Friendly Letter to Rev. Thomas Baldwin on Close Communionists. 12*mo,* 48 *pages.* *Concord, N. H.*, 1791

Very Rare Imprint.

Strong, Cyprian. Animadversions on the Substance of two Sermons by John Lewis. 12*mo,* 56 *p.* *Concord, N. H.*, 1793

Rush, Benjamin. An Inquiry into the Effects of Ardent Spirits upon the Body and Mind. 12*mo,* 32 *p. Scarce.* *Phila., n. d.*

Worcester, Sam'l. Sermon—The Messiah of the Scriptures—April 8, 1808, at Salem and Beverly. 12*mo,* 28 *p.* *Boston*, 1808

Lathrop, Joseph, Christ's Warning to Churches to Beware of False Prophets. 12*mo, uncut,* 60 *p.* *Amherst, N. H.*, 1804

2933 Miscellaneous. [*Twenty.*]

Miller, Samuel. Presbyterianism the Truly Primitive and Apostolical Constitution. 8*vo,* 98 *p.* *Phila.*, 1835

Judd, Thomas. An Essay on the Improvement in the Manufacture of Sugar adapted for Louisiana. 8*vo,* 36 *p., uncut. Scarce.* *Boston*, 1836

Import, Design, and Uses of Infant Baptism—Infant Baptism Scriptural and Reasonable. By Samuel Miller. 8*vo,* 122 *p.* *Phila.*, 1837

Subjects and Mode of Baptism.

Heyrick, Eliz. Immediate not Gradual Abolition. 36 *p.* *Phila.*, 1837

Parker, Theo. A Letter to the President of United States touching the Matter of Slavery. *8vo*, 120 *p*. *Very scarce.* *Boston*, 1848

The Anti-Slavery Record. May, 1836.

Southgate, H. Address delivered before the Missionary Frat. in Phillips' Acad., Andover, 31 *p*. 1834

Knox College. Rights of Congregationalists in. 93 *p*. *Chicago*, 1859

Roy, J. E. Manual of Principles, Doctrines, and Usages of Congregational Churches. *Chicago*, 1869

Reasons Assigned by a number of Ministers for Declaring themselves the True Reformed Dutch Church of United States. 12*mo*, 19 *p*. *Hackensack, N. J.*, 1822

A Treatise on Schism. *Balto.*

A Word to Sabbath Breakers. *N. Y.*, 1812

A Short and Easy Method to Perform well the Daily Actions of a Christian Life. 12*mo*, 24 *p*. *London*, 1764

Chipman, Samuel. Report of an Exam. of Poor Houses, Jails, &c., in New York State, and Berkshire County, Mass., &c. *8vo*, 96 *p*. *Albany*, 1834

Manning, James. Charge from the President of Brown University, September 2, 1789. 26 *p*., *8vo*. *Boston*, 1806

White, Daniel A. Address to the Merrimack Humane Soc., Sept. 3, 1805. *8vo*, 36 *p*. *Newburyport*, 1805

Mackenzie, Alex. Letter to the Rev. Samuel C. Aiken in Answer to his Sermon on Theatrical Exhib. *8vo*, 28 *p*. *Cleveland, O.*, 1836

Martin, S. Two Discourses. First—The Danger and Mischief of Self-Confidence. Second—Scripture Doctrine of Justification explained. Recommended to Moravian Sectaries. *8vo*, 78 *p*. *London*, 1760

2934 Miscellaneous. [*Twenty-One.*]

United States. Return of the whole number of Persons within the Several Districts of. Taken in 1791. *8vo*, *uncut.* /0 *Fine copy; very scarce.* *Wash. City*, 1802

——— The same. Taken in 1800.

General Theological Seminary Protestant Episcopal Church. Proceedings of Board of Trustees, June, 1828.

——— Introductory Address, March 11, 1822. By J. H. Hobart.

——— Letter from Professor Whittingham, June, 1838

——— B. T. Onderdonk's Address, June 30, 1837

——— H. U. Onderdonk's Address, June 29, 1838

——— S. A. McCoskry, Address, June 28, 1839

——— B. T. Onderdonk, Sermon, November 29, 1840

——— W. R. Whittingham, Sermon, December 15, 1839

——— W. R. Whittingham, Sermon, December 4, 1836

——— W. H. De Lancey, Address, June 25, 1841

Acts of the Diocesan Synod, at Exeter, England, June, 1851. *8vo*, 157 *p.* *N. Y.*, 1852

Review of the Apologies of Dr. Seabury and Mr. Haight. By a Churchman. *N. Y.*, 1843

Letter to the Clergy of Exeter, England. By Henry Lord Bishop. *N. Y.*, 1852

Political Tables Showing the Population of the Different States and the Return of Votes for 1824, 1826, and 1828, with Remarks. 12*mo*, 72 *p.* *N. Y.*, 1828

Peters, W. C. Burrowes' Piano Forte Primer. 12*mo*, 48 *p.* *Confederate pub.* *Richmond*, 1864

Reese, Levi R. Discoveries on the Origin, Universal Obligation, &c., of the Sabbath, delivered in the Capitol of the United States. 12*mo*, 51 *p.* *Balto.*, 1838

Religious Repertory for the Year 1814, Being a Choice collection of Original Essays, Curious and Interesting Documents, &c. 12*mo*, 69 *p.* *Cork*, 1814

Polwhele, R. Anecdotes of Methodism; added a Sermon on the Conduct that becomes a Clergyman. 12*mo*, 99 *p.* *Free.* *London*, 1800

Wesley, John. Minutes of Several Conversations at the 69th Conference in Leeds, July 27th 1812. 12*mo*, 84 *p.* *London*, 1812

5 2935 Miscellaneous. [*Ten.*]

Essay on the Rights and Duties of Nations with Reference to the Chesapeake Affair. By an American. *8vo*, 62 *p.*, *uncut.* *Boston*, 1807

New Hampshire. Report of Committee upon War Expenditures of the Towns and Cities in. *Concord*, 1866

Wilkes, Lieut. Charles. Defence of, to the Charge on which he has been Tried.

Pinckney. Lecture on the Goodness of God, June 24, 1838

Inquiry into the Causes of Public Distress. *8vo*, 52 *p.* *N. Y.*, 1834

Brief Survey of the Lottery System as Existing in the United States. *8vo*, 48 *p.* *Phila.*, 1833

New York. An Act to Organize the Militia of the State of, passed April 21, 1818, with Index. *8vo*, 46 *p.* *Albany*, 1818

——— In Assembly, No. 134, Message of Gov. Seward, in Relation to the Culture of Silk and Manufacture of Sugar from the Beet Root, February 12, 1840

——— Circular Letter from the General Republican Com. in Vindication of the Measures of General Government. *8vo*, 105 *p.* *Very scarce.* *N. Y.*, 1809

Channing, W. E. Discourse, June 15, 1814. *8vo*, *uncut.* *Boston.*

6 2936 Miscellaneous. [*Ten.*]

Onderdonk, B. T. Reply to Communication of Laymen. 16 *p.* *N. Y.*, 1844

Onderdonk, B. T. Review of Address in Respect to a late Ordination. By Observer. 23 *p.* *N. Y.*, 1843

——— Letter to, by Washington Plebs, with an Epistle to S. H. Tyng. 24 *p.* *Autograph of Onderdonk.* *N. Y.*, 1843

——— The Voice of Truth, No. 3.

——— The Trial Tried ; or, the Bishop and the Court at the Bar of Public Opinion. By Laicus. 24 *p.* *N. Y.*, 1845

——— Opinions of the Minority of the Court on the Trial of, &c. 8*vo*, 46. *p.* *N. Y.*, 1845

——— Statement of Facts and Circumstances connected with the Recent Trial of, &c., called "Bp. Onderdonk's Statement." 8*vo*, 31 *p.* *N. Y.*, 1845

Onderdonk, H. U. Considerations on Marriages Prohibited by the Law of God. 16 *p.* *Phila.*, 1841

Lewis, Isaac. Discourse on the Divinity of Jesus Christ. December 16, 1812, 8*vo*, 35 *p.* *Warren, R. I.*, 1812

——— Discourse—Public Thanksgiving. November 26, 1812. 8*vo*, 18 *p.* *Warren, R. I.*, 1812

2937 Miscellaneous. [*Nineteen.*]

Dawson, H. B. The Sons of Liberty in New York. 8*vo*, 118 *p.* *Poor copy.* *N. Y.*, 1859

Spear, Samuel T. The Nation's Blessing in Trial,—Sermon. /0 November 27, 1862. *Brooklyn.*

Thomson, John. An Address delivered July 4, 1810, at Newark. 12 *p.* *Poor copy.*

Remarks on the Practicability and Expediency of Establishing a Railroad from Boston to the Connecticut River. By N. Hale. 8*vo*, *uncut*, 71 *p.* *Boston*, 1827

Constitution of the Cape Cod Association, and Oration of Henry Scudder, at Boston, November 14, 1854. 8*vo*, 80 *p.*

Bath, N. H. Address, January 23, 1854, with an Historical Appendix. 8*vo*, 135 *p.* *Very scarce.* *Boston*, 1855

Report of Board of Directors on Internal Improvements on the Expediency and Practicability of a Railroad from Boston to the Hudson River; annexed Reports of Engineers with Plans and Profiles. 8*vo*, *uncut*, 195 *p.* *Boston*, 1829

Report of Finances, &c. of State of N. Y., for 1838. 71 *p.*

Report of Com. appointed to Submit a Plan for Supplying the City of Albany with Water. *Albany*, 1846

Fay, F. B. Speech on the License Billl, April 7, 1868. *Boston.*

High Prices. The Cause and the Remedy.

Archbishop Hughes in Reply to General Cass, and in Self-Vindication. 8*vo*, 34 *p.* *N. Y.*, 1854

70

Harrison, Wm. Henry. A Sketch of the Life and Public Services of. *8vo, 32 p. Very scarce.* *N. Y.*, 1836
Harper, Robt. G. A Letter from, to his Constituents. *8vo, uncut*, 16 *p. Wm. Hilliard Printer.* 1801
Hitchcock, Enos. A New Year's Sermon, delivered Jan. 1, 1797. *8vo*, 12 *p., uncut.* *Providence*, 1797
New England Manufacturers' Convention held at Worcester, Jan. 22, 1868, Proceedings of.
Message from the President of United States Transmitting a Roll of Persons having Office or Employment under U. S., February 16, 1802. *8vo, uncut.* *Wash.*, 1802
Sampson Against the Philistines; or, Reformation of Lawsuits. *8vo*, 96 *p., uncut.* *Phila.*, 1805
Address of the State Committee of Correspondence to the Citizens of Philadelphia, 1808.

☞ 2938 Miscellaneous. [*Twenty.*]

New York Public School Society. Address of Trustees, 1828
General Protestant Episcopal Sunday School Union. Sermon, July 29, 1830, by Charles Burroughs.
——— ——— Third Annual Report, June 25, 1829
——— ——— Sixth Annual Report, April 1, 1823
——— ——— Eleventh Annual Report, April 16, 1828
——— ——— Twelfth Annual Report, April 29, 1829
New York Prot. Episcopal Tract Society, Twentieth Annual Report.
——— ——— Address by Sam. R. Johnson.
Protestant Episcopal Church. Proceedings of Convention in New Jersey, June, 1801. *8vo*, 10 *p.* *Newark.* 1801
——— ——— Annual Conv. in New Jersey, Address by Bishop Doane, May 30, 1838
——— ——— General Conv. in Philadelphia, Sermon, by Bishop Meade, September 5, 1838
——— ——— Annual Conv. in New York, Sermon by M. Eastburn, October 4, 1838
——— ——— Annual Conv. in New Jersey, Episc. Address, May 29, 1839, by Bp. Doane.
——— ——— Third Annual Conv., Western New York, Sermon, by H. Gregory, Oct. 1, 1840
——— ——— General Conv. in New York, Sermon by Bp. McIlvaine, Oct. 12, 8411
——— ——— General Conv. in New York, October 6, 1841, Sermon by B. T. Onderdonk.

New York Female Union Society, First Report, April 9, 1817. 32 *p.*

—— —— Second Report, April 8, 1818. 52 *pages.*

—— —— Sixth Report, April 3, 1822. 40 *p.*

—— —— Seventh Report, April, 1823. 32 *p.*

2939 Miscellaneous. [*Twenty-five.*].

New York Society for Reformation of Juvenile Delinquents. Seventh and Eighth Reports. 1832, 1833

Johnson, W. L. Rectors' Christmas Offering for 1841–1842

New York Infant School Society, Constitution and By-Laws. May 23, 1827

Quincy, Josiah, Speech of, January 5, 1812, on Additional Military Force."

Osgood, David. Solemn Protest Against the Late Declaration of War. *Cambridge,* 1812

Perpetual War the Policy of Mr. Madison. By a New Eng. Farmer. *Boston,* 1812

Report of the Comptroller of the City Finances of New York, 1820

Casserly, P. S., to the Editor of the North American Review. 16 *p.*

Memorial on Personal Representation.

Facts and Observations on the Past and Present Situation and Future Prospects of the U. S., embracing a View of the Causes of the late Bankruptcies in Boston. 8*vo, uncut,* 54 *p.* *Phila.,* 1822

Hamilton. Address on the Tendency of our System of Intercourse with Foreign Nations. Nos. 1 and 5. *Phila.,* 1852

Electro-Magnetism as a Motive Power. *N. Y.,* 1839

Treaties Between the United States and Great Britain. *Boston,* 1815

Wirt, William. Celebration in Baltimore of the Triumph of Liberty in France with the Address. October 25, 1830. 42 *p.* *Fine copy.* *Balto.,* 1830

Waterman, A. G. Report of the Proceedings of Convention held in Independence Hall, July 6, 1852, for the purpose of Considering the Propriety of erecting one or more Monuments in Independence Square, Philadelphia. 8*vo,* 74 *p.* *Fine copy.* *Phila.,* 1852

Storrs, John. Sermon, January 2, 1848, in Middleborough, Mass.

Vindication of Mr. Randolph's Resignation. 8*vo,* 103 *p.* *Phila.,* 1795

Wayland, Francis. The Affairs of Rhode Island. Discourse, May 22, 1842. 8*vo,* 32 *p., valuable.* *Providence,* 1842

American Tract Society, 11th Annual Report, 1825. 8*vo,* 51 *p.*

—— —— Abstract of 15th Annual Report, May 13, 1840

—— —— 17th Annual Report, December 20, 1843. 72 *p.*

New York Religious Tract Society. 10th Annual Report. 1822

——— ——— 9th Annual Report, 1821

American Tract Society. 9th Annual Report, 1823. 72 *p.*

Philadelphia Sunday School Union. 6th Report, May 27, 1823. 87 *p.*

2940 Miscellaneous. [*Fourteen.*]

Northmen in America. Historical Sketches. Extracted from a Newspaper.

Redfield, W. C. The First Hurricane of September, 1853. 32 *pages.*

Watterston, George. A Memoir on the History, Culture, Manufacture, Use, &c., of the Tobacco Plant. 12 *pages, uncut, scarce,* *Washington,* 1817

Wilberforce, Wm. An Appeal to the Religion, Justice, and Humanity of the British Empire, in behalf of the Negro Slaves in the West Indies. 56 *pages.* *London,* 1823

Prescott, Oliver. A Dissertation on the Natural History and Medicinal Effects of the Secale Cornutum, or Ergot. With Plate. 8*vo, uncut,* 18 *pages, beautiful copy, scarce.* *Boston,* 1813

Slemons, Thomas. Oration. Pronounced at Mr. Thaddeus Broad's, July 4th, 1810, before the Republicans of Falmouth, (Me.) 16 *pages, verg scarce,* *Portland,* 1810

N. Y. Prot. Epis. S. S. Soc. Eleventh Annual Report. *N. Y.,* 1828.

Carey, M. Twenty-one Golden Rules to depress Agriculture, impede Manufactures, &c. 8*vo, uncut,* 60 *pages* *Salem,* 1824

Collyer, J. B. Sermon. June 30th, 1838. *Norwich, Eng.*

Chapin, Stephen. Two Sermons at Mount Vernon, N. H., November 26th, 1809; also appended: A Brief Sketch of the Life and Character of Rev. John Bruce, Minister of Mt. Vernon. 8*vo, uncut,* 39 *pages fine copy.* *Amherst, N. H.,* 1809

Church, J. H. The First Settlement of New-England. A Sermon delivered in Andover, April 5th, 1810, 8*vo,* 24 *pages, fine copy, very scarce.* *Sutton, Mass.,* 1810

Crowell, Seth. Some Polemical Remarks on the Principal Topics of the Calvinian System of Theology. 12*mo,* 23 *pages, uncut.* *Hudson, N. Y.,* 1805

Coast Survey. Reply by B. B. to the Official Defence of its Cost, Abuses, and Power. 8*vo,* 36 *pages.*

Congregational Churches. Manual of the Principles, Doctrines, and Usages. *Chicago,* 1869

2941 Miscellaneous [*Thirteen.*]

Evans, Oliver. To his Counsel, who are engaged in Defence of his Patent Rights for the Improvements he has Invented. 8*vo,* 55 *pages, scarce.*

Extracts from a Review of the Parliamentary and Forensic Eloquence of the U. S. 8*vo,* 31 *pages.* *Washington City,* 1834

Essex Junto and the British Spy; or Treason Detected. 8*vo*, 36 *pgs*, *uncut*. *Salem*, 1812

ELLERY, CHRISTOPHER A Defence against Calumny; or Haman in the shape of C. Ellery, hung upon his own gallows. Being the substance of certain publications, etc., refuting the accusations against John Rutledge. 8*vo*, 64 *pages*, *uncut*, *spicy*. *Printed for the Purchasers*, 1803.

Elder, Question. Geneva. 16 *pages*.

Emott, James. Speech of, Jan. 12th, 1813, on the War. 8*vo*, 35 *pages*. *Boston*, 1813

Elliott, Com. J. D. Speech of. Delivered in Hagerstown, Md., Nov. 14th, 1843. 8*vo*, 137 *pages*; *auto. of Elliott*. *Phila.*, 1844

Foye, M. W. Antiquity of the Church of England. 8*vo*, 24 *pages*. *Birmingham*, 1836

Furness, W. H. Discourse, Jan. 19th, 1840, on the loss of the Lexington. *Phila.*, 1840

Freemen, Awake! the Devil is in the Camp! 8*vo*, 24 *pages*; *curious*. *Phila.*, 1839

Fay, Francis B. Speech on the License Bill, April 7th, 1868. *Boston*.

Fisher, John D. Sketch of the Life and Character of. By Walter Channing. *Boston*, 1850

Foster, Eben B. Sermon at Instal. of W. C. Foster. 8*vo*. 34 *pages*. *Boston*, 1850

2942 Miscellaneous. [*Eleven*.]

Dorchester, (Mass.) Sermon, June 24th, 1827. By E. Richmond. 8*vo*, 16 *pages*.

——— Discourse, Sept. 30th, 1855. By Nath. Hall. 8*vo*, 27 *pages*.

——— The Limits of Civil Obedience. Sermon, Jan. 12th, 1851. By Nath. Hall. 26 *p*.

——— Sermon on the Death of Mrs. John Howe. Nov. 23d, 1844. 8*vo*, 16 *p*.

Devyr, Thos. A. Our Natural Rights. A Pamphlet for the People. 8*vo*, 50 *p*. *Williamsburg, L. I.*, 1842

De Grasse, Isaiah. A Sermon on Education. 8*vo*, 19 *p*. *N. Y.*, 1839

Dorr, Thos. W. The Merits of, and George Bancroft, as they are politically connected. 8*vo*, 41 *pages*. *Scarce*. *Boston*, 1844

David, J. C. Hierachy of the American Scientific, Educ. and Philos. Soc. No. 1. 16 *p*. *Phila.*, 1835

Decatur, Stephen. Correspondence between, and Com. James Barron, which led to the unfortunate meeting, March 22d, 1820. 8*vo*, 22 *p*. *uncut*. *Scarce*. *Bost.*, 1820

Duane, Wm. J. The Law of Nations investigated in popular manner. Addressed to the Farmers of the U. S. 8*vo*, 110 *pages*. *Phila.*, 1809

Duer, John, and Robert Sedgwick. An Examination of the Controversy between the Greek Deputies, &c. *8vo*, 179 *p. Scarce.* *N. Y.*, 1826

7 2943 Miscellaneous. [*Twelve.*]

Crane, E. D. Abstract of an Address on Transportation. Feb. 13th, 1868. *Boston*

Channing, W. E. Discourse delivered June 15th, 1814. *8vo, uncut*, 27 *pages.* *Boston*, 1814

Cobbett, William. Address to the Clergy of Mass., Nov. 13th, 1814; with a Prefatory to Certain Priests. By Jonathan. *8vo, uncut.* *Boston*, 1815

Channing, W. E. Letter to Henry Clay on Annexation of Texas. *8vo*, 72 *pages, uncut.* *Boston*, 1837

Cobbett, William. A Little Plain English on the Treaty, and on the Conduct of the Pres't. *8vo, uncut*, 111 *pages.* *Phila.*, 1795

Bell, Benj. Discourse on Ephesians v. 14. *8vo*, 24 *pages. Printed by Alden Spooner, in Windsor, Vt.* MDCCXCIII.

Very rare imprint.

Brenan, Rev. M. A Brief Statement of the Reasons which induced him to Renounce the Errors of the Church of Rome. Written by Himself. *8vo*, 32 *pages.* *Dublin*, 1825

Bouton, Nathl. Mem. Disc., on the 50th Anniv. of Concord Fem. Char. Soc., Jan. 26th, 1862. *8vo*, 40 *pages.* *Concord*, 1862

Beechwood Church, near Cohasset, (Mass.), Historical Sketch of. Jan. 15th, 1867. *8vo*, 20 *pages.* *Boston*, 1867

Buffalo. St. Paul's Cathedral. Historical Sermon, by Rev. William Shelton, Feb. 19th, 1867. *8vo*, 20 *pages.*

Blatchly, Cornelius C. An Essay on Fasting, and on Abstinence. *8vo*, 16 *pages, curious and interesting.* *New York*, 1818

Boardman, Henry, D. D. The Importance of Religion to the Legal Profession; with some remarks on the character of the late Chas. Chauncey. Discourse delivered October, 1849. *8vo, orig. cover, uncut*, 40 *pages.—Valuable.* *Philadelphia*, 1849

2944 Miscellaneous. [*Eighteen*].

Schlegel, J. F. W. Neutral Rights; or, an Impartial examination of the Right of Search, etc. *8vo, uncut*, 162 *p.* *Phila.*, 1801

Putnam, I. W. Farewell Sermon, March 15, 1835, in the North Church, Portsmouth, N. H. With a valuable Historical Appendix. *8vo*, 40 *p., fine copy, scarce.* *Portsmouth*, 1835

Randolph, John. Biography of, with a selection from his Speeches. By Lemuel Sawyer. *8vo*, 132 *p., fine copy.* *N. Y.*, 1844

Thoughts on the subject of Naval power in the U. S., etc. *8vo*, 35 *p.* *Phila.*, 1806

New York Dispensary. Annual Report of Bd. of Trustees of, Jan., 1832.

Pusey, E. B. Sermon the "Holy Eucharist." *N. Y.*, 1843

Vail, Alfred. Description of the Amer. Electro Magnetic Teleg., now in operation between Washington and Baltimore. *Illust.*, 8*vo*, 24 *p.* *Washington*, 1845

Peterson, Edw. Facts on Con'l. Intolerance and Ecclesiastical Despotism. *Providence*, 1845

Sandford, H. S. De lege Rhodia de Jactu. *Heidelbergae*, 1849

Woodbury's Tables and Notes on the Cultivation of Cotton, etc. 78 *p.* *Wash.*, 1836

Boston. Report of Com. on the Preservation of the Hancock House, June 3, 1863. 8*vo*, 14 *p.*

—— City Hospital. Address at Dedication, May 24, 1864, by T. O. Amory, Jr. 8*vo*, 45 *p.*

—— Metropolitan Police Bill. Argument of T. C. Amory against, March 16, 1863. 8*vo*, 31 *p.*

—— Miscellaneous Remarks on the Police of, as respects Paupers, Alms and Work House, For. and Domestic Mission. Soc., etc. 8*vo*, 42 *p.*, *uncut, very scarce.* *Boston*, 1814

—— Theatre. Description of the Scenery, etc. of the Grand Nautical Spectacle, called Black-Beard the Pirate, with all the Songs, Duetts, Glees and Chorusses, etc. 8*vo*, 12 *p.* *Boston*, 1811

—— Board of Trade, Public Interest and Private Monopoly. Address, Oct. 16, 1867, by Josiah Quincy. 8*vo*, 15 *p.*

—— State House, The Improvements of. The Investigations thereof investigated, etc. 8*vo*, 93 *p.* *Boston*, 1868

2945 Miscellaneous. [*Thirteen*].

Cleopatra. The Celebrated Statue of. *N. Y.*, 1837

Congregationalism. What it is.

Catholic Religion Vindicated, being an Answer to a Sermon preached by the Rev. Mr. Cuyler, in Pougkeepsie, July 30, 1812, in which Sermon, the religion of the Catholics was illiberally misrepresented as to require a vindication. By a Roman Catholic. 8*vo*, 58 *p.*; *fine copy, scarce.* *Printed for the Author*, 1813

Crawford, Joseph. The substance of a Sermon deliv. at the Funeral of Miss Nabby Frothingham, Feb. 24, 1809. 8*vo*, 36 *p.* *N. Y.*, 1809

Clarke, Adam. A Disssertation on the use and abuse of Tobacco. 8*vo*, 24 *p.* *Newburyport*, 1812

Creighton, James. The Advantages, Pleasure and Profit of Swearing in Common Conversation. 12*mo*, 12 *p.* *Newry*, 1812

Chickering, Jesse. A Statistical View of the Population of Mass., from 1765 to 1840. 8*vo*, 160 *p.*, *fine copy; valuable.* *Boston*, 1846

Buffalo Orphan Asylum. Report of Board of Trustees, June, 1854. *8vo, 24 p.*

BERKSHIRE JUBILEE. Celebrated at Pittsfield, Mass., Aug. 22, 23, 1844. Frontis. and Eng. *8vo, stiff paper, orig. cov.; 244 p.* *Albany*, 1845

Contains Hopkins' Sermon, Poem by Dr. William Allen, with valuable Historical Notes, Oration by J. A. Spencer, and a large appendix of great interest and value, and eight engravings of the principal Towns in the County, also an index.

Brownson, O. A. Sermon to Young People in Canton, May 24, 1835. *8vo, 18 p.* *Dedham*, 1835

Bancroft, Aaron. Sermon, Jan. 31, 1836. Fifty years ministry. *8vo, 44 p.; scarce.* *Worcester*, 1836

Brownson, O. A. Discourse on the Wants of the Times, May 29, 1836. *8vo, 23 p.* *Boston*, 1836

Butler, Benj. F. Plan for the Organization of a Law Faculty, and for a System of Instruction in Legal Science. *8vo, 40 p.* *N. Y.*, 1835

5* 2946 Miscellaneous. [*Twelve*].

BANGOR, Beaumaris and Snowdonia. Guide to, with a map, by John Smith. *8vo, 56 p.* *Liverpool*, 1829

Bowdoin College, Me. Address before the Benev. Soc. of, Sept. 5, 1826, by Samuel P. Neuman. *8vo, 29 p.* *Portland*, 1826

Bowdoin College. Laws of. *8vo, 28 p.* *Brunswick*, 1825

Brougham, Henry. Vindiciae Wyckeamicae: or, a Vindication of Winchester College, occasioned by his letter to Samuel Romilly, on charitable abuses, by W. L. Bowles. *8vo, 52 p., scarce.* *London*, 1818

BROWN, HON. NICHOLAS. A Discourse in commem. of the Life and Character of, deliv. Nov. 3, 1841, by Francis Wayland. *8vo, 30 p., valuable.* *Boston*, 1841

Buffalo Hospital of the Sisters of Charity. Discussion relative to, between Rev. John C. Lord and Bernard O'Reilly. *8vo, 38 p.* *Buffalo*, 1850

Emmons, Nathaniel. A Discourse concerning the Process of the General Judgment in which the modern Notions of Universal Salvation are particularly considered. *8vo, 94 p.; rough edges, scarce.* *Phila.*, 1791

Erskine, Hon. Thos. A View of the causes and consequences of the Present War with France. *8vo, 77 p.* *Phila.*, 1797

Everett, Edward. A Lecture on the Working Men's Party, delivered in Charlestown, Oct. 6, 1830. *8vo, 27 p.; uncut, valuable.* *Boston*, 1830

——— Speech of, March 9, 1826, in Com., on proposition to amend the Constitution. *8vo, 38 p.* *Boston*, 1826

——— Address before Phi Beta Kappa Soc. of Yale College, Aug. 20, 1833. *8vo, 35 p.; autog. of Everett.* *New Haven*, 1833

Emerson, Joseph. Letter to the Genessee Consoc. of N. Y. 8*vo*, 23 *p*. *Relates to his expulsion from the church for being a Mason.* *Boston*, 1829

2947 Pamphlets. Very scarce edition of Tom Paine's Political Tracts. [*Eight*].

COMMON SENSE: Addressed to the Inhabitants of America, written by an Englishman. 8*vo*. 77 *p*., *fine copy, rough edges, very rare.* 1*st Ed.* *Phila.: R. Bell*, 1776

——— Same as above. 8*vo*, 44 *p*. *Boston*, MDCCLXXVI.

——— Large additions to, with an appendix and an address to Quakers. 8*vo*, 44 *p*., *very scarce.* *Boston*, 1776

——— Same as No. 1. 8*vo*, 54 *p*.; *good copy. All the objectionable passages and words are omitted in this edition.* *London*, 1776

CANDIDUS. Plain Truth, addressed to the Inhabitants of America, containing Remarks on a late Pamphlet, intitled Common Sense. Second edition. 8*vo*, 47 *p*.; *fine copy.* *London*, 1776

WAKEFIELD, GILBERT. An Examination of the Age of Reason, or an investigation of true and fabulous Theology, by Thos. Paine. 8*vo*, 55 *p*.; *good copy.* *N. Y.*, 1794

PAINE, THOMAS. Agrarian Justice, opposed to Agrarian Law, and to Agrarian Monopoly. Being a plan for meliorating the condition of Man. 8*vo*, 32 *p*.; *fine copy, uncut.* *Phila.*, *n. d.*

A LETTER TO MR. PAINE on his late publication.

2948 Pamphlets. *Valuable.* [*Five.*]

GALLOWAY, JOSEPH; Speech of, one of the members for Phila. Co., in answer to John Dickenson, delivered in House of Assembly, Province of Pa., May 24, 1764. 8*vo*, 92 *pages*, *good copy, very scarce.* *London*, MDCCLXV

BRITISH COLONIES IN N. A. Considerations on the Measures carrying on with respect to. The Second Edition, with Additions and an Appendix. 176 *p*. *and* 45 *p*., 8*vo*, *good clean copy, scarce.* LONDON, n. d. (1774)

DULANY, DAN'L (of Maryland). Considerations on the Propriety of imposing Taxes in the British Colonies, etc. 8*vo*, 55 *p*., *scarce ed.* *New York: John Holt*, 1765

AMERICA. Treaty of Amity, Commerce, and Navigation. 8*vo*, 24 *p*., *uncut.* *Phil.*, 1795

AMERICA. Charters of the old English Colonies; with an Introduction and Notes. By Samuel Lucas. 8*vo*, 123 *pages*, *valuable doc.* *London*, 1850

2949 SERMONS on the Repeal of the Stamp Act. [*Seven.*]

STILLMAN, SAM'L. "*Good News from a far Country.*" Preached at Boston, May 17, 1766, upon the arrival of the important news of the Repeal, etc. 8*vo*, 34 *p*., *very fine copy.* BOSTON, MDCCLXVI

CHAUNCY, CHARLES. A Discourse on "*the Good News from a far Country*," delivered July 24th, 1766, a day of Thanksgiving. *8vo*, 32 *p.*, *fine copy*, *scarce.*
BOSTON, N. E., MDCCLXVI

EMERSON, JOSEPH. A Thanksgiving Sermon. Preached at Pepperell, July 24th, 1766. *8vo*, 37 *p.*, *fine copy*, *extremely scarce.* BOSTON, M,DCC,LXVI

PATTEN, WILLIAM. A Discourse delivered at *Hallifax*, in the County of *Plymouth*, July 24, 1766. *8vo*, *uncut* 22 *p.*, *very scarce.* BOSTON, N. E., MDCCLXVI

CUMINGS, HENRY. A Thanksgiving Sermon, preached at *Billerica*, November 27, 1766. *8vo*, 32 *p.*, *rough edges*, *fine copy*, *very scarce.* BOSTON, N. E., MDCCLXVII

A SHORT HISTORY of the Conduct of the Present Ministry with regard to the American Stamp Act. *8vo*, 21 *p.*, *uncut*, *fine copy*, *scarce.* LONDON : J. ALMON, 1766

AMERICAN STAMP-ACT, The NECESSITY of REPEALING, etc. demonstrated, or A PROOF that GREAT BRITAIN must be injured by that ACT. *8vo*, 31 *p.*, *good copy*, *very scarce.*
BOSTON: Printed and Sold by EDES and GILL, in Queen St., 1766

8 2950 PAMPHLETS, RELATING TO THE REVOLUTION. [*Seven.*]

FRISBIE, LEVI. An Oration delivered at Ipswich, April 29, 1783, on account of the Happy Restoration of Peace. *Sm. 4to*, *uncut*, 24 *p.*, *rare.*
BOSTON, IN AMERICA: Printed and Sold by E. RUSSELL, near Liberty Pole, MDCCLXXXIII

CANDIDUS. Plain Truth addressed to the Inhabitants of America, etc. *8vo*, 47 *p.*, *fine copy.* LONDON, MDCCLXXVI

OBSERVATIONS on the New Constitution and on the Federal and State Conventions. By a Columbian Patriot. *8vo*, 19 *p.*, *uncut.* s. l. s. a.

FEDERAL FARMER. Letters from, to the Republican. *8vo*, 40 *pages*, *uncut.* s. l. 1787

UNITED STATES in Congress assembled, April 27, 1784. Report of the Grand Committee on the arrears of Interest on the National Debt. *8vo*, 12 *p.*, *uncut*, *fine copy.*
BOSTON, MDCCLXXXIV

AMERICAN COLONIES. The Plain Question upon the Present Dispute with. *Sm. 8vo*, 24 *pages*, *fine copy*, *scarce.*
DUBLIN, 1776

DAY, THOMAS. Reflections upon the Present State of England and the Independence of America. The Fifth Ed., with Additions. *8vo*, 129 *pages*, *good copy*, *scarce.*
LONDON, 1783

SMITH, WILLIAM. A Sermon on the Present Situation of American Affairs, preached in Christ Church, June 23, 1775, at the Request of the Officers of the Third Battalion of the City of Philadelphia. *Sm. 8vo*, 24 *pages*, *scarce.*
London, MDCCLXXV

2951 Miscellaneous. [*Sixteen.*]

Carter, J. G. Address delivered at Plymouth, Mass., Consecration of "Plymouth Lodge," Sept. 6, A. L. 5826. *8vo*, 37 *pages.* *Plymouth*, 1826

Cumberland, Richard. Retrospection, a Poem, in familiar verse. *8vo*, 72 *p.* *Boston*, 1812

Crabbe, George. Review of. Philadelphia, October 3, 1808. 36 *pages.*

Caroline. Queen of Great Britain. An Impartial and Authentic Memoir of the Life of. Including every Proceeding in her Case, both in and out of Parliament. By E. Hamilton. 12*mo*, 38 *pages, elegant portrait.* *London*, 1820

Croly, George. The Angel of the World, an Arabian Tale; and Sebastian. 12*mo*, *uncut*, 100 *pages.* *New York*, 1821

Conjectures on original Composition in a Letter to the Author of Sir Chas. Grandison. *8vo*, 112 *pages.* *London*, 1759

Croswell, W. Description and Explanation of the Mercator Map of the Starry Heavens. *Boston*, 1810

Albany. Historical Reminiscences of the City. *8vo*, 18 *pages, uncut; with a view of the City.* s. l. n. d.

Alcott, Dr. Wm. Library of Health—*contains account of capture of General Prescott* by *Tak. Sisson, a colored man.* *8vo*, 31 *pages, uncut.* *s. l. n. d.*

America. A Letter to an English Gentleman, on the Libels and Calumnies on America, by British Writers and Reviewers. By James Athearn Jones. *8vo*, 43 *p., unb.* *Phila.*, 1826

Allen, Ethan. Sermon. Baltimore, August 6, 1863. 11 *pages.*

——— Sermon, Conv. Prot. Epis. Church, in Ohio. Gambier, Sept. 9, 1831. *8vo*, 12 *pages.*

——— Decennial Sermon in Dayton, Ohio. Oct. 25, 1840. *8vo*, 14 *pages.* *Baltimore*, 1863

——— Sermon, "Covenant of the Sabbath." s. l. n. d.

Abercrombie, James. Sermon, May 9, 1798, day of Fasting. *Sm. 8vo*, 38 *pages, fine copy.* *Phila.*, 1798

Abracadabra; or the Conceits of A. B. and C. By O. Davis. *8vo*, 16 *pages, uncut.* *Portland*, 1808

2952 Miscellaneous. [*Fifteen.*]

Boston Academy of Music. Address before, at the Opening of the Odeon. By Samuel A. Eliot. *8vo*, 17 *pages.* *Boston*, 1835

——— Peace Festival. Official Monthly Bulletin. No. 1. Feb., 1869.

——— Proceedings of the Const. Meeting. Nov. 26th, 1850. *8vo*, 46 *pages.* *Boston*, 1850

——— Reception and Entertainment of the Chinese Embassy. Aug., 1868. *8vo*, 77 *pages, beautifully printed document.* *Boston*, 1868

Boston. Mechanics' Institution. Address, Feb. 7th, 1827. By Geo. B. Emerson. *8vo, 24 pages.*

Brown University. Laws of, March, 1827. *Providence.*

Brereton, C. D. An Inquiry into the Workhouse System and the Law of Maintenance in Agricultural Districts. *8vo,* 124 *pages.* *Norwich, Eng.,* 182–

Burke, Edmund. Lessons to a young Prince, &c. ; with five copper plates. *8vo,* 68 *pages.* *N. Y.,* 1791

Austin, A. W. Opening Argument of, in Behalf of Jamaica Aqueduct Corp. Feb. 12th, 1867. 25 *pp.*

ALLEGHANIA : a Geographical and Statistical Memoir, &c. By James W. Taylor. *8vo,* 24 *pages, dble. col.* *St. Paul, Minn.,* 1862

ADAMS, J., AND THOS. JEFFERSON, Eulogy on. Pronounced in Hallowell, July, 1826. By Peleg Sprague. *8vo,* 22 *pp. Fine copy, scarce.* *Hallowell,* 1826

Amer. Educ. Soc. Discourse, May 26th, 1863. By Rev. Edwin Johnson. *8vo,* 17 *pp.,*

Alston, Philip W. An Address, at the Laying the Cornerstone of Immanuel Church, La Grange. *8vo, 9pp.* *Memphis,* 1840

ANDREW, JOHN A. Eulogy on, delivered by Edwin P. Whipple ; with an Appendix containing Proc. of City of Boston. *8vo, stiff covers,* 36 *pp.* *Boston,* 1867

Duffie, C. R. Eight Sermons Addressed to Children. *12mo,* 150 *pp.* *N. Y.,* 1829

2953 Miscellaneous. [*Thirteen.*]

ALLEN, PAUL. Noah : a Poem. *12mo, unbound, fine copy,* 103 *pp.* *Baltimore,* 1821

Anthon, Henry. The Churchman warned against the Errors of the Time. *8vo,* 66 *pp., dble. col.* *N. Y.,* 1843

St. Andrew's Soc. Constitution of, of New York : with a list of Officers and Members, since 1756. *8vo,* 38 *pp.* *N. Y.,* 1823

A. G. Address to Electors of 9th Cong. Dist. of Mass. *8vo,* 14 *pp.* 1860

Augustus, John. A Report of the Labors of, for the last ten years, in Aid of the Unfortunate. *8vo,* 104 *pp.* *Boston,* 1852

Albany. Report of the Com. of the Classis of, on Ministerial Support. *8vo,* 41 *pp.* *Albany,* 1854

ANDERSON, ELIZA. (Translation.) Military Reflections on Four Modes of Defence for the United States ; with a Plan of Defence, &c. By Max'an ***. *8vo. Fine copy.,* 42 *pp., scarce.* *Balto.,* 1807

ALLEN, ETHAN. Report of Com. under the Act providing for the Erection of a Monument over the Grave of. *8vo,* 7 *pp.* *Montpelier,* 1858

Ames, Fisher. The Speech of, in the House of Rep. of U. S., April 28th, 1796, in support of the Treaty, &c. *8vo, fine copy, uncut,* 52 *pp.* *Boston,* (1796.)

Appleton, Nathan, and John A. Lowell. Correspondence between, in relation to the Early History of the City of Lowell. 8*vo*, 19 *pages; important.* *Boston*, 1848

Appleton, Nathan, and John G. Palfrey. Correspondence between, Intended as a Supplement to Mr. Palfrey's Pamphlet on the Slave Power. 8*vo.* 20 *pp.* *Boston*, 1846

Appleton, Nathan. Labor; its Relations in Europe and the U. S. compared. 8*vo*, 16 *pp.* *Boston*, 1844

Allen, Ethan. Narrative of the Capture of Ticonderoga, his Captivity and Treatment by the British. Fifth ed., with notes. 8*vo*, 50 *pp., orig. covers, uncut, fine copy.* *Burlington*, 1849

2953*Miscellaneous. [*Fourteen.*]

Burke, Edmund. Two Letters addressed to a Member of Parl., on Proposals for Peace with France. 8*vo* 86 *pages.* *Phila.*, 1797

Bullock, Alex. H. Address of, to the Legis. of Mass. Jan. 3d, 1868. 8*vo*, 85 *pages.* *Boston.*

Burr, Aaron. Queries addressed by the Comm., 9th Dec., 1807, to Mr. Smith, with his Answers fully given. In relation to moneys paid, and projected empire in the South. 8*vo*, *uncut*, 38 *pp.* *Senate doc., Dec.* 31st, 1807.

Brush Hill, Milton, (Mass.) Five Reasons, &c.

Bird, F. W. "Look before You Leap," into Another Great Bore. Cape Cod Harbor. 15 *pp.* *Boston*, 1868. /2½

Benton, Thos. Speech of, in reply to Mr. Webster, relative to the Public Lands. 12*mo*, 74 *pp.* *Washington*, 1830

Collins, E. K. The Supremacy of the Seas; or, Facts, Views, &c., relating to the British and American Steamers. 8*vo*, 24 *pp.* *Washington*, 1851

Chandler, Samuel. The Notes of; considered in a Sermon. Jan. 16, 1734–5. 8*vo*, 58 *pp.* *London*, 1735

Congregational Polity; as Taught in the Word of God. By Rev. M. H. Wilder.

Congregationalism: its Proof; its Catholicity. By Samuel Wolcott.

Clubb, Stephen. A Journal containing an Account of the Wrongs, Sufferings, and Neglect experienced by Americans in France. 8*vo*, *uncut*, 60 *pp., scarce.* *Printed at Boston*, 1809

Confession of Faith put forth by the Elders and Brethren of many Congregations of Christians. 8*vo*, 42 *pp.* *First printed at London*, 1688

Casco, Bay. Chronicles of. 8*vo*, *frontis.*, 56 *pp.* *Portland*, 1850

Coolidge, J. I. T. Discourse, May 2d, 1858. 8*vo*, 17 *pp.* *Boston*, 1858

2954 BACON, THOMAS. FOUR SERMONS upon the Great and indispensable Duty of all CHRISTIAN MASTERS and MISTRESSES to bring up their NEGRO SLAVES in the Knowledge and Fear of GOD. PREACHED AT THE Parish Church of *St. Peter* in *Talbot* County, in the Province of MARYLAND. *8vo, Rox., gilt edges. Fine copy; scarce.* LONDON, MDCCL.

2955 BLOODGOOD, S. DE WITT. THE SEXAGENARY; or, Reminiscences of the American Revolution. *12mo, cloth,* 203 *p., with Index, very fine copy; extremely scarce.* *Albany,* 1833

This is the veritable production of a Farmer of Saratoga County. It was undertaken at the suggestion of Gov. De Witt Clinton. All anecdotes connected with the Revolution are now valuable to the Historian and Biographer. *Ed. Preface.*

2956 BRITISH POETS, WITH MEMOIRS OF THE AUTHORS, PREFACES AND NOTES. The whole thoroughly Revised and Corrected especially for this edition. Portraits on India paper. Now complete in 130 volumes. *Crown 8vo, hf. dk. gr. lev., gt. top, uncut, large paper. Only* 100 *copies printed.* BOSTON, 1865–6

This collection of the British Poets is the most Complete ever made, and consists of One Hundred and Thirty Volumes, including the following authors, all carefully edited by Professor Child, Professor Lowell and other eminent scholars:

Akenside	1 vol.	Milton	3 vols.
Beattie	1 vol.	Montgomery	5 vols.
Burns	3 vols.	Moore	6 vols.
Butler	2 vols.	Parnell and Tickell	1 vol.
Byron	10 vols.	Pope	3 vols.
Campbell	1 vol.	Prior	2 vols.
Chatterton	2 vols.	Scott	9 vols.
Churchill	3 vols.	Shakespeare	1 vol.
Coleridge	3 vols.	Shelley	4 vols.
Collins	1 vol.	Skelton	3 vols.
Cowper	3 vols.	Southey	10 vols.
Donne	1 vol.	Spenser	5 vols.
Dryden	5 vols.	Surrey	1 vol.
Falconer	1 vol.	Swift	3 vols.
Gay	2 vols.	Thomson	2 vols.
Goldsmith	1 vol.	Vaughan	1 vol.
Gray	1 vol.	Watts	1 vol.
Herbert	1 vol.	Kirke White	1 vol.
Herrick	2 vols.	Wordsworth	7 vols.
Hood	5 vols.	Wyatt	1 vol.
Keats	1 vol.	Young	2 vols.
Marvell	1 vol.	Ballads, English and Scotch.	8 vols.

2957 BRITISH ESSAYISTS. LARGE PAPER EDITION. Only 100 Copies Printed. In Thirty-eight volumes. *Cr. 8vo, hf. dk. gr. lev., gt. top, uncut, bound uniform with the Poets. Comprising:*

Tattler	4 vols.	Mirror	2 vols.
Spectator	8 vols.	Lounger	2 vols.
Guardian	3 vols.	Observer	3 vols.
Rambler	3 vols.	Looker on	3 vols.
Adventurer	3 vols.	World	3 vols.
Connoisseur	2 vols.	Idler	1 vol.
Index,	1 vol.		

BOSTON, 1865-6

2958 COLUMBUS. Personal Narrative of the First Voyage of, to America. From a Spanish Manuscript recently Discovered in Spain. Translated from the Spanish. *8vo, hf. crim. cr. lev. mor., gt. top, rough edges. Fine copy.* *Boston*, 1827

2959 FILLEY, WILLIAM. The Indian Captive ; or, The Long Lost Jackson Boy. Life and Adventures of, who was Stolen from his Home in Jackson, Mich., by the Indians, Aug. 3d, 1837, and his Safe Return from Captivity, October 19, 1866. After an absence of 29 years, with the Indian Tribes of the Rocky Mountains. Edited by J. Z. Ballard. *8vo, red Rox., gt. top, rough edges. Illus.*, 112 *p.* *Chicago*, 1867

2960 JOSSELYN, JOHN, Gent. New-England's RARITIES Discovered : in Birds, Beasts, Fishes, Serpents, and Plants of that Country. Together with the Physical and Chyrurgical Remedies wherewith the Natives Constantly use to Cure their Distempers, Wounds, and Sores. ALSO, A perfect Description of an Indian SQUA, in all her Bravery ; with a Poem not improperly conferred upon her. LASTLY, *A CHRONOLOGICAL TABLE* of the most remarkable Passages in that Country amongst the English. Illustrated with *CUTS*. 12*mo, Colophon Title, Dedication, Rarities,* 114 *p., and leaf of Advertisements. Very fine copy with large margins, and perfect in its orig. binding.*
London : Printed for G. Widdowes at the Green Dragon in St. Paul's Church-yard, 1672

2961 JOSSELYN, JOHN, Gent. AN ACCOUNT of two VOYAGES to NEW-ENGLAND. Wherein you have the setting out of a Ship, with the Charges ; The prices of all necessaries for furnishing a Planter and his Family at his first coming ; A Description of the Country, Natives, and Creatures, with their Merchantil and Physical use ; The Government of the Countrey as it is now possessed by the *English*, &c. A large Chronological Table of the most remarkable passages, from the first discovering of the Continent of America, to the year 1673.

Heart, take thine ease,
Men hard to please
  Thou haply might'st offend,
Though one speak ill
Of thee, some will
  Say better ; there's an end.

12*mo, Title, Dedication, &c. Relation,* 215 *p.* ; *Chronological Observ.,* 217–279 *;* 3 *p. advts. Pol. tree cf., tops closely trimmed in some few places.*
London : Printed for Giles Widdows, at the Green-Dragon, in St. Paul's Churchyard, 1674.

2962 KENTUCKY. A History of the Commonwealth of, from its exploration and Settlement by the Whites, to the Close of the Northwestern Campaign in 1813 ; with an Introduction, Embracing the Settlement of Western Virginia from the First Passage of the Whites over the Mountains of Virginia in 1736, to the Treaty of Camp Charlotte in 1774. By Mann Butler. Second edition, Revised and Enlarged by the Author. *8vo, hf. crim. cr. lev., gt. top, rough edges, beautiful copy ; very scarce. Cin.*, 1836

2963 LAY, WILLIAM, and CYRUS M. HUSSEY. A Narrative of the Mutiny on Board the Ship "Globe," of Nantucket, in the Pacific Ocean, Jan., 1824, and the Journal of a Residence of two Years on Mulgrave Islands ; with observations on the manners and Customs of the Inhabitants. *12mo, Rox., gt. edges. New London*, 1828

2964 LOSSING, BENSON J. THE PICTORIAL FIELD-BOOK OF THE REVOLUTION ; or, Illustrations by Pen and Pencil, of the History, Biography, Scenery, Relics and Traditions of the War for Independence. In two volumes. Second Edition. *Imp. 8vo, Rox., gt. top, uncut. New York*, 1860

2965 LOUISIANA. THE HISTORY OF, Particularly of the Cession of That Colony to the United States of America ; with an Introductory Essay on the Constitution and Government of the United States. By Barbé Marbois. *8vo, Rox., gt. top, uncut. Phila.*, 1830

2966 MARSHALL, CHRISTOPHER. PASSAGES FROM THE DIARY OF, Kept in Philadelphia and Lancaster during the Revolution. Edited by William Duane. Volume I., 1774–1777. *8vo, hf. crim. lev., gt. top, uncut. Phila.*, 1839

Only one volume published.

2967 MARYLAND. AN HISTORICAL View of the Government of, from its Colonization to the Present Day. Vol. I. By John V. McMahon. *8vo, Rox., gt. top, rough edges. Very fine copy, scarce. Baltimore*, 1831

Only one volume published.

2968 MASSACHUSETTS HISTORICAL SOCIETY. A DISCOURSE INTENDED TO COMMEMORATE THE DISCOVERY OF AMERICA BY CHRISTOPHER COLUMBUS. Delivered at Request of Society, on the 23d of October, 1792, being the Completion of the Third Century since that Memorable Event. To which are added FOUR DISSERTATIONS :

1.—On the circumnavigation of Africa by the Ancients.
2.—An Examination of the Pretensions of Martin Behaim to a discovery of America prior to that of Columbus, with a Chronological detail of all the Discoveries made in the 15th Century.
3.—On the question whether the Honey-bee is a Native of America?
4.—On the Color of the Native Americans, and the recent population of this Continent.

By Jeremy Belknap, *8vo, red Rox., gt. top, rough edges ; fine coy ; extremely scarce.* 132 *pp.*
Printed at the Appollo Press in Boston, by BELKNAP and HALL. MDCCXCII.

2968 McKENNEY, THOMAS L. Sketches of a Tour to the Lakes: of the Character and Customs of the Chippeway Indians, and of Incidents connected with the Treaty of Fond-du-Lac. Also a Vocabulary of the Algic, or Chippeway Language, formed in part, and as far as it goes, upon the basis of one furnished by the Hon. Albert Gallatin. Ornamented with 29 Engravings. *8vo, red Rox., gt. top, rough edges; scarce.* *Baltimore*, 1827

2969 MOORE, FRANK. The Rebellion Record. A Diary of American Events, with Documents, Narratives, Illustrative Incidents, Poetry, &c. In Twelve Volumes. Illustrated with over One Hundred and Fifty Portraits on Steel of the Prominent Generals, &c., of the War, and various Maps and Diagrams. *Imp. 8vo, Rox., gt. top, uncut.* *New York*, 1867–1869

2970 New Bath Guide; or Memoirs of the B–N–R–D Family, in a Series of Poetical Epistles. A New Edition. *8vo, hf. crim. cr. lev., gt. top, rough edges; fine copy. Illus. rather free.* *Lond.*, 1804

2971 NEW YORK. Letters on the Natural History and Internal Resources of the State. By Hibernicus. *8vo, Rox., gt. top, rough edges.* *New York*, 1822

2972 PAINE, THOMAS. The Political Writings of. To which is Prefixed a Short Sketch of the Author's Life. In two vols. *8vo, Rox,, gt. top, rough edges.* *Charlestown, Mass.*, 1824

2973 PARKMAN, FRANCIS. The Jesuits in North America in the Seventeenth Century. Being Part II. of a Series of Historical Narratives. *Imp. 8vo, Rox., gt. top, rough edges.* *Boston*, 1867

75 Copies printed.

2974 PIKE, Major Z. M. An Account of Expeditions to the Sources of the Mississippi, and through the Western Parts of Louisiana to the Sources of the Arkansas, Kans, etc., Rivers; during the years 1805, 1806, and 1807. And a Tour through the Interior parts of New Spain. Illustrated by Maps and Charts. *8vo, Rox. gt. top, rough edges. Port., fine copy, very scarce.* *Phila.*, 1810

2975 PUTNAM, ISRAEL. The Life and Heroic Exploits of. Illustrated with Plates from Original Designs. By Col. David Humphreys. *12mo, Rox., gt. edges.* *New York*, 1835

2976 SCHOOLCRAFT, HENRY R. Narrative Journal of Travels through the Northwestern regions of the United States, extending from Detroit through the great Chain of American Lakes, to the Sources of the Mississippi River in the year 1820. Embellished with a Map and 8 Copper Plate Engravings. *8vo, red Rox., gt. top, rough edges, with eng. title, fine, clean, perfect copy, with port. and Memoir of Schoolcraft inserted.* *Albany*, 1821

2977 SHERMAN and his Campaigns. A Military Biography. By Col. S. M. Bowman, and Lt.-Col. R. B. Irwin. *8vo, hf. dk. gr. lev., gt. top. uncut.* *New York*, 1865

2978 SOUTH CAROLINA AND GEORGIA. AN HISTORICAL ACCOUNT OF THE RISE AND PROGRESS OF THE COLONIES OF. In Two Vols. By Alexander Hewatt. *8vo, Rox., gt. top, uncut; beautiful copy, extremely scarce.*

PRINTED FOR ALEXANDER DONALDSON, LONDON, MDCCLXXIX

2979 STEUBEN, FREDERICK WILLIAM VON, THE LIFE OF. By Frederick Kapp. With an Introduction by George Bancroft. Second Edition. *8vo, cloth, rough edges. Portrait. New York,* 1859

2980 TRIALS. NARRATIVES OF REMARKABLE CRIMINAL TRIALS. By Lady Duff Gordon. *8vo, hf. dk. blue lev., gt. top, rough edges; fine copy. New York,* 1846

2981 VERMONT. THE NATURAL AND CIVIL HISTORY OF. By Samuel Williams. In two volumes. The Second Edition Corrected and much Enlarged. *8vo, hf. dk. blue lev., gt. edges; fine copy, with map. Burlington,* 1809

2982 WASHINGTON, GEORGE. OFFICIAL LETTERS to the Honorable American Congress, Writtten During the War. In two Volumes. *8vo, hf. dk. blue lev., gt. top. rough edges; fine copy. Lond.,* 1795

2983 WASHINGTON, GEORGE. THE LIFE OF. By David Ramsay. *8vo, Rox., gt. top, rough edges. Port. by Leney. Fine copy. New York,* 1807

2984 WASHINGTON, GEORGE, THE LIFE OF. By S. G. Arnold. *12mo, Rox., gt. tops, rough edges; fine copy,* 228 *pp. New York,* 1840

2985 WASHINGTON, GENERAL GEORGE, AN EULOGY ON. Pronounced at Boston, February 19, 1800, before the American Academy of Arts and Sciences. By John Davis. *4to, hf. dk. blue lev., wide backs and cors., gt. top, uncut,* 24 *pp.*

Boston, 1800. *Reprint* 1859, *to make good complete sets of the Memoirs of the Acad.*

2986 WASHINGTON, GEORGE. A COLLECTION OF THE SPEECHES OF THE President of the United States to both Houses of Congress, also the Addresses to the President, with his Answers. With an Appendix. *8vo, full dk. blue levant, gt. top; fine copy. Boston,* 1796

2987 WASHINGTON, GEORGE. LEGACIES OF. Being a Collection of the most approved writings of. With an Appendix containing a sketch of the Life of the Illustrious Patriot. *8vo, full cr. dk. blue levant, gt. edges; fine copy, excessively scarce.*

TRENTON, MDCCC.

2988 WASHINGTON; OR LIBERTY RESTORED. A POEM. By Thomas Northmore. *Full dk. blue olive green lev., gt. top, rough edges; very scarce. Balt.,* 1809

2989 WASHINGTON, GEORGE. Life of. Interspersed with Biographical Anecdotes of the most Eminent Men who effected the American Revolution. Port. By John Corry. *8vo, full dk. olive green lev., gt. top, rough edges, with the List of Subscribers.* *N. Y.*, 1809

2990 Wilkinson, Jemima, History of. A Preacheress of the 18th Century. Containing an Authentic Narrative of her Life and Character. By David Hudson. *8vo, hf. crim. lev., gt. top, rough edges. Fine copy.* *Geneva, N. Y.*, 1821

2991 WILLARD, SAMUEL. (*Pastor of a Church in Boston, in N. E.*) *The Peril* of the *TIMES Displayed;* or, The Danger of Mens Taking up with a Form of Godliness, But denying the Power of it. *12mo, full cr. crim. levant, gt. top.* *Boston: Printed by B. Green and J. Allen,* 1700

2992 Winslow, Edward. The Glorious Progress of the GOSPEL, amongst the Indians in New England, manifested By three Letters, under the Hand of that famous Instrument of the Lord, Mr. John Eliot, And another from Mr. Thomas Mayhew, Jr.; both Preachers of the Word, as well to the English as Indians in New England, &c. Together, With an Appendix to the foregoing Letters, holding forth Conjectures, Observations, and Applications. By I. D. (John Davenport) Minister of the Gospell. Published by Edward Winslow. *Sm. 4to, Title, Dedication, and 28 p. Beautiful copy, clean and perfect; excessively scarce, unbound.*

LONDON: Printed for Hannah Allen, in Popes-Head Alley, 1649.

2993 WINTHROP, JOHN (First Gov. of Mass.) A Journal of the Transactions and Occurrences in the Settlement of Massachusetts and the other New-England Colonies, from the year 1630 to 1644. And now first Published from a correct copy of the Original Manuscript. (By Noah Webster.) *8vo, full polished dk. blue, cf., gt. edge. Beautiful copy; very scarce.* Hartford: Printed by Elisha Babcock, MDCCXC.

Dedicated to the Posterity of John Winthrop.

"Mr. Winthrop kept a Journal of every important occurrence from his first embarking in America, in 1630, to the year 1644. This Manuscript, as appears by some passages, was originally designed for publication; and it was formerly consulted by the first compilers of New England History, particularly by Hubbard, Mather and Prince. On reading the work, the editor (N. Webster) found it to contain many curious and interesting facts relating to the settlement of Massachusetts and the other New England Colonies, and highly descriptive of the character and views of the first inhabitants. By consent of the descendants of Gov. Winthrop, proposals were issued for publishing a *small number of copies.*—Editor's Preface.

2994 WHEELER, CAPT. THOMAS. A THANKEFULL REMEMBRANCE OF GOD'S MERCY TO SEVERAL PERSONS AT QUABAUG OR BROOKFIELD. *Fo. 4to, red. cr. lev. mor., elegant dble green, with rich tooled borders around inside covers, fl. gt. back and French filleted pan. sides ; the whole dry cld., and the whole cleaned from foxy spots and other stains ; all ink removed and the whole dark sized and mending in do. as required. Magnificent copy, with large margins*, 52 *pp.*

CAMBRIDGE: Printed and sold by *Samuel Green*, 1676

When Gov. Hutchinson wrote his History of Mass,, in giving an account of the Expedition (Hist. Mass., Vol. I., 265), in which his ancestor sustained such an important part and lost his life, it does not appear that he has made any reference whatever to Captain Wheeler's Narrative, which he most likely would have done had he known of its existence. See No. 230 of this Catalogue. We give the following extract from the Preface—

"*I Purposing to Publish this ensuing Narrative of God's Providence* towards Capt. Hutchinson and myself and others, and the *Sermon* preached on the occasion hereafter, do Judge it expedient to give you a little further account of matters, occasioning the going of *Captain Hutchinson* and *myself* to Quabaug, and also of the *Motives* inducing me to the Publication of both to the world," etc.

We refer to W. E. Woodward's Catalogue, where this identical copy brought $72, unbound, and its condition was not very desirable ; but having passed through the hands of the best binder in England (F. Bedford), at an additional expense of $40, it is now, without any doubt, the finest copy in existence.

2995 ATALA ; OR, THE AMOURS OF TWO INDIANS in the Wilds of America. *8vo, hf. vellum, gt. edges. Frontis.* *Lond.*, 1802

2996 BELKNAP, JEREMY. AMERICAN BIOGRAPHY ; or, an HISTORICAL ACCOUNT of those PERSONS who have been distinguished in *AMERICA*, as

ADVENTURERS,	*DIVINES,*
STATESMEN,	*WARRIORS,*
PHILOSOPHERS,	*AUTHORS.*

AND OTHER REMARKABLE CHARACTERS, Comprehending a Recital of The EVENTS connected with their LIVES and ACTIONS. In Two Volumes. *8vo, dk. Rox., gt. top, rough edges. Splendid copy, and very scarce in this condition.*

PRINTED at *BOSTON* BY *ISAIAH THOMAS* AND *E. T. ANDREWS*, MDCCXCIV, and 1798.

2997 BENNETT, JAMES GORDON. THE LIFE AND WRITINGS OF Editor of the "New York Herald." *Sm. 4to, dk. Rox., gt. top.' rough edges*, 64 *pp., dble. col., with the orig. covers. Illus. with caricatures of Bennet as—"Ariel," "The Scottish Adventurer," "Puffing for Black-Mail," etc. All in fine condition.*

New York, 1844

A scurrilous pamphlet, now quite scarce.

A Thankefull REMEMBRANCE OF GODS MERCY To several Persons at Quabaug or BROOKFIELD:

Partly in a Collection of Providences about them, and Gracious Appearances for them: And partly in a Sermon Preached By *Mr.* EDWARD BULKLEY, Pastor of the Church of Christ at *Concord*, upon a day of Thanksgiving, kept by divers for their Wonderfull Deliverance there,

Published by Capt. *THOMAS VVHEELER.*

Psal. 107. 8. *Oh that men would Praise the Lord for his Goodness, and his Wonderfull Works to the Children of men,*

Psal. 111. 2. *The Works of the* LORD *are great, sought out of all those that Love him.*

C A M B R I D G E,
Printed and Sold by *Samuel Green* 1676.

2998 BERKELEY, GEORGE. A SERMON preached before the Incorporated Society for the *Propagation of the Gospel in Foreign Parts*, on *Friday, Feb.* 18, 1731. *8vo, hf. red lev., gilt top, uncut; very scarce*, 79 *pp*. LONDON, MDCCXXXII.

Besides the Sermon, there is also an Abstract of the Proc. of the Society, Reports from several of the Missionaries of South Carolina, Pennsylvania, New York, New Jersey, Connecticut, Rhode Island, Long Island, etc., with a list of the Members of the Society.

2999 BLUNT, JOSEPH. A HISTORICAL SKETCH OF THE FORMATION OF THE CONFEDERACY, Particularly with Reference to the Provincial Limits and the Jurisdiction of the General Government over Indian Tribes and the Public Territory. *8vo, red Rox., gt. top, rough edges. Fine copy.* *New York*, 1825

3000 BOSTON. SURVEY OF BOSTON AND ITS VICINITY. Showing the distance from the Old State House to all the Towns and Villages not exceeding fifteen miles therefrom; with a short Topographical Sketch of the Country, taken in the years 1818, '18, '19, '20. By John G. Hales. *Frontis. and map. 8vo, dk. Rox., gt. top, rough edges.* *Boston*, 1821

3001 BRACKENRIDGE, H. H. GAZETTE PUBLICATIONS. *8vo, hf. gr. lev., gt. edges; very scarce.* *Carlisle, Pa.*, 1806

Contains Historical account of Pittsburgh in 1786. Of the Indian War and Poems on Indian Treaties; and on Anthony Wayne. Sermon delivered to the American army a few days before the Battle of Brandywine. An Eulogium of the Brave Men who have fallen in the contest with Great Britain, delivered July 5, 1779. Poem to "Whiskey." "The Battle of Bunker's Hill." A Drama written a few weeks after this battle, performed by the youth of the academy on the eastern shore of Maryland of which Brackenridge was master. The prologue was written by Col. John Park of the American army, etc.

3002 BURR, AARON. REPORTS OF THE TRIALS OF, for Treason and for Misdemeanor, in preparing the means of a Military Expedition against Mexico, etc. To which is added an Appendix, containing the Arguments and Evidence, Etc., taken in Short-Hand by David Robertson. In Two volumes. *8vo, red Rox., gt. top, rough edges. Splendid Copy.* *Phila.*, 1808

3003 BURR, AARON. BURR'S CONSPIRACY exposed; and General Wilkinson Vindicated against the Slanders of his Enemies on that Important occasion. *8vo, red Rox., gt. top, rough edges; very scarce. Fine copy.* *Wash.*, 1811

3004 BURROUGHS, STEPHEN. MEMOIRS OF. Containing many incidents in the Life of this Wonderful Man never before published. Two Volumes in One. Curious Frontispiece. *12mo, hf. red tky., gt. edges. Fine copy.* *Boston*, 1835

3005 CANADA. THE BACKWOODS OF. Being Letters from the Wife of an Emigrant Officer. *12mo, hf. red tky., gilt edges. Illus.*

Contains considerable Indian History. *Lond.*, 1846

3006 CORNELIUS, ELIAS. THE LITTLE OSAGE CAPTIVE, an Authentic Narrative: to which are added some interesting letters, written by Indians. *12mo, hf. red t'ky., gilt top, rough edges, frontis., fine copy.* *York, Eng.*, 1824

This is not a romance, but the observations of one of the missionaries to the Choctaws, in 1817, in Arkansaw.

3007 CLARKE, McDONALD. Poems of. With Portrait after Inman. *8vo, full cr. crim. lev., gt. edges. Fine copy; extremely scarce.* *New York: J. W. Bell, MDCCCXXXVI.*

"The Book is pioneered by no parade of puffery. I despise it. No dazzling name of a distinguished publisher blazing on the title-page; none of the velvet trickery that smooths a *fashionable writer's* works into pic-nic patronage. Bell's undertaken to ring the death-bell of neglect, and if I can ring the Great Belle of my affections, shan't care if the Critics put my popularity to bed with a shovel. *In short, if the life of my poetry is wholesome, 'twill breathe, after the wild spirit that inspired it has been sobered* at the terrible tribunal of Eternity, and the weak hand that traced it, long wasted to ashes."—M'D. C. We give one of his poems in full, entitled—A Late Death at New London.—

Poor Kit is gone—
A funnier fellow never was born,
—Mirth must wear for the Captain, a double reefed weed—
Many a morn,
When a boy, in 1807,
Have I stood on Frink's stoop,
With New-London's jolliest group,
And haw, haw'd and he, he'd,
At his ripping fun.
* * * * *
Is it all done—done?—
Well—by the setting sun
He could laugh, as well as by the rising rays,
For his was an intellect, always a-blaze.
Here's a song to the olden days,
The memory of 1807—
Good Heaven! how Time waddles away,
But as long as the spirit doesn't get gray,
It matters not—'tis nature's lot—
To be forgot when the dim hour comes,
And not leave of Thought's luxuries, a few poor crumbs,
Is all that should make us sigh
When I come to die, may noble natures join,
And say, he could flush the World's heart like old wine,
And may some merry fellow,
On Mac's memory get mellow,
Pleasantly sit,
As I do, o'er dear old Kitt,
By the darkly setting sun.
Tell of the sumptuous fun
He had with Donald in his Bunkum days;
For posthumous praise,
That comes from the heart, and makes the tears start,
And waves the willow leaves over our sod,
Is grateful to man, and accepted of God.

—Page 195.

3008 DIBDIN, THOS. FROGNALL. Reminiscences of a Literary Life; with Anecdotes of Books, and of Book Collectors. Two Parts in Two Volumes. Frontispieces and a number of other elegant illustrations. *Large 8vo, full dk. green crushed lev., gt. tops, rough edges, rich inside borders, backs and covers richly tooled, fine copy, very scarce.*
LONDON: JOHN MAJOR, MDCCCXXXVI

This copy contains the Index, which having been published after the main work was issued, is seldom found in any copies.

3009 FLORIDA, EAST. Notices of, with an account of the Seminole Nation of Indians. By a recent traveller in the Province. *8vo, red rox. gilt top, uncut, fine copy.* *Charleston,* 1822

Contains also, a vocabulary of the Seminole Language.

3010 FOX, EBENEZER. The Adventures of, in the Revolutionary War, illustrated by elegant eng., from original designs. Portrait of Fox. *12mo, hf. red t'ky., gilt top, rough edges, veyr scarce.* *Boston,* 183

3011 GEORGIA. AN IMPARTIAL ENQUIRY INTO THE STATE and UTILITY OF THE PROVINCE of *Georgia.* *8vo,* 104 *p., full crim. cr. lev. gilt top, rough edges, rich inside borders, running title on back, paneled sides, etc.*

LONDON: Printed for W. MEADOWS, at the *Angel* in *Cornhill* MDCCXLI.

3012 ELDRIDGE, ELEANOR. MEMOIRS OF. In Two volumes. *Half gr. lev. gilt tops, with Portrait.* *Providence,* 1841

The subject of this memoir, was born of African and Indian parentage. Her mother was a native Indian of the Fuller Family of the tribe of the Narragansetts, and her father an African, who served in the Revol. army.

3013 ELIOT, John. THE LIFE OF. The Apostle to the Indians. *12mo, hf. dk. blue, lev. yellow edges, fine copy.* *Phila.,* 1829

3014 ELIOT, JOHN. MEMOIR OF, Apostle to the North American Indians. By Martin Moore. *12mo, hf. dk. blue lev., gilt top, rough edges, frontis.* *Boston,* 1842

"Not a whit behind the very chiefest apostles."

3015 GEORGIA. A VOYAGE TO, Begun in the Year 1735, CONTAINING, An Account of the Settling the Town of FREDERICA, in the Southern Part of the Province; and a Description of the SOIL, AIR, BIRDS, BEASTS, TREES, RIVERS, ISLANDS, &c., WITH the RULES and ORDERS made by the Honourable the TRUSTEES for that SETTLEMENT; including the Allowances of Provisions, Clothing, and other Necessaries to the Families and Servants which went thither.

ALSO A Description of the Town and County of *Savannah,* in the Northern Part of the Province; the Manner of dividing and granting the Lands, and the Improvements there: With an Account of the AIR, SOIL, RIVERS and ISLANDS in that Part.

By FRANCIS MOORE, *Author of* Travels into the Inland Parts of *Africa.* *8vo, full crushed crim. levant, gilt top, uncut, inside borders beautifully tooled, by Bedford, excessively scarce, fine copy,* 103 *pages.*

LONDON: Printed for JACOB ROBINSON, in *Ludgate Street,* 1744

3016 HENRY, JOHN JOSEPH. AN ACCURATE AND INTERESTING ACCOUNT of the Hardships and Sufferings of that Band of Heroes, who traversed the wilderness in the Campaign against Quebec in 1775. *8vo. full dk. blue, levant gilt edges, eleg't. rich inside borders, fine copy, very scarce.* *Lancaster,* 1812

3017 HEWES, GEORGE, R. T. TRAITS OF THE TEA PARTY; being a Memoir of George R. T. Hewes, one of the last of its survivors; with a History of that Transaction; Reminiscences of the Massacre, and the Siege, and other stories of old times. By a Bostonian. *12mo, full crushed crimson levant, gilt top, rough edges, inside borders, and covers richly tooled, extremely scarce and fine copy. Portrait of Hewes.* *New York,* 1835

Lossing in Vol. I., p. 499–502, of his "Field Book," mentions David Kinnison as the last survivor of the "Tea Party," who died in 1851, aged 115 yrs. Hewes died in 1843, aged 101 yrs. He was present at the Massacre in Boston on the 5th March, "and during the whole of it," "and was intimately acquainted with most of the circumstances which led to it," was also in Boston during the "Siege" or "hard times," "in a word, he happened to be one of that comparatively small class of persons who were situated, throughout the contest, and throughout the context of affairs connected with it, in the midst of them, and as it were, at the central seeing and hearing point." His military exploits were confined to the "*neutral ground* of Westchester, with the *Cow Boys, etc.*"

3018 HOPKINSON, FRANCIS. THE MISCELLANEOUS ESSAYS AND OCCASIONAL WRITINGS OF. In three volumes. *8vo, dk. rox., gt. top, rough edges. beautiful copy. Scarce. Phila.* MDCCXCII

3019 LIEBERKUHN, REV. SAMUEL. THE HISTORY OF OUR LORD AND SAVIOUR JESUS CHRIST: comprehending all that the Four Evangelists have recorded concerning him; all their relation being brought together in one narration, so that no circumstance is omitted, but that inestimable History is continued in one series, in the very words of Scripture. Translated into the DELEWARE INDIAN LANGUAGE, BY THE REV. DAVID ZEISBERGER. *8vo, full crim. cr. lev. elegant rich inside borders, gilt edges, beautiful copy, very scarce. New York*, 1824

3020 LONG ISLAND. THE HISTORY OF, FROM ITS DISCOVERY AND SETTLEMENT TO THE PRESENT TIME. With many important and interesting matters; including notices of numerous Individuals and Families; also a particular account of the different Churches and Ministers. In two volumes. Illustrated with Portraits Maps and Plates. Second Edition, revised and greatly enlarged. By Benjamin Thompson. *Large 8vo, full crimson, cr. lev. gt. tops, rough edges, rich inside borders, back and covers elegantly tooled, magnificent copy, and very scarce in this condition. New York*, 1843

3021 MASSACHUSETTS. THE HISTORY OF, from the First Settlement thereof in 1628, until the year 1760. In Two volumes. By Thomas Hutchinson, Esq. *8vo, dk., rox. gt. top., rough edges, remarkably fine copy, and exceedingly scarce in this condition.*

The Third Edition, with additional NOTES and CORRECTIONS PRINTED AT SALEM, FOR THOMAS AND ANDREWS. BOSTON, 1795

3022 MASSACHUSETTS BAY. THE HISTORY OF THE PROVINCE OF, from 1749 to 1774, comprising a detailed Narrative of the origin and early stages of the American Revolution. By Thomas Hutchinson. Edited by Rev. John Hutchinson. *8vo, dk. rox., gt. top, rough edges, forms the Third volume of Hutchinson's History.*
London: John Murray, MDCCCXXVIII

3023 MICHIGAN. HISTORY OF, from its earliest Colonization to the present time. By James H. Lanman. *12mo, hf. dk. blue lev., gt. edges. New York*, 1842

3024 NEW ENGLAND'S MEMORIAL. BY NATHANIEL MORTON. Fifth Edition, containing, besides the original work, and the supplement, large additions in Marginal Notes, and an Appendix, with a Lithographic copy of an Ancient Map. By John Davis. *8vo hf. crim. lev., gt. top, rough edges, backs beautifully tooled and lettered. Boston*, 1826

3025 NEW ENGLAND. LIVES OF THE CHIEF FATHERS OF:

Vol. I., The Life of JOHN COTTON. By A. W. McClure.

Vol. II., The Lives of JOHN WILSON, JOHN NORTON, and JOHN DAVENPORT. By A. W. McClure.

Vol. III., The Life of JOHN ELIOT, with an account of the Early Missionary Efforts among the Indians of New England. By Nehemiah Adams.

Vol. IV., The Life of THOMAS SHEPHERD. By John A. Albro.

Vol. V., The Lives of INCREASE MATHER and SIR WILLIAM PHIPPS. By Enoch Pond.

Vol. VI., The Life of THOMAS HOOKER. By E. W. Hooker.

In Six Volumes, *8vo, hf. vel., contents lettered diagonally on back, beautiful copy, gt. top, uncut.* *Boston,* 1846–'49

3026 NEW HAMPSHIRE. THE HISTORY OF. VOLUME I., COMPREHENDING THE EVENTS OF ONE COMPLETE CENTURY FROM THE DISCOVERY OF THE RIVER PASCATAQUA.
PHILADELPHIA, MDCCLXXXIV.

VOLUME II.—COMPREHENDING THE EVENTS OF SEVENTY-FIVE YEARS FROM MDCCXV to MDCCXC. Illustrated by a MAP.
BOSTON, MDCCXCI

VOLUME III.—CONTAINING A GEOGRAPHICAL DESCRIPTION OF THE STATE; WITH SKETCHES OF ITS NATURAL HISTORY, PRODUCTIONS, IMPROVEMENTS, AND PRESENT STATE OF SOCIETY AND MANNERS, LAWS AND GOVERNMENT. BY JEREMY BELKNAP. *8vo, dk. rox., gt. top, rough edges, excessively scarce in this condition, beautiful copy.*
BOSTON, MDCCXCII

3027 NEW HOLLAND AND THE CAROLINE ISLANDS. A Residence of Eleven years in, being the adventures of James O. Connell. Edited from his verbal narration. *12mo, hf. gr. t'ky., gilt top, rough edges, illust.* *Boston,* 1836

3028 NEW YORK CITY AND STATE. HISTORIC TALES OF OLDEN TIME; concerning the Early Settlement and Advancement of, etc. Illustrated with Plates. By John F. Watson. *8vo, hf. gr. t'ky., gt. edges. A. A. Smets' copy.* *New York,* 1832

3029 OREGON TERRITORY. A GEOGRAPHICAL AND PHYSICAL ACCOUNT of that Country and its Inhabitants, with outlines of its History and Discovery. By C. G. Nicolay. *12mo, hf. red t'ky., gt. edges, illust.* *London: Knight,* 1846

3030 OTIS, JAMES. THE LIFE OF, containing also, notices of some contemporary characters and events from the year 1760 to 1775. Portrait and plate. *8vo, red rox., gt. top, rough edges, fine copy.* *Boston,* 1823

3031 PENNSYLVANIA. THE HISTORY OF, IN NORTH AMERICA, FROM THE Original Institution and Settlement of that Province, under the first *Proprietor* and *Governor* WILLIAM PENN, in 1681, till after the year 1742; WITH AN INTRODUCTION RESPECTING, The Life of W. PENN, prior to the grant of the Province, and the religious Society of the People called *Quakers;* with the first rise of the neighboring Colonies, more particularly of *West-New Jersey,* and the Settlement of the *Dutch* and *Swedes* on *Delaware,* TO

WHICH IS ADDED, A brief Description of the said Province AND OF THE General State, in which it flourished, principally between the years 1760 and 1770. The whole including a Variety of Things, useful and interesting to be known, respecting that Country in early Time, etc. With an APPENDIX. BY ROBERT PROUD. In Two Volumes, with Portrait and Map. *8vo, full dk. gr. cr. lev., gt. edges, backs and covers richly tooled, rich inside borders, eleg't copy, scarce* *Philadelphia*, 1797–'98

3032 PORTSMOUTH, N. H. ANNALS OF, comprising a Period of Two Hundred Years from the First Settlement of the Town; with Biographical Sketches of a few of the most respectable Inhabitants. *8vo, rox., gilt top, rough edges, beautiful copy. Very scarce.* *Portsmouth*, 1825

3033 REVOLUTION. TALES OF THE REVOLUTION, being Rare and Remarkable passages of the History of the War of 1775. 12*mo, red rox., gilt top, uncut, scarce.* *New York*, 1835

Contains Arnold's Exped. up the Kennebec, naval maneuvres on the North River, Capture of Gen'l Prescott, Green's Retreat, The Whigs and the Wolves, Scenes in South Carolina, Narrative of Baroness Reidesel, etc.

3034 ROWLANDSON, MRS. MARY. A NARRATIVE OF THE Captivity, Sufferings and Removes OF——who was taken prisoner by the *Indians*; with several others, and treated in the most barbarous and cruel Manner by the vile *Savages*; with many other remarkable Events during her Travels. *Written by her own Hand for her private Use, and since made public at the earnest Desire of some Friends, and for the Benefit of the Afflicted. 8vo, full cr. crim. lev., gt. top, uncut, beautifully tooled inside borders and covers,* with a curious woodcut on title, of Mrs. Rowlandson at the door of her house resisting the attacks of the Indians, and another at the end, of the house in flames.

BOSTON: Reprinted and Sold by THOMAS and JOHN FLEET, at the *Bible* and *Heart*, Cornhill, 1791

3035 SANDERSON, JOHN AND ROBERT WALN, Jr. BIOGRAPHY OF THE SIGNERS TO THE DECLARATION OF INDEPENDENCE. In Nine Volumes. *8vo, dk. rox., gilt tops, rough edges, beautiful copy. Illustrated with Thirty Eng., all in fine, clean condition.* *Phila.*, 1820–'27

Gen'l. H. Dearborn's (of Mass.) copy, with autuograph.

3036 SCHOOLCRAFT, HENRY R. NOTES ON THE IRIQUOIS; or, contributions to the Statistics, Aboriginal History, Antiquities and General Ethnology of Western New York. *Roy. 8vo, red rox., gt. top, rough edges.* *New York*, 1846

3037 SOUTHOLD, L. I. GRIFFIN'S JOURNAL. First Settlers of Southold. The Names of the Heads of those Families, being only thirteen at the time of their landing; First Proprietors of Orient; Biographical Sketches, etc. By Augustus Griffin. *8vo, hf. crim. lev., gt. edges, fine copy, very scarce. Portrait.* *Orient, L. I.*, 1857

3038 **Stoddard Solomon**, Pastor to the Church of *Northampton, in* NEW ENGLAND. THE Safety of Appearing at the DAY OF JUDGMENT in the Righteousness of CHRIST, Opened and Applied. The Second EDITION Corrected. With some *Addition* by the AUTHOR. *8vo, hf. dk. blue lev., gt. edges; fine copy, very scarce.* *BOSTON: Re-printed for* D. HENCHMAN, *at his shop in Cornhill,* MDCCXXIX.

3039 ST. URSULA'S CONVENT; or The Nun of Canada. Containing Scenes from Real Life. In two Volumes. *12mo, hf. vellum, gt. edges; fine copy.* *Kingston, Upper Canada,* 1824

Said to be the first Novel published in Canada. Written by a young lady of "*Seventeen Summers.*" "The era to which this story relates was an eventful one, and may be reviewed with interest by many families, who, like the author, trace their descent in a manner similar to that of the principal personages of the Tale."

3040 SULLIVAN'S CAMPAIGN; NOTICES OF, OR THE REVOLUTIONARY WARFARE IN WESTERN NEW YORK. Embodied in the Addresses and Documents connected with the Funeral Honors rendered to those who fell with the gallant Boyd in the Genesee Valley, including the remarks of Gov. Seward at Mount Hope. *12mo, full crimson levant, elegant, rich inside borders, paneled sides, gt. edges. Frontis. Very fine copy.* 191 *pp.* *Rochester,* 1842

Contains an Oration, illustrative of the Revolutionary Warfare in Western New York, by Samuel Treat of Geneseo, embracing 91 pages. Very interesting notes included, also Letters of Moses Van Campen, John Salmon and others, survivors of Sullivan's Campaign.

3041 TRIALS. CELEBRATED TRIALS of all Countries, and Remarkable Cases of Criminal Jurisprudence. Selected by a Member of the Phila. Bar. *8vo, hf. vellum; fine copy.* *Phila.,* 1843

Contains over 88 Trials, among them, The Samuelston Witches in 1678, The Salem Witches, Capt. Kidd, etc.

3042 TRUMBULL, HENRY. HISTORY OF THE DISCOVERY OF AMERICA, of the Landing of our Forefathers, and of their most remarkable engagements with the Indians. To which is annexed the particulars of almost every important engagement with the Savages at the Westward, to the present day, including the defeat of Generals BRADDOCK, HARMER and ST. CLAIR, the CREEK and SIMINOLE War, etc. *8vo, hf. green levant, gilt edges, with curious plates of Indian battles and persecutions; the first edition; very scarce, and fine copy.* *Boston,* 1819

3043 UNCAS AND MIANTONOMOH; A HISTORICAL DISCOURSE, delivered at Norwich, July 4, 1842, on the occasion of the erection of a Monument to the Memory of Uncas. By William L. Stone. *12mo, hf. red Tky., gt. top, rough edges; fine copy.* *New York,* 1842

3044 VALE, G. FANATICISM; its Source and Influence, illustrated by the simple narrative of Isabella, in the case of Matthias, Mr. and Mrs. B. Folger, etc. A Reply to W. L. Stone. In Two Vols. *8vo, hf. gr. lev., gt. tops, uncut; curious.* *N. Y.,* 1835

For the Trial of Matthias see No. 2172.

3045 VERMONT. History of the State of. From its Earliest Settlement to the close of the Year 1832. By Zadock Thompson. 12*mo, dk. Rox., gt. top, rough edges; beautiful copy.*
Burlington, 1833

3046 WARREN, MRS. MERCY. History of the Rise, Progress and Termination of the American Revolution. Interspersed with Biographical, Political and Moral Observations. In Three Volumes. 8*vo, dk. rox., gt. top, uncut; fine copy.*
Boston, 1805

3047 WASHINGTON, GEORGE. The Life of. Interspersed with Biographical Anecdotes of the Most Eminent Men who effected the American Revolution. By John Corry. 8*vo, full crushed crimson levant, gt. edges, fine copy; scarce ed. with Index.*
London, 1800

3048 WASHINGTON'S Political Legacies. To which is Annexed an Appendix, Containing an Account of His Illness, Death and the National Tribute of Respect Paid to His Memory, with a Biographical Sketch of his Life and Character, His Will, and Dr. Tappan's Discourse, before the University of Cambridge. 8*vo, full crimson levant, gt. edges, beautiful tooling on covers and back, rich inside borders, elegant, clean copy; very scarce, with subscribers' names.*

NEW YORK: *Printed by* George Forman *for* C. Davis, *Water Street*, 1800.

3049 WILLIAMS, JOHN, (*Pastor of Church in Deerfield,*) and Mrs. MARY ROWLANDSON, (*of Lancaster.*) The Captivity and Deliverance of, who were taken, together with Families and Neighbors, by the French and Indians, and carried into Canada. Written by Themselves. 8*vo, full crimson levant, gt. edges, rich inside borders, elegant; very scarce edition, beautiful copy.* Brookfield: Printed by HORI BROWN, *Sept.*, 1811

3050 WILLIAMS, JOHN. Minister of the Gospel in Deerfield, *The Redeemed Captive Returning to* ZION. A Faithful History of *Remarkable Occurrences,* in the *Captivity and Deliverence* of, who, in the Desolation which befel that Plantation, by an Incursion of the *French* and *Indians*, was by *them* carried away, with his Family, and his Neighbourhood, unto Canada. Drawn up by Himself. Whereto there is annexed a Sermon, preached by him upon his Return, at the Lecture in *Boston, December* 5, 1706, On those Words, Luke 8. 39, *Return to thine own House, and shew how great Things God hath done unto thee.* The Fourth Edition. As also an Appendix, containing an Account of those taken Captive at *Deerfield, February* 29, 1703-4; of those killed after they went out of Town; those who returned; and of those still absent from their native Country; of those who were slain at that Time in or near the Town; and of the Mischief done by the Enemy in *Deerfield*, from the Beginning of its Settlement to the Death of the Rev. Mr. Williams, in 1729. With a Conclusion to the Whole, by the Rev. Mr. Williams, of *Springfield*, and the Rev. Mr. Prince, of *Boston*.

8*vo, full crushed crimson levant, gt. top, uncut, inside borders and covers beautifully tooled; beautiful copy, very rare,* 79 *pp.*

BOSTON: *Printed.*
NEW-LONDON: Re-printed by T. Green, 1758

3051 ZENGER, JOHN PETER. A BRIEF NARRATIVE OF THE CASE AND TRIAL OF, PRINTER OF THE NEW YORK WEEKLY JOURNAL, FOR A LIBEL.

In a free State, such as our's is, all Men ought to enjoy, and express their Minds freely." *4to, full dk. green lev., 53 pages, gilt top, uncut, inside borders richly tooled; superb copy, extremely scarce; by Bedford.*

NEW-YORK:

Re-printed by JOHN HOLT, at the *Exchange*, 1770.

This was the first attempt in New York to muzzle the press. Andrew Hamilton, of Philadelphia, was Zenger's Counsel; Zenger was acquitted, and the people, to express their approbation of the verdict, entertained Hamilton at a public dinner, and the Corporation presented him with the freedom of the city in a gold box. On his departure, he was honored with salutes of cannon.—*Lossing, Field Book, Vol. II.*, 580. Zenger was imprisoned thirty-five weeks; the excitement at his trial was intense. The following is the closing up of Mr. Hamilton's argument for the defence: "But to conclude, the question before the court, and to you, gentlemen of the jury, is not of small nor private concern; it is not the cause of a poor Printer, nor of *New York* alone, which you are now trying! No! It may in its consequence affect every free man that lives under a British government on the main of America. It is the best cause; it is the cause of Liberty; and I make no doubt but your upright conduct this day will not only entitle you to the love and esteem of your fellow citizens; but every man who prefers freedom to a life of slavery will bless and honour you, as men who have baffled the attempt of Tyranny; and by an impartial and uncorrupt verdict, have laid a noble foundation for securing to ourselves, our posterity and our neighbors, that, to which nature and the laws of our country have given us a right—the Liberty—both of exposing and opposing arbitrary power (in these parts of the world, at least,) by speaking and writing truth."

3052 ADAIR, JAMES. HISTORY OF THE AMERICAN INDIANS, &c. *4to, old calf binding, very clean copy, large margins, with map.*
See Title No. 5. *London*, MDCCLXXV

3053 ALLEN, COL. ETHAN. A NARRATIVE OF COLONEL ETHAN ALLEN'S CAPTIVITY, From the time of his being taken by the British near Montreal, on the 25th day of September, in the year 1775, to the Time of his Exchange on the 6th day of May, 1778, Containing, His Voyages and Travels, With the most remarkable Occurrences respecting himself, and many other Continental Prisoners of different Ranks and Characters, which fell under his Observation, in the Course of the same; particularly the Destruction of the Prisoners at N. Y. by General Sir William Howe, in the years 1776 and 1777—Interspersed with Political Observations. Written by Himself, and now published for the Information of the Curious of all Nations. [Motto.] *8vo, full dark blue crushed lev., gilt top, rough edges, beautiful copy, very scarce.* *Walpole*, 1807

3054 AMERICA. A COLLECTION of Interesting and Authentic PAPERS, relative to the DISPUTE between GREAT BRITAIN and AMERICA; shewing the CAUSES and PROGRESS of that MISUNDERSTANDING from 1764 to 1775. *Large 8vo, maroon Rox., gilt top, uncut, superb copy, extremely scarce.* LONDON: J. ALMON, MDCCLXXVII

3055 American Monthly Magazine and Critical Review. *8vo, unbound, 80 pages, good copy.* *New York,* 1818

Contains Rafinesque's "Farther account of Discoveries in Natural History in the Western States"—"Memoir on the Antiquities of the Western Part of New York," by De Witt Clinton—and an Obituary of Col. Jeremiah O'Brien, of Machias, Me., etc.

3056 ANDRE, MAJ. JOHN. Monody on. By Miss Seward. Fourth Amer. Ed. *8vo, full dark olive green levt., gilt top, edges uncut, very scarce, fine copy.* *Boston,* 1798

In same volume, AMELIA; or, the Faithless Briton: an Original American Novel, etc. *Boston,* 1798

3057 APES, WILLIAM. A Son of the Forest. The Experience of, comprising a notice of the Pequod Tribe of Indians. Written by himself. *12mo, full crushed crimson levant, gilt top, rough edges, beautiful copy.* *N. Y.,* 1829

3058 ——— Another copy. *Half dark blue levant, gilt edges.* *N. Y.,* 1829

3059 BOON, COL. DANIEL; Life and Adventures of. Comprising an account of his first excursion to Kentucky, in 1769, and of his various encounters with the Indians. Written by himself. To which is added a narrative of the most important incidents of his life, from the latter period until the period of his death. Annexed is an Eulogy on Col. Boon, by Lord Byron. *8vo, full dark maroon levant, gilt top, rough edges, very rare edition, 26 pages.* *Brooklyn,* 1823

3060 Bradley, Eliza. An Authentic Narrative of Shipwreck and Sufferings of. Curious Frontis. Written by herself. *8vo, half crim. tky., gilt edges.* *Boston,* 1820

3061 BRAINERD, REV. DAVID; Memoirs of—Missionary to the Indians, on the borders of New York, New Jersey, and Penn., chiefly taken from his own Diary. By Rev. Jon. Edwards. Including his Journal, for the first time incorporated with the rest of the Diary. By S. E. Dwight. *8vo, sheep fine copy.* *New Haven,* 1822

3062 BRANAGAN, THOMAS. Avenia; or, a Tragical Poem, on the oppression of the Human Species and Infringement of the Rights of Man. In Six Books. *8vo, half dark blue levant, very scarce.* *Phila.,* 1805

3063 BRANNAN, JOHN. Official Letters of the Military and Naval Officers of the United States, during the War with Great Britain in 1812. *8vo, full polished calf, gilt top, edges rough.* *Washington,* 1823

3064 BURR, AARON. The Two Principal Arguments of William Wirt on the Trial of, for High Treason, and on the Motion to Commit Aaron Burr for Trial in Ky. *12mo, full cr. tan colored levant, gilt edges.*

From the Press of Samuel Pleasants, Jr., Richmond, 1808

3065 *Clap*, Capt. *Roger*. MEMOIRS of, *Relating* ſome of GOD's Remarkable Providences to *Him,* in bringing him into *New-England*; and ſome of the Straits and Afflictions, the *Good People* met with here in their Beginnings. AND *Inſtructing*, Counſelling, Directing and Commanding his *Children* and Childrens Children, and Houſhold, to ſerve the LORD in their Generations to the lateſt Poſterity.

Heb. xi. 4.—*He being dead, yet ſpeaketh.*

12*mo, orig. covers, uncut, fine copy, very rare. Collation : Title page. Dedication by Thomas Prince,* 1 *leaf. Memoirs,* 34 *pages. Genealogical account of his family by James Blake, Jun.* 10 *pages.*

BOSTON in *New-England:*
Printed by *B. Green,* 1731.

3066 CLAP, CAPT. ROGER. Memoirs of—relating some of God's Remarkable Providences to Him, in bringing him into New-England; and some of the Straits and Afflictions the good people met with here in their beginnings. And Instructing, Counselling, Directing and Commanding his Children, and Children's Children, and household, to serve the Lord in their Generations to the latest Posterity. 8*vo,* 39 *pages, fine copy, very scarce.* *Boston,* 1807

3067 ——— ——— The same. 8*vo, orig. covers,* 36 *pages, fine copy, scarce.* *Pittsfield,* 1824

3068 COFFIN, ROBERT S. Oriental Harp. Poems of the Boston Bard. 8*vo, full cr. crim. levant, gilt edges, fine copy, eng. title and Port. inlaid.* *Providence,* 1826

"This is my own, my native land."

3069 COPWAY, GEORGE. The Traditional History and Characteristic Sketches of the Ojibway Nation. Illustrated by Darley. 8*vo, half crim. Tky., gilt edges.* *Boston,* 1851

3070 COVELL, LEMUEL. (*Missionary to the Tuscarora Indians.*) Memoir of. Also a Memoir of Alanson Covell. By Mrs. D. C. Brown. In Two Volumes. 8*vo, half dark green tky., gilt edges.* *Brandon, Vt.,* 1839

3071 DRAKE, SAMUEL G. Indian Biography, containing the Lives of more than two hundred Indian Chiefs: Also such others of that race as have rendered their names conspicuous in the History of North America from its first being known to Europeans to the present period. Giving at large their most Celebrated Speeches, Memorable Sayings, Numerous Anecdotes, and a History of their Wars. Illustrated. 8*vo, full cr. crim. levant, gilt top, rough edges, fine copy, rubric title.* *Boston,* 1832

3072 EDWARDS, CHARLES. **Feathers from my own Wings** Frontis. The Shade of Tecumseh. *8vo, fl. dk. olive gr. lev., gt. top, rough edges.* N. Y., MDCCCXXXII.

3073 ELIOT, REV. JOHN. MEMOIRS OF LIFE AND CHARACTER OF. By Martin Moore. *12mo, dk. blue lev. gt. edges.* *Boston*, 1822

3074 FISHER, WILLIAM. NEW TRAVELS among the Indians of North America; with a Dictionary of the Indian Tongue. Portrait. *8vo, hf. cr. dk. green lev., gt. edges; very scarce; fine copy.* *Phila.*, 1812

3075 FORT EDWARD, The Bride of, Founded on an incident of the Revolution. *8vo, hf. cr. crim. lev., gt. edges. Scarce, good copy.* *N. Y.*, 1859

3076 GILLELAND, J. C. HISTORY OF THE LATE WAR between the United States and Great Britain. Containing an Accurate Account of the most important Engagements by Sea and Land, interspersed with Geographical Sketches of the Country where the Principal Battles were fought. *8vo, hf. crim. tky., gt edges; fine copy.* Balto., 1817

3077 GOSDEN, THOMAS. IMPRESSIONS OF A SERIES OF ANIMALS, BIRDS, &c., illustrative of British Field Sports. From a Set of Silver Buttons. Drawn by A. Cooper, and engraved by John Scott on India paper. *8vo, full dk. olive green, gilt top.* *Lond., MDCCCXXI.*

3078 HAMILTON, ALEXANDER. A REVIEW OF DR. JOHN M. MASON'S ORATION ON THE DEATH OF GEN. HAMILTON. *8vo pamph., 10 p.; very scarce.*
New York, Printed by James Oram, 1807

First printed in the *Christian Observer*, 1805, and for the first time printed in this form. A very unjust and unfair criticism.

3079 HARRIOTT, LIEUT. JOHN. STRUGGLES THROUGH LIFE. Exemplified in the various Travels and Adventures in Europe, Asia, Africa, and America. In Two Volumes. *8vo, hf. dk. green, tky., gt. edges.* *New York*, 1809

3080 HEARNE, SAMUEL. JOURNEY FROM FORT PRINCE WALES, in Hudson's Bay, to the Northern Ocean, for the Discovery of Copper Mines and a Northwest Passage, performed between the years, 1769 and 1772. *12mo, full cr. crim. lev., gt. top; scarce, fine copy.* *Phila.*, 1802

3081 HUBBARD, WILLIAM. A NARRATIVE OF THE INDIAN WARS IN NEW ENGLAND, from the First Planting thereof in the year 1607 to the year 1677. *8vo, full dark crimson lev., gt. top, edges rough. Fine copy, very scarce edition.*
Printed at STOCKBRIDGE (*Mass.*), *by* HEMAN WILLARD, May, 1803.

3082 HUMPHREY, HEMAN. INDIAN RIGHTS AND OUR DUTIES. An Address delivered at Amherst, Hartford, &c., December, 1820. *12mo pamph., 23 pp.; scarce.* *Amherst*, 1830

3083 HOIKE UHANE. He Kamaiileo e Moawkaka ai ka uhane o Kanaka. Buke I. T. H. Gallaudet. Iunuhilia. *12mo, boards.* *Honolulu*, 1839

3084 MANE LANI. Ka ai na ka uhane, etc. *24mo, boards.* *Honolulu*, 1841

3085 WEHEWE HEHALA. Oia hoi ka Hulikanaka. *8vo, boards.* *Honolulu*, 1847

3086 LEE, MAJ.-GENL. THE LIFE AND MEMOIRS OF, Second in Command to General Washington, to which are added his Political and Military Essays. *8vo, full cr. crim. lev., gt. top, rough edges. Fine copy.* *N. Y.*, 1813

3087 LESLIE, CHARLES. A SHORT AND EASIE METHOD WITH THE DEISTS, etc. In a Letter to a Friend. The Eighth Edition. *8vo, full pol. calf; fine copy.* *Lond.*, 1723

3088 MAN'S WHOLE DUTY; OR, the RULE OF A Christian's Life AND conversation, containing plain and short Directions for Performance of the several Duties thereof—

"Only let your conversation be as becomes the Gospel of Christ." *Phil.* 1. 27.

24mo, full cr. dk. blue lev., gt. edges.

BOSTON: *B. Green, for Benj. Eliot*, 1718

3089 M'AFEE, ROBERT B. HISTORY OF THE LATE WAR IN THE WESTERN COUNTRY. Comprising a full Account of all the Transactions in that quarter, from the Commencement of Hostilities at Tippecanoe to the termination of the Contest at New Orleans. *Full dk. maroon lev., gt. top rough edges; fine copy; extremely scarce.* *Lexington, K.*, 1816

3090 MASSACHUSETTS. THE | CHARTER | GRANTED BY THEIR MAJESTIES | KING WILLIAM | AND | QUEEN MARY, | TO THE | INHABITANTS | OF THE | PROVINCE | OF THE | MASSACHUSETTS-BAY | IN | NEW-ENGLAND | . *4to. full cr. crim. lev., gt. top, rough edges. Fine copy.*

Boston in New England: Printed by B. Green, Printers to the Lieut.-GOVERNOUR and COUNCIL, for Benjamin Eliot, 1726.

3091 MATHER, COTTON. THE LIFE OF THE Very REVEREND and LEARNED COTTON MATHER, late Pastor of the *North Church* in BOSTON, who died February 13th, 1727–28.

"A Son honoreth his Father."

By SAMUEL MATHER. *8vo, full dk. mar. col. lev., gt. top, rough edges; beautiful copy; extremely scarce.*

BOSTON, *New-England:* Printed for SAMUEL GERRISH, in *Cornhill.* MDCCXXIX.

3092 MCCONNELL, J. L. Western Characters; or, Types of Border Life in the Western States. Illustrated by Darley. Frontis. *8vo, hf. crim. turkey; gilt edges.* *Redfield, N. Y.*, 1853

3093 MCCOY, ISAAC. HISTORY OF BAPTIST INDIAN MISSIONS. Embracing Remarks on the Former and Present Condition of the Aboriginal Tribes; their Settlement within the Indian Territory, and their Future Prospects. *8vo, hf. crim. turkey; gilt edges.* *Washington*, 1840

3094 McINTOSH, JOHN. THE ORIGIN OF THE NORTH-AMERICAN INDIANS; with a faithful description of their Manners and Customs, both Civil and Military; their Religion, Language, Dress, and Ornaments; to which is prefixed a brief view of the Creation of the World; the Situation of the Garden of Eden; the Antedeluvians, &c.; and some final observations on the origin of the Indians. Frontispiece, etc. *8vo, full mottled calf; fine copy.* *N. Y.*, 1844

3095 M'KENNY, THOS. L., AND HALL, JAMES. HISTORY OF THE INDIAN TRIBES OF NORTH AMERICA, etc. In Three Volumes. *Folio, hf. cr. crim. lev., elegant, by R. W. Smith. Bound up from the original numbers with the covers. A very fine copy.* *Washington*, 1838–44

See No. 1317, for a copy in Nos. as originally published.

3096 MAYHEW EXPERIENCE. INDIAN CONVERTS; OR, SOME ACCOUNT OF THE LIVES and Dying SPEECHES of a Considerable Number of the Christianized INDIANS of *Martha's Vineyard*, in *New England*. To which is added, Some Account of those ENGLISH MINISTERS who have successively presided over the *Indian* Work in that and the adjacent Islands. By Mr. *Prince*. *8vo, full cr. crim. lev., gt. top; fine copy, extremely scarce.* LONDON, MDCCXXVII.

3097 MORRIS, CAPT. CHARLES. A COMPLETE COLLECTION OF SONGS, BY CAPTAIN MORRIS. The Twelfth Edition, Revised, Corrected, and Enlarged. Portrait of Morris, in oval, holding a mask, and the following Lines beneath:

"When the fancy stirring Bowl,
Awakes its World to pleasure,
Glowing visions gild my Soul,
And life's an endless treasure."

8vo, unbound, 60 *pages. Part I,* 38 *pages, and Part* 2, 22 *pages. Fine copy.* *London*, 1790

Among the Poems contained in this Collection occurs the famous one entitled "Billy Pitt and the Farmer," narrating the adventures which befell "Billy," "Brittania's Prime Ruler," and "Harry, a staunch friend to Boston," as they were returning on a dark night from a cabinet meeting, with their "Skins full of wine." "Now so it fell out" "This pair were benighted" "And drove out of the road," etc., "Long lost in the dark were" "These *Lights* of the nation;" "But stumbled at last" "To a small habitation;" etc. "When Billy began for" "To make an oration," "As oft he had done," "To bamboozle the nation," etc. The Poem ends with this oft-quoted stanzas—

"Solid Men of Boston
Make no long orations;
Solid men of Boston
Banish strong Potations;
Solid men of Boston
Go to bed at sundown,
And never lose your way,
Like the loggerheads of London."

For a further account of Morris, see the Historical Magazine, Vol. 1, July, 1857, pp. 39 and 216-217. No mention is made, however, of this edition, which contains in all eleven poems, some of them exceedingly free, and ought never to have been printed.

3098 MEXICO, as it was and as it is: By Brantz Mayer. With numerous illustrations on wood, engraved by Butler. *8vo, hf. dark, blue levant. gt. edges. Beautiful copy.*
New York, MDCCCXLIV

3099 MICHIGAN. Historical and Scientific Sketches of. Comprising a series of Discourses delivered before the Historical Society of, etc., and other interesting Papers relative to the Territory. *8vo, hf. cr., crim. levant, gt. edges, very scare. Fine copy.* *Detroit*, 1834

3100 NEW AMSTERDAM. Affairs and Men of. In the time of Gov. Peter Stuyvesant. Compiled by J. Paulding. *8vo, hf. cr., dk. green lev., gilt edges.* *New York*, 1833

3101 NEW HAMPSHIRE. The History of. Comprehending the Events of one Complete Century, from the Discovery of the River Piscataqua. Containing also a Geographical Description of the State, etc. First Edition. In Three Volumes. Map. *8vo, full dk. blue, crushed lev. mor., gt. edges.* *Phila. and Boston.* 1784—1792

3102 NEWTOWN, N. Y. Annals of. Containing its History from its First Settlement, together with many interestings fact concerning the adjacent towns, etc. By James Riker, Jr. *8vo, cl. Fine copy. Maps.* *N. Y.*, 1852

3103 NORTH AMERICA. SUMMARY, Historical and Political of the first Planting, Progressive Improvements, and Present State of the *British* Settlements in North America. In Two Volumes. By Wm. Douglas. *8vo, full dk. blue, cr. lev., gilt edges. Very scarce edition.* Boston, MDCCXLIX.–1751

3104 OHIO. Journal of a Tour into the Territory North-West of the Alleghany Mountains; made in the Spring of 1803. With a Geographical and Historical account of the State of Ohio. Illustrated with original maps and views. By Thaddeus Mason Harris. *8vo, hf. crim. tky., gilt top, rough edges.*
Boston, 1805

3105 PATTIE, JAMES O. (*Of Kentucky.*) The Personal Narrative of, during an Expedition from St. Louis through the vast Regions between that place and the Pacific Ocean, and thence back through the City of Mexico to Vera Cruz, during journeyings of six years; in which he and his father, who accompanied him, suffered unheard of hardships and dangers, had various conflicts with the Indians, and were made captives, in which captivity his father died; together with a Description of the Country, and the various Nations through which they passed. Edited by Timothy Flint. *8vo, full cr. crim. lev., gt. top, edges rough. Fine copy, very scarce.* *Cincinnati*, 1833

3105*Another Copy. *Half cr. crim. lev., gt. edges.* *Cinn.*, 1833

3106 PRIEST, JOSIAH. STORIES OF THE REVOLUTION, with an Account of the Lost Child of the Delawares; Wheaton and the Panther. Plate. *Large 8vo, bds., uncut.* *Albany*, 1838

3107 REDFIELD: A LONG ISLAND TALE OF THE SEVENTEENTH CENTURY. *8vo, full dk. maroon, gt. top, edges uncut. Very scarce romance; full of Indian and Local incidents, etc.* *N. Y.*, 1825

3108 RICH, O. BIBLIOTHECA AMERICANA NOVA. A CATALOGUE OF BOOKS RELATING PRINCIPALLY TO AMERICA. Printed between the years 1500 and 1800. *8vo, full dk. blue cr. lev. mor., gt. top, rough edges. Contents lettered on the back.* *London*, 1853

This copy contains also the rare catalogue of Books, Bib. Amer. Vet., 1493–1700, and supplement printed in double colums, 24 pages: also, catalogue of books published in 1844—being duplicates of Mr. Rich's collection, 48 pages. Edward Everett's Report to the House of Representatives, submitting a list of MSS. and books relating to America, in possession of O. Rich. 24 pages. *Forming a unique volume.*

3109 BIBLIOTHECA AMERICANA NOVA. A CATALOGUE OF BOOKS RELATING TO AMERICA. Printed since the year 1700. Vol. I.—1701–1800, with Supplement. Part I.—1701–1800, and Index, 517 pages. *8vo, full dk. blue cr. lev. mor., gt. top, rough edges.* *London*, 1841

3110 BIBLIOTHECA AMERICANA NOVA. A CATALOGUE OF BOOKS RELATING TO AMERICA. Printed since the year 1700. Vol. II.—1801–1844. 402 pages. *8vo, full dk. blue cr. lev. mor. gt. top.* *London*, 1844

3111 SAMPSON, DEBORAH. THE FEMALE REVIEW; OR, MEMOIRS OF AN AMERICAN YOUNG LADY. WHOSE LIFE AND CHARACTER ARE PECULIARLY DISTINGUISHED—BEING A CONTINENTAL SOLDIER FOR NEARLY THREE YEARS IN THE LATE AMERICAN WAR, DURING WHICH TIME SHE PERFORMED THE DUTIES OF EVERY DEPARTMENT INTO WHICH SHE WAS CALLED, WITH PUNCTUAL EXACTNESS, FIDELITY AND HONOR, AND PRESERVED HER CHASTITY INVIOLATE, BY THE MOST ARTFUL CONCEALMENT OF HER SEX, WITH AN APPENDIX CONTAINING CHARACTERISTIC TRAITS BY DIFFERENT HANDS; HER TASTE FOR ECONOMY, PRINCIPLES OF DOMESTIC EDUCATION.

By a CITIZEN *of* MASSACHUSETTS—(*H. MANN.*) *8vo, hf. cf., orig. blue board binding, edges blue. In beautifnl condition, with the very rare portrait, half length in oval, and list of subscribers.*

DEDHAM: PRINTED BY NATHANIEL, AND BENJAMIN HEATON FOR THE AUTHOR. MDCCXCVII.

Collation: Portrait,—Title-Page,—Dedication, 1 Leaf,—Preface V. to XV.,—Review 17–258,—List of Sub., 3 leaves.

3112 SOUTH CAROLINA. THE HISTORY OF, from its first settlement in 1670, to the year 1808. In Five Volumes. By David Ramsay. *8vo, full crushed dk. blue levant, gt. top, uncut, with all the maps; magnificent copy, selected.* *Charleston*, 1809

3113 STONE, THOMAS T. SKETCHES OF OXFORD COUNTY. (Me.) *12mo, full levant, gt. top; very scarce.* *Portland*, 1830

Contains Lovewell's Fight and other incidents of early History of Maine.

3114 VERMONT, THE CONSTITUTION OF THE STATE OF—AS ESTABLISHED BY THE GENERAL CONVENTION ELECTED FOR THAT PURPOSE, AND HELD AT *WINDSOR*, JULY 2d, 1777, AND CONTINUED BY ADJOURNMENT TO DECEMBER 25, 1777.

8vo, pamph., 24 pages ; fine copy, cleaned, mended and put in excellent condition. (*Unbound*).

HARTFORD :
Printed by WATSON AND GOODWIN. (1778).

This document, which does not seem to be of much importance, if we look merely at the title, has, however, a very interesting history, and we subjoin the following extract from Ira Allen's History of Vermont. (See No. 2677). " The Council of Safety again paid attention to the Constitution, and made a preamble, stating the reasons why the citizens had rejected all connections with New York; but as there was not time, before the day assigned for the election, to print and publish the constitution, therefore the convention was summoned to meet at Windsor, in December, 1777; they met, revised the constitution, and appointed the first election to be on the 12th day of March, 1778. One difficulty was discovered by some members of the convention, who concluded the best way to evade it was, to keep it in as small a circle as possible; the difficulty *was, to establish the Constitution without the voice of the people*, further than was vested in the convention by their credentials, that authorized them to form a constitution, but were silent as to its ratification, and they had no ancient government to predicate their claims upon; besides intestine divisions and different opinions prevailed among the people, and even in the convention. To avoid discord, a large majority, in one instance, conformed to a minority, when deliberating on the articles of the constitution. As the people seemed inclined for a popular government, the constitution was so made, and for the better satisfying those who might choose any difference in the form of government, and as circumstances or increasing knowledge might make it necessary, a principle was established in the constitution, by which legal means might be taken to alter or amend the constitution once in seven years agreeable to the will of the majority of the freemen of the State, which, if perpetuated, would transmit to prosperity the same privileges of choosing how they would be governed, as the people of that day exercised from the inherent right of nature, without revolution or bloodshed. Had the constitution been then submitted to the consideration of the people for their revision, amendment, and ratification, it is very doubtful whether a majority would have confirmed it, considering the resolutions of Congress, and their influence at that time, as well as the intrigues and expense of the provincial Congress of New York, who endeavoured to divide and subdivide the people. *Under these circumstances the Convention appointed Ira Allen to see the constitution printed and distributed before the election. Mr. Allen returned from Hartford, in Connecticut, a few days before the time of the general election, with the Constitution printed, and dispersed it.* There was one (or more) in each town who coveted the honour of being a member in the first general assembly of the new State of Vermont. It was, therefore, their interest to induce their friends to attend the meeting, and take the freeman's oath. This was done, and representatives were elected, and attended the Assembly at Windsor, on the 12th of March, 1778, when and where the votes of the freemen for a Governor, a Lieutenant Governor, 12 Counsellors, and a Treasurer, were sorted and counted, and the persons who had the majority of votes for the respective offices, were declared duly elected. Thus the Constitution of the State of Vermont was put in force."

3115 THATCHER, B. B. INDIAN TRAITS. Being Sketches of the Manners, Customs and Character of the North American Natives. In Two Volumes. 12*mo, full cr. crimson levant, gt. top, rough edges, eng. title. Frontis.* *N. Y.*, 1836

3116 *TROJAN HORSE* OF THE PRESBYTERIAN GOVERNMENT UNBOWELLED. *Sm. 4to, full cr. dk. blue levant, gt. edges ; very curious.* LONDON, 1711

3117 TURNER, G. TRAITS OF INDIAN CHARACTER, etc. In Two Volumes. Port. inserted. 8*vo, full tan col. cr. levant, gt. top.* *Phila.*, 1836

See No. 2673.

3118 UNITED STATES. A HISTORY OF. Before the Revolution, with some account of The Aborigines. By Ezekiel Sanford. 8*vo, hf. cr. crimson levant, gt. edges, scarce ; fine copy.*

3119 MASSACHUSETTS, HISTORY OF. VOL. I.—FROM 1764 to JULY, 1775 : When General Washington took Command of the American Army. BOSTON, 1822

VOL. II.—FROM JULY, 1775, TO THE YEAR 1789, inclusive, when the Federal Government was established under the present Constitution. BOSTON, 1825

VOL. III.—FROM THE YEAR 1790 TO 1820. BOSTON, 1829
By Alden Bradford. *In three volumes.* 8*vo, dark Rox., gilt top, edges rough.*

☞ Bound Uniform in style with Hutchinson, Minot, and Barry. See Catalogue, Nos. 1285–2636–3021.

3120 OHIO HISTORICAL SOCIETY. A BRIEF TOPOGRAPHICAL DESCRIPTION OF THE COUNTY OF WASHINGTON. By J. Delafield, Jr. 8*vo,* 39 *pages, unbound. Good copy, very scarce. With plan of Campus Martius.* *New York*, 1834

3121 LORD NORTH'S ISLAND. Memoir on the Languages and Inhabitants of. By John Pickering. 4*to, red Rox., gilt top, rough edges,* 43 *pages.* *Cambridge*, 1845

Uniform in size and binding with No. 2647.

3122 GARDEN, ALEXANDER. ANECDOTES OF THE AMERICAN REVOLUTION, Illustrative of the Talents and Virtues of the Heroes and Patriots who acted the most conspicuous parts therein. Second Series. 8*vo, red Rox., gilt top, uncut.* *Charleston*, 1828

This copy belongs with No. 2615, as the Second Volume.

3123 BUSHNELL, CHARLES I. CRUMBS FOR ANTIQUARIANS. IN TWO VOLUMES, COMPRISING TEN PARTS, BEING THE COMPLETE SET BOUND UP FROM THE SHEETS, WITH THE BEAUTIFUL COLORED TITLE PAGES OF EACH VOLUME AND THE SPECIAL TITLE-PAGE TO EACH PART.

Volume I. Contains : 1.—An Historical Account of the first three BUSINESS TOKENS issued in the city of New York.

2.—Memoirs of SAMUEL SMITH, a Soldier of the Revolution, 1776–1786.

3.—Journal of SOLOMON NASH, A Soldier of the Revolution, 1776–1777.

4.—Memoirs of TARLETON BROWN, a Captain in the Revolutionary Army.

5.—A Narrative of the Life and Adventures of LEVI HANFORD, a Soldier of the Revolution.

6.—Journal of the Expedition against Quebec, under Col. BENEDICT ARNOLD, in the year 1775, by Major Return J. Meigs.

Volume II. Contains : 1.—The Narrative of Major ABRAHAM LEGGETT, of the Army of the Revolution.

2.—Narrative of the Exertions and Sufferings of Lieutenant JAMES MOODY in the Cause of Government, since the year 1776.

3.—The Narrative of JOHN BLATCHFORD, detailing his sufferings in the Revolutionary War while a Prisoner with the British.

4.—The Narrative of EBENEZER FLETCHER, a Soldier of the Revolution.

8vo, half dark green crushed lev. mor. gilt top, uncut by Bradstreet.

With Twenty-Six Illustrations, Portraits, Views of Old Buildings, &c. Of great interest to the Antiquary.

New York, 1859–1866

3124 PLYMOUTH (Mass.) HISTORY of THE TOWN OF, from its First Settlement in 1620, to the Present time, with a concise History of the Aborigines of New England and their Wars with the English. Second Edition, enlarged and corrected, with map. *8vo, half dark green crushed lev. morocco, gilt top, uncut, by Bradstreet. Very scarce in this condition.*

Boston, 1835

3125 WOODWORTH, SAMUEL. THE CHAMPIONS OF FREEDOM ; or, the Mysterious Chief : a Romance of the Nineteenth Century, founded on the Events of the War between the United States and Great Britain, which terminated in March, 1815. In Two Volumes. *8vo, full crushed dark green levant morocco, gilt top, rough edges. Very scarce.*

New York, 1816

3126 ANDRÈ, MAJOR. An Authentic Narrative of the Causes which led to the Death of. By Joshua Hett Smith. To which is added A MONODY on the Death of Major Andrè. By Miss Seward. *8vo, polished calf, gilt top, edges uncut, by Bedford, with portrait (being a remarkably brilliant impression) engraved by Hopwood, from a drawing by Major Andrè. Also, map and engraving of Sarcophagus in Westminster Abbey.*

London, 1808

It is not necessary to make any extended remarks in relation to this book, further than to speak of its condition, which is all that could be desired. Perfectly clean and spotless throughout.

> "Lamented youth! while with inverted spear
> The British legions pour th' indignant tear!
> Round the dropt arm the funeral scarf entwine,
> And in their heart's deep core thy worth enshrines;
> While my weak Muse, in fond attempt and vain,
> But feebly pours a perishable strain,
> Oh! ye distinguishable few! whose glowin lays
> Bright Phœbus kindles with his purest rays,
> Snatch from its radiant source the living fire,
> And light with Vestal flame your ANDRÈ'S HALLOWED PYRE!"

INDEX TO BOOKS.

The figures refer to the page of the Catalogue.

INDEX TO PAMPHLETS.

The figures refer to the No. of the Catalogue.

www.ingramcontent.com/pod-product-compliance
Lightning Source LLC
LaVergne TN
LVHW021105110826
845150LV00001B/176

9781425565527